1993

Discrepant Engagement addresses work by a number of authors nor normally grouped under a common rubric – black writers from the United States and the Caribbean and the so-called Black Mountain poets: Amiri Baraka, Clarence Major, Robert Duncan, Robert Creeley, Charles Olson, Edward Kamau Brathwaite, Wilson Harris, and others. Nathaniel Mackey examines the ways in which the experimental aspects of their work advance a critique of the assumptions that underlie conventional perceptions and practice. Mackey, arguing that the work of these writers engages the discrepancy between presumed norms and qualities of experience that such norms fail to accommodate, highlights their valorization of dissonance, divergence, and formal disruption. He advances a cross-cultural mix that is uncommon in studies of experimental writing, frequently bringing the works and ideas of the authors it addresses into dialogue and juxtaposition with one another. And he shows that parallels, counterpoint, and relevance to one another exist among writers otherwise separated by ethnic and regional boundaries.

Discrepant Engagement: Dissonance, Cross-Culturality, and Experimental Writing

CAMBRIDGE STUDIES IN AMERICAN LITERATURE AND CULTURE

Editor
Eric Sundquist, Vanderbilt University

Founding editor
Albert Gelpi, Stanford University

Advisory Board
Nina Baym, University of Illinois, Champaign–Urbana
Sacvan Bercovitch, Harvard University
Albert Gelpi, Stanford University
Myra Jehlen, University of Pennsylvania
Carolyn Porter, University of California, Berkeley
Robert Stepto, Yale University
Tony Tanner, King's College, Cambridge University

Books in the series

Continued on pages following the Index

Discrepant Engagement
Dissonance, Cross-Culturality, and Experimental Writing

NATHANIEL MACKEY

CAMBRIDGE
UNIVERSITY PRESS

Published by the Press Syndicate of the University of Cambridge
The Pitt Building, Trumpington Street, Cambridge CB2 1RP
40 West 20th Street, New York, NY 10011-4211, USA
10 Stamford Road, Oakleigh, Melbourne 3166, Australia

© Cambridge University Press 1993

First published 1993

Printed in the United States of America

Library of Congress Cataloging-in-Publication Data
Mackey, Nathaniel, 1947–
Discrepant engagement : dissonance, cross-culturality, and
experimental writing / Nathaniel Mackey.
p.   cm. – (Cambridge studies in American literature
and culture : 71)
Includes bibliographical references and index.
ISBN 0-521-44453-5
1. American literature – 20th century – History and criticism.
2. American literature – Afro-American authors – History and
criticism.   3. Caribbean literature (English) – Black authors –
History and criticism.   4. Literature, Experimental – United States –
History and criticism.   5. Literature and society – United States –
History –20th century.   I. Title.   II. Series.
PS221.M24   1993
810.9´005 – dc20   93-626
                                                          CIP

A catalog record for this book is available from the British Library.

ISBN 0-521-44453-5 hardback

Contents

148,706

Acknowledgments

The following essays have previously been published, most of them in a substantially different version: "The Changing Same: Black Music in the Poetry of Amiri Baraka" in *Boundary 2*, 6, 2 (Winter 1978); "To Define An Ultimate Dimness: The Poetry of Clarence Major" in *Black American Literature Forum*, 13, 2 (Summer 1979); "The World-Poem in Microcosm: Robert Duncan's 'The Continent'" in *ELH*, 47, 4 (Fall 1980); "Uroboros: Robert Duncan's *Dante* and *A Seventeenth Century Suite*" in *Robert Duncan: Scales of the Marvelous*, ed. Robert J. Bertholf and Ian W. Reid (New York: New Directions, 1979); "Robert Creeley's *The Gold Diggers*: Projective Prose" in *Boundary 2*, 6, 3/7, 1 (Spring/ Fall 1978); "New Series 1 (Folk Series): Edward Kamau Brathwaite's New World Trilogy" in *Caliban: A Journal of New World Thought and Writing*, 3, 1 (Spring-Summer 1979); "Limbo, Dislocation, Phantom Limb: Wilson Harris and the Caribbean Occasion" in *Criticism*, 22, 1 (Winter 1980); "Poseidon (Dub Version)" in *Wilson Harris: The Uncompromising Imagination*, ed. Hena Maes-Jelinek (Mundelstrup, Denmark: Dangaroo Press, 1991); "The Unruly Pivot: Wilson Harris's *The Eye of the Scarecrow*" in *Texas Studies in Literature and Language*, 20, 4 (Winter 1978); "The Imagination of Justice: Wilson Harris's *Ascent to Omai*" in *World Literature Written in English*, 22, 1 (Spring 1983); "Sound and Sentiment, Sound and Symbol" in *Callaloo: A Journal of Afro-American and African Arts and Letters*, 10, 1 (Winter 1987); "On Edge" in *Conjunctions*, 6 (Spring 1984); "Other: From Noun to Verb" in *Representations*, 39 (Summer 1992).

1

Introduction

And All the Birds Sing Bass

================

I

These essays address work by a number of authors not normally grouped under a common rubric – black writers from the United States and the Caribbean and the so-called Black Mountain poets for the most part. The latter became known by that name because of their association during the 1950s with Black Mountain College in North Carolina, the experimental college founded in 1933 by John Andrew Rice and other dissident professors dismissed from Rollins College in Florida. Not coincidentally, dissidence and experimentation figure prominently among the concerns touched on by these essays, and can be said to tie them together, though I make no large claims for a single, unifying argument running throughout. The title I have given this introduction lends itself to that tie while alluding to another Black Mountain, the one that gives its name to "Black Mountain Blues." Written by J. C. Johnson, the song was recorded by Bessie Smith in July 1930 (the same month and year Rice was hired at Rollins), and it begins:

> Back in Black Mountain a child will slap your face,
> Back in Black Mountain a child will slap your face,
> Babies cryin' for liquor and all the birds sing bass.

What I mean to suggest is that in the "bass notes" bottoming the work of these various writers – writers who, poet or novelist, black or white, from the United States or from the Caribbean, produce work of a refractory, oppositional sort – one hears the rumblings of some such "place" of insubordination.

Marginality might be another name for that "place." I have been concerned not only with the play between content and form but also with the impact of marginalized context on such play – the weight borne and the wobble introduced by positions peripheral to a contested center.

1

Nowadays, thanks to critical theory, the very notion of center is admitted to be problematic and, along with margin, increasingly relativized, but one finds Amiri Baraka making much the same point twenty-five years ago:

> ... there are now a great many young black writers in America who do realize that their customary isolation from the mainstream is a valuable way into any description they might make of an America. In fact, it is just this alienation that could serve to make a very powerful American literature, since its hypothetical writers function in many senses within the main structure of the American society as well. . . . Being black in a society where such a state is an extreme liability is the most extreme form of nonconformity available. The point is, of course, that this nonconformity should be put to use. The vantage point is classically perfect – outside and inside at the same time.[1]

And in another essay published about the same time, "The Myth of a 'Negro Literature,' " Baraka points to Bessie Smith and Billie Holiday as models black writers should turn to, cases in point of how black nonconformity should be used:

> No poetry has come out of England of major importance for forty years, yet there are would-be Negro poets who reject the gaudy excellence of 20th century American poetry in favor of disembowelled Academic models of second-rate English poetry, with the notion that somehow it is the only way poetry should be written. It would be better if such a poet listened to Bessie Smith sing *Gimme A Pigfoot*, or listened to the tragic verse of a Billie Holiday, than be content to imperfectly imitate the bad poetry of the ruined minds of Europe. (*H*, 113)

He quickly goes on to argue their relevance to white writers as well:

> For an American, black or white, to say that some hideous imitation of Alexander Pope means more to him, emotionally, than the blues of Ray Charles or Lightnin' Hopkins, it would be required for him to have completely disappeared into the American Academy's vision of a Europeanized and colonial American culture, or to be lying. (*H*, 113)

The implied correspondence between such music and "the gaudy excellence of 20th century American poetry" lends itself to the title I've chosen for this introduction, as do the references to Bessie Smith in *Man Orchid*, one of the works addressed in this book.

Still, the title is figurative. Indeed, rather than let this go unremarked,

I wish to call attention to it. The recourse to figurativity, to the fortuitous convergence "Black Mountain" affords, highlights the inadequacy of existing rubrics, brings the problematics of categorization to the fore. It will be seen that I frequently read the writers whose works these essays address in relationship to one another, bring their writings into dialogue and juxtaposition with one another. That such correspondence, counterpoint, and relevance to one another exist among authors otherwise separated by ethnic and regional boundaries is worth accenting in the context of current debates over canon formation and canon reformation. This fact is especially relevant to the current institutionalization of an African-American canon and the frequent assumption that black critics are to write only about black writers and that black writers are to be discussed only in relation to other black writers. Cornel West, in his essay "Minority Discourse and the Pitfalls of Canon Formation," offers a caveat with which I heartily agree. He argues that "the major twentieth-century Afro-American literary artists" have not been served well by such assumptions, that their contributions have tended to be diminished by too parochial an approach:

> Such diminishment takes place because these authors arbitrarily get lumped with a group of black writers or associated with a particular theme in Afro-American intellectual history, which obscures their literary profundity and accents their less important aspects.
>
> For instance, Toomer's ingenious modernist formal innovations and his chilling encounter with black southern culture in *Cane* are masked by associating him with the assertion of pride by the "new Negro" in the twenties. Ellison's existentialist blues novelistic practices, with their deep sources in Afro-American music, folklore, Western literary humanism, and American pluralist ideology, are concealed by subsuming him under a "post-Wright school of black writing." Baldwin's masterful and memorable essays that mix Jamesian prose with black sermonic rhythms are similarly treated. Toni Morrison's magic realist portrayal of forms of Afro-American cultural disruption and transformation links her more closely to contemporary Latin American literary treatments of the arrested agency of colonized peoples than with American feminist preoccupations with self-fulfillment and sisterhood. Last, Ishmael Reed's bizarre and brilliant postmodernist stories fall well outside black literary lineages and genealogies.[2]

Creative kinship and the lines of affinity it effects are much more complex, jagged, and indissociable than the totalizing pretensions of canon formation tend to acknowledge. My recourse to a figurative rubric admits that in our taxonomic practices, as Foucault has pointed out via Borges, we stand on poetic – that is, made-up – ground.

The problem, then, is not peculiar to African-American literature, however much the ghettoization to which black writers tend to be subjected exacerbates and gives a particular pungency to the more general problematics of categorization. We need not look far for another example. Casually applied to writers as different from one another as Charles Olson, Robert Creeley, and Robert Duncan, the Black Mountain rubric itself provides a good one. Olson complained in 1968: "I think that whole 'Black Mountain poet' thing is a lot of bullshit. I mean, actually, it was created by the editor, the famous editor of that anthology for Grove Press, Mr. Allen, where he divided – he did a very – but it was a terrible mistake made. He created those sections – Black Mountain, San Francisco, Beat, New York, New, Young, huh?"[3] The reference is to Donald M. Allen's *The New American Poetry: 1945–1960*, whose divisions, Allen himself admits, "are somewhat arbitrary and cannot be taken as rigid categories."[4] This becomes especially clear in the case of Duncan, whom Allen includes in the Black Mountain group while acknowledging that he could have been placed, with equal justification, in the San Francisco section. At a time when attention to the arbitrariness of the linguistic sign has occasioned epochal paradigm shifts in literary and cultural studies, surely the arbitrariness of the rubric warrants a grain of relativizing salt.

Some such grain is not inconsistent with key preoccupations that emerge in the essays that follow. The dialectical wholism espoused most notably by Robert Duncan and the Guyanese author Wilson Harris is especially germane. Duncan's idea of "a symposium of the whole," in which "all the old excluded orders must be included," nonetheless acknowledges that "not only the experience of unity but the experience of separation is the mother of man."[5] This leads to apprehensions regarding the unities we construct, a calling into question of the coherences we otherwise tend to take for granted. "Praise then the interruption of our composure," Duncan writes in the introduction to *Bending the Bow*.[6] We see an openness to disturbance not only in his readiness to quarrel with Olsonian doxy while at Black Mountain College but in the conception of a world-poem in which "there is no composure but a life-spring of dissatisfaction" (*BB, x*), a poem we see, as he puts it in "The Continent," "moving in rifts, churning, enjambing, / drifting feature from feature."[7]

The simultaneity of integrative and disintegrative tendencies attendant upon the pursuit of a wholeness admitted to be out of reach is a dynamic about which Harris too has had much to say. A man of mixed racial antecedents born in a country considered Caribbean though situated in South America, Harris is well aware of the arbitrariness of categories and of the exclusionary, conquistadorial uses to which classificatory schemes tend to be put. Sandra E. Drake, in her study *Wilson Harris and the Modern Tradition: A New Architecture of the World*, rightly identifies the hybrid, heterogeneous character of Harris's work with what the Cuban poet José Martí called "nuestra América mestiza" (our mixed America). His writings constitute, among other things, a long meditation on the legacies of conquest that have plagued not only the region from which he comes but, of course, the entire world, the subjugation and the marginalization of heterogeneity by self-centralizing, monolithic models. These legacies lie behind the much discussed and debated problem of Caribbean identity, a problem rooted in the imposition of models of sameness upon a reality characterized by hybridity, diversity, mix. In a 1985 interview, Harris responded to a question concerning "the search for identity, for wholeness," and "the theme of the broken individual" in Caribbean literature by suggesting the relevance of a centrifugal poetics. Key to this is his notion of the partial image, the therapeutic work of a play of images around the acknowledgment of a partiality one strives to overcome:

> Well, as I tend to see it at this point in time, there is a kind of wholeness, but one can't structure that wholeness. One knows it's there and one moves into it ceaselessly, but all the time one moves with partial images. Now the partial image has within it a degree of bias but it also represents a part of something else, so that there is a kind of ceaseless *expedition* into wholeness which has to do with the ways in which one consumes – metaphysically consumes – the bias in the partial image and releases that image as a part of something else which one may not be immediately aware of in that context – one may not be immediately aware of how the partial image links up with another partial image until the centre of being in an imaginative work breaks or moves and the illusory centrality of the partial image is enriched in creative paradox. So that I think in the Caribbean and in the South Americas, because of the residue of cultures and what has happened in the past, that kind of approach seems to be of significance.[8]

Harris situates his practice in what the Martinican writer Edouard Glissant calls the Other America. The partial image relativizes itself, very much in keeping with the relativization Glissant sees as the "realization" of a "new man":

> The issue . . . is the appearance of a new man, whom I would define, with reference to his "realization" in literature, as a man who is able to live the relative after having suffered the absolute. When I

say *relative*, I mean the Diverse, the obscure need to accept the other's difference; and when I say *absolute* I refer to the dramatic endeavor to impose a truth on the Other. I feel that the man from the Other America "merges" with this new man, who lives the relative; and that the struggles of peoples who try to survive in the American continent bear witness to this new creation.[9]

This passage occurs in an essay under the heading "Cross-Cultural Poetics." Harris has written a critical book called *The Womb of Space: The Cross-Cultural Imagination*. The book's aim is "to highlight variables of dialogue that tend to be suppressed in so-called normal classifications of fiction and poetry within regional scholarship."[10] I think of the mix these essays advance as a contribution to a cross-cultural poetics, plots upon an alternative map, one on which the Other America has begun to emerge.

II

Black music provides a reference point in several of these essays, most extensively in "The Changing Same: Black Music in the Poetry of Amiri Baraka," "Sound and Sentiment, Sound and Symbol," and "Other: From Noun to Verb." This is so in part because it does the same for some of the writers about whose work I have written. The outside/inside position Baraka refers to, for example, is nowhere more evident than in black music's infiltration of the dominant society, an infiltration that has been going on for some time. Reverend Samuel Davies, a white minister in the South during the colonial period, wrote effusively of the slaves' contribution to church services, their relegation to a segregated section notwithstanding:

> I can hardly express the pleasure it affords me to turn to that part of the Gallery where they sit, and see so many of them with their Psalm or Hymn Books, turning to the part then sung, and assisting their fellows who are beginners, to find the place; and then all breaking out in a torrent of sacred harmony, enough to bear away the whole congregation to heaven.

Similarly, Hector St. John de Crèvecoeur, the French immigrant who settled in New York in the mid-1700s, remarked in his *Sketches of Eighteenth-Century America*: "If we have not the gorgeous balls, the harmonious concerts, the shrill horn of Europe, yet we dilate our hearts as well with the simple Negro fiddle."[11] That black music, longer and more resoundingly than any other native product, has put the United States on the world-cultural map is by now a commonplace observation. For this and other reasons it serves many black writers as both a model and a highwater mark of black authority, a testament to black powers of self-styling as well as to the ability of such powers to influence others.

As we've seen in the passages quoted here, Amiri Baraka has long held black music to be a relevant model for a truly black writing, for a truly American writing. "The Changing Same: Black Music in the Poetry of Amiri Baraka" looks at the ways in which his writings embrace the music as a liberatory index of possibility, as a stimulus to an extramusical pursuit of innovative authority – poetic and political authority. The essay deals with the presence of black music in his writing not only as content – references to songs, musicians, musical practices, and so forth – but also as form – technical and stylistic tendencies deriving from an attempt to emulate the music. The essay also situates Baraka's work and its relationship to black music in the context of the cultural and social movements of which he was a part from the late fifties to the mid-seventies – the bohemian scene in Greenwich Village and the "New American Poetry," Black Nationalism, and the "Black Arts Movement," his more recent Marxist-Leninist position.

During that first period – the late fifties through the mid-sixties – Baraka was involved with the various "schools" of the "New American Poetry," Beat to Black Mountain. He is, then, among other things, a bridge figure, the only black writer associated with the Black Mountain group – M.L. Rosenthal, in *The New Poets*, discusses his first two volumes of poetry in Chapter IV, "The 'Projectivist' Movement"[12] – and, as he himself would later complain, the only black writer included in Donald Allen's anthology. In *The Autobiography of LeRoi Jones* he writes of this involvement in terms of overlapping marginalities:

> I had come into poetry from a wide-open perspective – anti-academic because of my experience, my social history and predilections. Obviously, as an African American I had a cultural history that should give me certain aesthetic proclivities. . . . The open and implied rebellion – of form and content. Aesthetic as well as social and political. But I saw most of it as Art, and the social statement as merely our lives as dropouts from the mainstream. I could see the young white boys and girls in their pronouncement of disillusion with and "removal" from society as being related to the black experience. That made us colleagues of the spirit. . . . the connection could be made because I was black and that made me, as Wright's novel asserted, an *outsider*. (To some extent, even inside those "outsider" circles.)[13]

His characterization of the poetic tendencies with which he was involved insists upon the link between ethnicity and formal innovation, social marginality and aesthetic marginality (a link that Werner Sollors, in *Beyond Ethnicity*, argues has not been sufficiently acknowledged in traditional notions of literary "growth"[14]):

> The various "schools" of poetry we related to were themselves all linked together by the ingenuous. They were a point of departure from the academic, from the Eliotic model of rhetoric, formalism, and iambics.
>
> Under the broad banner of our objective and subjective "united front" of poetry, I characterized the various schools: the Jewish Apocalyptic; biblical, long crashing rhythms of spiritual song. *Howl* and *Kaddish* are the best examples. Kerouac's "Spontaneous Bop Prosody" is an attempt to buy into the "heaven in the head" of religious apocalypse, which Ginsberg inherited from his rabbinical sources (and his historical models, Christopher Smart, Blake, Whitman). It is a hyped-up version of Joyce with a nod in the direction of black improvisational music. . . .
>
> The Black Mountain people linked me to a kind of Anglo-Germanic School, more accessible than the academics, but still favoring hard-edged, structured forms. Olson and Creeley were its twin prophets, but Olson had the broader sword, the most "prophetic" stance. His concerns touched me deeply. Creeley was closer to the William Carlos Williams style – sparse and near-conversational, though much more stylized than Williams and influenced by Mallarmé in his tendency toward using the language so denotatively it became abstract in its concreteness. (ALJ, 158)

The voice of discontent Baraka hears in black music, what he terms its "anti-assimilationist" sound, relates it to Black Nationalism and to Marxist-Leninist dissent as well as to, as we see here, Beat/bohemian "revolt."

The impact of black music on U.S. culture at large is particularly evident in the tradition of which Baraka partakes, the music's longstanding status as a symbol of dissent, of a divergence from conventional attitudes and behavior. Prod and precedent for nonconformist tendencies, the music has repeatedly been embraced by centrifugal impulses within white society (all too often, however, with condescending, romantic-racist, appropriative attitudes that have done nothing to radically challenge the country's founding racial assumptions). This embrace has tended to promote divergent aesthetic practices in a variety of art forms. The Jazz Age and the Beats offer the best known examples, but the Projectivists can be seen to have been touched as well. Olson, in the interview from which I quoted earlier, remarked: "And that there was a poetics? Ha ha. Boy, there was no poetic. It was Charlie Parker. Literally, it was Charlie Parker. He was the Bob Dylan of the Fifties" (*M*, 71). Robert Creeley, whose book of stories *The Gold Diggers* is the subject of one of these essays, noted in 1966:

> I have, at times, made reference to my own interest when younger (and continuingly) in the music of Charlie Parker – an intensive variation on "foursquare" patterns such as "I've Got Rhythm." Listening to him play, I found he lengthened the experience of time, or shortened it, gained a very subtle experience of "weight," all some decision made within the context of what was called "improvisation" – but what I should rather call the experience of possibility within the limits of his materials (sounds and durations) and their environment. . . . There's an interview with Dizzy Gillespie . . . in which he speaks of rhythm particularly in a way I very much respect. If *time* is measure of *change*, our sense of it becomes what we can apprehend as significant condition of *change* – in poetry as well as in music.[15]

And in prose. Though "Robert Creeley's *The Gold Diggers*: Projective Prose" deals primarily with the relationship of Creeley's stories to Projectivist poetics, the affinity between the latter and black improvisatory music on which the Baraka essay touches is touched on again, albeit lightly, in the attention to the "bop" aspects of Creeley's prose, its syncopated, "offbeat" quality, the stuttering or stumbling displacements by which it proceeds.

The interplay between writing and music is given a more extended treatment in "Sound and Sentiment, Sound and Symbol," an essay that deals with work by Jean Toomer, William Carlos Williams, Ralph Ellison, and Wilson Harris. Arguing that these instances of writing that alludes to or seeks to ally itself with music do so as a way of reaching toward an alternate reality, the essay treats music as a form of social and epistemological dissent. It gives further attention to the sense of stuttering, stumbling, and limping broached in the Creeley and Baraka essays, that of them as marks of both damage and philosophic divergence (deprivation on the one hand, epistemological dilation or would-be dilation on the other). In this divergence and dissent one hears the voice of the orphan, the outsider, the excluded. Music and the writing that embraces it are something like the *icno-cuicatl* or orphan song of ancient Mexico, which, as Gordon Brotherston explains, "explores feelings of cosmic abandonment and the precariousness of mortal life before the unknown."[16] This includes abandonment and precariousness in their most immediately social aspects as well. Moreover, writing that emulates music is orphan song in another sense: Words are of the realm of the orphan insofar as they are severed from that to which they refer. (Think of Addie Bundren's mistrust of language in Faulkner's *As I Lay Dying:*" . . . words that are not deeds, that are just the gaps in people's lacks, coming down like the cries of the geese out of the wild darkness in the old terrible nights, fumbling at the deeds like orphans to whom are pointed out in a crowd two faces and told, That is your father, your mother."[17]) The notion of orphan song the essay advances relies heavily on Steven Feld's *Sound and Sentiment*, a study of the way in which the Kaluli of Papua New Guinea conceptualize music and poetic language. Central to this is their myth of a boy who, denied kinship, social sustenance, turns into a bird, a kind of fruitdove called a *muni* bird. The essay examines the connection between the orphan's ordeal of being left out and the writer's or the musician's recourse to divergent practices and precepts, "outside" practices and precepts. Jack Spicer, in a passage that could serve as an epigraph to the essay, gets at this connection in his poem for Charlie Parker: "So Bird and I sing / Outside your window."[18]

The voice of "the boy who became a *muni* bird," the voice of the orphan, figuratively embodies and continues a concern we see in some of the earlier essays: the sounding of an apocalyptic undertone or note, the "bass note" I referred to earlier, a note of alarm at the exclusions by which coherencies tend to be supported. All the writers dealt with in these essays, in differing ways and to varying degrees, have recourse to this note. An awareness of the exclusions to which the ordering impulse, whether collective or individual, is prone leads them to an attempt to allow for, include, or at least allude to what is excluded. A line from Ralph Ellison's *Invisible Man* that I quote in "Sound and Sentiment, Sound and Symbol" says it well: "The mind that has conceived a plan of living must never lose sight of the chaos against which that pattern was conceived."[19] I quote it in an earlier essay as well, "To Define An Ultimate Dimness: The Poetry of Clarence Major." This piece looks at the ways in which a "return of the repressed" enters Major's work of the early seventies both as content or theme and as form/deformation, working its disruptions into what the poems say and into the way – grammatically, syntactically, typographically – they say it.

Major is best known, perhaps, as a novelist. As Charles Johnson notes in *Being and Race: Black Writing since 1970*: "For twenty years Major and his colleagues in the Fiction Collective, a cooperative publishing venture started in the early 1970s by a handful of 'experimental' writers (among them Ronald Sukenick, Jonathan Baumbach, and Raymond Federman), have been on the cutting edge of nontraditional fiction in America."[20] The Surfictionist project with which he is associated aims to foreground the constructedness of the work, to make the arrangements and the premises whereby it proceeds unignorable, opaque, something not to be looked through (overlooked) but looked into, looked at. This process

more often than not short-circuits reader expectations regarding character, plot, representation, and so forth, thus bringing to the fore –
opening up to scrutiny – the assumptions on which those expectations
rest. (The self-reflexivity of such an undertaking, the calling into question
of the conventions of traditional narration, is not unlike Wilson Harris's
exploration, in *The Eye of the Scarecrow*, of "the void in conventional
memory" or his pursuit, in *Ascent to Omai*, of a "novel history.") We
thus never lose sight not only of chaos but of the stopgap ordering devices
we concoct. A similar aim informs Major's early poetry, where we see
an insistence on the "arrangedness" not only of the poem but of language
inside and outside the poem as well as of the reality to which language
and poem are commonly said to refer. In this regard, the poems anticipate
the practices and proclamations of the recently much discussed
$L = A = N = G = U = A = G = E$ poets, though I'm not aware that any of
these poets have had anything to say about Major's work.

The "creative brutality" Major resorts to wants to make way for
attitudes and impulses marginalized by the will to order. A base of
discontent underlies this project, which can never not problematize itself,
never not be in touch with the ethic of disturbance on which it rests.
The obvious differences in texture and tone between Major's work and
that of Robert Duncan notwithstanding, a similar ethic is articulated in
the latter, with which the two essays following "To Define An Ultimate
Dimness" deal. Duncan speaks of "a lifespring of dissatisfaction in all
orders" (*BB, x*). He declares in "The Propositions": "There is a disturbance in the House." And in "The Structure of Rime IX": "I crave the
visible disturbers."[21]

The disturbance, the self-problematizing portent looked into in "Uroboros: Robert Duncan's *Dante* and *A Seventeenth Century Suite*" is what
Harris calls "the omen of unity," the specter of ceaseless, unsettling
supplementation and revision prompted by an uncontainable whole. Alan
Bass, whose comments on Derrida's "double science" I bring to bear on
the issues of originality, indebtedness, and repetition raised by Duncan's
work, writes: ". . . there can be no 'full' unity, no unity without something missing, something that calls for the production of a supplementary
'unity' . . . "[22] This problematic is likewise at work in the self-reflexivity
and the apocalyptic portent shown in "The World-Poem in Microcosm:
Robert Duncan's 'The Continent' " to be active in Duncan's espousal of
an open poetics. "The Continent" underscores the sense of marginality
as an awareness of exclusion, the apprehension of an uncaptured inclusiveness, the inexhaustibility of an incontinent whole:

> The artist of the margin
> works abundancies

and sees the theme is much too big
to cover all o'er . . . (RB, 172)

These two essays deal as well with the ways in which tradition enters
Duncan's work, the self-conscious way in which he constructs and re-
constructs tradition, brings the past and the present to bear upon one
another. His insistent interweaving of an ensemble of histories and con-
temporaneities – literary, sociopolitical, personal, and so forth, even, as
we see in "The Continent," geological – relates work and world, the
world-poem, in ways with which current concerns with intertextuality
may someday catch up. The ominous reminders tradition issues in Duncan's work, the dark note it sounds, comply with a psychoanalytic/depth-
psychological accent upon that which tends to be kept down, disruptive
contents of which the "Under- / earth currents" in "The Continent"
figuratively speak. In "Apprehensions," a companion-poem to "The
Continent," Duncan speaks of "myth / that Freud says lies in our blood,"
aiming to "open Night's eye that sleeps in what we know by Day" (RB,
pp. 37 and 30). A later poem, addressing the Vietnam War, he calls
"Bring It Up from the Dark." The inclusionist aspiration of his open
poetics encourages a descent into the depths, an excavatory descent into
the unconscious, individual and collective both. This is true of Harris
too, whose uses of Jung receive some attention in "Limbo, Dislocation,
Phantom Limb: Wilson Harris and the Caribbean Occasion" and whose
affinities with Jungian psychologist James Hillman are touched on in the
essay on *Ascent to Omai*. It is also true of Olson, for whom Jung was
similarly important. He writes in *The Maximus Poems*:

> . . . below below - below
> is a factor of being, <u>underneath</u>
>
> is a matter this is like the vault
>   you aren't all train
> of Heaven . . . [23]

III

The two Caribbean writers whose work I have addressed, Harris and
the Barbadian poet Edward Kamau Brathwaite, are likewise artists of
the margin – in several more senses than one. Born in a region whose
plantation/colonial history relegated it to the fringes of a Eurocentric
map, they wrestle with legacies of domination and with senses of cultural
and historical nonentity imposed from outside. They are of the margin
from a U.S. perspective in a further sense: What little attention writers
from the anglophone West Indies get in the United States goes to those,

most notably Derek Walcott and V. S. Naipaul, who work in a more conventional vein. Brathwaite and Harris tie the reclamation of what the latter calls "eclipsed perspectives" to divergent, refractory practices on the formal and stylistic levels. My discussions of their work largely examine this tie. "New Series 1 (Folk Series): Edward Kamau Brathwaite's New World Trilogy" looks at Brathwaite's valorization, in his trilogy *The Arrivants*, of the African presence in the Caribbean. The essays on Harris's work discuss his pursuit of a "novel history," a new novel and a new historical sense intent on breaking the spell of an "idolatrous realism." Like Brathwaite's excavation of the Caribbean's black legacies, Harris's insistence on "an act of memory" recalls and corroborates Edouard Glissant's observation: "Because the collective memory was too often wiped out, the Caribbean writer must 'dig deep' into this memory, following the latent signs that he has picked up in the everyday world" (CD, 64). This both Brathwaite and Harris do. They too "sing bass," bring up what's under.

In Brathwaite's case, as I have already noted, this "what" is in large measure the Africanity of the West Indies. "Africans and their descendants," David Lowenthal writes, "have outnumbered all other West Indians since the 1650s"[24] – a fact that has tended to be forgotten in discussions of Caribbean identity. Such discussions have typically lamented a lack of cultural coherence, advancing a conflictual prognosis built on the concept of a "plural society," a concept that, Brathwaite writes in *The Development of Creole Society in Jamaica 1770–1820*, "is based on an apprehension of cultural polarity, on an 'either/or' principle, on the idea of people sharing common divisions instead of increasingly common values."[25] Historian as well as poet (he studied history at Cambridge and has taught history at the University of the West Indies since the late sixties), Brathwaite too laments the polarizations that have stood in the way of West Indian identity, obstructed the process he calls creolization. He has not, however, forgotten the black majority, the contributions, real and potential, of the Afro-creole folk culture that has been undervalued if not entirely left out of the West Indian equation. The "critique of the pyramid" and the accent on "grounding" we see in *The Development of Creole Society in Jamaica 1770–1820* we also see in *The Arrivants*. The hierarchical disequilibrium in power and prestige between Euro-creole minority and Afro-creole majority, the effacement of the culture of the latter by that of the former, accounts for the thwarting of what he takes to be "a natural built in drive or gravitational tendency towards cultural autonomy":

> Cultural autonomy demands a norm and a residential correspondence between the "great" and "little" traditions within the society.

Under slavery there were two "great" traditions, one in Europe, the other in Africa, and so neither was residential. Normative value-references were made outside the society. Creolization (despite its attendant imitations and conformities) provided the conditions for and possibility of local residence. It certainly mediated the development of authentically local institutions, and an Afro-creole "little" tradition among the slave "folk." But it did not, during the period of this study, provide a norm. For this to have been provided, the Euro-creole elite (the one group able, to some extent, to influence the pace and quality of creolization) would have had to have been much stronger, culturally, than it was. Unable or unwilling to absorb in any central sense the "little" tradition of the majority, its efforts and its continuing colonial dependence merely created the pervasive dichotomy which has been indicated in this study. (*DCS*, 309)

The larger political and cultural project of which his poetry is meant to be a part we grasp in the paragraph with which the book concludes:

With political power now in the hands of the black majority of the population, it remains to be seen whether the society will remain conceived of as "plural" – the historical dichotomy becoming the norm – or whether the process of creolization will be resumed in such a way that the "little" tradition of the (ex-)slaves will be able to achieve the kind of articulation, centrality, prestige and influence – assuming, that is, that it is not by now too debased – that will provide a basis for creative reconstruction. Such a base, evolving its own residential "great" tradition, could well support the development of a new parochial wholeness, a difficult but possible creole authenticity. (DCS, 311)

Accordingly, he writes of his "realization that the home – the true imaginative and spiritual home – of the 'rootless' Afro-American and West Indian was in Africa" in the liner notes to his recording of *Rights of Passage*[26] – a move into "unmentionable black" related, like Baraka's, to the social and political changes of the fifties and sixties.

Brathwaite tells of his discovery of a physical, meteorological link between Africa and the West Indies upon his return from Ghana in the early sixties. The annual drought that descends upon the islands he realized to be a continuation of the African harmattan, the dry, hot Saharan wind that thus became "inspiration" for the poems that followed:

And returning myself to the West Indies in 1962, I became aware that the islands themselves were as much geographical extensions of Africa as they were Atlantic outriders and off-shoots of the

American continent. There was, in fact, a remarkable physical and meteorological link with West Africa largely ignored by or invisible to geographers and totally missing from our common consciousness. It was this: in December to about February every year, a drought visits the islands. The green canefields take the golden deciduous crispness of scorched parchment. The blue sky burns muted. The dry air rivets the star nights with metallic cold. It is our tropical winter. This dryness, unexplained, is put down to "lack of rain."

But living in St. Lucia at this time, I watched this drought drift in towards the island, moving in across the ocean from the east, obscuring Martinique, obscuring sails beating towards Castries. And I suddenly realized that what I was witnessing – that milky haze, that sense of dryness – was something I had seen and felt before in Ghana. It was the seasonal dust-cloud, drifting out of the great ocean of Sahara – the *harmattan*. By an obscure miracle of connection, this Arab's nomad wind, cracker of Fante wood a thousand miles beyond, did not die on the seashore of West Africa, its continental limit; it drifted on, reaching the New World archipelago to create our drought, imposing an African season on the Caribbean sea. And it was on these winds too, and in this season, that the slave ships came from Guinea, bearing my ancestors to this other land.

And so the poem grew . . . [27]

This is a good example of the act of "appropriating a *de facto* situation by endowing it with a figurative meaning" that Harris, who, like Brathwaite, challenges "conventional memory," encourages in his essay "History, Fable and Myth in the Caribbean and Guianas." In this and other writings dealt with in "Limbo, Dislocation, Phantom Limb" we see Harris's version of a "creative reconstruction" that reassesses Caribbean possibilities, finding prospects and promise where others have mainly dwelt on deprivation, dead end. Coming from South America and having worked as a land surveyor for many years, Harris brings to the question the added dimension of the Guyanese interior, a sense of continental expanse and of the enigmas of the tropical bush. He also brings a concern with Amerindian traditions, a "digging down" into the cultural and mythological legacies of the Caribs, the Arawaks, the Macusis, and others.

"The Unruly Pivot: Wilson Harris's *The Eye of the Scarecrow*" and "The Imagination of Justice: Wilson Harris's *Ascent to Omai*" examine Harris's practice in two novels that reflect upon themselves and upon their relationship to conventional novelistic procedures, offering a cri-

tique, by both precept and example, of such procedures. Against a backdrop of social and familial disarray, each novel advances a radical revision
of what Harris terms "the novel of persuasion," the nineteenth-century
realist novel whose rise, he argues, "in its conventional and historical
mould coincides in Europe with states of society which were involved
in consolidating their class and other vested interests."[28] The differences
between twentieth-century Caribbean and nineteenth-century European
states of society, he contends, demand a renovation of the premises on
which the novel rests.

Worth particular mention, especially relating to the dark note to which
I made reference earlier, is the repudiation of "a certain canon of clarity"
found in *Ascent to Omai*. We see this repudiation's relevance to marginality
suggested by the fact that the self-reflexive novelist/judge offers his critique in the form of marginalia (while poking fun at the nineteenth-
century convention of addressing the reader):

> "*Dear Reader*, (THE JUDGE WROTE HALF IN THE MARGIN
> OF HIS BOOK AND HALF ON A VACANT CARD). My
> intention, in part, is to repudiate the vicarious novel – vicarious
> sex-mask, death-mask – where the writer, following a certain canon
> of clarity, claims to enter the most obscure and difficult terrain of
> experience without incurring a necessary burden of authenticity,
> obscurity or difficulty at the same time."[29]

He goes on to insist upon the task of "immersing ourselves in language
as omen" – an insistence consonant with Duncan's line in "Food for Fire,
Food for Thought": "Language obeyd flares tongues in obscure matter"
(*OF*, 95). Harris's work, like that of not only Duncan but the other
writers these essays deal with, moves, with considerable regularity, into
moments of obscurity, opacity, the "ultimate dimness" to which Major
refers. These are writers whose work is often difficult – the indeterminacy
and resistance to explanation in a Creeley story (whose form he calls "an
egg of obdurate kind"[30]), the runelike character of an Olson poem, and
so forth.

Glissant, like Harris, repeatedly raises this issue. The "theory of particular opacities" he espouses in the piece from which I quote in "On
Edge" not only encourages a tolerance of obscurity but argues its
necessity:

> For the attempt to approach a reality so often hidden from view
> cannot be organized in terms of a series of clarifications. We demand
> the right to obscurity. Through which our anxiety to have a full
> existence becomes part of the universal drama of cultural transfor-
> mation: the creativity of marginalized peoples who today confront

the ideal of transparent universality, imposed by the West, with secretive and multiple manifestations of Diversity. . . . Repetition of these ideas does not clarify their expression; on the contrary, it perhaps leads to obscurity. We need those stubborn shadows where repetition leads to perpetual concealment, which is our form of resistance. (CD, 2 and 4)

What I wish to underscore before concluding this introduction is that this willingness to risk obscurity diverges not only from mainstream notions of clarity but also from the prescription of such notions, in the name of political urgency, to writers from socially marginalized groups. A comment made by Dudley Randall regarding Baraka typifies the equation of political relevance with accessibility: "Originally writing in the obscure Greenwich Village idiom, his recent identification with the black masses has caused him to write with more clarity and force."[31] And, indeed, Baraka, the most politically active of the writers with whom these essays deal, has, as Werner Sollors puts it, "preferred the risk of losing artistic complexity"[32] to that of inaccessibility. But compare Glissant on the question of audience:

We realize that literature in these conditions cannot be an object of pleasure or reassurance. Now this raises the question of *the one for whom the work is written*. A generous tendency in our works tempts us to place ourselves from the outset "within reach" of those who suffer social or cultural alienation. A justifiable tendency insofar as we have a concrete effect on the symptoms of this alienation. But an almost elementary statement of our needs, if it is valuable in our daily struggle, can also prevent us from seeing the deeper structures of oppression which must nevertheless be brought to light. This act of exposure, paradoxically, is not performed each time in an open and clear way. Western thought has led us to believe that a work must always put itself constantly *at our disposal*, and I know a number of our folktales, the power of whose impact on their audience has nothing to do with the clarity of their meaning. It can happen that a work is not written *for someone*, but to dismantle the complex mechanism of frustration and the infinite forms of oppression. Demanding that in such a situation they should be immediately understandable is the same as making the mistake of so many visitors who, after spending two days in Martinique, claim they can explain to Martinicans the problems in their country and the solutions that need to be implemented. (CD, 107).

My view is that there has been far too much emphasis on accessibility when it comes to writers from socially marginalized groups. This has resulted in shallow, simplistic readings that belabor the most obvious aspects of the writer's work and situation, readings that go something like this: "So-and-so is a black writer. Black people are victims of racism. So-and-so's writing speaks out against racism." It has yet to be shown that such simplifications have had any positive political effect, if, indeed, they have had any political effect at all. As I argue in the last essay in this book, "Other: From Noun to Verb," the ascription of only the most obvious orders of statement to the work of black writers, the confinement of the work to racial readings that tell us only what we already know, is a symptom of the social othering such readings presumably oppose.

Failures or refusals to acknowledge complexity among writers from socially marginalized groups, no matter how "well-intentioned," condescend to the work and to the writers and thus, hardly the solution they purport to be, are a part of the problem. Allied with such simplistic readings is the tendency to overlook variance and divergent approaches in the writing from such groups, especially to overlook writing that defies canons of accessibility. The clear, polemical, sloganeering Baraka is better known and more widely validated, despite the controversies his work has aroused, than the obscure, introspective LeRoi Jones, just as Gwendolyn Brooks's "We Real Cool" is thought to be more genuine than "The Anniad." The poetry of Melvin Tolson, the poetry and plays of Jay Wright and such work as William Melvin Kelley's *Dunfords Travels Everywheres* and N. J. Loftis's *Black Anima* tend to become margins within the margins, receiving much less attention and validation than they deserve. It thus becomes easy and potentially self-fulfilling to characterize writing from socially marginalized groups in the most sweeping, totalizing terms, to posit a homogeneity of approach and inclination. Ron Silliman, for example, writes:

> Progressive poets who identify as members of groups that have been the subject of history – many white male heterosexuals, for example – are apt to challenge all that is supposedly "natural" about the formation of their own subjectivity. That their writing today is apt to call into question, if not actually explode, such conventions as narrative, persona and even reference can hardly be surprising. At the other end of this spectrum are poets who do *not* identify as members of groups that have been the subject of history, for they instead have been its objects. The narrative of history has led not to their self-actualization, but to their exclusion and domination. These writers and readers – women, people of color, sexual minorities, the entire spectrum of the "marginal" – have a manifest political need to *have their stories told*. That their writing should often appear much more conventional, with the notable difference

as to whom is the subject of those conventions, illuminates the relationship between form and audience.[33]

There are, however, writers from socially marginalized groups who do both – tell their stories while calling such conventions into question, tell their stories *by* calling such conventions into question. The distinction between a formally experimental center and a formally conventional periphery distorts and grossly oversimplifies matters. Just as there are writers from "groups that have been the subject of history" who adhere to convention, there are writers from groups that have been its object who do not. The essays that follow will have the salutary consequence, I hope, of reminding us that experimental writing, the aesthetic margin, is not the domain solely of those from socially nonmarginalized groups. All of these writers – Harris and Major, say, no less than Creeley and Olson – have sought new ways to show us not only what we don't see but that we don't see, the constructs by which we are both blinded and enlightened.

IV

The title of this book is taken from one of the essays on Wilson Harris's work, "Poseidon (Dub Version)." It is an expression coined in reference to practices that, in the interest of opening presumably closed orders of identity and signification, accent fissure, fracture, incongruity, the rickety, imperfect fit between word and world. Such practices highlight – indeed inhabit – discrepancy, engage rather than seek to ignore it. Recalling the derivation of the word *discrepant* from a root meaning "to rattle, creak," I relate discrepant engagement to the name the Dogon of West Africa give their weaving block, the base on which the loom they weave upon sits. They call it the "creaking of the word." It is the noise upon which the word is based, the discrepant foundation of all coherence and articulation, of the purchase upon the the world fabrication affords. Discrepant engagement, rather than suppressing or seeking to silence that noise, acknowledges it. In its anti-foundational acknowledgment of founding noise, discrepant engagement sings "base," voicing reminders of the axiomatic exclusions upon which positings of identity and meaning depend.

Jacques Attali, to whose book *Noise: The Political Economy of Music* I refer in "Other: From Noun to Verb," offers a relevant definition:

A noise is a resonance that interferes with the audition of a message in the process of emission. . . . Noise, then, does not exist in itself, but only in relation to the system within which it is inscribed. . . . Information theory uses the concept of noise . . . in a more general

way: noise is the term for a signal that interferes with the reception
of a message by a receiver, even if the interfering signal itself has
a meaning for that receiver.[34]

Noise is whatever the signifying system, in a particular situation, is not
intended to transmit, be the system a poem, a piece of music, a novel,
or an entire society. Open form (itself a discrepant, oxymoronic for-
mulation, not unlike Williams's "variable foot") is a gesture in the direction of noise. Baraka's valorization of "honking" by rhythm and blues
(R&B) saxophonists, Major's "remarkable verb of / things," Duncan's
invocation of "disturbance," Creeley's bebop-influenced deviation from
expected narrative accents, Olson's insistence that things "keep their
proper confusions," his advocacy of "shout" as a corrective to discourse,
Brathwaite's "calibanisms," and Harris's "language as omen" all in their
distinctive ways validate noise. The discrepant openings they advance
bespeak, in varying degrees, what Leonard Barrett calls cultural dissonance, "the social and cultural incongruities which the society feel are
responsible for its alienation whether real or imagined." Writing about
the Rastafarians of Jamaica, Barrett suggests that in their music, whether
ritual Nyabingi or popular reggae, we "detect in the lower beats deep
structural dissonance which mirrors the social conflicts within the society."[35] The open practices and aspirations of the writers dealt with in
this book, I have been insisting, do likewise. "Dissonance / . . . leads to
discovery," Williams writes.[36]

Discrepant engagement, rather than suppressing resonance, dissonance, noise, seeks to remain open to them. Its admission of resonances
contends with resolution. It worries resolute identity and demarcation,
resolute boundary lines, resolute definition, obeying a vibrational rather
than a corpuscular sense of being, "a quality," as Major puts it, "of
which sharp contact is / the qualification, a remarkable verb quiver."[37]
To see being as verb rather than noun is to be at odds with hypostasis,
the reification of fixed identities that has been the bane of socially marginalized groups. It is to be at odds with taxonomies and categorizations
that obscure the fact of heterogeneity and mix. "Poseidon (Dub Version)"
brings discrepant engagement to bear upon questions of representation,
naming, and identity in a context of cultural mix inherited from colonizing projects, arguing that it dispels or seeks to dispel the specter of
inauthenticity that haunts post-colonial hybridity, dislodges or seeks to
dislodge homogeneous models of identity and assumptions of monolithic
form. But, as I have already indicated and by titling the book as I have,
discrepant engagement is relevant not only to writers from recently de-
colonized regions such as Harris and Brathwaite. It pertains to and is
symptomatic of a postmodern/postcolonial suspicion of totalizing par-

adigms, a suspicion of which Williams's admonition "Waken from . . . this dream of / the whole poem" (P, 234), Major's caveat with regard to "control versions of any / coherence"[38] or Olson's dissatisfaction with having "lived long in a generalizing time"[39] is no less an instance than Harris's comments on the partial image or Brathwaite's audition of "some- / thing torn // and new."[40]

Still, because of preconceptions regarding who belongs where and with whom, which have been shaped and reinforced by existing rubrics and academic practice, there are readers who will find the mix of writers dealt with in this book incongruous and problematic. In this respect, the book's title refers to its own practice, its willingness to engage what will be seen by some as an unlikely or an unsanctioned fit, a non-fit. Though I have attempted in this introduction to offer some of my senses of how these essays and the writers with whose work they deal fit together, I have also offered its fortuitous, figurative title, "And All the Birds Sing Bass," as a discrepant note meant to call attention to the problematics of rubric-making, a caveat meant to make the act of categorization creak. Such creaking is always present, even in the case of more customary groupings – groupings that appear unproblematic, proper, only because we agree not to hear it. It is my hope that this book lives up to its title, that it avails itself of resonances and dissonances, the interstitial play between fit and non-fit, the non-totalizing drift a book of essays affords. It is my hope that in addition to making sense it makes noise.

2

The Changing Same

Black Music in the Poetry of Amiri Baraka

Consistency is one of the last words one would use in characterizing Baraka's thinking during the first two decades of his career. Coming into his earliest prominence as a member of the Beat/Black Mountain avant-garde of the fifties and sixties, he wrote in 1959, still calling himself LeRoi Jones: "For me, Lorca, Williams, Pound and Charles Olson have had the greatest influence. Eliot, earlier. . . . " He went on to name Philip Whalen, Gary Snyder, Michael McClure, Frank O'Hara, Ron Loewinsohn, John Weiners, Robert Creeley, and Allen Ginsberg as some of the "young wizards . . . that everybody calling himself poet can learn from."[1] Seven years later in an essay called "Poetry and Karma," having in the interim abandoned Greenwich Village for Harlem and the "New American Poetry" for the "Black Arts Movement," he writes of his earlier influences and associates:

> White poetry is like white music (for the most part, and even taking into account those "imitations" I said, which are all as valid as W. C. Williams writing about Bunk Johnson's band. Hear the axles turn, the rust churned and repositioned. The death more subtly or more openly longed for. Creeley's black box, Olson's revivification of the dead, Ginsberg's screams at his own shadowy races or the creepier elements completely covered up with silver rubied garbage artifacts and paintings and manners and ideas. . . .[2]

Such openness not only to change but to about-faces of the most explosive kind is typical of his career, an openness he himself acknowledges in "The Liar":

> Though I am a man
> who is loud
> on the birth

of his ways. Publicly redefining
each change in my soul, as if I had predicted
them,
  and profited, biblically, even tho
  their chanting weight,
        erased familiarity
        from my face.[3]

Qualifications if not outright repudiations of earlier stances have thus
come to be expected. *Black Magic*, the collection of poems written between 1961 and 1967, opens with "An Explanation of the Work," written
in 1968, which more or less dismisses the work up to about 1965, calling
it "a cloud of abstraction and disjointedness, that was just whiteness."[4]

Hard Facts, comprised of poems written between 1973 and 1975, announces yet another change of direction. At the height of his Black
Nationalist phase Baraka was fond of countering any mention of Marxist
theory by insisting that socialism is contrary to the nature of whites and
thus unattainable by them in any form other than intellectual abstraction,
whereas black people, being by their very nature communistic (generous,
nonexploitative, etc.), have no need of any such theories. In the course
of an interview conducted by Marvin X in 1968 for instance:

> White boys always come out and say, "Oh, don't you think there'll
> be a socialistic solution to the world's problems?" Well, you know,
> that's irrelevant bullshit. It'll be a Black solution to the world's
> problems. Whatever they gonna do it will be Black. You can say
> what that is only when you're in it. When white people speak about
> socialism they're really theorizing. I mean, they're giving you a
> theory that they've never realized: like socialism. They try to force
> something on their nature that they're not ready for as a being, as
> a species – with its unnatural worth. But we don't have to call it
> anything but Black, 'cause that's what it is – being Black. They
> call it socialism because they have to find a theory to justify within
> their alien psyches.[5]

Yet on the back cover of *Hard Facts* we find a portrait of Marx, Engels,
Lenin, Stalin, and Mao and read in Baraka's introduction:

> The work and study, should be work active work toward making
> revolution, toward seeing the masses of people in this society 1st
> build a revolutionary vanguard party, a new communist party, an
> anti-revisionist party, a party guided by the science of Marxism-
> Leninism-Mao-Tse-Tung Thought, and then led by that party
> smash the bourgeois state machine and seize state power to turn
> the means of producing wealth, the land, factories, machines, min-

eral wealth, from private property owned by a handful of super-billionaires to state owned public property under the dictatorship of the proletariat. That is the work we are putting forth.

He explicitly disowns his earlier nationalist position as a "subjective mystification." Subjecting it to a class analysis, he calls it "an ultimately reactionary nationalism that served no interests but [those of] our newly emerging Black bureaucratic elite and petit bourgeois." He argues that the legitimate nationalist aspirations of black people can be realized only through socialist revolution.[6] There are other changes as well. One notes another name change, for example: the dropping of the Muslim title *Imamu* (meaning "teacher"), bringing to an end his affiliation with Islam. The poem "When We'll Worship Jesus" twice associates Allah with Christ, long a villain in Baraka's work:

> jesus aint did nothin for us
> but kept us turned toward the
> sky (him and his boy allah
> too, need to be checkd
> out!) (HF, 7)

In addition, two poems attack Kenneth Gibson, whom he helped get elected mayor of Newark in 1970. One thing, however, has not changed. Black music continues to be respectfully invoked, serving in *Hard Facts*, as in earlier work, as a harbinger of change:

> hung out with any and all thats bad and mad and wont
>   be had. In with
> all and all with in, out here stomping in the streets for the
>   trumpeting
> dynamic of the people themselves – new and renew –
>   Our Experience
> Nows the time, charley parker sd, Now's the time. Say
>   do it, do it, we gon
> do it (HF, 25)

In this essay I will be discussing black music in its dual role of impulse (life-style or ethos as well as technique) and subject matter in Baraka's work, exploring its usefulness as a focal point for pulling together disparate strands of Baraka's thought. His early attraction to Projectivist and Beat poetics, for instance, bespeaks an attitude that he and other spokesmen for those poetics repeatedly called upon jazz to exemplify. Kerouac, Ginsberg, Creeley, McClure, and others glowingly referred to bop improvisation as a technique from which poets could learn. Even Olson, for whom music was not of prime importance, remarked in a letter to Cid Corman in the early fifties: "How does – or is there – an analogy to (as i'd gather any of us do) to jazz?"[7] Black music for Baraka, however, comes eventually to express the very spirit that leads to his repudiation of Olson et al. – the Black Nationalist ferment of the middle and late sixties. This ferment, in his particular case, is itself impelled by certain attitudes and impulses that also motivated his Beat/Projectivist writings and with which this repudiation is thus not entirely inconsistent. What he rejects is an alleged failure of the Beat and Black Mountain writers to live up to the extra-literary (especially political) implications of their poetics – implications they themselves often insist upon in their pursuit of a relevance wider than the aesthetic.

Warren Tallman alludes to this extra-literary aspiration when he remarks in his preface to *The Poetics of the New American Poetry*: "And whatever else the poets in this volume may or may not have in common all demonstrably are seeking a new or re-newed writing in hopes of a new or renewed world."[8] Olson's insistence that "the projective involves a stance towards reality outside a poem as well as a new stance towards the reality of the poem itself,"[9] and Jack Spicer's assurances that "the objective universe can be affected by the poet"[10] attest to the importance of the notion of poetry as an agent of change and revelation to the poetic movement of which Baraka was – and remains – a part. The persistence of his celebration of black music has to do with the persistence of a "will to change" (Olson's phrase) common to his Projectivist, Black Nationalist, and Marxist periods, a will that the music evokes and exemplifies. "There is a daringly human quality to John Coltrane's music that makes itself felt, wherever he records," Baraka writes in the liner notes to *Coltrane Live at Birdland*. "If you can hear, this music will make you think of a lot of weird and wonderful things. You might even become one of them."[11]

II

Blues People, Baraka's socio-historical reading of black music published in 1963, is the most appropriate work with which to begin. The product of such black self-consciousness as would later give rise to his nationalist stance, the book also exhibits the impact upon his thought of Projectivist aesthetics as well as that of the Beat ethic. In addition, the thesis and methodology of the book anticipate his conversion to Marxist theory. *Blues People*'s most repeatedly insisted upon theme, that is, shares with Marxist thought the conviction that cultural expression is determined by and thus reflective of the social, political, and economic realities of the context in which it is produced:

It seems possible to me that some kind of graph could be set up using samplings of Negro music proper to whatever moment of the Negro's social history was selected, and that in each grouping of songs a certain frequency of reference could pretty well determine his social, economic, and psychological states at that particular period . . . The most expressive Negro music of any given period will be an exact reflection of what the Negro himself is. It will be a portrait of the Negro in America at that particular time.[12]

The book thus has to do with the various transformations – from African to Afro-American, slave to citizen, rural to urban – undergone by black people in the United States and the attendant transformations of Afro-American music.

Underlying the great amount of attention given to changes in the black stance and situation is the deeper conviction that a continuum exists within which the threat of dilution, co-optation, or amalgamation by the dominant white culture has been and continues to be repelled. A black *position*, one of alienation and resistance (which in *Black Music* he will call "the changing same"), becomes a kind of "unmoved mover" at the root of black America's transformations: "The Negro's music changed as he changed, reflecting shifting attitudes or (and this is equally important) *consistent attitudes within changed contexts*" (BP, 153). Baraka's nascent Marxism, together with a more explicitly Beat contempt for middle-class American mores and a soon-to-be-nationalist espousal of the black cultural continuum, manifests itself again in the class analysis he offers of the early development of New Orleans jazz. He stresses the fact that the segregation laws passed at the turn of the century forced the black middle class of that time – the Creoles, *gens de couleur*, and mulattoes – into closer association with the working-class black people from whom they had held themselves apart. This resulted in middle-class musicians being influenced by the blues, the music of the working class, the music that, in their emulation of white culture and their acquisition of European instrumental techniques, they had previously looked down upon. The interactions between these two social strata led to the beginnings of jazz: "The black rhythmic and vocal tradition was translated into an instrumental music which utilized some of the formal techniques of European dance and march music" (BP, 139). The idea of a conflict between the working-class estrangement articulated in the blues and the assimilationist aspirations of the bourgeoisie – "the *freedman-citizen* conflict" – dominates Baraka's understanding of the forces at work within subsequent developments in jazz:

The important idea here, though, is that the first jazzmen were from both sides of the fence – from the darker blues tradition and

a certain fixed socio-cultural, and most of the time economic, stra-
tum, and also from the "white" Creole tradition and its worship
of what were certainly the ideals of a Franco-American middle class.
. . . This meant that as jazz developed after the early twenties in this
country, it could only be a music that would reflect the socio-
cultural continuum that had developed within Negro America from
blackest black to whitest white. The jazz player could come from
any part of that socio-cultural spectrum, or at least combine sufficiently the older autonomous blues tradition with the musical
traditions of the Creoles or the ragtime orchestras of the North.
And thus, jazz could not help but reflect the entire Black society.
(Such a thing as a *middle-class blues singer* is almost unheard of. It
is, it seems to me, even a contradiction of terms.) (BP, 139–140)

That his own sympathies lie with the "blackest black" end of the
spectrum is made clear by references to the black middle class as "vague,
featureless Americans," as well as by the recurrence of such passages as
the following: "It was the growing black middle class who believed that
the best way to survive in America would be to *disappear* completely,
leaving no trace at all that there had ever been an Africa, or a slavery,
or even, finally, a black man" (BP, 124). Such disparagement of the
bourgeoisie, as I've already noted, has partly to do with the anti-
Establishment posture of the Beat Generation of which Baraka was a
part. That the book is very much a Beat interpretation of black music
is evidenced by the fact that Baraka resorts to a parallel between the
Beats and the bebop musicians after whom they patterned themselves
several times in the final chapter:

> When the moderns, the *beboppers*, showed up to restore jazz, in
> some sense, to its original separateness, to drag it outside the main-
> stream of American culture again, most middle-class Negroes (as
> most Americans) were struck; they had passed, for the most part,
> completely into the Platonic citizenship. The willfully harsh, *anti-
> assimilationist* sound of bebop fell on deaf or horrified ears, just as
> it did in white America. My father called me a "bebopper" in much
> the same way as some people say "beatnik" now. (BP, 181–182)

Or again: "Bebopper jokes were as popular during the forties as the
recent beatnik jokes" (BP, 190). Reference is also made to Jack Kerouac's
professed desire "to be considered a jazz poet / blowing a long blues in
an afternoon jam / session," as well as to Ginsberg's notion of a "bop
prosody." The Beat romance of alienation, nonconformity, and revolt
has much to do with the book's celebration of a black estrangement from
"the rudimentary sterility" of American life. But however much more

Baraka's gravitation toward blackness has to do with an idea of negation than with the *blackness* of blackness, the transition from this Beat separatism to a black cultural-nationalist separatism is not a very difficult one (unless, of course, you happen to be white).

The idea of black music as, in its most authentic, undiluted forms, the issue of a willful dissociation from mainstream American culture – as in fact "a form of social aggression" – is absolutely central to *Blues People* and other works in which use is made of the black musical tradition: "Negro music is *always* radical in the context of formal American culture" (BP, 235). Baraka refers to John Coltrane, Sonny Rollins, and others as "this new generation's private assassins,"[13] and the association of the music with acts of subversion, sabotage, and revolution or, at the very least, contempt carries over into his poetry, his fiction, and his plays. In *Dutchman*, he has Clay tell Lula that what Bessie Smith and Charlie Parker are saying through their music is "Up you ass, feeble-minded ofay! Up you ass."[14] In "The Screamers," one of the stories in *Tales*, R&B saxophonist Lynn Hope and his band, honking the same riff over and over again, lead a crowd of "five or six hundred hopped-up woogies" on a march through the ghetto, laughing, dancing, yelling and obstructing traffic:

> We screamed and screamed at the clear image of ourselves as we should always be. Ecstatic, completed, involved in a secret communal expression. It would be the form of the sweetest revolution, to huckle-buck into the fallen capital, and let the oppressors lindy hop out. We marched all the way to Spruce, weaving among the stalled cars, laughing at the dazed white men who sat behind the wheels.[15]

Also in *Tales*, "Now and Then," a thinly veiled story about saxophonist Albert Ayler and his brother, trumpeter Don, begins:

> This musician and his brother always talked about spirits. They were good musicians, talking about spirits, and they had them, the spirits, and soared with them, when they played. The music would climb, and bombard everything, destroying whole civilizations, it seemed. And then I suppose, while they played, whole civilizations, actually *were* destroyed. Leveled. The nuns whimpered with church spears through their heads. Blind blond babies bled and bled. (T, 117)

The best example of how such ideas figure into the poems is "Rhythm & Blues," a poem dedicated, significantly, to Robert Williams, the head of the Monroe, North Carolina, branch of the NAACP who in 1959 came into national prominence by organizing a black rifle club and advocating armed resistance to Ku Klux Klan attacks. Williams was eventually forced into exile – first to Cuba, then to China – by a trumped-up kidnapping charge. Baraka's comments on R&B in *Blues People* help shed light on the poem, especially his remarks on the practice of "honking" among R&B saxophonists:

> The point, it seemed, was to spend oneself with as much attention as possible, and also to make the instruments sound as unmusical, or as non-Western, as possible. It was almost as if the blues people were reacting against the softness and "legitimacy" that had crept into black instrumental music with the advent of swing. In a way, this is what had happened, and for this reason, rhythm & blues sat as completely outside the mainstream as earlier blues forms. (BP, 172)

A deliberate affront to the dominant culture's canons of musicality, "honking" challenges and delegitimates that culture's distinction between music and noise, its imposition of hegemonic expectations as to what constitutes acceptable sound. "Honking" strikes a deliberately discordant "note." Its recourse to what would otherwise be thought of as noise marks the divide between black and white, accenting the dissonant relations within a white-supremacist society, the discrepant rift between racist practices and professed democratic ideals. Baraka's dedication of "Rhythm & Blues" to Williams advances an analogy between R&B's contestation of mainstream aesthetic values and Williams's advocacy of black resistance to racist assault. The poem, like the music, voices a reaction, that of the poet's growing discontent with "the softness and 'legitimacy' " of his participation in the predominantly white "New American Poetry." (In reference to Donald Allen's anthology he writes in "Poetry and Karma": "Only LeRoi Jones in the New American Poetry, 1945–60. *The* Negro! Whose poetry then, only a reflection of what the rest of the E-X-C-L-U-S-I-V-E club was doing" [RR, 25].) The poem speaks contemptuously of "the deadly idiot of compromise / who shrieks compassion, and bids me love my neighbor," couching its description of integrationist forgiveness in musical terms:

>   Such act as would give me legend, "This is the man who saved us
> Spared us from the disappearance of the sixteenth note, the
>   destruction
> of the scale. This is the man who against the black pits of despair-
>   ing genius
> cried, "Save the Popular Song." (DL, 46)

But he envisions himself possibly going against the grain of the black musical assault upon Western values and institutions – represented here by the sixteenth note, the scale, and the popular song (about all of which more will be said in Section III) – only to go on to reject that possibility:

> I am not moved. I will not move to save them. There is no
> "melody." Only the foot stomped, the roaring harmonies of need.
>   The
> hand banged on the table, waved in the air. The teeth pushed
>   against
> the lip. The face and fingers sweating. "Let me alone," is praise
>   enough
> for these musicians. (DL, 46–47)

"Rhythm & Blues" is also a good example of the way in which Baraka subjects himself to the sort of class analysis characteristic of *Blues People*. An idea that he insists upon not only in *Blues People* but in the essays "The Myth of a 'Negro Literature,' " "A Dark Bag," and "Philistinism and the Negro Writer" is that black literature tends to be a less accurate or authentic depiction of the black condition than does black music. The reason for this, he argues, is that black literature has been dominated by middle-class writers seeking to advertise, by way of their writing, their qualification for admission into – and their *willingness* to enter – mainstream American life. Black music, on the other hand, has for the most part not been harmed by any such quest for prestige, refinement or, finally, whiteness. A passage from "Philistinism and the Negro Writer" states it best:

> Most of what could be called the Negro's formal attempt at "high art" was found in his music, and one of the reasons . . . was that it was only in music that the Negro did not have to respect the tradition outside of his own feelings – that is, he could play what he felt and not try to make it seem like something alien to his feelings, something outside of his experience. In most cases the Negro writers who usually wanted to pursue what "they" classify as "high art" were necessarily middle-class Negroes, and the art that these middle-class Negroes made tended to be an art that was, at best, an imitation of what can only be described as white middle-class literature.[16]

This equation of literary aspirations with a necessarily assimilationist desire for upward mobility is at work in the third and final section of "Rhythm & Blues." Baraka has acknowledged his own middle-class background in a number of places; for example, his biographical note in the anthology *New American Story*: "Went to school in Newark in guise of skinny prim middle class Negro, i.e., lower middle class American. . . . "[17] In light of his middle-class background and his involvement in an almost exclusively white literary movement, his writing of poetry seems to him symptomatic of exactly the sort of integrationist status-seeking he argues has been the tendency among too many black writers. "Rhythm & Blues" concludes with a resolution to repudiate this tendency, to abandon poetry and align himself with the black musician's contempt for and attack upon mainstream culture. The poem ends on an apocalyptic note:

> I am deaf and blind and lost and will not again sing your quiet
>   verse. I have lost
> even the act of poetry, and writhe now for cool horizonless dawn.
>   The
> shake and chant, bulled electric motion, figure of what there will
>   be
> as it sits beside me waiting to live past my own meekness. My
>   own
> light skin. Bull of yellow perfection, imperfectly made, im-
>   perfectly
> understood, except as it rises against the mountains, like sun
> but brighter, like flame but hotter. There will be those
> who will tell you it will be beautiful. (DL, 47)

While Baraka's early association with such poets as Ginsberg, Dorn, and O'Hara may have conflicted with the politics – the *ethno*politics – of his understanding of black music, there was little if any such antagonism on the aesthetic plane. He himself writes of a "feeling of rapport between the jazz of the forties, fifties, and sixties with the rest of contemporary American art" in *Blues People*: "There are aesthetic analogies, persistent similarities of stance that also create identifiable relationships. And these relationships seem valid whether they are found in the most vital contemporary American poetry or the best new American painting" (BP, 233). In fact, his description of the music of Ornette Coleman and Cecil Taylor, with its emphasis on "total area" as the determinant of form, is highly suggestive of the Projectivist notion of "composition by field":

> Their music does not depend on constantly stated chords for its direction and shape. Nor does it pretend to accept the formal considerations of the bar, or measure, line. In a sense, the music depends for its form on the same references as primitive blues forms. It considers the *total area* of its existence as a means to evolve, to move, as an intelligently shaped musical concept, from its beginning to its end. This total area is not merely the largely artificial considerations of bar lines and constantly stated chords, but the *more* musical considerations of rhythm, pitch, timbre, and melody. (BP, 226)

There is also the analogy here between this increased "musicality" – that is, aurality (as against the essentially graphic insistence of the bar) – and

the increased orality of much recent poetry with its attendant redefinition
of poetic measure and line. Also worth noting is Taylor's acquaintance
with and professed admiration for this poetry. "In the broader sense,"
Nat Hentoff wrote in 1965, "Taylor continues moving in multiple directions of interests outside music that invariably become absorbed in
his music. He has become acutely knowledgeable about poetry, his current favorites including Robert Duncan, LeRoi Jones, Charles Olson,
and Robert Creeley."[18] Taylor's liner notes to his album *Unit Structures,*
"Sound Structure of Subculture Becoming Major Breath/Naked Fire
Gesture," begin with a phrase that recalls the title of one of Duncan's
books, *The Opening of the Field,* a title that in turn recalls the synonymy
of "composition by field" with "open verse" in Olson's essay "Projective
Verse": "The first level or statement of three an opening field of question,
how large it ought or ought not to be." He goes on to assert that "form
is possibility," espousing an open, exploratory approach to form not
unlike that of the poets to whom he alludes.[19]

The most obvious of the "persistent similarities" among, say, Olson's
or Baraka's poetry, the painting of Jackson Pollock, and the music of
Coleman or Taylor is their exaltation of process. Baraka's belief, stated
repeatedly throughout the essay "Hunting Is Not Those Heads on the
Wall," is that process is more valuable than its products, its *artifacts*:

> The academic Western mind is the best example of the substitution
> of artifact worship for the lightning awareness of the art process.
> Even the artist is more valuable than his artifact, because the art
> process goes on in his mind. But the process itself is the most
> important quality because it can transform and create, and its only
> form is possibility. The artifact, because it assumes one form, is
> only that particular quality or idea. It is, in this sense, after the fact,
> and is only important because it remarks on its source.[20]

He goes on to speak of "the *verb process,* the doing, the coming into
being, the at-the-time-of" as the reason "we think there is particular
value in live music, contemplating the artifact as it arrives, listening to
it emerge." The closeness of improvised music to the primacy of process
is the quality Baraka strives for in his poems. His appreciation of black
music has to do with a spiritualistic bias against the artifactual. In *Blues
People* he attributes the retention of links with the African past in religion,
music, and dance to the non-artifactuality of these aspects of culture:

> Only religion (and magic) and the arts were not completely sub-
> merged by Euro-American concepts. Music, dance, religion, do
> not have *artifacts* as their end products, so they were saved. These
> nonmaterial aspects of the African's culture were almost impossible

to eradicate. And these are the most apparent legacies of the African past, even to the contemporary black American. (BP, 16)

Significantly, the whitening of the black musical continuum during the swing era is spoken of as a tendency away from process toward artifactuality. Chapter 10 of *Blues People* is entitled "Swing – From Verb to Noun" ("Worship the verb," he says in "Hunting Is Not Those Heads . . . "), and at one point we read: "Beiderbecke's slight, reflective tone and impressionistic lyricism was the most impressive example of 'the artifact given expression' in jazz" (BP, 154).

These ideas concerning process are important to understanding the synonymy of blackness with spirituality during Baraka's nationalist phase. Having come to see artifact worship, a preoccupation with *things*, as the dominant characteristic of the Western mind, he sees the prominence of the African and the Afro-American in the more spiritual, "nonmaterial" areas of music, dance, and religion as the sign of an opposing dispensation, one more in keeping with the reality of process and change. He comes to see black people as having privileged insight as well as input into the working out of alternative courses for the future. A poem that expresses this spiritualization and, to a lesser extent, ethnicization of "the will to change" is "History As Process":

> The thing, There As Speed, is God, as mingling
> possibility. The force, As simple future, what
>
> the freaky gipsies rolled through Europe
> on.
>
> (The soul.)

And at the end:

> . . . strumming my head
> for a living. Bankrupt utopia sez tell me
> no utopias. I will not listen. (Except the raw wind makes
> the hero's eyes close, and the tears that come out are real.)
> (BMP, 38)

The poem specifically names a dark-skinned, marginalized people whose music, flamenco, *cante jondo*, has been likened to the blues. The likeness is not lost on Baraka, as the lines "strumming my head / for a living" attest, recalling the guitar's prominence both in flamenco and in country blues.[21] The Gypsies' mobile, non-sedentary way of life exemplifies the openness to the unexpected, to process and possibility, the poem advocates.

III

During the sixties, assertions were often made to the effect that jazz groups provided glimpses into the future. What was meant by this was that black music – especially that of the sixties, with its heavy emphasis on individual freedom within a collectively improvised context – proposed a model social order, an ideal, even utopic balance between personal impulse and group demands. Cecil Taylor would write in the poem "Aqoueh R-Oyo": "Each Ensemble member as an active / community agent attempting a special / social function (human)."[22] The musicians' exhilaration at contributing to evolving musical orders rather than conforming to an already existing one seemed to anticipate the freedom of some future communalist ethic. In *Black Nationalism and the Revolution in Music*, Frank Kofsky quotes Malcolm X's reference to the black musician's improvisational ability as an index of what black people could do in the social, economic, and political realms "if given intellectual independence":

> He [the black person] can come up with a philosophy that nobody has heard of yet. He can invent a society, a social system, an economic system, a political system, that is different from anything that exists or has ever existed anywhere on this earth. He will improvise; he'll bring it from within himself.[23]

Bill Mathieu, in a review of Roscoe Mitchell's *Sound*, stresses a communalist impulse he hears in the music: "There is emerging the sense of the holy tribal family as the primal artistic source."[24] In a review of Lester Bowie's *Numbers 1 & 2* he returns to this point, quoting Carl Rogers at the review's beginning:

> The recent San Francisco *Oracle* quotes Carl Rogers in an article on the future: "Intensive group experience is perhaps the most significant social invention of this century. Whatever forms will proliferate out of these groups in the coming decades, men will discover new bases of intimacy which will be highly fulfilling. There will be experiments with ways in which a whole person will communicate himself to another whole person. We will discover that security resides not in hiding oneself, but in being more fully known."

He then goes on to speak of Bowie's music as an instance of such experimentation, remarking at some length on a tuning-in process to which he applies the term *agreement*:

> In this music I hear the musicians making themselves fully known to each other. But the means are new . . .

In the old days, musicians used themes, rhythmic and harmonic inventions, expressive coloring, as the language of group play. These aspects are still present, but other work is done in other ways. The most important of these let us call *agreement*. The quality of agreement has always been a factor in making group music. Now, however, this aspect has become the illuminating aesthetic of contemporary music.

How is the new agreement new?

First, the new agreement is not *about* the music. It happens *above* the music, and the music flows on down from it.

. . . It occurs beyond the pitches, and is a tuning-in process (but not to individual musicians). It's a condition of life, not art; its artistic expression comes only *after* its realization in the life of the musician.

The music on this record is the audible expression of the musicians' states of agreement. . . . Like Rogers said, whole persons are communicating themselves to other whole persons.[25]

Somewhat similarly, McCoy Tyner, the pianist for John Coltrane's quartet, once remarked, "Everyone plays his personal concept, and nobody tells anyone else what to do. It is surprisingly spontaneous, and there's a lot of give and take, for we all listen carefully to one another. From playing together, you get to know one another so well musically that you can anticipate."[26]

Baraka's writings on black music share with those of critics like Mathieu this tendency to discern inklings of an Edenic, open state or condition, though the terms of his particular sense of "agreement" are more insistently tribal or nationalist – that is, black. The music's communalist impulse is understood by him in terms of the synonymy of blackness with collectivity that characterizes the interview from which I've already quoted. Accordingly, he interprets the interest in and experimentation with collective improvisation among the newer musicians as a return to the African ethic, a departure from which he takes the growth of the jazz solo to have been:

Albert Ayler has talked about his music as a contemporary form of collective improvisation (Sun-Ra and John Coltrane are working in this area as well). Which is where our music was when we arrived on these shores, a collective expression. And to my mind, the *solo*, in the sense it came to be represented on these Western shores, and as first exemplified by Louis Armstrong, is very plain indication of the changed sensibility the West enforced.

The return to collective improvisations, which finally, the West-oriented, the whitened, say, is chaos, is the *all-force* put together,

and is what is wanted. Rather than accompaniment and a solo voice,
the miniature "thing" securing its "greatness." Which is where the
West is. (BM, 194–195)

Something like the observation that this openness – "a condition of life,
not art" – proceeds from an agreement that exists *above* the music also
gets made in terms of blackness (understood to be synonymous with
spirituality as well). These notions of black communality carry the weight
of a wished-for release from egocentricity, from the solipsism so rhap-
sodically lamented in poems like "The Death of Nick Charles," "*An
Agony. As Now*," or "A Guerrilla Handbook":

> Convinced
> of the man's image (since
> he will not look at substance
> other than his ego. . . . (DL, 66)

Since Baraka views egocentrism as the result of acculturation into whiteness, blackness represents a liberating concern for as well as openness to
others. The target of the black-musician-as-saboteur thus becomes the
Western cult of individualism. The music is an assault upon the ego.
"New Black Music," he writes in 1965, "is this: Find the self, then kill
it" (BM, 176). (There is a John Coltrane album entitled *Selflessness*,
appropriately enough.)

As if in preparation for the coming communalist ethic, Baraka's poems
during the early sixties involve practices comparable to the surrealist
dérèglement de sens as well as to the music's assault on the self.[27] Like the
surrealists – the analogy is enhanced by the fact that Baraka, as did Breton,
Aragon, and others, now espouses Communism – Baraka sought in these
poems a derangement of the ratiocinative ego. Like black surrealist Aimé
Césaire, moreover, he saw this derangement as a plunge into previously
repressed black ancestral strata. Césaire, in an interview conducted by
Haitian poet René Depestre in 1967, remarked on the writing of *Notebook
of A Return to My Native Land*:

> And my thinking followed these lines: Well then, if I apply the
> surrealist approach to my particular situation, I can summon up
> these unconscious forces. This, for me, was a call to Africa. I said
> to myself: it's true that superficially we are French, we bear the
> marks of French customs; we have been branded by Cartesian phi-
> losophy, by French rhetoric; but if we break with all that, if we
> plumb the depths, then what we will find is fundamentally black.[28]

The sense of "a plunge into the depths" is exactly what's evoked by
Baraka's early poem "The Bridge," though the poem relies on musical

terminology rather than surrealist imagery. The title refers to that portion of a jazz composition that leads the players back to the main melody line, referred to by musicians as the tune's "head." Baraka makes punning use of both terms, *bridge* and *head*, allowing his having "forgotten" the latter to suggest an experience of ego-loss, his having strayed beyond the former – "I can't see the bridge now, I've past / it" – to suggest, again, a lostness that results in drowning, absorption in "unmentionable black." The poem in full:

> I have forgotten the head
> of where I am. Here at the bridge. 2
> bars, down the street, seeming
> to wrap themselves around my fingers, the day,
> screams in me; pitiful like a little girl
> you sense will be dead before the winter
> is over.
>
> I can't see the bridge now, I've past
> it, its shadow, we drove through, headed out
> along the cold insensitive roads to what
> we wanted to call "ourselves."
> "How does the bridge go?" Even tho
> you find yourself in its length
>
> strung out along its breadth, waiting
> for the cold sun to tear out your eyes. Enamoured
> of its blues, spread out in the silk clubs of
> this autumn tunc. The changes are difficult, when
> you hear them, & know they are all in you, the chords
>
> of your disorder meddle with your would be disguises.
> Sifting in, down, upon your head, with the sun & the insects.
>
> (Late feeling) Way down till it barely, after that rush of
> wind & odor reflected from hills you have forgotten the color
> when you touch the water, & it closes, slowly, around your head.
>
> The bridge will be behind you, that music you know, that place,
> you feel when you look up to say, it is me, & I have forgotten,
> all the things, you told me to love, to try to understand, the
> bridge will stand, high up in the clouds & the light, & you,
>
> (when you have let the song run out) will be sliding through
> unmentionable black.[29]

On a strictly musical level "The Bridge" evokes the tendency toward defamiliarization among players of what was then – the poem was written sometime between 1957 and 1961 – beginning to be called "the new thing." This tendency involved a departure from – even outright abandonment of – bebop's reliance on the recurring chords referred to as "the changes" of a particular piece. Rather than basing their improvisations on the chord structure of the tune's head, the "new thingers" began to venture into areas not so patly related to the harmonics of the piece being played. To listeners accustomed to recurrent reminders of a tune's head in the form of the soloist's confinement to the changes, the new music seemed structureless and incoherent. These "nonchordal" excursions were often put down as unmelodic ("Save the Popular Song") or as evidence of the musicians' confusion. The players were frequently said to sound *lost*. What Baraka does in "The Bridge" is make a poem of this charge – "I have forgotten the head / of where I am" – making this "confusion" suggest a descent into the black subconscious, into "unmentionable black." "The Bridge" is still, however, a poem that *refers* to rather than *enacts* the sort of derangement I have been discussing. We find in it very little of the "difficulty in focusing on its controlling insights" M.L. Rosenthal sees as the characteristic defect in Baraka's first two books of poems.[30] The poem's "controlling" musical conceit remains very much in view throughout.

Rosenthal, as have others, remarks on "the structural similarity of some of its [*Preface to a Twenty Volume Suicide Note*'s] pieces to jazz improvisation" and observes: "The spiraling, dreaming movement of associations, spurts of energetic pursuit of melody and motifs, and driftings away of Jones's poems seem very much an expression of a new way of looking at things, and of a highly contemporary aesthetic, of a very promising sort."[31] He fails, however, to appreciate the connection between this "jazz" aesthetic and the "difficulty in focusing" he finds so disappointing. This "difficulty" is not so much a defect as a principled outgrowth of the African aesthetic underlying black music and Baraka's poetry. In *Blues People* Baraka quotes a passage from Ernest Borneman's "The Roots of Jazz" that is worth quoting again, a passage that ventures a description of the African aesthetic in language and music:

> While the whole European tradition strives for regularity – of pitch, of time, of timbre and of vibrato – the African tradition strives precisely for the negation of these elements. In language, the African tradition aims at circumlocution rather than at exact definition. The direct statement is considered crude and unimaginative; the veiling of all contents in ever-changing paraphrases is considered the criterion of intelligence and personality. In music, the same tendency towards obliquity and ellipsis is noticeable: no note is attacked straight; the voice or instrument always approaches it from above

or below, plays around the implied pitch without ever remaining any length of time, and departs from it without ever having committed itself to a single meaning. The timbre is veiled and paraphrased by constantly changing vibrato, tremolo and overtone effects. The timing and accentuation, finally, are not *stated*, but *implied* or *suggested*. The denying or withholding of all signposts. (BP, 31)

In the course of his liner notes to Archie Shepp's *Four for Trane*, Baraka applauds a certain "tendency towards obliquity" in the playing of altoist John Tchicai (whose solos he elsewhere describes as "metal poems"): "John Tchicai's solo on 'Rufus' comes back to me again. It slides away from the proposed" (BM, 160).

Baraka's poems, especially those in *The Dead Lecturer*, likewise tend to slide away from the proposed, to refuse to commit themselves to any single meaning. The beginning of "The Measure of Memory (The Navigator," for example, leads one to expect some sort of theodicy (if the existence of evil is that to which "The presence of good" is the "answer"), but by the second line conceptualization has given way to a stream of images the relationship or relevance of which to the poem's opening assertion is nowhere made explicit:

> The presence of good
> is its answer (at the curb
> the dead white verb, horse
> breathing white steam
> in the air)
> > Leaving, into the clocks
> sad lovely lady fixed by words
> her man
> her rest
> her fingers
> her wooden house
> set against the rocks
> of our nation's
> enterprise.

The second stanza follows from the first – in the sense of being logically or thematically related – only in that its image of disappearance echoes that of "leaving" in the poem's sixth line:

> That we disappear
> to dance, and dance
> when we do,
> badly.

The third stanza follows from the second in that it continues to describe what "we" do, but the discontinuity between it and the fourth stanza is not only tolerated by Baraka but accentuated by the double line he inserts between them:

> And wield sentiment
> like flesh
> like the dumb man's voice
> like the cold environment
> of need. Or despair, a trumpet
> with poison mouthpiece, blind player,
> at the garden of least discernment; I
> stagger, and remember / my own terrible
> blankness and lies.

> The boat's prow angled at the sun
> Stiff foam and an invisible cargo
> of captains. I buy injury, and decide
> the nature of silence. Lines and speed
> decay in my voice. (DL, 40–41)

The image of the boat in this final stanza recalls the word *navigator* in the poem's title, but what does it or any of the poem's other images and assertions have to do with the proposition that "the presence of good / is its answer?" The connective is neither logic nor discourse, but the poet's voice. Adhering to and putting into practice Olson's *dictum* that "in any given poem always, always one perception must must must MOVE, INSTANTER, ON ANOTHER,"[32] the poem has a mercurial, evanescent quality, as though it sought to assassinate any expectations of traceable argument or logical flow. This is exactly the quality Baraka praises in Shepp's "Rufus," going on in the liner notes to *Four for Trane* to speak of the music in terms more commonly applied to poems:

> But Archie's tune "Rufus" moved me most (although they are all so good, so deep, so satisfying). "Rufus" makes its "changes" faster. *Changes* here meaning, as younger musicians use that word to mean "modulations," what I mean when I say *image*. They change very quickly. The mind, moving. (BM, 160)

The mind, moving. Poems like "The Measure of Memory (The Navigator" seek to circumvent stasis, to be true to the mobility of thought, perception and the play of unconscious forces. Their "tendency towards obliquity" is a gesture that pushes the limits of what we take to be meaningful. "Poetry aims at difficult meanings," Baraka writes. "Meanings not already catered to. Poetry aims at reviving, say, a sense of meaning, or meaning's possibility and ubiquitousness" (BMP, 41).

This gesture proceeds in part from an anti-rationalist feeling that is also anti-Western, a conviction that implicates Western rationality in a range of exclusionary practices – not only epistemic but political (racism, class oppression, colonialism), exclusions in one realm complicit with those in the other. The dreamish, arational quality of Baraka's poems is of a piece with his contempt for the confusion of rationality with rationalization ("Bankrupt utopia sez tell me / no utopias"). Hence his espousal of "insanity," the ultimate irrationality, in the form of a black dadaistic uprising in the poem "BLACK DADA NIHILISMUS" and in the essay "Philistinism and the Negro Writer." In the latter he remarks:

> For myself, I aspire to the craziness of all honest men, that is, the craziness that will make a man keep talking even after everyone else says he shouldn't. Perhaps one way Negroes could force institutionalized dishonesty to crumble, and its apologizers to break and run, would be to turn crazy, to bring out a little American Dada, Ornette Coleman style, and chase these perverts into the ocean where they belong.[33]

The mention of Ornette Coleman is no haphazard one, but fits into a consistent ethnomusicological scheme that views Western musical theory and practice as manifestations of a rationalist ethic. Ortiz Walton, in his essay "A Comparative Analysis of the African and the Western Aesthetics," comments: "Bach completed the process of rationalizing the scale by tempering it."[34] Similarly, Baraka finds the most striking illustration of this rationalist bent in the diatonic tempered scale, making pointed use of the term *tempered*'s extra-musical connotations. The practice among black musicians such as Coleman of interjecting shrieks, slurs, growls, groans, moans, and other illegitimate "notes" into their playing he hears as a rejection of the Western worship of reason:

> the Eastern Colored peoples' music demands, at least, that many many half, quarter, etc. tones be sounded, implied, hummed, slurred, that the whole sound of a life get in . . . no matter the "precision" the Europeans claim with their "reasonable" scale which will get only the sounds of an order and reason that patently deny most colored peoples the right to exist . . . The Black musicians who know about the European tempered scale (Mind) no longer want it . . . (BM, 194, 199)

This rejection creates room for feeling, allowing more uninhibitedly emotional statements. "Music should make you *feel* . . . the point of living seems to me [to be] to get at your actual feelings, as, say, these musicians want always to get to theirs. If you can find out who you are ... then you can find out what you feel. Because we *are* our feelings, or our lack of them" (BM, 160–161).

At its worst, Baraka's praise for the emotively expressive veers towards the anti-intellectualism – which, coming from an intellectual, sounds rather lame – of pieces like "New-Sense," in which he sets up an opposition between the expressive and the reflective:

> The thinkers try. The extremists, Confucius says, shooting past the mark. But the straight ahead people, who think when that's what's called for, who don't when they don't have to. Not the Hamlet burden, which is white bullshit, to always be weighing and measuring and analyzing, and reflecting. The reflective vs. the expressive. Mahler vs. Martha and the Vandellas. It's not even an interesting battle. (T, 96)

In its best aspects this anti-intellectualism is not so much a repudiation of thought as an effort to rethink, to as it were *un*think the perversions of thought endemic to an unjust social order – rationalization, "institutionalized dishonesty" and so forth. The anti-reflective position, that is, having been arrived at by way of reflection, represents an instance of dialectical thinking. Fredric Jameson describes two contrary but complementary components of dialectical thinking, the second of which applies to Baraka's celebration of the nonreflective:

> when common sense predominates and characterizes our normal everyday mental atmosphere, dialectical thinking presents itself as the perversely hairsplitting, as the overelaborate and the oversubtle, reminding us that the self-evident draws its force from hosts of buried presuppositions. When, on the other hand, after the fashion of intellectuals, we begin to work our way up through a series of abstractions, each one progressively further and further away from the real itself, pervaded as we do so by an uneasy suspicion that the whole teetering construction stands as a monument not to new laws of nature, but rather to the rules of some private mental hobby, then dialectical thought comes as a brutal rupture, as a cutting of the knots that restores us suddenly to the grossest truths, to facts as unpleasantly common as common sense itself. Indeed, these two apparently antithetical effects of dialectical awareness largely correspond ... to the respective dialectics of Hegelianism and Marxism.[35]

An ongoing oscillation between these two impulses – or two alternate modes of a single impulse – makes for the characteristic unrest of Baraka's thought. The unrest itself bespeaks a desire to transcend conditionality, the very desire whose futility the poem "Jitterbugs" points out, illustrating the materialist branch of dialectical thought:

> The imperfection of the world
> is a burden, if you know it, think
> about it, at all. Look up in the sky
> wishing you were free, placed so terribly
> in time, mind out among new stars, working
> propositions, and not this planet where you
> cant go anywhere without an awareness of the hurt
> the white man has put on the people. Any people. You
> cant escape, there's no where to go. They have made
> this star unsafe, and this age, primitive, though yr mind
> is somewhere else, your ass aint. (BMP, 92)

This repudiation comes of Baraka's desire for some such transcendence – or, if not transcendence, room at least in which to challenge the conditions whose limits one cannot escape.

The obliquity, the sliding away from the proposed we find in many of Baraka's poems ("Jitterbugs" is not one of them) complies with a fugitive, perhaps idealist impulse, as though "the mind, moving" might, if not outmaneuver such constraints, at least register the need or desire to do so. Such obliquity, such would-be escape, betrays a sense of the world as determined and conditioned, meaning as determined and conditioned, what can be said or thought as well as what can be done hemmed in by prohibitions. Obliquity or angularity (a word used frequently in reference to the music of Thelonious Monk, Andrew Hill, Eric Dolphy, and others) challenges the epistemic order whose constraints it implicitly brings to light. This it does by insisting upon the partial, provisional character of any proposition or predication, by advancing a vigilant sense of any reign or regime of truth as susceptible to qualification. It thus calls into question the order by which it is otherwise conditioned on the basis of conditionality itself. Baraka hears a spirit of interrogation and discontent in the most moving of black music, especially that of John Coltrane, whom he calls "the heaviest spirit." Of the version of Billy Eckstine's "I Want to Talk about You" on the *Coltrane Live at Birdland* album he writes:

> instead of the simplistic though touching note-for-note replay of the ballad's line, on this performance each note is tested, given a slight tremolo or emotional vibrato (note to chord to scale reference), which makes it seem as if each one of the notes is given the possibility of "infinite" qualification, i.e., scalar or chordal expansion . . . threatening us with those "sheets of sound," but also prov-

ing that the ballad as it was written was only the beginning of the story. (BM, 66)

A similar "testing" can be heard in many of Baraka's poems, giving them a hesitant, stuttering quality suggestive of a discomfort with any pretense of definitive statement. What this "testing" projects is a world of uncertainties and redefined possibilities, a world of shifting, unsettled boundaries in which any gesture toward definition is unavoidably tentative, self-conscious, and subject to revision. This "uncertainty principle" often takes the rather obvious form of a preponderance of questions, as in "The Clearing," where repetitions of and variations upon the questions "Where are the beasts?," "What bird makes that noise?," "Were you singing?," and "What song is that?" occur throughout:

> Your voice down the hall. Are
> you singing? A shadow song
> we lock our movement
> in. Were you singing?
> down the hall. White plaster
> on the walls, our fingers
> leave their marks, on
> the dust, or tearing
> the wall away. Were you
> singing? What song
> was that? (TVSN, 30)

Another characteristic use of repetition has much the same effect. While not a repetition of outright questions as in "The Clearing," the repetition of such phrases as "or pain," "the yes," and "flesh or soul" in "*An Agony. As Now.*" suggests a state of astonishment if not one of confusion. Each repetition, followed by a staccato burst of imaged evocation, gives the sense of wrestling with definition, a sense of anxiety regarding the possibility of arriving at a stable sense of what these phrases mean:

> It can be pain. (As now, as all his
> flesh hurts me.) It can be that. Or
> pain. As when she ran from me into
> that forest.
>   Or pain, the mind
> silver spiraled whirled against the
> sun, higher than even old men thought
> God would be. Or pain. And the other. The
> *yes.* (Inside his books, his fingers. They

are withered yellow flowers and were never
beautiful.) The yes. You will, lost soul, say
"beauty." Beauty, practiced, as the tree. The
slow river. A white sun in its wet sentences.
Or, the cold men in their gale. Ecstasy. Flesh
or soul. The yes. (Their robes blown. Their bowls
empty. They chant at my heels, not at yours.) Flesh
or soul, as corrupt. Where the answer moves too quickly.
Where the God is a self, after all. (DL, 15–16)

Something of a stumbling or a stuttering effect results. The sense of
encountering obstruction or of being caught in a rut is heightened by
the dead-end options – the word *or* occurs twelve times in the poem –
created by posing the same word as an alternative to itself ("Or pain...
Or pain... Or pain"). This effect is a salient feature of the playing of
those black musicians Baraka most admires. (Listen, for example, to
Sonny Rollins's "Green Dolphin Street," Coltrane's "Amen," or John
Tchicai's "Everything Happens to Me."[36]) In some poems, in fact, the
use of repetition is almost purely musical, in that sound seems to take
precedence over sense:

> say day lay day may fay come some bum'll
> take break jake make fake lay day some bum'll
> say day came break snow mo whores red said they'd
> lay day in my in fay bed to make bread for jake
> limpin in the hall with quiverin stick (BMP, 169)

Another statement Baraka has made about Coltrane can be applied to
such gestures as these:

> One night he played the head of "Confirmation" over and over
> again, about twenty times, and that was his solo. It was as if he
> wanted to take that melody apart and play out each of its chords
> as a separate improvisational challenge. And while it was a mar-
> velous thing to hear and see, it was also more than a little fright-
> ening; *like watching a grown man learning to speak* . . . and I think that's
> just what was happening. (BM, 59; emphasis added)

Baraka too, in such instances as those we've just addressed, seems to
have gone back to the beginning, to be learning to speak or relearning
to speak – *un*learning modes of speech that impede the speech he is
reaching toward.

IV

*What is encumbered sings to
change its meaty box. The dirt
is full of music.*

"OK Shoot!"[37]

Black music is the meeting ground for two contending forces in Baraka's thought. An acknowledgment, on the one hand, of the importance to life and art of the contingent manifests itself in the sociological orientation of *Blues People* and much of *Black Music*. On the other hand, something like a mystic's respect for the other-worldly aspirations the music so often expresses both informs many of the essays in *Black Music* and accounts for a drive toward indeterminacy in Baraka's poems. Black music, owing to a liminality that situates it somewhere between the reality away from which it recoils and the ideal toward which it aspires (and thereby makes it suggestive of both), is the appropriate unifying focus for these two forms of attention. While the poems aspire to the apparent conditionlessness of the music, *Blues People* and *Black Music* have to do with the dialectical attachment of that conditionlessness to specific social, economic, and political conditions. The music, Baraka goes so far as to say, is both conditioned and unconditioned, "harnessed and not harnessed":

> The hard, driving shouting of James Brown identifies a place and image in America. A people and an energy, harnessed and not harnessed by America. JB is straight out, open, and speaking from the most deeply religious people on this continent.
>
> The energy is harnessed because what JB does has to go down in a system governed by "aliens," and he will probably never become, say, as wealthy, etc., that is he will never reap the *material* benefits that several bunches of white folks will, from his own efforts. But the will of the expression transcends the physical-mental "material," finally alien system-world it has to go through to allow any "benefits" in it. Because the will of the expression is spiritual, and as such it must transcend its mineral, vegetable, animal, environment. (BM, 185)

And of the more esoteric "new thing" he remarks: "The new music began by calling itself 'free,' and this is social and is in direct commentary on the scene it appears in. Once free, it is spiritual. But it is soulful before, after, any time, anyway. And the spiritual and free and soulful must mingle with the practical, as practical, as existent, anywhere" (BM, 193).

Baraka's poetry, like the new music, began by calling itself "free."
"MY POETRY," he wrote in 1959, "is whatever I think I am . . . I CAN
BE ANYTHING I CAN . . . I *must* be completely free to do just what I
want, in the poem."[38] This declaration of poetic freedom is likewise
social, a commentary on the context in which it is made. So assertive
an espousal of poetic freedom suggests the absence of such freedom
outside of poems. It may have been this absence Baraka had in mind in
1960 when he remarked: "I'm always aware, in anything I say, of the
'sociological configuration' – what it *means* sociologically. But it doesn't
have anything to do with what I'm writing at the time."[39] He seems at
this point to have believed in poetry as an actual, though fleeting, transcendence of material constraints, yet only a few years later he insists in
"Green Lantern's Solo":

> . . . Can you understand
> that nothing is free! Even the floating strangeness of the poet's
>   head
> the crafted visions of the intellect, *named, controlled*, beat and
>   erected
> to work, and struggle under the heavy fingers of art. (DL, 68)

He not only discerns the "sociological configuration" from which the
freedom-thrusts of black music emerge, but comes to acknowledge the
contingencies his poetry's obliquity seeks to deflect.[40] In fact, the poems
become increasingly concerned with explicit statements regarding these
contingencies, creating a tension between such directness and any attempts to "slide away from the proposed." Such attempts all but disappear from the poems of the early seventies, poems such as those in *It's
Nation Time*, poems like "Afrikan Revolution":

> We are for world progress. Be conscious of your
> life! We need food. We need homes; good
> housing – not shacks. Let only people who want to
> live in roach gyms live in roach gyms
> We do not want to live with roaches. Let
> Nixon live with roaches if he wants to. He
> is closer to a roach. What is the difference
> between Nixon and a roach?
> Death to bad housing
> Death to no work
> We need work. We need education. . . . [41]

This contentment with the explicit and the sloganistic, though inconsistent with "the denying or withholding of all signposts" Borneman posits,

articulates the message, the "enraged sociologies" (T, 77) Baraka hears in black music.

The poems in *Hard Facts* appear to signal an arrest of this trend toward utter directness, a return to the blend of the explicit with the oblique characteristic of *Black Magic*, a work in which one finds statements as straightforward as "President Johnson / is a mass murderer" (BMP, 93) or "The white man / at best / is corny" (BMP, 162), along with images as indecipherable as that of "a black toe sewn in their throats" (BMP, 154). The poems in *Hard Facts* are generously laced with unambiguous sloganeering: "Fight for the dictatorship until it is reality. The dictatorship of the proletariat, the / absolute control of the state by the working class" (HF, 31). They also allow the warp of such lines as "In rag time, slanting / stick legs, with a pocket full of / toasted seaweed" (HF, 12). Baraka appears to be attempting an accord between the conflicting claims of the accessible and the esoteric ("the spiritual and free and soulful must mingle with the practical").[42] This is the synthesis he envisions a future black music achieving:

> But here is a theory stated just before. That what will come will be a *Unity Music*. The Black Music which is jazz and blues, religious and secular. Which is New Thing and Rhythm and Blues. The consciousness of social re-evaluation and rise, a social spiritualism. A mystical walk up the street to a new neighborhood where all the risen live. (BM, 210)

(Except the raw wind makes / the hero's eyes close, and the tears that come out are real.)

3

To Define an Ultimate Dimness

The Poetry of Clarence Major

The aesthetic underlying Clarence Major's poetry has to do with an ethic best expressed in Ralph Ellison's *Invisible Man*: "The mind that has conceived a plan of living must never lose sight of the chaos against which that pattern was conceived."[1] Technically as well as thematically, Major's poetry seeks to be some such bearing in mind of "chaos," of that which what he calls "control versions of any / coherence"[2] attempt to exclude. Major has spoken of the influence of Freudian ideas on his work, particularly on his first two novels, *All-Night Visitors* and *NO*. It seems fair, then, to speak of the oppositional impulse in his poetry as a gesture on behalf of the repressed or ignored areas of experience and awareness, on behalf of civilization's discontents. Major is explicit about his own discontent with Christianity in particular, a prime contributor to the repressiveness of Western civilization:

> Christianity is something with which I have been at war almost all my life. When I was a kid I believed the things I was told about God and the devil. . . . These feelings about Christianity are in my work because I agonized with these things in my own experience of growing up, these problems of good and evil and sex. I think that's why there's so much sex in *All-Night Visitors*. . . . Christianity's view toward sex exists because of the great self-hatred that's so embedded in Christian teaching. Look at St. Paul's doctrine of Original Sin. I can see it in everything around us: sex is something that's nasty and something to hide. *All-Night Visitors* was a novel I had to write in order to come to terms with my own body. I also wanted to deal with the other body functions. In *NO* I was trying to exploit all the most sacred taboos in this culture, not just sexual taboos, but those related to the private functions of the body and that's where they all seem to center.[3]

Such attitudes as these, I will be arguing in this essay, inform Major's poetry as well as his novels. Before attending to the technical disruptions in his poems – their unconventional syntax, violations of grammar, typographical irregularities, and so forth – I will discuss how his iconoclastic impulse asserts itself thematically, how it figures in the content of the poems.

Major's quarrel with social strictures, especially where they take the form of Christian taboos and beliefs, is especially visible in three poems: "I Was," "Inscription for the 1st Baptist Church as It Comes Out on Saturday to Park," and "Holyghost Woman." "I Was," the shortest as well as easiest of the three, can be quoted in full:

> I said I was the night
> to try to be it. Magic
> a collision of black
>
> music, midnight allies
> when I said I screwed
> a girl, late at night.
>
> While a Baptist Church
> talked thru its loud
> speaker. I said it all. (SL, 60)

A relatively straightforward poem, it asserts Major's identification with those outlawed powers and proclivities symbolized by "the night" and proclaims his opposition to orthodox religiosity. The Baptist Church figures into the second of these poems as well, as its title indicates. The poem's final stanza suggests a connection between the hierarchical structure of the church (the "high up the totem pole" ascendancy of the speakers over the congregation) and what Freud calls an upward displacement of libido ("thorns of these ages of flesh," "their insensible love songs"):

> thru eerie smiles of irongray faces on wooden benches
> where the certain thorns of these ages of flesh held
> the bold, gentle speakers high up the totem pole safe
> from skepticism even reinforced by the practical paper-
> plates not to mention their insensible love songs[4]

"Holyghost Woman" equates the would-be transcendence of the body with a deceitful social mobility, an upward mobility hypocritically aimed at material comfort. Such words as *deception, commercial, material, flirting,* and *cajolery* help characterize Sister Patty Johnson's piety as a ploy used to exploit unsuspecting believers:

pre-
tending not to BE
not even flesh wind talked in her way of
looking transient: DECEPTION spoke out of
stride, the petty quiver
                    HIGHER!!!
coming on as flat devotion to a   :cause (SM, 19)

And at the end:

SO BLACK & SOFT gentle honeysweet trusting these
humble people I know so
well & ready to give to her, a woman called Sister
Patty Johnson (ex-slave to nothing but MOTION:)
        EVERYTHING: in the midday of silver leaves
from the moment of the front porch, EVERY-
THING they had to give she ATE, hard. (SM, 19)

In "Holyghost Woman" the persistence of appetite in someone who
pretends to have risen above it ("she ATE, hard") is pointed out in order
to undercut pretensions to bodilessness. Major's work invests heavily in
an insistence upon eating as a reminder of human animality, the ines-
capability of the demands of the bodily, appetitive side of human nature.
This is especially clear in *All-Night Visitors*:

I see this poor Mexican, with fifteen kids at home, dig, and here
he is at the Chicago stockyard, Department: BEEF KILL, he's at
the hatchet-door, it's a gate, not a door; and these dumb cows keep
coming . . . The blade comes down, and I am putting the tender,
well-done steak into my mouth, the acutely sensitive interior of
my mouth, almost throbbing with anticipation, I'm also sweating
and melancholy, the blade comes down, WHAM!!!! takes off the
cow's head very neatly . . . and I'm chewing now, chewing, grinding my teeth into the secreting meat. . . . I am as involved in this
savage activity as any animal of gluttony would be, the membraney
walls of myself reacting, responding to it.[5]

Major is particularly attentive to the violence to which human appetites
give rise, the profoundly simple fact that we kill in order to feed ourselves.

He tends to be impatient with any attempt to suppress recognition of this fact, to apply a cosmetic to what this says about being human. In "The General Sense of Self," he speaks of civilization's efforts at bolstering up the human at the expense of the animal, rationalizing human behavior and motivation, as mere "excuses":

> soaked in repressed rhythms
> our life myths
> are sunk in the useless riddle of
> the emptiest excuses
>
> these wornout and yet desperate artifacts
> not enhancing our humanity   yet remain
> imperishable as the idea of
> killing food   killing for dreams (SL, 25)

Particularly symptomatic of such "desperation" is the great emphasis American society places on hygiene and cosmetics, especially deodorants, air fresheners, and such – the various aids designed to neutralize or "civilize" the sense of smell, the most "primitive" of the senses. That odors having to do with the body and with bodily processes are the prime target of these aids further implicates them in a social ruse whose aim is a facade of bodilessness. Some of Major's poems address the fact that, as he says in "Self World," "these monsters, they use deodorant, / and brush their teeth / And do not know / anything . . . " (SL, 35). In "The Backyard Smelled of Deodorant and Talc," the perfumed air at a picnic signifies an attempt to disguise or domesticate the Id, to

> cut the uncertain   portion of the
>   self
>   back   into something be-
>   tween   smiles & popped cans . . . (SM, 11)

As do the "practical paper- / plates" in "Inscription to the 1st Baptist Church . . . ," the fact that the picnic is an occasion for eating belies any transcendence of the body or of appetite. The poem ends on a note suggesting that we "do not know / anything," that we comfortably presume to have risen above animality in an age of supermarkets and packaged meats, able to avoid coming face-to-face with the bloodshed which feeds us:

> we are summer meat, spirit eating baked
>   life summer   outdoor funeyes we have
> unwilling
>   some of us even unable to
> kill

what we digest
>   now in picnic (SM, 11)

"Conflict," another poem that makes use of the idea of perfumery or
deodorization as a suppression of the body, is significant in that it shows
Major appropriating one of society's preoccupations in order to critique
society, taking over the terms of that preoccupation and inverting their
customary usage. He confounds the floral scents of which soaps and
perfumes are made with the Baudelairean figure "flowers of evil." Viewing this suppression of "offensive" smells as an evil, he answers the
commercial image of a soap-cleansed and therefore lovable body with
the "fishy," genital odor of actual erotic love:

> the heart of sweetheart smelling
> Purex product beauty soap, dye drying
> me. Of love, the fishy odor of a boat (SM, 12)

The poem goes on to speak of another, perhaps more subtle, even immaterial odor:

> I remember, also   I knew a long time
>   the strong stink mortal insult of those
> big baggy men without sense
>   in their eyes
> standing on the trolley coming
>   where they were going. That against the
> nostrils. (SM, 12–13)

If these "baggy men" are junkies (as the word *baggy*, alongside the image
of eyes "without sense," suggests), this passage suggests that society's
castoffs carry the truly offensive odor of social ills and injustices, that
they are the "flowers" of society's evil. Major's attention, informed by
his awareness of how psychical exclusions underwrite social exclusions,
gravitates toward the marginal, unacknowledged, or outlawed realms of
society and of consciousness – toward, in fact, a redefinition of the terms
good and *evil*.

This redefinition results in a poem such as "The Unfaithful Wife: A
New Philosophy," in which the conventional morality by which the
adulterous woman would be condemned is questioned to the point of
being turned around. The poem celebrates rather than condemns the
woman's breach of that morality, while making fun of the husband's
conformity to it:

>   . . . well. seems
> coke hash grass anything was a
> bigger success than you tho you

> were a steady husband a good
> father a provider and a trusty
> pillow coke was adventure
>
> and he'd be gone next day for-
> ever which was
> the magic of it for her memory[6]

"The Exhibition" likewise applauds a woman's repudiation of conventional expectations, snidely addressing the woman's husband and again
citing an affection for cocaine as a measure of the woman's rebellion:
"think you knew all / along coke / had your wife in a / cultural corner."[7]
Major's identification with those who venture outside the closed circle
of conventional mores is further indicated by a poem like "Private Line"
(PL, 24), in which the speaker is the "other man" in an adulterous
triangle. Similarly, in "Kitchen Chair Poem #5" the love the speaker
professes for an apparent prostitute compares favorably with that which
he feels for his wife:

> . . . like this dude said who just came
> out of prison, giggling. Man I can't even afford
> to look, with my eyes, funny
> but how could i tell him
> her love had hit me the hardest? with my wife
> standing inside my skull. (SL, 22)

The stance of the outsider, the cynical observer, assumed in many of
Major's poems aims at unmasking conventional pretensions, unveiling
the unmentionable dysfunctions conventional ideals attempt to keep covered. "Possession and Madness," for example, touches upon the sado-
masochistic powerlusts that twist most male-female relationships, along
with the sexual impairment that often goes along with them:

> Sweet, she sees her
> self   taking him:
>   in, as he loses
>
> his vital force, in
>   HER
>
> She tells me this
>
>   How she feels in
> her mornings   why he
> stands under her
> nylon brush,   an

> unreciprocal thing:
> he, too, talks to me.
> says she can't come.
>   never has (PL, 23)

Similarly, attention tends to be sneeringly focused on exactly those facts of life that give the lie to collective as well as personal myths of well-being, as in "Motion Picture" (PL, 15), which reminds the affluent person it addresses of the racial oppression that supports that affluence; "Author of an Attitude" (PL, 12), which reminds the woman for whom it's intended of her egotism; or "Vietnam" (SL, 44), which confronts the complacency of the American way of life with the turmoil it promotes abroad.

II

The technical disruptions found in Major's poems are generated and underscored by the iconoclastic stance we see at work on a thematic level. Major's targets tend to be the institutionalized blindnesses that buttress consensus. That any definition of reality, any world view, is compounded of both seeing and not-seeing, blindness as well as vision, is the axiom from which his technical disruptions proceed. In a comment made in the course of an interview in 1973 he insisted upon the indefinability of reality, remarking to the interviewer, John O'Brien:

> I think that you should stop when you use the word "reality" because reality itself is very flexible and really has nothing to do with anything. I don't think that reality is a fixed point that theories adjust around. Reality is anything but a fixed point. (DF, 137)

This insistence upon the wrongness or unreality of any system or theory, coupled with the recognition that language itself is a system, a set of conventions and agreed-upon procedures fully implicated in the maintenance of certain assumptions about the world, leads to an assertion of the need for what Major calls "a new kind of creative brutality" (SM, 33) in one's approach to the use of that system. In the linguistic realm, just as in the ethical realm – as a poem like "The Unfaithful Wife" illustrates – breaks with conventional behavior are to be encouraged. One can call this impulse dissociative, as it seeks to dissociate itself from the seductions of a hegemonic world-view, to loosen the syntactical and grammatical threads that knit that world-view together. Robert Kelly, in the "prefix" to The Mill of Particulars, quotes a passage that articulates the intent of this impulse: "Through manipulation and derangement of ordinary language (parole), the conditioned world is changed, weakened in its associative links, its power to hold an unconscious world-view (consensus) together."[8]

To question language's access to reality, its claims to being intimate with anything other than its own occasion – to regard it, that is, as an essentially self-appointing *arrangement* of correspondences, projected onto in order to be retrieved from the world or reality it thereby claims to be reporting – is to have already begun the work of dissociation. "All words are lies," Major comments, "when they, in any arrangement, pretend to be other than the arrangement they make" (DF, 126–127). The referentiality of language thus undermined, "meaning", that peculiarly linguistic imposition upon the world, is viewed as affording no guarantee of accurate insights into actual relations in the non-linguistic world. It provides an assurance of certain rules of order having been complied with, certain maneuvers known as grammar having been successfully completed, but possibly nothing more. To the extent that the ordinary notion of "meaning" reifies the successful passage through permissible channels, thereby elevating the skillful negotiation of the grammar's resistances to the status of truth, it entails another eclipse of reality by convention. For this reason, Major, in "Dismal Moment, passing," implicates "meaning" in the "laundering" of reality of which, as we've seen, hygiene, cosmetics, and sexual repression are other examples:

> . . . I think of my mother when I think
> of nature, her beliefs. Those lies, in space
> hanging there to arrange
> human minds like suffixes to structures,
> like societies. Or meaning like a sheet flapping
> on a back porch, people might still
> wash things, hang them up to dry. . . . (SM, 9)

Two of Major'a poems address language's – and therefore poetry's – presumptions to be about things outside itself ("about" both in the sense of having those things as its subject matter and of being "on all sides" of them, having them covered or contained). "Beast: a new song" offers the figure of a tiger imprisoned in the "cage" of language, a prisoner of the "captions" or words imposed upon it by humans:

> tiger pacing on unable to capsize
> his direction trapped in minds
> of human captions labor of his
> sway up down thru absolute by
> absolute in absolute beyond
> even the absolute cage language
> of this absolute song. (SM, 32)

Given the Freudian insistence of so much of Major's work, it is hard not to think of this tiger as representing repressed animal instincts from which society attempts to protect itself. Again, as in "Dismal Moment, passing," Major notes the role language plays in this repression. In "My Child," the pre-linguistic, pre-definitional, pre-taxonomic *innocence* this animal world suggests is represented by childhood. Major cautions himself against the presumption of making the child his subject (of *subjecting* her, placing her under his own control, as well as of making reference to her as subject matter). He reminds himself of her autonomy, that she exists independently of both him and the poem, that she does not need them:

> her curls, like black sparkling things
> out of the interruptions of music or
> endemic structure of just things, are simply
> there, not even needing this poem, nor
> me: a mirror, coming in my love to what I vainly
> interpret as some vague property, a shadow of my-
> self... (SL, 10)

The end of the poem complies with this warning, honoring the caveat the poet issues himself by abruptly falling silent:

> ... her 3 year old rendition of the world is
> not inferior to anybody's, her play accepts
> the debt of herself, the simple undefined reality
> of this − .(SL, 10)

The reader is made to feel the indefinability, the unwordedness of certain aspects of the world. The poem deliberately draws a blank at the end, short-circuits its own propositionality in order to be consistent with its self-critique, to desist from its infringement on the child's wordless "being-there."

While acknowledging the ability of words, by way of agreed-upon, prearranged equations, to conjure impressions of the physical world, Major defines his intention as one of *occupying* rather than projecting outward from the "arrangedness" or arbitrariness of language, thereby calling attention to that arbitrariness as a world, a form of life even, peculiar to itself: "What I try to do is achieve a clear and solid mass of arrangements, an entity, that passes for nothing   except flashes of scenes and impressions we all know − much outside the particular shape of its own 'life' " (DF, 127). Habit and familiarization tend to efface the arbitrariness of conventional arrangements, to render the fact of their having been arranged more and more transparent. In order to overcome as well as critique this tendency, Major strives for highly idiosyncratic

arrangements, their idiosyncrasies – grammatical, syntactical, and typographical – not only defying convention but serving to make their
"arrangedness" harder to overlook or to take for granted; indeed, blatant.
An example:

> getting to her
> even in the frustrated riddle
> of technology
> :that (   ) theoretically
> protects her in
> her
> !inscrutable "history" (SL, 67)

This passage, with its variable margins and its idiosyncratic punctuation
(the colon and the exclamation mark placed at the beginning of their
respective lines, the empty parentheses, the absence of punctuation in
places we'd normally expect it), is typical of Major's work. Poems such
as "Float Up" go even further in the direction of typographical peculiarity, certain words or entire lines being printed in italics, others totally
in upper-case letters, others in boldface. An apparently capricious use of
punctuation – in this instance, parentheses, colon, slash, exclamation
mark, and comma – can again be noted:

> my EYE
>
> knows the TEAR-STAINED (face
>
> my) *sister*
>
> BE: HIND   /Glass
>
> a **moving!** window
>
> **going carefully along tracks**
>
> AWAY, to a kind of unreal protection (SM, 59)

Here we have an attempt to raise arbitrariness to the level of an ethic.
Charles Olson once remarked: "There's no artificial way to be arbitrary.
There's only one way – moral."[9] Similarly, Amiri Baraka: "The point
of life is that it is arbitrary, except in its basest forms. Arbitrariness, or
self-imposed meaning, is the only thing worth living for."[10]
   The "morality" of these gestures, their honesty, consists of an open
display of the willfulness or whimsicality that brings them into being.
They bring to the surface the arbitrariness more conventional procedures
suppress. Rather than abide by a deceptively referential transparency –
a presumably natural correspondence between words and things whereby
we look through but not *at* language – these gestures insist upon a certain

density, the opaqueness of a network of signs that more likely block than facilitate access to an "outside" world. The dredging up of this density requires that discourse – that set of rails meant to insure the smooth running to and fro of acceptable predications – and, along with it, its "lubricants," the rules of grammar, syntax, and semantics, be either jammed or dissected. In Major's work both things are done, the first as a way of undoing discourse's claim to thoroughness, the second its pretensions to continuity. By dissection I mean the practice of interrupting or cutting up the flow of an utterance by the insertion of periods, commas, colons, and other such marks of punctuation where one doesn't normally expect them:

> ceremonial objects decorate the
> *in*direct-lit D I N S of very
> smooth, people. i burn
> the invitations and stay into
> my. own touch. (CC, 16)

Or:

> . . . the deity
> growing inside
> her own. spirit, from
> a tiny spirit, place called
> Elquis. no
> one's heard of. . . (CC, 17)

The same thing is frequently done to individual words, as in the case of "BE:HIND" in the first-quoted "Float Up," and Major's use of the slash in such instances as "-o/p/ening" (SM, 39) and "clash/ ing" (SL, 26). The effect of this is the introduction of a choppy, staccato quality that thickens or "clouds" an otherwise limpid, possibly hypnotic flow. These interruptions or dissections serve as reminders of an inescapable segmentality, the discontinuity within as well as between words that calls to our attention the corresponding gap between words and things. This discontinuity, the space between words, is often visibly rendered on the page:

> My people are in centers, who
> see columns and touch   concrete. Cab
> drivers, heavy, . (SM, 70)

What I refer to as jamming works in somewhat the opposite way, run-on rather than halting, the effect of density it achieves being one of overload, interference. What it more specifically dismantles is the notion of the sentence as a completed thought, showing the sentence thus conceived to be at best an artificial holding action. This run-on tendency is an attempt to more accurately graph the quickness of thought, its disregard for grammatical obstructions. One of the more simple examples occurs in "The Design":

> ... I am tired of the
> apartment is dull a place but it comes
> to this each ... (SL, 11)

In this case the word *apartment* is the point at which two distinct predications – "I am tired of the apartment" and "The apartment is dull" – flow into one another, the single word serving as both the object of *tired* and the subject of *is*. The first predication is jammed or interfered with by the second in the sense that by the time we get to the concluding terms of the one we're also into the initial terms of the other: "the / apartment." Another example:

> If I were adequately armed
> And the kind of decision that makes
> Or breaks the settlement of
>   human arms and human galilees
> Would finally mean rejection of Myself (SL, 54)

Here the failure to follow the *if*/imperfect clause of the first line with a *then*/conditional clause gives the impression of nothing if not an incomplete, jammed, or cut-into thought. Since the fifth line begins with the conditional *would*, the obvious monkey wrench is the *And* of the second line. What it does is make the four lines it introduces seem to be more in collision with or an interruption of the first than would the word *then*, which our grammar has us prepared to hear as a smoother transition in this situation, a logical connective that honors the integrity of each clause.

Another example of jamming is "Overbreak," a poem that describes while enacting what it does. Its very title suggests a jammed, congested condition – "over" as in overload, "break" as in a breaking-point, bursting-point. The run-on quality is attested by the fact that the poem, consisting of 49 lines and 328 words, is presented as one long utterance that neither begins with a capitalized word nor ends with a period, punctuated almost exclusively by commas, the exceptions being a colon in one instance and a dash in two others. The poem makes use of no periods at all, indicating an absence of full stops. This run-on quality is referred to in the poem itself as a "verb" quality or a "verb quiver," an ongoingness that makes a point of the kinetic nature of the world and of consciousness, the primacy of flux: "there is a remarkable verb of / things" (SM, 16). The sense of dispersal and agitation to which this "quiver" gives rise is reinforced by the occurrence in the poem of such words as *infected, perturbation, cluttered, excitement, devilment, breakdown, delirium, reel, scattered*, and *thrills*. The "verb" quality makes for a murkiness or lack of definition, a promiscuous overlap of one thing with another which erases clear demarcations. This is said to give a more accurate, "more loyal" picture than do the discriminations language normally affords:

> ... there is
> a quality of which sharp contact is
>   the qualification, a remarkable verb quiver
> like some hypothesis, an
>   irony, a quest, a breakdown, out
> of delirium yet continues to enrich hedges
>   of the self, definition or cause to become
> somewhat more loyal – a description. A REEL OF DESCRIPTION
>   (SM, 16–17)

The poem earlier speaks of an attempt, which would appear to be its own, "to define an ultimate dimness," an attempt at "the wedding of the conscious and the unconscious" of which Major elsewhere speaks (DF, 127). The poem's concern with psychological as well as linguistic marginality is brought out by such phrases as "hedges / of the self" and "a sexual assessment baited / in the brain of riddles," as well as by the words *breakdown* and *delirium*. The poem ends with a passage whose density will not be reduced but whose concerns do appear to touch upon, however unsharply, the problematic nature of socially and linguistically upheld dichotomies, especially moral ones:

> a paradox of evil devouring the
> electricity of our flesh, the near-
>   ly acceptable tangibility of
> goodness ... (SM, 16)

Such dichotomies, having violated psychic wholeness, have to be violated in return:

> ... contact the energy myth taboo all
> this dimness beneath the rhythm, scattered and
>   colored, in social fires and thrills so
> slow they burn the skin tight around the brain, quick
>   dichotomy – good or evil & company, the
> sense of a world smashed and re-realized, over & like
>   nothing touchable in the particular land-
> or inscape we know, in all its contradictions saves
>   us yes saves us no here in this
> sustained instant, as we turn in a tacit polarity (SM, 17)

Major's poetry's technical disruptions, informed by a stance of estrangement and dissent, embody a desire to *un*speak – to silence, to make "tacit" – the polarities that normally govern behavior and thought.

III

I would like to venture a few reflections on the predicament of Major's poems, which is that of avant-garde aspirations generally. It is also the predicament of readers such as myself who are sympathetic to the poems. I should not let this essay end without having said that I find it difficult, problematic, to claim to enjoy these poems. This is not to say that I don't respond to such images as "nurtured waves" (SM, 16) or "absentminded earth" (SM, 61), to the grace of such a passage as

> ... My arms at my side. I
> will never be this or that old man feeding birds.
>   They scatter trash, they scatter
> the sound, the color it creates in the exact
>   time it takes to frighten them always
> caught my eye. . . . (SM, 15)

It is not to say that I don't respond to entire poems, such as "Air" (*SL*, 38), "Egyptians" (SL, 50), or the just-discussed "Overbreak." What I mean is that Major, as is evident in the poems' oppositional thrust, is not particularly concerned with providing enjoyment, nor, I would think, with being applauded as having done so. I'm not absolutely certain of this, of course. Perhaps he *is* so concerned. But part of what I see as his predicament is that he should not be. To begin a poem with the line "She knew more about me *than* let us say" (SL, 16) is to announce a desire to frustrate rather than appeal to the reader's expectations. Unless one likes asking the unanswered question " '*Than* let us say' what?" there is no particular enjoyment to be gotten from this. Nor is it irrelevant that the poem in which this occurs is called "Isolate" and tells of wanting to be alone:

> Here she was everything to me, after the crude
> Cramming of Nothing; but now
> I want isolation. I told her what.
> She said, then isolate motherfucker (SL, 16)

The stance of alienation from which the disruptions I have been discussing proceed makes for a problematic relationship between the work and its audience and between the poet and possible "fellow travellers" as well.

Without going so far as to reduce the poetry's attitudes and disruptions to an antisocial or nonconformist bent, to a pursuit of estrangement as an end in itself, it is possible to see how a desire for "isolation" can lead to a persistent flight from companionship or consensus – even nonconformist companionship or nonconformist consensus. In this regard it is instructive and intriguing to read Major's comments on the Beat movement in his essay "Eldridge Cleaver: And White Writers." Given the sorts of attitudes that recur throughout his work, one might expect Major to feel some degree of kinship or affinity with the Beats' celebration of unorthodoxy, rebellion, sexual freedom, and so forth. I share his impatience with their romanticization of "the Negro," with the inaccuracy of labels, with the popularization that eventually co-opted their stance of revolt, and with the crutch the sense of a "movement" can be used to provide, but I'm still surprised to come across the following:

> . . . the best poets critics novelists of these years worked outside the Beat circle. People like Margaret Randall, John Berryman, Walter Lowenfels, Kenneth Patchen, Gil Orlovitz, W. S. Merwin, Marvin Bell and Sandra Hochman. . . . (I like the deep roots of good poems in books by dudes like Galway Kinnell – who was never a bigmouth.) (DF, 109–111)

I'm not certain what the aesthetic by which these writers are judged "the best" has in common with that which informs a passage of his own such as:

> this rubbermetalglass mathematical mobile, Ford
>   outshining/ growing into distance / timing
>   oozing, discharging, trickling
>   BANG! !
>   (unconscious
>   CRASH! !
> death)   (SL, 63)

One cannot help feeling that one (if not both) of these passages amounts to an act of bad faith. Major's poetry, if on the basis of nothing more than the way it looks on the page, would appear to share more with the "New American Poetry," which he dismisses as "an illusion at sea" (DF, 108), than with that of those poets he designates "the best." Why so emphatic a dissociation from the very trends to which his own work is most related? A desire for "isolation"? He does tell us that "the weak ones need movement[s] always: they can't make it on their own" (DF, 110). So what are we to make of his membership in The Fiction Collective?

Major's is a persistent unrest, the discontent to which marginality gives rise. The pervasiveness of this air of uneasiness renders "enjoyment" beside the point – or, at the very least, subject to quotation marks. It also results in Freudian thought, with which Major's discontent so largely agrees, becoming a target of that discontent. Major remarked to John O'Brien:

> I regret . . . in my haphazard education my exposure to Freudian psychology because it has left its effect in my thinking. Since I finished *NO* I found myself weeding out so much of it. I can't reject it all because we live in a technological world where we have certain ways of dealing with reality. But that's one thing that I regret about *NO*. I noticed the Freudian influence there and it's very disturbing. That whole sensibility is probably present in my earlier work, too, and it's a sensibility that I want to forget. I don't want to get trapped in terminology. I worry that, despite the fact that *NO* came from the gut level, a large part of it seems to be caught in the sensibility of Freudian psychology. (DF, 137)

The susceptibility of his attitudes and opinions to systemization – Freudian, Beat, "New American," or whatever – to, indeed, the sort of intellectualization to which I have subjected them in this essay, is a fact that troubles Major's work. Attempting to free itself from the shackles of consensus and discursive thought, to get to the marrow of individual, instinctual impulse, it finds itself involved in a new discourse, a new consensus. The vigilance of its discontent, of a desire for "isolation" (a desire to be without precedent or peer), leads Major, in the poem "Conflict," to dismiss the importance of three forerunners of and possible influences on his stance of disaffection:

> air of stale milk, I was under
> the influence of power flow   the
>   mouth of the 3 flowers of evil
>
>   Rimbaud
>   Baudelaire
>   Verlaine)
>
> not myself here except I know
> (*I knew* beyond sense of the French
> decadents example
>
>   .   .   .
>
>   . . . I
>   claim that knowledge, outside the fragments
>   of V, B & R.. (SM, 12–13)

These lines provide another example of Major's insistence upon the primacy and radical honesty of individual experience, his feeling that "the only way to be revolutionary is to begin from one's deepest motivations" (DF, 108). That "one's deepest motivations" might have something in common with those of others can prove annoying, however, and Verlaine, Baudelaire, and Rimbaud have to be kept at a distance.

Major's poetry exhibits a certain refractoriness, as though it wanted to surround itself with "No Trespassing" signs. This quality seems related to a nostalgic, even narcissistic desire for something like the uncompromised naiveté of childhood. He writes of Richard Wright, for example:

> I try to imagine the type of work Richard Wright would have done had he developed into another type of person. As a child he wrote a story that was of "pure feeling." In his later work there was always some ideology behind everything. I like to play with the idea that original innocence might have saved him from many hallucinations had he been able to save it. (DF, 71)

The desire for a "gut" level of "pure feeling" and "original innocence" is a futile one, doomed to frustration if one is to work within language at all. What is language, after all, if not a social pact (an ideology), the basis, in fact, of all other social pacts? Even the dissociative assault on language is finally a testimony to its importance and power – is, quite simply, a *linguistic* assault on language. Baraka once wrote:

> A compromise
> would be silence. To shut up, even such risk
> as the proper placement
> of verbs and nouns. . . . [11]

But we are not much given to silence. A certain use of language that, in short-circuiting predication, approximates silence is as close as we get. The futility of its fight against language, against the omnivorousness of ideation, leads me to say of Major's poetry what he tells us John A. Williams said of *All-Night Visitors*. It too "gives off a kind of gentle helplessness and anger with no place to go" (DF, 135). To make more triumphant claims for such work is to miss its point.

4

The World-Poem in Microcosm
Robert Duncan's "The Continent"

===========

The drama of our time is the coming of all men into one fate, "the dream of everyone, everywhere."
                                    Robert Duncan, *The H.D. Book*

I

During an interview conducted by George Bowering and Robert Hogg in 1969, Robert Duncan remarked: "I'm always immensely conservative of everything, I want to keep the whole thing going"[1] – "the whole thing" being the retrospect yet ongoing integrity of both his own body of work and that of, as he elsewhere puts it, "the generations of poets that have likewise been dreamers of the Cosmos as Creation and Man as Creative Spirit," the larger Work of which his own is but a part. Duncan's "conservatism," his sense of himself as "not an experimentalist or an inventor, but a derivative poet,"[2] has caused him to acknowledge himself, sometimes a little defensively, as something of an anomaly among the Black Mountain poets: "Of the poets publisht in *Origin*, noticeably I'm the only one who would think of Edith Sitwell as a major poet and who frequently will be writing in the high Edith Sitwell manner. Edith Sitwell's notebooks had been one of the things that really expanded my mind and got me engaged with the Romantics" (I, n.p.). Or, similarly, in the course of his remarks to Ann Charters as to what Black Mountain was like when he arrived to teach there in 1956:

> Students at Black Mountain at that time would have, let's say, a library of ten books. They'd have the *Cantos*, *Paterson*, Charles' work and mine. . . . There'd be no Henry James, no Joyce. It was thought pretty wicked to read *Finnegans Wake*. Charles felt stronger than Pound about the betrayal of *Finnegan*. These books may have been in the library, but I'm not sure. The first entertainment I gave

at Black Mountain – because I knew how Charles felt about *Finnegan* – was to read it, and everybody turned up but Charles. No Virginia Woolf; she'd be thought of as genteel. There'd be Jung. That came from Charles, but it was temperamentally across the board. That meant no Freud.[3]

Pretty much from the beginning Duncan felt himself to be at odds with the insularity of the Black Mountain movement. Just as he'd begun by confronting the College with Joyce's outlawed *Wake*, he'd later, for example, insist that Michael Rumaker, then a student at the College, be required to read Henry James before receiving a degree.

The back cover of the first Australian edition of *The Venice Poem*, obviously seeking to relate Duncan's work to a British Commonwealth audience, quotes a reviewer in *The Times*: "If Olson gives us breadth, scale; then Duncan gives depth which goes way, way back down into tradition, the ultimately English tradition." It also quotes a review in *The Australian*: "Robert Duncan is the Shelley of our age." The unlikeliness of such comments being made about Paul Blackburn, Amiri Baraka, Robert Creeley, or Olson himself is one mark of Duncan's uniqueness within the movement with which he is most often associated. Many of Duncan's works and attitudes invest in and pay respect to established figures in the English literary canon – Milton, Hopkins, Shelley, Coleridge, and the Metaphysicals among others – to a degree that, given the sometimes anglophobic American-Adamism of his Black Mountain associates, borders on heresy. Poems like "From Richard Burton's *Anatomy of Melancholy*," "Variations upon Phrases from Milton's *The Reason of Church Government*," "Shelley's *Arethusa* set to new measures," "Variations on Two Dicta of William Blake," and those in *A Seventeenth Century Suite* have few, if any, counterparts in the work of other Black Mountain poets.

Duncan's amenability to the influence of the English tradition is simply one manifestation of the "conservatism" that at times makes him devil's advocate for a somewhat Eliotic "historical sense." In "Passages 24," written in 1965, in fact, he goes against the anti-Eliot backlash characteristic of post-War American poetics and acknowledges Eliot – whom Olson called "the reverend reverse"[4] – as one of his masters:

> and now that Eliot is dead, Williams and H.D. dead,
> Ezra alone of my old masters alive, let me
>   acknowledge Eliot was one of them, I was
> one of his, whose "History has many
>   cunning passages, contrived corridors"
> comes into the chrestomathy.[5]

Coming from a Black Mountain poet, this amounts to a confession. But the tradition or "historical sense" Duncan draws upon and thereby conserves is vastly more inclusive than Eliot's and in many crucial aspects not at all "ultimately English." His friendly relations with the English canon and his acknowledgment of Eliot don't indicate a conservatism so much as an inclusionist impulse. This impulse militates against the biases of received wisdoms and party lines, be they orthodox or heterodox, conservative or avant-garde.

Coexistent with Duncan's better known quarrels with conventional poetics and orthodox proprieties – in the essay "Ideas of the Meaning of Form," for example – has been a tendency to call into question or to apply a grain of salt to many of the pet pronouncements, *dicta*, and doxologies of the "New American Poetry" of which he is considered to be a part. Of Olson's insistence on open form he remarks: "I'm not going to take Charles's alternatives, I'm not going to take the closed form versus the open form because I want both, and I'll make open forms that have closed forms in them and closed forms that are open" (I, n.p.). And of Creeley's endlessly repeated assertion that his use of language is non-referential, that his writing has no subject: "Well, but then that's balderdash. His subject seems to be a very special kind of Creeley predicament."[6] The multidirectionality of Duncan's critical sense can be seen in the fact that while reading the interview from which this last remark is taken one comes across critiques and qualifications not only of poets like James Dickey, William Stafford, and Robert Bly but also of Creeley, Olson, Denise Levertov, and Allen Ginsberg:

> The whole thing has to have an architecture. It's got a character armor, to use the Reichian term, and in that I am identifiably Protestant. Ginsberg's melting down, or breaking down, and wanting to disappear, or Burroughs' tendency to the same effect, was very disturbing to me. Are we really going to dissolve all the boundaries? So I was in direct conflict. When we came to our poetry conference in Vancouver in 1963, I was frequently on the floor challenging Ginsberg's position. And a lot of it was concerning his position on the poem. Mine would be the Constructivist poem, the poem as a work of art, and I very well understood where Ginsberg was in that. I knew about the prohibition that you shouldn't *make* a poem from the *Zohar*. You should pour forth God's voices, and that I went exactly against. Fine, go ahead and pour forth that God voice, but let's distinguish that from the poem. A poem, for me, is a mystery in making. (TNAP, 66)

Likewise, Jerome Rothenberg and Robert Kelly's phrase "deep image" comes under fire: "Concerning deep image our critique and my witticism right away was: one inch deep, two feet deep, how deep? It's like, what is important and what trivial? In my sense of things, there is nothing trivial, so that everything has to have depth since it relates throughout" (TNAP, 70). This comment, like his explanation that he called himself "a poet, self-declared, manqué" in 1953 "not to deny the depths, but to affirm that the shallows too, and all our water-works, belonged to the sea,"[7] again brings to light Duncan's catholic, holistic, inclusionist aspirations. Ekbert Faas, the interviewer in this instance, notes this impulse when he remarks: "It seems to be one of the most important characteristics of your open form poetry and poetics that you try to integrate everything. You integrate rhetoric and you integrate closed form" (TNAP, 82). Duncan's poetics is open, then, in the sense of being, or at least seeking to be, inclusive. Or as he himself puts it: "As a matter of general principle I don't understand that anything in writing is prohibited" (TNAP, 60).

Duncan has taken an often critical look at not only his contemporaries but his predecessors as well, even those to whom he feels greatly indebted and from whom his own work, in part at least, derives. Even while considering himself one of "the sons of Pound and Williams" (Olson's phrase), he has been quick to acknowledge the biases and the limitations of both. Much of *The H.D. Book*, Duncan's massive work of ancestor-worship, has to do with shedding light on his forebears' blind spots, with looking askance at and holding himself apart from their particular exclusions. Thus, of the absence of Christ from Pound's work: "At the thought of Jesus, Pound has all the furious fanaticism of the Emperor Julian; he is a pagan fundamentalist. Aphrodite may appear to the poet, and even Kuanon, but not Mary; Helios and even Ra-Set may come into the poem, but not Christ."[8] He similarly criticizes Williams's " 'American' thing," anxious to dissociate Williams's "genius" – those aspects of Williams's work most conducive to and in accord with his own intents and aspirations – from Williams's American-Adamic sense of himself:

Picturing himself as defending something betrayed by Eliot, and by Pound in his admiration of Eliot, Williams posed against the internationalism of *The Waste Land* the authenticism of the American speech. . . . Against the cinematographic time-flux, he meant to take with a vengeance the camera eye of still photography, the locality in time. . . . At heart, Williams' genius as a poet lay not in the local condition, in the isolated percept, the "American" thing or speech, but in the heritage Eliot – Jacob to his Esau – had stolen from him, in the world-poem where the wives of an African chief, a red basalt grasshopper recalling Chapultepec, Toulouse-Lautrec, Madame Curie working the pitchblende, Sappho, and Peter

Brueghel were to enter in. *The Waste Land* had stolen a march on *Paterson*, but by the time the first volume of *Paterson* appeared twenty-four years later Williams had brought his early poem to a fullness that was to be a challenge to the poets to come as *The Waste Land* was not.[9]

Duncan's description of himself as simply a derivative poet is belied by the strikingly contentious character of his relationships to the poets, both present and past, from whom his work is derived. There is very little of the diffidence or passivity the word *derivative* suggests either about his pronouncements, about his poetics, or about his poems. The corrections and admonitions he offers in response to the attitudes and the works of others issue from a will not simply to be inclusive but to include *himself*, to make room for his own highly original, albeit syncretic, contribution: "... the aesthetics of Pound and Williams in their negative response to Whitman seem to me a regression in poetics. *Especially for me because it puts me in a threatened position*" (TNAP, 68; emphasis added).

II

"The Continent" is a poem that directly relates to and proceeds from these sorts of issues. The poem is the concluding piece in *Roots and Branches*, the book Duncan designates as a return to what he calls a rhetoric of Romantic elevation, a mode incorporating the rhapsodic, the elegiac, the fabulous, and so forth, "the high Edith Sitwell manner" of which his conversion to Olson's poetics had made him feel ashamed:

> ... noticeably it takes me some time to begin to bring back into my poetry without too much shame the old rhetoric I had of earlier forms. One of my reactions as I came along the line of this strong natural feeling we had in the fifties, that we were in a firmer esthetic and what was a cleaner and more meaningful form, was that I had quite a bit of shame about *Heavenly City, Earthly City* and I couldn't read it aloud any longer, and I never republished it until I came to admit, and admitting was not only admitting, it was seeing, yes, this is part of the whole. So that I guess in *Roots and Branches* you have a returning to a rhetoric of earlier form. (I, n.p.)

One of the factors making for his embarrassment would have been the impact upon the Black Mountain movement of Williams's insistence on the use of an American vernacular, of down-to-earth diction and of everyday patterns of speech. Duncan's impatience with Williams's " 'American' thing or speech," which he elsewhere in *The H.D. Book* calls "Williams's regular-guy voice," has much to do with the threat it posed to his more rhetorical bent. His sense of shame, that is, tends to mingle with a sense of defiance, just as he tends to be both inclusive and contentious at the same time. He tells, for example, of having been inspired by Williams's adverse reaction in the late forties to a group of poems of his, *Domestic Scenes*:

> When I wrote *Domestic Scenes* I kept making these poems I could send to Williams as a little homage or something; they were filled with domestic scenes, filled with things around like buses, and paraphernalia of the contemporary world. I sent them off to Williams, and oh, what a blast back I got about it; there was no American language in there. Of course I have never written in American language, nor did I ever in my whole life. But that letter was in itself an inspiration, because then with vengeance I wrote *Medieval Scenes*. I mean I just decided to write: Okay, no American language! I wrote it straight on, so those two sequences were a funny play around Williams. (I, n.p.)

The poems in *Medieval Scenes*, as the title suggests, revel "with vengeance" in precisely what Williams could rail against as anachronistic diction and outmoded lore.

I'm not sure Duncan ever really, even temporarily, left the rhetoric behind, but the poem in *Roots and Branches* that most overtly expresses his sense of having done so, and of thereby having it as something to which he could now return, is called "Returning to the Rhetoric of an Early Mode." The poem celebrates the greenness of an earth and a foliage-, flower-, and fruit-bearing tree that are both in fact its own rhetorical flourish:

> If I think of my element, it is not of fire,
> of ember and ash, but of earth,
> nor of man's travail and burden
> to work in the dirt, but of the abundance,
> the verdant rhetorical. Servant of the green,
> the Gardener of the Hesperides returns,
> sometime no more than pompos of the poem,
> a claim I made on some modal prince
> I thought I had seen so real he was mine
> received in the music-magic of Sitwell or of Stevens,
> robed round in sound, rich as a tree
> in full foliage of metaphor, flower and fruit. (RB,
>   89)

Such phrases as "the abundance,/the verdant rhetorical," "green panic," and "all verdant thought" are recalled by the invocation of the "mother of the Lady Verdure" in "The Continent," which begins:

> Under-
> earth currents, Gaia, Hannahanna,
> mother of the Lady Verdure
> all dresst in green
> her leafy graces, in margins
>
> the writ illumined, wreathed round
> with pomegranate
> split for in-betweens of jeweld hive
> red seed upon red seed,
> ripe peach, pear, apple cut
> to show the core,
>
> vine tendril into talon curls,
> faces in the fruit occur. (RB, 172)

Though the line here is considerably more stripped down than that of "Returning . . . " and its manner less rhetorical in that its thrust is more pictographic than declarative, its picture of plenitude, of cornucopic abundance, and its musicality hark back to the earlier poem. While "The Continent" isn't a rhetorical poem in the sense in which "Returning . . . " and the early poems in *The Years As Catches* are, it does have to do with and seeks to celebrate the dream-swollen world to which the more overtly rhetorical poems bear witness.

"The Continent" appears to be an attempt to include within the boundaries of the same poem both the fable- or myth-world of the earlier rhetoric and a here-and-now colloquialness worthy of Williams. One encounters the slanginess or hipness of "In Iowa they do not dig / the swarming locale," the ungrammatical Americanness of "They do not remember the body of / them waters," and the folksiness of "it's a caution / to see their faring." It is as though Duncan had set out, again with a vengeance, to make use of specifically American forms of speech. Much of the poem could in fact be called "a funny play around Williams," as Williams's work is blatantly alluded to at various points. Just as the phrase that brings Section I of the poem to a close, "against the / run to the mythic sea, the fabulous," recalls the title of Book IV of *Paterson*, "The Run to the Sea," the opening lines of Section II, with their description of Earth as "murmurer," bring to mind the phrase "Earth, the chatterer," also in *Paterson*.[10] Similarly, the final stanza of Section II echoes and alludes to Williams:

> I'm not so old but I can put
> the thought away, my foot
> before my foot,
> climbing the hill as if for rime

> my teeth are gnashing, and again
> the thought returns
> that we conquer life itself to live,
> survive what we are. (RB, 173)

With the phrase "my foot / before my foot," this passage recalls Williams's figure of walking or dancing, a figure he uses throughout *Paterson* or in such a poem as "Heel & Toe to the End" to speak of poetic meter. Its last three lines both echo ("the thought returns") and answer the following lines from *Paterson*:

> The thought returns: Why have I not
> but for imagined beauty where there is none
> or none available, long since
> put myself deliberately in the way of death? (P, 30–31)

The line midway through Section II, "a sparrow smasht upon the sidewalk," alludes to Williams's poem "The Sparrow," and the first few lines of Section III continue with the allusion. Williams describes the flattened bird as:

> a wisp of feathers
> flattened to the pavement,
> wings spread symmetrically
> as if in flight,
> the head gone,
> the black escutcheon of the breast
> undecipherable,
> an effigy of a sparrow,
> a dried wafer only[11]

From this Duncan derives:

> The head crusht sideways, the wings
> spread out
> as if embracing the sidewalk, too close
> for shadow,
> the immediate! (RB, 174)

Finally, the second half of Section III also alludes to Williams:

> How bright the sun
> surrounds them,
> and day by day they
> sun themselves
> turning

> a day's eye turning as the sun passes
> over head. (RB, 174)

This echoes Williams's lines in *Paterson*:

> It is all for
> pleasure . their feet . aimlessly
> wandering
>
> The "great beast" come to sun himself (P, 70).

But what exactly is Duncan doing with these allusions and derivations? It seems to me that he's doing a number of things: celebrating, having fun with, and even correcting or reclaiming Williams. The extent to which these allusions focus on *Paterson*, the work in which, Duncan argues, Williams the dreamer of the world-poem triumphs over Williams the feet-on-the-ground American realist, suggests an effort to recover Williams from the widely held sense of him as the down-to-earth, no-nonsense "regular-guy" of American poetry. Duncan's answer at the end of Section II to Williams's question "Why have I not . . . put myself . . . in the way of death?" echoes his own assertion in "Apprehensions," one of the earlier poems in *Roots and Branches*: "To survive we conquer life or must find / dream or vision" (RB, 36). "Apprehensions," a poem upon which "The Continent" in several ways relies, opens with the line "To open Night's eye that sleeps in what we know by Day" (RB, 30), a line that not only says a great deal about Duncan's intentions but also explains the phrase "day's eye" and the recurrence of the words *day* and *sun*. Section III of "The Continent," that is, allies Williams's demotic aspirations, his desire to be "of the people," with a daylit or sunlit sense of things, with a reality principle ("a day's eye" or "what we know by Day") that militates against dream, against vision, against "the fabulous" – against the "Night's eye" Duncan's rhetoric serves. The crushed sparrow, brought down to the ground and no longer capable of flight, symbolizes a shadowless and depthless immediacy of perception, while the exclamation "the immediate!" recalls Williams's use of that term to suggest a uniquely American stance. In his essay "The American Background," Williams writes:

> These transplanted men were at the same time pushing back a very necessary immediate knowledge of the land to be made theirs.
>
> *   *   *
>
> Franklin, coming down from New England, saw things in a different way from that of Virginia. His talent, primarily technical, with the bearing which all technical matters have upon the immediate, took him quite apart from his will in the right direction.

*   *   *

One might go on to develop the point . . . that the American addition to world culture will always be the "new," in opposition to
an "old" represented by Europe. But that isn't satisfactory. What
it is actually is something much deeper: a relation to the immediate
conditions of the matter in hand, and a determination to assert them
in opposition to all intermediate authority.[12]

As we have seen, however, Duncan's most approving sense of Williams dissociates him from "the great beast," from a one-sidedly sunlit
or daylit version of the world and from his self-declared " 'American'
thing." He sees him as a fellow "artist of the margin," and this marginality is a part of what he applauds. He could very easily be referring to
the inconclusive character of *Paterson*, to Williams's inability to confine
the poem to its original four-book scheme, when he writes in Section I:

> The artist of the margin
> works abundancies
>
> and sees the theme is much too big
> to cover all o'er, a decorative frieze
> out of earthly proportion to the page (RB, 172)

Yet "The Continent" is a poem that does resort to the theme of an
American ethic, though it does so only by way of Duncan's holding
himself apart from that ethic. In fact, he holds himself apart or "of the
margin" exactly on the basis of what, in large part owing to Williams,
has become a pet obsession for many American poets – the idea of locality.
Looking "east, east, east" from his birthplace and homeground, the San
Francisco Bay area, he writes of middle America:

> The mid-Western mind
> differs in essentials
> – another time zone.
> In Iowa they do not dig
> the swarming locale, this port of
> recall. There's no
> Buddhist temple in the mid-West town. (RB, 172-173)

Against the heartland insularity of the mid-West Duncan poses "the
swarming locale," the cosmopolitan heterogeneity of San Francisco, an
international port. The absorption in "the immediate!" that Williams
views as typically American and to which Section III of the poem alludes
is presented here as a case of American-Adamic amnesia. The mid-West's
lack of use for "this port of / recall," after being implicated in a spiritual

isolationism that has no use for Buddhism, is elaborated upon in the lines
that follow:

> Earth drains down the Old Man River and runs out
> in swamps and shallows of the Caribbean.
>
> They do not remember the body of
> 　　them waters
> but stand with feet upon the ground
> 　　against the
> run to the mythic sea, the fabulous. (RB, 173)

Here, then, is that characteristically "American," feet-on-the-ground
aversion to the myth-world to which Duncan's rhetoric inclines, an
aversion to "the mythic sea" recalling Williams's complex, contradictory
sense of "the sea" at the end of Book IV of *Paterson*, where, while
repeating that "the sea is not our home," he also says: "The sea *is* our
home whither all rivers / (wither) run" (P, 234–236). Williams refers to
the sea as "where the day drowns," leading Duncan to equate it with
myth, the death of "what we know by Day." That Williams also speaks
of the sea as "nostalgic" tallies with Duncan's sense that the aversion to
"the body of / them waters" is an act of amnesia. "They do not remember" suggests a resistance to the past and to tradition implied by Williams's equation of the sea with the Greek-mythological sea-mother
Thalassa and with "the dead, enwombed again." The desperate, repeated
(and rhetorical) insistence that "the sea is not our home" expresses,
among other things, a desire to be free of memory, to assume "a relation
to the immediate conditions" unencumbered by tradition, precedents left
by the dead.

While Williams's repeated evocation of Thalassa suggests a specific
cultural heritage and mythological tradition from which American "immediacy" seeks to liberate itself, "the sea," as Duncan appropriates it for
"The Continent," is more transcultural than culture-specific – "mythic"
in exactly that sense. His postulation of a "mythic sea, the fabulous"
derives in part from the use of the sea as a trope in the depth psychology
of Carl Jung, Erich Neumann, and others, where it symbolizes the collective unconscious, a global, shared repository of which correspondences among scattered myths are taken to be evidence. Though Freudian
rather than Jungian psychology is central to Duncan's intellectual orientation, depth psychology, as an outgrowth of the trauma of two world
wars, is analogous to the world-poem of which Duncan writes – a would-
be world-mending, the making (would-be making) of a world-mind.
More importantly, Jung was of central importance to Olson, whose myth
of "Pacific man" the poem goes on to echo in Section IV, a myth that

uses the sea, the Pacific Ocean, as the occasion and the symbol for a new
ethic, a newly arrived-at equanimity, a "NEW HISTORY." Duncan
returns to the association of San Francisco with what could be called an
oceanic sense, playing upon its proximity to Olson's "mythic sea," the
Pacific:

> ... Here
> our West's the Orient,
> our continent the sea. (RB, 174)

Olson proposes his myth of "Pacific man" in the concluding chapter
of *Call Me Ishmael*, which was for him what *In The American Grain* was
for Williams – a "historical grammar," call it, of the poetics of his American myth:

> ... the Pacific gives the sense of immensity. She is HEART SEA,
> twin and rival of the HEARTLAND. The Pacific is, for an Amer-
> ican, the Plains repeated, a 20th century Great West.... With the
> Pacific opens the NEW HISTORY.... The movement into it dur-
> ing the 19th century, of which Melville was a part, makes the third
> great shift. Melville felt the movement as American. He understood
> that America completes her West only on the coast of Asia.

Taking Ulysses, to whom he says Homer gave "the central quality of
the men to come: *search, the individual responsible to himself*," as the prototype of Western man, Olson argues that while Homer's Ulysses corresponds to the Mediterranean-centered phase of Western history and
Dante's to the Atlantic-centered phase, the death of Melville's Ahab
represents the death of the individualist ethic and ushers in its replacement
by that of "the NEW HISTORY" and of "Pacific man":

> The third and final odyssey was Ahab's. The Atlantic crossed, the
> new land America known, the dream's death lay around the Horn,
> where West returned to East. The Pacific is the end of the UN-
> KNOWN which Homer's and Dante's Ulysses opened men's eyes
> to. END of individual responsible only to himself. Ahab is full
> stop.[13]

Though patently Eurocentric not only in its literary antecedents but also
in its inattention to the claim of native populations to the sobriquet
"Pacific man," Olson's myth seeks to announce an end to the ruthless,
imperial impulse that brought Europeans to the Americas. Olson
strongly implies not only a communal ethic as characteristic of "Pacific
man" (playing on *pacific*'s alternate meaning of "peaceful"), but also,
taking off on Frederick Jackson Turner's famous thesis, an exploration
of inner space – what the Buddhist temple in "The Continent" stands

for – as his "West," his new frontier. Duncan, likewise alluding to
Turner, as well as to the Continentalist movement of the 1840s, converts
geographical fact into poetic shorthand and asserts that the continent to
be crossed in our time is "the mythic sea," a neglected or repressed
interiority, the psychic realm.

It is not difficult to see how the sense of San Francisco as a hub of
international influences, the Golden Gate to the Pacific and to the Orient
and so forth, alongside Olson's view of the new communalism of "Pacific
man," accords with and supports the idea of a world-poem. "The Continent" makes additional reference to this idea by way of the use Duncan
makes of Alfred Wegener and Tuzo Wilson's theory of continental drift.
Wegener, a German meteorologist, first put forth the theory in 1912,
arguing that 200 million years ago all the continents of the world were
joined together as a single supercontinent. He suggested that due to forces
having to do with the rotation of the earth this land mass broke apart,
opening up the Atlantic and Indian oceans. The novelty of his hypothesis
was its contention that if masses of earth could move vertically in response
to vertical pressures they must also be able to move laterally. Most
physicists at that time found the mechanics of Wegener's proposal unlikely, but in the early sixties Tuzo Wilson put together a variety of
evidence supporting while somewhat modifying Wegener's theory. The
disruption and migration of continents could be explained by the behavior
of what are called convection currents. These, the "under-earth currents"
at the beginning of "The Continent," conduct heat up from the earth's
core by way of its mantle, moving laterally as well as up and down.
Using these with other findings, Wilson argues "that about 150 million
years ago, in mid-Mesozoic time, all the continents were joined in one
land mass and that there was only one great ocean."[14] Duncan thus writes
in Section VI of "The Continent," echoing Wilson:

> . . . There is only
> the one continent, the one sea (RB, 176)

The Wilson-reconstructed map of the world at the time of Pangaia (Wegener's name for the supercontinent), which later appears on the cover
of Olson's *Maximus Poems IV, V, VI*, serves in Duncan's mind as a
symbol of world unity and the global inclusiveness of the world-poem.

Section V is the poem's most exemplary enactment of the world-
poem idea. The universalist ethic at the core of this idea, epitomized by
such statements as Pound's famous assertion that "all times are contem-
poraneous to the mind," dictates the sort of imaginative participation in
and sense of solidarity with so-called primitive beliefs we find in lines
such as:

> Gaia! Time's mother too
> must wear guises,
> hop on one leg
> and hide her head in a hut,
> dance with the rest among the maskt guys. (RB, 175)

Here, like the nearly extinct Carib Indians – who whenever there is an earthquake say, "The Earth-Mother dances!" – Duncan characterizes the phenomenon of "under-earth" dislocations, of which earthquakes and continental drift are two dramatic manifestations, as a ritual dance in which the Earth – Time's (Kronos's) mother in ancient myth – herself takes part. (The passage also resonates with a possibly "local" reference to San Francisco's quake-prone history.) Such passages as this put into practice the conviction Duncan states in *The H.D. Book*: "We go now to the once-called primitive – to the bush man, the child, or the ape – not to read what we were but what we are."[15] The three stanzas that follow this passage, written, they themselves tell us, on the day before Easter, give a small inkling of the global reach of the Resurrection myth, "the dream of everyone, everywhere":

> It's still Saturday
> before Easter
> and Love's hero lies
> in the nest of our time.
>
> In Banyalbufar the little doll of the Virgin
> once more meets the sorrowing procession,
> the black-clad walkers
> before the green of April, and looks upon
> His corpse they carry forth
> to meet her.
>
> Effeminized, the soul is Sleeping Beauty
> or Snow White who waits
> for Sunday's kiss to wake her. (RB, 175-76)

The geographical distance between San Francisco and Banyalbufar collapses, as does the vertical, hierarchical distance between the presumed height or depth of the archetypal (Resurrection) and the presumed lowliness or shallowness of the fairy tale (Sleeping Beauty, Snow White). Within the crucible of Duncan's inclusionist alchemy, scientific theory, aboriginal belief, religious myth, children's lore, and so forth are all melted down and flow together as one ongoing dream of "the Cosmos as Creation and Man as Creative Spirit." This melting down allows him the opening lines of Section VI:

> There is only the one time.
> There is only the one god. (RB, 176)

Beginning with the third line of Section VI, the poem returns to Williams and his " 'American' thing," having by now provided the context by which that "thing" is to be revised. In Book III of *Paterson*, Williams likens the poetic imagination to a cleansing fire. The fire that destroyed the Paterson Library near the turn of the century serves as a metaphor for an Adamic contempt for tradition, the "defiance of authority" he declares beauty to be. The figure of a burning page accordingly mirrors the creative workings of the poet's mind as it confronts the past:

> The night was made day by the flames, flames
> on which he fed – grubbing the page
> >   (the burning page)
> like a worm—for enlightenment (P, 141)

Duncan takes over this figure in the lines:

> There's only the one promise
>
> and from its flame
> the margins of the page flare forth.
> There's only the one page,
>
> the rest remains
> in ashes. . . . (RB, 176)

In so doing, he deprives Williams's impulse toward renewal of its self-declared "Americanness." The Adamic wish for a return to the beginning of things or for a new beginning, whether symbolized by Christ's or Osiris's resurrection, the "discovery" of the New World, Sleeping Beauty's awakening, or whatever, is "the one promise," "the dream of everyone, everywhere," that unites the world. It cannot be laid claim to as the private property of any nation, sect, or group. Very much in the tradition of humanity's age-old dream of renewal, Williams's "Americanness," its aversion to "the mythic sea" notwithstanding, is itself a myth – and not a particularly new one at that.

III

Tuzo Wilson warns that Pangaia should not be thought of as having been primeval, a Unity at the origin of things from which the world has since fallen. He points out that the coming together of the various continents was preceded by a period (or periods) of disunity and that an ongoing oscillation between varying degrees of unity and disunity is a more accurate picture of geohistory (see fn 14):

> It is not suggested that this continent was primeval. That it was in fact assembled from still older fragments is suggested by two junction lines: the ancient mountain chain of the Urals and the chain formed by the union of the Appalachian, Caledonian and Scandinavian mountains may have been thrown up in the collisions of older continental blocks. Before that there had presumably been a long history of periodic assembly and disassembly of continents and fracturing and spreading of ocean floors, as convection cells in the mantle proceeded to turn over in different configurations.

Duncan alludes to this ancient chain in Section V:

> In the far, the Appalachians
> belong to time before our time
> the Urals are a part of. (RB, 175)

These lines indicate Duncan's awareness of Wilson's warning, and, by extrapolation, his acknowledgment of the oscillatory, dialectical dynamic that accounts for both unity and disunity, assembly and disassembly. Thus, the final lines of the poem, while insisting upon unity, give the last word to separation:

> . . . There is only
> the one continent, the one sea –
>
> moving in rifts, churning, enjambing,
> drifting feature from feature. (RB, 176)

These lines pertain not only to the world-poem idea of unity but also, where they have to do with rifting and fragmentation, to a problematic regarding form to which the inclusionist aspiration gives rise.

This problematic has to do with the fact that the inclusiveness to which the world-poem aspires, the unity to which it seeks to lend itself, exists not as a state but as a process, is dynamic rather than static, an ongoing, not-yet-accomplished fact. The inclusionist aspiration is then at odds with what form is normally taken to be. It relates to form in the same way that the infinite relates to the finite, the unbounded to the bounded, eternity to time. As Duncan says very early in the poem, "the theme is much too big / to cover all o'er " This is the lesson Williams learned in his inability to end *Paterson*, as did Pound in the *Cantos*. Duncan, finding precedent in these two works, has sought to redefine form, to think of it not as containment but as flow. In his essay "Changing Perspectives in Reading Whitman" he argues for what he terms totalism or ensemblism and contrasts this with the more conventional notion of form:

For the New Criticism of the 1930s and 1940s, it was most important that the poet not put on airs. The dominant school of that
time thought of form not as a mystery but as a manner of containing
ideas and feelings; of content not as the meaning of form but as a
commodity packaged in form. It was the grand age of Container
Design; and critics became consumer researchers, wary of pretentious claims and seeking solid values. Ideas were thought of as
products on the market.

But Whitman's ideas flow as his work flows. He knows that
thought is a melody and not something that you manufacture.[16]

That "The Continent" in a quite self-reflexive way has to do with this
question of form becomes more evident as one reflects on the etymology
of the word *continent*, which derives from the same Latin word as does
contain: continere, meaning "to hold or keep together." The title of the
poem, on one level at least, refers to the would-be containment to which
the conventional sense of form aspires. (In Duncan's case this containment
would be taken in the sense not only of a coherence or "holding together"
but also − *continent* meaning "self-restrained, temperate" as well − of
keeping his rhetoric in check, of not "putting on airs.") What Duncan
shows us by the end of the poem, however, is this continent, this coherence or containment, doing just the opposite of what it is supposed
to do: "moving in rifts, churning, enjambing, / drifting feature from
feature."

At the end of his introduction to *Bending the Bow* Duncan writes that
"there is no composure but a life-spring of dissatisfaction in all orders
from which the restless ordering of our poetry comes" (BB, x). In "The
Continent" the fact that the very ground on which we stand − the symbol
and presumed guarantor of stability, stasis, and composure, *terra firma* −
is subject to quakes and continental drift underscores this sort of contention, the "life-spring of dissatisfaction" taking the form of convection
currents, the "under-earth currents" at the poem's beginning that betoken
a fluidity that opposes containment. The "dissatisfaction" here is that of
a totalist, cosmic aspiration whose service of Unity requires that it oppose
and disrupt any lower-case unity, that it eschew the hubris of conclusive
form. The rifting, the fragmentariness of both the poem and the supercontinent to which it refers is symptomatic of this Cosmic aspiration.
As Duncan suggests in "Apprehensions," quoting Paul-Henri Michel's
"Renaissance Cosmologies," fragmentation on the terrestrial plane is the
paradoxical caveat of a higher Unity:

> *"Whenever the subject is not the earth*
> *but the universe viewed as a whole"*
>   *"divergences appear"* (RB, 32)

The rifting of Pangaia thus becomes a symbol in the Renaissance *discordia concors* tradition. One manifestation, that is, of both the worldliness of the world-poem (the fact that it conforms to rather than transcends the fate to which all earthly things are prone) and the cosmicity to which it can do no more than allude is its openness to inconclusiveness and fragmentation.

The formal consequence of this openness is a heterogeneity and a dispersiveness that makes Duncan's poetry rich in echoes and anticipations. Duncan has stated that he doesn't seek to homogenize experiences in the poem (TNAP, 78), to smooth away jagged edges and so forth, but to leave the poem open to whatever might make its way in. He often refers to the art of collage in explicating his poetics, and in one of the earlier poems in *Roots and Branches*, "Nel Mezzo Del Cammin Di Nostra Vita" (RB, 21–24), Simon Rodia's Watts Towers are used to symbolize the poem as bric-a-brac, the poetics of piecing together what comes to hand. Some examples of the dispersive character of Duncan's work have already been seen, the rapport between "Apprehensions" and "The Continent" being a good illustration of the fact that Duncan's poems are best read as overlapping rather than self-contained. Each poem, as Duncan says, is both open and closed, self-contained to a certain extent but still subject to resonances (somewhat like the vibrations of sympathetic strings on a sitar) from other poems, both Duncan's and those of other poets. Just as the lines "There is only the one time. / There is only the one god" in "The Continent" echo the line "There is only one event" in "Apprehensions" (RB, 41), the latter poem additionally anticipates the former by way of its image of "the earth turning" (RB, 39) – compare "The Continent": "a wave / Earth makes in turning" (RB, 176) – phrases like "the swarming earth" and "the dead and the unborn that swarm in the floods" (RB, 42–43) – compare "The Continent": "the swarming locale" – and passages like:

> Compressions, oppressions – the horde gathering
>   in the poorest lands,
> shifting the weight of continents. And continents
>   are only what giants must be. (RB, 36)

Or:

> so that there is a continent of feeling beyond our feeling,
>   a big house of the spirit,
> indians and cowboys taking over the english-styled garden.
>   (RB, 37)

The frontier theme that exists latently in "The Continent" is more explicit in such lines in "Apprehensions" as:

    But it was my grandfather who made that trek
    after the war into the Oregon Territory
    and my grandmother who entered the dragon West (RB, 36)

Other examples of reverberation, involving poems earlier than "Apprehensions" as well as poems more recent than "The Continent," could very easily be given. These brief examples, alongside earlier examples of the way in which "The Continent" leans not only on "Apprehensions" but on "Returning to the Rhetoric of an Early Mode," Williams's work, Olson's work and so forth, should suffice to show what is meant by dispersiveness.

    A certain amount of repetition, of variation on certain images, themes, and turns-of-phrase is to be encountered in the work of almost every poet. Duncan's work, however, makes use of reverberation to a degree uncommon enough to establish it as a deliberate, self-conscious maneuver. By dissolving the boundaries between poems, by having his poems echo one another so insistently, Duncan puts aside the notion of the discrete, self-contained poem in favor of the field concept, a practice meant to give inklings of synchronicity, the "one event" or "one time" the world ultimately is. Duncan has pointed out that for him the field concept is synonymous with the idea of eternity (I, n.p.). In the Tree diagram of the Kabbalistic tradition to which he often refers, the complement of the sefirah *Nezah*, Eternity, is *Hod*, Reverberation – a fact that agrees with his use of dispersiveness to suggest a coherence transcending sequential divisions. The reverberations are like the experience of *déjà vu*, "something in which time is suddenly revealed to be other than it is" (I, n.p.). The paradox, the *discordia concors*, again, is that dispersiveness is used to suggest coherence, recurrence, or reverberation (time repeating itself) to suggest the eternal, the illusoriness of time. Insofar as the poem has to do with this transcendental, paradox-inducing coherence, its title refers to the "continent of feeling beyond our feeling" in "Apprehensions," of which Pangaia remains a suitable symbol.

    The paradoxicality has to do with the hierarchical view of the universe that is being put forth. The fragmentariness of the world-poem betokens the fact that the Unity to which it alludes is taken to be not-of-this-world, unattainable, that any pretense of having achieved such coherence, any work that fails to let its fragmentariness show, is hubristic. The fragmentariness of the world-poem partakes of the humility that befits any earthly act. Yet this humility, like that of prayer, is an upward-reaching one, and the attribution of Unity to a necessarily *higher* realm may be differently stated so as to attribute a fallenness or (where we have to do with convection currents, earthquakes, and such) a faultedness to the terrestrial plane. The latent or lurking theme of a Fall accounts for one aspect of "The Continent" with which I've yet to deal, certain lines of an ominous or portentous nature. These lines bring into the poem the apocalyptic theme encountered in the sections of *The H.D. Book* that have to do with the world-poem. In these sections Duncan characterizes the twentieth century as a time of great crisis, the most dramatic sign of this being the two world wars. The communalism of the world-poem emerges as a dialectical response to the manifest disunity of a world at war, while one of its themes is the apocalyptic portent of that disunity:

> These poems where many persons from many times and many places begin to appear – as in *The Cantos, The Waste Land, Finnegans Wake*, the War Trilogy, and *Paterson* – are poems of a world-mind in process. The seemingly triumphant reality of the War and State disorient the poet who is partisan to a free and world-wide possibility, so that his creative task becomes the more imperative. The challenge increases the insistence of the imagination to renew the reality of its own.[17]

The apocalyptic portent, while understated, is unmistakably present in "The Continent." This portent takes the form of certain undertones (or, more appropriate to this particular poem, undercurrents) that cast a shadow of doom over what are otherwise hopeful themes, those of Unity and Resurrection. At the beginning of Section II, for example, the first of the three words used to characterize Earth, *murther*, despite its similarity in sound to *mother*, is actually a dialect variant of *murder*. The word that follows, *murmurer*, seems to be ominously referred back to in Section IV where the "pang" made "in the heart of things" might very well be a murmur:

> In the heart itself a pang
> as if the very Day moved northward
> over the face of the waters. (RB, 174)

And the third word, *demurrer*, given the ring of the courtroom one of its meanings carries, suggests judgment and retribution, while its meaning of "one who objects or takes exception" casts Earth in the role of spoiler. Likewise, at the beginning of Section IV the shear-waters, small soot-black birds related to the storm petrel and the albatross and thought to forebode calamitous weather, seem to be harbingers of some disruption:

> These figures: a snake-coil of water,
>   a bird-wheel in the sky,
> to the great wheel of sooty shear-waters
>   passing north

> counter-clockwise as far as the
> > horizon
> between shore and the islands
>
> make their announcement
> in the heart of things . . . (RB, 176)

In Section V, as we've seen, the world is pictured awaiting Easter Sunday's "kiss" of Resurrection, a new dawning of Love:

> Time zone by time zone
>
> across the continent dawn so comes
> breaking the shell of flowers
> a wave
> Earth makes in turning
> a crest
> against tomorrow breaks. (RB, 176)

The "wave / Earth makes in turning" recalls the tidal wave attendant upon the birth of Aphrodite, and while the "time zone by time zone" advance of dawn makes one think of Earth's "turning" as her daily rotation, the fact that earthquakes are the cause of tidal waves suggests that this "turning" is the "dance" – Duncan's way of referring to a quake – she does in stanza three. Finally, the last two lines of the poem, with their image of Pangaia's rifting, put the finishing touch on an apocalyptic mood in which revival or renewal is anticipated, though overshadowed by the prospects of an initiatory catastrophe. The promise of "the green of April," that is, carries with it the warning we read in *The Opening of the Field*: "death is prerequisite to the growth of grass."[18]

These portents are the thematic complement of the poetics' insistence on openness, noncontainment, or dis-closure, an insistence that can itself be termed apocalyptic, given the term's derivation from the Greek verb meaning "to uncover." On another level, these portents, coming as they do in the final poem in *Roots and Branches*, anticipate "the great theme of War" (BB, 114) to which Duncan, inspired and outraged by U.S. aggression in Vietnam, turns in *Bending the Bow*, the volume that follows *Roots and Branches*. In the poems having to do with the Vietnam War the critique of American-Adamism we see subtly at work in "The Continent" finds a less literary occasion and becomes considerably more explicit:

> . . . this secret entity of America's hatred of Europe, of Africa, of
> > Asia,
> the deep hatred for the old world that had driven generations of
> > America out of itself . . . (BB, 82)

R.W.B. Lewis, in his study *The American Adam*, refers to the opponents of the Adamists, whom he calls the party of Hope, as the party of Memory. Duncan's "conservatism," his emphasis on the respect owed the past by the present, the old world by the new, puts him solidly in this latter group. In 1967 at a seminar on "Parable, Myth and Language" Duncan spoke of being "overtaken by myth," the myth of Christ in particular, in a way which relates both to this critique of the United States and to what in "The Continent" is called a "run to the mythic sea":

> My experience as a poet is that my reality depends on the reality of Christ. It's very clear in my work. I wasn't born and raised a Christian. When I spoke of myth overtaking you, I began to see that I will have to incur some of the rather grievous difficulties that poets who are overtaken by the myth of Christ have. Poetry is an effort to protect yourself against these things overtaking you. I think America will have no redemption until it suffers what all of humanity suffers. I think we have to come into an abyss of human suffering and share what, as a matter of fact, all of humanity shares. All this I see entirely in the figure of Christ as if it were overtaking me. . . . [19]

The "coming of all men into one fate" taught by this myth of Christ is the coming of all men into "rather grievous difficulties," and the wave that "time zone by time zone" overtakes the world on the day of Christ's Resurrection in "The Continent" portends exactly that. While the "one promise" to which the world-poem aspires is redemption or renewal, the "one fate" it portends is the achievement of that renewal through duress and suffering, indeed holocaust: "and from its flame / the margins of the page flare forth." Being overtaken by myth, what Duncan means by "the / run to the mythic sea" in "The Continent" and by "the rush, the being carried away" in "Returning to the Rhetoric of an Early Mode" (RB, 90), is both a remembering and a paying of dues to a history of ordeal, the communality of "what all of humanity suffers." As he writes in "Apprehensions":

>   . . . this is myth
> that Freud says lies in our blood, Dragon-wise,
> to darken our intelligence.
>
>   We remember it all.
> The sinister children at table reject their food,
>   spewing up bits,
> member by member remember, part by part
>   the cast, a bit in the play,
> of the eyes, of the dice, of design toward crisis. (RB, 37)

5

Uroboros

Robert Duncan's Dante *and*
A Seventeenth Century Suite

Robert Duncan's answer to the possible charge against *Dante* and *A Seventeenth Century Suite* that their occasion is too insistently bookish can be gathered from his essay "A Critical Difference of View."[1] Responding to two reviews that appeared in *Poetry* – one of Charles Tomlinson's *A Peopled Landscape* by Hayden Carruth, the other of Louis Zukofsky's *Found Objects* by Adrienne Rich – he takes Rich to task for criticizing Zukofsky's allusions to and quotations from the work of others. The essay begins with Duncan quoting the following passage from Rich's review:

> . . . committed to an enormous, self-conscious struggle with language and tradition . . . Zukofsky brings to the battle some inherited stratagems of Pound (heavy use of allusion and quotation) and Williams (a short, breath-phrased line, too often here a one-word line). One wonders if nature – instinctual wisdom – might not have led him to drop the greaves and breastplate of those great old warriors and to step, finally, light and self-exposing, into the fray.

Aware of his own susceptibility to this critique, Duncan makes no attempt to disguise the stake his work has in his rallying to Zukofsky's defense. He questions Rich's inclination to decide for *all* poets what their aims and intentions should be:

> I would not want to go on record against Miss Rich's wish for "the coming honestly and uniquely by the 'torsion' of grace and ungainliness, casualness and splendor" in a poem – it sounds terrific; but I do have a certain understanding that my own task in poetry is something other and less than what Miss Rich is so sure is "clearly the task of all today" etc. . . . What is most probably at issue is that . . . Miss Rich does not have any great concern for the poetry of

Pound or of Williams and what is certainly at issue is that she would
reprove those of us who have had and do have such a concern. Is
she an entirely original poet beholden to the work of no poets
before her? I am unacquainted with her work so I cannot say. But
given that Miss Rich does indeed write in the high "torsion" that
proceeds from no communal forms but from "instinctual wisdom"
even as in Eden before the Fall, I do not grant that her natural grace
has given her any understanding of what should be the task of Louis
Zukofsky or should have been the task of Williams or is to be the
task of me.

No communal forms. Duncan's answer to the charge of bookishness
Rich makes against Zukofsky invokes a concern with community that
is central to *Dante* and *A Seventeenth Century Suite*, a concern that is
enacted by these works' allusiveness, their conscious indebtedness to
Dante's prose and to seventeenth-century English poetry, respectively.
Completing an Uroboroslike circuit of justification, the poetry and its
poetics are one. This means that throughout *Dante* and throughout *A
Seventeenth Century Suite* poetry (to echo Charles Olson) is preoccupation
with itself. This preoccupation, especially in *Dante*, insists that poetry
and community coincide:

> In nothing superior
>
>   to his manhood   Dante
>
> – Shakespeare likewise –
>
>   the great poet
>
> nowhere makes us feel inferior
>
>   but there grows in the soul
>
> in reading   space and time
>
> Life writing   in each mind
>
>   teems:
>
>   his mind
>
> ours   sublime community.[2]

These are not the first of Duncan's works in which the idea of poetry as
community occurs. In his introduction to *Bending the Bow* we read of a
"commune of Poetry." This commune, he makes clear, is none other
than Creation, the Cosmos itself:

All my common animal being comes to the ox in his panic and, driven by this speech, we imagine only man, *homo faber*, has, comes into a speech words mean to come so deep that the amoeba is my brother poet . . . I'd like to leave somewhere in this book the statement that the real "we" is the company of the living, of all the forms Life Itself, the primal wave of it, writing itself out in evolution, proposes. Needs, as our poetry does, all the variety of what poets have projected poetry to be.[3]

This variegated Poem is beyond the reach or apprehension of any single poet. But, through an act of imagination that Dante calls "apprehension by means of the potential intellect," the individual consciousness proceeds by way of intuitions and intimations of a Whole in whose service its partiality, its particularity, exists. Its inability to encompass that Whole takes the form of a "darkness" conducive to – a muse or motivation for – the postulation of "light":

In the poem this very lighted room is dark, and the dark alight with love's intentions. *It* is striving to come into existence in these things, or, all striving to come into existence is It – in this realm of men's languages a poetry of all poetries, *grand collage*, I name It, having only the immediate event of words to speak of It. In the room we, aware or unaware, are the event of ourselves in It. (BB, vii)

This "poetry of all poetries" qualifies empirical achievement, rendering it incomplete, each "completed" poem simply further evidence of the ongoingness and the inexhaustibility of Creation: " . . . now the poet works with a sense of parts fitting in relation to a design that is larger than the poem. The commune of Poetry becomes so real that he sounds each particle in relation to parts of a great story that he knows will never be completed" (BB, vi).

Dante repeats and offers different versions of such assertions as these. Compare this last-quoted passage with the following lines:

> how many essential parts of the story we belong to
>   we will never know;
>
> and only in the imagination of the Whole
> the immediate percept is
>   to be justified – Imagining
>   this
>   pivot of a totality
>   having

> no total thing in us, we so
> live beyond ourselves
>
> – and in this   unitive. (GW, 106–107)

The iterative, derivative character of *Dante* and *A Seventeenth Century Suite*, Duncan repeating himself repeating others, calls into question the canons of originality and "instinctual wisdom" central to Rich's critique of Zukofsky. The title of this essay refers to Duncan's tendency to return to the sources of his poetics, to cycle and recycle the characteristic assertions of that poetics in work after work, repeating himself as he repeats those from whose work his own assertions derive. The figure of Uroboros, the tail-eating serpent suggesting unity and wholeness in ancient tradition, is compounded of ominous as well as "unitive" connotations in the poetic tradition from which Duncan's work more immediately derives. William Carlos Williams makes use of the figure in *Paterson* to convey a sense of having come full-circle, a sense that is darkly inflected by suggestions of exhaustion. In one such passage he quotes a line from one of his earliest poems, "The Wanderer: A Rococo Study," in a self-reflexive, performative gesture:

> the serpent
> its tail in its mouth
> "the river has returned to its beginnings"
> and backward
> (and forward)
> it tortures itself within me[4]

This, the final appearance of the figure in *Paterson*, is haunted, qualified, and complicated by earlier passages in which a quasi-Uroboros figure has to do with self-torture, self-cannibalization: "the shark, that snaps / at his own trailing guts" and "fish / swallowing / their own entrails" (P, 234, 259). That "it tortures itself" within him articulates an ominous, agonistic sense of the figure that is relevant to *Dante* and *A Seventeenth Century Suite* as well. In these works, that is, Duncan seems to be saying, at several levels, what Charles Olson said at the Berkeley Poetry Conference in 1965: "I have arrived at a point where I really have no more than to feed on myself."[5]

A sense of exhaustion and limitation, along with a somewhat confessional note, enters these works, a sense that is contrapuntal to the poetics' promise of an escape from closure. The experience of limitation is a recurring concern, as when *A Seventeenth Century Suite* acknowledges limits that impede community, limitations on the ability to share:

> I do not   as the years go by   grow tolerant
> of what I cannot share and what

> refuses me.   There's that in me as fiercely beyond
>   the remorse that eats me in its drive
> as Evolution is   in
> working out the courses of what will last. (GW, 83)

In contradistinction to such admissions as this, declarations regarding a
"boundless Source" project a cosmic Poem, a freedom from limitations
dialectically related to the experience of limits:

> O starry Net of Lives
> outflung!   And our little lives at last
>   among them realized!   Elohim-Cloud of bright
> expectancies,   quickening hunger for worlds
>   out of boundless Source seeking its bounds,
> the ground of all Immensities,   tremendous thruout,
>   agony of striving energies thruout, devouring
>   self thruout!   our little household and its
> inner court of our repose found hidden there. (GW, 91–92)

Bounds and unboundedness conspire with one another, the experience
of one inspiring the idea of the other. Duncan's repeated recourse to the
work of predecessor poets as sources for his own work attests to limits
dialectically related to a theme of unboundedness found in his and their
work. His having to do with sources leads to the idea of a transcendent
Source.

Following Dante, Duncan asserts that the Source gains access to us
through speech. He begins *Dante* by quoting from and elaborating upon
De Vulgari Eloquentia:

> "We will endeavor,
> the word aiding us from Heaven,
>   to be of service
> to the vernacular speech"
>
>   – from "Heaven" these
>
> "draughts of the sweetest honey-milk",
>
>   *si dolcement*
>
> from the language we first heard
>
>   endearments   whisperings
>
>   infant song and reverie
>
> a world we wanted   to go out into,
>
>   to come to ourselves   into,

> organizations in the sound of them
> verging upon meaning,
>> upon "Heaven" (GW, 95)

One of the cornerstones of Duncan's poetics is the idea of language, both written and spoken, as a communal, community-making act. "To write at all," he remarks in "Rites of Participation," "is to dwell in the illusion of language, the rapture of communication that comes as we surrender our troubled individual isolated experiences to the communal consciousness."[6] However, the commune instituted and maintained by the rules of grammar, syntax, and semantics contracts the non-anthropomorphic commonality to which a more primal, "vulgar" eloquence offers access. In the course of an unpublished interview conducted by L.S. Dembo in 1967, Duncan observed that the concern with meaning from which these rules derive has the effect of binding us to an adult, oppressively human order, the social order. But rapt attention to sound, the music or utterance-impact in words, he goes on to remark, moves us into the animal, cosmic realm of the child:

> Meaning is us. That's man, you know. The thing we think we're dealing with in language. But when you get into poetry and you become more excited about the sound, that's already got beyond what you think is your very human area. You share it with animals, babies and so forth. And that one then, I would say, is the larger area of the poem. . . . After all, the universe shares with the poem . . . projections of space and things that are sounds.

Positing this latter use of language as "primary, / natural and common, / being 'milk' " (this last word evoking both nurse and nightsky, the galaxy, the Milky Way), he writes, again in the opening poem of *Dante*:

> From the beginning,   color
> and light, my nurse;   sounding waves
> and air, my nurse;   animal presences,
> my nurse;   Night, my nurse
>
> out of hunger,   instinctual
> craving,   thirst for "knowing",
>
> toward oracular teats. (GW, 96)

The second poem in *Dante* takes up the idea of grammar as an instance of social coercion, a secondary impulse, an imposition aimed at domesticating humanity's inborn animality and cosmicity:

> Secondary is the grammar of
> constructions and uses, syntactic
> manipulations, floor-plans,

> spellings and letterings of the word,
>   progressions in writing, stanzas,
>   conservations and disturbances in meaning (GW, 96)

And at the poem's conclusion:

> Insufferable
> are those masters of grammar
> who have denied their illiterate nurses.
>
> Out of dry dugs of their own?
>
> Clonkt lightning! (GW, 98)

The line of argument running through the early poems in *Dante* retraces that of the comment to L.S. Dembo just quoted, emphasis moving from meaning by way of sound through the animal/child realm to the world at large. The third poem begins:

> I know a little language of my cat, though Dante says
> that animals have no need of speech and Nature
> abhors the superfluous.   My cat is fluent.   He
> converses when he wants with me.   To speak
>
> is natural.   And whales and wolves I've heard
> in choral soundings of the sea and air
> know harmony and have an eloquence that stirs
> my mind and heart – they touch the soul. . . . (GW, 98)

And the fifth poem:

> Everything speaks to me!   In faith
> my sight is sound.   I draw from out
>   the resounding mountain side
> the gist of majesty.   It is at once
>   a presentation out of space
> awakening a spiritual enormity, and still,
>   the sounding of a tone
> apart from any commitment to some scale.
>
>   The sea
> comes in on rolling surfs
>   of an insistent meaning,   pounds
> the sands relentlessly,   demanding
>   a hearing.   I overhear
> tides of myself all night in it. (GW, 100–101)

The reversion to and repetition of what are by now patently Duncanesque assertions deepens the sense of exhaustion and limitation that enters these works. Duncan, that is, appears to have come, as Olson said *he* had, to where there's none other than himself to feed upon. What is interesting is that this should have occurred in the context of works given over to variations upon the work of others. It underscores Duncan's insistence upon calling himself a derivative poet, pointing up the fact that the self upon which he feeds has been largely constituted of his borrowings from others, his feeding upon others.

A Seventeenth Century Suite Duncan describes as "imitations, derivations & variations upon certain conceits and findings made among strong lines," lines found in Robert Southwell's "The Burning Babe," George Herbert's "Jordan (I)" and "Jordan (II)," Ben Jonson's *Hymenai*, John Norris of Bemerton's "Hymn to Darkness," and Sir Walter Raleigh's "What Is Our Life?" His method throughout the *Suite* is to quote in full the seventeenth-century poem in question (with the exception of *Hymenai*) and to follow it with his own variations upon specific themes, phrases, and images found in the poem. Raleigh's poem, for example, begins: "What is our Life? a play of passion, / Our mirth the musicke of division. . . . " Duncan's variation not only echoes its opening question but also updates its answering figure of life as theatrical performance with a figure of life as cinematic projection: "What does this life most seem? But shadows upon / a moving picture screen . . . " (GW, 70–71). *Dante* he describes as études drawn from Dante's prose, specifically *De Vulgari Eloquentia, De Monarchia*, the *Convivio*, and the epistles. A process of communion that dissolves the distinction between Dante and himself informs his sense of what these "studies" are about: " 'Gists', yes, I have meant these études to come from and to return to create gists of my intentions in Dante's intentions. . . . His is not a mind researcht in the lore of another time, for me, but immediate, everlastingly immediate to the presence of the idea of Poetry. . . . I draw my 'own' thought in reading Dante as from a well-spring" (GW, 94). Duncan has been saying this for decades, so the work is clearly not about novelty any more than about the anachronistic or the antiquarian. The concern is with where the timely and the "timeless" coincide, with where phylogeny recapitulates ontogeny and the individual life is but a localization of generic traits and characteristics. This is the gist of many lines in *A Seventeenth Century Suite*:

> faltering in our resolve,   resolute in faulty cause,
>   heirs of ancient accusations,   hidden in our bones
> long-plotted designs of our poor demise.
>
> Our persons are but closets that such skeletons conceal
>   our species dreads,   as in our graves
> we lay down the law and return

the grievous courses of our lives
   to swell the sentence after our parts are done. (GW, 71)

The pun on the word *sentence* bears directly upon the concern with grammar, syntax, and semantics one finds in *Dante*, where the same punning use of the word occurs:

a felt architectonics then of the numinous
   that drives us beyond us, thruout,
      tries us in the sentence . . . (GW, 97)

The phrase "tries us in the sentence" makes a verdict of guilty a foregone conclusion, the "trial" itself a punishment. The "crime" would seem to be limits:

It was very like that coming to know
   my mother was at war with what I was to be;
and in the Courts of Love I raged that year
   in every plea declared arrogant
      and in contempt of Love.

I do not   as the years go by   grow tolerant
   of what I cannot share . . . (GW, 83)

The sense of limits and exhaustion deepens into the death-wish that enters these works. Death comes not only as a disclosure of mortality –

In death alone   we are sincere.
We'll not return to take our bows or read reviews.
   There's   nor night nor day,
nor reward nor punishment,   nor heaven nor hell,
   where all is done   and our mortality at last
made evident,   we are in earnest and have left the play.
      (GW, 72) –

but also as a dis-closure of limits. Thus, in the final poem in *Dante*:

Open out like a rose
   that can no longer keep its center closed
   but practising for Death, lets go,

lets go,   littering the ground
   with petals of its rime . . . (GW, 131)

In the variations on Jonson's *Hymenai*, this opening-out is both an epochal and an individual apocalypse:

Slow, slow, even as time alone erodes the matter,
   I turn and turn upon my life.

Tho I resist the learning,   the drive to study it out
     returns.

> *   *   *

In the old stories, the protagonist learns

what Time has to do with him. And in his true

          identity burns within the learning.

     He serves the years.
There comes an overturning of his Age. (GW, 84–85)

Predecessors from Duncan's earlier work exist for these two passages as well. The first recalls the second half of "Sonnet 4":

> sure as the rose scattering its petals to prepare is sure
> for the ripeness near to the perfection of the rose.
>
> I would know the red *thee* of the enclosure
> where thought too curls about, opens
> out from, what's hid,
>
> until it falls away, all the profuse allusion let go (BB, 3)

The second recalls instances throughout *The H.D. Book* where Duncan writes of the impact of the Second World War on the poetry of H.D., Williams, and Pound. His suggestion is that the crisis manifested by the war, the sense of an age in crisis, acquires a particularly personal relevance for the three of them because of their advancing age:

> Was it that the war – the bombardment for H.D., the imprisonment and exposure to the elements for Ezra Pound, the divorce in the speech for Williams – touched a spring of passionate feeling in the poet that was not the war but was his age, his ripeness in life. They were almost "old"; under fire to come "to a new distinction."
>   Where the fullness of their age was also the fullness of an historical age, as if the Second World War were a trouble of the times, unprepared or prepared for its old age?[7]

Duncan, in *Dante* and *A Seventeenth Century Suite*, is reading his own life, work, and times in a manner identical to that in which he reads those of H.D., Williams, and Pound. The Uroboros impulse in these works is something that has characterized Duncan's writing from the start: an inclination to understand his own experience and artistic practice in the light of precedents found in the work of others.

II

Adrienne Rich's discomfort with Zukofsky's bookishness, her desire that he "step, finally, light and self-exposing, into the fray," reminds us that the literature of the United States is a post-colonial literature. The Adamic presence, the appearance of unindebted immediacy she demands of Zukofsky and "of all today" has been called for before and will continue to be called for. This call is part of the legacy of post-colonial anxiety regarding tradition, one of the marks left by the struggle against cultural inheritances viewed as alien, outmoded and inhibiting, a threat to New World self-definition. A continuing bias in favor of directness, immediacy, the apparent absence of mediating tradition, reflects the fact that the United States was the first post-colonial society to develop a national literature, doing so in part by equating tradition with subjugation, viewing it as an impediment to authentic expression.

It is this bias, the erasure or would-be erasure of tradition, " 'instinctual wisdom' even as in Eden before the Fall," that Duncan is at odds with. His strenuous foregrounding of tradition answers Adamic presence by insisting upon the presence of tradition, the problematics of tradition, as inescapable, something not to be overlooked. He proceeds with a post-colonial resolve of another sort, one that demystifies tradition not by avoiding it but by engaging it head on. He shows tradition to be porous rather than impermeable, to be fissured and incomplete rather than comprehensive and monolithic. He shows that its fissures and its incompleteness leave room for variation and invention, the intervention of contemporary energy and inspiration. Diverging from triumphalist, monumentalist uses of tradition, he stresses its acknowledgment of frailty and fallibility, "our mortality at last / made evident." His strategy is similar to that of Guyanese writer Wilson Harris, whose context and situation are much more recently and recognizably post-colonial.

The concerns of Harris's essay "The Phenomenal Legacy" are in many ways the same as those that hold our attention here: community, inheritance, collapse, revelation. In his discussion of tradition, "the phenomenal legacy of the old in the new," Harris is careful to insist upon a ground more imposing than the cultural/conquistadorial, a ground underlying tradition, ontogenetic, on which "one virtually becomes a species of nature." Phenomenal legacy, the disclosure of this ground, assumes as one of its forms an obduracy, a durability, whose manifestation is a function of crisis, an obduracy that appears to invite ordeal. Harris argues that wholeness is at issue in this tendency toward crisis, investing the idea of unity with an aura as of something ominous, threatening. Access to this ground entails a negative capability (he quotes Keats at the beginning of the essay) that is confessional in its disclosure of "the irony of self-sufficiency," ironic in its admission of an otherness residing in the self. The self is permeable, as is tradition:

> In the medium of art and science one becomes susceptible to a species of unpredictable arousal, one virtually becomes a species of nature which subsists on both mystery and phenomenon, participating an otherness akin to the terrifying and protean reality of the gods. It is within this instant of arousal that abolishes the "given" world that one's confession of weakness has really begun: a confession that because of mortality, the mortality of all assumptions, there is and must be an inherent device of consciousness which looks beyond the fortress of self-created things towards a paradoxical womb through which we are being cautioned that a fantastic originality exists as the omen of unity.[8]

We begin to get a sense of why *Dante* and *A Seventeenth Century Suite* should be at once among the most derivative and among the most confessional of Duncan's works. *It is within this instant of arousal that abolishes the "given" world that one's confession of weakness has really begun.*

Here, however, the confessional is not restricted to the autobiographic, as it is in M.L. Rosenthal's sense. The self-obsession of the poets dubbed confessional by Rosenthal, the investment in individual ordeal bordering on exhibitionism, partakes of the Adamic valorization of direct, unmediated experience, Adamic assumptions regarding the uniqueness of individual predicament and sensibility. Duncan takes a more mixed, more mediated approach. As it relates to *Dante* and *A Seventeenth Century Suite*, confessionality is also mediumistic – in the compound, conjunctive sense of channeling voices from the past and of engaging the medium qua medium, consciously and self-reflexively engaging issues pertaining to poetics and poetic tradition. The derivative nature of the work in itself constitutes a confession. Hence the aura of subjectivity surrounding the term *confessional* needs to be replaced by a sense of susceptibility, of being subject-to. The "species of unpredictable arousal" Harris remarks upon revises – radically calls into question – the notions of self subjectivity implies. Likewise, in *Dante* Duncan speaks of a "restitution / of my self from every loss of me" (GW, 121). In the poem following the one in which these lines appear he acknowledges his indebtedness to Robert Adamson, Pound, Whitman, Shelley, Rossetti, and William Morris before questioning the limits of identity and authorship:

> Go, my songs, then in zealous
>   liberality,   no longer mine,
> but now the friendship of the
>   reader's heart and mind

> divine;   find out,
> as if *for*,   in every soul
> its excellence,   as if *from* me
>   set free.   "*My*" songs?
>
> the words were ever ours each thought
> his own . . . (GW, 122)

There is also, however, the more familiar confessional tone:

> In my youth, not unstaind
> and in much ignoble;   in manhood,
> struggling to ring true   yet
> knowing often my defection from
> these graces Dante lists
> proper to Man: temperance, courage,
> love, courtesy,
> and loyalty . . . (GW, 130)

The mix of the autobiographical and the mediumistic makes for the connection between the arrogance or insensitivity of which Duncan at points accuses himself and the otherness of which the poems claim to be a transmission. Several lines quoted earlier come to mind:

> . . . There's that in me as fiercely beyond
> the remorse that eats me in its drive
> as Evolution is   in
> working out the courses of what will last. (GW, 83)

The sense of a larger identity "fiercely beyond" the claims of individual identity, personhood, poses a threat to the senses of fellow-feeling those claims promote. The communal aspirations of *Dante* and *A Seventeenth Century Suite* are haunted by the possibility that Uroboros amounts to no more than an inflated solipsism – communion not with *others* but with an Other that is simply a trope for the self or the clan. The haunting and the communal aspirations comply with a dialectical unity, "the omen of unity," posed against but also inclusive of the bounded, self-embracing unity of Uroboros. The "Uroboric" circle will torment itself, will thus be broken at points by a disclosed (ideally, dis-closed) solipsism, as when, in *Dante*, Duncan quotes his own accuser:

> "*. . . and you, I know from other occasions, are apt
> to get caught up in one of your talking jags when
> you don't listen to anyone else and it becomes
> exhausting to listen to you . . .*" (GW, 103)

But not so "simply" a trope. No matter how nonchalantly stated, the fact is that life enigmatically turns upon an absence. Duncan's friend and fellow poet Robin Blaser, writing of what he calls "the practice of out-side" in Jack Spicer's work, speaks of a duplicity, a doubling or a folding back, a tropicality or a reversibility that, bearing the brunt of an irre-ducible mystique, composes the world:

> Jack used an Orphic methodology, as if the cosmos or love had fallen into hell. The experience is tropic – in the turn, hell is dis-covered and the true and the false begin to play. And, unfortunately, as Jack says, the dictation will be true and false... because as a proposition of an ultimate duplicity in the real itself, the dictation will be wild and playful, a disappearance and an appearance, an invisibility and a visibility exchanging their powers in the heart.

This disappearance or invisibility, "manifested" in language's ability to negate, is the also literal phenomenon of death:

> ... death is an interrogation close to the world because it is not ourselves. Death and ghostliness in this work must be seen not as a choice against life or even a helplessness within it but as a literal pole, where life is present to a point and then suddenly absent from an articulation. The curious thing about language and experience, which haunts Jack's work, is that they are so immediately reversible. And as a friend said, discussing this essay with me, if you don't have knowledge of that reversal, then you don't have the heart of it.[9]

As the apparently literal intrusion of an all too figurative Other ("ap-parently" because death itself attests to the duplicity that is the crux of figuration), death, at a number of points in *Dante* and *A Seventeenth Century Suite*, becomes a wished-for reassurance that otherness is not merely a manner of speaking. ("The grave's a comfort if we come to that.") But the truth of duplicity is that nothing is ever *merely* what it is, that the literal itself is already figurative as well as prefigured. Among the evidences of an all-pervading figurativity is the medium of language itself, the translatability between language and experience. We say "lit-eral," meaning actual, factual, speaking figuratively.

In both *Dante* and *A Seventeenth Century Suite* Duncan is concerned with the relevance of texts from the past to present-day occurrences, particularly those of a catastrophic, disastrous nature, such as the Vietnam War. A prime example of this occurs in *A Seventeenth Century Suite* where, as does Denise Levertov in "Advent 1966," he sees the napalmed children of Vietnam prefigured in Southwell's "The Burning Babe":

> *"A pretty Babe"* – that burning Babe
>   the poet Southwell saw –
> a scorching, a crying, that made his cold heart glow,
>   a fuel of passion in which
> the thought of wounds delites the soul.
>
>   *   *   *
>
> I cannot imagine, gazing upon photographs
>   of these young girls,   the mind
> transcending what's been done to them.
>
>   From the broil flesh of these heretics,
> by napalm monstrously   baptised
>   in a new name,   every delicate and
> sensitive curve of lip and eyelid
>   blasted away,   surviving . . .
>   eyes?   Can this horror be calld their
> *fate?* . . . (*GW*, 75)

Here, as throughout both works, bookishness and worldliness pervade one another, implicitly arguing the impossibility of an Adamic, unindebted, fully constituted presence. As in the following passage from *Dante*, the poems attest to a marriage, more for worse than for better, between the present and the past:

> out of the side-lesions of Congress:
> the bills and appropriations breeding their trade,
> the mounting flow of guns, tanks, planes, fires, poisons, gases,
> fragments of metal tearing flesh from flesh, thermonuclear
>   storings,
> outpourings of terror   even unto Zion
> that now swells and bursts asunder,
>
> the remnants of the old Jehovah, Lord of Hosts, of that rule of
>   Jealousy and Wrath
> the Father proclaimd,
> advance, divided against Itself,
> the two identities
> Yaweh and Allah in one   conflagration,
> America's industries feeding the abscess. (GW, 126–127)

This marriage, having both a world and a poetic text in which to articulate itself, is the prophecy-fulfilling susceptibility of the present to the past, the subjection of presence to an absence, an Other, announced in and figured by the past. Small wonder, then, that intimations of apocalyptic change ("othering") and of annihilation ("absenting") run through the poems.

The "double science" of Jacques Derrida designates the coinherence of "worldly" and "bookish" by the term *textuality*:

> Derrida proposes to elaborate a "double science," a "science" in which each concept, each term carries within it the principle of its own death. Once one has determined the totality of what is as "having been" made possible by the institution of the trace, "textuality," the system of traces, becomes the most global term, encompassing all that is and that which exceeds it.[10]

The most global term. As do *Dante* and *A Seventeenth Century Suite* in a more implicit way, the "double science" eschews notions of absolute origin, absolute originality, substituting a "notion of an origin other than itself, here called 'trace,' [which] makes it impossible to locate any origin, ever to constitute a full presence." The "double science" attributes the persistence of insufficiency, non-original originality, indebtedness (Duncan's "the burden of our spectral need, the / debt, the mounting dues" in *A Seventeenth Century Suite*) to the trace, "a kind of writing before writing as we know it," an inscription prior to, "fiercely beyond," presence. "Writing as we know it" locates and thus loses the trace, relinquishing the absence, the otherness of it, an absence it can at best report – and thus also not, in a sense, relinquish. The Uroboros impulse, the iterative nature of originality ("the river has *returned* to its beginnings"), takes into its mouth a tail that behaves like a phantom limb:

> The disappearance of an origin implied in this enlarged conception of writing (writing as *différance*, the word invented by Derrida to connote production of spatial and temporal difference), also entails an enlarging of the concept of repetition.
>
> . . . the thing itself, in its identical presence, is "duplicitous" (true and not-true), is doubled, doubles itself, as soon as it appears, or rather it appears as the possibility of its own duplication: it *repeats* itself, its origin is its repetition. (*VC*, 347–348)

The derivative character of *Dante* and *A Seventeenth Century Suite*, their reliance on earlier work, that of Duncan himself as well as others, confesses in an unusually relentless way the "onticity" of dependence, the indebtedness of being to an otherwise absent, iterative Source.

6

Robert Creeley's
The Gold Diggers
Projective Prose

<hr>

*She could not offer herself up; she only told of herself in a preoccu-
pation which was its own predicament.*
                                                Djuna Barnes, *Nightwood*

Despite having said that he "would rather be a 'writer' than a 'poet' or
a 'novelist,' "[1] and repeated assertions that he feels equally given to prose
as to poetry, Robert Creeley is known primarily as a poet. He is more
specifically thought of as a Black Mountain poet, though this designation,
with its suggestion of sprawling, open-ended structures à la Charles
Olson and Robert Duncan, seems at odds with the clipped, "minimal"
poems he has for the most part written. Creeley himself seems to have
sensed that his characteristic terseness is rather out of line with the "open"
practices of the poets with whom he's usually associated. In 1968 in a
postscript appended to the transcript of remarks he made at the Van-
couver Poetry Conference of 1963, he commented apropos the drift of
those remarks: "I had trusted so much to thinking, apparently, and had
gained for myself such an adamant sense of what a poem could be for
me, that here I must have been signaling to myself both a warning and
the hope of an alternative" (CP, 41). He goes on to thank "Allen Ginsberg
. . . Robert Duncan, Charles Olson, Denise Levertov, and the many others, who were wise, as they say, long before myself" for their part in
the breakthrough signaled by *Pieces* the following year.

Creeley, as his own sense of indebtedness suggests, wasn't alone in his
dissatisfaction with his pre-*Pieces* poems. Duncan remarked in 1969:
"There was nothing for me to take hold of in a mythology in the poetry,
and the early Creeley was very stubbornly restrictive in his areas of oper-
ation . . . "[2] Levertov, in her review of *Pieces*, comments that even in light
of the new, more explorative direction seemingly hinted at by "The
Door," an uncharacteristically long earlier poem dedicated to Duncan,

Creeley went on writing mostly more *conclusive* poems: many of them are of a ravishing perfection, but sometimes it has seemed as if that perfection were a limitation, a sealing off when one wanted him to go on, to go further, not to be obsessed with refining what he had already done impeccably.[3]

Pieces she calls "Creeley letting his hair down . . . a breaking open." It's very interesting that Creeley himself views his prose, the novel *The Island* and the earlier collection of stories *The Gold Diggers*, as having paved the way for this opening up. He remarked to Lewis MacAdams during an interview:

That novel opened up a great deal of possibility for me. I remember Duncan saying, after he'd read it, "This really changes the whole formal occasion for you. Both rhythmically, and in the order of statement you previously had." And I think he's right. I think it permits poems like "The Finger" to be written. . . . And honestly, by the time I get to "The Finger" now, now the information is transformed. In the writing, and in the experience that the writing is getting to. And that's what was happening in that damn novel. (CP, 164–65)

("The Finger," one of the poems in *Pieces*, Levertov refers to as "a poem that does relate pretty closely to 'The Door.' ") Duncan seems to have felt similarly about *The Gold Diggers* – that the stories were out in front of the poems, if in no other sense than that he could "get to" them quicker:

. . . much of the tone of Creeley was one that I was not quick to pick up on. But Creeley's short stories I could read aloud and did in 1953, I guess, at a reading we had at that point, it sort of got Creeley across to the San Francisco poetic community. Again of course because of the punctuation in the short stories, you could carry across in the rhythms, and I realized that Creeley was the only artist since Lawrence, as far as I was concerned, in the short story. And I knew if a man could write short stories that way I must be wrong wrong wrong about the poetry. (I, n. p.)

Olson too seems to have been more excited by Creeley's stories than by his poems. In his letters to Cid Corman early in the fifties he calls Creeley "the most important narrative writer to come on in one hell of a time" and "the push beyond Lawrence," and insists that "Creeley's work is extremely important exactly as the push beyond the fictive."[4] But one looks in vain for any such reference to the poems. Or compare the almost autistic tentativeness of his review of *For Love*, in which he resorts to such pseudo-statement as "Creeley has had the wit to make the short poem do what any kind of a poem might be imagined to do if it was doing what a poem might,"[5] with the tone of confident endorsement, the more typically Olsonian assertiveness of his "Introduction to Robert Creeley," which has to do with the stories: "I take it there is huge gain to square away at narrative now, not as fiction but as RE-ENACTMENT. . . ."[6]

One of the most noticeable things about Olson's "Introduction" is the perfect consistency between the principles he brings to bear upon and sees exemplified in Creeley's stories and the basic tenets of his own Projectivist poetics, the articulation of which he worked out largely in his correspondence with Creeley. Creeley's narratives come off sounding like projective verse. The assertion in "Projective Verse" that "man is himself an object," for example, is echoed in the "Introduction" by the insistence that "the writer, though he is the control (or art is nothing), is, still, no more than – but just as much as – another 'thing,' and as such, is in, inside or out" (HU, 128). There are other such echoings as well. Overall, Olson argues that Creeley's prose performs the Projectivist act of *situating* its controlling intelligence in the midst of the objects to which its attentions attend:

> It is human phenomenology which is reinherited, allowed in, once plot is kissed out. For the moment you get a man back in, among things, the full motion and play comes back (not parts extricated for show or representation) but the total bearing, each moment of the going – as it is, for any of us, each moment, anywhere. (HU, 128)

So if the designation "Black Mountain poet" is taken to refer to more than the fact of residence at Black Mountain College – is taken, that is, to be synonymous with "Projectivist poet" and to involve the formal predilections and "stance towards reality" thus implied – Creeley's claim to it would appear to rest, on the basis of Olson's, Duncan's, and his own testimony, as much, if not indeed more, upon his prose as upon his poems.

Creeley's "Notes for a New Prose," which first appeared in the second issue of *Origin* in 1951, has much to do with the relationship between poetry and prose. With something like Olson's assertion that "narrative writing is . . . wholly waiting for the advance of verse" (LO, 60), Creeley vindicates, as it were, the "poetic" potentialities of prose. Intent on liberating prose from a subservience to fact, to empirical phenomena, he argues that prose be given poetry's permission to register thought, "to project supposition, as fact." His quarrel is with a "realist" aesthetic whose "reality" is too narrowly conceived to accent the mind's play within its composition. He insists that prose, no less than poetry, is the projection of ideas:

> It is, then, that we are still confused by the idea of "reality" in prose. We do not as yet get the basic fact, that reality is just that which is believed, just as long as it is, believed. Poets are more used to this thing. . . . So how could a prose catch up? Difficult to make the competition actual. It isn't. . . . prose is the *projection* of ideas, in time. This does not mean that the projection must be an "actual" one, date by date, etc. The word is law, is the creator, and what it can do, is what any prose can do. There is nothing more real, in essence, about a possible prose than there is about any possible poetry. The ordering of *conjecture* will remain as "real" as the ordering of fact, given the right hand.[7]

Worth particular note, in light of the charge of premature closure made against Creeley's poems, is his insistence upon the inconclusive or anti-conclusive nature of prose. The new prose he advocates is projective not only in the epistemological and psychological senses indicated by the emphasis he places upon conjecture, but also in the sense of being extensible, tending toward openness. In this latter respect he sees more of a contrast than a convergence between poetry and prose, arguing that poetry, in its ability to compress, tends toward stasis, while prose eschews conclusion, moves for a furtherance of content, extends it:

> Poetry, as the formulation of content, in stasis; prose, as the formulation of content, in a progression, like that of time. This is a simple way of putting it. But sufficient to show that while poetry depends on the *flux contained*, held within the form, in stasis, prose may intend such a limiting but cannot justify one. It has no beginning or end. It has only the length it happens to have. . . . Just here is the key to its possible reach, that, in spite of itself, it has to continue, keep going – cannot stop. . . . it is, by nature, against conclusions. . . . (CE, 466–467)

Ironically, it appears that Creeley found prose more amenable than poetry to the demands of an open poetics. However applicable or inapplicable as a universal principle, such, he later comes to argue, has been the truth of his particular case. In the course of his "colloquy" with Linda Wagner in 1965 he returned to the subject of the differences between poetry and prose:

> . . . for me personally poetry is an intense instant which is either gained or lost in the actual writing. Prose is much more coming and going, though my own habits in writing prose are very much

like those I do have in writing poetry. . . . Prose allows me a tentativeness which I much enjoy at times because it's a need. That
is, I don't want to anticipate the recognition of what's involved so
that prose gives me a way of feeling my way through things.
Whereas poetry again is more often a kind of absolute seizure,
a demand that doesn't offer variations of this kind. (CP, 107,
109–10)

There is a danger, of course, of exaggerating differences, of pitting Creeley's narratives against his poems. The point is that aside from their
intrinsic interest (the fact that they are some of the best writing Creeley
has done and arguably some of the best by any recent narrative writer),
the stories in *The Gold Diggers* are interesting also in relation to Creeley's
and Olson's Projectivist poetics.

A good deal of similarity in fact exists between the poetry and the
prose. They both show Creeley to be a master of compression and both,
very exactingly measured, have as one of their most salient features
Creeley's habit of breaking each utterance into smaller, somewhat staccato bits (by way of a caesura at each line break in the poems and an
almost percussive use of commas in the prose). One finds in the stories,
that is, the same "practiced stumbling" Duncan attributes to the poems
(I, n.p.). For example:

> I would have gone, or as I think, I should have in spite of it, simply
> slipped out, when the others weren't looking, just left and waited
> for her outside. I can't see that she would have been hurt. That is,
> I would think, or think I would have that right to, that it would
> make no difference to her, that is, that she would understand my
> going, seeing that it had begun to tire me, even became painful to
> stay. I think of it so, being such, that no difference could be in it,
> since she was enjoying it, or so it seemed. (GD, 30–31)

This "stumbling" is shared on the thematic as well as the stylistic level.
Duncan, in the course of his remarks apropos "practiced stumbling,"
refers to Creeley's attraction to Robert Graves's *The White Goddess*, a
book that he reviewed in *Poetry* in 1959 (CE, 240–243). There is no better
illustration of this theme and this attraction than the very poem Creeley
dedicates to Duncan, "The Door," whose lines "The Lady has always
moved to the next town / and you stumble on after Her" are probably
the source of Duncan's phrase. This poem recalls Graves not only in its
regard for the Lady but also by way of its title. Graves too has written
a poem entitled "The Door," which Creeley in fact quotes in his review
of *The White Goddess*.

One passage in particular from *The White Goddess* stands out as relevant to Creeley's theme of woman-as-Muse. "Man is a demi-god," Graves writes. "He always has either one foot or the other in the grave; woman is divine because she can keep both feet always in the same place, whether in the sky, in the underworld, or on this earth."[8] A certain "surefootedness" characterizes women as portrayed by Creeley, as opposed to an insistent awkwardness, a tendency to stumble, on the part of the men. The women in his tales strike one as much more solid, much more situated and at home with things than the men, who tend to be like Italo Svevo's Zeno, crippled by excessive thought (as when Zeno, reflecting on the complicated coordination of fifty-four distinct muscles in the simple act of taking a step, finds himself almost unable to walk, reduced to a limp). In a binarism that is not innocent of sexist equations (man = mind, woman = matter), the female characters function as foils for the ruminations of the men. This is especially the case in "The Lover," "The Dress," "In the Summer," and "The Party":

> Of uncleanliness, he was saying, there are, one must come to think, a good many kinds. Of more, put it, than dirt on the hands.
>
> The wind shifted, slightly, pulling them down the lake and in toward the dock which he saw now as a line, black, on the water, lying out and on it.
>
> Not one, he said, not one sense would give you the whole of it, and I expect that continues what's wanted.
>
> But they sat quiet, anyhow, the woman at the far end, slumped there, and the length of her very nearly flat on the canoe's bottom. The man kept upright, the paddle still in his hands, but he held it loosely, letting it slap at the water, lightly, as the waves lifted to reach it.
>
> Nothing important, she said. Nothing to worry about, and what about tonight? We forgot that.
>
> He began to paddle again, but slowly, and looked back at her reluctantly, almost asleep.
>
> That doesn't please you, she said. You seem determined not to enjoy yourself. (GD, 55)

The sense of women as somehow privileged or blessed, somehow exempt from the ruminative lostness, the mind-at-large-within-the-quandary-of-itself that afflicts the men, gives rise at times to paranoid feelings of contempt. In "The Lover," for example, the male protagonist complains, "I don't do a goddamn thing, but think, do I?" and tells himself, "Stop thinking about it. Get out of it. Let go." Yet he resents and in his mind lashes out against his wife's apparent contentment, her presumed immunity to the ordeals of consciousness:

... talk, damn you, talk, he thought, say something, that makes sense, that won't leave me always alone, here or there, or nowhere I have chosen for myself, as I am now, here or there, but nowhere I would be. And the cats, he thought. The shell. The need for necessity, to have dependents. She liked them, she fed them. They were hers. And it was useless not to be angry anymore because he was and expected he would be, for a long time, that it would continue to be her that he didn't want or like or didn't want to have close to him, and always busy, he thought. Always busy. And could, then, scream, get away from me, you common thing! But she had rolled off and away, or he had, and lay there thinking, what was I thinking of. (GD, 70–71)

Similarly, the speaker in "The Unsuccessful Husband" at various points expresses a fear of his wife's cunning and surreptitious power: "And I wonder even now if her weakness, so persuasive in its own way, was not, after all, just another trick. . . . I had lived with my wife too long not to realize the infinite resources at her disposal . . ." (GD, 18). "The Gold Diggers," "A Death," and "The Boat" are also stories in which a controlling female presence figures, the last somewhat violating the pattern, however, in that a woman, Mrs. Peter, is the one who shoulders the burdens of thought: "Do I now think what I think because I think other people have thought it" (GD, 111).

The blurb on the back cover of New American Story asserts that "Robert Creeley's protagonists are caught in the exacerbated sensibilities of their own minds." This is true. Creeley's tales tend to have been given rise to by certain knots of sensibility. Such knots, in any event, seem to be what they're about. Which is not to say that any definite sense of issue or "plot" tends to emerge, even given the phrase "knots of sensibility" as an abiding malaise. Creeley has repeatedly warned against too easy an assumption of what the word *subject* entails: "I find myself increasingly less able to explain why it is that I write something. I have no sense of subject more than some elemental one concerned with the need for distinction and the fact we are all alive. The story, as it were, comes with its own occasion, and orders me as much as I may it."[9] Or as the male speaker puts it at the beginning of "In the Summer": "I am not saying that it was ever to the point or that a purpose could be so neatly and unopposedly defined. Or that twenty-one or so years ago, on that day, or on this, he was then, or is now, there or here, that we could know him and see him to be what he is. I don't much care for that" (GD, 75). Some such disavowal of "subject" allows an indeterminacy to dictate what courses the tales might take:

The story has no time finally. Or it hasn't here. Its shape, if form can be so thought of, is a sphere, an egg of obdurate kind. The only possible reason for its existence is that it has, in itself, the fact of reality and the pressure. There, in short, is its form – no matter how random and broken that will seem. The old assumptions of beginning and end – those very neat assertions – have fallen away completely. . . . (GD, 7)

This indeterminacy, the randomness or brokenness of the world it seeks to disclose, is what aggravates or "knots" the protagonists' minds.

"A Death" illustrates this tendency well, the characteristic coyness as to what is at issue. A distinct tension pervades the piece, though whatever events have given rise to this tension are left undisclosed:

But what was to be done with James. His wife thought she knew, and yet he was strangely moved. The children were happy, they played behind them with the toys they had brought in the basket. So she attacked him directly, and asked him, what was it. He said he did not know.

Is it your sister, she said, and looked down, and away, to the form still clear to them, a white odd shape on the top of the sea. He answered that he did not think it was. She said, you must see the difficulties. He was not sure that he did. (GD, 39)

Nor are we, the readers, sure that we do. Some sense of rivalry between the wife and the sister appears to exist (even if nowhere other than in the wife's imagination), but the details of it, much less the reasons for it, are never quite gone into or spelled out. Such ellipsis or understatement actually increases the tension, in much the same way that undiscussed anxieties tend to grow more intense. When James's sister and her son Amos take their nude swim, we are told quite casually that "James fumbled in his embarrassment" and that he "coughed, he wanted not quite to see," but Creeley avoids stating outright or seeming to make a big point of the fact that James is upset with his sister's daring. In fact, the probable cause of his discomfort, her nakedness, is never explicitly referred to as such. Neither the word *nude* nor the word *naked* is ever used, and the apparent impropriety of any such explicitness, the apparent unmentionability of her nakedness, is perfectly consistent with and instrumental to the air of repressed, inarticulate emotion to which the story gives rise. The reader is informed of James's sister's decision to swim naked in a very offhand and oblique manner, in such a way that her nudity is made incidental to the words that are used:

> Taking off their clothes, she put them in a pile, and then put a stone
> on top of it. Amos giggled. She had forgotten the bathing-suits,
> and they were in the basket, high up on the hill with the others.
> Even so she slipped into the water quietly, and calling softly to
> Amos, drew him in after her. (GD, 37)

The fact that this nude swim catalyzes a whole host of anxieties, resentments, and frustrations is allowed to sneak up on us (and on the
characters in the story as well). When the man in the boat sees James's
sister – or, more to the point, sees her nakedness – we are told that "at
that even James was angry," but still no such explanation as that James's
prudish, possibly incestuous protectiveness causes his anger is offered.
In the next paragraph the sister is described as smiling after this swim
and "not ashamed," the implication clearly being that in the minds of
James and his wife she should have been. Finally the wife's questions
"And the boat?" and "Did you see the boat?" – really meaning the *man*
in the boat – and James's noticing "the tight thigh, and the brown, close
flesh," beneath his sister's raised skirt brings things to a head: "She saw
the faces all in front of her, and if she cried out at them, she was still in
love with everything" (GD, 41).

The indeterminacy in such a story as "A Death" can be said to involve
the absence of an "objective correlative" (to further overwork an over-
worked notion). The emotions portrayed seem in excess of – or at least
incongruous with – the facts presented. (Why all the fuss over a naked
swim?) This would seem to be the point of the quotation from García
Lorca that serves as an epigraph to the story: *Vestida con mantos negros
piensa que el mundo es chiquito y el corazón es inmenso* . . . (Dressed in black
clothes she thinks the world is tiny and the heart is immense . . .). In
other words, feelings (*el corazón*) are finally larger than the facts (*el mundo*)
to which they attach themselves, and the absence of an "objective correlative" is not so much an artistic defect as a fact of life. No such naive
adequation as Eliot advocates in fact exists. The lack of such adequation
is what forces the mind (or heart) back upon itself, away from (by way
of) the world and into the knot of self-apprehension. Creeley is thus
careful not to be presumptive as to which facts are to be seen as the
source of the emotions he depicts. One can, of course, argue that James's
and his wife's anxieties and James's sister's climactic outburst all derive
from the stresses and strains of the recent death of the sister's husband.
But it is worth noting that, even though the story's title leads one to
expect otherwise, Creeley seems bent on discouraging any such focusing
on that death, any such taking of it as subject or underlying explanation.
No outright mention of it is made until the story's next-to-last sentence,
and even there it's given no more weight than the obvious fact that

James's sister knows it's her brother's wife who has just asked about the boat: "Did you see the boat, his wife asked. She knew it was her brother's wife. She knew her own husband was dead" (GD, 41).

Creeley seems less interested in depicting the emotions with which the story has to do as the issue of any conclusively determinable source than in insisting upon the *diffuseness* of feelings and of possible sources of feeling. He makes use of a field, rather than a focal, approach. The most readily acceptable explanations of why James, his wife, and his sister feel and behave as they do – that the recent death has put them all on edge or even that James cares for his sister in some way of which his wife is jealous – are suspect and thus to be played down exactly because they are so readily acceptable, so pat. The fact that at the time of the writing of these stories Creeley was listening to and influenced by Charlie Parker, Dizzy Gillespie, Miles Davis, and other bebop musicians is not without significance. Bebop altered the rhythmic order and the habits of expectation it inherited, cultivating a variability of accent and emphasis, introducing new patterns and possibilities of insistence. Likewise, Creeley's narratives have a certain syncopated, "offbeat" quality in that their emphases and accents tend to fall other than where one would expect. Notwithstanding its title, "A Death" pays no direct attention to its ostensible subject. Nor are the sorts of psychologizings one might expect indulged in. Unexpected transitions or abrupt changes of reference typify the prose:

> But what was so simple about it. Make me happy, she said. Don't please think of her. James was very much in the middle and began to know it. He knew love was not multiple, or could not be here divided. He said, be patient with her. He let it all rest on kindness.
>
> The water around them changed all that, on their bodies, very much on their bodies. Amos jumped up, shrieking, and she loved him more than she admitted. Look, she said. The small fish darted out, past their white feet, and then back again to the darker places. But Amos had seen them. It was lovely. (GD, 38)

Here, literally before we know it, "them" is no longer James and his wife but James's sister and Amos.

The further point insisted upon by this "offbeat" prose is that not only are things not always where we look for them, they are not altogether where we find them either. Or, to borrow, as Creeley or Olson might, the language of physics, not only is a thing or event a corpuscle (discrete, particulate, local), it is also a wave (continuous, tumescent, dispersed). Again, *the diffuseness of feelings and of possible sources of feeling.* Creeley forsakes the flatness of explanation, of any reductive attribution of causes, for a vigilantly non-presumptive, open apprehension, allowing the multiplicity of forces and influences that impinge upon an event to make their presences felt. The reactions to a nude swim, say, are implied to be the issue of events (psychic as well as empirical events) other than the swim itself. The feelings that manifest themselves in response to the swim do not so much issue *from* that event as issue *through* it, their ultimate sources as much a mystery as those of life itself. Thus the speakers in Creeley's tales tend to approach things cautiously, to express themselves tentatively so as to give this mystery its due, dissociating themselves from the "certainties" entertained by the crowd:

> Other people, although I don't for a moment believe that what they say is true, at least claim a continuity in their lives, a going up or a coming down. The rise or fall which they maintain is their way of saying that they have lived and even those who stay in the middle suppose that they narrowly missed worse or very nearly achieved better. For me this does not apply, and I find it very hard to believe that it does even for others. (GD, 15)

Or again:

> It's all right, or right is what they have said, that it's all right, but myself, I don't find their answers or even what they answer, to say it's all right. To her, or myself, or anyone, or even looking straight down at it, after it happens, what happens? (GD, 47)

The preponderance of such qualifications as "I think," "so to speak," "like they say," and "I expect" bespeaks the provisional, non-definitive character of the assertions being made. "A reality, before it becomes our own, is often tricky and can be easily mistaken," the speaker in "3 Fate Tales" remarks (GD, 52).

Olson's regard for Creeley's stories had much to do with a disdain for presumption. The "offbeat," unsettled rhythms of Creeley's prose, the near stutter (or stumble) he gets from his use of the comma, mime a sense of apprehension, a nervousness or jitteriness not unlike that which Olson attributes to the Maya in "Human Universe": "It was better to be a bird, as these Maya seem to have been, they kept moving their heads so nervously to stay alive, to keep alerted to what they were surrounded by . . . " (HU, 12). This nervous alertness is the gist of the field approach Olson espoused, that one not be "so astonished he can triumph over his own incoherence, he settles for that, crows over it, and goes at a day again happy he at least makes a little sense" (HU, 3). Creeley's protagonists tend to deny themselves the comforts and numbing assurances of any presumed or ready-made coherence. They instead approach experience with something like the *humilitas* to which Olson refers in "Projective Verse" (HU, 60). For example:

> A few nights ago I wrote down some of this, thinking, trying to think, of what had happened. What had really happened like they say. It seemed, then, that some such effort might get me closer to an understanding of the thing than I was. So much that was not directly related had got in and I thought a little noting of what was basic to the problem might be in order. That is, I wanted to analyze it, to try to see where things stood. I'm not at all sure that it got to anything, this attempt, because I'm not very good at it. But you can look for yourselves. (GD, 23)

The speaker in this story, "Mr Blue," not only eschews omniscience, but goes on to question his knowledge of those aspects of his life we would expect him to be most knowledgeable about:

> But perhaps that's where I'm wrong, that I have that assumption, that I think I know what she is like. Strange that a man shouldn't know his wife but I suppose it could be so, that even having her around him for five years, short as they are, he could still be strange to her and she to him. I think I know, I think I know about what she'd do if this or that happened, if I were to say this to her, or something about something, or what people usually talk about. It's not pleasant doubting your own knowing, since that seems all you have. (GD, 25)

Creeley's third-person narratives likewise shy away from any pretense of omniscience, offering very little comment upon or interpretation of the facts they report.

The stories are often, in fact, similar in atmosphere and spirit to the French "New Novel." Creeley's seeming concern not with *why* things happen but *that* they happen recalls Alain Robbe-Grillet's remark: "But the world is neither significant nor absurd. It *is*, quite simple."[10] Likewise, his reluctance to engage in explications of motive, to rationalize or render actions transparent, has much in common with Nathalie Sarraute's *Tropisms*, where an insistence upon a pre-conscious, practically vegetative motility qualifies any "understanding" of human behavior.[11] Creeley too is bent on evoking that primordial, mindless irritability we share with the simplest forms of life:

> Then she got into the bed, and lay down, coming to him, then, but nothing, he thought, and heard it, the cry, and got up himself to run to the door, pulling at it, and yelled, what, seeing the boy sitting straight in the bed, staring, and crying, screaming, the sound driving in on him as he came.

What, he yelled, what, what, what, and got hold of the boy,
by one arm, dragging him clear of the blanket, then bringing his
own hand back, hard, to slap him, the head jerking back, and down.
But useless, the screaming now louder, and he felt it useless, picking
the boy up, to cradle him, holding him, and walking beside
the bed's length, the moon still against them, a light, he said, and
went back to the other room to find her waiting with the candle.
(GD, 97)

What *The Gold Diggers*'s "Frenchness" has to do with Open Field poetics
is this: Both attempt a withholding of any anthropomorphic or solipsistic
coverage of experience. Robbe-Grillet speaks of getting back to "hard,
dry objects . . . as alien as ever," just as Olson does of allowing objects
"to keep . . . their proper confusions." The admission that opens the field
is the acknowledgment of obduracy as a component of experience, an
otherness unamenable to appropriation. Thus the speaker in "3 Fate
Tales" remarks: "I think we deal with other wisdoms, all more real than
our own, which is to say, I think we have to do with others" (GD, 49).
And the male speaker of "In the Summer": "I am not sure that I speak
now, even for myself, that I have not become the fact of much more
than I intend" (GD, 80).

In reference to the Sumerians and the Maya, Olson spoke of "a disposition toward reality which understood man as . . . force in field of
force containing multiple other expressions."[12] An Open Field aesthetic,
he argued, would bring this "disposition" to bear upon writing, and it's
clear that he saw Creeley's stories as an instance of this. *The Gold Diggers*
allowed him the assertion that "narrative can take up that aspect of verse
which is its multitude" (HU, 127), its admission of "multiple other
expressions." The title story, in fact, reads like a deliberately graphic
exemplification of this field approach. The setting in which the story
takes place, that is, is literally an open field, and Creeley immediately –
in the first paragraph in fact – stresses the unintentionality or unpredictability, the *otherness* of what can happen there:

West of the mountains, the land rides out on a flat and open plain
and continues for more miles than any one man ever knows of.
The light is high, it comes from the farthest point of the sun. If
you put a man here, already you find him lonely. If you put two,
then what happens is not so much what either one man decides on,
but what happens to them no matter. (GD, 119)

Here two men live and shovel the ground for gold with a tractorlike
machine. One of the two has gone into the city some distance away and
returns with the story of a woman with whom he went to bed while

there. The weirdness of the tale is that the other man, the one who stayed behind, becomes helplessly caught up in his own idea of what this woman was like: "He thought of each thing, and could not even say who he was, or whether this had happened to him, or had not" (GD, 121). The next day while driving the machine he sees the woman, who after a moment floats clear of the ground and then disappears. That evening his sharing of this incident with his partner ends with his falling to his knees crying and the latter attempting to bring him back to himself by dangling a garment of some sort – the woman's presumably, and most likely lingerie ("the odor incredible but certain") – before his face:

> He went forward, grabbing at the cloth. The other man fell down still holding it, and then sat, on the floor. He kicked at him, and the other fell over completely and rolled flat on the floor, then quiet. The room was quiet. He bent over and picked up the table, and lifting it as high as he could, he let go. (GD, 126)

There the story ends.

Olson, in his "Introduction to Robert Creeley," distinguishes two possible narrative stances, one in which "the narrator stays OUT, functions as pressure not as interpreting person," and the other in which the narrator is a "total IN . . . taking on himself the job of making clear by way of his own person that life is preoccupation with itself" (HU, 127). He argues that Creeley's stories are of the second type. It seems to me, however, that the tales in *The Gold Diggers* are of both types. One of the striking things about "The Gold Diggers" is the narrator's withholding of any interpretive comment (aside from the remark that "what happens is not so much what either one man decides on, but what happens to them no matter"). As in "A Death," no such explication as would familiarize the events, relieve them of their haunting peculiarity, is offered or allowed to intrude. Rather than clarifying or sorting things out, Creeley seems bent on furthering a certain opaqueness, on allowing events "to keep . . . their proper confusions." This is especially evident in his use of pronouns (as in the just-cited use of *them* taken from "A Death"):

> One of them came up to him. He saw her head nodding under a high light, and some of it fell off the hair, glancing down to the glass in his hands. She was smiling at him or trying to also, and her hand had come forward enough to find his own. Speaking to her, his mouth was like the substance of his whole body, and twisted itself to answer. The low phrases continued, marking again and again each act of the meeting.
>
> In her room she went completely into him, against his own will tearing at him, so that he left her, he thought, unconscious. The

obscenities were now actual, they surrounded him. He thought of each thing, and could not even say who he was, or whether this had happened to him, or had not. When he made supper, because the other man was too tired and hardly ate it, he went in a daze, and even the food which the other had brought was almost something he could not taste. (GD, 121)

Though we don't find it out until the fourth and last sentence of this second paragraph, the third *him* ("they surrounded him") no longer refers to the man who had gone into town but to the one who stayed behind. (We know this because "the other" who brought the food has to have been the one who made the trip to the city.) This confusion of *him*'s, however, is perfectly proper to a tale in which one man so totally appropriates the experience of another as to be put upon by a vision. Similarly, in the first paragraph an abrupt, unannounced shift of reference takes place: "Speaking to her, his mouth was the substance of his whole body, and twisted itself to answer. The low phrases continued, marking again and again each act of the meeting." Here two distinct instances of speaking, the man's answering the woman in the bar in the city and his later relating of the incident at home, are allowed to merge, thus confounding the two time/space frames. This too is appropriate, of course, in that in the mind of the other man the two frames are the same.

There are in fact, to my reading, more stories of the first than of the second type in *The Gold Diggers*. Of the sixteen stories, only five ("The Unsuccessful Husband," "Mr Blue," "3 Fate Tales," "The Seance," and "The Dress") appear to be of the "NARRATOR IN" sort. "Mr Blue" is the best example of this, the one to which Olson specifically refers. But Olson's distinction between these two narrative stances is finally more misleading than useful, insofar as it perpetuates the objective/subjective dichotomy Creeley wants to put aside. In "A Note on the Objective" he comments:

A useless fight. However right it may be to damn the use of the subjective method as an excuse for emotional claptrap, it's apt to push us away from any understanding of the subjective in a more basic character, i.e., "belonging to, or of, or due to, the consciousness. . . . " Impossible to write anything, lacking this relation of its content to oneself. Put another way: things have to come in before they can go out.

Perhaps best to junk both terms, or at least to understand this necessary balance, one with the other. We can't stand outside our content and at the same time we can't eat it like an apple, etc. And perhaps, finally, more to the point than either of these two stances is that one which maintains: a man and his objects must both be presences in this field of force we call a poem. (CE, 464)

Or a story. One of the most notable characteristics of Creeley's narrators, even when they're as introverted or introspective as in "Mr Blue," is a tense awareness of the possibility that things exist apart from the orderings of the mind. Creeley's tales, whether rendered as first-person or as third-person narrative, are "subjective" or "IN" in the sense of registering the movements and contents of consciousness, but also "objective" or "OUT" in that this registration constantly checks itself, avoids losing awareness of the possible breach between actuality and thought. Conjecture is never allowed to lose consciousness of itself as such. In the first two paragraphs of the third of the "3 Fate Tales," for example, the phrase "I think" occurs five times, "I am not sure" twice, and "I would hope" once (GD, 49). This is typical of the air of tentativeness and critical self-consciousness that pervades Creeley's prose, the disdain for presumption I've already mentioned. The proliferation of qualifiers even in the reporting of what would otherwise seem incontestable is another sign of this, as in "The Suitor":

> Staggering back along what *he took to be* the path, he thought, long roads are happy roads, and continued. Somewhere inside the shape now looming beside him, *like they say*, was also the woman he loved, or *had taken himself to*, as she had *apparently* also taken him to. (GD, 129; emphasis added)

Thus "Mr Blue" opens with the speaker announcing his intention to keep any "subjective" responses in check – "I don't want to give you only the grotesqueness, not only what it then seemed" (GD, 23) – to remain faithful to "what had really happened." His three assertions apropos dwarfs and the nature of size are offered with no small amount of self-effacement: "I'm not at all sure that it got to anything, this attempt, because I'm not very good at it." The tone throughout is humble, even apologetic, and his desire not to impose upon his audience all but ties him in knots:

> My wife is also large. . . . But she is not so much large as large-boned. A big frame. I sound as though I were selling her, but I'm not. I mean, I don't want to sound like that, as though I were trying to impress you that way. It is just that I don't want to do. That is, make you think that I am defending her or whatever it is that I may sound like to you. In short, she is an attractive woman and I don't think I am the only one who would find her so. (GD, 24)

This passage not only charts the movement of the speaker's thoughts but also registers the impact upon the rhythms of those thoughts of his apprehension of the other inhabitants of the field or space in which this articulation takes place. The allowance he makes for the sensibilities of his audience exemplifies a decentralizing impulse, a field approach, his admission that not only other things but also other minds exist. This making evident of the impingement and impact of otherness upon consciousness, of a space occupied by other people, other things, even other places and other times, is what Warren Tallman means when he says of Creeley that "rather than think thoughts he thinks the world."[13]

The sensibility thus disclosed is a knotted one, yes, but to accuse it of solipsism is to retard rather than advance critical discourse.[14] The people in these tales so vigilantly reach out for the world, so relentlessly worry about the possible gulf between mind and world, as to make their tension the dialectical "knot" that unites the two. Or to quote Tallman again: "Creeley is lost enough, his writing testifies, but he is lost on the near side of thought, in this world." How else to account for the specificity of his observations, the amazing grace of his stumbling prose?

> I looked, a flash, sideways, as it then happened. Looked, he looked at me, cut, the hate jagged, and I had gone, then, into it and that was almost that. But she said, then, she had seen him, earlier, that same day, as he was standing by a store, near the door, I think, as it had opened, and she, there, across the street, saw him motion, the gesture, then, a dance, shuffle, the feet crooked, and the arms, as now, loose, and it was before, as before, but not because of this, that made it, or I thought, so made it, was it, or it was that thing I hung to, when, the show over, they motioned us out, and I pushed a way for her out through the crowd. (GD, 31–32)

7

That Words Can Be On The Page

The Graphic Aspect of Charles Olson's Poetics

An issue of *Boundary 2* devoted to "the oral impulse in contemporary American poetry" contains an interview with Jerome Rothenberg conducted by William Spanos. Spanos's remarks at a number of points illustrate the danger of too heavy an investment in academic distinctions. Insisting upon an opposition between the oral and the visual built upon the more familiar distinction between orality and literacy, Spanos is led to question the use by Rothenberg, presumably an oral poet, of figures of speech having to do with vision in describing his sense of what orality entails. The opposition, a false one, is concocted of the tension between two differing "perspectives on reality," the will toward openness and the will toward closure, to which the terms *oral* and *visual* have been forcibly made to apply. Spanos, alluding along the way to Heidegger, Sartre, Merleau-Ponty, Joseph Frank, Wilhelm Worringer, and Marshall McLuhan, can make the assertion that "the eye-oriented perspective on reality . . . is essentially a coercive activity, the motive of which is to *shape* and thus to achieve aesthetic distance from or psychic repose in the shapelessness of experience."[1] What he is in fact talking about is a philosophical stance, not the act of seeing, a stance for which that act is a metaphor. Speech and vision, as Rothenberg points out, "aren't separated in real life," and even the fact that they are distinct functions involving distinct organs doesn't justify speaking of them as opposites. In what sense, that is, are speech and vision mutually exclusive, opposed to one another? Don't they in fact coexist? Wouldn't it be more accurate to insist on blindness, rather than speech or hearing, as the opposite of vision?

Spanos does offer an assurance that he doesn't "prefer blind poets with ears to earless poets with eyes" and goes on to explain: "My emphasis on the voice/ear – like McLuhan's as well as the phenomenologists' – has its source in my desire to recover the vitality of the 'vulgar' senses narcotized by the primacy of the 'spiritual' eye throughout the history of Western civilization" (B, 545). Yet if by " 'spiritual' eye" he means abstraction, ideation, his own consignment of orality and visuality, which have to do with nothing so much as with sensory experience, to the realm of ideas and philosophical stance perpetuates the narcotization he claims to oppose. Still, the equation of orality with a philosophical stance or dispensation is not something for which Spanos can be held accountable by himself. The apologetics with which various poets have justified the "oral impulse" on epistemological grounds are obviously among the contributors to this conflation. Spanos quotes, in the course of opening the interview, a Heideggerian passage from Charles Olson's "Human Universe":

> We have lived long in a generalizing time, at least since 450 B.C. And it has had its effects on the best of men, on the best of things. Logos, or discourse, for example, has, in that time, so worked its abstractions into our concept and use of language that language's other function, speech, seems so in need of restoration that several of us got back to hieroglyphics or to ideograms to right the balance. (The distinction here is between language as the act of the instant and language as the act of thought about the instant.)[2]

There is also, however, a more sensual aspect to Olson's emphasis on orality, one that justifies itself with reference to "the hunger of people merely to hang their ears out and hear" (*HU*, 75) rather than to philosophical trends. Yet even this passage makes it clear that the oral and the visual are not locked inside the either/or dilemma on which Spanos wants to insist. Otherwise, why would Olson speak of going to hieroglyphics and ideograms, with their primarily visual impact, as a means of restoring speech? Emphasis needs to be put on his use of the term *balance*. (More on the connection of hieroglyphics and ideograms to the open, "oral" stance in Section II.)

The rush to canonize orality as a radical departure from the values of an "eye-oriented" civilization runs the risk of obscuring the attention paid by recent poets to the way the poem appears on the page. This "graphicity," moreover, hardly at odds with the "oral impulse," has to a significant extent been meant to assist in carrying out its demands. Olson, in "Projective Verse," an essay that with its emphasis on breath and voice amounts to a manifesto for a more oral poetry, stresses the usefulness of the typewriter as a scoring device:

> It is the advantage of the typewriter that, due to its rigidity and its space precisions, it can, for a poet, indicate exactly the breath, the pauses, the suspensions even of syllables, the juxtapositions even

of parts of phrases, which he intends. For the first time the poet
has the stave and the bar a musician has had. For the first time he
can, without the convention of rime and meter, record the listening
he has done to his own speech and by that one act indicate how he
would want any reader, silently or otherwise, to voice his work.
(HU, 57–58)

Robert Duncan, in a similar vein, speaks of his work's "careful notations
of typewriter spaces as musical rests" and of his use of "two, four, and
six line spaces between stanzas and between sections to designate time
intervals in the articulation of the poems."[3] Robert Kelly also resorts to
an analogy with musical notation to explain his use of multiple, shifting
margins: "The ordinary left-hand margin avails as the base-line or 'tenor,'
to which all pitch transformations (signalled in my work by indentation
and 'dropped' lines) return as norm, at the start of a 'new line.' The use
of margin as notation or musical reference precludes the use of indentation
for intellectual 'organization of parts.' "[4]

It would be naive to assume that all the experimentation by poets of
this century with line breaks, multiple margins, orthography, typogra-
phy, and so on, has exclusively to do with an adherence to the poem's
musical demands. Were this the case one might be justified in characterizing the graphic impulse as an effort toward systematization, fixity,
and closure, and thus toward a domestication of the volatility of speech,
an attempt to imprison by rendering repeatable the instantaneity of an
oral articulation. (Olson himself provides evidence for such a charge with
the remark in "Projective Verse":

> It is time we picked the fruits of the experiments of cummings,
> Pound, Williams, each of whom has, after his way, already used
> the machine as a scoring to his composing, as a script to its vo-
> calization. It is now only a matter of the recognition of the con-
> ventions of composition by field for us to bring into being an open
> verse as formal as the closed, with all its traditional advantages.
> [HU, 58]

This passage led Robert Bly, who seems to have been making a career
of attacking Olson at one point, to condemn "the formalist obsession
which Olson embodies."[5]) There is often something purely sensuous,
intuitive, or gratuitous about the way a poem is arranged on the page,
having less to do with musical specifications than with that very quality
of openness, spontaneity, and even whimsicality often associated with
an "oral" stance. There seems to be a good deal of arbitrariness at work
in the graphic impulse, a principle of tolerance, at the very least, for its
disruptive, de-formalist thrust, often outright celebration of it. It is ex-

actly this whimsical, "oral" quality in the graphic experiments among younger poets that caused William Carlos Williams to complain to Cid Corman:

> We have no measure by which to guide ourselves except a purely intuitive one which we feel but do not name. I am not speaking of verse which has long since been frozen into a rigid mold signifying its death, but of verse which shows that it has been touched with some dissatisfaction with its present state. It is all over the page at the mere whim of the man who has composed it. This will not do.[6]

The graphic impulse is not in and of itself either formalist or disruptive, but a tool available to either inclination. The work of Williams himself bears this out. The early poem "Rain" makes use of unusual spacings between lines as well as shifting margins and what Kelly calls dropped lines:

> As the rain falls
> so does
>   your love
>
> bathe every
>   open
> object of the world[7]

The gist of the poem is one typical of Williams: Love is that quality of cleansed, purified perception that renews the world, bestowing upon it the grace of an attention to concrete particulars, an almost worshipful regard for "the thing itself." Crucial to "the spring wash" that is love is an appreciation of the individual word as a thing itself, an awareness of the concrete particularity of each word as indeed something physical on the printed page. The poem's graphic peculiarities thus have more of a thematic than a musical justification. The frequent isolation of single words, for example, is meant to heighten their visibility as individual entities worthy of our attention. What Williams is disrupting is the tightness of a more conventional arrangement of the poem, a tightness that would stress each word's value not as an entity in and of itself but as a placeholder, a cog in some larger pattern (sentence, phrase, line, and so on). That the spacing employed in the poem is meant to further an arousal of the love that attends to each word or each worldly object as a thing in and of itself is explicitly stated:

>   the world
>
> of spring

> drips
>
> so spreads
>
> the words
>
> far apart to let in
>
> her love

Love is the disruption of pattern, an assault on whatever routine narcotizes perception. The poem's content extends into its form in that we see this disruption enacted on the page.

The use of graphic features for more formalist ends in Williams's work can be seen in the triadic arrangement he so often used in the later poems:

> Daffodil time
> is past. This is
> summer, summer!

This arrangement is generally thought of as Williams's scoring of the "variable foot," each of the three lines or part-lines constituting a "foot." But the notion of a "variable foot" is an oxymoron. Its conjunction of the idea of fixity with that of flexibility is mirrored in Williams's bestowal of a visual regularity upon the irregular measure of his "American idiom." "A certain regularity in the actual putting of the words on the page does wonders for a poem in making it acceptable to the eye and to the mind," he remarked in a letter to Denise Levertov.[8] Whereas he could have begun each "foot" at the left-hand margin –

> Daffodil time
> is past. This is
> summer, summer! –

Williams chose to stagger the margins, I imagine, because of the greater degree of deliberateness in doing so, the consequent gain in evidence of intentionality. The triadic arrangement calls attention to its "arrangedness" more emphatically than does the more familiar return to the left-hand margin. Thus in this instance Williams uses the arrangement of the words on the page as a means of tempering the impression of patternless extemporaneity the poem might otherwise give.

So much, then, for the oral-as-open versus graphic-as-closed opposition. Any such rigid alignment overlooks the fact that audibility, like visibility, can be made the vehicle of closed as well as open inclinations. (I say inclinations as I'm not certain that openness can be other than a tendency.) Neither orality nor "graphicity" is monolithic, the epistemological stance so often attributed to the former notwithstanding. In the remainder of this essay I will be examining the importance and various uses of the latter in Charles Olson's poetics, looking at the variety of attitudes and assumptions from which it proceeds.

II

> *but when the bird swooped past,*
> *that first evening,*
> *I seemed to know the writing,*
>
> *as if God made the picture*
> *and matched it*
> *with a living hieroglyph*

H.D., Helen in Egypt

In the essay "Human Universe," Olson speaks of getting "back to hieroglyphs" as a means of restoring "language's other function, speech." By "speech" he means something more than the act of speaking, however, focusing upon that act, which unfolds in time, primarily as a means of insisting upon language's beingness, its temporality or phenomenality, upon the fact that language indeed exists *in* the world. Notwithstanding the attempts of discourse to transcend or disburden itself of the world of phenomena, to attain to a Platonic realm of eternal Ideas, language, Olson insists, is itself a phenomenon. (Hence Robert Creeley's remark in his introduction to Olson's *Selected Writings*: "Camus despairs of his inability to fit experience to possible orders of language, whereas Olson would insist that language be returned to its place *in* experience, neither more nor less than any other act."[9]) The particular hieroglyphs to which Olson himself "got back" were those of the ancient Maya of the Yucatan peninsula. "Human Universe" grew largely out of the time he spent in Campeche studying the glyphs. It is to this experience that he alludes in the essay as his having "been living for some time amongst a people who are more or less directly the descendants of a culture and civilization which was the contrary of that which we have known and of which we are the natural children" (HU, 61). The ancient Maya represented an alternative to the reign of abstraction he argues against, epitomizing for him a certain quality of attention, an orientation that refuses to depreciate the phenomenal world or to take it for granted, a non-anthropomorphic, ecologically informed stance he described to Creeley as "a disposition toward reality which understood man as only force in field of force containing multiple other expressions" (SW, 113).

Force in field of force. In the Maya Olson found precedent for the Open Field stance proposed in "Projective Verse," and both in his "Mayan

Letters" to Creeley and in "Human Universe" he refers to the Mayan glyphs as a form of verse:

> . . . men were able to stay so interested in the expression and gesture of all creatures, including at least three planets in addition to the human face, eyes and hands, that they invented a system of written record, now called hieroglyphs, which, on its very face, is verse, the signs were so clearly and densely chosen that, cut in stone, they retain the power of the objects of which they are the images. . . .
> (HU, 7)

He seems to have been particularly attracted to the fact that the glyphs are a transitional form of writing situated between the visual mimeticism of pictographic script and the more abstract and arbitrary semantics of phonetic writing. "Mayan writing," he wrote in a funding proposal in 1951, "is a hieroglyphic system in between the pictographic and the abstract (neither was it any longer merely representational nor had it yet become phonetic)." [10] He no doubt saw a best-of-both situation embodied in what he also referred to as "sculptured writing." The glyphs "retain the power of the objects of which they are images" not only by way of their pictoriality but also by virtue of the solidity and palpability they share with the objects they represent.

Throughout the proposal for funds he submitted to the Viking Fund and Wenner-Gren Foundation Olson repeatedly emphasizes the "double nature" of Mayan writing, seeing it as "inextricable from the arts of its own recording (sculpture primarily, and brush-painting)," an instance of "writing . . . as a plastic art":

> . . . I have called the study, and the book I plan to be sum of the work here, "The Art of the Language of Mayan Glyphs." The "art" is a matter of the fact that a glyph is a design or composition which stands in its own space and exists – whether cut in stone or written by brush – both by the act of the plastic imagination which led to its invention in the first place and by the act of its presentation in any given case since. Both involved – I shall try to show – a graphic discipline of the highest order.
>
> Simultaneously, the art is "language" because each of these glyphs has meanings arbitrarily assigned to it, denotations *and connotations* . . . and because they are put together, are "written" over a whole stone . . to make the kind of sense we speak of as language.
> . . . (A, 95–96)

What he saw narrowed if not overcome by the glyphs is the chasm between pictorial representation and linguistic representation that Michel Foucault describes in *The Order of Things*:

> . . . the relation of language to painting is an infinite relation. It is
> not that words are imperfect, or that, when confronted by the
> visible, they prove insuperably inadequate. Neither can be reduced
> to the other's terms: it is in vain that we say what we see; what
> we see never resides in what we say. And it is in vain that we
> attempt to show, by the use of images, metaphors, or similes, what
> we are saying; the space where they achieve their splendour is not
> that deployed by our eyes but that defined by the sequential ele-
> ments of syntax.[11]

The gulf between these two spaces has been particularly troublesome to
American poetry's Adamic aspirations. One finds American poets repeatedly trying to close the gap between the said and the seen. The quest
for a primordial, Edenic immediacy in poetry has manifested itself in
theoretical assertions to the effect that language in its primal state partakes
of the visibility of the material world. Emerson, to cite a nineteenth-
century example, is typical of this tendency, making use of etymology
to insist upon language's "rootedness" in the world of concrete, visible
things:

> Every word which is used to express a moral or intellectual fact,
> if traced to its root, is found to be borrowed from some material
> appearance. *Right* means *straight; wrong* means *twisted. Spirit* pri-
> marily means *wind; transgression,* the crossing of a *line; supercilious,*
> the *raising of the eyebrow.*[12]

Still, the gulf persists, etymologies notwithstanding. The spoken word,
however much it denotes or is derived from a visible fact, remains invisible, and the written word, though visible, is not identical to the visible
fact to which it refers (or even, in the case of phonetic script, imitative
of it).

In *The Pound Era* Hugh Kenner points out the indebtedness to Emerson's emphasis on visuality of Ernest Fenollosa's *The Chinese Written
Character as a Medium for Poetry,*[13] an important text, thanks to Ezra
Pound, for the poetics of the "New American Poetry." Strong parallels
exist between Olson's celebration of the Mayan glyphs and Fenollosa's
celebration of Chinese notation. In both cases the Saussurian principle
of the arbitrariness or conventionality of the linguistic sign is contended
with (though neither Olson nor Fenollosa explicitly quarrels with Saus-
sure). Throughout Fenollosa's essay the characteristics of Chinese script
are attributed to natural fact rather than human convention:

> . . . Chinese notation is something much more than arbitrary sym-
> bols. It is based upon a vivid shorthand picture of the operations
> of nature. In the algebraic figure and in the spoken word there is

no natural connection between thing and sign: all depends upon sheer convention. But the Chinese method follows natural suggestion.[14]

Olson likewise sees the Maya as having followed "natural suggestion." Their "obedience to the phenomenal world," he asserts, is clearly visible in the glyphs themselves:

> . . . this people's vaunted brilliance about time and its recording (their invention of the concept of zero, their observations of the movements of Venus, the moon, the sun, their calendar) is not to be divided from their exactness about all the solid things which nature offered them and which, seized as they seized them and transposed them into language, gives that language its exceptional subtleties and exactitudes. (A, 97)

Such assertions bespeak an anxiety regarding the conventionality of language. Emerson, Fenollosa, and Olson fear the possibly solipsistic character of cultural invention, the danger of becoming "uprooted" from the natural world. Hence the stress on etymology as a possible corrective. Thoreau, tellingly, speaks of wanting "something which no *culture*, in short, can give" (his emphasis), asking:

> Where is the literature which gives expression to Nature? He would be a poet who could impress the winds and streams into his service, to speak for him; who nailed words to their primitive senses, as farmers drive down stakes in the spring, which the frost has heaved; who derived his words as often as he used them – transplanted them to his page with earth adhering to their roots.[15]

One finds the same imagery, the same emphasis on earth and roots, in one of Olson's early poems, "These Days":

> whatever you have to say, leave
> the roots on, let them
>
> dangle
> And the dirt
>
> > just to make clear
> > where they came from[16]

The Adamic sense of language is a self-supportive myth, an "invocation to the Muse," a theory of inspiration. What it describes is not so much language as a stance toward language, a stance thought to be conducive to the making of poems. As Fenollosa is quick to admit, the "subject is poetry, not language." That poetry should be vivid and that

vivid poetry is born of a trusting, attentive respect for the physical world
are the essential points being made. A mistrust of language's capacity
for abstraction leads to an insistence on the accountability of words to
concrete actions and things. Thus Olson in "Tyrian Businesses":

> There may be no more names than there are objects
> There can be no more verbs than there are actions[17]

This mistrust translates anxiety into a belief in the essential linguisticity
of the world, the "living hieroglyph" to which H.D. refers. Williams in
"The Botticellian Trees" speaks of "the alphabet of / trees," evoking the
Druidic Beth-Luis-Nion and a sense of words as, again, rooted in the
actual earth. Robert Kelly, in similar fashion, writes:

> Soaked siena linden leaves
> after a whole winter on the porch roof,
>   fallen twigs
>   writing the old language,
> the language that was never spoken,
>
>   only read, first learned to read.
> Primacy of Text.[18]

The world, to this sense of things, *is* language (just as the animals that
presented themselves to Adam *were* their names), a field of signification
on the order of the Medieval "Book of Nature." The Adamic mistrust
of abstraction leads to a demand that poetry disclose the reciprocity
between language and the world, that poets be true to ideation's imbed-
dedness in the world (for example, Williams's famous "no ideas but in
things"), the intrinsic textuality without which language would not exist.
The word *idea*, Olson points out, comes from the Greek verb *idein*, "to
see" (HU, 65).

The sense of language as native to the natural world contributes to a
conviction that poetry can partake of a force that is not human in any
solipsistic sense, not cultural in opposition to natural, but both. Williams
speaks of "the enlargement of nature which we call art," arguing that
"the excitement of it is that you no longer copy but *make* a natural object.
(Something comparable to nature: an other nature.) You yourself become
the instrument of nature – the helpless instrument" (SE, 302–303). Louis
Zukofsky calls this process objectification: "the apprehension satisfied
completely as to the appearance of the art form as an object."[19] Olson
calls it objectism: "the necessity of a line or a work to be as wood is, to
be as clean as wood is as it issues from the hand of nature, to be as shaped
as wood can be when a man has had his hand to it" (HU, 59). What he
extols in the Mayan glyphs is the coexistence of cleanliness and shape-

liness, the achievement of objectification, a constructed naturalness. The stress upon "the art form as an object" is crucial to an understanding of both the glyphs and the graphic dimension of these poets' work. Olson, in his funding proposal, argues that the writing of poetry puts him in a privileged position with regard to appreciating the Mayan glyphs:

> The value of the writing to my work here would seem to be a matter of the insights which follow from the practice of it as a profession, particularly such graphic verse as a contemporary American poet, due to the work of his immediate and distinguished predecessors, does write. (A, 96)

The glyphs in turn exert an influence on his poems. He discussed a book that was to be called *The Transpositions* in a letter to Cid Corman in 1952:

> THE TRANSPOSITIONS are the
> least known and the least done, but they are a project I have
> been at now for years (they are, chiefly, from the Mayan
> glyphs and from the Sumerian). . . .
> (Such a volume wld be
> a chance to establish a body of discipline from stone & clay
> which wld, for my taste, be of more use than translations
> from the Provencal or the Japanese.
> It wld, in fact, be chips from the wood I work
> most for my own proper verse.)[20]

Though this volume never materialized, the impact of the Mayan glyphs on Olson's poetics can still be seen in the graphic idiosyncrasies of much of his "own proper verse."

III

Objectification as defined by Zukofsky depends upon a quality of which Olson's "obedience to the phenomenal world" is reminiscent. He calls it sincerity. The significance he attaches to *shape* in defining this quality is likewise echoed by Olson's insistence that a work "be as shaped as wood can be." "In sincerity," Zukofsky writes, "shapes appear concomitants of word combinations. . . . Writing occurs which is the detail, not mirage, of seeing, of thinking with the things as they exist, and of directing them along a line of melody. Shapes suggest themselves, and the mind senses and receives awareness." He describes objectification as "the arrangement, into one apprehended unit, of minor units of sincerity – in other words, the resolving of words and their ideation into structure," adding that "each word in itself is an arrangement . . . each word possesses objectification to a powerful degree" (P, 12–13). Olson's objectism derives from Zukofsky's notion of objectification, an important feature of this derivation being an expansion of the emphasis on shape to include the visual as well as the aural, the graphic as well as the melodic. The graphic impact of Olson's verse resides largely in a saliency of visual shape to which either term, *objectism* or *objectification*, can be applied.

One of the most immediately noticeable features of Olson's work, the use of large pages in *Maximus Poems, IV, V, VI* and *The Maximus Poems, Volume Three*, of large areas of blank space and the isolation of individual words or small clusters of words, derives from something like Zukofsky's conviction that "each word in itself is an arrangement... each word possesses objectification." The following poem, for example, takes up, along with its date of composition, an entire 8″ × 11″ page of *Maximus Poems IV, V, VI*:

> tesserae
> commissure (MP, 269)

The showcasing of these two words, the insistence that two words are in fact sufficient to make a poem, is the issue of a sensibility for which not only does "each word possess objectification" but, as Emerson said, "every word was once a poem." As in Williams's "The Rain," but to an even greater extent, the use of blank space highlights each word as an object in and of itself. "The word / is image," Olson says in "ABCs" (CP, 172), and elsewhere he asserts that "any of us intend an image as a 'thing,' never, so far as we know, such a non-animal as symbol" (HU, 65). Here he echoes Williams's characterization in 1931, the year in which Zukofsky's "Sincerity and Objectification" appeared, of "the principal move in imaginative writing today – that away from the word as symbol toward the word as reality" (SE, 107).

The idea of words as objects lends itself, as we've already seen, to the idea of poems as objects as well. One of the meanings of Williams's "no ideas but in things" is that a poem is first of all a thing, a constructed natural object, and only secondarily a platform for ideas, that objectification rather than ideation makes it a poem. Creeley, as a footnote to Williams's oft-quoted dictum, comments that "things are made out of words." The sense of words as physical things, building blocks or bricks, can be seen in Olson's often masonlike way of addressing them. It is no coincidence that both *tesserae* and *commissure* pertain to masonry. His concern with the appearance of the poem on the page, the arrangement of the words on the page, led him to devote a two-page letter to Corman in 1951 to a variety of anxieties regarding the handling of spacing, overhung lines, indentations, and so forth in the imminent first issue of *Origin*:

> you haven't sd anything abt proofs – and it begins to
> get close to April 15. Is it hopeless? If so, please, go over all

olson with someone, will you? that is, watch carefully for (1) the
spacing, that, it keep the same proportions I get fr this machine
(print or varitype space is different, and it is the feeling of the
equivalent proportion that i am after)

& (2) – what is always a trouble – that, my line is often so long,
it overhangs, in type, and so, I have always the headache that,
tradition calls for the overhung line to go all the way back to the
left margin, when, for my effects such is disastrous: it should,
any overhung line, be placed at the *right* margin, the end of the
word or phrase coinciding with the end of the line which it is
organically a part . . .

O, yes, (3) indentations, that is, the other spacing problem, the
        space I intend fr left to right: this is always being
        tampered with, by printers – please, here, too, see,
        that the relative proportions are accomplished, yes?
        (LO, 39)

This concern with the visual impact of the poem persists in Olson's later
work and, if anything, intensifies. In the work of the sixties, in *Maximus
Poems IV, V, VI* and *The Maximus Poems, Volume Three*, one finds him
occasionally on the borders of concrete poetry, as in the latter, where
there is a poem in the shape of the number 7 (MP, 589).

Olson's tendencies toward a "sculptured writing," as I have already
suggested, can best be appreciated in relation to objectism, his sense of
what an object does. In "Human Universe" one encounters his impatience with what he variously calls comparison, symbology, and description – "Art does not seek to describe but to enact" (HU, 10) – and
his desire to apprehend "the thing itself":

    . . . to compare is to take one thing and try to understand it by
    marking its similarities to or differences from another thing. Right
    here is the trouble, that each thing is not so much like or different
    from another thing . . . but that such an analysis only accomplishes
    a description, does not come to grips with what really matters: that
    a thing, any thing, impinges on us by a more important fact, its
    self-existence, without reference to any other thing, in short, the
    very character of it which calls our attention to it, which wants us
    to know more about it, its particularity. (HU, 5–6)

This passage articulates his interest in a seductive opaqueness, a density, a
fundamental allure he sees at the crux of our experience of things. An appreciation of the blunt, non-relational character of objects carries over into
his sense of meaning, the "thingness" to which his poems aspire, an equa-

tion of meaning with being: "That which exists through itself is what is called meaning."[21] The emphasis on "self-existence," on meaning that is non-referential or self-referential, on an enactive, non-reductionist art in which things "keep . . . their proper confusions" (HU, 56), contributes to – is used by Olson to justify – the enigmatic character of much of his work. An Olson poem frequently puzzles us, but in doing so "wants us to know more about it." Matthew Corrigan highlights both the graphic and the cryptic qualities of Olson's poems by referring to them as runes ("a secret, a mystery" – *Webster's New Collegiate Dictionary*):

> It is a stroke of genius to put on the cover of *Archaeologist of Morning* a reproduction of a Lingsberg Rune. So many of Olson's poems are fragments as this stone is fragment and are impenetrable to anything but the eye (Olson would crucify me on that *anything*). . . . His craft may have taken its chief sense of itself from the archaeological: rootings and scrapings. Reading Olson can deteriorate into cryptology (the game of). Sometimes the effort is worth it, sometimes not. The incredible thing, though, is the way he causes you to make sense of it; by which time (and effort) he has you in his world.[22]

The hermeticism of Olson's work tends to be tempered by a visual intelligibility ("impenetrable to anything but the eye"), a sense of coherence that resides in shape rather than message or paraphrasable statement, a sense impressed upon the reader by the placement of the words on the page. (Williams's comment to Levertov comes to mind.) This visual impression can serve to entice the reader into the poem, to allay for a crucial moment whatever doubts might be had as to the fruitfulness of repeated readings. An example:

<pre>
          wonis kvam
     HARBOR the back
     of the Cape bump
     Lobster Cove   bump
     Goose Cove run   bump
     Mill River – right there Alewife

          or Wine
          Brook
          in Winter
     Time   GRAPE   VINE

     HOEK   wyngaer's

     HOEK   Dutch

     bottom   Svenska
</pre>

bottom   ladder

of the Cut water

ran up hill from bump

on earth's

tit (MP, 410)

It is possible to be swayed by the shapeliness of this poem. Even without understanding in any paraphrasable way what the poem is about, the specifics of what is being referred to, or the point thus being made, one gets a sense of meaning from the way the poem looks. Intentionality, again, best gets at what this meaning entails. The evident care with which the words have been arranged gives the impression that Olson had something in mind, that this something is there in the poem to be elicited through repeated readings. The shapeliness of the poem excites and sustains inklings of an underlying intent, semantic as well as graphic. Another example:

Cyprus
the strangled
Aphrodite - Rhodes

Crete
-the Mother Goddess
fr Anatolia
Phrygian Attis

Malta: Fat Lady

Spain (MP, 263)

The word *commissure*, the second of the two words comprising the poem I cited earlier, comes from masonry and refers to a juncture, a joint, seam, or closure. It indicates the importance of joinings, fit, in Olson's work. Thus in *Maximus Poems IV, V, VI*:

All night long
I was a Eumolpidae
as I slept
putting things together
which had not previously
fit (MP, 327)

The frequent precedence fit takes over predication in Olson's verse – truth "is bare / of every quality / but connection," Kelly writes[23] – is one of the contributors to its lack of easy access. This has to do with

what he calls "the replacement of the Classical-representational by the
primitive-abstract" (HU, 96). A useful sense of what the latter entails can
be gotten from William Bronk's poem "The Beautiful Wall, Macchu
Picchu," which contrasts the "abstract austerities" of the Incan wall with
the representationality of Greek sculpture. The second of the poem's two
stanzas has to do with the Incas, the first with the Greeks:

> Looking at stones the Incas laid, abstract
> austerities, unimitative stones,
> so self-absorbed in their unmortared, close
> accommodation, stone to different stone,
> exactly interlocked, deep joined,
> we see them say of the world there is nothing to say.
> Who had to spend such easing care on stone
> found grace inherent more as idea than in
> the world, loved simple soundness in a just joint,
> and the pieces together once though elsewhere apart.[24]

Olson's poetry likewise appears at times to "say of the world there is
nothing to say" – at least that such is the case if by "say" one means
discourse, for the poems do speak to us nonetheless. It's not so much
that there's nothing to say as that there are other, non-discursive things
to say, other, non-discursive ways of speaking. This brings us back to
one of the central contentions of "Human Universe," that "discourse
has arrogated to itself a good deal of experience that needed to stay put"
(HU, 4).

The "primitive-abstract" valorization of fit embodied in the wall at
Macchu Picchu partakes of an analogy with masonry not applicable to
Olson's work alone. Gary Snyder in *Myths and Texts* calls poetry "a
riprap on the slick rock of metaphysics," elsewhere describing riprap as
the "work of picking up and placing granite stones in tight cobble patterns
on hard slab."[25] The middle section of Kelly's *The Mill of Particulars* is
called "A Book of Building" and makes a muse of commissure:

> She makes her presence known
> by joint,
>   fuck of images first revealed,
> Mars & Venus dangled in one net
> with background of mosaic leaves,
> holy marriage, opposites in bed,
> she is lady
>   (if she is lady)
> of associations,

> capable of magnetic parts, ultimate
> building for its own sake. (M, 77)

The masonlike putting together of words to achieve graphic presence recognizes shape as a quality through which objects announce what Olson calls their "self-existence." One could argue that such masonry (the term's suggestion of the Freemasons, of secrecy, hermeticism, and initiation, should be kept in mind) is typical of "the eye-oriented perspective on reality," a blatantly "coercive activity, the motive of which is to *shape*." I don't, however, see any reason to attribute its "coerciveness" to its visual nature. Shape can be aural as well as visual, "coercion" carried out in the realm of sound as well as of sight. Much of what we normally speak of as poetic form (meter, rhyme, assonance, and so forth) has to do with the shapely organization of sound, as does Zukofsky's notion of sincerity. In the case of the graphic qualities at which we have been looking, one finds form perceivable in visual relationships as well. Even traditional versification, the simple fact of lineation that distinguishes poetry from prose, is an attempt to render aural shape visible.

The shapeliness of Olson's poems tends toward the idiosyncratic, each poem bringing into being a unique instance of the myriad possibilities to which the poet strives to remain open. The pursuit of shape is consistent with the poetry's open aspirations, Projectivism's exploratory bent manifesting itself in the often desultory, nomadic sprawl into which the words extend:

> of the
> Pragmatism (secular
> cosmology, not   materials
> theology of most (or highest – hypissimus
>
>   Tower
>   of Ziggurat Mount hypsistos
> Purgatory "Heaven"
>   in that 7, or Colored
>   such
>
>   but
>   saecula
> saeculorum
>   conditioned – limited
>   Necessity is essential to an end (boundary Time 82,000,000,000
>   or condition (conditio   years
>   founded – Creation
>   indispensable
> of this age   saeculum   a race, age, the world . . . (MP, 456)

Passages like this graphically embody the instantaneity of thought, the multiple margins and highly variable line-lengths contributing to a ruminative, improvisatory effect. One notes a jaggedness, an irregularity of outline not unlike that of a polygraph tracing ("Let my poems be a graph / of me," Amiri Baraka writes[26]). The passage has an almost jittery look, a shape suggestive of that aliveness to the unfolding of experience Olson attributes to the Maya. Such aliveness is the gist of the open stance, Olson's insistence that form has to be fought for rather than conformed to, vigilantly sought from one moment to the next. He attempts to register the ongoingness of search and discovery in the very way the poem appears on the page.

The anti-conformist impulse of Olson's graphic experimentations can be seen most clearly in his attempts to disrupt the sense of uniform, homogeneous space afforded by print. One of the poems in *The Maximus Poems, Volume Three* is reproduced in handwritten form (MP, 479). Less radical but still effective is the use of skewed lines and skewed margins in "Letter, May 2, 1959" (MP, 150), "Later Tyrian Business" (MP, 206), and a number of other poems (MP, 404, 438, 466, 498–499). While such gestures obviously have to do with a discontent with the rigidities of print, to interpret them as symptomatic of a one-sided, "oral" repudiation of literate culture is to oversimplify Olson, the incredible allusiveness of whose work bespeaks an undeniable bibliophilic bent. One of the several bibliographies he put together is in fact entitled "The Advantage of Literacy Is That Words Can Be on the Page."[27] One of the most significant features of the quest for an open poetics is the effort to circumvent the closure of either/or propositions. In Olson's case, one encounters an inclusiveness in which the oral and the graphic coexist, each in its own way furthering an attempt, to use Spanos's words, "to recover the vitality of the 'vulgar' senses" – not only the ears, but the eyes as well.

8

New Series 1 (Folk Series)
Edward Kamau Brathwaite's
New World Trilogy

Barbadian writer Edward Kamau Brathwaite's *The Arrivants: A New World Trilogy* consists of three books of poetry published in separate volumes during the late sixties: *Rights of Passage* (1967), *Masks* (1968), and *Islands* (1969). The trilogy highlights New World Africanity, its prospects and its predicaments, focusing mainly upon the West Indies but ranging widely both geographically and across time. *Rights of Passage*, the most synoptic and panoramic of the three books, takes a "wide-angle" approach that extends to four continents, going as far back in time as the migration of West African peoples from the east, yet touching upon events as recent as the Bay of Pigs invasion. *Masks* and *Islands* take a more focused approach. The former, set entirely in Africa, deals with African history, myth, and cultural practices, drawing largely upon Brathwaite's eight-year residence in Ghana as an education officer. *Islands* focuses in a similar way on the Caribbean, drawing upon its history, its cultural heritage, and aspects of Brathwaite's life and recollections. Cultural and geographical dislocation, slavery, the plantation system, colonialism, and their continuing repercussions in the present are among the issues the trilogy addresses, as are the status of the African inheritance and the possibility of a genuine post-coloniality, cultural and material self-possession among the formerly enslaved and colonized people of the West Indies.

The most concise yet thoroughgoing entrance into the crux of *The Arrivants*'s concerns I find to be an assertion made by Guyanese author Wilson Harris. In his essay "The Question of Form and Realism in the West Indian Artist" Harris argues that the very topography of the West Indies, "a comparatively bare world... where the monumental architecture of the old world is the exception rather than the rule," forces upon the West Indian artist an apprehension of vulnerability, of the human person in the ambivalent grip of an enabling frailty. "This cosmic frailty (which is man)," he remarks, "brings a terrifying authority into human affairs," an authority of which the failure as well as the efficacy of those powers known as gods constitutes a disclosure. Of the early history of the Americas Harris writes:

> Immigration from Asia produced the American Indian. He built an amazing civilization but his gods failed him. Perhaps gods will always fail men. The failure of these primitive gods, who were rooted in real conditions, in forests or river, in birth and death, in fertility and agriculture, points the way to the necessity for new human values after the fetish. Man will never pass beyond prehistoric conditions until all his gods have failed, and their failure which puts him on the rack, opens up the necessity for self-knowledge and for the scientific understanding of his environment.[1]

This point concerning the necessary failure of the gods is the one I would like to repeat, pursue, and bring to bear upon Brathwaite's trilogy.

I

Man will never pass beyond prehistoric conditions until all his gods have failed, and their failure which puts him on the rack, opens up the necessity for self-knowledge.... In the first two poems in *Rights of Passage*, the first book of the trilogy, two such failures of the gods – or, in Brathwaite's stronger language, betrayals by the gods – occur. The setting in "Prelude," the first poem, is West Africa prior to the European invasion, West Africa in the immediate wake of the trans-Sahara migrations. The insistence throughout is upon the need for building ("So build build / again the new / villages"), the poem ending with a prayer that God's blessings be upon the newly erected structures ("So grant, God / that this house will stand") as well as the negative or negating response to that prayer, destruction of the village by fire:

> Grant, too, warm fires, good
> wives and grateful children.
>
> But the too warm fire flames.
> Flames burn, scorch, crack,
> consume the dry leaves of the hot
> house. Flames trick the seasons,
> worms, our neighbours' treacheries,
> our bars, our bolts, our prayers,
> our dogs, our God. Flame,
> that red idol, is our power's
> founder: flames fashion wood; with powder,
> iron. Long iron

runs to swords,
to spears, to burnished points
that stall the wild, the eyes, the whinneyings.

Flame is our god, our last defence, our peril.

Flame burns the village down.[2]

The god in question, though he remains nameless in the text, is Ogun,
the Yoruba orisha of iron and fire, patron of warriors, hunters, and smiths
("our power's / founder: flames fashion wood; with powder, / iron").
In the second poem, "New World A-Comin'," having to do with the
arrival of the Europeans and the consequent enslavement of millions of
Africans, Ogun's betrayal takes the form of the invaders' firearms (their
technological superiority) and the chains with which the captives are
bound:

> And the fire, our
> fire, fashioning locks,
> rocks darker than iron;
> fire betrayed us once
> in our village; now
> in the forest, fire falls
> us like birds, hot pods
> in our belly. Fire
> falls walls, fashions
> these fire-
> locks darker than iron,
> and we filed down the path
> linked in a new
> clinked silence of iron. (A, 10–11)

These two poems initiate the recurrence of a constellation of figures
– iron, fire, forge, urbanization, clink (or clank), "progress," and so forth
– that intimates that the historical material in the trilogy defines an epoch
presided over by Ogun, something like the degenerate Age of Iron told
of by the Greeks. Of urbanization in the West Indies Brathwaite writes
in "Mammon":

> Now slave no more
> now harbour-
> less no more, he forges
> from his progress'
> flames, new iron masters;
>
> brilliant concrete crosses –
> look – he bears – to crucify his freedom.
> So he must cut the cane-

fields of Caymanas down,
of Chaguaramas down:
the soil too soiled

with whip, with toil,
with memory, with dust; replacing them with soil-

less, stain-
less, name-
less stalks

of steel like New
York, Paris,
London town. (A, 75–76)

And of alienation in London in "The Emigrants":

In London, Undergrounds are cold.
The train rolls in from darkness
with our fears

and leaves a lonely soft metallic clanking
in our ears. (A, 54)

Here the "soft metallic clanking" recalls the "new / clinked silence of iron" in "New World A-Comin'." Not until *Islands*, the third book of the trilogy, however, does the orisha appear by name. The poem "Ogun," a portrait of Brathwaite's uncle, relies heavily upon a conception of the god as prototypical artisan, handyman, technician:

My uncle made chairs, tables, balanced doors on, dug
out coffins, smoothing the white wood out

with plane and quick sandpaper until
it shone like his short-sighted glasses. (A, 242)

Viewed in this light, the iron-and-fire motif becomes the trilogy's way of speaking not only of Ogun but of the technological motive or imperative he thus embodies, a technological drive that is one of the defining attributes of human beings and of human history (as when we speak of *homo faber*, man the toolmaking animal).

As Thoreau pointed out, the toolmaking facility carries a risk, that of becoming tools of the tools we concoct. There is also the related danger of becoming tools to other people (means rather than ends, reversing Kant's imperative). The betrayal by Ogun has the significance of a technology gotten out of hand and become demonic ("O Lord / O devil / O fire / O flame"), and of the latter predicament as well, the slave's predicament, the slave in the eyes of the master amounting to something of a hammer, an axe, a hoe. Brathwaite underscores the status of *tool* to which enslaved Africans were reduced by punningly entitling a section of *Rights of Passage* "The Spades." The specter of man becoming the tool of his own tools, human beings the tools of other human beings, exemplifies a duplicity, a reversibility about which *The Arrivants* has a great deal to say. As the title *Rights of Passage* implies, the work is strongly concerned with change, catastrophic change in particular, the explosive, inexplicable abruptness with which blessing turns into curse, God-the-Protector into God-the-Chastiser:

> . . . God sen' ev'ry month
>
> a new moon. Dry season
> follow wet season again
> an' the green crop follow the rain.
>
> An' then suddenly so
> widdout rhyme
> widdout reason
>
> you crops start to die
> you can't even see the sun in the sky;
> an' suddenly so, without rhyme,
>
> without reason, all you hope gone
> ev'rything look like it comin' out wrong.
> Why is that? What it mean? (A, 68–69)

The Roman god of beginnings, thus of change and renewal as well, was two-faced Janus – a fact that agrees with Brathwaite's sense of a duplicity, a likelihood of betrayal, at work within time. In one of the poems in *Islands*, the Akan trickster-creator Ananse embodies the idea of treachery as a condition of creation:

> black, iron-eye'd eater, the many-eye'd maker,
> creator,
> dry stony world-maker, word-breaker,
> creator . . . (A, 167)

The verb *forge* – getting back to Ogun – meaning both to fashion and to counterfeit, provides a linguistic symptom of this duplicity: "he forges / from his progress' / flames, new iron masters." Janus proves to be especially relevant to the trilogy's treatment of the notion of the Americas as a New World, a new beginning. Brathwaite's awareness of beginning's two faces points out the losses underlying the advance brought to mind by "new." Of Columbus he writes:

> But did his vision
> fashion, as he watched the shore,
> the slaughter that his soldiers
>
> furthered here? . . .
>
>   *   *   *
>
> Now he was sure
> he heard soft voices mocking in the leaves.
> What did this journey mean, this
>
> new world mean: dis-
> covery? Or a return to terrors
> he had sailed from, known before? (A, 53)

The New World was no heaven for the Africans either. The Middle Passage, alluded to by the title *Rights of Passage*, is invested throughout the poems with an aura of ritual initiation, a rite of passage whose epiphany or point seems to have been the unveiling of the gods' mockery of man. In the title, ironically, *rights* takes the place of *rites*, the irony residing in the fact that the Middle Passage meant a loss, not an acquisition, of rights (except in the case of certain Europeans, though even there it was a matter of "property rights," more privilege than rights proper, human rights).

An ironic recognition of the two-sidedness of history, of the fact that regression accompanies progress, defeat accompanies triumph, down accompanies up, informs Brathwaite's attention to the underside of human events. This downward cast of attention makes the trilogy something like a series of digging songs. The first section of *Rights of Passage* is called "Work Song and Blues," and one such relevant song, a type of work song found in Jamaica, is the digging song, a call-and-response form employed by laborers in the field that incorporates the periodic clanks of pickaxes hitting the earth.[3] Reminders of *toil* very much like these clanks occur throughout the trilogy, as in "Folkways" where the clank is that of steel against stone:

> steel
> hits the rock
> and the broad blade
> shivers, eye
> sockets bulge and
> burn with the
> shock, sweat
> silvers the

> back until I feel
> bad, mother . . . (A, 31)

And so on, recurringly, even until the next-to-last poem of the last book, *Islands*:

> . . . here is his hoe and his rude implements
>
> on this ground
> on this broken ground. (A, 266)

   The Arrivants is a digging song in the further sense that it recalls the figure of the poet as archaeologist we find in such work as Pablo Neruda's *The Heights of Macchu Picchu*, Charles Olson's *Mayan Letters* and *Archaeologist of Morning*, Ernesto Cardenal's *Homage to the American Indians*, and Armand Schwerner's *The Tablets*. The stance from which Brathwaite's "dig" proceeds has a particular affinity with *Macchu Picchu*, the work in which Neruda, confronting the remains of the Incan city, cries out in solidarity with the workers without whose miseries it could not have been built, "Let me have back the slave you buried here!" He interrogates a monumentality achieved at the expense of those least remembered:

> I question you, salt of the highways,
> show me the trowel; allow me, architecture,
> to fret stone stamens with a little stick,
> climb all the steps of air into the emptiness,
> scrape the intestine until I touch mankind.
> Macchu Picchu, did you lift
> stone above stone on a groundwork of rags?[4]

Likewise, Brathwaite focuses on what went on with Tom, his archetypal slave. This proceeds from his apprehension of historiography's traditional blind spots, the evasions inherent in the notion of history as unequivocal ascent. The upward aspiration that is tied to this notion is nowhere more evident than in those structures that project humanity's desire to immortalize itself: Chichen Itza, the Gothic cathedral, the Pyramids at Giza, the wall at Macchu Picchu, and so forth. In contrast to such edifices as these, as well as to their twentieth-century counterpart, the skyscraper ("stain- / less, name- / less stalks / of steel"), Brathwaite shows us where Tom lived, "his whole / tight house no bigger than your /sitting room," its modesty the epitome of those whose lives historiography overlooks:

> . . . brittle leaves, green speechless
>
> fritters, only mock
> this shack's dilapidation and the hopes of one
> whose life here, look

how snapped, how
broken, will not be
recorded on our cenotaphs or

books. (A, 72)

Brathwaite's archaeology excavates reminders of the oppressed, those
pushed under by a supposedly upward march of events. He shows the
"groundwork of rags" on which the New World was built. "These are
the *deepest* reaches of time's long / attack," he writes of Tom's cabin's
dilapidations (A, 70; emphasis added).

II

And their failure which puts him on the rack, opens up the necessity for self-
knowledge. . . . For Tom, whose ordeal "on the rack" – "ruined on this
rock / of God," as he puts it – follows directly upon the betrayal by
Ogun, this knowledge of self at times takes the form of guilt, self-
accusation. Rememberer as well as reminder, Tom recalls the satisfactions
of an autonomous African past:

the paths we shall never remember
again: Atumpan talking and the harvest branches, all the tribes of Ashanti dreaming the dream
of Tutu, Anokye and the Golden Stool, built
in Heaven for our nation by the work
of lightning and the brilliant adze: and now nothing (A, 13)

Under the influence of his captors' religion, he adopts a typically Christian interpretation of his "fall." Even the younger generation's awareness
and resultant critiques of the passivity-inducing effects of his religious
feelings – "they hate the hat / in hand / the one- / roomed God / I praise"
– serve as symptoms, to his view of things, of a deeply-rooted sinfulness:

These my children?
God, you hear them?

What deep sin
what shattered glory?

What harsh logic
guides their story?

When release
from further journey? (A, 21)

In his role of historian, Brathwaite, like Tom (whom he calls a *persona*),
is himself a rememberer. Aware of the guilts as well as the glories to be
found in the past, he moves, at certain points in his treatment of African

history, as if to uncover the "deep sin" that would account for the diaspora. In "The New Ships," the question of culpability, the Africans' complicity with the catastrophe that befell them, comes up toward the end:

> our elders,
> kola-nut-
>
> chewing,
> showing
> gums stained,
>
> tarnished
> with drugs'
> greed, love of
>
> profit, for-
> got the grey
> gods of anger
>
> who warned
> against smiling
> hands groping
>
> for markets, not
> wor-
> ship; for-
>
> got the long wars
> brought us here
> in the gossip
>
> of who pleases
> Portuguese
> best, sneezes
>
> snuff. (A, 129)

The question of culpability, however, is most often treated as exactly that – a question. In "Sunsum" the Ashanti proto-priest Anokye is asked to explain the Golden Stool's failure to repel the whites:

> Why did our gold, the sun's
> *sunsum*, safe against termites, crack
>
> under the white gun
> of plunder, bright bridge-
> head of money, quick bullet's bribe?

Why did the god's
stool you gave us,
Anokye,

not save us from pride,
foreign tribes' bibles,
the Christian god's hunger

eating the good of our tree;
flesh of my brothers' flesh
torn to feed ships,

profit's sea?
too proud?
too loud

in our white teeth
of praises?
too rich?

too external?
too ready
with old ceremonial? (A, 149–150)

Thus a kind of uncertainty principle vies with the reducibility afforded by guilt, an uncertainty having to do with the many-sidedness of
experience.

Just as the African's contribution to their own enslavement is only
one of numerous, perhaps innumerable historical factors, the hat-
holding, penitence-ridden Christian is only one of the various aspects of
Tom. "The *persona*, Tom," Brathwaite points out, "also undergoes a
series of transformations – from ancestor to slave to prophet to Uncle
Tom, and is finally translated into an image of the past out of which the
future springs."[5] The term *persona*, Latin for mask, here refers not only
to a literary device. Tom's "*persona*-hood" also speaks of a basic fact of
the Afro-American experience, the existentiality of dissimulation with
which, for example, Paul Laurence Dunbar deals: "We wear the mask
that grins and lies, / It hides our cheeks and shades our eyes. . . ."[6] This
fact, furthermore, participates in the cosmic principle that informs the
betrayal by the gods. What apter illustration of duplicity, the Janus principle, than the mask, a sort of second face? Hence the importance of the
second book of the trilogy. Evoking the wood-carving genius for which
Africa is famous, *Masks*, having so largely to do with ritual and lore as
well as with history, implies a connection between this genius and the
variety of guises the New World African has had to assume. Tom's
stoical placidity, then, is as much the issue of his ancestry and its mask-

making propensity as of an alien, conquest-imposed Christian disposition.

This mask-making bent bodies forth the specter of an apocalyptic interiority, an inner, unmanifest realm "out of which the future springs." The poems "Ogun" and "Anvil" define this realm as one of sublimated rage. "Ogun" portrays Brathwaite's uncle carving a block of wood:

And as he cut, he heard the creak of forests;

green lizard faces gulped, grey memories with moth
eyes watched him from their shadows, soft

liquid tendrils leaked among the flowers
and a black rigid thunder he had never heard within his hammer

came stomping up the trunks. And as he worked within his
    shattered Sunday shop, the wood took shape: dry shuttered

eyes, slack anciently everted lips, flat
ruined face, eaten by pox, ravaged by rat

and woodworm, dry cistern mouth, cracked
gullet crying for the desert, the heavy black

enduring jaw; lost pain, lost iron;
emerging woodwork image of his anger. (A, 243)

"Anvil" gives us a close-up of Tom, stressing the mask-like quality of his face and making the apocalyptic undertones even more pronounced than in "Ogun":

                    ... and underneath

        the wire mesh
        of wrinkled skin, the unloosed, untied
        skull of holocaust wreathes

        its revenging smile, breathes
        its revolted smoke of branded hide,
        of tong-sequestered flesh;

        beneath
        the docile smile, lies
        this unbridle'd monster's breath:

        hot, shot with sulphur, sour with its grief,
        waiting for time to die,
        for eyes

        to close, for history to wither. (A, 249)

The poem goes on to remark upon Tom's refusal to act on his rage:

> So he chose otherwise.
> Foolish or wise,
> his hand upon his
>
> hatred's anvil,
> he did not strike
> the white
>
> slave master down;
> the promptings of his
> tragic hammer
>
> held him dumb;
> the forge
> throbbed fury
>
> yet he let the fear-
> ful flare cool down . . . (A, 250–251)

A sense of dialectical inevitability makes past repression the promise of insurrection in the future, Tom's passivity a paradoxical reserve of messianic fury. Recalling the poem "Leopard" that immediately precedes it, "Anvil" uses the caged cat as a metaphor for Tom's inner being, and concludes by putting a question to its readers:

> His terror, caged, still
>
> paces, turns
> again and
>
> paces. Time
> ticks
>
> still.
> Which one
>
> of you
> with doubt-
>
> ing, peer-
> ing faces,
>
> will return
> to where this

future paces
and dare

to let it out? (A, 252–253)

Tom's terror, his aversion before the "terrifying authority in human affairs" of which Harris writes, is in part the other-worldly aspiration of the saint. The characteristic of the world from which this aspiration seeks release is the co-contamination of opposites – wars fought in the name of peace and so forth – the very duplicity the trilogy so often accentuates. While respecting Tom's saintly predilections, Brathwaite himself extols a refusal to be intimidated by the undeniable perils, moral and physical, of worldly endeavor. Over against a desire for innocence, we find a tough-minded acceptance of taint, man's inevitable collusion with the squalor as well as the beauty of the world:

For man eats god, eats life, eats world, eats wickedness.
This we now know, this we digest and hold;
this gives us bone and sinews, saliva grease and sweat;
this we can shit. And that no doubt will ever hit
us, the worm's mischance defeat us, dark roots
of time move in our way to trip us; look, we dance. (A, 116)

Similarly, in "Eating the Dead," having invoked the trickster Ananse as accomplice and brother – "I need your speed / and your enduring cunning" – he *invites* the violation of any innocence he might possess:

. . . Slaughters
of my innocence I must take on to bleed the fetters

of my tribe. I must devour it all like a bank,
cell by cell, vault by vault, blinding to the void . . .

        *   *   *

. . . I can show
you what it means to eat
your god, drink his explosions of power

and from the slow sinking mud of your plunder, grow. (A, 221)

We thus come to a further ramification of *The Arrivants* as digging song: The poet's acceptance of life's "earthy" truths and his invocation of chthonic powers. The earth, as in all primal vision, is recognized as nourishment, nutriment, source: "mud is a milk of darkness that feeds / orchids, roots that scramble outward like spiders" (A, 232). As in the passage quoted ("look, we dance"), rootedness in the things of the earth participates in a specifically African cultural inheritance epitomized by dance. The intimacy between the ground and the dancer's feet repeatedly serves as a sign of such rootedness:

> and we dance
> on the firm
> earth; cer-
> tainties, farms,
> tendrils un-
> locking; wrong's
> chirping lightning
>
> no longer harms
> us; birds echo
> what the earth
> learns; and the earth
> with its mud, fat
> and stones, burns
> in the tun-
> nelling drum
> of our hot
> timeless
> morning,
> explo-
> ding dimensions
> of song. (A, 117–118)

A later poem, "Tano," makes the merger of ethnicity (cultural memory, roots, ancestral tree) with "telluricity" more explicit:

> . . . Buttocks balance
> the earth; spine
>
> fuses the drum-
> beats to move-
>
> ment; lights twinkle to life
> in their root tips; the
>
> tree rises
> again and you rise
>
> with its trunk and its move-
> ment of branches; leaves
>
> hear again what the distance is
> saying; and my mem-

> ory bends, curves, nods
> head and crouches
>
> feeding the dust at the soles
> of its feet as it dances. (A, 154–155)

Brathwaite's "earthiness" has to do with a repudiation that is similar in spirit to Jimmy Cliff's "The Harder They Come" and the Wailers' "Get Up, Stand Up." It is a repudiation of Tom's "pie-in-the-sky" expectations and the Christian source of those expectations, a source with which the invocation of African gods is meant to dispense: "Keep ya Cross / keep ya Christ / keep ya nun dem" (A, 256). Like René Depestre in *A Rainbow for the Christian West*, he proposes the orishas of Haitian *vodoun* as a more viable dispensation:

> find me the rage
> and I will raze the colony
> fill me with words
> and I will blind your God.
>
> *Att*
> *Att*
> *Attibon*
> *Attibon Legba*
> *Attibon Legba*
> *Ouvri bayi pou' moi*
> *Ouvri bayi pou' moi* . . . (A, 224)

These last four lines – "Attibon Legba, open the door for me" – invoke the orisha of crossroads and gateways, Legba, the link between the human and divine orders and thus the first to be invoked in the *vodoun* rites.

A poem that epitomizes not only this gravitation toward the Afro-Haitian gods but Brathwaite's sense of his work's indebtedness to the earth as well is "Vèvè," the next-to-last poem in *The Arrivants*. The *vèvè*, the symbolic design made on the ground to invoke the orishas at the start of the *vodoun* rites, becomes a figure for the act of writing, the poetic rite:

> So on this ground,
> write;
> within the sound
> of this white limestone *vèvè*,
>
> talk
> of the empty roads,
> vessels of your head,
> claypots, shards, ruins.

> And on this sailing ground,
> sprinkled with rum, bitten
> with the tenor of your open wound,
> walk
>
> walk
> the hooves will come, welcomed
> by drumbeats, into your ridden head . . . (A, 265)

On this ground. Brathwaite's muse, the state of grace toward which the writing aspires, can be summed up with the Rastafarian term *grounding*[7]: grounding, that is, in the multiple sense of an unevasive apprehension of actual conditions, an appreciation of the African subsoil of Caribbean culture, a sense of communion and solidarity with the masses, and, lastly, an end to the latter's migrant status ("release / from further journey").

The first three of these connotations have already been dealt with to some extent. With regard to the first, it should also be noted that the hard realities of the world come, in the course of *Islands*, to be embraced as occasions for song, the cause for celebration being that these realities can be endured, to say nothing of song itself as a survival tactic. Thus the preponderance of imagery suggestive of hardness, that of the world and that of the people who endure it: bone, rocks, coral, and so on. Again, from "Eating the Dead":

> But if to live here
> is to die
> clutching ashes
>
> the fist tight
> the skull dry
> I will sing songs of the skeleton
>
> I will return to the pebble (A, 219)

Likewise, Brathwaite sees in the polyp's oysterlike ability to convert irritants (pebbles, bits of sand) into embryonic coral the more general phenomenon of adversity assuming the role of muse, summoning reserves of creative endurance and resistance. In "Coral":

> A yellow mote of sand dreams in the polyp's eye;
> the coral needs this pain.
> Look closely:
> the pearl has limestone ridges . . . (A, 232)

That the poems themselves issue from an adjustment to pain is attested to by "Dawn," where the image of salt carries connotations of bitterness, adversity, and affliction. The poem ends with Brathwaite's vision of his words' source, a vision of woundedness, hurt, and victimization:

> and I see you, my wound-
> ed gift giver of sea
> spoken syllabels: words salt on your lips
> on my lips . . . (A, 238)

The relationship of this vision of source to a sense of communion and solidarity with the masses is readily apparent, the "you" to whom the lines are addressed being an everyman/underdog figure. The masses in the West Indies being predominantly of African descent, the second of these senses of grounding relates as well. With this in mind, I have borrowed the title of this essay from Charles Mingus. Fishing for a title for a composition during a recording session, Mingus answered his own question "What could replace *Opus*?" (what could replace the Eurocentric, elite connotations the word carries) with the tentative "New Series 1 . . . *Folk* Series."[8] What I mean to suggest by this title is the feeling of oneness with the West Indian masses *The Arrivants* evokes. This feeling is nowhere more evident than in such stylistic properties as the poems' strikingly oral thrust, the preponderance of assonance, alliteration, and percussive effects:

> Click lock
> your fire-
> lock fore-
> arm fire-
> arm flashed
> fire and our firm
> fleshed, flame
> warm, fly
> bitten warriors
> fell. (A, 9)

These stylistic features, the extraordinary rhythms and syncopated cadences in particular, embody an African or neo-African aesthetic. A poem in which we see not only a stylistic evocation of allegiance with the masses but also their desire for groundedness, "release / from further journey," is "Cane." As are two other poems in the trilogy, "Rites" and "The Dust," "Cane" is written entirely in West Indian patois, Brathwaite's way of letting the people speak. We hear their anxieties, resentments, and aspirations:

> an' de hearsin' dark
> that darken de sky

> is de dark o' de dead
> o' de desert an' all dem
> travellin' years: tramp
>
> o' foot, stamp
> o' cotton, an' we root-
> less, waterless years.
>
> But we want to stop
> as others have stop
> want to stan'
>
> as others have stood;
> want to rest, want to build
> want to bless the Lord
>
> as the rest, as the others
> have done. (A, 226–227)

This brings to mind such grounding as that at the end of *Rights of Passage*:

> . . . So
> Noah
>
> stepping
> softly on the brown
> loam, returns
> to the firm
> earth
> his home . . . (A, 83)

This is the millennium the masses await.

III

Harris writes of the Amerindian gods as having been "rooted in real conditions, in forests or river, in birth and death, in fertility and agriculture," as having been grounded. He goes on to suggest that the failure of these gods had to do with an illusory transcendence of such conditions, a prime expression of which can be found in what García Lorca calls "the extra-human architecture" of the city:

> The great civilization of the American Indian, which was based on an agricultural norm, is a vivid example of an architecture of values made manifest from original conditions devoid of illusory masses or materials. Matter truly bore the imprint of genius, not the dead stamp of industrialization or the taboo of spirituality removed from

sensuous direction. This was an assertion of human greatness truly epic in dimension. To realize it, is to be aware of the diminutive man of the cities of the world today and the tragic ancestry of his gods which failed him with the rising tide of individualism that exploited those gods, thereby exposing an early deception whose intrinsic hollowness once followed communal patterns and was thereby able to wear the mask of man's self-torture and fear without failing under the strain.

Individualism has unmasked the original hollowness, and in that disillusionment the real rhythms of the human being are innately strengthened and discovered, the complexity of value is shown to be – flesh and blood, not spirit and stone. (TWS, 17)

Harris points to the Aztec civilization in particular as having valorized "spirit and stone," noting that "its failure was accelerated by contact with the individualism of an alien power" but also that intrinsic contradictions took their toll: "The priests of the Aztecs sacrificed living hearts torn out of the breast of human beings. This horrible contradiction was the result of man becoming the toy of his religion. A contradiction developed between man who built a world, and the world he built which made him helpless" (TWS, 19).

Octavio Paz, examining the same Aztec legacy, has written a "critique of the pyramid." He views – and opposes – the pyramid as *the* embodiment of the Aztec world-view, a hierarchical view of the world built on sacrifice:

The pyramid is an image of the world; in turn, that image of the world is a projection of human society. . . . The pyramid assures the continuity of time (both human and cosmological) through sacrifice: it is a life-generating space. . . . The [solar] cult demanded that the gods be fed human blood in order to keep the universe operating. A sublime and frightening idea: blood as the animating substance of the motion of the worlds. . . . [9]

His point is that the pyramid is still with us: "The critique of Mexico begins with the critique of the pyramid." Brathwaite, looking at contemporary West Indian life, also sees and critiques a pyramidal social order, the many being sacrificed to the upward aspirations of the few. In "O Dreams O Destinations" he writes:

but now our islands' leaders:
clever caught democracy of laymen preachers,
lawyers, pupil teacher teachers,

typists, skilled hospital
porters; each in his Wal-

ter Mitty world a wild Napoleon with dir-
ty hands; each blind

to that harsh light and vision that had once
consumed them; eager now, ambitious,

anxious that their single-
minded fames should rise

up uncorrupted from the foundry flames
of time's unblemished brasses, while the

supporting poor, famished upon their simple
politics of fish and broken bread . . . (A, 60–61)

This is one of the senses in which the "prehistoric conditions" of which
Harris writes persist. Brathwaite goes on to examine some of the "prehistoric" roots of this predicament in the anthropological investigations
that in large part comprise *Masks*. His own "critique of the pyramid,"
Masks delves into African traditions, finding the notion of vertical mobility tied to sacrifice.

The first instance of this occurs in the book's second poem, "The
Making of the Drum." In its role of communicant with subterranean
and extraterrestrial powers the drum serves as a vehicle for vertical aspirations. The first section of the poem has to do with the killing of a
goat to provide the drum's skin, which is described in terms of sacrifice:

we have killed
you to make a thin
voice that will reach

further than hope
further than heaven, that will
reach deep down to our gods where the thin
light cannot leak . . . (A, 94)

A later poem, "The Golden Stool," deals with the idea of nationhood,
the Ashanti nation of which the Stool is the symbol. Identification with
the nation is a mode of self-transcendence, verticalization, which, again,
entails sacrifice:

For the tribe's
sake, the priests cried:

die: for the Stool's
honour, shrine's wealth,

lean slaver's health
of money. Do not seek

> to find in the smoke's
> mask of battle, your own
>
> face, coward's eyes,
> truth of fear.
>
> For the tribe's
> sake, the priests cried:
>
> die . . . (A, 145)

Throughout the trilogy Brathwaite is concerned with the recurrence of exile throughout the African and New World African experiences. The epigraph to *Rights of Passage* comes from the sixteenth chapter of *Exodus*: "And they took their journey from Elim. . . . " The Middle Passage and such contemporary problems as the emigration of West Indians in search of employment and education overseas are presented as continuations of a legacy of migration extending back into the shadowy, uncertain prehistory of the African peoples. Brathwaite explains:

> The seeds of *Rights of Passage*, however, were planted during the eight years I lived and worked in Ghana. This experience (which is more fully recorded in a second long poem, *Masks*) brought me to the realization that the home – the true imaginative and spiritual home – of the "rootless" Afro-American and West Indian was in Africa, though the peoples of Africa were themselves immigrants – tribes who had also had knowledge of journeys – in the case of the West Africans, from somewhere within the Sahara and perhaps beyond, into the forests of Guinea, Ashanti and the lower Niger. The journey across the Atlantic on the infamous "Middle Passage" of slavery was therefore only another stage of this *diaspora*.[10]

"The Forest" is a poem that has to do with these early migrations. Having journeyed from the east, the migrants in the poem recall the austerity of Egypt and its pyramidal regime, from which they seek relief in the forest, Harris's "real conditions":

> But the lips remember
> temples, gods and pharaohs,
>
> gold, silver ware; imagination
> rose on wide unfolded wings.
>
> But here in the dark,
> we rest:
>
> time to forget
> the kings;

time to forget
the gods.

That fat man
with the fire-

light's grease
that dances

on his belly –
belly button

bunged – is he
the king

or glutton?
He lives

on human
blood

and dies
in human

blood;
our empire's

past of stone
and skulls

demands it.
And Ra,

the sun
god's gold,

demanded blood
to make it

sacred.
Time to forget

these kings.
Time to forget

these gods. (A, 113–114)

This as well, the leveling of the pyramid ("I will raze the colony"), is the grounding toward which *The Arrivants* points. Aware of its possibly being another motivating fiction, Brathwaite nonetheless allows this enfjvisioned "rest" to temper the brunt of history's trickster dynamic, the conceivably endless oscillation between arousal and frustration.

The tensions involved are obvious and perhaps inescapable. Roland Barthes has remarked:

> It seems that this is a difficulty pertaining to our times: there is as yet only one possible choice, and this choice can bear only on two equally extreme methods: either to posit a reality which is entirely permeable to history, and ideologize; or, conversely, to posit a reality which is *ultimately* impenetrable, irreducible, and, in this case, poetize. In a word, I do not yet see a synthesis between ideology and poetry (by poetry I understand, in a very general way, the search for the inalienable meaning of things).[11]

But what "the inalienable meaning" of duplicity, betrayal, portends is that there is no *inalienable* meaning, however much grounding provides an image of one. "Man's inhumanity to man," the specter of otherness verticality supports, advances alienability as a condition of being, a condition grounding seeks to resist. There remains, that is, the search for such meaning, alienability being likewise a condition of search, a search that is no less the job of ideology than it is of poetry, *The Arrivants* tells us. What the trilogy advances is a search to which there is no end or alternative, though its muse persists in promising one. Another face of this very muse, remember, the unevasive apprehension of actual conditions, forebodes betrayal. Hence the epigraph to *Islands*, taken from James Baldwin's *Tell Me How Long the Train's Been Gone:*

> It was as though, after indescribable, nearly mortal effort, after grim years of fasting and prayer, after the loss of all he had, and after having been promised by the Almighty that he had paid the price and no more would be demanded of his soul, which was harboured now; it was as though in the midst of his joyful feasting and dancing, crowned and robed, a messenger arrived to tell him that a great error had been made, and that it was all to be done again.

That Brathwaite, at the end of *Islands*, the end of the trilogy, can nonetheless look forward to "waking / making / . . . some- / thing torn / and new" (A, 269–270) attests to the tough, sophisticated resilience it is the job of rites of passage to instill. Such resilience is foremost among the "rights" trickster history's betrayals underwrite and bestow.

9

Limbo, Dislocation,
Phantom Limb
Wilson Harris and the Caribbean Occasion

. . . in a context such as the Caribbean and the Americas . . . the life of situation and person has an inarticulacy one must genuinely suffer with and experience if one is to acquire the capacity for a new relationship and understanding.

Wilson Harris

She succeeded in getting rid of the scaffolding of the song, to make way for a furious and fiery duende, *companion of sandladen winds, that made those who were listening tear their clothes rhythmically, like Caribbean Negroes clustered before the image of St. Barbara.*

Federico García Lorca

I

García Lorca's "Theory and Function of the *Duende*" affords a useful route into Wilson Harris's work. Lorca, in his now famous essay, suggests that "the *duende* is a power and not a behaviour, . . . a struggle and not a concept" and that "every step that a man . . . takes toward the tower of his perfection is at the cost of the struggle he maintains with a *duende*." He goes on to offer the example of Pastora Pavón, *La Niña de los Peines*, an Andalusian flamenco singer. One night while singing in a tavern in Cádiz, *La Niña*, disturbed by the audience's indifference to her technical brilliance, is forced to abandon virtuosity, to sing, as Lorca puts it, "without voice":

La Niña de los Peines had to tear her voice, because she knew that she was being listened to by an *élite* not asking for forms but for the marrow of forms, for music exalted into purest essence. She had to impoverish her skills and aids; that is, she had to drive away her muse and remain alone so that the *duende* might come and join

162

in a hand-to-hand fight. And how she sang! Now she was in earnest, her voice was a jet of blood, admirable because of its sincerity, and it opened like a ten-fingered hand in the nailed but tempestuous feet of a Christ by Juan de Juni.[1]

The *duende* is both an omen and a goad. It insists upon the insufficiency, the essential silence of mere technical eloquence, stretching the singer's voice to the breaking point. This pursuit of a meta-voice, of an acknowledged and thus more authentic "silence" beyond where conventional elocution leaves off, this impoverishment or tearing of the voice, corresponds to what Harris, quoting the Barbadian poet Edward Kamau Brathwaite, refers to as "tunelessness," the essential condition of the Caribbean's "orchestra of deprivation." Such numinous embrace as that of *La Niña* by the muse of dispossession, by the realization of one's having been silenced by presumptions of mastery, standards and canons of control, is what is repeatedly invoked throughout Harris's work: "The creative human consolation – if one dwells upon it meaningfully today – lies in the search for a kind of inward dialogue and space when one is deprived of a ready conversational tongue and hackneyed comfortable approach."[2] To embark upon this "inward dialogue" is to abandon one's conventional tongue. Such abandonment provides the occasion for, in Lorca's words, "the constant baptism of newly created things," what Harris calls "the Well of Silence."[3]

The term *duende*, as the inclusion of Lorca's essay in Donald Allen and Warren Tallman's *The Poetics of the New American Poetry* indicates, has made a place for itself in the vocabularies of many of the United States' more explorative poets. The relevance of the idea of *duende* to these poets' Adamic intentions is obvious in light of Lorca's assertion that "the appearance of the *duende* always presupposes a radical change of all forms based on old structures," that "it gives a sensation of freshness wholly unknown, having the quality of a newly created rose." The term can thus serve to bring to bear upon Harris's work the notion of place as a persistent muse among American writers (by "American" I refer to both North and South America, not merely the United States), more specifically the notion of the Americas as a New World, at odds with traditional structures, conventions, and forms. In the Americas, more than anywhere else, the occasion of place has provided the pretext for a poetics. This has been true primarily of those writers espousing and in search of an *open poetics*, the American condition being celebrated as one of marginality and unsettledness. Wilderness, whether that of the frontier West in the United States and Canada or that of the tropical bush in Central and South America, has served as a symbol of and inspiration for yet to be discovered poetic practices, for a break with established procedures and forms. What place means in American poetics is most often the quality of not having been wholly domesticated or mapped. (Lorca: "To help us seek the *duende* there is neither map nor discipline.") Robert Kelly, for example, has written: "What sustains us / is the empty landscape / the land we have not touched, / the primal temple."[4]

Wilson Harris, who worked for several years as a government surveyor in the heartland bush of his native Guyana, has very much concerned himself with the Caribbean occasion, the impact of place, of a typically American "yet-to-be-inhabited-ness," upon consciousness and the arts in the Caribbean. In his essay "The Question of Form and Realism in the West Indian Artist" he stresses the openness or emptiness of the Caribbean landscape, a bareness he views as conducive to "an original conception of values":

> What is the position that the West Indian artist occupies? He lives in a comparatively bare world – mountains, jungles, rivers – where the monumental architecture of the old world is the exception rather than the rule ... the very bareness of the West Indian world reveals the necessity to examine closely the starting point of human societies. The diminution of man is not entirely accomplished and a relationship between man and the paradoxes of his world becomes evident as a relationship which can still have momentous consequences. (TWS, 13–14)

Harris's approach is explorative, prospective, even hopeful – "the diminution of man is not entirely accomplished" – and invests in the Caribbean's relative lack of what he sees to be dubious attainments after all, the inhibiting structures that characterize a more settled, more conventional world. The bareness of an environment that is unencumbered by such structures, of "the land we have not touched," is embraced as a blessing, the birthing ground for "the revelation of original and authentic rhythms." The hinterland plays a prominent part in virtually all of Harris's novels, confronting his protagonists with enabling perils whereby their diminished, conventional consciousnesses are enlarged:

> Fenwick found himself at a nightmare loss for words. He was often repelled and fascinated by his camp attendant's calculating and yet spontaneous industry. It evoked in him a sensation of curious and abnormal helplessness as if a great distance stood between himself now and the faithful amenities of every past and truly harmonious domestic world, whatever loyal contrivances he had managed to establish. The jungle remained an eternal primitive condition. Everything and everyone could become threatening, even strangely privileged and demanding.[5]

The disorientation given rise to by the terrain can become the occasion for an immaterial transcendence or transformation as well. Fenwick, Harris writes, "liked to think of all the rivers of Guiana as the curious rungs in a ladder on which one sets one's musing foot again and again, to climb into both the past and the future of the continent of mystery" (SL, 19–20).

Place, as the foregoing indicates, corresponds to or is made to be suggestive of states of mind. The "monumental architecture" occupying the old world landscape is the embodiment, both literal and symbolic, of rigid, ingrained habits of thought. C.L.R. James has commented on Harris's work in the context of the critique of these habits of thought undertaken by three European philosophers in particular, Heidegger, Jaspers, and Sartre, arguing that "Harris is to be seen as a writer of the post war period who is in the full philosophical tradition":

> ... Heidegger, in my opinion, and Jaspers and Sartre, are aware
> that the European preoccupation or acceptance of the material basis
> of life, a fixed assumption – that has broken down. That is the
> significance of Heidegger, Jaspers and Sartre ... Harris is saying
> that in the Americas, in Central America and in the West Indies,
> that has never been. There has never been that fixed assumption
> of things, that belief in something that is many centuries old and
> solid. That is why he is saying what I interpret as the *dasein*, the
> "being there". I find it profoundly important and viable especially
> for people who live in these territories.[6]

To the extent that Harris, like these philosophers, sees any "fixed assumption of things" (and, correspondingly, the "monumental architecture" by which it is symbolized) as an impediment to open, authentic consciousness, architectural and technological bareness, "underdevelopment," serves as a positive symbol in his conception of Caribbean prospects – that of an *opportune* deprivation or dispossession. In this context, then, such terms as *deprivation* and *dispossession* are subject to quotation marks. The possibility of fulfillment in the midst of presumed and even manifest deprivation is a recurrent insistence throughout Harris's works. It is his commitment to and exploration of this possibility that set him apart from the dominant view of the Caribbean situation (or predicament, as that dominant view is more likely to call it).

The problematics of the Caribbean situation have to do with a history of colonialist and, more recently, neo-colonialist exploitation. This history has resulted in the continuation of patterns of dependency established with the inception of the plantation system three centuries ago. Despite so-called independence, the nations of the Caribbean find themselves dependent upon outside powers – the United States and the former colony-holding nations of Europe – for military "protection" as well as such essentials as food and manufactured goods. Their physical resources and economic institutions have been developed for and dominated by outsiders, and they suffer the adverse trade balances in which their export economies result. Dependency likewise manifests itself in the cultural realm, the area with which Harris is concerned. As David Lowenthal in *West Indian Societies* writes: "If Europe dominates West Indian political and economic life, in terms of culture the West Indies are also Old World appendages. No other ex-colonies are so convinced they are British or French or cling more keenly to their European heritage."[7] It has thus become customary to speak of the West Indies almost wholly in terms of cultural deprivation or cultural parasitism. In an essay called "The Unresolved Constitution" Harris cites two authors in particular who exemplify this tendency, Jamaican novelist and sociologist Orlando Patterson and Trinidadian novelist V.S. Naipaul. In their writings a litany of such terms as *historylessness, rootlessness*, and *chaos* has to do with the presumed lack of cultural traditions native to the Caribbean.

Harris argues that such writers reveal their own dependencies or parasitisms by clinging to so simplistic an interpretation of Caribbean culture, that the standards by which they judge the West Indies void are taken from Europe. Naipaul, who has argued that "a literature can grow only out of a strong framework of social convention" and that the Caribbean lacks any such indigenous framework, simply imitates, Harris argues, the conventional English novel. Harris accuses him of mimicry and of insulating himself, by way of borrowed conventions, against the very condition – conventionlessness – about which he writes:

> The contemporary English Novel . . . possesses a coherent design based on a social evolution and contract or bridge of generations. That this is something native to a particular social landscape – that in fact it has never claimed to subsume world literature – far less the imagination of man – is something that arouses the deepest uneasiness in the educated colonial from the British West Indies who wants – above everything else – to escape from humiliating reality into a style akin to first-class citizenship at the heart of Empire. . . . [I]t seems to me that if a writer employs a "coherency" based on the English social model to describe a native world which he himself goes to great lengths to declare invalid and non-historic or parasitic and mimic he gains a commanding strength (which is nevertheless illusion) over the material he describes that may entertain or divert people who have, in fact, no real experience or perception of what he is talking about.[8]

Such an approach lacks *duende*. Which is to say that it forsakes the anguished ground in which a tradition true to the Caribbean must root itself, what Harris means by a descent into voicelessness, a "confrontation in depth":

> The constitution of history as it affects the Caribbean and the Guianas is one which the creative writer is profoundly qualified to explore, I believe, provided he can suffer again through his work the ancestral torment of finding his tongue seized again as if he had become a dumb thing without voice or language. . . . It is easy enough to pronounce on "historylessness," oppression etc. – once one stands above it within an order of insulation – once one does not creatively descend into the disorder of it, suffer creatively the disorder of it: an escape route which may well prove the best of two worlds and permit a skillful short-circuiting of real crisis or confrontation in depth. The art in short not of alienation as it is popularly called but of insulation.

Throughout such remarks as these Harris is adamant that the opportunities afforded by the Caribbean "void" or "incoherency," opportunities for experimentation and possible innovation, for "the constant baptism of newly created things," not be overlooked. The very predicament that is so often lamented or railed against he wants to embrace as the occasion for an Adamic "centreing process, an internal representation of alien, however forbidding, particulars rather than an external representation of familiar hopelessness, stalemate and feud." He calls for the creative rejection of what he insists are oversimplifications, of the pressures on the writer "to make national and political and social simplifications of experience" (TWS, 30). Such an oversimplification he takes Patterson's "historylessness" to be:

> . . . what he is doing is to underscore "history" and point up to a "historylessness" within centuries of oppression. The danger of this – if danger it can be called – is that if inflated into a monolithic trumpet to wage war against philistinism and bankruptcy, it may react with poetic justice by bolstering up through glaring oversimplification, the very philistinism it sets out to destroy – if in fact it does set out to destroy anything at all. . . . [T]he clown of history is not *without* history but in fact is pregnant with a native constitution – the "lost" ages of men.

Thus: "If I were asked to give in four words . . . the direction in which I would like the West Indian novel to move, my reply would be towards *an act of memory*."

II

In the essay "History, Fable and Myth in the Caribbean and Guianas"[9] Harris quotes Merleau-Ponty's assertion that the freedom of the artist or the philosopher "consists in appropriating a *de facto* situation by endowing it with a figurative meaning beyond its real one." One of the essay's recurring contentions is that historians of the Caribbean, native and foreign alike, have failed to exercise such freedom, "that a cleavage exists . . . between the historical convention in the Caribbean and Guianas and the arts of the imagination." The essay points to a possible closing of that gap, toward an art (as well as act) of memory: "I believe the possibility exists for us to become involved in perspectives of renascence which can bring into play a figurative meaning beyond an apparently real world or prison of history . . . I believe a philosophy of history may well lie buried in the arts of the imagination." The essay embodies, methodologically, the point Harris wishes to make: that a native tradition of imaginative response to cultural dislocation or "historylessness" does in fact exist and that this tradition provides models and cues for the Caribbean artist. Harris's act of memory consists of reassessing the Caribbean past in such a way as to find precedent for "a profound art of compensation," an art that, refiguring the past and the present, prefigures or seeks to prefigure the future. Certain features of the past are endowed as figures by a self-reflexive muse.

Harris brings his art of memory to bear upon specific aspects of the Caribbean's Amerindian and African cultural inheritances, vestiges of and variations upon certain ritual practices, historical anecdotes, symbols, and myths. The figurativity of his approach is readily seen in his evocation of what he calls "a *limbo* gateway between Africa and the Caribbean." His highly resonant use of the term *limbo* has first of all to do with the West Indian dance in which the dancer maneuvers his or her way underneath a bar that is gradually lowered. The outspread, spiderlike sprawl of the limbo dancer's limbs relates the dance to the Africa-derived Anancy tales. These tales dealing with Anancy, a cunning trickster-god in the form of a spider, are widely known in the Caribbean, very much a part of the region's folklore. Harris also points out that limbo is said to have been born in the holds of the slave ships during the Middle Passage, brought into being by the extreme lack of space. This connection with the Middle Passage and thus with the idea of a liminal or in-between state enhances the play on limbo-as-purgatory Harris wants to be "born" in mind. Another pun, this one on the word *limb*, which the term *limbo* contains, brings in the idea of the phantom limb related to amputation or, in this context, geographical and cultural (yet another pun) dislocation. Finally, the phantom limb comes to be associated with the "rowdy" bands Harris recalls from his youth in Georgetown, a form of guerrilla theater in which "some of the performers danced on high stilts like elongated limbs while others performed spreadeagled on the ground." Thus a network of resonances and poetic associations yokes a cultivation of the unusually low (limbo) with a compensatory extension into un-accustomed height ("rowdy" stilts).

What Harris is attempting with this figurative act of memory, his own spectral or phantom remembering of a dismembered past, is to free the Caribbean of a reductionist historiography that imprisons it in its deprivations. He is attempting to recall and bring to light a tradition of folkish cunning, of imaginative, Anancy-like response to those deprivations:

> It has taken us a couple of generations to begin – just begin – to perceive, in this phenomenon, an activation of subconscious and sleeping resources in the phantom limb of dis-membered slave and god. An activation which possesses a nucleus of great promise – of far-reaching new poetic synthesis.
>
> For *limbo* (one cannot emphasize this too much) is not the total recall of an African past since that African past in terms of tribal sovereignty or sovereignties was modified or traumatically eclipsed with the Middle Passage and within generations of change that followed. *Limbo* was rather the renascence of a new corpus of sensibility that could translate and accommodate African and other legacies within a new architecture of cultures. For example the theme of the phantom limb – the re-assembly of dismembered man or god – possesses archetypal resonances that embrace Egyptian Osiris, the resurrected Christ and the many-armed deity of India.

And further on:

> . . . the *limbo* dance becomes the human gateway which dislocates (and therefore begins to free itself from) a uniform chain of miles across the Atlantic. This dislocation or interior space serves therefore as a corrective to a uniform cloak or documentary stasis of imperialism. . . . Once we perceive this inner corrective to historical documentary and protest literature which sees the West Indies as utterly deprived, or gutted by exploitation, we begin to participate the genuine possibilities of original change in a people severely disadvantaged (it is true) at a certain point in time.
>
> The *limbo* dance therefore implies, I believe, a profound art of compensation which seeks to re-play a dismemberment of tribes (*note again the high stilted legs of some of the performers and the spider-anancy masks of others running close to the ground*) and to invoke at the

same time a curious psychic re-assembly of the parts of the dead god or gods. And that re-assembly which issued from a state of cramp to articulate a new growth – and to point to the necessity for a new kind of drama, novel and poem – is a creative phenomenon of the first importance in the imagination of a people violated by economic fates.

Harris goes on to relate limbo to *vodun*, the Haitian possession rites derived from West Africa. The point he stresses, quoting Pierre Verger and Harold Courlander on African *vodun* and Haitian *vodun* respectively, is that the latter lacks the former's orthodoxy, the insularity that tribal custom and authority maintain: "African *vodun* is a school of ancestors: It is very conservative. Something of this conservative focus remains very strongly in Haitian *vodun* but there is an absorption of new elements which breaks the tribal monolith of the past and re-assembles an inter-tribal or cross-cultural community of families." The insularity of the various African peoples brought to the New World – Ibo, Arada, Nago, Congo, and so on – was broken or dislocated by the Middle Passage. Harris views this breakage, this amputation, as fortunate, an opportune disinheritance or partial eclipse of tribal memory that called creative forces and imaginative freedoms into play. He relates the word *vodun* to the word *void*, to the emptiness or "historylessness" left by the collapse of tribal coherency and sanction, the dissolution of ancestral rule. Limbo and *vodun* are characterized by a phantom extension into the novel "in-articulacy" brought about by the Middle Passage, into imaginative reas-semblings, resourceful acts of *bricolage*. Throughout all of this Harris is making a case for the imagination: " . . . the apparent void of history which haunts the black man may never be compensated until an act of imagination opens gateways between civilizations, between technological and spiritual apprehensions, between racial possessions and disposses-sions. . . . *Limbo* and *vodun* are variables of an underworld imagination – variables of phantom *limb* and *void* and a nucleus of stratagems in which *limb* is a legitimate pun on *limbo, void* on *vodun*."

Charles Olson, lecturing at Black Mountain College during the fifties in a course he called "The Special View of History," said of Yeats's *A Vision* by way of characterizing his own "special view":

(The messengers who came to Yeats through his wife's voice as a medium, and through whose instructions he wrote the Vision – a spiritualistic Spenglerism of time – Yeats was honest enough to quote in these words, "We come to bring you images for your verse.") It may turn out in the end that this dogmatic system of mine is no more.[10]

Harris's "philosophy of history...in the arts of the imagination" is likewise intimate with and committed to his own poetic work. As with Yeats and Olson, his view of history contributes figures to that work. Merleau-Ponty, in the passage Harris quotes, points out that "the act of the artist or philosopher is free, but not motiveless." The motive underlying Harris's figurative reconstruction of the Caribbean heritage is his need to find his own work prefigured in what he brings back from the past, to bring back images for – and of – the strikingly poetic, image-laden novels he writes. The phantom limb/Osirian phallus conceit of which he makes use in "History, Fable and Myth...," for example, can also be found in the novel *Ascent to Omai*.[11] Other such overlaps between Harris's critical and theoretical writings and his novels abound. His treatment of Odysseus's flight from Circe in the essay "The Writer and Society" (TWS, 52–54) is brought to mind in *The Waiting Room* by the recurrence of words and images pertaining to ships and sailing and to deafness and/or blindness. An example:

> The uncertainty of shape or direction – ancient vessel, model of creation, ark or covenant –...acted like a hidden spur as well as naked pole, a dynamic and static concretion to which one surrendered oneself as to a "black" pilot, weathered masthead, phantom of flesh within but beyond the sound of flesh, echo of self-regard, song of the sirens.... One embraced and was held in turn by this "deaf" mast to which one was truly bound and secured within the elements of distraction....[12]

That Harris's critical and theoretical writings are of a piece with his novels should come as no particular surprise though, especially in this day when poetry and fiction so often comment upon themselves. Nor should it come as a surprise that his exploration of the Amerindian legacy, like his exegesis of limbo and *vodun*, brings to light exactly such images and gestures as his own novels emulate and feed upon.

Harris looks in particular at the bush baby legends of the ancient Caribs, the cannibalistic aborigines after whom the region is named. Having conquered the Arawaks, the original inhabitants of the area, the Caribs themselves eventually fell victim to another wave of conquest, this one by the Spanish. The bush babies were wraiths, apparitions that rose out of the pots in which they cooked their Arawak victims. Harris argues that these wraiths "carried...overtones of eclipse at the hands of Spain..., overtones also of a new dawn":

> We know from investigations into the psychology of the *victim* (conducted, for example, in post-Hiroshima Japan) that it is he, the victim, very often, whose consciousness is infused with omens of

the future (apocalyptic omens are often of this kind in a *victor/victim* syndrome). It is as though the guilt of the victor stands on the threshold of a creative breakthrough in the darkening consciousness of the victim as prelude to the birthpangs of a new cosmos. It is not inconsistent, therefore, that we may discern, in the rubble of the Carib past, signs akin to a new ominous but renascent consciousness at the time of the Spanish conquest.

The bush babies are the annunciation of and symbol for what he terms "the native or host consciousness," the dawning of a new consciousness in which conquest gives way to accommodation as the model for human behavior and motivation:

> The overtones and undertones of host native – or a native consciousness – could have occupied little more than a latent threshold in the Carib/Latin world of the 16th century. For that was an age whose over-riding character – as in the centuries to follow – remained rooted in notions of conquest. What I would suggest, however, is that this over-riding character of conquest (the Caribs themselves were conquerors of the ancient West Indies before Spain, England, France, Holland came on the scene) was in a state of subconscious erosion. And I also feel that this latent threshold – this inner erosion of a certain dominant mould or character of conquest – this inner secret of the native (inner divergence of the native from a consolidated given pattern which is the tyranny of history) – is fundamental to the originality of the Guianas and the Caribbean and to a renascence of sensibility.

Thus the bush baby syndrome further articulates the need for an imaginative "inner time," an "inner divergence" from the apparent hegemony of realist/materialist history in the Caribbean: " . . . the Carib or Carnival 'immortal child' was an inner omen which diverged from the immediate realism of the day. Such a divergence exposed latencies or sleeping resources. Those resources of inner divergence need to be converted in our age, I feel, into an original threshold in a West Indian architecture of consciousness."

In another essay dealing with the Amerindian inheritance, "The Phenomenal Legacy," Harris is more explicit regarding the connection between his own writing and the omens or imperatives he elicits from the Caribbean past. He insists that he is not formulating or seeking to impose upon anyone a preconceived theory or an aesthetic blueprint but that his insights and assertions come from the actual act of writing: "My approaches . . . are not intellectual, but rather part of a hard and continuous wrestling within the medium of my own work, a process more akin to something active and unpredictable rather than planned and theoretical."[13] He points out as well that his involvement with the Amerindian past is an involvement "not with these aborigines as such, but with the aboriginal fact of conquest" (E, 44), and then goes on to insist on the need for an imaginative participation in the *brokenness* of the Amerindian legacy, for a vicarious, phantom penetration of an analogous broken state, "the necessity to enter a transformative area of assumptions beneath one's safe crust of bias" (E, 44):

> For the subject which is being approached exists in a void and therefore one needs to participate in it, I believe, with an art of fiction, an imaginative fluidity that is as close as one can possibly come to existing now, with immediacy, in a form that has already been broken in the past. It is here that one starts to concede and enter upon those alternative realities ("phenomenal legacy") which may lead to a new scale or illumination of the meaning of "community." Such a willingness to participate imaginatively borders upon a confession of weakness, and this, therefore, paradoxically, supplies the creative wisdom or potential to draw upon strange reserves and perspectives one would otherwise overlook or reject, detached as we feel we are within an absolute tower of strength (false tower of strength). (E, 45)

This "confession of weakness" is the artistic counterpart of the "erosion of conquest" of which Harris finds portents in the bush baby myths. What he is doing is insisting that the Caribbean artist descend into the consciousness of the conqueror-turned-conquered, into that shock-induced awareness of ephemerality (of what he calls "the mortality of all assumptions") and the consequent need for a new dawn that overcame the Caribs. The Caribbean artist should cultivate a similar apprehension of the provisionality of all structures and institutions, of the fact that no set of conventions, no "coherency," constitutes a final conquest of "the perennial, essentially human or natural fact of obscure, sometimes catastrophic change, life-in-death, death-in-life" (E, 44). One must vigilantly question, that is, the conquistador – the "safe crust of bias," the "false tower of strength" – within oneself.

Harris's two books of retellings of Amerindian myths, *The Sleepers of Roraima* and *The Age of the Rainmakers*, can be taken to be exemplary of the approach he advocates. That he is not encouraging acts of protest on behalf of the vanquished is made evident by such passages as "Hunter and hunted. Could they be one and the same in the end?"[14] and "the conquistador pass had changed hands frequently."[15] Instead, his concern is with "gateway conceptions of community" (AR, 61), with "a conception of the native as a curious host of consciousness" (AR, 38). The divergence of Harris's treatment of the aborigine from the more familiar romantic and/or protest treatments is evident in his highly idiosyncratic, highly specialized use of the term *native*. In the tale of the bush baby Yurokon, for example, he writes: "He began to age into the ancient Child of Legend. It was a story he had been told from the beginning – that he was the last Carib and the first native. . . . " (SR, 68). The term *native* appears to signify a certain racelessness or triblessness, what Harris refers to in the "History, Fable and Myth" essay as "the inner universality of Caribbean man." Significantly, Yurokon is said to have appeared "when the revolution of conquest was over" (SR, 68), underneath "the broken sky of conquest" (SR, 72). That he represents a universality that subsumes hunter and hunted is indicated by the reference to him as "victor-in-victim":

> As the Caribs withdrew across the ridge of the land and began to descend into a continent of shadow, each knot of ash linked them to the enemy. And Yurokon was the scarred urchin of dreams, victor-in-victim; over the centuries he remained unageing (ageless) as a legend, a curious symptom or holocaust of memory, whose burnt-out stations were equally embryonic as a cradle, fugue of man, unchained chain of fires. (SR, 75)

Fugue of man. Harris insists upon a contrapuntal play of opposites that is antithetic to conquistadorial agendas and regimes. In another essay, "The Native Phenomenon," he warns against "the tactic of fascism which battens on fear of contrasts" (E, 50), while positing "a universal host capacity to sustain contrasts" and "a play of contrasts" (E, 53–54). In the prefatory note to "The Age of Kaie" he writes: "I have attempted in this story to interpret the rainmaking fabric of the Macusis [a people native to regions of Guyana and Brazil] as a conception of opposites which has largely been obliterated by histories of conquest – Carib, Spanish, French, English, etc." (AR, 15). The story itself speaks of the Macusis' "need to reconcile the twin elements" (AR, 24) and of a "betrothal of opposites" (AR, 20). This fugue or betrothal is the "unwritten symphony" (SR, 63) Yurokon plays on his flute, the "music at the beginning of the end of an age" (SR, 76) – an age of conquest.

III

> . . . *on alto, he assembles long lines that roll and plunge as they accumulate to some personal critical mass, then he rams that mass with furious force into the barrier that begins with what the horn will not do. He implies beyond the horn. He tries to sneak through the limitations at some swift, flat angle. He tries to stroke through them, head-on. He makes you hurt with knowing how he felt inside that*

range, with listening to the faith he had in his bones and ligaments and muscles and breath.

Mack Thomas, on Eric Dolphy

The heart-searching rhythms born of North American Negro music have been described as "raucous."

Wilson Harris

As Harris points out in "The Native Phenomenon," a correspondence exists between Yurokon and Carroll, the black boatman in Harris's first novel *Palace of the Peacock*. Once the crew has undergone its "second death" and entered the Palace of the Peacock, a city of gold similar to El Dorado located in the hinterlands of Guyana and Brazil, Carroll (who has played the guitar from time to time throughout the expedition) becomes the mouthpiece for a music symbolizing universal fulfillment, "an invocation of indestructible harmony at the heart of the cosmos" (E, 54). The Palace of the Peacock is related to the *cauda pavonis* or peacock's tail, which Harris discusses in his Jungian/alchemical reading of the bush baby myth in "History, Fable and Myth in the Caribbean and Guianas":

> . . . we can look back at the Carib "immortal child" of dreams with the aid of alchemical symbolism for which, as you may know, there are three stages, namely, first of all the *nigredo* or blackness – sometimes called the *massa confusa* or unknown territory (not to be equated superficially with the colour *black* but with an undiscovered realm), secondly, the *albedo* or whiteness (again not to be equated superficially with the colour *white* since it means an inner perspective or illumination, the dawn of a new consciousness), thirdly, *cauda pavonis* or the colours of fulfillment we can never totally realise.
>
> The immortal wraith which the Caribs glimpsed as they crouched over their campfires and consumed a morsel of the enemy carried therefore overtones of eclipse at the hands of Spain (akin to *nigredo*), overtones also of a new dawn (akin to *albedo*) and of a host native (akin to *cauda pavonis* or rainbow peacock).

The kinship between Yurokon and Carroll (Harris calls them cousins) has to do with the fact that they both represent "the native or host consciousness." It is important to keep in mind, however, that the music for which each becomes a vehicle is itself a symbol – a *"metaphoric symphony"* Harris calls the music of Yurokon's flute (E, 53; emphasis added) – a way of speaking of a truth that cannot be embodied. This symbolic music is Harris's writing's way of speaking of an extrapolation beyond itself, just as in Jungian psychology the Self is said to project images of a wholeness it struggles in vain to embody in thought. Jung, to whose writings on alchemy Harris has repeatedly alluded and referred, writes of "the indescribable and indeterminable nature of this wholeness," explaining that "wholeness consists partly of the conscious man and partly of the unconscious man. But we cannot define the latter or indicate his boundaries."[16] Harris likewise defines *cauda pavonis*, the Palace of the Peacock, as something "we can never totally realise."

Such recourse to metaphor betrays an estrangement, a distance, that the metaphor – the word is derived from a verb meaning "to carry over" – seeks to overcome. The use of metaphor is then a "confession of weakness," the recognition of a chasm one wishes to cross, to be carried across. In the very text of *Palace of the Peacock* Harris alludes to this chasm. The narrator notes an incongruity between the sound Carroll's lips appear to be making, a whistle, and the sound he in fact hears, one like that of an organ. The chasm, the incongruity, is that which separates heaven from earth: "Carroll was whistling. A solemn and beautiful cry – unlike a whistle I reflected – deeper and mature. Nevertheless his lips were framed to whistle and I could only explain the difference by assuming the sound from his lips was changed when it struck the window and issued into the world."[17] This music, a metaphor for cosmic unity somewhat like "the harmony of the spheres," through its metaphoricity "confesses" an estrangement from the wholeness it intimates. The narrator finds the music, just as Jung does wholeness, indescribable and indeterminable, and his attempt to evoke it is marked by a tentative, rather hesitant movement that whenever it asserts immediately qualifies itself:

> It was an organ cry almost and yet quite different I reflected again. It seemed to break and mend itself always – tremulous, forlorn, distant, triumphant, the echo of sound so pure and outlined in space it broke again into a mass of music. It was the cry of the peacock and yet I reflected far different. I stared at the whistling lips and wondered if the change was in me or in them. I had never witnessed and heard such sad and such glorious music. (PP, 147)

The music itself breaks. It is as if Harris wanted to show the metaphor cracking under the weight – the "indestructible harmony at the heart of the cosmos" – it is being made to carry. But the music also mends itself; in the same way, I'd venture to say, that a phantom limb "mends" an amputation. The music/metaphor can be said to be the phantom limb with which the novel reaches toward a wholeness to which it can only *refer*, the cosmic fulfillment we at once intuit and are "cut off" from.

The specter of this wholeness in relation to which all expression or manifestation has to be deemed incomplete haunts the world of Harris's works. A similar incongruity between an act of producing sound and the sound produced occurs in *The Secret Ladder* when Fenwick first encounters Poseidon, the descendant of a runaway slave living in the swamps being surveyed by Fenwick's crew:

> Poseidon addressed Fenwick at last. His mouth moved and made frames which did not correspond to the words he actually uttered. It was like the tragic lips of an actor, moving but soundless as a picture, galvanized into comical association with a foreign dubbing and tongue which uttered a mechanical version and translation out of accord with the visible features of original expression. (SL, 24)

The un-Africanness of the name Poseidon, despite its allusion to Leo Frobenius's African researches, heightens the sense of schism and incongruity. What Harris is attempting to suggest is a sundering or "a play of contrasts" at the heart of things. Insofar as Poseidon represents Adamic seed or primogenitorship ("the Grand Old Man of our history" and "the black king of history" are what he's called in the text), the passage constitutes either a refusal to invest the ancestral past, as is commonly done, with connotations of Edenic wholeness – in which case Poseidon represents not a Golden Age of unity à la Adam Qadmon but "a form that has already been broken in the past" – or a reminder of Fenwick's and our own estrangement from (and thus the unintelligibility to us of) whatever unity Poseidon does represent. These two readings essentially amount to the same thing – an insistence upon the elusiveness or irretrievability of wholeness, upon *différance*. This elusiveness is further suggested by the fact that in three novels, *Palace of the Peacock, The Whole Armour*, and *Tumatumari*, the Amerindians (again, possibly suggestive of some ancestral or aboriginal wholeness) are *in flight*: " . . . shattered tribe. A terrible broken family. *On the run!* They were running, running, I tell you. Full retreat. Full flight. God knows who started it. You would think the blasted tiger of hell was chasing them."[18]

Harris's acknowledgment of and struggle with this elusiveness make for the rapport I've been attempting to suggest between his writings and Lorca's idea of the *duende*. Just as Lorca extols the brokenness of *La Niña's* voice, Harris accords brokenness, breakage, symptomatic as well as symbolic of incompleteness, the status of cosmogonic truth: "Yurokon held the twine in his hands as if with a snap, a single fierce pull, he would break it *now* at last. Break the land. Break the sea. Break the savannah. Break the forest. Break the twig. Break the bough" (SR, 69). Harris's prose has itself become more broken. Here, for example, is a passage from one of his more recent novels, *Companions of the Day and Night*:

It was time to take stock of others as hollow bodies and shelters into which one fell. Hollow newspaper into which one fell, newsworthy sacrifice, wrinkled skin. FIRING SQUAD OF RAIN. Headline. Heartline. STOCKMARKET SHELTER, CITY RAINS. Deadline. CANVAS REQUIRED, SACRIFICE REQUIRED.

For centuries it seemed to him now he had been ascending, sliding, falling into rain inch by inch, into shelters of paint, shelters of stone. Sacrificed paint. Sacrificed stone. Lament for the dying sun. This was the altar of his malaise, Idiot shelter, Idiot fascination, fall into the sculptures of the greatest men (upon whom? from whom? times rained).[19]

Comparing this with the passages I quoted from the earlier novels *Palace of the Peacock* and *The Secret Ladder*, one immediately notes an increased reliance on sentence fragments and one- or two-word bursts. The more recent prose is more agitated, more impatient it seems. Its urgency furthers a certain rowdiness or raucousness – something Derek Walcott has referred to as "audacious" – that typified Harris's work from the very beginning. A sometimes strained, obsessional energy brings Harris's writing, even in its earlier, less choppy phase – in which phase just the opposite tendency, the unusual length and the complexity of the sentences, conveys this energy – close, to my hearing at least, to that raspy, "unmusical" quality a flamenco singer or a horn player like Eric Dolphy or Anthony Braxton often gets. (Carroll's music, interestingly, is likened to the cry of a peacock, a sound not particularly known for its euphonious qualities.) This stridency or raspiness is both an acknowledgment of and a doing battle with limitation ("the barrier that begins with what the horn will not do"), a "confession of weakness," and a phantom reach beyond incompleteness.

IV

"So on this ground, / write . . . / on this ground / on this broken ground," writes Edward Kamau Brathwaite.[20] These lines have to do with the Caribbean condition – fragmentation, dislocation, and so forth. The "broken ground" is the island topography itself, the separation of the islands from one another as though they were remnants of some larger, sundered whole. It is also the ground of other breakages and a metaphor for such breakages – the broken, alienated labor of slaves and descendants of slaves, the ecological breakdown or depletion of the soil due to decades of mono-crop agriculture, the break, albeit partial, with old world homelands, old world histories, old world continuities and "coherencies," the

further breakage brought about by the collision of cultures under cir-
cumstances of enmity and coercion. These lines also have to do with
writing, and if one calls to mind the Derridean idea that the very possibility of writing signifies and is indebted to a cosmogonic severance
known as *différance*, one is prepared to understand "this broken ground"
in the way that Harris does. The Caribbean's brokenness participates in
a larger-than-local problematic, the universal human predicament Harris
calls "cosmic frailty" (TWS, 20), an ontological estrangement or weakness the Caribbean writer, having no historically sustained "coherency"
as insulation or defense, is in a position to confess. The problem of large-
scale emigration from the Caribbean, for example, the fact that every
year an enormous number of West Indians leave home in search of
economic, educational, cultural, and other opportunities abroad, is not
simply a manifestation of the dependency situation peculiar to the Caribbean but is endowed by Harris, himself an emigrant now living in
England, with suggestions of a universal condition of exile. In Idiot
Nameless's "Manifesto of the Unborn State of Exile" in *The Eye of the
Scarecrow* then:

> The education of freedom . . . begins with a confession of the need
> to lose the base concretion men seek to impose when they talk of
> one's "native" land (or another's) as if it were fixed and anchored
> in place. In this age and time, one's native land (and the other's) is
> always *crumbling:* crumbling within a capacity of vision which re-
> discovers the process to be not foul and destructive but actually the
> constructive secret of all creation wherever one happens to be. (ES,
> 101–103)

With such insistent reach beyond the simply local, such vigilant qualification of nominal roots and nominal nativity, Harris claims that much-
contested ground, universality. This is ground to which writers from
colonized or recently colonized regions are not expected or encouraged
to lay claim, and the claim is further handicapped by the suspicion with
which universalizing assertions tend to be greeted these days. Largely
because of the imperial projects to which such assertions have been tied
in the West, we rightly regard them skeptically. But when the claim to
the "secret of all creation" is made by a writer from a region victimized
by such projects and when the claim is made in contestation of such
projects, advancing an erosion rather than a consolidation of scaffolding
and support – when the claim, that is, is made with so much *duende* –
we had better listen.

10

Poseidon (Dub Version)

Though supplanted by Zeus, Poseidon continued to exercise his empire over the entire earth, as is proved . . . by the titles Homer gives him, such as Enosichthon — "earthshaker." Poseidon was indeed, the god of earthquakes.

New Larousse Encyclopedia of Mythology

"I am not deaf, Bryant," Fenwick could not help himself crying out. "I understood Poseidon perfectly today." He knew that he lied, but his vanity and self-possession had been strangely shaken.

Wilson Harris, The Secret Ladder

The European became aware of the fact that the life he had built on the agony of the colonized man, the Mayas, the Incas, the Toltecs — the Africans and others — was losing its assurance. Fanon has intimations of the psychic meaning of this earthquake. It is about the brutality and heroism and the uncertain future to come.

John La Rose

The Dogon of West Africa, for whom weaving is cosmogonic, refer to their weaving block as the "creaking of the word." We read in *Conversations with Ogotemmeli*, Marcel Griaule's well known account of the catechism into which he was inducted by the Dogon:

It remained only to speak of the Word, on which (he said) the whole revelation of the art of weaving is based.

"The Word," said the old man, "is in the sound of the block and the shuttle. The name of the block means 'creaking of the word.' Everybody understands what is meant by 'the word' in that connection. It is interwoven with the threads: it fills the interstices in the fabric . . ."[1]

What this means is not only that our purchase on the world is a weave but also that the word is a rickety witness, the telltale base on which our sense of that weave sits. *Fabric* echoes *fabrication*, as both go back to a root that has to do with making. The creaking of the word calls attention to the constructedness of the hold on the world fabrication affords. It carries the seeds of a self-critique, a caveat bearing upon the axiomatic, rickety fit between world and word.

It is only fitting, poetically just, that this notion of anti-foundational noise, the reminder of uninsured fit, should emerge in the course of an ethnographic encounter. Since Griaule's day, ethnography, like other disciplines within the so-called human sciences, has been increasingly unable not to hear its own creaking, the "crisis of representation" to which George Marcus and Michael Fischer devote a chapter in their book *Anthropology as Cultural Critique:*

> The key feature of this moment, then, is the loosening of the hold over fragmented scholarly communities of either specific totalizing visions or a general paradigmatic style of organizing research. . . .
>
> The part of these conditions in which we are most interested is what we call a crisis of representation. This is the intellectual stimulus for the contemporary vitality of experimental writing in anthropology. The crisis arises from uncertainty about adequate means of describing social reality. In the United States, it is an expression of the failure of post-World War II paradigms, or the unifying ideas of a remarkable number of fields, to account for conditions within American society, if not within Western societies globally, which seem to be in a state of profound transition.[2]

They go on to relate this crisis to social and political changes, attentive in particular to the impact of geopolitical power shifts:

> This trend may have much to do with the unfavorable shift in the relative position of American power and influence in the world, and with the widespread perception of the dissolution of the ruling post-war model of the liberal welfare state at home. Both the taste for totalizing frameworks and the predominance in many academic disciplines of general models of stability in the social and natural order seemed to have coincided with the previously more confident and secure national mood. The current exhaustion of this style of theorizing merely points up the politicized context in which post-World War II intellectual trends have been shaped all along.[3]

James Clifford, in the introduction to his and Marcus's *Writing Culture,* points to the breakdown of colonialism, noting, like John La Rose paraphrasing Fanon in one of the epigraphs prefacing this essay,[4] its contribution to the West's loss of assurance. This contribution he sees having been joined by those of an array of intellectual trends that tend to be grouped under the rubric "theory":

> The critique of colonialism in the postwar period – an undermining of "The West's" ability to represent other societies – has been reinforced by an important process of theorizing about the limits of representation itself. There is no way adequately to survey this multifarious critique of what Vico called the "serious poem" of cultural history. Positions proliferate: "hermeneutics," "structuralism," "history of mentalities," "neo-Marxism," "genealogy," "post-structuralism," "post-modernism," "pragmatism"; also a spate of "alternate epistemologies" – feminist, ethnic, and non-Western. What is at stake, but not always recognized, is an ongoing critique of the West's most confident, characteristic discourses. Diverse philosophies may implicitly have this critical stance in common.[5]

What these critiques amount to is a creaking of the word, a confessional dissonance implicating representation in the very conflicts and complications it seeks to contain. The self-consciousness, self-scrutiny, and suspicion that characterize current approaches to modes of representation, the loss of faith in metanarratives, dominant paradigms, and so forth, attest to a foundational crisis, the "bottomless extremity" that Wilson Harris mentions early on in *The Secret Ladder*.[6]

Marcus and Fischer speak of "experimental writing in anthropology." Clifford touches upon the "literary qualities" of ethnography, putting "literary" aside in favor of "artisanal" but going on to speak nonetheless of "ethnographic fictions" and "the poetic dimensions of ethnography." What this may help to remind us is that the insights that inform this crisis derive substantially from the self-inquisitive (and/or -incriminating) testimony of much of the literature of the past one hundred years. It is no coincidence that the first book by the author of *Orientalism* was a study of Joseph Conrad's work. Nor should we be surprised that literature continues to partake of what it often opts, as in Harris's case, to view not only as crisis but as constitutive condition:

> The morning fire of the sun was now clear risen: a large patch of blue had been stitched between the trees. An air of enormous artifice rested everywhere, the gnarled shadow of cloaked branches, naked leaves pinned fortuitously to the sky, these worn materials of earth stretched almost to the limits of enduring apprehension. Fenwick wanted to brush his thoughts aside. They were needling him into

supplication, making him conscious of the immaterial thread of awareness he possessed of the nature of himself, and other creatures and men. All was an artifice of mystery to which one addressed oneself often with idle and pretentious words. The shape of mystery was always invisibly there, each representation the endless source of both humility and parody. Nothing lasted that did not show how soon it would crumble again. . . . (195)

The Secret Ladder presumes no transparent mediation. Even the bush, commonly taken to epitomize the natural, the nakedly organic, is here said to be cloaked, clothed, fabricked. The words admit to their weave. Harris has written of an "eclipse of the word" in Conrad's *Heart of Darkness*, of "a *cry* that is *mute*" in Marlow's "compassionate lie."[7] Creak, rickety weave, ups the ante on eclipse.

The confessional opacity of Harris's writing, the endlessly sounded note of apprehension regarding the ruses and misconceptions endemic to acts of representation, is indissociable from the colonial encounter – is, that is, one of the repercussions of and responses to that encounter. The colonizing adventure, the exploitative encounter between the West and its others, we know to be a key component of the representational tradition that is being called into question. Harris's repudiation of the realist novel – rooted in the awareness that, as he puts it, "the rise of the novel in its conventional and historical mould coincides in Europe with states of society which were involved in consolidating their class and other vested interests"[8] – participates in a politicized context in which the West's exploited, misrepresented others contest their misrepresentation. Where the word is inflected with legacies of conquest and oppression, as in the region where Harris was born and of which he writes, the creaking of the word is an opening, an opportune alarm sounded against presumed equivalence, presumed assurances of unequivocal fit. This opening, in which the apparatuses of representation come under inspection, entails, among other things, discrepant engagements of word and image, deployments of word and image that are at variance with their ostensible report, at variance with an ostensible rapport between word and image, signifier and signified.

I would like to look a bit more closely at discrepant engagement in *The Secret Ladder* (*discrepant* comes from a root meaning "to rattle, creak"), particularly as it pertains to Poseidon, the descendant of a runaway slave encountered by Fenwick and his crew. One is struck, first of all, by the name, which is hardly one we'd have expected for the embodiment of African survival, African presence, "the black king of history" (154). The discrepant play between African and Greek, African and European, is called attention to by the text itself, as Fenwick writes in a letter to his mother: "He has a Greek name – Poseidon. Lord knows who gave him this!" (170). He comes back to this in referring to "this creature Poseidon, the black man with the European name" on the next page. The un-Africanness of the name is only partly what is at issue. Were Poseidon and his followers descendants of a maroon community founded in the seventeenth or eighteenth century, we might be justified in looking for such names as those found among, say, the Saramaka of Suriname: Abátelí, Kandámma, Otjútju, and so forth.[9] Richard Price writes in his introduction to *Maroon Societies*:

> Maroons indeed drew on their diverse African heritages in building their cultures. But unlike other Afro-Americans, who were unable to pass on integrated patterns of traditional culture, maroons could and did look to Africa for deep-level organizational principles, relating to cultural realms as diverse as naming their children on the one hand, or systems of justice on the other.[10]

But we also learn from Price that the establishment of viable maroon communities did not occur in British Guiana, the setting of *The Secret Ladder*, that maroon enclaves there "were wiped out by the end of the eighteenth century."[11] The act of marronage at the root of Poseidon's presence in the Canje took place only two generations back and was a solitary rather than a collective undertaking. By the first half of the nineteenth century, the time of Poseidon's grandfather's escape into the bush, European names had replaced African names within the slave community.

So Kenneth Ramchand is partly correct when he writes: "For Harris, 'the black man with the European name' is not an anomaly."[12] It is, indeed, the normativeness, brought about by the slave trade, of Africans bearing European names throughout the Americas that has given rise to the preoccupation with and problematizing of the relationship between name and named among African Americans.[13] The normative European name, a consequence and thus a symptom/symbol of cultural and geographical dislocation, cultural and geographical captivity, comes under erasure in such gestures as the adoption of African names and the well known Black Muslim practice of replacing the "slave name," the European surname, with an X. Titles like James Baldwin's *Nobody Knows My Name*, Archie Shepp's "Call Me By My Rightful Name," and Audre Lorde's *Zami: A New Spelling of My Name* reflect a related concern with the implications of naming, as does Edward Kamau Brathwaite's concept/neologism "nam."[14] Toni Morrison's attentiveness in novel after novel to names and acts of naming accords a tellingly prominent place to misnaming or inversive naming (a neighborhood situated in the hills but known as the Bottom,[15] a man with "milky white" skin called Tar

Baby,[16] a street on which a doctor lives known as Not Doctor Street[17]), accenting a discrepancy between name and named so as to signify on[18] the act of naming and, by implication, the context in which that act takes place. She heightens the contradictions in order to make a point, to make several points. The discrepant relationship between name and named synecdochically recalls the history of dispossession that haunts the act of naming for the African American. It is in the context of this New World African preoccupation with and problematizing of the act of naming that Harris's choice of the name Poseidon has to be seen.

A black man with a European name is no anomaly, but Poseidon is not just any European name. It is not a common one among either whites or blacks. The name creaks, calls attention to itself, in a way that, for example, Bryant, another European name borne by a black character in the novel, does not. It blatantly stands out, blatantly doesn't fit. A black man named Poseidon (any man named Poseidon, for that matter) *is* an anomaly, and the anomalous name, like the inversive name,[19] both fits and doesn't fit. It signifies by not fitting, fits in that it signifies. That the name is Greek and mythological is obviously important. This echoes, inversively, Alejo Carpentier's *The Lost Steps*, where Yannes's comment concerning Rosario uses Greek nomination to apprise the narrator of the gulf between the bush and the cultural baggage he has brought along: "She no Penelope."[20] That the name doesn't fit signifies the alterity of the way of life Rosario represents. Its invocation signifies the tenacity of Greco-discrepant expectation. In *The Secret Ladder* the name Poseidon does likewise. Greek nomination belies a failed escape, failed flight from Greco-expectant paradigms.

Harris, the humor in whose work has not been sufficiently noted, has a bit of fun with this during the conversation with Stoll in which Fenwick speaks of his encounter with Poseidon:

> "I met someone in the river. The meeting disturbed me in a way I had never been troubled before."
> "I don't understand."
> "I realized at the time – in a way I had never seen it before – that we'll all sink or swim together."
> "Sounds like Greek to me, Mr. Fenwick."
> "Possibly it is," Fenwick smiled. "Maybe even further back than that, the mystery of a lost continent. . . . " (192)

This mention of "a lost continent" recalls two telling episodes in the history of European expeditions into the non-European world. One remembers, first, that the Bahamas owe their name to Christopher Columbus having thought of them as remnants of the lost continent Atlantis, the story of which, in written form, first appears in Plato's *Kritias* and

Timaios. Columbus took the islands to be the remains of something the bulk of which was below the sea or, in Spanish, *baja mar* – hence, Bahamas. This was only the beginning of an "Atlantean revival," a series of further "footnotes to Plato" that would, in one form or another, associate the New World with the old Atlantis well into the nineteenth century. This "revival" would include Guillaume de Postal's suggesting in 1561 that one of the new continents be called Atlantis and John Swan writing in 1644 that "America was sometimes part of that great land which *Plato* calleth the Atlantick island," a theory that was accepted by Buffon in the eighteenth century and by Alexander von Humboldt in the nineteenth.[21]

Atlantis, according to Plato, was presided over by Poseidon, a connection that was not lost on Leo Frobenius, the German ethnographer whose expeditions into Africa are also brought to mind by Fenwick's mention of "a lost continent." Influenced heavily by Heinrich Schliemann's excavation of Troy, Frobenius, whose best known devotees were Léopold Sédar Senghor and Ezra Pound, was convinced he had found the remnants of Atlantis among the Yoruba of Nigeria. Janheinz Jahn notes in his sympathetic but not uncritical essay *Leo Frobenius: The Demonic Child*:

> Schliemann took myth literally, contrary to the preconceptions of his time. "The significance of his performance," writes Frobenius, "lies in the fact that he regarded the accounts of old Homer as supported by history, whereas scholarship until then had considered them to be mythical and 'simply imaginative.' Following such conviction he first regarded the hill Hissarlik as the location of Old Troy and began excavations." Likewise Frobenius would later take tradition literally and would excavate proofs of African history. The parallels to Schliemann probably drove him consciously or unconsciously to raise the significance of his discovery to Homeric proportions. Troy – that was the *Iliad*, but what was Ife? An unknown African provincial town. That could not be true. Out of it Frobenius conjured up his Atlantis.[22]

Thus the titles *En Route to Atlantis*, a travel report published in 1911, and *Atlantis*, a collection of African oral tales in twelve volumes published between 1921 and 1928. Thus, too, Frobenius's reference to the Yoruba sea-god Olokun, a terra-cotta head of whom he excavated during his 1910–1912 expedition, as "the Poseidon of the Atlantic Ocean." Jahn comments critically on Frobenius's "bold fantasies" and on the limitations his Greco-Atlantean preoccupations imposed on his research:

As curious as it may sound, the father of African archaeology had never practiced African archaeology. He had looked for Greek heads in Ife, for the cultural products of the people of Atlantis. In his eyes the head of the Yoruba sea-god Olokun was the head of Poseidon. That a later archaeologist like Bernard Fagg would be able to excavate a Nok culture, a native predecessor of Ife, would never have occurred to him. . . . He saw no African, but Greek beauty in the excavated *terra-cottas*: "Out of these scanty fragments spoke harmony and vitality, the expression of a gracefulness in form directly recalling the ancient Greek mind, the proof of a non-Negroid pure race which had resided here from time immemorial."[23]

He goes on to lament the fact that Frobenius "fell to using the vocabulary of racialism," calling him "a pacesetter of fascism" while crediting him, nonetheless, with "a significant contribution to the liberation and decolonization of Africa." This is not the place to dwell upon or to attempt to unravel the contradictory strands running through Frobenius's project. The point is that its Greco-expectant aspects exemplify a tradition of colonizing reverie to which Fenwick's mix of confession and warning clearly applies: "To *misconceive* the African, I believe, . . . is to misunderstand and exploit him mercilessly and oneself as well" (171).

Colonizing reverie, colonizing misconception, was, of course, brought to bear on the Americas as well. The association of the New World with Atlantis by Columbus and others is a case in point, as is the search for cities of gold, El Dorado and others, a tradition of which we are reminded by the name of Fenwick's dinghy: "Fenwick had named his dinghy *Palace of the Peacock* after the city of God, the city of gold set somewhere in the heart of Brazil and Guiana" (151). This is also, of course, the name of Harris's first published novel, the first in the quartet of which *The Secret Ladder* is the fourth, and it alerts us to the reflexive, metafictional dimension of his work – another way in which the novel creaks. The setting and the crew's activity lend themselves to this reflexive dimension: "watching the river and being watched in turn by one's reflection" (144). Textuality is underscored by the titles of the three "books" into which the novel is divided: "The Day Readers," "The Night Readers," and "The Reading." (Looking at the books on Fenwick's bookshelf, Stoll goes on in the passage quoted above to say, "I see you're partial to *all* the fables" [192].) Like *Palace of the Peacock, The Secret Ladder*, while set in the twentieth century, resonates with a history of conquistadorial incursion that reaches back hundreds of years. As in the choice of the name Donne for the conquistador figure in *Palace*, it brings to the forefront an awareness of the poetico-fictive constructs that accompanied

such incursion. In so doing, it acknowledges itself to be an heir to tex-
tualizations of the New World that were occasioned by the colonial/
conquistadorial enterprise. It opens that tradition up to inspection, strug-
gling to intimate an alternative, to extricate even as it implicates itself.

Reflexivity, metafictionality, advances a warning the text issues to
itself, a reminder that it not presume to have escaped the discourses it
ostensibly critiques. In this it complies with the confessional impulse
upon which Harris repeatedly, in such essays as "The Complexity of
Freedom," places emphasis:

> There is no decision or originality of gesture and freedom of move-
> ment that can be authentic unless as it arises to consciousness it
> confesses to how it is still masked, in some degree, by the very
> conditions from which it arises, by past education or propaganda,
> past or present securities and anxieties, by the historical restriction
> it partially breaks. And as it so confesses it points intuitively to the
> reality of freedom, the complexity of freedom, as an unfathomable
> decision that varies with the cloak of age or biased history it
> unravels.[24]

Poseidon, at whom Fenwick looks "as if he saw down a bottomless
gauge and river of reflection" (155), is an omen of unfathomability, an
omen of "uncapturable essence" (246). (The same can be said of his Greek
– presumably Greek – namesake, of whom W.K.C. Guthrie writes:
"Poseidon is a god who is generally supposed to be Greek in origin,
though as to the meaning of his name there is truth in the remark of
Roscher which may be rendered, 'they have multiplied the interpretations
but not increased the certainty.' "[25]) It is upon Fenwick's first encounter
with him that the novel's descriptive machinery is most noticeably
stressed, put under a strain, resorting to while revising image after rickety
image to advance a mixed-metaphorical conceit whose chimerical essence
remains beyond its reach. Poseidon is alternately endowed with attributes
recalling fish, lamb, snake, and gorgon, a monstrous, annunciative mix
from which Fenwick recoils in disarray:

> Fenwick adjusted his eyes. He could no longer evade a reality that
> had always escaped him. The strangest figure he had ever seen had
> appeared in the opening of the bush, dressed in a flannel vest,
> flapping ragged fins of trousers on his legs. Fenwick could not help
> fastening his eyes greedily upon him as if he saw down a bottomless
> gauge and river of reflection. He wanted to laugh at the weird
> sensation but was unable to do so. The old man's hair was white
> as wool and his cheeks – covered with wild curling rings – looked
> like an unkempt sheep's back. The black wooden snake of skin

peeping through its animal blanket was wrinkled and stitched together incredibly.

"Poseidon!" Fenwick asked, feeling himself turning to stone.
He did not trust his own eyes like a curious fisherman, playing for
time, unable to accept his own catch, trying to strip from the
creature who stood before him – the spirit with which he himself
had involuntarily invested it. This was no god of the swamps, no
leviathan of the depths, he protested. This was an old bent artifice
of a man, clothed in the changing witness of age and lamb's snow,
shading his buried eyes from the glare of the sun – after the clotted
memory of darkness – in order to see clearer the two men sitting
on the water before him. (155–156)

What follows is one of the novel's most multiply aspected instances of
discrepant engagement. Poseidon speaks, but the shapes and movements
his lips make are said not to fit the words that emerge:

Poseidon addressed Fenwick at last. His mouth moved and made
frames which did not correspond to the words he actually uttered.
It was like the tragic lips of an actor, moving but soundless as a
picture, galvanized into comical association with a foreign dubbing
and tongue which uttered a mechanical version and translation out
of accord with the visible features of original expression. (156)

Tellingly, his words are not reported. The text appears to harbor questions regarding its ability to do him justice. Neither here nor elsewhere
in the novel are Poseidon's words directly reported. His alterity is such
as to be rendered mute in counterpoint with a prolixity that constantly
threatens to carry Fenwick away, the rhetorical bent – "flood of expression" (183), "tide of excess" (184), "dramatic inflation" (228) – he repeatedly labors to keep in check.

The implications of such divergence between word and frame, the
discrepant play between frame and "foreign dubbing," are extremely
far-reaching. Such play speaks to questions of identity in the context of
cultural mix brought about by colonial/conquistadorial projects, the
specter of inauthenticity haunting the hybrid inheritance of formerly
colonized regions. Discrepant engagement dislodges or seeks to dislodge
homogeneous models of identity, assumptions of monolithic form, purist
expectation, redefining "the features of original expression." Since *The
Secret Ladder*'s publication in 1963, "dubbing" has acquired new meaning
and additional resonance from the well known musical practice that
assumes a similar non-essentialist approach and confirms the novel's
uncanny diagnostic aplomb. The practice of dubbing that emerged in

Jamaican recording studios during the late sixties opens every original up to variation, "versioning":

> On the dub the original tune is still recognisably there but it is broken up. The rhythm might be slowed down slightly, a few snatches of song might be thrown in and then distorted with echo. The drums and bass will come right up to the listener and demand to be heard. Dermott Hussey, a Jamaican record producer, explains what modern dub is like: "The dub now is just the bare bones, the rhythm played, bass line of course overemphasised."[26]

Finding virtue in necessity ("Dubbing Is A Must" is the title of a tune by Pablo Moses), dub accents mix, adaptation, improvisation, using echo and reverb, as Timothy White puts it, "to enhance the 'haunted house' effect."[27] It gave rise to the related practice of "talk over," in which a monologue is part spoken, part sung (but mostly spoken) by a dj/performer over the "version" mix.

In so insistently rattling its frame, calling attention to its framing devices (the repeated play on the Gorgon myth, the seven days of creation, Poseidon's association with horses, and so forth), *The Secret Ladder* adopts an analogous bare-bones approach. It bares its devices to disclose a skeletal essence that turns out to be neither naked nor an essence but a further investiture, not an inner but an outer skeleton, reverberant shell. (Hence "astronomical crab" and the stolen turtle [223–235] on which the plot so decidedly turns: shell ex machina.) Its discrepant reverberations, bare-bones riffing on history and myth, inhabit the haunted house we call culture with maroon mercuriality, rare getaway spin:

> The fire of desire that had been lit emphasized the black void of the night and the black face of the judge, godless now as well as godlike, lying mute and uncreated amongst them. Their formless outcry stirred not even a quiver on his lips, neither imitation nor resonance, and the fire that flickered within and without his countenance, streaked him only with the premature coming of the dawn, the false or early dawn dubbed upon the cheeks of men. It signified the lie in their hopes as well as the creation of a jewel of light without self-evident generation or action. (252)

11

The Unruly Pivot
Wilson Harris's The Eye of the Scarecrow

But I experienced once more the resulting chaos I knew, loss of orientation, the unruly pivot around which revolves the abstract globe in one's head.

Wilson Harris

I

Wilson Harris must be one of the most daring authors writing in English. Born in 1921 in British Guiana (since become, with independence in 1966, Guyana) and now living in England, Harris has published, in addition to poetry, criticism, and two books of retellings of native Caribbean myths, a series of highly unusual novels. The sixth of these, *The Eye of the Scarecrow*, can be said to be the pivot, the unruly pivot, on which Harris's work turns decidedly self-reflexive. I say "decidedly" because this novel is not necessarily the first in which the insights offered pertain as much to the writing itself as to the ostensible subject of that writing, the characters and the events that occupy the work. *Palace of the Peacock*, Harris's first novel, the tale of a boat crew's fatal journey upriver through the Guianese jungle, reads on a more subtle level as an extended comment on its own genesis and intended impact.[1] It is not accidental that the fulfillment the members of the crew experience in the paradisiacal Palace of the Peacock is described in aesthetic terms, in terms of a sad and glorious all-enthralling music. Given the distinctly poetic and musical character of Harris's prose, one is justified in feeling that when the narrator at the end remarks, "This was the inner music and voice of the peacock I suddenly encountered and echoed and sang as I had never heard myself sing before,"[2] the music is the novel itself. The plausibility of such a reading – of viewing the crew's adventure as a journey into the apotheosis of poetry – is enhanced by the fact that the boat's skipper, who is not

191

only the novel's chief protagonist but something of the narrator's alter ego as well, is named Donne. And as though that were not enough, his poet namesake is explicitly evoked by the epigraph to Book III, two lines from John Donne's "Hymn to God My God, in My Sickness."[3]

Somewhat similarly, *Heartland*, Harris's fifth novel, has to do with the growth in consciousness of Zechariah Stevenson, and concludes with a postscript comprised of fragments of three poems written by Stevenson and found in the half-burnt resthouse in which he is last seen before his disappearance in the heartland jungle. These three poems, it turns out, are taken from Harris's privately printed book of poems *Eternity to Season* (1954), thus making a case for the identification of Stevenson with the novel's author and for a reading of the novel as a self-reflexive treatment of the theme of "the growth of the poet's mind." When I say that with *The Eye of the Scarecrow* Harris's work turns *decidedly* self-reflexive, I mean that what operates as a latent impulse in the earlier novels surfaces in this sixth one as a dominant thrust.

A definite continuity exists between *The Eye of the Scarecrow* and the five novels that precede it, in that all six have to do with journeys beyond the boundaries of conventional consciousness, journeys into a jungle representing the marginality of authentic thought. Harris's novels typically involve a consciousness-altering "confession of weakness"[4] brought about by a crisis or catastrophe of some kind. The crew in *Palace of the Peacock*, Mohammed, Ram, Beti, and Oudin in *The Far Journey of Oudin*, Cristo, Sharon, and Magda in *The Whole Armour*, Fenwick and Bryant in *The Secret Ladder*, and Stevenson in *Heartland* all undergo a collapse of their customary ways of perceiving the world. In *The Eye of the Scarecrow*, however, this "confession of weakness" and its attendant journey into unconventionality pertain more explicitly to artistic conventions. Very early in the novel the narrator "confesses" his inability to conform to the conventions of what he later calls "idolatrous realism":

> Much as I would like to recall – like a ghost returning to the past – the identical map of place which shattered in a moment I cannot. . . . This effort of memory still cannot restore more than an assumption of an essential fabric of person and thing. . . . The fact is I find myself conferring the curious baptism of living imagination upon helpless relics, relics which thereby lose a smothering or smothered constitution and character. For if I were to attempt to confine or draw an exact relationship or absolute portrait of what everything was before the stroke fell and created a void in conventional memory, I would have succumbed to the dead tide of self-indulgent realism. On the other hand, to travel with the flood

of animated wreckage that followed after, is a different matter, a trusting matter in which I am involved.[5]

This inability makes for the book's unruliness.

The Eye of the Scarecrow, that is, is a novel that exasperates conventional expectations as to plot and characterization. In fact, its plot, if it can be said to have one, revolves around the collapse of the materialist assumptions on which traditionally linear, mimetic narration is based. This collapse is symbolized in the novel by the crash of an airplane, a "reconnaissance machine," in the jungle outside a place called Raven's Head. It is this crash that creates the "void in conventional memory." The crash, in some sense the denouement or climax of the novel (though Harris, true to the book's unconventional cast, calls it an "anti-climax"), is arrived at by way of a meandering, associational movement to which the book's diary format readily lends itself. Form is of a piece with content in that the novel, written as a series of journal entries, structurally embodies the fragmentariness for which the crash and a recurrence of manifesto-like assertions apologize. The book is an act of faith ("a trusting matter in which I am involved") – and this in more than one sense. It concludes with the word *amen* and is prefaced by a passage from *Ecclesiastes*: "There is no man that hath power over the spirit to retain the spirit." Its fragmentariness and repudiation of "idolatrous realism" have to do with a religious unwillingness to invest entirely in the things of the empirical world, a recognition of the empirical realm's inability to retain – to *contain* – the spirit. The impossibility of reducing even empirical reality to some static, fixed representation testifies to an indomitability or an unruliness which intimates the spirit's domain: "The truth is – *I can't remember*. Evolution. Revolution. Regeneration. Collapse. All I can honestly say is that the potential fragments of recollection before and after GOD KNOWS WHAT are *alive* in a way I never suspected before" (ES, 100–101). Or again: "the flood of *animated* wreckage" (emphasis added).

The novel's plotlessness, its inability or refusal to represent experience in an acceptably reductive, realist manner, proceeds from a gnostic estrangement from the world that realism wants to portray. Typical of this estrangement is the following passage that insists upon the nothingness of the phenomenal world:

No wonder the ghostly idiot stranger and spectator in one's own breast plunged into awareness of how deprived one was of root and reality – started prompting one to wonder indeed whether the blossoming casket in clear view carried rags of nothing within, or the wheat of something without, resembling a shattered loaf for this or that non-existent stomach. (ES, 20)

At another point the narrator speaks of becoming "a religious stranger to all previous knowledge of emotion" (ES, 41). Gnostic estrangement regards the world as a misbegotten lapse into materiality, the issue of "the law of an unlawful beginning" (ES, 48), a demiurgic mistake. To be born into it is to suffer exile from the "treasure of immateriality" (ES, 32), from one's true residence in the spirit. Hence the recurrence throughout *The Eye of the Scarecrow* of the word *misconception* and its implication that to be born is not so much to have been conceived as to have been *mis*conceived:

> Indeed, long ago, in the tragic misconceived beginning (one now dreams to return to with a different paradoxical vision of hope) one chose to purchase the manufacture of despair, unwittingly it may be true, and tasted in this bargain a growing hoard of sensibility one conceived as self-sufficient and original, the newfound coin and cement of freedom, instantaneous harvest which seemed truly ambitious, truly right, anything but a miserly or incongruous investment in one's own human prolongation of misery. (ES, 35)

Gnosis is the undoing of this misconception, a going back beyond birth to become the "Child in a womb of ancestral fantasy whose every unborn move is a refusal to bow to an inventory of mechanical fates" (ES, 89). Such return to the womb is symbolized by the expedition to Raven's Head, "to the lost womb of a mining town, nine months journey from Water Street into the jungle of conception" (ES, 48). When one notes the nine months difference between the date of the initial journal entry, 25–26 December 1963, and that of the concluding "Postscript of Faith in Dark Room of Identity," 25 September 1964, one sees that the novel itself is the trip to Raven's Head, its writing Harris's gnostic act.

The crash of the "reconnaissance machine," as I have already suggested, is the novel's self-reflexive image of its disruptive drift, of its dismantling of what Harris calls "the novel of persuasion":

> The nineteenth-century novel has exercised a very powerful influence on reader and writer alike in the contemporary world. And this is not surprising after all since the rise of the novel in its conventional and historical mould coincides in Europe with states of society which were involved in consolidating their class and other vested interests. . . . The novel of persuasion rests on grounds of apparent common sense: a certain "selection" is made by the writer, the selection of items, manners, uniform conversation, historical situations, etc., all lending themselves to build and present an in-

dividual span of life which yields self-conscious and fashionable moralities. The tension which emerges is the tension of individuals – great or small – on an accepted plane of society we are persuaded has an inevitable existence.[6]

There is no such inevitable existence, Harris insists. Thus his work has much to do with catastrophe, cataclysm, the undermining of any sense of a stable, self-sufficient order of things, especially where that order is of a social, political sort. In the Author's Note written in 1973 to preface the paperback edition of the novel, Harris responded to the question of the book's relationship to political and economic developments in British Guiana between the 1920s and the year 1964 when the book ends by speaking of a predicament in which "the imagination is cornered by the very claims of historical narrative to be identical with universality" and of "the necessary breakdown of historical and economic categories." He goes on to argue that man "seems therefore to possess a passion to caricature history in his own body" and that "from this ground of loss one undermines given categories."

His refusal to identify the boundaries of reality with those of social, political, and economic events has led Harris to condemn the protest novel as a simple extension of the novel of persuasion. The protest novel, he argues, perpetuates the same materialist assumptions as those that uphold the social order it seeks to reform. By appealing to no reach of experience beyond the social, the economic, and the political, the protest novel invests in the sense of deprivation it seeks to end. Harris concerns himself not with protest but with the exploration of unapparent levels of "fulfillment" (the term he counterposes to *persuasion* and *consolidation*),[7] as in his second novel *The Far Journey of Oudin*, about which Kenneth Ramchand, much to the point being made here, remarks:

> Two versions of Oudin's life take shape: There is the socially re-alistic figure who suffers as a slave in an oppressive social order, and who dies having covenanted even his unborn child to the grasp-ing Ram; and there is the godlike inheritor of the kingdom who fulfills destiny by abducting the virgin Beti, a bride and prize cov-eted by Ram. The two Oudins are evoked with equal credibility, both stories residing in the same events. Like Blake in the two "Holy Thursday" poems, Harris shows and responds to the co-existence of different conditions – the meek being overwhelmed by the earth, but inheriting it at the same time. Through imaginative fictions it is possible to remember that no social order is inevitable and ultimate, and that the "individual span of life" need not be identified with the most oppressive of its possibilities.[8]

In *The Eye of the Scarecrow* the refusal of such identification takes the form of Anthrop's "miraculous" ability, in the midst of an economic depression, to come up with his rent each month. The narrator, on one of his grandfather's rent-collecting missions, peers into Anthrop's apartment and glimpses "the subterranean anatomy of revolution . . . the treasure of immateriality" (ES, 31–32). It is here that the second of the book's recurrent quotations of Christ's words to Simon Peter occurs: "In my Father's house are many mansions." There is more to experience, Harris asserts, than that which meets the eye. The ability of the Anthrops – who are referred to as a "family of symbolic tenants" – to pay their monthly rent serves to sabotage any social-realist appropriation of their ordeal. In one of the novel's numerous self-reflexive moments, this monthly "miracle" is likened to the freedom of art, an animacy and unruliness, a spiritedness, the liveliness and aliveness peculiar to creative work:

> And there was Anthrop, after all, the head of one family, who miraculously, it seemed, overcame circumstance and settled with him on each occasion he visited. In truth my grandfather was beginning almost to enjoy (though he would never have confessed this) the paradox of it all in the way an artist may grow in awe of the train of his unpredictable material when it becomes capable of the unique momentum of acquiring its own godlike stamp and redeeming character of life. (ES, 31)

A "miraculous" realism is what Harris's work is after: "an open dialogue within which a free construction of events will emerge in the medium of phenomenal associations all expanding into a mental distinction and life of their own" (ES, 13).

II

The specifics of the book's "curious baptism," the nonlinear but highly resonant meanderings to which it gives rise, are of a peculiar enough sort, I think, to warrant a somewhat lengthy summing up of what goes on. The novel is divided into three "books." Book I, entitled "The Visionary Company," is made up of journal entries, the first dated 25–26 December 1963, the last 1 March–7 May 1964. The narrator, writing in London, recollects events from his childhood and youth in British Guiana between the years 1929 and 1948, the year of the Guiana Strike. These recollections have largely to do with a number of visionary experiences: the "incredible image of a scarecrow" the narrator momentarily glimpses on his friend L–'s face; the dream of a windowless secret apartment in what appears to be either his grandfather's lodge or L–'s engineering office, this black room turning out to be the "revolutionary goal" he pursues; "the scarecrow of shadow alighting for a flashing moment" upon the funeral procession for a group of slain strikers as the procession merges or collides with a possibly empty "poor man's hearse" driven by two laughing riders; intimations of a hanging in his grandfather's garden; a rent-collecting visit, during the economic slump of the twenties, to a tenement range owned by his grandfather, where none of the tenants, because of the depression, are able to pay the rent – none, that is, except Anthrop, whose face "self-reverses" the image of his twin infants into that of the two laughing hearse riders; and so forth. On a slightly more literal level, an account is given of the narrator's premeditated/involuntary pushing of L– into the East Street canal, this incident reverberating throughout the novel's repeated concern with the paradox of a compulsory freedom.[9] Book I concludes with evocations of the narrator's mood and thoughts upon his release, in 1932 at the age of eleven, from the hospital following a month's convalescence in the wake of a nearly fatal illness.

Book II is called "Genesis" and takes up where Book I leaves off, in the garden one afternoon a month after the narrator's return from the hospital, where he and L– fashion figures out of lumps of mud. A breasted mother-figure molded by L– sparks a drift of dreamlike transformations wherein the narrator's recollected glimpse of his mother through the partly open door of her room, weeping and being spoken to by his grandparents, recalls the visit to Anthrop's room and the glimpse of his half-naked wife, a twin infant at each breast, through the open door. That night the narrator dreams of his own funeral and of Anthrop's unexpected encounter with his (Anthrop's) twin brother, a wealthy civil engineer who resembles L–'s father, rumor having it that L–'s dead mother had all along been engineer Anthrop's secret mistress. The narrator wakes to find his own mother on the bed beside him, having come in response to the cry he let out while asleep, and sees that she too has been weeping over the news of the drowning of his stepfather, an engineer, in a jungle in the interior. It turns out that the narrator's actual father, also an engineer, was convicted of and executed for murder in this very jungle at about the same time the narrator was being born in 1921, and that the stepfather's expedition there eleven years later was in part an attempt to uncover facts that would prove that the father had been framed. Some years later (in 1944 it appears, though this is not altogether clear – perhaps 1948), the narrator sets out for this jungle with L–, the engineer in charge of the expedition, to relocate a lost mining town called Raven's Head, where enormous gold deposits are expected to be found. (L–'s motives are mercenary and technical while the narrator's search is for proof of his father's innocence.) The second half of

Book II has to do, in typically elliptical fashion, with this expedition, especially the narrator's and L–'s sexual sharing of the whore Hebra, the tooth-mother namesake of Raven's Head. (The town is also, that is, known as Hebra's Town – as Hebra is also known as Raven's Head.)

Book III, "Raven's Head," opens with the horse and carriage (in which sit an old man and a young boy) of the Ancient of Days at the north gate, the Gateway of Fear, into Raven's Head. Something frightens the horse, causing it to rear and come close to turning the carriage over. Approaching the town through the south gateway, Hebra's Gate, on the other hand, the driver of a motor-driven vehicle runs over a cow, killing it but also demolishing the vehicle, and is taken in by the old man and the young boy (the former "clothed now in shepherd's rags" and the latter his grandson), who share their evening meal with him. The driver turns out to be an engineer, with a sense of self-possession reminiscent of L–'s, a sense of self-possession, however, to which the collision does irreparable harm: "the necessity had now been born (the driver groaned with distaste) to feed himself and clothe himself upon eyes of mineral substitution; the artist's mask, the animal or plant of camouflage and vision" (ES, 73) – the Eye of the Scarecrow, in short. The writing continues with a diary entry dated 30 July 1964, the first dated entry since Book I, in which the crash of a reconnaissance vehicle ("car, plane, call it what you will") carrying the narrator and L– north of Raven's Head is brought to light. As a result of this crash and the presumed death of the narrator, L– is put on trial and convicted of murder, his jealous quarrel with the narrator over Hebra the day before the crash constituting the most damaging piece of evidence against him. The narrator in the meantime takes nine months to find his way through the jungle, arriving just in time to prove that he is not in fact dead, much less murdered, and thus bring about L–'s release from the prison hospital. The writing moves now into a series of visions: a descent into the Raven's Head canal, a confrontation with a shoe salesman, and so forth. This is followed by a letter dated 14–15 August 1964 addressed to L– at Raven's Head, containing Scarecrow's confession to strangling Hebra and signed "Idiot Nameless"; in turn followed by a meditation on murder, consciousness, freedom, and space. Next, a "Manifesto of the Unborn State of Exile" in the form of another letter to L–, in which the narrator holds forth on language, poetry, memory, and the need for a "crumbling of the will" into self-exile; followed by a section called "The Black Rooms" in which passages from Book I and Book II are quoted, and finally a "Postscript of Faith in Dark Room of Identity" in the form, again, of a letter to L–, ending on the subject of prayer and in the form of a prayer ("Amen. Amen."), signed "Idiot Nameless" and dated 25 September 1964.

So ends the novel. Many questions remain unanswered and the various threads of possible plot are left unresolved. Resolution, in fact, has given way to resonance, the writing repeatedly declaring its occasion to be the demise of any resolute sense of what occurred. In this way the book is relentlessly circular and anticlimactic, insistent to the end upon the "void in conventional memory" to which it owes its form. One important aspect of this breakdown or void is the feature that most strongly illustrates the substitution of resonance for resolution in the novel, Harris's dismantling of the notion of character. The novel of persuasion, he tells us, is preoccupied with valorizing the sovereign, self-contained individual:

> The consolidation of character is, to a major extent, the preoccupation of most novelists who work in the twentieth century within the framework of the nineteenth-century novel.... As a result "character" in the novel rests more or less on the self-sufficient individual – on elements of "persuasion" (a refined or liberal persuasion at best in the spirit of the philosopher Whitehead) rather than "dialogue" or "dialectic" in the profound and unpredictable sense of person which Martin Buber, for example, evokes. (TWS, 28–29)

In *The Eye of the Scarecrow*, on the other hand, the narrator describes the breakdown of his previous ("persuasive") view of people. He began, he says, to move away from the sense of each person as being self-contained and consistently what he or she appeared or was supposed to be:

> And I began to discover a force of obsession in things I had only dimly dreamt before (it seemed to me now) to question, things and persons I had accepted too easily (it seemed now, once again) for what they were supposed to be and what they were instinctively supposed not to be. Things and persons whose life of obsession lay less within themselves and more within myself, within my lack of a universal conception. (ES, 53)

The puzzling resonances that recur throughout the novel have to do with the fact that, as in, say, Bergman's *Persona* or Altman's *Three Women*, identities overlap.

Take the relationship between L– and the narrator for example, a relationship that is at first described by way of a contrast recalling the opposition between self-sufficiency on the one hand and unpredictability on the other:

> L– and I . . . were to enjoy the enigma of being related. . . . He would acquire a reputation for sober and matchless good sense, judgment, responsibility while I would be the striking unpredictable one. He

would never come to blame anyone for the evil which happened
to him – as I was often religiously inclined to do. (ES, p. 40)

This contrast is exemplified by the incident in which the narrator pushes
L– into the East Street canal. While the narrator is quick to suggest that
he did so at the prompting of some force outside his control, L– does
just the opposite in assuming responsibility for something he in fact did
not do: "When asked by my grandfather to tell what had actually happened he declared he had suddenly slipped and fallen of his own accord.
He did not dare to dream anyone (least of all myself) had in reality given
him the slightest push" (ES, 26). L–, then, is the "self-sufficient individual," impervious, as far as he's concerned, to all outside influence and
thus willing to take the blame for whatever befalls him:

> And if indeed any further blame was necessary, the misjudgement
> or misconception of reality – he agreed – then he – because of his
> insusceptibility to a continuing motion or cause outside of himself
> (or, in other words, because of his susceptibility to himself as his
> own faulty agent) – must suffer the blame, in terms of his own
> absolute logic of context, solely, in the numb fixture of himself.
> He was trapped within the riddle of his own leaden machinery –
> the riddle of the fixed instincts. (ES, 58)

The self-reflexivity of the novel again reveals itself in that Harris appears
to be using L– and the narrator to personify two opposing novelistic
tendencies (the persuasive and the dialectical, respectively), as well as the
differing senses of character to which these tendencies give rise.

But rather than consolidate (as he would put it) the differences between
L– and the narrator, Harris gradually, consistent with his commitment
to dialogue and dialectic, advances a sharing of characteristics between
the two, a confounding of identities. Although the driver who runs into
the cow in Book III remains nameless, his presumption of his own self-
sufficiency and his inability to concede the possibility of having been
"pushed" into what has occurred very much recall L–:

> . . . he bargained to rule himself – and be ruled by himself – by
> allowing of no sensible proportion except in his own standing or
> stumbling experience of it. And for this reason he did not know
> how to begin to accept the possibility that he was being counselled
> or pushed, wittingly and unwittingly, fairly and unfairly, by some-
> one and something other than himself. (ES, 69)

However, the trauma of his collision with the cow initiates a conversion,
Harris's description of which makes significant use of the words *persuasion*
and *dialogue*: "And yet – now for the first time he was not so sure. The

counsellors of past and present generations might possess . . . an element of indistinct dialogue which survived within their vociferous arts of force and persuasion" (ES, 69). The driver, who, again resembling L–, is an engineer, undergoes a trial of faith that opens up a certain artistic impulse, the very impulse of which Harris or the narrator would have *The Eye of the Scarecrow* be an instance. He is described not only as at last acknowledging the possibility of his having been pushed, but also as envisioning the necessity of himself becoming the one who pushes, becoming the narrator or like the narrator:

> He would turn then, out of a curious despair, to someone or something he may have always unconsciously disregarded and despised, someone or something he would find himself driven now to push into the religious obscurity of moon or canal, the realm or depth of place he could not yet truly visualize for himself; someone who would appear surprisingly intact and whole, residual but unaffected by the landscape of fact, totally without – at that stage – the consciousness of having been actually set in motion or conscripted or wounded by another in the way the driver himself had once been free of such a dubious conviction. (ES, 73–74)

Meanwhile, the narrator grows less and less able to distinguish himself from L–. As early as Book II he acknowledges, in his dream of L–'s mother, his own susceptibility to self-censure, a characteristic presumably monopolized by L–:

> I pushed her and she fell into these uninspired arms, the engineer of depth, and dissolved into the scaffold of one drowned reflective self to my sudden indescribable horror. I heard myself shout (though scarcely able to believe my own ears) that it was all my fault. (ES, 46)

Later, in describing the events surrounding and subsequent to the crash in Book III, he has trouble getting his pronouns right:

> Was it he who crept and crawled that last mile to save me or I to unlock him? I still like to think it was I who saved L–'s life, and not he mine, in the nick of time. . . . For on that afternoon when I (it was on the tip of my tongue to say *he*) succeeded – more dead than alive – in finding a way through the jungle, nine months after I had been left for dead, I arrived in time to prove to the authorities I was a living soul and not the dead beast they swore they had seen.
>
> L– was released from the prison hospital (which was all that was standing between him and execution), the conviction against him quashed. The violent quarrel we had had over the woman Hebra

the day before I was killed, so it was consistently reported, had weighed heavily against me (my mind still wanders in a trap); I should have said – against him. (ES, 77–78)

The two pages following this passage aggravate this confusion. The description of a descent (the narrator's presumably) into the Raven's Head canal cannot help but recall L–'s earlier plunge into the East Street canal. Like the earlier plunge, this one is described as having been involuntary:

> I saw myself moving away from myself within a dimension over which I appeared to have little control. . . . I was situated, I discerned, not beneath but above the northern gateway of Raven's Head canal and I recalled – as I became aware of biting into the food in my mouth – how I had walked away helplessly and fearfully from myself only a moment ago, descended into the canal, crossed an ageless pit, and recrossed back to where now once again I stood. (ES, 79–80)

By this point the question of identity is acknowledged to be an open, unanswerable one: "Whoever I was . . . " (ES, 80). The unmistakable resonances and resemblances between events, however, raise the question of whether L– and the narrator might be different aspects of the same person, or perhaps separate but interchangeable persons.

Toward the end of the novel the narrator, in one of his letters to L–, affirms this possibility, introducing in doing so, however, a further extension of the range of possible identifications:

> It is as if sometimes (I hope you will forgive me) I have an involuntary but acute awareness of changing places with you. And for a fraction of an instant I am filled with a terrible dread of place and of standing irrevocably in your shoes. (ES, 100)

The last three words of this passage resound with Harris's repeated punning on the word *stepfather* throughout the novel, on the fact that the narrator, in undertaking the expedition to Raven's Head, is following in his father's (as well as his stepfather's) footsteps – *in his shoes*. The implication is that in doing so he becomes a surrogate father (a *step*father) to himself:

> L– and I suddenly stumbled upon the faint but "timeless" footprints of a self-created self – the step-father for whom my mother wept (as if she had been weeping for *me* as well as for *him* all the time). . . . he had set foot into the past in search of proof of another's (or was it my own?) disfigured innocence. (ES, 47–48)

Thus the words *in your shoes* in the letter to L– serve to strengthen earlier suggestions that the stepfather, like L–, may be no more than the narrator's self-projection. In Book II there is a passage in which the narrator not only confuses himself with his stepfather but also describes the stepfather's expedition to Raven's Head in terms that recall L–'s descent into the East Street canal:

> I was influenced as well by my mother's reflection embodied within an unreasoning tradition of fear: fear that my unwelcome (stepfather's) attachment to her (was it true or not that he had been my own father's engineering colleague and friend?) may have compelled him in order to win from the family of his adoption their everlasting gratitude and affection – to leave his well-ordered camp and *plunge* into the closed forbidden jurisdiction of the past in search of my open gauge and sceptical grain of fact. (ES, 56)

The phrase "in search of my open gauge" recalls the fact that the narrator pushes L– into the canal in order to measure (to use L– *as a gauge* with which to measure) the water's depth. Again similar to L–, the stepfather is described as having been "compelled," pushed, into his "plunge" into Raven's Head. Not to mention the fact that the stepfather, like L–, is an engineer. It would thus appear that all three of them, the stepfather, the narrator, and L– are interchangeable: "self-revolving parts in endless dialogue" (ES, 70).

The foregoing should suffice to make the point that the concept of character operative in *The Eye of the Scarecrow* is quite antithetical to that of the conventional novel. The proliferation of resemblances and overlaps is in fact more dizzying in the sustained text of the novel than the foregoing discussion suggests. Harris has spoken of a "possible revolution in the novel – *fulfillment* rather than *consolidation*" (TWS, 28). By this he means that rather than consolidate character he seeks to diffuse or disperse it, to treat it as projective, expansive, and dynamic rather than contractive, contractual, and static. He prefers the term *person* to the word *character*:

> In the epic and revolutionary novel of associations the characters are related within a personal capacity which works in a poetic and serial way so that a strange jigsaw is set in motion like a mysterious unity of animal and other substitutes within the person. Something which is quite different to the overelaboration of individual character within the conventional novel. (TWS, 38)

His use of the term is meant to convey an archetypal, phylogenic wholeness in which the full range of what it is to be human is identified with – not unlike the concept of the Universal Man one encounters in the spiritualist traditions (Adam Qadmon in the *Qabala*, Wang among Taoists, Manu in the Hindu *Vedas*, El-Insānul-kāmil in Sufi belief, and so

on) – the "universal conception" represented by Anthrop and the transcendence of individual identity represented by Idiot Nameless. What
this involves is a sense of self vastly more inclusive than that of the
individual defined by societal norms and social interactions, the dimension of character, that is, to which the novel has traditionally limited
itself. *In my Father's house are many mansions.*

III

The novel's repeated insistence upon "many mansions" suggests a variegated existence – "variegated blood," "mansions of blood" (ES, 83,
91) – which fulfills itself according to no fixed, uniform scale of values
but is instead a complex occasion of events that intimates riches whose
proper assessment or enjoyment lies in "the strength to remain within
the gratifying spirit of anomaly" (ES, 34). The sense of fulfillment to
which Harris commits his work is a negative, paradoxical one, rooted
in a numinous experience of "deprivation" – "one simulates dying in
order to live" (ES, 23) – akin, as I have already suggested, to the estrangement or allogenesis of gnosticism. Henri Corbin, in whose *Avicenna and the Visionary Recital* one encounters the idea of gnostic
estrangement ("The sense of being a Stranger is certainly the dominant
feeling in every gnostic, the feeling that gives his consciousness its power
of exaltation"), makes a comment that I find applicable to Harris's work.
Elaborating upon the gnostic's experience of estrangement, Corbin introduces the notion of "dualitude," a notion that accords well with Harris's preponderant use of the words *dialogue* and *twin* throughout the
novel (Anthrop's twin infants and his wealthy twin brother, L– and the
narrator referred to as Hebra's twins, "the dreamer's twin obsession,"
"the true beginnings of possible dialogue," and so on):

> At the moment when the soul discovers itself to be a stranger and
> alone in a world formerly familiar, a personal figure appears on its
> horizon, a figure that announces itself to the soul personally because
> it symbolizes with the soul's most intimate depths. In other words,
> the soul discovers itself to be the earthly counterpart of another
> being with which it forms a totality that is dual in structure. The
> two elements of this dualitude may be called the ego and the Self,
> or the transcendent celestial Self and the earthly Self, or by still
> other names. It is from this transcendent Self that the soul originates
> in the past of metahistory; this Self had become strange to it while
> the soul slumbered in the world of ordinary consciousness; but it
> ceases to be strange to it at the moment when the soul in turn feels
> itself a stranger in this world.[10]

Corbin refers to this figure as the Guide, the initiatic glimpse of whom awakens the soul to its coexistent other life. In Harris's novel this harbinger of otherness is referred to as the Scarecrow and is the *it* in the passage describing the unnamed driver's conversion following his collision with the cow:

> It was clothing him with the necessity of acknowledging the cloak of otherness, retirement into so little and obscurity of movement into so much: the conviction drove him – and had been driving him all along though he had never seen it – into a sphere of reduction and an arm of extensive feeling; the meeting ground of two, and he was indelibly associated with *one*. . . . It was both sliding rule and sliding scale of place with a reflex not merely of its own but of unpredictable room for transaction between TWO. (ES, 74–75)

The Scarecrow is a complicated and, in a sense, contradictory figure, in that it simultaneously announces and annuls the ego's estrangement. The narrator, for example, acknowledges his "awareness of changing places with" L– only after Scarecrow has come forth: "His confession it is which frees us now to make ours — if we wish" (ES, 85). The Scarecrow alerts the ego to its separation from the world, advancing such alienation as evidence of the ego's simultaneous though unconscious communion with the Self. This communion thus becomes conscious, the rift between the ego and the world subsides in the face of the all-consuming unity of the Self, the nominal individual become "Idiot Nameless." The Scarecrow is the transcendent synthesis of every thesis and antithesis constitutive of worldly dialogue, IT the transcendent conjunction of whatever terms engage as TWO. Harris accordingly describes the Scarecrow as looking in two directions at the same time:

> It was a strange company – TWO and IT – though who it was no one could say: a crumbling scarecrow perhaps, the key to . . . ? *It* possessed nevertheless a backbone and a single eye which turned and looked – without appearing to make any effort to see – both ways in the same blank crude instant. (ES, 75)

The Scarecrow's complexity is a consequence of the fact that it serves as a figure of mediation (between the ego and the world, the ego and the Self, the Self and the world, unity and separation, one and two, L– and the narrator, and so on), as well as that it is both mediator and mediated outcome. Mediation is suggested by the very fact of what a scarecrow is: a thing disguised as a person, a man-thing. The suggestion is furthered by the fact that what supports the scarecrow is two sticks in the form of a cross, an archetypal symbol of the intersection of and the mediation between two contrasting realms – the celestial and the earthly most often – symbolized by its vertical and horizontal lines. The cross is also suggestive of Christ, a mediator in the sense of being a man-god as well as God's messenger among men. Several passages in the novel bring out the analogy between the Scarecrow and Christ. Shortly following a passage concerning "the innocent unborn" soul's indictment for murder, the narrator remarks: "But would not someone always be found – in the midst of the 'dead' seal and ransom of everything – to subscribe – without even knowing how or why – to the 'living' mutilation of the scarecrow?" (ES, 87). The phrase "without even knowing how or why" recalls Christ's insistence that his crucifiers knew not what they did. The Scarecrow is later described as dying something of a martyr's death: "Poor Scarecrow! it was his confession – he said he strangled her – which saved my neck. . . . the Scarecrow (with which I had invested myself as if I were now intent on breaking through from within) accepted the sentence of death passed on him" (ES, 84, 89). Finally, the narrator says to L– at one point: "Someone had died for us, you said" (ES, 103). As a Christlike figure, the Scarecrow mediates between guilt and innocence, complicity and estrangement, and is "the conjunctive witness" (ES, 70) to both immanence and otherness, disclosing otherworldliness at the earthly level.

The Scarecrow, then, is not so much a thing as a process – a dialectical process whose dynamics obscure distinctions to evoke an "almost unendurable unity, silence and sacrifice" (ES, 47). This unity, notwithstanding the fulfillment that it is, is described in terms of deprivation or annihilation, since it involves the collapse or sacrifice of one's ordinary sense of reality. This is a persistent motif in Harris's work, so it is not surprising to find some of the most succinct expressions of it as early as *Palace of the Peacock*: "The unceasing reflection of themselves in each other made them see themselves everywhere save where they thought they had always stood" (PP, 100). Or: "All he knew was the misty sense of devastating thoroughness, completion and endless compassion – so far-reaching and distant and all-embracing and still remote, it amounted to nothingness again" (PP, 129). Hence in *The Eye of the Scarecrow*:

> an equation – destined to salvage a certain area of recollection – began to form – the sweep of nothing equals everything. Or to put it in a personal nutshell – the extinction or rekindling of one confirms a witness either way which equals two.
>
> The CRASH – which I am now aware demolished not only their conventional presence but my fixed senses as well of room and absence from them – broke through to a passage of long-lost existence wherein the total deprivation of every clipped assumption

of relative circumstance took ages to grow into the living fable of
reality. (ES, 78–79)

The paradoxical equation of plenitude with emptiness, all with nothing,
is typical of the literature of mysticism and spirituality, Harris's con-
versance with which is evident throughout his work. A passage from a
Taoist text, *The Secret of the Golden Flower*, serves as the epigraph to
Genesis of the Clowns; the title of his fourth novel, *The Secret Ladder*,
echoes *la secreta escala* of St. John of the Cross's poem "Noche Oscura";
a quotation from Paulinus of Nola is one of the epigraphs to Book III
of *The Eye of the Scarecrow*; and so on. The equation of fullness with
emptiness signifies the obliteration of the ego and its subject–object perceptions of the world during the experience of undifferentiated Being.
St. Teresa's "swoon," the anonymous fourteenth-century mystic's
"cloud of unknowing," and the Buddhist "Void" are analogues of what
Harris variously calls "the crash," "the dark room of identity," and "the
unborn state of exile" – an experience of ego-loss and "loss of orientation"
to which Keats's more literary "Negative Capability" also applies. (Harris refers to Keats's self-professed lack of an "identical nature" at the
beginning of his essay "The Phenomenal Legacy.") Hence the narrator
writes to L–: "The key to my present meaning lies in a crumbling of the
will which may be seen in another sense as the breakdown of a series of
tyrannous conception or misconception – the cruel strength of individual
legacy" (ES, 68). This "crumbling of the will" is enacted in and through
language. Harris's writing *does* that of which the Scarecrow, which is
also described as crumbling, is merely a symbol.

A crumbling of the will enacted in and through language is repeatedly
evoked in Octavio Paz's *The Bow and the Lyre*, a book whose insights
and assertions are so consistently in line with Harris's as to amount to
an unwitting gloss on the latter's work.[11] For Paz, as for Harris, poetry
is a call to and from otherness, a vocation of otherness, poetic inspiration
epitomizing a uselessness of the will which hurls one beyond oneself,
hurls one, as he puts it, "to the other shore" (see ES, 79–80, for Harris's
use of the same image): "The will is inextricably mingled with other
forces . . . at the moment of poetic creation. Freedom and fatality ren-
dezvous in man" (BL, 107). Language itself is one of these "other forces."
Paz argues that while the ordinary sense of language misconceives it as
a tool at the disposal of its user's will, the poet submits to language as
to a master. Poetry highlights the plastic, sonorous, and affective values
of words, values that are rendered secondary by the instrumental view
of language. It also cultivates and lends itself to what Paz insists is language's "original nature," a plurality of meanings, the possibility of a

word meaning two or more things at the same time. This he refers to as returning words "to the plenitude of their nature," though it also seems to annul or deny meaning and sense. Here is another face of the conjunction of plenitude and deprivation, submission to the polysemous fullness of the word entailing an eclipse of common, univocal meaning. Harris refers to this fullness/eclipse as "the Well of Silence" (ES, 95).

The "Manifesto of the Unborn State of Exile" is perhaps the apex of *The Eye of the Scarecrow*'s self-reflexivity, and what it has to say about language is essential to an understanding of Harris's style. Language is held to be the medium for the enactment and expression of what the Scarecrow represents, a visionary capacity for multiple perspectives:

> The subtle logic of image and transformation in consciousness of all one's apparent and stable and persuasive functions is the meaning of language. For language because of its untrappable source transforms – in a terrifying well-nigh unendurable perspective – every subjective block and fixture of capacity. *In my Father's house are many mansions.* (ES, 95–96)

"Many-mansioned" fullness corresponds to the Palace of the Peacock, the alchemical *cauda pavonis*, which Harris describes as "the colours of the peacock which may be equated with all the variable possibilities or colours of fulfillment we can never totally realise."[12] (The journey to Raven's Head to "the unborn state of exile" is also an alchemical quest for lost gold deposits on L–'s part and for regeneration or "disfigured innocence" on the narrator's part.)

The most obvious example of Harris's submission to the word's plurality of meanings is the recurrent punning one encounters throughout the novel, plays on the words *stepfather, premise, conception, misconception,* and *conviction* being the most prominent. There are others, however, as when the narrator "deciphers" the name of his nurse: "Her name was Cromwell or Crumbwell or the crumb (of reality) – WHICH – MAKES – WELL" (ES, 22). This anticipates the untrappable grain spoken of in the "Manifesto of the Unborn State of Exile," the untrappable crumb that makes the Well of Silence. Later, the word *execution* is invested with more than one meaning as L–'s use of it in the sense of a technical feat or accomplishment coincides with the narrator's thoughts about his father's hanging. L– and the narrator are inspecting a bridge the narrator's stepfather built:

> . . . he [L–] was pointing to the engineering merits of the bridge, the excellence and height of the site, the outcrops of rock in which the steel cable on either side was embedded. . . . (I myself was staring into the river and I wondered if it was upon the very plank on

which I stood *he* had been trapped, *stunned*). The execution was perfect, L– said. The remark struck me in a flash: I gave an incredible start (as if I had been immersed very deeply, thinking, but *not* of my stepfather's bridge at all) and pulled my gaze away from the water. The bridge was both a trapdoor and a poem. (ES, 49–50)

The narrator's obsession with his father's execution later tinges the word *sentence* in such a way that it refers to the imposition of a punishment or penalty as well as to a unit of speech. He says of L–:

> ... he fulfilled the most negative role of all – the self-imposed ratification of every closed sentence I could not truly accept and which I found myself helplessly probing in order to uncover wherein lay the movement of original compassion, the furthest point and agency of reason and the source of an active responsible *spiritual* (L– loathed the word) tradition still. (ES, 59)

This particular instance of punning has the added significance of connecting the narrator's nonacceptance of worldly justice (his father's presumed guilt) with Harris's discontent with the "closed" or "persuasive" sentence.

Harris's labyrinthine sentences, that is, stylistically embody the narrator's quest for innocence or immortality, for an open "movement of original compassion." These sentences tend to be more spatial than linear, rarely content with confining themselves to a single line of argument or exposition, but instead allowing for tangential pursuits of counterpoint, qualification, periphrasis, apposition, elaboration, and so forth, suggesting eternity, immortality, by threatening to never end:

> But even as I struggled to find a way of new conviction other than the ancient riddle of protest I knew the changeless ground of it all would yield ultimately, of its own accord, when it succeeded in marrying the fearful strength of the past to the infant freedom of choice which was still weak in the conviction of the present and the future: my own impulsive rein of eagerness and repulsive light of action grew brutally fitful and restrictive as the uncertain spring of day – I was *pushing* her (I was aware of a contrary rebuke and stillness in the heart of crude action) – *pushing* her, nevertheless, even as I had involuntarily pushed him, her son, into the canal and to the brink of his (and her) total self-acceptance, total responsibility for my bewildered self belonging to both sides of the blanket, illegitimate one of present speculation and legitimate reinforcement to escape from the prison of past knowledge. (ES, 45–46)

Harris's tendency to extend rather than restrict a sentence's range of meaning is also evident in the fact that he often interjects an alternate word that, rather than being synonymous with the word whose place in the sentence it is allowed to share, introduces an altogether different, if not opposite, meaning or sense. Often the choice of the alternate word seems to be primarily a matter of similarity of sound: "Anything to circumscribe their own fear of explosive nature in one and to relieve (or relive) their helplessness through another" (ES, 78). One finds the same reliance on homophony in such pairings as that of *invented* with *inverted* (ES, 90) and *prison* with *person* (ES, 91). Here, of course, *relieve* and *relive* function as antonyms. Such conjunctions of conflicting meanings exemplify the Scarecrow's ability to look in opposite directions at the same time and are a characteristic feature of Harris's prose. Hence one reads of "a wayward flock, wayward yet still shepherded" (ES, 13), "a strange inviting and yet curiously uninviting thought" (ES, 49), "something which was much more and so much less than any vision of responsibility" (ES, 54), "the bodily (or bodiless) mystery of mysteries" (ES, 69), a "vulnerable (or was it invulnerable?) carriage of secrets" (ES, 70), a "swollen, still shrunken square of flesh" (ES, 91), and so forth.

Harris's *cauda pavonis* evokes its "almost unendurable unity" also by way of what he refers to in the Metaphysical poets as "a range of potency of association in which nothing is ultimately alien." At one point Donne says to the narrator in *Palace of the Peacock*, "Every boundary line is a myth" (PP, 17). What Harris's "subtle logic of image and transformation" does is precisely violate or transgress (hence the recurrence of the word *trespass* throughout *The Eye of the Scarecrow*) the conventional boundaries between things, persons, places, and so on. Images such as that of "beaked eyes" (ES, 64) or that of a "dripping mist or sweat of proportion" (ES, 94) recall Surrealism in their abrupt yoking together of disparate phenomena. What Harris calls *"pace* and *new dimension* in a certain kind of imaginative fiction" in his Author's Note is the ability to move nimbly through what are otherwise taken to be discontinuous realms of experience: "it was filled with a rust-coloured light like ammunition fired from distant stars, naked metallic rose, neither iron nor bronze nor gold: the sleep of an immaterial unsupported element: the armour of the poor" (ES, 22–23). Related to this quickness and extensive reach of image is Harris's ability to confer, in an almost casual way, cosmic and archetypal significance upon whatever he describes. Thus one encounters "celestial furniture," "the scissors of the universe," and "a backcloth of stars" (ES, 44), a "supernatural driver" and a "supernatural horse" (ES, 63) or "numinous boulders" (ES, 68). Eternity is always nearby:

> The incident occurred within a stone's throw of the ancient and modern riverwall, and the timeless river stood waiting to be dis-

cerned like a dark floating ball on which the lighted shadow of its own interior had formed itself into ships whose cargo was no less than the motion of the earth. (ES, 64)

Language, Harris repeatedly insists, is the medium that allows such lightninglike leaps and such instantaneous bestowals of otherness as when L–'s clothing, as he is pulled out of the East Street canal, is described as "wrinkled into the alien folds of another skin" (ES, 26). Language is the vehicle (perhaps the "reconnaissance vehicle" the narrator declines to be specific about) of a visionary projection through time and space – of exile, dislocation, and ultimate reunion, and of an othering that makes the narrator "a ghost returning to the past." The narrator, that is, dies into language and becomes Idiot Nameless, negatively capable of giving birth to his multifaceted Self. In place of a presumably "objective" train of events or configuration of facts to which the writing could be made to refer, Harris insists upon the factuality of the writing itself, upon writing as a *live* medium:

The medium of language, the poet's word (and this is essentially every man's true expression), is much more than a question of emotional and intellectual usage or documentary coinage. In fact to hint at a *medium* is to embrace a vision of patterns and capacities beneath and beyond every conventional game of one-sided meaning. (TWS, 21)

Alain Robbe-Grillet's remark that writing "is not a testimony offered in evidence concerning an external reality, but is its own reality" and his comment on his novel *Jealousy* are relevant here:

. . . it was absurd to suppose that in the novel *Jealousy* . . . there existed a clear and unambiguous order of events, one which was not that of the sentences of the book, as if I had diverted myself by mixing up a pre-established calendar the way one shuffles a deck of cards. . . . there existed for me no possible order outside of that of the book. The latter was not a narrative mingled with a simple anecdote external to itself, but again the very unfolding of a story which had no other reality than that of the narrative, an occurrence which functioned nowhere else except in the mind of the invisible narrator, in other words of the writer, and of the reader.[13]

This is the point made by the "Black Rooms" section of *The Eye of the Scarecrow*, the section in which Harris quotes passages from earlier points in the novel. (The title suggests the windowless apartment the narrator calls his "revolutionary goal" in Book I.) In doing so he seems to be insisting upon the irreducibility and the substantiality of the linguistic medium in which the novel has its being, reifying its linguistic events as exactly that – events. Such refusal to view writing as subservient to what is normally thought of as reality is exemplified further by Harris's Author's Note, which, reminiscent of "The Black Rooms," concludes with a lengthy quotation from the text of the novel, Harris again insistent that the reader deal with the density of the linguistic reality of which the book is composed, that no relief be sought outside the novel's primordially linguistic occasion, "the reality of the original Word, the Well of Silence."

IV

The Eye of the Scarecrow initiates the mining of an intensely self-conscious vein in Wilson Harris's work. The act of writing is not transparent, a pane of glass to be overlooked, looked through, but instead calls attention to itself. For this reason most of the novels that follow it involve writers (nonprofessionals but nevertheless writers) as their protagonists. *The Waiting Room* takes the form of a "logbook" written by its heroine, Susan Forrestal, just as *Companions of the Day and Night* is presented as the posthumous publication of selections from the diaries and writings of one Idiot Nameless, a tourist whose dead body has been found at the base of the Pyramid of the Sun at Teotihuacán in Mexico. Victor in *Ascent to Omai* writes poems, as did his father Adam, one of whose compositions, "Fetish," is introduced as evidence in his defense during his trial for arson. Even the judge has literary intentions, seeking, as he puts it, "to repudiate the vicarious novel."[14] In *Black Marsden* Clive Goodrich, who turns up again as the editor of Idiot Nameless's manuscripts in *Companions of the Day and Night*, makes regular entries in a diary he calls his "book of Infinity." Though the narrator usually refers to Goodrich as "he," it becomes obvious at various points that he and Goodrich are one and the same. The novel oscillates between third-person and first-person narration. At one point it is suggested that Goodrich's "book of Infinity" is a continuation of *The Eye of the Scarecrow*:

> My notes are corrections and revisions of an early "diary of Nameless" in order to build a new eye of the Scarecrow or stage or theatre of essences occupied by a phenomenon of personality reaching back into the slate of childhood. Upon that slate Clive Goodrich is a given existence and other buried traumatic existences as well wrestling one with the other to express a caveat or unknown factor, an intuitive fire music within the hubris of assured character, assured rites of passage into death or namless town. . . . My book is not autobiographical. I lose myself in it, you see. (BM, 94, 96)

In these novels the writing insistently announces itself as the locus of a process of "self-abandonment and self-recognition" (ES, 108), a multi-phasic projection of a spectral presence/ancestral absence, of what Harris calls – and quotes from his own evocation of which to conclude his Author's Note – "the dazzling sleeper of spirit":

> The dazzling sleeper of spirit, exposed within the close elements, the refraction and proximity of sun and water, awoke all too sud-denly and slid, in a flash, like speechless gunfire, from crown to toe, along the slowly reddening whiteness of the sand, turning darker still like blood as it fell; and ultimately black as the river-bottom descended, vanishing into a ripple, a dying footfall again, darting across the deep roadway of water and rising once more, distinct web or trace of animation upon a flank of stone. (ES, 49)

12

The Imagination of Justice
Wilson Harris's Ascent to Omai

What Leopardi in Ezra Pound's translation calls the "concord"
wherein "the arcane spirit of the whole mankind turns hardy
pilot" . . . persuades me that he has best imagined reality who has
best imagined justice.

W.B. Yeats

I

Ascent to Omai continues Wilson Harris's exploration of a reality not only haunted but oddly haloed by a specter of justice. This exploration of the enigmatic and problematical character of both "reality" and "justice" goes back at least as far as *The Whole Armour* and has its other most explicit occasion in *The Eye of the Scarecrow*. Throughout *The Whole Armour* one repeatedly feels oneself summoned, as Mattias is at one point said to have felt summoned, "to discern a deep, ancient, irrational logic on the most troubling question of all mankind – the meaning of individual innocence and guilt."[1] The question of Cristo's innocence or guilt in the killing of Sharon's suitor receives no definitive answer. Instead, it becomes more deeply removed from the possible presumption of any such answer by way of a refractedness in which Magda's ruses and would-be acquittal of her son coexist with her acceptance of his guilt. "I know Cristo better than judge and jury roll in one," she says (WA, 19), challenging the authority and wisdom of conventional justice, only to mock Sharon's belief in Cristo's innocence later: " 'Innocent?' Magda almost spat. She was furious. 'Because he's alive he's innocent? I suppose everybody else innocent too' " (WA, 82). She seems to agree with Abram, who answers Cristo's claim of innocence by remarking drily, "Nobody innocent" (WA, 23).

At the end of Book One of *The Whole Armour* Cristo realizes that one of the conditions of Magda's helping him escape is that he falsely confess to having killed Abram:

> Cristo stared at her, feeling bound and gagged before her theatrical and blinding performance – more real than life itself. Save that even the flickering reflex of knowledge of ultimate escape from a pure dramatic ordeal and dream was absent in this case. Indeed everything was so *real* the truth itself paled into a shattering insignificance. He felt that she would never release him until he had utterly condemned and surrendered himself. (WA, 28–29)

That in order to escape prosecution for a killing of which he claims to be falsely accused he has to confess falsely to another killing initiates a train of ironies, overlaps, and upsets that, throughout the rest of the book, confirm while complicating even further an "irrational logic" that both affirms and affronts the propriety of judgment: " 'I want to escape at any price,' Cristo confessed piteously, turning away from her and feeling shamed to the core, accepting the fabulous injustice of guilt. . . . 'All right,' he cried. 'I killed him. I killed Abram' " (WA, 29). The phrase "fabulous injustice" occurs several times in the book. The word *fable* occurs even more often, as when Sharon "lifted her hands, pushing away all tigerish responsibility and flight and acceptance of guilt, the fable and wilderness of inhumanity" (WA, 83). These recurrences insert a warning as well as a question mark into an otherwise stable, straightforward equation that identifies truth with empirical fact, for a fable is an admittedly fictitious narrative that nevertheless exemplifies or embodies a truth (or what, in any case, it asserts to be one). No easy ratio any longer obtains, agitated as both sides of the equation are by the possible conspiracy between "fable," "fact," and "truth" that breathes throughout the novel: " '*Tiger!*' Magda was startled and rooted to the ground. '*Tiger!*' the grotesque truth flashed on her face like a ruling fable of the land" (WA, 36–37).

The preponderance of such phrases as "a ruling fable of the land," "white fables of . . . the mixed ancestral legendary land" (WA, 78), and "the fable of his sleeping land and home" (WA, 86) implicates *terra firma*, the very image to which we resort to attribute a bedrock, no–nonsense solidity and support to empirical reality, in an aspect of experience that unsettles the line between fact and fiction. Thus the recurrence throughout the novel of such words as *theatrical, performance, fantasy, hallucination, disguise, pretension, camouflage, ritual, cue, mask, illusion, drama, fabricate, deception, hypocrisy, superstition, misconception, ruse, hoax,* and *masquerade.* Magda is twice described as "the queen of fate," her work as "a hazardous, ungrateful profession involving constant and extravagant deceptions and traps" (WA, 47). The question of justice, the problematic need to establish a ratio between innocence or guilt and events in the world, is implied throughout *The Whole Armour* to be intimate with and inextricable from this disruptive, enigmatic aspect of experience. Cristo, on his way to asserting that "history is a fable," says as much to Sharon while describing the Caribs and the Africans he claims to have come across in the bush:

> "They were running again, I tell you. All the shapes you can ever see in your mind's eye. Every black ancestor and bloodless ghost. What had they done to be running like that, Sharon?" he demanded of her, speaking to no one in particular. "What were they guilty of? I was one of them, a morose witness shadow, *one of a crowd of fictions*. I was dreaming. No, God knows, I was never so wide-awake. . . . " (WA, 125, emphasis added)

The recurring apprehension on the part of the characters in *The Whole Armour* that they are involved in a fable points not only to the complex of social fictions (collectively upheld and reinforced biases, expectations and judgments) in which they find themselves entangled, but possibly to the novel itself. The possibility that the book in which we encounter them is the "ruling fable" so insistently alluded to anticipates the more explicit self-reflexivity that characterizes *The Eye of the Scarecrow* and *Ascent to Omai*. When Cristo describes the fable he takes history to be as "all mixed up in my head on all sides like a grotesque tumbled pack of cards" (WA, 126), it is as though he were looking ahead to *Ascent to Omai*, where the judge writes or sketches his "novel history" on a deck of cards. The meditation on justice that is interwoven with *The Whole Armour*'s latent self-reflexivity surfaces again in *The Eye of the Scarecrow*, intimate and again tied up with questions concerning the relationship of fiction to the world. The narrator's voyage into the interior, the nine-month journey to Raven's Head that corresponds to the nine-month writing of the journal entries and letters that comprise the book, constitutes a repudiation of "idolatrous realism" undertaken, we're told, "in search of proof of another's (or was it my own)? disfigured innocence."[2]

The journey to Raven's Head anticipates and has much in common with Victor's journey to Omai, an expedition into the interior not unlike Cristo's forty days and forty nights in the bush. Like Victor, the narrator of *The Eye of the Scarecrow* is the son of a man who has been tried and found guilty of a crime. In both cases the son's desire to revise the judgment passed on his father involves an indictment of conventional realism's endorsement of and complicity in the assumptions that perpetuate such judgments. *The Whole Armour*, *The Eye of the Scarecrow*, and *Ascent to Omai* can be read as something of a trilogy in which the unjust fictional quality or "fabulous injustice" of social judgments

(collective oversimplifications embodied in mores, ritual, rumor, industry, art, and other institutions) is brought to a crisis that increasingly
reflects on the art of fiction itself. The susceptibility of experience to
novelistic treatment is implicated in a larger fiction-making process that
reduces the complexity of experience to a tidy set of prejudices, preconceptions, or prejudgments, a set of foregone conclusions:

> Magda's wake for her wayward son, Cristo, they felt, was a conces-
> sion to outraged proprieties – foreshadowed for long years in whis-
> pered jealous secrets projected upon her, the compulsive mistress
> of men, by timid and cruel wives and women. It had seemed a
> foregone conclusion that Cristo – educated in a remarkable way
> out of *their* pockets – wearing airs *they* could not afford – should
> be involved in stabbing a man in a brawling feud over a woman.
> (WA, 49–50)

The insistence throughout *The Whole Armour* on the fabulous, fictional
character of Cristo's predicament (its rootedness in collective preconceptions that acquire the impact of a predestined fate) carries over into
The Eye of the Scarecrow's repudiation of conventional realism in the name
of an "ultimate uprooting of all preconception" (ES, 27) and a "refusal
to bow to an inventory of mechanical fates" (ES, 89). Both carry over
into the proposal in *Ascent to Omai* to write a "novel history" – new
history and new novel both – as a way of reopening Adam's trial.

II

Roland Barthes's essay "Dominici, or the Triumph of Literature" could
easily serve as a preface to *Ascent to Omai*. The indictment it makes of
bourgeois realism's complicity in the privileging of certain ruling assumptions agrees with the recognition that the novel is a seat of social
judgments that informs the equation of "novel history" with "new courtroom OH MY."[3] Writing about the 1952 trial in which Gaston Dominici,
an eighty-year-old farmer, was convicted of three murders, Barthes
argues:

> it is in the name of a "universal" psychology that old Dominici has
> been condemned: descending from the charming empyrean of bour-
> geois novels and essentialist psychology, literature has just con-
> demned a man to the guillotine. . . . Now that particular
> psychology, in the name of which you can very well today have
> your head cut off, comes straight from our traditional literature,
> that which one calls in bourgeois style literature of the Human
> Document. It is in the name of the human document that the old

Dominici has been condemned. Justice and literature have made an alliance, they have exchanged their old techniques, thus revealing their basic identity, and compromising each other barefacedly. Behind the judges, in curule chairs, the writers. . . . [4]

That the judge in *Ascent to Omai* is also a novelist has to do with this "alliance" or "basic identity." In his essay "Tradition and the West Indian Novel" Harris makes a point similar to Barthes's, commenting on what he terms "the novel of persuasion" and its investment in "fashionable judgements" that maintain and reinforce the social order to which it owes its birth. He argues that it upholds and perpetuates assumptions that arose and "coincide[d] in Europe with states of society which were involved in consolidating their class and other vested interests."[5] His own work is concerned with dismantling "the novel of persuasion," with divesting the novel of its stake in conventional judgments and foregone conclusions.

The novelist-judge in *Ascent to Omai*, then, seeks to revise an earlier judgment made in keeping with accepted conventions, the guilty verdict passed on Adam, a welder accused of sabotage. The reopening of Adam's trial, the writing of a "novel history," is an act of conscience on his part, an act of compassion brought on by the impending crisis or crash at Omai. Like the quest for "the movement of original compassion" in *The Eye of the Scarecrow*, the new trial is an act of filial preoccupation, for the judge turns out to be Adam's son Victor: "Victor now saw that the judge sitting there was himself – cheek pressed to velvet glove and upholstery of the aircraft. He (Victor) toyed now with a writing-pad upon which he drew the outline of a novel history (his father's trial) through the witnesses he (the judge) had interrogated forty years ago" (AO, 52). The "novel history" is referred to as "a courtroom of truth – a drama of soul . . . gestation of the soul" (AO, 42–43), for it undertakes an understanding of psyche more complex than that of the psychology that Barthes describes and indicts:

> It is an adjectival psychology, it knows only how to endow its victims with epithets, it is ignorant of everything about the actions themselves, save the guilty category into which they are forcibly made to fit . . . Utilitarian, taking no account of any state of consciousness, this psychology has nevertheless the pretension of giving as a basis for actions a pre-existing inner person, it postulates "the soul": it judges man as a "conscience" without being embarrassed by having previously described him as an object. (M, 45)

It is to this presumptuous, callous aspect of the court that Adam objects: "I challenge the constitution of this court. Too one-sided I say. How

can it have *personal* authority over me when it cannot *feel*. . . . This court
– apart from the blasted witnesses who don't give a damn anyway – is
not mine, does not feel my existence at all" (AO, 59–60).

Ascent to Omai, the "novel history" that Judge/Victor writes, is an
attempt to hear and give expression to Adam's objection. His challenge
is taken up in the novel – taken seriously in Judge/Victor's sketches – in
a way in which it wasn't during the original trial. Given a weight it
wasn't given then, it now activates an unprecedented movement in the
court, a self-inquisitive, self-reflexive impulse on the judge's part that
simultaneously unravels and further enfolds a "court-within-a-court-
within-a-court" (AO, 122). Adam's appeal to a higher court, his claim
that *"the court which now tries him stands under the jurisdiction of another, far
wiser, far greater"* (AO, 58) – the goldmining claim he stakes with a bit
of debris from the airplane/courtroom crash that "looked like the wreckage of his own factory – the one he had burnt down" (AO, 48) – is itself
an act of sabotage. A disruption of business-as-usual, his challenge mo-
tivates Judge/Victor to interrogate the conventional courtroom and the
conventional novel in a single gesture:

> It was here for the first time, in fact, that he began indeed to question
> his own synthetic authority and to wonder how much truth lay in
> Adam's claim for a higher courtroom of original feeling rather than
> quasi-feeling, a court which could sift the entrenched reality of
> world-historical ruling intransigence, world-historical error, self-
> sufficient historical model, self-sufficient historical myth. . . .
> (AO, 61)

The "novel history" that Judge/Victor sketches is an attempt to evoke
this higher court, to intimate an eclipsed, oppositional courtroom that
is not in retreat from complication and thus not incapable of compassion.

Without losing sight of the possible seduction of the arts by the dominant assumptions of a particular age or social order, Harris remains
confident in their ability to break through such assumptions and fixations.
In "Interior of the Novel: Amerindian/European/African Relations," an
essay published in the same year in which *Ascent to Omai* appeared – its
title suggests the journey into the interior so central to *Ascent to Omai*
and *The Eye of the Scarecrow*, the exploration of a novel-within-a-novel-
within-a-novel corresponding to the "court-within-a-court-within-a-
court" – Harris remarks: "I am only too well aware of the disablement
of the arts, the irrelevance of the arts, in an age dedicated to materialism
and violence. And yet – having confessed to this – what may be better
constituted than the arts to visualize the irrelevant disabled of mankind,
the irrelevant dead, the irrelevant beaten, the irrelevant blind?"[6] It is this
"irrelevance" that Judge/Victor seeks to activate. Tellingly, the term

crops up in *Ascent to Omai* in the form of an objection by the prosecuting counsel that Judge/Victor overrules:

> "My lord," said the prosecuting council, "the man on trial is a welder, a porknocker, a very ordinary though skilled Columbian/ Guianese/Albuoystonian/El Doradonne/Alias upon Alias *ignorant* labouring man. I think the line of inquiry adopted by defence counsel is completely irrelevant . . . He has put words already into his client's mouth. . . ."
>
> The judge polished off the horn he had been drawing on his pad. "Irrelevant, yes," he said, "but therein lies its curious aptness in this trial. . . . " (AO, 66)

A refusal to endorse the "ruling fable" by complying with accepted procedure, the defense counsel's line of argument is irrelevant in the positive sense of initiating a departure from an entrenched world-view, actively out to divest itself of a conformist relevancy. Unwilling to ratify such a world-view by catering to the expectations it generates, the defense counsel avails himself of the opportune irrelevancy of the arts.

That a case is being made for an iconoclastic art becomes more apparent when the defense counsel, following Judge/Victor's overruling of the prosecuting counsel's objection, introduces "Fetish," a poem written by Adam, into the proceedings, noting that "one is involved at a certain level in an abnormal irrelevancy as Fetish indicates" (AO, 67). The introduction of this piece of evidence brings Judge/Victor's liberalism to a crisis, challenging his patronizing view of Adam. The prospect of Adam's speaking for himself rather than being spoken for by others is at first more than he can handle, but it eventually converts him to what are later in the novel termed "canons of obscurity" (AO, 122):

> he was still unprepared to face the fact that the untutored prisoner himself could speak out of the subconscious, on his own behalf, like a dead portrait consistent with its own voice of nothingness in order to blast the pretensions of all who made a living by dubbing those, whose cause they espoused, with their own noises of emancipation or tyranny.
>
> If he (the untutored prisoner speaking now through Fetish) had to be dubbed and gagged like the picture of a slave on a wall, *better to be truly obscure* when he croaked through his welded lips than to wear a false light or coherent function of robot on his brow, dawn of a uniform callous. (AO, 68–69, emphasis added)

By this point "irrelevant" has become roughly synonymous with "obscure," for "Fetish," from its opening lines on – "Drowned darkness / is the pursuit of stains like flowers" – diverges from overt intelligibility or easy access, enacting while implicitly commenting on a corrosive obscurity bent on dissolving (to quote Barthes again) "a terror which threatens us all, that of being judged by a power which wants to hear only the language it lends us" (M, 46).

Responding to the prosecuting counsel's objections to the poem, the defense counsel comments on the poem's assault on "tidy self-indulgent rationalizations," attributing a liberating impulse to its deviation from conventional clarities: "Fetish is a poem about disintegration – you perceive the implicit foundation or lack of foundation very well – but you are unable to see you are being *assisted*, as it were, to break the callous you deplore. . . . Fetish seeks to break this *tidiness* because, in fact, it's all part of a callous or callouses of conceit we plaster upon everything" (AO, 72–73). The same could be said of *Ascent to Omai*, as is evident later when Judge/Victor, a convert to Adam's "canons of obscurity," appropriates the nineteenth-century convention of addressing the reader, doing so, however, only to repudiate convention:

> *"Dear Reader,* (THE JUDGE WROTE HALF IN THE MARGIN OF HIS BOOK AND HALF ON A VACANT CARD). My intention, in part, is to repudiate the vicarious novel – vicarious sex-mask, death-mask – where the writer, following a certain canon of clarity, claims to enter the most obscure and difficult terrain of experience without incurring a necessary burden of authenticity, obscurity or difficulty at the same time. No matter his material stems from centuries of inequality, repression, oppression, etc. All this must serve as a prophylactic in the name of emancipation or industry. . . . " (AO, 96)

Judge/Victor's court, we begin to see, aspires to compassion in its root sense of a *suffering with* the often obscure complexity of the matters it seeks to sift. Its resistance to an oversimplified grid or presumptuous clarity has to do with an effort not to aggrandize its calibrations into static assumptions. Harris uses the courtroom setting both to portray the novel as a seat of social judgments and to articulate a poetics that looks beyond or sees through its conventional character. Not unworthy of note is the fact that one such articulation, a statement advocating language as a vehicle of psyche, lays stress on the word *irrelevant*. He writes of the pencils Judge/Victor sketches with:

> Those pencils *spoke* by illumining the curious disintegration of the past and invoking through the granular sensation of images – the dust of memory, the rubbish heap of landscape – a sequence of words allied not simply to pictures but to the very brokenness of all fabric inherent in vision. *Language for him, therefore, was a vision*

of consciousness as if what one dreams of in the past is there with a new
reality never so expressive before because nothing stands now to block
the essential intercourse of its parts, however mute, however irrelevant.
(AO, 78)

It is in this surprised and surprising brokenness that "the irrelevant disabled of mankind, the irrelevant dead, the irrelevant beaten, the irrelevant
blind" bear dark, exacting witness.

III

Judge/Victor, in his address to the "gentle reader" whose outline he
sketches, goes on to assert that "incurring a necessary burden of authenticity" entails "immersing ourselves in language as omen, as an
equation of experience" (AO, 96). On a certain level the pronouncements
on language and novelistic procedure that occur in *Ascent to Omai* apologize for and rationalize the difficulties presented by Harris's style, potentially taming its obscurities by offering a set of intelligible, coherent
precepts that, exactly because they "explain" or justify the obscurities,
run the risk of being dwelt on or seized upon with disproportionate
attention by the clarity-seeking reader. The novel's self-reflexivity itself
runs the risk of serving as a "prophylactic," insulating the "gentle reader"
against the very difficulties it advertises and promotes. This is an alive,
active risk, but one that the pronouncements themselves can be read as
taking into account. On another level, that is, these pronouncements
insist that the obscurities be dealt with directly, insist on the need for
"immersing ourselves in the actual difficulty" (AO, 96). The precepts
they offer are both imperative and apologetic, with a thread of warning
woven in as well. This accounts in part for Harris's tactic of quoting
lengthy passages from earlier sections of the novel in the early pages of
Book Three, a practice that first appeared in *The Eye of the Scarecrow*,
toward the end of which earlier passages are quoted in the wake of a
manifesto endorsing language as "one's medium of the vision of consciousness" (ES, 95). In doing so, Harris returns us to and reimmerses
us in a manifest "poetry of original and precarious features" (AO, 96)
rather than discursive proclamations that merely propose one.

In the essay "Interior of the Novel" Harris writes of a "danger of self-
enchantment or *hubris*" in which "prize and penalty . . . are closely interwoven" (E, 17). Something like this danger, I have been suggesting,
haunts the self-reflexivity of such works as *Ascent to Omai*, whose apologetics border on self-congratulation even while alluding to a threshold
they admit not being able to reach. The courtroom setting of *Ascent to
Omai* amounts to an admission that throughout the novel self-

endorsement and self-interrogation put one another on trial. This is the exemplary ordeal of the imagination of justice. Harris argues in "Interior of the Novel" that "a certain *caveat* should inform the imagination: a *caveat* which unceasingly appoints *losses* within *gains*. As such . . . it voids its own focus of conscription to preserve an unfulfilled goal, a balance of natures within which a continuous vigilance, submerged and buoyant, prevails or attempts to prevail" (E, 12). In *Ascent to Omai* he speaks of "a scale of balances that subsists *through* disintegration not *upon* disintegration . . . an ideal balance which, in the nature of things, is the frailest but most enduring spirit of art in that it moves within and beyond one's grasp to balance *loss* with *gain*" (AO, 102). Both the imagination of justice and the justice of the imagination revolve around such an appointment or would-be balance between gains and losses, prize and penalty, congratulation and caution.

The difficulties in which Harris's style immerses us grow largely out of a vigilant determination not to fall into one-sidedness, the crime of which Adam accuses the court in the original trial. The result is a mercurial, somewhat agitated quality in which retreat complicates advance and vice versa, doing complicates undoing and vice versa, questions complicate pronouncements, and so forth. The site of this "continuous vigilance," the sentence, relates with punning inversion to the hubris of the conventional court's judgment of and passing sentence on Adam: "So that sentence having been passed in the very entrenched nature of things, wherein then lay the possibility of parole, genuine parole, true parole from the whole forlorn prisonhouse of adventure, claim of Adam, backside of the moon, OH MY?" (AO, 51). We recall that "parole" is at root a manner of speaking, so that, as in *The Eye of the Scarecrow*, a quest for "the movement of original compassion" carries into a grammatology that rejects or attempts to reject the "closed sentence" (ES, 59). The quest is for a new sentence, a manner of speaking more alive to ambiguity, dialectics, and dislocations, a peculiar way with words that aspires to justice and in which the sentence tries not to be the tool of any foregone conclusion.

The at times obscure but opportune "irrelevance" cultivated by *Ascent to Omai*, which is perhaps the most difficult of Harris's novels, is an attempted deviation from a canonical realism. The novel's struggle against an entrenched naturalism, its introduction of a disturbance into "the very entrenched nature of things," is made reference to a number of times by the phrase "*opus contra naturam* " Victor first encounters it as an "*enigma and epitaph,*" an inscription, on his way to Omai:

OH MY was a mushroom settlement far beneath the spectral watershed of Guyana, Amazon/Orinoco. Some said it was really

> OMAI – an Amerindian root word – subconscious foreboding. Others that a clown like Victor had invoked the substitution OH MY/OMAI. To forge a treaty of sensibility. English/Amerindian. Conqueror/Conquered.   Free/Enslaved.   Richman/Porknocker. Translation of the stigmata of the watershed. Was it a mirage of the senses, ruined faculty but therapeutic lighthouse, *opus contra naturam?*
>
> OPUS CONTRA NATURAM. Victor stopped to read this inscription upon an outcrop of volcanic material. (AO, 20)

The phrase occurs again in relation to a revision or would-be revision of Adam's trial and the sentence that was passed on him:

> This was the prison of reality (or irreality) in which Adam dwelt. Futuristic robot. Ruined porknocker. Insensible soul, insensible in-surrection, insensible bone, insensible nerve. It was as if he had already ceased to exist and Victor's journey in search of him pos-sessed an order of fatality – "immaterial" adventure of the soul, *opus contra naturam.* (AO, 41–42)

These passages are themselves telling cases in point of the mutable, tele-graphic flux of images and implications in Harris's writing, an urgent, sometimes anxious mutability bent on unsettling the neat but inert fix-ations of one-sided statement.

James Hillman's *Re-Visioning Psychology* is a book whose concerns and principal insights have much in common with Harris's. There are nu-merous passages throughout the book that could serve as glosses on *Ascent to Omai*. Drawn to and drawing his insights from many of the areas to which Harris is also attracted, such as alchemy and the Renais-sance art of memory, Hillman writes that his book "is about soul-making,"[7] a statement that could also be made of *Ascent to Omai*, where we find such expressions as "cradle of the soul" (AO, 28), "drama of the soul" (AO, 42), "adventure of the soul" (AO, 42), "trial of the soul" (AO, 43), and "gestation of the soul" (AO, 43). Hillman speaks of "a psychology of soul that is based in a psychology of image" (RP, xi), and we reflect on the weight being carried by images in *Ascent to Omai*. The term *pathologizing* he coins is a useful one: "I am introducing the term *pathologizing* to mean the psyche's autonomous ability to create illness, morbidity, disorder, abnormality, and suffering in any aspect of its be-havior and to experience and imagine life through this deformed and afflicted perspective" (RP, 57). He goes on to suggest that "pathologizing is a psychic activity per se" (RP, 79), and we recognize this as what is going on in the various images of breakdown, disintegration, and ca-tastrophe that recur throughout Harris's work. The impending crash in

Ascent to Omai (reminiscent of the crash at Raven's Head in *The Eye of the Scarecrow*) is one such image. Hence the punning translation of "Omai" into apocalyptic dread or foreboding "Oh my." The soul-making import of pathologizing is suggested by Harris when he speaks of "disease as a therapeutic omen of identity" (AO, 82), a suggestion unconsciously in agreement with Hillman's sense of "the God in the disease" or that "Gods reach us through affliction" (RP, 105). "My client," the defense counsel says of Adam, "is obviously a very sick man" (AO, 60).

Hillman, as does Harris, makes use of the phrase *"opus contra naturam,"* and what he has to say sheds light on *Ascent to Omai*. The phrase occurs in his discussion of alchemy, a soul-making activity to whose lore and symbolism Harris frequently refers. (He speaks of a "metamorphosis of metals" at one point [AO, 36], and we recall that Adam's claim to a higher court is entwined with his claim to being "gilded man," a native of Manoa/El Dorado, and with the goldmining claim he stakes on Omai ridge.) Hillman writes:

> Freeing the psyche from its material and natural view of itself and the world is an *opus contra naturam*, a work against nature. Essential to changing the soul's viewpoint are the experiences of pathologizing, for they express the decomposition of the natural; they present images that do not and cannot take place in the natural world. Although working with natural materials such as urine, quicksilver, or antimony, alchemy changed these substances into fantasies. It recognized the substantial nature of fantasy and the fantasy aspect of all natural substances. This was its true *opus contra naturam*: the transmutation, within the alchemist himself, of the natural viewpoint into the imaginal viewpoint. (RP, 91)

It is as though the soul, "naturalized" at birth into an alien world, declared itself a citizen of no such place by way of these images. This too is an aspect of Adam's claim: "I sought to *unmake* myself to *make* something I had lost before I was born. The land that is nowhere. Manoa" (AO, 58). The fact that Adam is a welder is relevant in this context not only because it involves work with metals, but also because these pathologizing, denaturalizing images often entail a yoking or welding together of otherwise incongruous elements as in Surrealism. On the first two pages of the novel we encounter images of "rags of gold," "falling up a ladder," and "ragged trousers of leaves . . . blue rather than green, blue leaves within a forest of cloud" (AO, 15–16).

Making and unmaking are confounded in Adam's case, and for this reason both his work as welder and the act of sabotage of which he is accused stand as metaphors or self-reflexive projections of Harris's practice in *Ascent to Omai*. It is Adam's claim and his poem "Fetish," we recall, that instigate Judge/Victor's attempt at a "novel history." The case for an alternate reality Harris makes throughout his writings is buttressed and bodied forth by an *opus contra naturam* that disassembles and reorganizes the features of the world as we most commonly know it. This in itself is a subversive, catastrophic, apocalyptic activity, so that in addition to images of breakdown, disaster, and collapse we get images that partake with a vengeance of an unlikely, outlandish quality. One such image is that of a mirror planted in Victor's side, the goad of reflection he flashes into Adam's eyes each day as he emerges from work. This mirror is referred to variously as "the chasm in his side" (AO, 23), "the robot in his side" (AO, 23), the "door in his side" (AO, 28), the "spear in his side" (AO, 34), "the millionaire rooms in his side" (AO, 36), and so forth – a variousness crucial to a use of image to avoid one-sided statement. This recourse to an imaged, equivocal prose contributes to an *opus contra naturam* in that it also serves to subvert the naturalizing, self-justifying tendency of the novel's self-reflexive pronouncements and apologetics, the danger of hubris that haunts or inhabits the propositionality toward which they tend. Someone will no doubt write in more technical detail someday on the way in which, throughout Harris's writing, highly charged, ambivalent, polysemous images intervene, so to speak, to rescue a passage from the foregone conclusions or patness of meaning into which it might otherwise drift:

> It dawned on him like pinpoint and stab that he was involved in a grotesque battle with the constable of the watershed, the ruined porknocker of space. And that the bombardment which he suffered (as protagonist or antagonist), mist or rain, gold or sand, sky or leaf, walking tree, slate or cloud was a meteoric flock flying through the eye of the void – implosive characteristic – even as it appeared to congeal or pause and encircle the tombstone of history like a radiant constellation, tail or fan. (AO, 21–22).

An image worthy of closer attention is that of stone or rock, which occurs with great persistence and variation throughout *Ascent to Omai*. It is a figure whose elaboration not only exemplifies Harris's *praxis* of image, but one that mediates or attempts to mediate the risky intimacy of loss with gain, penalty with prize, humility with hubris – a risk or an intimacy for which it in fact stands or works as a symbol. Late in the novel we encounter a highly denaturalized, pathologizing image – that of a bleeding, singing stone. The passage in which this occurs has to do with Victor's memory of nearly being run over by a car when he was three and a half years old:

It was a narrow shave: the car had stopped an inch from his brow where he had fallen on the ground unhurt save for a sharp cut on his knee from a stone in the roadway.

It was a minor bruise actually though with the car almost on top of him he felt he had been cut to rib and heart and that the stone itself *bled*. It was curious but in the hubbub of passersby and the outcry of the driver of the car, a nothingness had enveloped him, like a muffled drum in the sun, a singing stone, something faint, voiceless *and yet he could hear it distinctly*. (AO, 91)

This image carries the accumulated import of earlier instances in the novel where stone is either endowed with or dialectically participates in a diametrically fluid state or condition of feeling. The book's earliest mention of stone – that of the two rocks that, dislodged by the "ruined figure" ascending Omai ridge, strike Victor on the brow – conforms to the commonplace equation of stone with an absence of feeling. Hence the phrase "stone of insensibility" (AO, 16). As we move deeper into the novel, however, the simplicity of such an equation is soon disrupted by more ambivalent, complex castings of the image.

Mention is made, for example, of a French landowner who as a child accidentally hit and killed his brother with a stone. His remorse leads to repentance and an act of charity, thus implicating stone in a capacity for feeling and reformation:

There were the estates of a French landowner of the eighteenth century – La Penitence, Le Repentir (now the site of a cemetery in Georgetown) – all named by him to endorse a secret contract of remorse arising out of the death of his younger brother which he had unintentionally caused. He had flung a sharp stone in the heat of a game, a child's game, somewhere in France, which on striking his brother down arose afresh into the boot of exile. . . . His last will and testament bequeathed a calculated sum to relieve the plight of orphans and turned the stone of death inside/out as it were. (AO, 19–20)

This tendency continues with Harris investing in the multiple senses of the name Magdalene, grafting its archeological and geological connotations (involving minerals, rocks, and tools from a certain level in the earth) onto the associations and derivations having to do with Mary Magdalene (the application of the name to reformed prostitutes, as well as the root it provides for the word *maudlin* by way of depictions of Mary weeping):

Felt his eyes fill with mineral tears, sandstone, earthstone, greenstone, rainbow, slate, sanctification of vacancy. Empty tomb.

The stratification of rock-epitaph he now appeared to possess (like an ingrained faculty, *camera obscura*) resembled (as in an abstract painting) a procession of witnesses, witnesses of the soul.

The first of these – teardrop of glass – shook and moved its location. Like a dew-drop, ear-ring. Exquisite fossil. Magdalene of geology. It had taken ages of transference, evolution of fin, evolution of feather – ages of the riddle of lust – penetrations and modifications – to effect this chasm of daring, bridge of sight, bridge of sound, chasm of love. (AO, 27)

On the next page a reference is made to "the Magdalene of Compassion." Harris is hinting at a symbiotic knot that bridges the chasm between sensitivity and insensitivity, a dialectic in which feeling builds upon numbness or the affront to feeling, and vice versa. Twice he quotes from Matthew 16: 18, where Christ announces, "On this Rock I shall build my Church" (AO, 26, 33). Even the colloquial epithet "stone-drunk," applied to Adam at various points, appears to partake of this conjunction of feeling with non-feeling, "drunk" fluidity with rigid "stone." At one such point he is described as "stone-drunk, crazed by grief" (AO, 30), tying the numbness he seeks in liquor to his feelings over the death of his wife.

That this repeated conjunction of stoniness and fluidity (stone/blood, stone/tear, stone/liquor) implies an alchemical wedding of opposites becomes more evident when we come to the phrase "*lapis* of ambivalences" in yet another passage involving a mingling of liquid and rock: "Through the window of his aeroplane the lost city of Manoa had become like a pool in the clouds in which a stone, *lapis* of ambivalences, had fallen, and concentric rings representing frontiers of memory spread across the sea of the atmosphere" (AO, 89). The stone, an unlikely image of transmutation or transformability, is haloed throughout by intimations of the alchemist's *lapis*, the Philosopher's Stone. Its unlikeliness is highly appropriate, much like that of lead as a potential source of gold. The subject as well as the symbol of an alchemizing process, the "stone of insensibility" mutates into a "stone of love": "It was in this confrontation of opposites, these ruined prepossessions, that one glimpsed the moderation of the stone of love capable of replacing, like a Christian goal, the Gorgon classical unforgiving or unforgiven extremity" (AO, 100). This, at any rate, is the hopeful side of the image, but by no means the only one, for the stone embodies warning as well as hope, caution as well as wish, hauntedness as well as halo. Victor's tossing of stones into Albuoystown canal – akin to the figure of Manoa as a pool into which a stone has fallen – is said to "symbolize a state of precocity and *malaise* – equations of loss/gain" (AO, 93). The breakthrough which each ripple/horizon or ripple/epitaph represents – renewed capacity or emotional resilience through penetrations of trauma – is compounded and complicated with numbness: "As his pebbles fell into the canal he watched the ripples expand; and always as each horizon died, he would feel a numbness at heart" (AO, 93).

Harris's deployment of the image of stone projects a would-be transmutability or balance, yet the image untamably admits to a possibility of hubris or numbness that haunts any such attempt at equilibration. The attempt to imagine justice as an attribute of reality – a manifestly unjust reality moreover – is fraught with the risk of justification, the risk of glib, unfeeling assurances invested in a providential acquittal of the world: "And he saw these – the objects around him – so unemotionally and lucidly that a strange *hubris* overtook him: an assumption of painless comedy enacted everywhere" (AO, 41). The image of stone darkly attests to this condition of "sublime immunity" (AO, 54) or "mathematics of euphoria" (AO, 55), a further numbness, inflation, or hubris toward which an unself-critical assumption of justice tends. The imagination of justice in *Ascent to Omai* differs from and attempts to correct that of its worldly, institutionalized counterparts by reminding itself of the risk it runs of a lapse into rock-hard judgment, rock-hard presumptions, rock-hard justification. Adam, we're told at one point, "suspects everything" (AO, 64) – which would appear to include his own actions, for we find that he attempted to put out the very fire which he had set.

The imagination of justice in Harris's writing vigilantly works to undermine the possibility of hubris, even while admitting that one can do no better than an "ironic acquittal" – to use the expression coined in *Black Marsden* – from such a possibility. We see the vigilant, revisionary aspect of such an undertaking at work when Marsden reflects on a dream he has had: "The depersonalization of the human or cosmic desert in one's dreams is a kind of ironic acquittal from the charge of hubris. . . . Acquittal, therefore, from hubris is nothing more than the revitalized life of the imagination to re-assess blocked perspectives and to begin to digest as well as liberate contrasting figures." In order to be true to this insight, however, he has to go on to caution himself: "It was stimulating and sobering. Indeed the very stimulation was a caution. In describing or gloating upon his dream, had he not partially betrayed it and succumbed to an order of self-congratulation or inflation?"[8] The haunting, haloing complexity of "ironic acquittal" endorses a principle of non-exemption to which Harris refers as "poetic justice": "A very important contribution to criticism of art was made by Engels, and later reaffirmed by Georg Lukács. . . . This contribution, which to my mind reacts with poetic justice on many of the theories of Lukács himself, is that creative work may, and often does, have entirely different meanings to what the author hopes . . . " (TWS, 7). Harris writes similarly with regard to Orlando Patterson's notion of "historylessness" in an essay entitled "The Unresolved Constitution."[9] In each case "poetic justice" brings the author of an observation under the jurisdiction of that observation, making him subject to the judgment he passes. It is in keeping with this notion of poetic justice that Judge/Victor sees that he himself is on trial: "He felt himself and the prisoner now truly in the same abnormal ill-defined dock" (AO, 53). *Ascent to Omai*, the "novel history" he writes, likewise puts itself on trial. That this trial amounts to a tryout is conveyed by the emphasis put on its tentative, provisional quality, as though it were at all points subject to revision. The novel is described as a series of sketches, and in order to highlight the factor of randomness and chance the sketches are said to be made on cards, each of which is subject to reversal: "The judge . . . flicked the pages of his book like an expert gambler with currencies of time – obverse and reverse. On one side *judge* on the other *judged*. On one side again *father* on the other *son*. On one side still again *ancient* on the other *modern*" (AO, 86).

It is not inappropriate to conclude in this context by noting that W.B. Yeats revised the passage that serves as an epigraph to this essay. In the 1937 edition of *A Vision* the passage that had appeared in the 1924 edition is considerably recast, noticeably more cautious and qualified:

> if sometimes, overwhelmed by miracle as all men must be when in the midst of it, I have taken such periods [the periods into which history is divided in *A Vision*] literally, my reason has soon recovered; and now that the system stands out clearly in my imagination I regard them as stylistic arrangements of experience comparable to the cubes in the drawing of Wyndham Lewis and to the ovoids in the sculpture of Brancusi. They have helped me to hold in a single thought reality and justice.[10]

Such mingling of sobriety and daring is consistent with the caveat or "continuous vigilance" Harris says should inform the imagination. Likewise, we look at *Ascent to Omai*, especially the sketch that appears on page 90, and we see "stylistic arrangements of experience" arbitrating an ideal but elusive, alive but elusive balance.

13

Sound and Sentiment, Sound and Symbol

Senses of music in a number of texts is what I would like to address –
ways of regarding and responding to music in a few instances of writings
which bear on the subject. This essay owes its title to two such texts,
Steven Feld's *Sound and Sentiment: Birds, Weeping, Poetics and Song in
Kaluli Expression* and Victor Zuckerkandl's *Sound and Symbol: Music and
the External World*. These two contribute to the paradigm I bring to my
reading of the reading of music in the literary works I address.

Steven Feld is a musician as well as an anthropologist and he dedicates
Sound and Sentiment to the memory of Charlie Parker, John Coltrane,
and Charles Mingus. His book, as the subtitle tells us, discusses the way
in which the Kaluli of Papua New Guinea conceptualize music and poetic
language. These the Kaluli associate with birds and weeping. They arise
from a breach in human solidarity, a violation of kinship, community,
connection. *Gisalo*, the quintessential Kaluli song form (the only one of
the five varieties they sing that they claim to have invented rather than
borrowed from a neighboring people), provokes and crosses over into
weeping – weeping that has to do with some such breach, usually death.
Gisalo songs are sung at funerals and during spirit-medium seances and
have the melodic contour of the cry of a kind of fruitdove, the *muni*
bird.[1] This reflects and is founded on the myth regarding the origin of
music, the myth of the boy who became a *muni* bird. The myth tells of
a boy who goes to catch crayfish with his older sister. He catches none
and repeatedly begs for those caught by his sister, who again and again
refuses his request. Finally he catches a shrimp and puts it over his nose,
causing it to turn a bright purple red, the color of a *muni* bird's beak.
His hands turn into wings and when he opens his mouth to speak the
falsetto cry of a *muni* bird comes out. As he flies away, his sister begs
him to come back and have some of the crayfish but his cries continue

and become a song, semi-wept, semi-sung: "Your crayfish you didn't give me. I have no sister. I'm hungry. . . . " For the Kaluli, then, the quintessential source of music is the orphan's ordeal – an orphan being anyone denied kinship, social sustenance, anyone who suffers, to use Orlando Patterson's phrase, "social death,"[2] the prototype for which is the boy who becomes a *muni* bird. Song is both a complaint and a consolation dialectically tied to that ordeal, where in back of "orphan" one hears echoes of "orphic," a music that turns on abandonment, absence, loss. Think of the black spiritual "Motherless Child." Music is wounded kinship's last resort.

In *Sound and Symbol*, whose title Feld alludes to and echoes, Victor Zuckerkandl offers "a musical concept of the external world," something he also calls "a critique of our concept of reality from the point of view of music." He goes to great lengths to assert that music bears witness to what is left out of that concept of reality, or, if not exactly what, to the fact that something *is* left out. The world, music reminds us, inhabits while extending beyond what meets the eye, resides in but rises above what is apprehensible to the senses. This co-inherence of immanence and transcendence the Kaluli attribute to and symbolize through birds, which for them are both the spirits of the dead and the major source of the everyday sounds they listen to as indicators of time, location and distance in their physical environment. In Zuckerkandl's analysis, immanence, and transcendence meet in what he terms "the dynamic quality of tones," the relational valence or vectorial give and take bestowed on tones by their musical context. He takes great pains to show that "no material process can be co-ordinated with it," which allows him to conclude:

> Certainly, music transcends the physical; but it does not therefore transcend tones. Music rather helps the thing "tone" to transcend its own physical constituent, to break through into a nonphysical mode of being, and there to develop in a life of unexpected fullness. Nothing but tones! As if tone were not the point where the world that our senses encounter becomes transparent to the action of nonphysical forces, where we as perceivers find ourselves eye to eye, as it were, with a purely dynamic reality – the point where the external world gives up its secret and manifests itself, immediately, *as symbol*. To be sure, tones say, signify, point to – what? Not to something lying "beyond tones." Nor would it suffice to say that tones point to other tones – as if we had first tones, and then pointing as their attribute. No – in musical tones, being, existence, is indistinguishable from, is, pointing-beyond-itself, meaning, saying.[3]

One easily sees the compatibility of this musical concept of the world, this assertion of the intrinsic symbolicity of the world, with poetry. Yeats's view that the artist "belongs to the invisible life" or Rilke's notion of poets as "bees of the invisible" sits agreeably beside Zuckerkandl's assertion that "because music exists, the tangible and visible cannot be the whole of the given world. The intangible and invisible is itself a part of this world, something we encounter, something to which we respond" (SS, 71). His analysis lends itself to more recent formulations as well. His explanation of dynamic tonal events in terms of a "field concept" is not far from Charles Olson's "composition by field," and one commentator has brought *Sound and Symbol* to bear on Jack Spicer's work.[4]

The analogy between tone-pointing and word-pointing is not lost on Zuckerkandl, who, having observed that "in musical tones, being, existence, is indistinguishable from, is, pointing-beyond-itself, meaning, saying," immediately adds: "Certainly, the being of words could be characterized the same way." He goes on to distinguish tone-pointing from word-pointing on the basis of the conventionally agreed-upon referentiality of the latter, a referentiality writers have repeatedly called into question, frequently doing so by way of "aspiring to the condition of music." "Thus poetry," Louis Zukofsky notes, "may be defined as an order of words that as movement and tone (rhythm and pitch) approaches in varying degrees the wordless art of music as a kind of mathematical limit."[5] Music encourages us to see that the symbolic is the orphic, that the symbolic realm is the realm of the orphan. Music is prod and precedent for a recognition that the linguistic realm is also the realm of the orphan, as in Octavio Paz's characterization of language as an orphan severed from the presence to which it refers and which presumably gave it birth. This recognition troubles, complicates, and contends with the unequivocal referentiality taken for granted in ordinary language:

> Each time we are served by words, we mutilate them. But the poet is not served by words. He is their servant. In serving them, he returns them to the plenitude of their nature, makes them recover their being. Thanks to poetry, language reconquers its original state. First, its plastic and sonorous values, generally disdained by thought; next, the affective values; and, finally, the expressive ones. To purify language, the poet's task, means to give it back its original nature. And here we come to one of the central themes of this reflection. The word, in itself, is a plurality of meanings.[6]

Paz is only one of many who have noted the ascendancy of musicality and multivocal meaning in poetic language. (Julia Kristeva: "The poet

... wants to turn rhythm into a dominant element ... wants to make language perceive what it doesn't want to say, provide it with its matter independently of the sign, and free it from denotation."[7])

Poetic language is language owning up to being an orphan, to its tenuous kinship with the things it ostensibly refers to. This is why in the Kaluli myth the origin of music is also the origin of poetic language. The words of the song the boy who becomes a *muni* bird resorts to are different from those of ordinary speech. Song language "amplifies, multiplies, or intensifies the relationship of the word to its referent," as Feld explains:

> In song, text is not primarily a proxy for a denoted subject but self-consciously multiplies the intent of the word.
>   ... Song poetry goes beyond pragmatic referential communication because it is explicitly organized by canons of reflexiveness and self-consciousness that are not found in ordinary talk.
>   The uniqueness of poetic language is unveiled in the story of "the boy who became a *muni* bird." Once the boy has exhausted the speech codes for begging, he must resort to another communication frame. Conversational talk, what the Kaluli call *to halaido*, "hard words," is useless once the boy has become a bird; now he resorts to talk from a bird's point of view ... Poetic language is bird language.[8]

It bears emphasizing that this break with conventional language is brought about by a breach of expected behavior. In saying no to her brother's request for food the older sister violates kinship etiquette.

What I wish to do is work *Sound and Sentiment* together with *Sound and Symbol* in such a way that the latter's metaphysical accent aids and is in turn abetted by the former's emphasis on the social meaning of sound. What I'm after is a range of implication that will stretch, to quote Stanley Crouch, "from the cottonfields to the cosmos." You notice again that it is black music I'm talking about, a music whose "critique of our concept of reality" is notoriously a critique of social reality, a critique of social arrangements in which, because of racism, one finds oneself deprived of community and kinship, cut off. The two modes of this critique that I will be emphasizing Robert Farris Thompson notes among the "ancient African organizing principles of song and dance":

> ... *suspended accentuation patterning* (offbeat phrasing of melodic and choreographic accents); and, at a slightly different but equally recurrent level of exposition, *songs and dances of social allusion* (music which, however danceable and "swinging," remorselessly contrasts social imperfections against implied criteria for perfect living).[9]

Still, the social isn't all of it. One needs to hear, alongside Amiri Baraka listening to Jay McNeely, that "the horn spat enraged sociologies,"[10] but not without noting a simultaneous mystic thrust. Immanence and transcendence meet, making the music social as well as cosmic, political and metaphysical as well. The composer of "Fables of Faubus" asks Fats Navarro, "What's *outside* the universe?"[11]

This meeting of transcendence and immanence I evoke, in my own work, through the figure of the phantom limb. In the letter that opens *From A Broken Bottle Traces of Perfume Still Emanate* N. begins:

> You should've heard me in the dream last night. I found myself walking down a sidewalk and came upon an open manhole off to the right out of which came (or strewn around which lay) the disassembled parts of a bass clarinet. Only the funny thing was that, except for the bell of the horn, all the parts looked more like plumbing fixtures than like parts of a bass clarinet. Anyway, I picked up a particularly long piece of "pipe" and proceeded to play. I don't recall seeing anyone around but somehow I knew the "crowd" wanted to hear "Naima." I decided I'd give it a try. In any event, I blew into heaven knows what but instead of "Naima" what came out was Shepp's solo on his version of "Cousin Mary" on the *Four for Trane* album – only infinitely more gruffly resonant and varied and warm. (I even threw in a few licks of my own.) The last thing I remember is coming to the realization that what I was playing already existed on a record. I could hear scratches coming from somewhere in back and to the left of me. This realization turned out, of course, to be what woke me up.
>
> Perhaps Wilson Harris is right. There are musics which haunt us like a phantom limb. Thus the abrupt breaking off. Therefore the "of course." No more than the ache of some such would-be extension.[12]

I will say more about Wilson Harris in Section V. For now, let me simply say that the phantom limb is a felt recovery, a felt advance beyond severance and limitation that contends with and questions conventional reality, that it is a feeling for what is not there that reaches beyond as it calls into question what is. Music as phantom limb arises from a capacity for feeling that holds itself apart from numb contingency. The phantom limb haunts or critiques a condition in which feeling, consciousness itself, would seem to have been cut off. It is this condition, the non-objective character of reality, to which Michael Taussig, following Georg Lukács, applies the expression "phantom objectivity," by which he means the veil by way of which a social order renders its role in the construction of reality invisible: "A commodity-based society produces such phantom objectivity, and in so doing it obscures its roots – the relations between people. This amounts to a socially instituted paradox with bewildering manifestations, the chief of which is the denial by the society's members of the social construction of reality."[13] *Phantom*, then, is a relative, relativizing term that cuts both ways, occasioning a shift in perspective between real and unreal, an exchange of attributes between the two. So the narrator in Josef Skvorecky's *The Bass Saxophone* says of the band he is inducted into: "They were no longer a vision, a fantasy, it was rather the sticky-sweet panorama of the town square that was unreal."[14] The phantom limb reveals the illusory rule of the world it haunts.

II

Turning now to a few pieces of writing that allude to or seek to ally themselves with music, one sense I'm advancing is that they do so as a way of reaching toward an alternate reality, that music is the would-be limb whereby that reaching is done or that alerts us to the need for its being done. The first work I will look at is Jean Toomer's *Cane*. Though *Cane* is not as announcedly about music as John A. Williams's *Night Song*, Thomas Mann's *Doctor Faustus*, or any number of other works one could name, in its "quieter" way it is no less worth looking at in this regard. First of all, of course, there's the lyricism that pervades the writing, an intrinsic music that is not unrelated to a theme of wounded kinship of which we get whispers in the title. Commentators have noted the biblical echo, and Toomer himself, in notebooks and correspondence, referred to the book as *Cain* on occasion. His acknowledged indebtedness to black folk tradition may well have included a knowledge of stories in that tradition that depict Cain as the prototypical white, a mutation among an earlier people, all of whom were up to that point black: "Cain he kill his brudder Abel wid a great big club . . . and he turn white as bleech cambric in de face, and de whole race ob Cain dey bin white ebber since."[15] The backdrop of white assault that comes to the fore in "Portrait in Georgia," "Blood-Burning Moon," and "Kabnis" plays upon the fratricidal note struck by the book's title.

Indebted as it is to black folk tradition, *Cane* can't help but have to do with music. That "Deep River," "Go Down, Moses," and other songs are alluded to comes as no surprise. Toomer's catalytic stay in Georgia is well known. It was there that he first encountered the black "folk-spirit" he sought to capture in the book. Worth repeating is the emphasis he put on the music he heard:

> The setting was crude in a way, but strangely rich and beautiful.
> I began feeling its effects despite my state, or, perhaps, just because

of it. There was a valley, the valley of "Cane," with smoke-wreaths during the day and mist at night. A family of back-country Negroes had only recently moved into a shack not too far away. They sang. And this was the first time I'd ever heard the folk-songs and spirituals. They were very rich and sad and joyous and beautiful.[16]

He insisted, though, that the spirit of that music was doomed, that "the folk-spirit was walking in to die on the modern desert" and that *Cane* was "a swan-song," "a song of an end." The elegiac weariness and weight that characterize the book come of a lament for the passing of that spirit. In this it is like the music that inspired it, as Toomer pointed out in a letter to Waldo Frank:

> ... the Negro of the folk-song has all but passed away: the Negro of the emotional church is fading. . . . In my own . . . pieces that come nearest to the old Negro, to the spirit saturate with folk-song . . . the dominant emotion is a sadness derived from a sense of fading. . . . The folk-songs themselves are of the same order: the deepest of them, "I aint got long to stay here."[17]

So, "Song of the Son":

> Pour O pour that parting soul in song,
> O pour it in the sawdust glow of night,
> Into the velvet pine-smoke air to-night,
> And let the valley carry it along.
> And let the valley carry it along.
>
> O land and soil, red soil and sweet-gum tree,
> So scant of grass, so profligate of pines,
> Now just before an epoch's sun declines
> Thy son, in time, I have returned to thee,
> Thy son, I have in time returned to thee.
>
> In time, for though the sun is setting on
> A song-lit race of slaves, it has not set;
> Though late, O soil, it is not too late yet
> To catch thy plaintive soul, leaving, soon gone,
> Leaving, to catch thy plaintive soul soon gone.
>
> O Negro slaves, dark purple ripened plums,
> Squeezed, and bursting in the pine-wood air,
> Passing, before they stripped the old tree bare
> One plum was saved for me, one seed becomes
>
> An everlasting song, a singing tree,
> Caroling softly souls of slavery,

What they were, and what they are to me,
Caroling softly souls of slavery.[18]

Cane is fueled by an oppositional nostalgia. A precarious vessel possessed of an eloquence coincident with loss, it wants to reach or to keep in touch with an alternate reality as that reality fades. It was Toomer's dread of the ascending urban-industrial order that opened his ears to the corrective – potentially corrective – counterpoint he heard in Georgia. In the middle section of the book, set in Northern cities, houses epitomize a reign of hard, sharp edges, rectilinear pattern, fixity, regimentation, a staid, white order: "Houses, and dorm sitting-rooms are places where white faces seclude themselves at night" (C, 73). The house embodies, again and again, suffocating structure: "Rhobert wears a house, like a monstrous diver's helmet, on his head . . . He is sinking. His house is a dead thing that weights him down" (C, 40). Or: "Dan's eyes sting. Sinking into a soft couch, he closes them. The house contracts about him. It is a sharp-edged, massed, metallic house. Bolted" (C, 57). Compare this with Kabnis's fissured, rickety cabin in the south, through the cracks in whose walls and ceiling a ventilating music blows:

> The walls, unpainted, are seasoned a rosin yellow. And cracks between the boards are black. These cracks are the lips the night winds use for whispering. Night winds in Georgia are vagrant poets, whispering. . . . Night winds whisper in the eaves. Sing weirdly in the ceiling cracks. (C, 81, 104)

Ventilating song is what Dan invokes against the row of houses, the reign of suffocating structure, at the beginning of "Box Seat":

> Houses are shy girls whose eyes shine reticently upon the dusk body of the street. Upon the gleaming limbs and asphalt torso of a dreaming nigger. Shake your curled wool-blossoms, nigger. Open your liver lips to lean, white spring. Stir the root-life of a withered people. Call them from their houses, and teach them to dream.
>
> Dark swaying forms of Negroes are street songs that woo virginal houses. (C, 56)

Thirty years before the more celebrated Beats, Toomer calls out against an airtight domesticity, a reign of "square" houses and the domestication of spirit that goes with it, his call, as theirs would be, fueled and inflected by the countering thrust of black music.

Not that the beauty of the music wasn't bought at a deadly price. Its otherworldly reach was fostered and fed by seeming to have no home in this one ("I aint got long to stay here"). What the night winds whisper is this:

White-man's land.
Niggers, sing.
Burn, bear black children
Till poor rivers bring
Rest, and sweet glory
In Camp Ground. (C, 81, 85, 103)

The singing, preaching, and shouting coming from the church near Kabnis's cabin build as Layman tells of a lynching, reaching a peak as a stone
crashes in through one of the windows:

A shriek pierces the room. The bronze pieces on the mantel hum.
The sister cries frantically: "Jesus, Jesus, I've found Jesus. O Lord,
glory t God, one mo sinner is acomin home." At the height of
this, a stone, wrapped round with paper, crashes through the window. Kabnis springs to his feet, terror-stricken. Layman is worried.
Halsey picks up the stone. Takes off the wrapper, smooths it out,
and reads: "You northern nigger, its time fer y t leave. Git along
now." (C, 90)

Toomer put much of himself into Kabnis, from whom we get an apprehension of music as a carrier of conflicted portent, bearer of both
good and bad news. "Dear Jesus," he prays, "do not chain me to myself
and set these hills and valleys, heaving with folk-songs, so close to me
that I cannot reach them. There is a radiant beauty in the night that
touches and . . . tortures me" (C, 83).

Cane's take on music is part and parcel of Toomer's insistence on the
tragic fate of beauty, the soul's transit through an unsoulful world. This
insistence begins with the very first piece in the book, the story of
"Karintha carrying beauty," her soul "a growing thing ripened too
soon." The writing is haunted throughout by a ghost of aborted splendor,
a specter written into its much-noted lament for the condition of the
women it portrays – woman as anima, problematic "parting soul." These
women are frequently portrayed, not insignificantly, singing. The mark
of blackness and the mark of femininity meet the mark of oppression
invested in music. Toomer celebrates and incorporates song but not
without looking at the grim conditions that give it birth, not without
acknowledging its outcast, compensatory character. "Cotton Song," one
of the poems in the book, takes the work song as its model: "Come,
brother, come. Lets lift it; / Come now, hewit! roll away!" (C, 9). Like
Sterling Brown's "Southern Road," Nat Adderley's "Work Song," Sam
Cooke's "Chain Gang," and Edward Kamau Brathwaite's "Folkways,"
all of which it anticipates, the poem excavates the music's roots in forced

labor. Music here is inseparable from the stigma attached to those who make it.

This goes further in fact. Music itself is looked at askance and stigmatized in a philistine, prosaic social order: "Bolted to the endless rows of metal houses. . . . No wonder he couldn't sing to them" (C, 57). Toomer's formal innovations in *Cane* boldly ventilate the novel, a traditional support for prosaic order, by acknowledging fissures and allowing them in, bringing in verse and dramatic dialogue, putting poetry before reportage. This will to song, though, is accompanied by an awareness of song's outlaw lot that could have been a forecast of the book's commercial failure. (Only five hundred copies of the first printing were sold.) *Cane* portrays its own predicament. It shows that music or poetry, if not exactly a loser's art, is fed by an intimacy with loss and may in fact feed it. This comes out in two instances of a version of wounded kinship that recurs throughout the book, the thwarted communion of would-be lovers. Paul, Orpheus to Bona's Eurydice, turns back to deliver an exquisitely out-of-place poetic address to the doorman, then returns to find Bona gone. Likewise, the narrator holds forth poetically as he sits beside Avey in the story that takes her name, only to find that she has fallen asleep. A play of parallel estrangements emerges. His alienation from the phantom reign of prosaic power – the Capitol dome is "a gray ghost ship" – meets her detachment from and immunity to prepossessing eloquence:

> I talked, beautifully I thought, about an art that would be born, an
> art that would open the way for women the likes of her. I asked
> her to hope, and build up an inner life against the coming of that
> day. I recited some of my own things to her. I sang, with a strange
> quiver in my voice, a promise-song. And then I began to wonder
> why her hand had not once returned a single pressure. . . . I sat
> beside her through the night. I saw the dawn steal over Washington.
> The Capitol dome looked like a gray ghost ship drifting in from
> sea. Avey's face was pale, and her eyes were heavy. She did not
> have the gray crimson-splashed beauty of the dawn. I hated to
> wake her. Orphan-woman. . . . (C, 46–47)

III

Beauty apprised of its abnormality both is and is not beauty. (Baraka on Coltrane's "Afro-Blue": "Beautiful has nothing to do with it, but it is."[19]) An agitation complicates would-be equanimity, would-be poise. "Th form thats burned int my soul," Kabnis cries, "is some twisted awful thing that crept in from a dream, a godam nightmare, an wont

stay still unless I feed it. An it lives on words. Not beautiful words. God
Almighty no. Misshapen, split-gut, tortured, twisted words" (C, 110).
The tormenting lure of anomalous beauty and the answering dance of
deformation – form imitatively "tortured, twisted" – also concern the
writer I would like to move on to, William Carlos Williams. The har-
assed/harassing irritability that comes into the "Beautiful Thing" section
of *Paterson* recalls Kabnis's "Whats beauty anyway but ugliness if it hurts
you?" (C, 83). In black music Williams heard the "defiance of authority"
he declares beauty to be, a "vulgarity" that "surpasses all perfections."[20]

Williams's engagement with black music was greatly influenced by
his sense of himself as cut off from the literary mainstream. At the
time the two pieces I would like to look at were written, Williams
had not yet been admitted into the canon, as can be seen in the omission
of his work from the *Modern Library Anthology of American Poetry* in
1945, at whose editor, Conrad Aiken, he accordingly takes a shot in
Man Orchid, the second of the two pieces I'll discuss. His quarrel with
T.S. Eliot's dominance and influence doesn't need pointing out, except
that it also comes up in *Man Orchid*. Seeing himself as a victimized
poet, Williams celebrated the music of a victimized people. In a gesture
that has since been overdone ("the white negro," "the student as
nigger," analogies between "women and blacks"), he saw parallels
between their lot and his own. This can also be seen, though in a
slightly more subtle way, in the first of the two pieces I would like
to turn to, "Ol' Bunk's Band."

Both pieces grew out of Williams's going to hear New Orleans trumpeter Bunk Johnson in New York in 1945. A revival of interest in Johnson's music was then going on, and Williams caught him during a three-
and-a-half-month gig at the Stuyvesant Casino on the lower East Side.
He soon after wrote "Ol' Bunk's Band," a poem whose repeated insistence "These are men!" diverges from the dominant culture's denial
of human stature to black people. He goes against the grain of accepted
grammar in such things as the conscious "vulgarity" of the triple negative
"and / not never / need no more," emulating a disregard for convention
he heard in the music. The poem in full:

> These are men! the gaunt, unfore-
>   sold, the vocal,
> blatant, Stand up, stand up! the
>   slap of a bass-string.
> Pick, ping! The horn, the
>   hollow horn
> long drawn out, a hound deep
>   tone –

> Choking, choking! while the
>   treble reed
> races – alone, ripples, screams
>   slow to fast –
> to second to first! These are men!
>
> Drum, drum, drum, drum, drum,
>   drum, drum! the
> ancient cry, escaping crapulence
>   eats through
> transcendent – torn, tears, term
>   town, tense,
> turns and back off whole, leaps
>   up, stomps down,
> rips through! These are men
>   beneath
> whose force the melody limps –
>   to
> proclaim, proclaims – Run and
>   lie down,
> in slow measures, to rest and
>   not never
> need no more! These are men!
>   Men![21]

The "hound deep / tone," reminding us that Johnson played in a band known as the Yelping Hound Band in 1930, also conjures a sense of underdog status that brings the orphaned or outcast poet into solidarity with an outcast people. The repeated assertion "These are men!" plays against an implied but unstated "treated like dogs."

Threaded into this implicit counterpoint are the lines "These are men / beneath / whose force the melody limps," where *limps* reflects critically upon a crippling social order. The musicians do to the melody what's done to them, the social handicap on which this limping reports having been translated and, in that sense, transcended, triumphed over. Williams anticipates Baraka's more explicit reading of black music as revenge, sublimated murder. Looking at *Paterson*, which hadn't been underway long when "Ol' Bunk's Band" was written, one finds the same complex of figures: dogs, lameness, limping. In the preface to Book One the image conveyed is that of a pariah, out of step with the pack:

> Sniffing the trees,
> just another dog
> among a lot of dogs. What

else is there? And to do?
The rest have run out –
after the rabbits.
Only the lame stands – on
three legs. . . . (P, 11)

This leads eventually to the quote from John Addington Symonds's *Studies of the Greek Poets* that ends Book One, a passage in which Symonds comments on Hipponax's choliambi, "lame or limping iambics":

> . . . Hipponax ended his iambics with a spondee or a trochee instead of an iambus, doing thus the utmost violence to the rhythmical structure. . . . The choliambi are in poetry what the dwarf or cripple is in human nature. Here again, by their acceptance of this halting meter, the Greeks displayed their acute aesthetic sense of propriety, recognizing the harmony which subsists between crabbed verses and the distorted subjects with which they dealt – the vices and perversions of humanity – as well as their agreement with the snarling spirit of the satirist. Deformed verse was suited to deformed morality. (P, 53)

That Williams heard a similar gesture in the syncopated rhythms of black music is obvious by Book Five, where, after quoting a passage about Bessie Smith from Mezz Mezzrow's *Really the Blues*, he makes his well known equation of "satiric" with "satyric":

a satyric play!
All plays
were satyric when they were most devout.
Ribald as a Satyr!

Satyrs dance!
all the deformities take wing. (P, 258)

This would also be a way of talking about the "variable foot," less an aid to scansion than a trope – the travestied, fractured foot.

Williams here stumbles upon, without naming and, most likely, without knowing, the Fon-Yoruba orisha of the crossroads, the lame dancer Legba. Legba walks with a limp because his legs are of unequal lengths, one of them anchored in the world of humans and the other in that of the gods. His roles are numerous, the common denominator being that he acts as an intermediary, a mediator, much like Hermes, of whom Hipponax was a follower. (Norman O. Brown: "Hipponax, significantly enough, found Hermes the most congenial god; he is in fact the only personality in Greek literature of whom it may be said that he walked with Hermes all the days of his life."[22]) Like Hermes's winged feet,

Legba's limp – "deformities take wing" – bridges high and low. Legba presides over gateways, intersections, thresholds, wherever different realms or regions come into contact. His limp a play of difference, he is the master linguist and has much to do with signification, divination, and translation. His limp the offbeat or eccentric accent, the "suspended accentuation" of which Thompson writes, he is the master musician and dancer, declared first among the orishas because only he could simultaneously play a gong, a bell, a drum, and a flute while dancing. The master of polyrhythmicity and heterogeneity, he suffers not from deformity but multiformity, a "defective" capacity in a homogeneous order given over to uniform rule. Legba's limp is an emblem of heterogeneous wholeness, the image and outcome of a peculiar remediation. *Lame* or *limping*, that is, like *phantom*, cuts with a relativizing edge to unveil impairment's power, as though the syncopated accent were an unsuspected blessing offering anomalous, unpredictable support. Impairment taken to higher ground, remediated, translates damage and disarray into a dance. Legba's limp, compensating the difference in leg lengths, functions like a phantom limb. Robert Pelton writes that Legba "transforms ... absence into transparent presence,"[23] deficit leg into invisible supplement.

Legba's authority over mix and transition made him especially relevant to the experience of transplantation brought about by the slave trade. The need to accommodate geographical and cultural difference placed a high premium on his mediatory skills. He is thus the most tenaciously retained of the orishas among New World Africans, the first to be invoked in *vodoun* ceremonies, be they in Haiti, Cuba, Brazil, or elsewhere. There is little wonder why Williams's work, concerned as it is with the New World as a ground for syncretistic innovation, would be paid a visit by the African bridge between old and new. What he heard in Bunk Johnson's music was a rhythmic digestion of dislocation, the African genius for enigmatic melding or mending, a mystery of resilient survival no image puts more succinctly than that of Legba's limping dance.

Legba has made more straightforward appearances in certain works written since Williams's time, showing up, for example, as Papa LaBas (the name he goes by in New Orleans) in Ishmael Reed's novels. Or as Lebert Joseph in Paule Marshall's *Praisesong for the Widow*, a novel whose third section is introduced by a line from the Haitian invocation to Legba and in which one comes upon such passages as: "Out of his stooped and winnowed body had come the illusion of height, femininity and power. Even his foreshortened left leg had appeared to straighten itself out and grow longer as he danced."[24] One of his most telling appearances in the literature of this country, though, is one in which, as in Williams's work, he enters unannounced. In Ralph Ellison's *Invisible Man* one finds adumbrations of Legba that, bearing as they do on the concerns addressed here, deserve more than passing mention.

Invisible Man, like *Cane*, is a work that draws on black folk resources. While collecting folklore in Harlem in 1939 for the Federal Writers' Project, Ellison was told a tale that had to do with a black man in South Carolina who, because he could make himself invisible at will, was able to harass and give white people hell with impunity.[25] This would seem to have contributed to the relativizing thrust of the novel's title and its long meditation on the two-way cut of invisibility. On the other side of invisibility as exclusion, social death, we find it as revenge, millenarian reversal. The prominence of Louis Armstrong in the novel's prologue brings to mind Zuckerkandl's discussion of the case music makes for the invisible, as invisibility is here both social and metaphysical. The ability to "see around corners" defies the reign of strict rectilinear structure lamented in *Cane* by going outside ordinary time and space constraints. Louis horn, apocalyptic, alters time (and, with it, space):

> Invisibility, let me explain, gives one a slightly different sense of time, you're never quite on the beat. Sometimes you're ahead and sometimes behind. Instead of the swift and imperceptible flowing of time, you are aware of its nodes, those points where time stands still or from which it leaps ahead. And you slip into the breaks and look around. That's what you hear vaguely in Louis' music.[26]

This different sense of time one recognizes as Legba's limp. It leads to and is echoed by a later adumbration of Legba, one in which Ellison hints at a similarly "offbeat" sense of history, one that diverges from the Brotherhood's doctrine of history as monolithic advance. Early on, Jack describes the old evicted couple as "already dead, defunct," people whom "history has passed . . . by," "dead limbs that must be pruned away" (IM, 284). Later "dead limbs" plays contrapuntally upon Tarp's contestatory limp, a limp that, as he explains, has social rather than physiological roots. It was caused by nineteen years on a chain gang:

> You notice this limp I got? . . . Well, I wasn't always lame, and I'm not really now 'cause the doctors can't find anything wrong with that leg. They say it's sound as a piece of steel. What I mean is I got this limp from dragging a chain. . . . Nobody knows that about me, they just think I got rheumatism. But it was that chain and after nineteen years I haven't been able to stop dragging my leg.
> (IM, 377–378)

Phantom limb, phantom limp. Tarp goes on, in a gesture recalling the protective root Sandy gives Frederick Douglass in the latter's *Narrative*, to give Invisible Man the broken link from the leg chain he dragged for nineteen years. Phantom limb, phantom limp, phantom link: "I think it's got a heap of signifying wrapped up in it and it might help you remember what we're really fighting against" (IM, 379). This it does, serving to concentrate a memory of injustice and traumatic survival, a remembered wound resorted to as a weapon of self-defense. During his final confrontation with the Brotherhood, Invisible Man wears it like a set of brass knuckles: "My hand was in my pockets now, Brother Tarp's leg chain around my knuckles" (IM, 462).

IV

"The trouble has been," Charles Olson writes, "that a man stays so astonished he can triumph over his own incoherence, he settles for that, crows over it, and goes at a day again happy he at least makes a little sense."[27] Ellison says much the same thing toward the end of *Invisible Man* when he cautions that "the mind that has conceived a plan of living must never lose sight of the chaos against which that pattern was conceived" (IM, 567). This goes for both societies and individuals, he points out. Legba's limp, like Tarp's leg chain, is a reminder of dues paid, damage done, of the limbs that have been "pruned away." It is a reminder of the Pyrrhic features every triumph over chaos or incoherence turns out to possess. The specter of illusory victory and its corollary, the riddle of deceptive disability or enabling defeat, sit prominently among the mysteries to which it witnesses. "No defeat is made up entirely of defeat," Williams writes (P, 96).

In *Man Orchid*, the second piece that grew out of Williams's going to hear Johnson's band, the stutter plays a significant role. What better qualification of what can only be a partial victory over incoherence? What limping, staggering, and stumbling are to walking, stuttering and stammering are to speech. "*To stammer* and *to stumble*, original *stumelen*, are twin words," Theodore Thass-Thienemann points out. "The use of the one and the same phonemic pattern for denoting these two different meanings is found in other languages too. Stammering and stuttering are perceived as speech *im-pedi-ments*."[28] The stutter enters *Man Orchid* largely because of Bucklin Moon, the author of a novel called *The Darker Brother*. Moon was at the Stuyvesant Casino on the night of 23 November 1945, the second time Williams went to hear Johnson's band. He ended up joining Williams and his friends at their table, among whom was Fred Miller, editor of the thirties proletarian magazine *Blast* and one of the co-authors of *Man Orchid*. Because of his novel and his knowledge of black music, Moon was incorrectly taken by them to be black, though Miller asked Williams in a letter two days later: "Would you ever think that Bucklin Moon was a Negro, if you passed him – as a stranger – in the street? He looks whiter than a lot of whites."[29] Moon evidently spoke with a stutter whenever he became nervous and unsure of himself, which was the case that night at the Stuyvesant Casino. Miller goes on to offer this as a further peculiarity: "A stuttering or stammering Negro is a pretty rare bird indeed: your darker brother is articulate enough, when he isn't too frightened to talk." Like Legba's limp, Moon's stutter would come to symbolize a meeting of worlds, a problematic, insecure mix of black and white.

At the Stuyvesant Williams suggested that he and Miller publish an interracial literary magazine. Miller was enthusiastic at the time but soon lost interest. He suggested within a couple of weeks, however, that he and Williams collaborate on an improvisatory novel that was to be written as though they were musicians trading fours: "You write chap. I, send it to me, I do the 2d Chap., send mess back to you, you do 3 – and so on." Williams liked the idea and *Man Orchid* was launched. They spent the next year working on it, off and on, bringing in a third collaborator, Lydia Carlin, in March. The work was never completed, and what there is of it, forty pages, remained unpublished until 1973. It is going too far to call it a novel and outright ludicrous to call it, as Paul Mariani does, "Williams's black novel," but the piece is interesting for a number of reasons, not the least of them being its anticipation of the bop-inspired attempts at collaborative, improvisatory writing that became popular among the Beats a decade later.[30]

Wray Douglas, *Man Orchid*'s black–white protagonist, is based in part on Bucklin Moon and intended to embody America's yet-to-be-resolved identity. As Williams writes: "To resolve such a person would be to create a new world" (MO, 77). But other than his presumed black–white mix and his stutter not much of Moon went into the figure. Wray Douglas is clearly his creators' alter ego, the narrated "he" and the narrator's "I" in most cases the same. Want of resolution and the stubborn problematics of heterogeneity are what *Man Orchid* most effectively expresses, the latter symptomized by the solipsistic quality of the work and the former a would-be flight from the resolute self (false resolution) that the solipsism indulges even as it eschews. Two white writers sit down to create a black protagonist whose model is another white writer. The ironies and contradictions need not be belabored.

The stutter thus becomes the most appropriate, self-reflexive feature of an articulation that would appear to be blocked in advance. Williams's and Miller's prose in *Man Orchid* both stutters and refers to stuttering. Here, for example, is how Williams begins Chapter 1:

> Is it perchance a crime – a time, a chore, a bore, a job? He wasn't
> a musician – but he wished he had been born a musician instead of

a writer. Musicians do not stutter. But he ate music music wrinkled his belly – if you can wrinkle an inflated football. Anyhow it felt like that so that's what he wrote (without changing a word – that was his creed and always after midnight, you couldn't be earlier in the morning than that). All good writing is written in the morning.

Is *what* perchance a crime? (One) (or rather two) He ate and drank beer. That is, he ate, he also drank beer. A crime to be so full, so – so (the thing the philosophers hate) poly. So p-p-poly. Polypoid. Huh? (MO, 77)

Thinking, perhaps, of the use of singing in the treatment of stuttering, Williams identifies writing with the latter while looking longingly at music as the embodiment of a heterogeneous wholeness to which his writing will aspire, an unimpeded, unproblematic wholeness beyond its reach. Miller's contribution to *Man Orchid* is likewise touched by a sense of writing's inferiority to music. Early on, referring to Bessie Smith's singing, he asks: "What were the little words chasing each other like black bits of burnt leaves across the pages he held – [compared] to that vast voice?" (MO, 79). Two pages later he answers:

> More printed words like black bits of burnt leaves. They had the right keyhole, those guys, but the wrong key. The only words that could blast like Bunk's horn or smash like John Henry's hammer were the poet's, the maker's, personal, ripped out of his guts: And no stuttering allowed. (MO, 81)

Throughout *Man Orchid*, however, the writer's emulation of the musician causes rather than cures the stutter. Imitating the spontaneity of improvisatory music, Williams and Miller approach the typewriter as a musical keyboard on which they extemporize "without changing a word." Wrong "notes" are left as they are rather than erased, though the right ones do eventually get "played" in most cases. This results in a repetitiveness and a halting, staccato gesture reminiscent of a stutterer's effort to get out what he wants to say. Thus Williams: "American poetry was on its way to great distinction – when the blight of Eliot's popular verse fell pon – upon the gasping universities – who hadN8t hadn8T hadn't tasted Thames water for nearly a hundred years" (MO, 82). By disrupting the fluency and coherence available to them Williams and Miller attempt to get in touch with what that coherence excludes, "the chaos against which that pattern was conceived." This friendly relationship with incoherence, however, constitutes a gesture toward but not an attainment of the otherness to which it aspires, an otherness to which access can only be analogically gotten. *Man Orchid*, to make the obvious point, is a piece of writing, not a piece of music. Nor, as I have already noted, is the color line crossed. The stutter is a two-way witness that on one hand symbolizes a need to go beyond the confines of an exclusionary order, while on the other confessing to its at best only limited success at doing so. The impediments to the passage it seeks are acknowledged if not annulled, attested to by exactly the gesture that would overcome them if it could.

One measure of *Man Orchid*'s flawed embrace of otherness is the prominence in it of Williams's all too familiar feud with Eliot, a feud into which he pulls Bunk Johnson. Johnson's music is put forth as an example of an authentic American idiom, "the autochthonous strain" (MO, 85) whose dilution or displacement by "sweet music" paralleled and anticipated that of a genuine "American poetry [which] was on its way to great distinction" by *The Waste Land*:

> Eliot would not have been such a success if he hadn't hit a soft spot. They were scared and rushed in where he hit like water into the side of a ship. It was ready for it a long time. Isn't a weak spot always ready to give way? That was the secret of his success. Great man Eliot. They were aching for him, Aiken for him. He hit the jackpot with his popular shot.
>
> But long before that, twenty years earlier ol' Bunk Johnson was all washed up. Sweet music was coming in and jazz was through. But I mean THROUGH! And when I say through, I mean through. Go ahead, quit. See if I care. Take your band and go frig a kite. Go on back to the rice swamps. See if I care. Sell your ol'd horn. See if I care. Nobody wants that kind of music any more: this is a waste land for you, Buddy, this IS a waste land! I said Waste Land and when I sez Waste land I mean waste *land*.
>
> . . . Thus American poetry, which disappeared about that time you might say, followed the same course New Orleans music had taken when sweet music displaced it about in 1906 or so. (MO, 83–84)

Fraternity with Johnson is less the issue than sibling rivalry with Eliot, a literary quarrel in which Johnson has no voice but the one Williams gives him. What it says is simple: "Black music is on Williams's side." (The Barbadian poet Edward Kamau Brathwaite provides interesting counterpoint, picturing Eliot and black music as allies when he notes the influence of Eliot's recorded readings in the Caribbean: "In that dry deadpan delivery, the riddims of St. Louis . . . were stark and clear for those of us who at the same time were listening to the dislocations of Bird, Dizzy and Klook. And it is interesting that on the whole, the Establishment couldn't stand Eliot's voice – far less jazz!"[31])

The possibility that otherness was being appropriated rather than engaged was recognized by Miller, and for him it became an obstacle to going on. When he began to voice his misgivings Williams brought in Lydia Carlin, who not only added sexual otherness to the project but a new form of ethnic otherness as well, in that, though she herself was English, one of the two chapters she contributed was about a Polish couple, the Czajas. Her two chapters are much more conventional, much less improvisatory than Williams's and Miller's and tend to stand apart from rather than interact with theirs. Her taking part in the project did nothing to solve the problem, and as late as Chapter 7 Miller is asking:

> Now returning to this novel, Man Orchid. Why the orchid? –
> to begin with. There's the old, tiresome and at bottom snobbish
> literary assumption that the Negro in America is an exotic bloom.
> Negro equals jungle. Despite the fact that he has been here longer
> than the second, third, even ninth generation Eurp European –
> Negro equals jungle. Then why doesn't the ofay bank president of
> German descent equal Black Forest? The Rutherford doctor of
> Welsh descent equal the cromlechs? or Welsh rarebit? (MO, 111)

As bad if not worse is the fact that the choice of that particular orchid because of its phallic appearance plays upon a stereotypic black male sexuality. The distance from this to Norman Mailer's "Jazz is orgasm" is not very great, which is only one of a handful of ways in which *The White Negro* bears upon this predecessor text.

Miller, though he could agonize as in the passage just quoted, was no more free than Williams was of stereotypic equations. To him Johnson and his music represent a black essence that is unself-conscious and non-reflective: "Only the Bunks're satisfied to be Bunks, he told himself enviously. Their brain don't question their art. Nor their left hand their RIGHT. Their right to be Bunk, themself" (MO, 79). The vitiation of "black" non-reflective being by "white" intellectuality is largely the point of his evocation of Wray Douglas and the trumpeter Cholly Oldham. The latter he describes as having "too much brain for a musician." Oldham stutters when he plays and wants to be a painter:

> There was between Cholly and Bunk – what? a difference of thirty,
> thirty-five years in age, no more. But the difference otherwise!
> Hamlet son of Till Eulenspiegel. Showing you what the dry rot of
> intellectuality could do to the orchid in one generation. Progress (!
> Up from Slavery. That night-colored Hamlet, he wants to paint
> pictures now. (MO, 82)

Black is nonreflective, white cerebral. So entrenched are such polarizations as to make the notion of a black intellectual oxymoronic. In May, Miller wrote to Williams that it had been a mistake to model their protagonist on Bucklin Moon: "I don't know enough about him and his special type, the colored intellectual (although I've been acquainted with and've liked lots of ordinary Negro folk, laborers, musicians et al)" (MO, 73). Small wonder he questioned the idea of an interracial magazine by writing to Williams:

> Is there sufficient Negro writing talent – of the kind we wd. have no doubts about, AS talent, on hand to balance the white talent? I don't believe any more than you that publishing second-rate work with first-rate intentions would serve any cause but that of bad writing. (MO, 68)

To what extent was being looked upon as black – as, even worse, that "rare bird," a black intellectual – the cause of Moon's nervousness that night at the Stuyvesant? Could a sense of distance in Williams's and Miller's manner have caused him to stutter? Miller's wife recalls in a letter to Paul Mariani:

> Moon began with easy speech and there was talk at first of the interracial magazine but Moon soon took to stammering. To me Williams was always a warm congenial person, but he would become the coldly analytical surgeon at times and the effect it had on those around him at such a time was quite devastating. (MO, 67)

That "coldly analytical" scrutiny would seem to have been disconcerting, making Williams and Miller the agents of the disarray about which they would then go on to write – as good an example as any of "phantom objectivity," the social construction of Moon's "mulatto" self-consciousness.

What I find most interesting about *Man Orchid* is that it inadvertently underscores a feature that was then coming into greater prominence in black improvised music. With the advent of bebop, with which neither Williams, Miller, nor Carlin seem to have been much engaged, black musicians began to assume a more explicit sense of themselves as artists, conscious creators, thinkers. Dizzy Gillespie would don a beret and a goatee, as would, among others, Yusef Lateef, who would record an album called *Jazz for the Thinker*. Anthony Braxton's pipe, wire-rim glasses, cardigan sweater, and diagrammatic titles are among the present-day descendants of such gestures. The aural equivalent of this more explicit reflexivity would come at times to resemble a stutter, conveying senses of apprehension and self-conscious duress by way of dislocated phrasings in which virtuosity mimes its opposite. Thelonious Monk's mock-awkward hesitancies evoke an experience of impediment or impairment, as do Sonny Rollins's even more stutterlike teasings of a tune, a quality Paul Blackburn imitates in "Listening to Sonny Rollins at the Five Spot":

> There will be many other nights like
> me standing here with someone, some
> one
> someone
> some-one
> some
> some
> some
> some
> some
> some
> one
> there will be other songs
> a-nother fall, another – spring, but
> there will never be a-noth, noth
> anoth
> noth
> anoth-er
> noth-er
> noth-er
>   Other lips that I may kiss,
> but they won't thrill me like
>   thrill me like
>   like yours
> used to
>   dream a million dreams
> but how can they come
> when there
>   never be
> a-noth – [32]

Though Williams and Miller insist that Bunk Johnson doesn't stammer, the limp he inflicts on the melody is ancestral to the stutter of Monk, Rollins, and others.

As among the Kaluli, for whom music and poetry are "specifically marked for reflection," the black musician's stutter is an introspective gesture that arises from and reflects critically upon an experience of isolation or exclusion, the orphan's or the outsider's ordeal, the "rare bird's" ordeal. Like Tarp's leg chain, it symbolizes a refusal to forget damage done, a critique and a partial rejection of an available but biased coherence. Part of the genius of black music is the room it allows for a telling "inarticulacy," a feature consistent with its critique of a predatory coherence, a cannibalistic "plan of living," and the articulacy that upholds it. *Man Orchid*, where it comes closest to the spirit of black music, does so by way of a similar frustration with and questioning of given articulacies, permissible ways of making sense. In Chapter 6 Williams attempts to make racial distinctions meaningless, the result of which is part gibberish, part scat, part wisdom of the idiots ("the most foolishest thing you can say... has the most meaning"). His inability to make sense implicitly indicts a white-dominated social order and the discourse of racial difference by which it explains or makes sense of itself:

> Not that black is white. I do not pretend that. Nor white black. That there is not the least difference is apparent to the mind at a glance. Thus, to the mind, the eye is forever deceived. And philosophers imagine they can have opinions about art? God are they dumb, meaning stupid, meaning philosophers, meaning schools, meaning – learning. The limits of learning are the same as an egg to the yolk. The shell. Knowledge to a learned man is precisely the sane – that's good: sane for same – the same as the egg to the hen. No possibility of interchange. Reason, the shell.
>
> No matter how I try to rearrange the parts, to show them interchangeable, the result is always the same. White is white and black is the United States Senate. No mixing. Even if it was all black it would be the same: white. How could it be different? (MO, 100–101)

The very effort to talk down the difference underscores the tenacity of the racial polarization *Man Orchid*'s liberal mission seeks, to some degree, to overcome – a tenacity that is attested to, as we have seen, in other ways as well, not the least of them being the authors' preconceptions.

V

The play of sense and nonsense in Wilson Harris's *The Angel at the Gate* is more immediately one of sensation and non-sensation, a complex mingling of endowments and deprivations, anesthetic and synesthetic intuitions. One reads, for example, late in the novel:

> Mary recalled how deaf she had been to the voice of the blackbird that morning on her way to Angel Inn and yet it returned to her now in the depths of the mirror that stood beside her. Half-reflected voice, shaded sound, silent echo. Was this the source of musical composition? Did music issue from reflections that converted themselves into silent, echoing bodies in a mirror? Did the marriage of

reflection and *sound* arise from deaf appearance within silent muse
(or was it deaf muse in silent appearance) from which a stream of
unheard music rippled into consciousness?[33]

In dialogue with and relevant to such a passage is a discussion in Harris's
The Womb of Space that touches upon Legba as "numinous shadow."
Harris writes of "metaphoric imagery that intricately conveys music as
the shadow of vanished but visualised presences": "Shadow or shade is
alive with voices so real, yet strangely beyond material hearing, that they
are peculiarly *visualised* or 'seen' in the intricate passages of a poem.
Visualised presence acquires therefore a *shadow and a voice* that belongs to
the mind's ear and eye."[34] Music described in terms pertaining to sight
is consistent with inklings of synesthetic identity that run through *The
Angel at the Gate*. It is also part and parcel of Harris's long preoccupation,
from work to work, with an uncapturable, ineffable wholeness, a heterogeneous inclusiveness evoked in terms of non-availability ("silent
echo," "unheard music") and by polysemous fullness and fluency ("a
stream . . . rippled").

The Angel at the Gate's anesthetic-synesthetic evocations recapitulate,
in microcosm, the translation between media – aural and visual, music
and writing – it claims to be. The intermedia impulse owns up to as it
attempts to advance beyond the limits of a particular medium and is a
version of what Harris elsewhere calls "a confession of weakness."[35] The
novel acknowledges that its particular strength can only be partial and
seeks to "echo" if not enlist the also partial strength of another art form.
Wholeness admitted to be beyond reach, the best to be attained is a
concomitance of partial weaknesses, partial strengths, a conjunction of
partial endowments. This conjunction is facilitated by Legba, upon
whom *The Womb of Space* touches as a "numinous frailty" and a "transitional chord." In *Da Silva da Silva's Cultivated Wilderness*, an earlier
novel that likewise leans upon an extraliterary medium, the painter da
Silva's advertisement for a model is answered by one Legba Cuffey,
whose arrival infuses paint with sound: "The front door bell pealed it
seemed in the middle of his painting as he brooded on past and future.
The sound of a catch grown sharp as a child's cry he thought in a line
of stroked paint."[36] In this case painting, like music in *The Angel at the
Gate*, is an alternate artistic arm with which the novel extends or attempts
to extend its reach. "So the arts," Williams writes in *Man Orchid*, "take
part for each other" (MO, 85).

Music figures prominently at the end of Harris's first novel, *Palace of
the Peacock*, where Legba's limp, the incongruity between heaven and
earth, is marked by the refractive obliquity and bend of a passage from
one medium to another. The annunciation of paradise takes the form of

a music that issues through the lips of Carroll, the black namesake singer whose father is unknown but whose mother "knew and understood . . . [that his] name involved . . . the music of her undying sacrifice to make and save the world."[37] The narrator notes a discrepancy between the sound Carroll's lips appear to be making and the sound he hears: "Carroll was whistling. A solemn and beautiful cry – unlike a whistle I reflected – deeper and mature. Nevertheless his lips were framed to whistle and I could only explain the difference by assuming the sound from his lips was changed when it struck the window and issued into the world" (PP, 147). The deflection from apparent sound reveals not only the insufficiency of the visual image but that of any image, visual, acoustic, or otherwise. Heaven is wholeness, meaning that any image that takes up the task of evoking it can only fail. Legba's limp is the obliquity of a religious aspiration that admits its failure to measure up to heaven, the bend legs make in prayer. As in the *Paradiso*, where Dante laments the poem's inability to do heaven justice by calling it lame, the narrator's evocation of Carroll's music is marked by a hesitant, faltering gesture that whenever it asserts immediately qualifies itself. It mimes the music's crippling, self-correcting attempts to register as well as redeem defects. The music repeatedly breaks and mends itself – mends itself as a phantom limb mends an amputation:

> It was an organ cry almost and yet quite different I reflected again. It seemed to break and mend itself always – tremulous, forlorn, distant, triumphant, the echo of sound so pure and outlined in space it broke again into a mass of music. It was the cry of the peacock and yet I reflected far different. I stared at the whistling lips and wondered if the change was in me or in them. I had never witnessed and heard such sad and such glorious music. (PP, 147)

This is the ongoingness of an attempt that fails but is repeatedly undertaken to insist that what it fails to capture nonetheless exists. Legba's limp is the obliquity of a utopian aspiration, the bend legs make preparing to spring.

Inability to capture wholeness notwithstanding, *Palace of the Peacock* initiates Harris's divergence from the novel's realist-mimetic tradition. The accent that falls upon the insufficiency of the visual image is consistent with the novel's earlier suggestions of an anesthetic-synesthetic enablement that displaces the privileged eye[38]: "I dreamt I awoke with one dead seeing eye and one living closed eye" (PP, 13–14). And again: "I had been blinded by the sun, and saw inwardly in the haze of my blind eye a watching muse and phantom whose breath was on my lips" (PP, 16). That accent encapsulates Harris's quarrel with the cinematic pretense and the ocular conceit of the realist novel, a documentary stasis against which he poses an anesthetic-synesthetic obliquity and rush. This obliquity (seeing and/or hearing around corners, in Ellison's terms) is called "an angled intercourse with history" in *The Angel at the Gate* (AG, 113), the medium for which is the Angel Inn mirror, described at points as "spiritual" and "supernatural." Mary Stella is said to perceive the world "from a meaningfully distorted angle in the mirror" (AG, 113), a pointed subversion of the mirror's conventional association with mimesis. Angularity cuts with a relativizing edge: "How unreal, yet real, one was when one saw oneself with one's own eyes from angles in a mirror so curiously unfamiliar that one's eyes became a stranger's eyes. As at the hairdresser when she invites one to inspect the back of one's head" (AG, 21).

Late in the novel Mary Stella's "automatic codes" are said to have "propelled her pencil across the page of a mirror" (AG, 122) – clear enough indication that the novel sees itself in the Angel Inn mirror, that reflection and refraction are there the same. Angled perception is a particular way of writing – writing bent or inflected by music. *The Angel at the Gate* is said to be based on Mary Stella's automatic writings and on notes taken by her therapist Joseph Marsden during conversations with her, some of which were conducted while she was under hypnosis. In the note that introduces the novel mention is made of "the musical compositions by which Mary it seems was haunted from early childhood," as well as of "a series of underlying rhythms in the automatic narratives" (AG, 7). Like the boy who became a *muni* bird, Mary Stella, an orphan from the age of seven, resorts to music in the face of broken familial ties – those with her parents in the past and in the present her troubled marriage with Sebastian, for whom she's "the same woman broken into wife and sister" (AG, 13). Louis Armstrong's rendition of "Mack the Knife," the song her mother frequently sang during her early childhood, animates a host of recollections and associations:

> . . . the music returned once again coming this time from an old gramophone her mother possessed. It was "Mack the Knife" sung and played by Louis Armstrong. The absurdity and tall story lyric, oceanic city, were sustained by Armstong's height of trumpet and by his instrumental voice, hoarse and meditative in contrast to the trumpet he played, ecstatic cradle, ecstatic childhood, ecstatic coffin, ecstatic grieving surf or sea.
>
> . . . Stella was shivering. The fascination of the song for her mother was something that she grew up with. Mack was also the name that her father bore. Mack was her mother's god. And her mother's name? *Guess*, Stella whispered to Sebastian in the darkened studio. Jenny! It was a random hit, bull's eye. It struck home. Jenny heard. She was weeping. It came with the faintest whisper of the

sea, the faintest whisper of a flute, in the studio. Mack's women were the Sukey Tawdreys, the sweet Lucy Browns, of the world. Between the ages of four and seven Stella thought that the postman was her father. Until she realized that he was but the middleman between her real father and Jenny her mother. He brought the letters from foreign ports with foreign stamps over which Jenny wept. On her seventh birthday the last letter arrived. Her father was dead, his ship sunk. It was a lie. It drove her mother into an asylum where she contemplated Mack clinging for dear life to sarcophagus-globe even as she vanished into the arms of god, bride of god.

Stella was taken into care by a Social Welfare Body and placed in an orphanage in East Anglia. (AG, 44–45)

Mary Stella's automatic narratives, prompted by her thirst for connection and "her longing to change the world" (AG, 46), instigate patterns of asymmetric equation into which characters named Sukey Tawdrey, Mother Diver, Lucy Brown, and so forth enter. The song, it seems, populates a world, an alternate world. Her music-prompted hand and its inscription of far-flung relations obey intimations of unacknowledged wholeness against a backdrop of social and psychic division. "To be whole," we are told at the end, "was to endure . . . the traffic of many souls" (AG, 126).

The novel's concern with heterogeneous wholeness invokes Legba repeatedly – though, significantly, not by that name. As if to more greatly emphasize Legba's association with multiplicity, Harris merges him with his trickster counterpart among the Ashanti, the spider Anancy, tales of whose exploits are a prominent part of Caribbean folklore. An asymmetric equation that relates deficit leg to surplus legs, lack to multiplicity, brings "a metaphysic of curative doubt" (AG, 78) to bear upon appearances. Apparent deficiency and apparent endowment are two sides of an insufficient image. When Sebastian discovers Mary Stella's attempt at suicide "his legs multiplied" (AG, 14), but later "there was no visible bandage around his ankle but he seemed nevertheless as lame as Anancy" (AG, 33). Other such intimations occur: Marsden described as a cane on which "something, some invisible presence, did lean" (AG, 29), Sebastian asking of the jockey who exposed himself to Mary Stella, "Did he, for instance, possess a walking stick?" (AG, 50), and Jackson, Mary Stella's "authentic messenger" (AG, 125), falling from a ladder and breaking his leg. The most sustained appearance occurs when Mary Stella happens upon the black youth Anancy in Marsden's study. The "funny title" of a book has brought him there:

> . . . He turned his eyes to the desk. "The door was open and I saw the funny title of that book." He pointed to the desk.
> "Sir Thomas More's *Utopia*," said Mary, smiling against her

fear and finding her tongue at last. "I put it there myself this week."
His eyes were upon hers now. "I put it . . ." she began again, then
stopped. "I brought you here," she thought silently. "*Utopia was
the bait I used.*" The thought came of its own volition. It seemed
irrational, yet true. There was a ticking silence between them, a
deeper pull than she could gauge, a deeper call than she knew, that
had sounded long, long ago, even before the time when her father's
great-great-grandmother had been hooked by an Englishman to
bear him children of mixed blood. (AG, 26–27)

Mary Stella's pursuit of heterogeneous relations carries her out as well
as in. She discovers an eighteenth-century black ancestor on her father's
side. That discovery, along with her perusal, in Marsden's library, of
seventeenth- and eighteenth-century parish accounts of money spent to
expel children and pregnant women, several of them black, arouses her
desire for a utopian inclusiveness, the "longing to change the world"
that "baits" Anancy. The world's failure to comply with that desire leads
her to distance herself from it, to practice a kind of cosmic displacement.
Her schizophrenia involves an aspect of astral projection, as she cultivates the "capacity to burn elsewhere" (AG, 85) suggested by her middle
name: "Ah yes, said Stella, I am a mask Mary wears, a way of coping
with truth. We are each other's little deaths, little births. We cling to
sarcophagus-globe and to universal cradle" (AG, 44).

Displacement and relativizing distance account for the resonances and
agitations at work in the text, an animated incompleteness whose components tend toward as well as recede from one another, support as well
as destabilize one another. The pull between Mary Stella and Anancy is
said to arise from "a compulsion or infectious Cupid's arrow . . . related
to the target of unfinished being" (AG, 26). Some such pull, together
with its other side, aversion, advances the accent on relationality that
pervades the novel and has much to do with Harris's distinctive style.
The sought-after sense of dispersed identity makes for staggered equa-
tional upsets and elisions in which words, concepts, and images, like the
characters, are related through a mix of contrast and contagion. The
musicality of Harris's writing resides in its cadences, imaginal concaten-
ations, and poetic assurance, but also in something else. *The Angel at the
Gate* offers a musical conception of the world whose emphasis on animate
incompleteness, "unfinished being," recalls Zuckerkandl's analysis of
tonal motion:

> A series of tones is heard as motion not because the successive tones
> are of different pitches but because they have different dynamic
> qualities. The dynamic quality of a tone, we said, is a statement of
> its incompleteness, its will to completion. To hear a tone as dynamic

quality, as a direction, a pointing, means hearing at the same time beyond it, beyond it in the direction of its will, and going toward the expected next tone. Listening to music, then, we are not first *in* one tone, then in the next and so forth. We are, rather, always *between* the tones, *on the way* from tone to tone; our hearing does not remain with the tone, it reaches through it and beyond it. . . . pure betweenness, pure passing over. (SS, 136–137)

A mixed, middle ground that privileges betweenness would seem to be the realm in which Harris works. He alludes to himself as a "no-man's land writer" at one point (AG, 23) and later has Jackson say, "I must learn to paint or sculpt what lies stranded between earth and heaven" (AG, 124). An "attunement to a gulf or divide between sky and earth" (AG, 123) probes an estrangement and a stranded play in which limbs have to do with limbo, liminality, lift:

The women were dressed in white. They carried covered trays of food and other materials on their head. There was a statuesque deliberation to each movement they made, a hard-edged beauty akin to young Lucy's that seemed to bind their limbs into the soil even as it lifted them very subtly an inch or two into space.

That lift was so nebulous, so uncertain, it may not have occurred at all. Yet it was there; it gave a gentle wave or groundswell to the static root or the vertical dance of each processional body. (AG, 122)

What remains to be said is that to take that lift a bit further is to view the outsider's lot as cosmic, stellar. Social estrangement is gnostic estrangement and the step from Satchmo's "height of trumpet" to Sun Ra's "intergalactic music" is neither a long nor an illogical one. In this respect, the film *Brother from Another Planet* is worth – in what will serve as a closing note – mentioning briefly. That it shares with *The Angel at the Gate* a theme of cosmic dislocation is obvious enough. That the Brother's limp is the limp of a misfit – the shoes he finds and puts on don't suit his feet – is also easy to see. An intermedia thread is also present and bears on this discussion, especially the allusions to Dante (the Rasta guide named Virgil) and *Invisible Man* (the Brother's detachable eye), where it would seem the film were admitting a need to reach beyond its limits. What stronger suggestion of anesthetic-synesthetic displacement could one want than when the Brother places his eye in the drug dealer's hand? Or than the fact that the movie ends on a seen but unsounded musical note as the Brother gets aboard an "A" train?

14

On Edge

I came here with apprehensions about the title "A Symposium of the Whole."[1] This probably has to do with living in Santa Cruz, where so many "holistic" enterprises of one sort or another get heavily advertised in various newspapers and on the bulletin boards around town. The prospect of coming all the way here just to get more of that didn't seem all that inviting, so one of the things I immediately did was think about alternate titles. I found I was more drawn to the idea of an edge than to the idea of a whole. This morning, then, I was pleased to hear Nathaniel Tarn speak of Mr. Hyde "trying to get a word in edgewise,"[2] since one sense of what I would call "A Symposium of the Edge" is that there the otherwise excluded do exactly that – get a word in edgewise.

With the idea of an edge I mean to offer a possible correction to a too simple reading of Robert Duncan's phrase "symposium of the whole." In the same chapter of *The H.D. Book* in which the phrase is found Duncan writes: "Not only the experience of unity but the experience of separation is the mother of man."[3] To bring separation back into the picture is to observe that the edge is a cutting edge, the "mother of my cutting" Jay Wright refers to in *The Double Invention of Komo*. Edges figure prominently in Wright's book, an extended poem based largely on Bambara ritual motifs: knife's edge, axe's edge, and such assertions as "Each word is my knife's incision" and "What is true is the incision."[4] The old and new truth of the incision is that one is profoundly and inescapably cut off and cut into by differences. The edge is where differences intersect, where we witness and take part in a traffic of partialities, where half-truths or partial wisdoms converse, contend, interlock.

I would like to underscore this idea of an interface by returning to one of the papers given at the Ethnopoetics Symposium in 1975. The Martinican writer Édouard Glissant had some things to say that merit repeating. Toward the end of his talk, "Free and Forced Poetics," he remarks:

Finally, my exposé has sufficiently demonstrated that if certain communities, oppressed by the historical weight of dominant ideologies, long to convert their speech into a shout, rediscovering thereby the innocence of primitive ethnos, our task is rather to transform the shout we once uttered into a speech which continues it, thus discovering, albeit intellectually, the expression of a finally liberated poetics.[5]

Glissant is rightly, if I may say so, edgy – wary of "certain communities" whose comfortable hold on "speech" allows them the indulgence of prioritizing "shout." The danger of such a prioritization becoming a one-way choice against "speech" leads him to say, somewhat hopefully: "I believe that ethnopoetics can go both ways." I think it is imperative that it go both ways, an aspect of which would be that the very enterprise of ethnopoetics confront its First World specificity, its First World partiality, confront the fact that its valorization of the "shout," as Glissant makes clear, grows out of a particular history and is not necessarily universal, not, for example, terribly relevant to the historical imperatives facing the community to which Glissant belongs. One of the things he warns against is overlooking differences: "In opposition to a universalizing and reductive humanism, we must develop widely a theory of particular opacities."

One way to do this is to sharpen the edge along which the excluded have their say. In a sense, we have just done so in listening to Glissant, whose remarks on "speech" and "shout" can be heard as cuttingly or contrapuntally contending with, say, the endorsement of "shout (tongue)" at the expense of "discrimination (logos)" in Charles Olson's "Human Universe,"[6] a seminal essay in ethnopoetics' valorization of the oral. (While Olson makes "speech" synonymous with "shout," it needs to be noted, Glissant uses it to mean "discourse" or "discrimination.") Glissant is not alone or atypical. It is instructive to listen to others who, like him, come from communities we tend to think of as oral. Their remarks on the orality versus literacy question provide an antidote to the either/or, too easy infatuation with the oral that ethnopoetics might lapse into.

Amiri Baraka, for example, in his introduction to Arthur Pfister's book of poems, *Beer Cans, Bullets, Things & Pieces*, is careful not to dissociate black people from literacy, as is often done, even as he extols the oral. We hear from him too that whatever taint may be attached to literacy has more to do with the alien "weight of dominant ideologies" to which Glissant alludes than with anything intrinsic to writing:

We talk about the oral tradition of African People, sometimes positively, many times defensively (if we are not wised up), and it's always as a substitute for the written. What this is is foolfood, because we were the first writers, as well . . . Thor is the God of writing, its inventor, an African. It is headstretching to contemplate that the same God translated reduced to manhood and shot up to Greek demigodhood as Hermes . . . to the Romans' Mercury, shd end up with the Scandinavians as a God of War. Having made the strange conversion from Inventor of language and poetry and medicine (via residence as a Graeco-Roman pickpocket) to the wodan god of war.[7]

Similarly, in Ishmael Reed's novel, *Mumbo Jumbo*, we see a repudiation of simpleminded endorsements of orality. Jes Grew, an African-rooted music and dance "epidemic" spreading across the United States, is said to be *in search of its text*: "Jes Grew was an influence which sought its text . . . If it could not find its Text then it would be mistaken for entertainment."[8] Or we can go back to the nineteenth century, where Frederick Douglass reminds us that, however much literacy might be the prisonhouse that First World reappraisals of the oral say it is, there is a prisonhouse of orality too, a much more "literal" one in fact. In Douglass's *Narrative* we hear one of his former owners, a Mr. Auld, say to his wife while forbidding her to teach Douglass to read and write: "Learning would *spoil* the best nigger in the world. Now if you teach that nigger how to read, there would be no keeping him. It would forever unfit him to be a slave."[9]

We cannot even begin to talk about the whole without observing that ideologies of dominance cut us up and cut us off. I was gratified to hear an admission of this in Nathaniel Tarn's use of the Dr. Jekyll/Mr. Hyde dichotomy. W.E.B. DuBois in 1903 coined his famous term "double-consciousness" in discussing an inner division he took black people in this country to be peculiarly afflicted with. What I was gratified to hear in Tarn's talk was its validation of a notion I've held for some time, which is that everyone, black and white, has a case of "double-consciousness" and that the black "double-consciousness" DuBois was talking about is very much an effect of First World "double-consciousness," white duplicity, of the kind of split that divides Dr. Jekyll from Mr. Hyde. Somewhat related to this, I notice what might be called a double standard at work in Edmond Jabès's remarks. I find his comments fascinating, but I have to differ with his view that there is something particularly tragic about Aimé Césaire and Léopold Senghor writing in French rather than, presumably, an African language, a language "of their own." If language is the subversive, unsettling force, the engine of displacement he tells us it is, then none of us are at home in it and certainly no one owns it. If language generally, not just a particular language, is catastrophic rather than grounded, then Césaire and Senghor are no more uprooted in French than they would be in Wolof. If, as Maurice Blanchot says, "to stay within language is always to be already outside,"[10] then Césaire and Senghor are no more exiled in French than Jabès or Blanchot.

I once heard David Antin remark that there's no such thing as a native language, no such thing as a native speaker. What I took him to mean by this is that language undoes any ostensible ground and that we have to part with notions of a sedentary relationship to it, that we have to part with attitudes of "native" simplicity, "native" complacency, "native" gullibility, and so forth. One isn't born speaking one's so-called native language but has to be taught it. To remember this is to keep the weirdness of language in mind. This would seem to be the point of Blanchot's comment, as well as of much of what Jabès had to say. I would also relate the "antinativist" view to William Burroughs's idea of language as "a virus from outer space," as well as to Jack Spicer's notorious "Martians." To see language as extraterrestrial is to accent its groundlessness. But this too is old news. Most of the "natives" to whom a simplistic relationship to language has been attributed have long testified to language's essential strangeness, its prodigiousness and possible treachery. Among the Yoruba, the linguist and master of languages who serves as messenger between humans and Olorun, the Owner of the Sky, is none other than Eshu, the orisha of chance, accident, and unpredictability, the trickster. Among the Dogon, it is the fox, the "deluded and deceitful son of God," who acquires the gift of speech by violating his mother, the earth, and is thereafter called upon by diviners to reveal the designs of God (just as Eshu is said to be the best friend of Orunmila, the orisha of divination).

Jerome Rothenberg's maxim in *Technicians of the Sacred* bears repeating: "Primitive means complex."[11] If ethnopoetics is to amount to something other than the First World's assurance of its own complexity (a weary assurance of its own complexity) seeking out refreshing, picture-postcard simplicities elsewhere, it has to keep that in mind. We can learn from the words of Wilson Harris, whose work repudiates simplistic nativity, both with regard to language and with regard to place: "In this age and time, one's native land (and the other's) is always *crumbling*: crumbling within a capacity of vision which rediscovers the process to be not foul and destructive but actually the constructive secret of all creation wherever one happens to be."[12] And in the same "Manifesto of the Unborn State of Exile" he remarks of language:

> Language is one's medium of the vision of consciousness . . . language alone can express (in a way which goes beyond any physical

or vocal attempt) the sheer – the ultimate "silent" and "immaterial"
complexity of arousal . . . the original grain or grains of language
cannot be trapped or proven. It is the sheer mystery – the impossibility of trapping its own grain – on which poetry lives and thrives.
And this is the stuff of one's essential understanding of the reality
of the original Word, the Well of Silence. Which is concerned with
a genuine sourcelessness, a fluid logic of image. So that any genuine
act of possession by one's inner eye is a subtle dispersal of illusory
fact, dispossession of one's outer or physical eye.

A subtle dispersal of illusory fact. This I would give the name the Dogon
give their weaving block, the "creaking of the word." That language
creaks testifies to the rickety, telltale base on which its word-weave, its
"fabrication," rests.

15

Other

From Noun to Verb

Cultural diversity has lately become a much-discussed topic.[1] I would like to emphasize that cultural diversity *is* cultural, that it is a consequence of actions and assumptions that are socially – rather than naturally, genetically – instituted and reinforced. The inequities the recent attention to cultural diversity is meant to redress are in part the outcome of confounding the social with the genetic, so we need to make it clear that when we speak of otherness we are not positing static, intrinsic attributes or characteristics. We need instead to highlight the dynamics of agency and attribution by way of which otherness is brought about and maintained, the fact that other is something people do, more importantly a verb than an adjective or a noun. Thus, I would like to look at some instances of and ways of thinking about othering – primarily othering within artistic media, but also othering within the medium of society, touching upon relationships between the two. Artistic othering has to do with innovation, invention, and change, upon which cultural health and diversity depend and thrive. Social othering has to do with power, exclusion, and privilege, the centralizing of a norm against which otherness is measured, meted out, marginalized. My focus is the practice of the former by people subjected to the latter.

The title "Other: From Noun to Verb" is meant to recall Amiri Baraka's way of describing white appropriation of black music in Chapter 10 of *Blues People*. In that chapter he discusses the development of big-band jazz during the twenties and thirties by Fletcher Henderson, Duke Ellington, Jimmie Lunceford, and others and the imitation and commoditization of it by white musicians like Jimmy and Tommy Dorsey, Artie Shaw, Charlie Barnet, and Benny Goodman (who became known as the "King of Swing"). He calls the chapter "Swing – From Verb to Noun." Typical of the way he uses the verb/noun distinction is this remark: "But for most of America by the twenties, jazz (or *jass*, the noun, not the verb) meant the Original Dixieland Jazz Band (to the hip) and Paul Whiteman (to the square)."[2] Or this one:

> *Swing*, the verb, meant a simple reaction to the music (and as it developed in verb usage, a way of reacting to anything in life). As it was formalized, and the term and the music taken further out of context, *swing* became a noun that meant a commercial popular music in cheap imitation of a kind of Afro-American music. (BP, 212–213)

"From verb to noun" means the erasure of black inventiveness by white appropriation. As in Lukács's notion of phantom objectivity, the "noun," white commodification, obscures or "disappears" the "verb" it rips off, black agency, black authority, black invention. Benny Goodman bought arrangements from black musicians, later hired Fletcher Henderson as his band's chief arranger and later still brought black musicians Teddy Wilson, Lionel Hampton, Charlie Christian, and Cootie Williams into his band, but for the most part black musicians were locked out of the enormous commercial success made of the music they had invented. The most popular and best paid bands were white and the well-paying studio jobs created by the emergence of radio as the preeminent medium for disseminating the music were almost completely restricted to white musicians.

"From verb to noun" means, on the aesthetic level, a less dynamic, less improvisatory, less blues-inflected music and, on the political level, a containment of black mobility, a containment of the economic and social advances that might accrue to black artistic innovation. The domain of action and the ability to act suggested by *verb* is closed off by the hypostasis, paralysis, and arrest suggested by *noun*, the confinement to a predetermined status Baraka has in mind when he writes: "There should be no cause for wonder that the trumpets of Bix Beiderbecke and Louis Armstrong were so dissimilar. The white middle-class boy from Iowa was the product of a culture which could *place* Louis Armstrong, but could never understand him" (BP, 153–154). This confinement to a predetermined status (predetermined stasis), the keeping of black people "in their place," gives rise to the countering, contestatory tendencies I'll be talking about as a movement from noun to verb.

My topic, then, is not so much otherness as othering, black linguistic and musical practices that accent variance, variability – what reggae musicians call "versioning." As Dick Hebdige notes: " 'Versioning' is at the heart not only of reggae but of *all* Afro-American and Caribbean musics: jazz, blues, rap, r&b, reggae, calypso, soca, salsa, Afro-Cuban, and so on."[3] When Baraka writes of John Coltrane's recording of Billy

Eckstine's "I Want to Talk About You," he emphasizes what could be called Trane's versioning of the tune, what I would call his othering of it:

> ... instead of the simplistic though touching note-for-note replay of the ballad's line, on this performance each note is tested, given a slight tremolo or emotional vibrato (note to chord to scale reference) which makes it seem as if each one of the notes is given the possibility of "infinite" qualification. . . . proving that the ballad as it was written was only the beginning of the story.[4]

Trane himself spoke of his desire to work out a kind of writing that would allow for "more plasticity, more viability, more room for improvisation in the statement of the melody itself."[5] His lengthy solos caused some listeners to accuse him of practicing in public, which, in a sense that is not at all derogatory, he was – the sense in which Wilson Harris calls one of his recent novels *The Infinite Rehearsal*.

Such othering practices implicitly react against and reflect critically upon the different sort of othering to which their practitioners, denied agency in a society by which they are designated other, have been subjected. The black speaker, writer, or musician whose practice privileges variation subjects the fixed equations that underwrite that denial (including the idea of fixity itself) to an alternative. Zora Neale Hurston writes of the gossipers and storytellers in *Their Eyes Were Watching God*:

> It was the time for sitting on porches beside the road. It was the time to hear things and talk. These sitters had been tongueless, earless, eyeless conveniences all day long. Mules and other brutes had occupied their skins. But now, the sun and the bossman were gone, so the skins felt powerful and human. They became lords of sounds and lesser things. They passed nations through their mouths.[6]

Hurston is one of the pioneer expositor-practitioners of a resistant othering found in black vernacular culture. In her essay "Characteristics of Negro Expression,"[7] published in the thirties, she writes: "What we really mean by originality is the modification of ideas ... So if we look at it squarely, the Negro is a very original being. While he lives and moves in the midst of a white civilization, everything he touches is reinterpreted for his own use." Baraka's valorization of the verb recalls a similar move on her part thirty years earlier, her discussion of "verbal nouns" as one of black America's contributions to American English. She emphasizes action, dynamism, and kinetics, arguing that black vernacular culture does the same: "Frequently the Negro, even with detached words in his vocabulary – not evolved in him but transplanted on his tongue by contact – must add action to it to make it do. So we have 'chop-axe', 'sitting-chair', 'cook-pot' and the like because the speaker has in his mind the picture of the object in use. Action." She goes on to list a number of "verbal nouns," nouns and adjectives made to function as verbs, and "nouns from verbs," verbs masquerading as nouns. *Funeralize, I wouldn't friend with her,* and *uglying away* are among her examples of the former, *won't stand a broke* and *She won't take a listen* among those of the latter.

The privileging of the verb, the movement from noun to verb, linguistically accentuates action among a people whose ability to act is curtailed by racist constraints. I prefer to see a connection between such privileging and such curtailment than to attribute the former, as Hurston occasionally does, to black primitivity. Language is symbolic action, frequently compensatory action, addressing deprivations it helps its users overcome. The privileging of the verb, the black vernacular investment in what Hurston calls "action words," makes this all the more evident. The sort of analysis found in the passage from *Their Eyes Were Watching God* that I quoted is brought to bear on the movement from noun to verb in a piece that Hurston published in the early forties, "High John de Conquer."[8] The High John the Conqueror root that plays so prominent a role in African-American hoodoo is here personified and figured as a key to black endurance and resilience, "the secret of black song and laughter." In the title and throughout the piece Hurston elides the last syllable of *conqueror*, as is frequently done in black speech. In doing so, honoring the vernacular in more senses than one, she changes *conqueror* to *conquer*, noun to verb, practicing what she expounds upon in "Characteristics of Negro Expression."

Hurston presents High John de Conquer as an inner divergence from outward adversity, the ability of enslaved Africans to hold themselves apart from circumstance. "An inside thing to live by," she calls it. She relates High John de Conquer to a propensity for laughter, story, and song, to black liberties taken with music and language. He embodies mastery of sound and mastery through sound, "making a way out of no-way." High John de Conquer moves quickly, as mercurial as he is musical: "His footsteps sounded across the world in a low but musical rhythm as if the world he walked on was a singing-drum. . . . He had come from Africa. He came walking on the waves of sound." He embodies music, storytelling, and laughter as a kind of mobility, a fugitivity which others the slaves' condition:

He walked on the winds and moved fast. Maybe he was in Texas when the lash fell on a slave in Alabama, but before the blood was dry on the back he was there. A faint pulsing of a drum like a goat-

skin stretched over a heart, that came nearer and closer, then some-
body in the saddened quarters would feel like laughing and say,
"Now, High John de Conquer, Old Massa couldn't get the best
of *him*. . . ."

Hurston writes of the song High John de Conquer helps the slaves find:
"It had no words. It was a tune that you could bend and shape in most
any way you wanted to fit the words and feelings that you had."

The bending and shaping of sound, black liberties taken with music
and language, caused Lucy McKim Garrison, one of the editors of *Slave
Songs in the United States*, to write in 1862:

> It is difficult to express the entire character of these negro ballads
> by mere musical notes and signs. The odd turns made in the throat,
> and the curious rhythmic effect produced by single voices chiming
> in at different irregular intervals, seem almost as impossible to place
> on the score as the singing of birds or the tones of an Aeolian Harp.

Another of its editors, William Allen, likewise wrote:

> What makes it all the harder to unravel a thread of melody out of
> this strange network is that, like birds, they seem not infrequently
> to strike sounds that cannot be precisely represented by the gamut,
> and abound in "slides from one note to another and turns and
> cadences not in articulated notes." . . . There are also apparent ir-
> regularities in the time, which it is no less difficult to express
> accurately.

Henry G. Spaulding wrote in 1863: "The most striking of their barbaric
airs it would be impossible to write out." The compilers of the Hampton
spirituals, M.F. Armstrong and Helen W. Ludlow, wrote similarly a
decade later: "Tones are frequently employed which we have no musical
characters to represent. . . . The tones are variable in pitch, ranging
through an entire octave on different occasions, according to the inspiration of the singer."[9] One could go on and on with similar statements.
Western musical notation's inability to capture the tonal and rhythmic
mobility and variability such quotes remark upon confirms the fugitive
spirit Hurston identifies with High John de Conquer. "It is no accident
that High John de Conquer has evaded the ears of white people," she
writes, punning on while poking fun at the use of accidentals by Garrison,
Smith, and others to approximate the flatted or bent notes of the African
American's altered scale.

Fugitive spirit has had its impact upon African-American literary practices as well. As fact, as metaphor, and as formal disposition, the alliance
of writing with fugitivity recurs throughout the tradition. One recalls

that in 1829 George Moses Horton hoped to buy his freedom with money made from sales of his book of poems, *Hope of Liberty*. One thinks of the role played by literacy in Frederick Douglass's escape, of Harriet Jacobs's denunciations of the Fugitive Slave Law, of the importance of the slave narratives to the anti-slavery movement. W.E.B. DuBois referred to the essays in *The Souls of Black Folk* as "fugitive pieces," and the impact of fugitive spirit can also be found in the work of William Melvin Kelley (the mass exodus in *A Different Drummer*, the bending and reshaping of language in *Dunfords Travels Everywheres*), Ishmael Reed (Quickskill in *Flight to Canada*), Toni Morrison (the flying African in *Song of Solomon*, the "lickety-split, lickety-split" at the end of *Tar Baby*, Sethe's escape in *Beloved*), and others. Ed Roberson, for example, in a recent poem called "Taking the Print":

> See night in the sunlight's starry reflection
> off the water   darkening the water
> by contrast.
> > The dark hiding in the water
> also hid us in the river at night
> Our crossing guided by the internal sight
> on our darkness
> > the ancient graphis
> and -from this passage of abductions and escapes-
> this newer imprimatur of the river
> cut deep in the plate.
> > see in the river the ripples'
> picture on the surface of the wind the lifting of the
> image
> has taken at the deeper face
> > the starry freedom
> written in the milky rivery line that pours
> the brilliance of that image from a depth only black
> night fleeing across this land
> > has to voice.[10]

An especially good example of the movement from noun to verb's identification or alliance with fugitive spirit is Aimé Césaire's 1955 poem "The Verb 'Marroner'/ for René Depestre, Haitian Poet."[11] Written in response to Louis Aragon and the French Communist Party's call for a return to traditional poetic meters and forms, which Depestre supported in the journal *Présence Africaine*, the poem insists upon openness, experimentation, and formal innovation:

> Comrade Depestre
> It is undoubtedly a very serious problem

the relation between poetry and Revolution
the content determines the form

and what about keeping in mind as well the dialectical
backlash by which the form taking its revenge
chokes the poems like an accursed fig tree

The poem announces and enacts its poetics under the sign of a neologistic
verb. Césaire invokes the history of fugitive slaves in the Caribbean, the
runaway Africans known as maroons who escaped the plantations and
set up societies of their own. The French noun for this phenomenon,
marronage, is the basis for the word, the verb *marroner*, Césaire invents,
an act of invention exemplifying the independence for which the poem
calls. The coinage has no English equivalent. Clayton Eshleman and
Annette Smith translate it "escape like slaves":

Is it true this season that they're polishing up sonnets
for us to do so would remind me too much of the sugary
juice drooled over there by the distilleries on the mornes
when slow skinny oxen make their rounds to the whine
of mosquitoes

Bah! Depestre the poem is not a mill for
grinding sugar cane absolutely not
and if the rhymes are flies on ponds
                              without rhymes
                  for a whole season
away from ponds
                              under my persuasion
let's laugh drink and escape like slaves

Such invention in Césaire's work, such othering of and taking of
liberties with French, has been referred to as "a politics of neologism."[12]
A similar practice can be found in the work of another Caribbean poet,
Edward Kamau Brathwaite, who writes of Césaire: "His fabulous long
poem *Cahier d'un retour au pays natal (1939)* evolved the concept of *ne-
gritude*: that there is a black Caliban Maroon world with its own aesthetics
(*sycorax*), contributing to world and Third World consciousness."[13]
Brathwaite's recently completed second trilogy, comprised of *Mother
Poem, Sun Poem*, and *X/Self*, is characterized by a versioning of English he
calls "calibanization," a creolization "that comes into conflict with the cultural imperial authority of Prospero."[14] One of the remarkable features
of the work, one of the features any reader will come away from it unable to forget, is its linguistic texture – not only what is done with words
but what is done to them. Brathwaite makes greater use of West Indian

nation-language (the term he puts in place of "dialect" or "patois") than in the first trilogy, *The Arrivants*, but what he is doing goes further than that. In his use of "standard" English as well he takes his cue from the vernacular, subjecting words to bends, breaks, deformation, reformation – othering.

Brathwaite concludes the next-to-last poem in *The Arrivants* with the lines "So on this ground, / write; / . . . on this ground / on this broken ground."[15] Nation-language, what some would call broken English, partakes of that ground. "Calibanization" insists that in West Indian folk speech English is not so much broken as broken into, that a struggle for turf is taking place in language. "It was in language," Brathwaites has written, "that the slave was perhaps most successfully imprisoned by his master, and it was in his (mis-)use of it that he perhaps most effectively rebelled. Within the folk tradition, language was (and is) a creative act in itself."[16] This tradition of black liberties taken with language informs *Mother Poem, Sun Poem*, and *X/Self* with the weight of a history of anti-imperial struggle, a weight felt in so small a thing as the word. As in the anagrammatic "derangement" Shakespeare had recourse to in fashioning *Caliban* from *cannibal*, the puns, malapropisms, odd spellings, neologisms, and strained meanings Brathwaite resorts to speak of disturbances outside as well as inside the language, social disruptions the word is thus made to register.

Changing *militia* to *malitia* is one small instance of this.[17] As in this instance, most of Brathwaite's "calibanisms" underscore senses of malice and malaise, emphasize the hurt put on the land and on the people by slavery, the plantation system, colonialism, capitalism. The words partake of that hurt. It shows in the language both as referent and as a telling misuse inflicted on English, an abuse that brings that referent more emphatically to light. *The panes of his eyes* becomes *the pains of his eyes* (SP, 6), *the games we played* becomes *the games we paid* (SP, 19), *landscape* becomes *landscrape* (SP, 55), *the future* becomes *the few- / ture* (SP, 87). *Huts* becomes *hurts* and *hillsides* turns into *hillslides*:

> but those that drone their lorries all day up the sweating
>   hill to the factory of mister massa midas
> those mindless arch
>
> itects that cut the cane
> that built their own hurts on the hillslide (SP, 61)

Brathwaite avails himself of and takes part in a revolution of the word that has long been a part of Caribbean folk culture, a reinvention of English of the sort one hears in Rastafarian speech, where *oppressor* gets replaced by *downpressor*, *livicate* takes the place of *dedicate*, and so forth.

But a revolution of the word can only be a beginning. It initiates a break while remaining overshadowed by the conditions it seeks to go beyond. The shadow such conditions cast makes for a brooding humor that straddles laughter and lament, allows no easy, unequivocal foothold in either. Oppositional speech is only partly oppositional. Cramp and obstruction have to do with it as well. In Brathwaite's recent trilogy we not only get the sorts of pointed, transparent wordplay I just quoted, but something more opaque and more disconcerting, not resolved as to its tone or intent. Brathwaite revels in a sometimes dizzying mix of parody and pathos, embrace complicated by a sense of the bizarre and even bordering on embarrassment here and there. His otherings accent fugitive spirit and impediment as well, the predicaments that bring fugitive spirit into being:

> but is like we still start
> where we start/in out start/in out start/in
>
> out since menelek was a bwoy & why
> is dat & what is de bess weh to seh so/so it doan sounn
>   like
>
> brigg
> flatts nor hervokitz
>
> nor de pisan cantos nor de souf sea
> bible
>
> nor like ink. le & de anglo saxon
> chronicles
>
> &
>
> a fine
> a cyaan get nutten
>
> write
>
> a cyaan get nutten really
> rite
>
> while a stannin up here in me years & like i inside a me
>   shadow
>
> like de man still mekkin i walk up de slope dat e slide
> in black down de whole long curve a de arch

i

pell

ago (X, 85–86)

Brathwaite helps impeded speech find its voice, the way Thelonious Monk makes hesitation eloquent or the way a scat singer makes inarticulacy speak. This places his work in the New World African tradition of troubled eloquence, othered eloquence, I'm here sketching. Here, that is, trouble acts as a threshold. It registers a need for a new world and a new language to go along with it, discontent with the world and the ways of speaking we already have. A revolution of the word can only be a new beginning, "beating," as Brathwaite puts it, "its genesis genesis genesis genesis / out of the stammering world" (SP, 97).

My reference to Monk, as Hurston would say, is no accident. Indeed, had Hurston written "Characteristics of Negro Expression" later, she might have included "Rhythm-a-ning" and "Jackie-ing," two Monk titles, in her list of "verbal nouns." In her section on asymmetry ("Asymmetry," she begins it by saying, "is a definite feature of Negro art") she might have quoted Chico O'Farrell's comments on the advent of bebop in the forties:

> . . . it was such a new thing, because here we were confronted for the first time with phrases that wouldn't be symmetrical in the sense that string-music phrasing was symmetrical. Here we were confronted with phrases that were asymmetrical. They would come in into any part of the phrase they felt like, and, at first, also the changes threw us off completely because it was a complete new harmonic – not new, but we'll say unusual harmonic concept that was so alien to what we had been doing. To us it was such a drastic change that I think anything that came afterwards wasn't as drastic as that particular first step from swing to bop. I think in a sense bop probably marks the real cut-off point of the old concept of swinging. I don't mean in the sense of swinging – we were still swinging – but the concept of the square structure of the music as to this new particular way of playing and writing.[18]

The bebop revolution of which Monk was a part – Ellington called it "the Marcus Garvey Extension" – was a movement, in its reaction to swing, from noun to verb. It was a revolution that influenced a great number of writers, Brathwaite included, as can be seen, among other places, in his early poem "Blues."[19] Its impact upon Baraka's work and thought can be seen not only in Blues People but also in the poetics, the valorization of the verb, in the 1964 essay "Hunting Is Not Those Heads

On The Wall."[20] There he espouses a poetics of process, arguing: "The clearest description of now is the present participle . . . Worship the verb, if you need something." Halfway through the essay he mentions Charlie Parker, having earlier remarked: "I speak of the *verb process*, the doing, the coming into being, the at-the-time-of. Which is why we think there is particular value in live music, contemplating the artifact as it arrives, listening to it emerge." The sense he advances that "this verb value" is an impulse to "make words surprise themselves" recalls the popular description of jazz as "the sound of surprise."

The white appropriation and commercialization of swing resulted in a music that was less improvisatory, less dependent upon the inventiveness of soloists. The increased reliance upon arrangements in the Fletcher Henderson mold led to a sameness of sound and style among the various bands. In *Blues People* Baraka quotes Hsio Wen Shih's comments regarding the anthology album *The Great Swing Bands*, a record Shih refers to as "terrifying" due to the indistinguishability of one band from another. It was against this uniformity that bebop revolted. "Benny Goodman," Howard McGhee recalls, "had been named the 'King of Swing'. . . . We figured, what the hell, we can't do no more than what's been done with it, we gotta do somethin' else. We gotta do some other kind of thing" (SB, 314). ("Some other stuff," a common expression among black musicians, would become the title of an album by Grachan Moncur III in the sixties.) Mary Lou Williams said of her first meeting with Monk in the thirties: "He told me that he was sick of hearing musicians play the same thing the same way all the time."[21] Monk himself summed up his music by saying: "How to use notes differently. That's it. Just how to use notes differently."[22] It is no accident that bebop was typically performed by small combos rather than big bands as was the case with swing. It accentuated individual expression, bringing the soloist and improvisation once more to the fore.

Baraka emphasizes nonconformity in his treatment of bebop in *Blues People*, stressing what he terms its "willfully harsh, *anti-assimilationalist* sound" (BP, 181). The cultivation of a unique, individual style that black music encourages informs and inspires his attitudes toward writing. In his statement on poetics for the anthology *The New American Poetry 1945–1960* he echoes Louis Armstrong's ad-libbed line on a 1949 recording with Billie Holiday,[23] calling it "How You Sound??" The emphasis on self-expression in his work is also an emphasis on self-transformation, an othering or, as Brathwaite has it, an X-ing of the self, the self not as noun but as verb. Of the post-bop innovations of such musicians as Albert Ayler and Sun Ra, he writes: "New Black Music is this: Find the self, then kill it" (BM, 176). To kill the self is to show it to be fractured, unfixed. The dismantling of the unified subject found in recent critical theory is old news when it comes to black music. I've seen Bukka White break off singing to exhort himself: "Sing it, Bukka!" Charles Mingus's autobiography begins: "In other words, I am three."[24] A recent composition by Muhal Richard Abrams has the title "Conversation With the Three of Me." Craig Harris remarks of the polyrhythmicity of one of his pieces: "It's about cutting yourself in half."[25]

Our interest in cultural diversity – diversity within a culture as well as the diversity of cultures[26] – should lead us to be wary of hypostasis, the risk we take with nouns, a deadend that will impede change unless "other," "self," and such are "given the possibility of 'infinite' qualification." Wilson Harris, whose novel *The Infinite Rehearsal* I referred to earlier, has written of "qualitative and infinite variations of substance clothed in nouns," arguing that "nouns may reveal paradoxically when qualified, that their emphasis on reality and their inner meaning can change as they are inhabited by variable psychic projections."[27] In his new novel *The Four Banks of the River of Space* he speaks of "the instructive bite of music" on the way to suggesting that "breaking a formula of complacency" consists of "becoming a stranger to oneself."[28] As Monk's tune "Jackie-ing" tells us, even a so-called proper noun is a verb in disguise – present-participial, provisional, subject to change. John Gilmore, tenor saxophonist with Sun Ra's band for some thirty years, tells a story about the time he spent with Art Blakey's Jazz Messengers in 1965. After about a month, he says, the music was at so inventive a level that one night in Los Angeles, following one of his solos, trumpeter Lee Morgan looked over at him and asked: "Is that you, Gilmore?" Morgan then took a solo that caused Gilmore to ask the same thing of him: "Lee, is that you?"[29]

II

The "nounization" of swing furthered and partook in a commoditization of music that, in the West, as Jacques Attali points out, had been developing since the 1700s. "Until the eighteenth century," he writes in *Noise: The Political Economy of Music*, "music was of the order of the 'active'; it then entered the order of the 'exchanged.'"[30] The process was completed in the twentieth century, he argues, with the birth of the recording industry and its exploitation of black musicians: "Music did not really become a commodity until a broad market for popular music was created. Such a market did not exist when Edison invented the phonograph; it was produced by the colonization of black music by the American industrial apparatus" (N, 103). The transition from "active" to "exchanged," verb to noun, reflects the channeling of power through music it is the point of the book to insist upon:

Listening to music is . . . realizing that its appropriation and control is a reflection of power, that it is essentially political. . . . With music is born power and its opposite: subversion. . . . Music, the quintessential mass activity, like the crowd, is simultaneously a threat and a necessary source of legitimacy; trying to channel it is a risk that every system of power must run. . . . Thus music localizes and specifies power, because it marks and regiments the rare noises that cultures, in their normalization of behavior, see fit to authorize. (N, 6, 14, 19–20)

Attali is at all points alive to the shamanic roots of music, its magico-prophetic role, no matter how obscured those roots and that role tend to be by the legal, technological, and social developments he goes to great lengths to analyze and describe.

The idea of music as a conduit of power, a channeler of violence, a regulator of society, is particularly visible – unobscured – among the Carib-speaking Kalapalo of the Upper Xingu Basin in Brazil. Ellen B. Basso, in her study *A Musical View of the Universe: Kalapalo Myth and Ritual Performances*, deals with their ideas regarding sound and what she terms "orders of animacy," a hierarchic taxonomy at the top of which the Kalapalo place entities known as "powerful beings." These beings are nonhuman, though they sometimes appear in human form, and, Basso points out, "they are preeminently and essentially musical":

Powerful beings are different from concrete historical figures because they and their acts are "always" and everywhere. . . . This multiplicity of essence or "hyperanimacy" is coupled on the one hand with a multiplicity of feeling and consequent unpredictability and on the other with a monstrous intensity of some feeling or trait; hence powerful beings are dangerous beings. . . . Their hyperanimacy and multiplicity of essence are perhaps what is deeply metaphorized by their association with musical invention.[31]

Music represents the highest degree or level of animacy, hyperanimacy, and in their musical performances the Kalapalo model themselves upon their images of powerful beings, aspiring to the condition of powerful beings. They seek both to endow themselves with and to domesticate hyperanimate power. Basso writes:

. . . music (or more exactly, musical performance) is identified by the Kalapalo as having controlling force over aggressive, transformative, and wandering power; it is also a manifestation of that power. The ability of music to control and channel aggression, to limit hyperanimacy in ways that are helpful to people, has further consequences for understanding its importance within ritual contexts. This is because in such contexts of use, political life – the relations of control that some people effect over others – achieves its most concrete and elaborate expression. (MV, 246)

I would like to highlight two features of Kalapalo thought and practice concerning music, and bring them to bear, by way of analogy, upon the minstrel show, a form of theatrical performance unique to the United States that emerged during the 1820s and reached its apex between 1850 and 1870. An appropriation of the slave's music and dance by white men who blackened their faces with burnt cork, going on stage to sing "Negro songs," perform dances derived from those of the slaves, and tell jokes based on plantation life, the minstrel show is an early instance of the cannibalization of black music to which we saw Attali refer. "Minstrelsy," Robert C. Toll observes in *Blacking Up: The Minstrel Show in Nineteenth-Century America*, "was the first example of the way American popular culture would exploit and manipulate Afro-Americans and their culture to please and benefit white Americans."[32] The first of the two aspects of Kalapalo thought and practice I would like to highlight is the fact that powerful beings are associated with darkness and with the color black, that for ritual performances the Kalapalo shaman darkens himself with pot black as a way of becoming, Basso explains, "less visibly human and appearing more like a powerful being" (MV, 248). Blacking up, the white minstrel practice of donning blackface makeup, amounts to a pseudo-shamanic performance in which the power of black musicality is complimented yet simultaneously channeled, caricatured, and contained. As is not the case for the Kalapalo shaman, for the white minstrel "less visibly human" means less than human, even as the appeal and the power of the music are being exploited.

Minstrelsy reveals the ambivalent, duplicitous relationship of nineteenth-century white Americans not only to black people but to music and language as well. The second aspect of Kalapalo thought and practice I would like to highlight relates to this, having to do with the distinctions the Kalapalo make among calls, speech, and music, and among degrees of animacy. Human beings share with entities of lesser animacy the ability to emit calls and with entities of greater animacy, powerful beings, the ability to speak and to make music, but it is speech that is regarded as quintessentially human. Speech is the form of sound by which humans are characterized and symbolized in the taxonomic order, music the form with which powerful beings are identified. Interestingly, calls as well as music are considered more truthful, more trustworthy than speech:

> . . . human beings can express truthful and empirically motivated feelings best through *itsu* [calls]. Pain of varying degrees of intensity, deep sadness, shame, joy, sexual passion, frustration with

oneself, indeed, the entire range of human emotion is expressed most succinctly (and by implication as truthful feeling) this way.

Human beings are distinguished from other *ago* [living things], however, by their ability to speak, and it is through language that they are most commonly symbolized and distinguished from other categories of entities. . . . But language allows people to do something very different from animals. Human beings were created by a trickster, whose name "Taugi" means "speaks deceptively about himself". . . . Hence human beings are in essence deceitful beings because of their ability to speak. Therefore, people are capable not only of truthfully expressing their feelings, but – and this is the unmarked understanding of human speech for the Kalapalo – of creating an illusory screen of words that conceals their true thoughts. (MV, 67–68)

Music, the Kalapalo believe, is more to be trusted than speech because, rather than masking the mental, powerful beings "in J.L. Austin's sense . . . are performative beings, capable of reaching the limits of awareness of meaning by constructing action through a process that is simultaneously mental and physical" (MV, 71).

Calls and music both put sound in the service of sentience. In this they differ from speech, which valorizes the sentence, the humanly constructed realm of meaning, grammaticality, predication. The minstrel show, in its recourse to music (the slave's music, moreover, in which calls, cries, and hollers played a prominent part) and in its "translation" of that music into songs of sentiment (Stephen Foster's "Old Folks at Home," "Massa's in de Cold, Cold Ground," and so forth), critiqued even as it exemplified the deceptiveness of language. The implicit critique, the recourse to music and to sentimentality, to songs that advertised themselves as innocent of ambiguity, insincerity, or circumlocution, was accompanied by an explicit critique. This took the form of the stump speech and its malapropisms, the heavy reliance upon wordplay and puns in minstrel humor and such routines as the following, called "Modern Language":

Bones: How things have changed of late. A man can't depend on anything. A man must discount his expectations by at least 80 per cent.

Midman: In other words, "never count your chickens before they are hatched."

Bones: That sort of language is not up to the four hundred. You should say that this way: Never enumerate your feathered progeny before the process of incubation has been thoroughly realized.

Midman: That does take the rag off the bush.
Bones: Wrong again. You should not say that. You should say:
That removes the dilapidated linen from off the shrubbery.[33]

While the stump speech poked fun at black people's alleged insecure hold on language, such humor as this poked fun at language itself, at language's – especially elevated language's – insecure hold on the world. Minstrelsy, under cover of blackface, was able to vent apprehensions regarding the tenuousness of language, even as it ridiculed its target of choice for a supposed lack of linguistic competence. In regard to language as in other matters, the minstrel show allowed its audience to have it both ways.

One of the reasons for minstrelsy's popularity was what Alexander Saxton terms "the flexibility of standards which flourished behind the fake facade of blackface presentation."[34] That facade made it permissible to refer to such topics as homosexuality and masturbation, which were taboo on the legitimate stage, in the press, and elsewhere. Sentimental songs and female impersonation, as did the blackface facade, allowed performers and audience alike access to a world of emotion that was otherwise held to be off-limits. Minstrelsy's wide appeal had largely to do with the illusion of escape from conventional strictures it afforded, the degree to which it spoke to a white, predominantly male imaginary. Minstrel star George Thatcher's description of his feelings after seeing his first minstrel show as a boy alerts us to the deep psychic forces at work (and also, incidentally, sheds light on the title of John Berryman's *Dream Songs*, which, dedicated to Thomas D. Rice, the "father" of black-face minstrelsy, makes use of the minstrel figure Bones): "I found myself dreaming of minstrels; I would awake with an imaginary tambourine in my hand, and rub my face with my hands to see if I was blacked up. . . . The dream of my life was to see or speak to a performer" (BU, 33).

The influence of blackface minstrelsy extended well into the present century, having an impact upon vaudeville, musical comedy, radio, movies, television, and other forms of popular culture. It tells us a great deal regarding the obstacles in the way of a genuine multiculturality or cross-culturality, a genuine, non-exploitative cultural exchange. Toll recounts that in 1877 Bret Harte and Mark Twain wrote a minstrel play based on a poem of Harte's about the "heathen chinee." On opening night Twain explained to the audience: "The Chinaman is getting to be a pretty frequent figure in the United States and is going to be a great political problem and we thought it well for you to see him on the stage before you had to deal with the problem." Toll goes on to remark that Twain's is a clear and accurate statement of one of minstrelsy's functions: "Although on the surface they just sang songs and told jokes about peculiar people, minstrels actually provided their audiences with one of the only

bases that many of them had for understanding America's increasing
ethnic diversity" (BU, 169). This base, however, was an impediment
rather than an aid to cultural diversity, a strategy of containment through
caricature designed to consolidate white privilege and power. The minstrel made use of music to channel power in the service of "orders of
animacy" in which whites came out on top, to uphold unequally dis-
tributed orders of agency in which violence, albeit under control, was
never out of the picture. Saxton remarks of a minstrel song: "This 'comic-
banjo' piece, as it was described, appeared in a songster published in
New York in 1863. Geographically and emotionally, it was only a block
or two from a song such as this to the maiming and lynching of blacks
on the sidewalks of New York during the draft riots of the same year"
(23).

The subject of cultural diversity and the goal of a healthy cross-
culturality are haunted by the specter of such appropriation as the minstrel
legacy represents. We should not be surprised that not only pop-cultural
but also high-cultural and avant-garde venues number among its haunts.
I'm thinking, for example, of Gertrude Stein's early piece "Melanctha,"
described by her in "Composition as Explanation" as "a negro story."
Katherine Mansfield, reviewing the book in which "Melanctha" appears,
Three Lives, heard sentences overwhelmed by sound and sentience, much
to her alarm. Moreover, she heard it as a minstrel band, a channeling of
black musicality into prose:

> . . . let the reader go warily, warily with *Melanctha*. We confess we
> read a good page or two before we realised what was happening.
> Then the dreadful fact dawned. We discovered ourselves reading
> in *syncopated time*. Gradually we heard in the distance and then
> coming uncomfortably near, the sound of banjos, drums, bones,
> cymbals and voices. The page began to rock. To our horror we
> found ourselves silently singing "Was it true what Melanctha said
> that night to him" etc. Those who have heard the Syncopated
> Orchestra sing "It's me – it's me – it's me" or "I got a robe" will
> understand what we mean. *Melanctha* is negro music with all its
> maddening monotony done into prose; it is writing in real ragtime.
> Heaven forbid Miss Stein should become a fashion.[35]

The analogue to what Mansfield misapprehends as black-musical mo-
notony, Stein's notorious use of repetition advances a critique of language
that is not unrelated to the one we see in the minstrel show. Under cover
of blackness, she issues an avant-garde caveat regarding the trustwor-
thiness of the linguistic sign and of the discursive, ratiocinative order it
promotes. The search for and the nature of "understanding" are pointedly

at issue in the story, especially in the relationship between impulsive, sensation-seeking Melanctha and reflective, respectability-minded Jeff:

> "Yes I certainly do understand you when you talk so Dr. Campbell. I certainly do understand now what you mean by what you was always saying to me. I certainly do understand Dr. Campbell that you mean you don't believe it's right to love anybody." "Why sure no, yes I do Miss Melanctha, I certainly do believe strong in loving, and in being good to everybody, and trying to understand what they all need, to help them." "Oh I know all about that way of doing Dr. Campbell, but that certainly ain't the kind of love I mean when I am talking. I mean real, strong, hot love Dr. Campbell, that makes you do anything for somebody that loves you." "I don't know much about that kind of love yet Miss Melanctha. You see it's this way with me always Miss Melanctha. I am always so busy with my thinking about my work I am doing and so I don't have time for just fooling, and then too, you see Miss Melanctha, I really certainly don't ever like to get excited, and that kind of loving hard does seem always to mean just getting all the time excited. That certainly is what I always think from what I see of them that have it bad Miss Melanctha, and that certainly would never suit a man like me. . . . "[36]

On a typical page of dialogue between the two, the word *certainly* occurs as often as twenty times. Such repetition undermines the word, underscoring the uncertainty in which the two of them are immersed. Words are treated as though, rather than sticking, as Jack Spicer put it, to the real, they were continually slipping from it. Repetition compulsively moves to make up for that slippage, accenting all the more the words' insecure grip on the world. Not unlike the Kalapalo, Jeff at one point complains that "the ordinary kind of holler" would offer "much more game," much more forthright expression (TL, 127). The story strongly suggests that the order of what the Kalapalo term *itsu is* where "understanding" most unproblematically resides:

> And now the pain came hard and harder in Jeff Campbell, he groaned, and it hurt him so, he could not bear it. And the tears came, and his heart beat, and he was hot and worn and bitter in him.
> Now Jeff knew very well what it was to love Melanctha. Now Jeff Campbell knew he was really understanding. (TL, 145)

"Melanctha" recalls minstrelsy in that Stein uses one form of marginality, blackness, to mask another, to mask two others in fact – the avant-garde linguistic experimentation that we just noted (experimental writing being relegated to the fringes by middlebrow, if not outright philistine American predilections) and, albeit much less evident, lesbianism. Janice Doane and Carolyn Copeland argue that "Melanctha," as the latter puts it, "is not really a story about the ethnic reality of Negroes,"[37] that the story reworks material from the earlier novel *Q.E.D.* "Melanctha" is *Q.E.D.* done in blackface. Doane writes that "the lesbian affair of *Q.E.D.* is converted into the heterosexual affair of the 'Melanctha' story."[38] Copeland says the same at greater length:

> It will be recalled that *Q.E.D.*, written in 1903, concerned three homosexual women involved in a triangle. When one considers the trouble Theodore Dreiser had with *Sister Carrie* during that same period, it is not surprising that Gertrude Stein dropped the homosexual elements from her story before using the material again. Some very important elements of *Q.E.D.*, however, would have become problematic in a simple shift from homosexual to heterosexual in the story, and these elements must be discussed briefly.
>
> In *Q.E.D.* Adele and Helen together undergo a full and complete series of sexual experiences, and obviously they are not married when they experience them. It is important to Adele's full realization of how completely "out of rhythm" she and Helen are that they not be married. Adele must be able to walk away from the experience with no ties such as marriage to complicate it. At the turn of this century in America the only background against which a writer could portray premarital sexual relationships without having an outraged white, middle-class public to contend with was one dealing with Negroes. It was part of the white man's view of the black man that they were sexually promiscuous. If Gertrude Stein wished to drop the homosexual elements and make them heterosexual, her choice of Negroes instead of whites allowed her to retain as much as possible of the important extramarital elements involved. And this is exactly what she did. (24–25)

Orders of marginality contend with one another here. It is instructive that blackness is the noun-mask under whose camouflage two other forms of marginality gain an otherwise blocked order of animacy or agency, an otherwise unavailable "verb-ness." We are again at the sacrificial roots of the social order, the ritual murder of which music, Attali argues, is the simulacrum. Under cover of scapegoat blackness, the otherwise marginal cozies up to the center.[39]

I say this not to encourage turf wars among marginalized groups and/or individuals, but to raise a question. Wilson Harris writes of marginality in a way that is as promising as it is challenging. "Extremity or marginality, in my view," he writes, "lifts the medium or diverse experience to a new angle of possibility. . . . It involves us in a curiously tilted field in which spatial pre-possessions and our pre-possessions are dislodged . . . marginality is a raised contour or frontier of habit in the topography of the heart and mind."[40] I think of this tilt[41] as arising to contend with another form of tilt – that of unevenly allotted orders of agency, the unfair playing field, as it's commonly put. I think of the tilt of Edgar Pool's tenor saxophone in John Clellon Holmes's novel *The Horn*:

> Edgar Pool blew methodically, eyes beady and open, and he held his tenor saxophone almost horizontally extended from his mouth. This unusual posture gave it the look of some metallic albatross caught insecurely in his two hands, struggling to resume flight. In those early days he never brought it down to earth, but followed after its isolated passage over all manner of American cities, snaring it nightly, fastening his drooping, stony lips to its cruel beak, and tapping the song.[42]

The idiosyncratic tilt of "isolated originality," modeled on Lester Young:

> It was only one of many bands he worked those years, the tireless jumping colored bands that flourished like a backwash after the initial wave of swing. But already he was blowing strange long lines, rising out of the section, indrawn and resolute, to stand before the circling dancers, tilt the big horn roofward from his body, and play his weightless, sharply veering phrases over the chunking of unsubtle drums. In those days, no one heard. (89)

I also, however, think of another tilt we see in the novel, that of a whisky bottle "tilted into the coffee as he [Pool] spiked it generously" (194) during the last night of an alcoholic binge, the last night of his life. The tilt of entropy, exhaustion, disillusionment. Hence, my question: Which tilt will it be? In order for the latter not to prevail, the discourse on cultural diversity will have to acknowledge both.

By this I mean that we need more than content analyses based on assumptions of representationality. The dislocating tilt of artistic othering, especially as practiced by African-American artists, deserves a great deal more attention than it has been given. While the regressive racial views of white writers like Stein and Ezra Pound tend to be regarded (if they're regarded at all) as secondary to their artistic innovations, black writers tend to be read racially, primarily at the content level, the noun level, as responding to racism, representing "the black experience." That black writers have been experimentally and innovatively engaged with the medium, addressing issues of form as well as issues of content, tends to be ignored. The ability to influence the course of the medium, to *move* the medium, entails an order of animacy granted only to whites when it comes to writing. The situation with regard to music is a bit better, black musicians having been acknowledged to be innovators, even though their white imitators enjoy commercial success and critical acclaim greatly disproportionate to their musical contributions. The non-recognition of black artistic othering is symptomatic of the social othering to which black people are subjected, particularly in light of the celebration accorded artistic othering practiced by whites. This is a disparity the discussion of cultural diversity should be addressing.

Perhaps we can increase not only the quantity but also the quality of attention given to African-American art and cultural practices. Perhaps we can make it possible for the music of Henry Threadgill or David S. Ware to be as widely known as that of Wynton Marsalis, Ed Roberson's *Lucid Interval as Integral Music* or Will Alexander's *The Black Speech of the Angel* to win the sort of acclaim accorded Rita Dove's *Thomas and Beulah*, Amiri Baraka to be as well known for *The Dead Lecturer* as for *Dutchman*. If we are to do so, we must, à la Césaire, confront the neo-traditionalism that has taken hold of late with a countertradition of marronage, divergence, flight, fugitive tilt. Henry Dumas put it well in "Black Trumpeter": "the wing praises the root by taking to the limbs."[43]

Notes

CHAPTER ONE

1 LeRoi Jones, *Home: Social Essays* (New York: Morrow, 1966), p. 164. Hereafter referred to as H.

2 Cornel West, "Minority Discourse and the Pitfalls of Canon Formation," *The Yale Journal of Criticism*, I, 1 (Fall 1987), 198–199.

3 Charles Olson, *Muthologos: The Collected Lectures and Interviews*, Volume II, ed. George F. Butterick (Bolinas: Four Seasons Foundation, 1979), p. 71. Hereafter referred to as M.

4 *The New American Poetry: 1945–1960*, ed. Donald M. Allen (New York: Grove Press, 1960), p. xii.

5 Robert Duncan, "Rites of Participation," in *A Caterpillar Anthology*, ed. Clayton Eshleman (Garden City: Doubleday, 1971), pp. 24, 39.

6 Robert Duncan, *Bending the Bow* (New York: New Directions, 1968), p. ix. Hereafter referred to as BB.

7 Robert Duncan, *Roots and Branches* (New York: Scribner's, 1964), p. 176. Hereafter referred to as RB.

8 Wilson Harris, "Interview," *Kunapipi*, VIII, 2 (1986), 30–31.

9 Edouard Glissant, *Caribbean Discourse: Selected Essays*, trans. J. Michael Dash (Charlottesville: University Press of Virginia, 1989), pp. 147–148. Hereafter referred to as CD.

10 Wilson Harris, *The Womb of Space: The Cross-Cultural Imagination* (Westport and London: Greenwood Press, 1983), p. xx.

11 Davies and Crèvecoeur quoted in Eileen Southern, *The Music of Black Americans: A History*, 2nd Edition (New York: Norton, 1983), p. 59.

12 M.L. Rosenthal, *The New Poets: American and British Poetry since World War II* (New York: Oxford University Press, 1967), pp. 189–192.

13 Amiri Baraka, *The Autobiography of LeRoi Jones* (New York: Freundlich Books, 1984), pp. 156–157. Hereafter referred to as ALJ.

14 Werner Sollors, *Beyond Ethnicity: Consent and Descent in American Culture* (New York: Oxford University Press, 1986), pp. 237–258.

15 Robert Creeley, "Notes Apropos 'Free Verse,' " in *Naked Poetry: Recent*

American Poetry in Open Forms, ed. Stephen Berg and Robert Mezey (Indianapolis and New York: Bobbs-Merrill, 1969), pp. 186–187.

16   Gordon Brotherston, *Image of the New World: The American Continent Portrayed in Native Texts* (London: Thames and Hudson, 1979), p. 263.

17   William Faulkner, *As I Lay Dying* (New York: Vintage Editions, 1987), p. 160.

18   Jack Spicer, *One Night Stand and Other Poems* (San Francisco: Grey Fox Press, 1980), p. 80.

19   Ralph Ellison, *Invisible Man* (New York: Random House, 1952), p. 438.

20   Charles Johnson, *Being and Race: Black Writing Since 1970* (Bloomington and Indianapolis: Indiana University Press, 1988), pp. 57–58.

21   Robert Duncan, *The Opening of the Field* (New York: Grove Press, 1960), pp. 36 and 71. Hereafter referred to as OF.

22   Alan Bass, " 'Literature'/Literature," in *Velocities of Change: Critical Essays from MLN*, ed. Richard Macksey (Baltimore and London: Johns Hopkins University Press, 1974), p. 348.

23   Charles Olson, *The Maximus Poems* (Berkeley, Los Angeles and London: University of California Press, 1983), p. 335.

24   David Lowenthal, *West Indian Societies* (New York: Oxford University Press, 1972), p. 39.

25   Edward Brathwaite *The Development of Creole Society in Jamaica 1770–1820* (Oxford: Oxford University Press, 1971), p. 310. Hereafter referred to as DCS.

26   Liner notes, *Rights of Passage*, Record One (Argo PLP 1110).

27   Ibid.

28   Wilson Harris, *Tradition, the Writer and Society* (London and Port of Spain: New Beacon, 1967), p. 29.

29   Wilson Harris, *Ascent to Omai* (London: Faber and Faber, 1970), p. 96.

30   Robert Creeley, *The Gold Diggers and Other Stories* (New York: Scribner's, 1965), p. 7.

31   Dudley Randall, "Three Giants Gone," *Negro Digest*, XVII, 1 (November 1967), p. 87.

32   Werner Sollors, *Amiri Baraka/LeRoi Jones: The Quest for a "Populist Modernism"* (New York: Columbia University Press, 1978), p. 261.

33   Ron Silliman, "Poetry and the Politics of the Subject," *Socialist Review*, XVIII, 3 (July–September 1988), 63.

34   Jacques Attali, *Noise: The Political Economy of Music* (Minneapolis: University of Minnesota Press, 1985), pp. 26–27.

35   Leonard Barrett, *The Rastafarians: Sounds of Cultural Dissonance* (Boston: Beacon Press, 1977), p. 167.

36   William Carlos Williams, *Paterson* (New York: New Directions, 1963), p. 207. Hereafter referred to as P.

37   Clarence Major, *Symptoms and Madness* (New York: Corinth, 1971), p. 16.

38   Clarence Major, *Swallow the Lake* (Middletown: Wesleyan University Press, 1970), p. 28.

39   Charles Olson, *Human Universe and Other Essays* (New York: Grove Press, 1967), p. 3.

40 Edward Brathwaite, *The Arrivants: A New World Trilogy* (Oxford: Oxford University Press, 1973), p. 270.

CHAPTER TWO

1   *The New American Poetry:1945-1960*, ed. Donald M. Allen (New York: Grove Press, 1960), p. 425.

2   LeRoi Jones, *Raise Race Rays Raze* (New York: Random House, 1971), p. 23. Hereafter referred to as RR.

3   LeRoi Jones, *The Dead Lecturer* (New York: Grove Press, 1964), p. 79. Hereafter referred to as DL.

4   LeRoi Jones, *Black Magic* (Indianapolis and New York: Bobbs-Merrill, 1969). Hereafter referred to as BMP.

5   Marvin X, "Everything's Cool . . . : An Interview with LeRoi Jones," *Black Theatre*, No. 1 (1968), 18.

6   Amiri Baraka, *Hard Facts* (Newark: Congress of Afrikan People, 1976), pp. i–v. Hereafter referred to as HF.

7   Charles Olson, "Memorial Letter," *Origin*, No. 20 (January 1971), 42.

8   *The Poetics of the New American Poetry*, ed. Donald M. Allen and Warren Tallman (New York: Grove Press, 1973), p. ix.

9   Ibid., p. 185.

10 Ibid., p. 230.

11 LeRoi Jones, *Black Music* (New York: Morrow, 1967), p. 67. Hereafter referred to as BM.

12 LeRoi Jones, *Blues People* (New York: Morrow, 1963), pp. 65, 137. Hereafter referred to as BP.

13 *Blues People*, p. 228. Compare *Black Music*, p. 55, on Sonny Rollins's quartet: "Assassins is what I have been calling this group privately. *The Assassins*."

14 LeRoi Jones, *Dutchman & The Slave* (New York: Morrow, 1964), p. 35.

15 LeRoi Jones, *Tales* (New York: Grove Press, 1967), p. 79. Hereafter referred to as T.

16 *Anger, and Beyond*, ed. Herbert Hill (New York: Harper and Row, 1966), p. 54.

17 *New American Story*, ed. Donald Allen and Robert Creeley (New York: Grove Press, 1965), p. 267.

18 Nat Hentoff, "The Persistent Challenge of Cecil Taylor," *Downbeat*, Feb. 25, 1965, p. 40.

19 Liner notes to *Unit Structures* (Blue Note BST 84237).

20 LeRoi Jones, *Home:Social Essays* (New York: Morrow, 1966), p. 174.

21 The influence of Federico García Lorca, which Baraka acknowledges in *The New American Poetry*, is perhaps behind the implied rapport between Gypsy marginality/spirituality and Afro-American marginality/spirituality, given Lorca's celebration of Gypsies, in *Gypsy Ballads*, such essays as "Deep Song" and "Theory and Function of the *Duende*," and elsewhere, and of Afro-Americans, most notably in *Poet in New York*. His statement in the essay on *duende*, "All that has dark sounds has *duende*," which has also been translated "All that has black sounds has *duende*," has particularly strong

ethnic resonance and relevance for an Afro-American poet with an inclination toward music. Langston Hughes was one of the first translators of *Gypsy Ballads*, and Bob Kaufman quoted, alluded to, and paid homage to Lorca in such poems as "Lorca" and "The Ancient Rain." Baraka's early poem "Lines to García Lorca" begins with an epigraph taken from an Afro-American spiritual, suggesting an affinity between Afro-American culture and the ethos and aesthetics Lorca espoused – an affinity Lorca himself suggested, though not without an exoticizing touch, in *Poet in New York*. See *New Negro Poets: USA*, ed. Langston Hughes (Bloomington: Indiana University Press, 1964), p. 55.

22 Liner notes to *Air Above Mountains* (Inner City IC3021).

23 Frank Kofsky, *Black Nationalism and the Revolution in Music* (New York: Pathfinder Press, 1970), p. 66.

24 *Downbeat*, June 15, 1967, p. 35.

25 *Downbeat*, May 2, 1968, p. 26; Mathieu's italics.

26 C.O. Simpkins, *Coltrane: A Biography* (New York: Herndon House, 1975), p. 124.

27 *Arsenal: Surrealist Subversion*, No. 3 (Spring 1976), contains, in addition to poems by Cecil Taylor and Joseph Jarman, an essay by Franklin Rosemont, "Black Music and the Surrealist Revolution," which deals with the affinity between revolution, "surrealist subversion" and black music.

28 Aimé Césaire, *Discourse on Colonialism* (New York and London: Monthly Review Press, 1972), p. 68.

29 LeRoi Jones, *Preface to a Twenty Volume Suicide Note* (New York: Totem Press/Corinth Books, 1961), pp. 25–26. Hereafter referred to as TVSN.

30 M.L. Rosenthal, *The New Poets* (New York: Oxford University Press, 1967), p. 191.

31 Ibid., p. 190. Compare Paul Blackburn in David Ossman's *The Sullen Art* (New York: Corinth Books, 1963): "Kerouac, for instance, borrows jazz forms a good bit, and with a fair amount of success in terms of that kind of music, I think. In *Mexico City Blues*, when he reads three or four choruses together, they work in terms of a poem, and will balance out. Some carry material over and some don't. I think it's an interesting concept. It's not the easiest – but Kerouac works the form very well. I don't know anyone, aside from Roi Jones, who even touches on that kind of thing at all" (p. 23).

32 "Projective Verse," *Human Universe and Other Essays* (New York: Grove Press, 1967), p. 53.

33 *Anger, and Beyond*, p. 53.

34 *The Black Aesthetic*, ed. Addison Gayle, Jr. (Garden City: Doubleday, 1971), p. 155.

35 Fredric Jameson, *Marxism and Form* (Princeton, N.J.: Princeton University Press, 1971), pp. 308–09.

36 On the albums *Sonny Rollins on Impulse!* (Impulse! A-91), *Sun Ship* (Impulse! AS 9211), and the New York Art Quartet's *Mohawk* (Fontana 881 009 ZY), respectively.

37 *Black World*, May 1973, p. 40.

38 *The New American Poetry*, p. 424.

39   *The Sullen Art*, p. 81.

40   Worth noting are several condemnations of the use of poetry (or literacy) as a form of escapism. In *The Slave* Walker says to Easley, "Yeah, well, I know I thought then that none of you would write any poetry either. I knew that you had moved too far away from the actual meanings of life . . . into some lifeless cocoon of pretended intellectual and emotional achievement, to really be able to see the world again. What was Rino writing before he got killed? Tired elliptical little descriptions of what he could see out the window" (pp. 76–79). Similarly, Baraka says of Louis Zukofsky in "Poetry and Karma": "Those dits and das, Morse again. To tell us what??? that all of it is not coming in. Like Zukofsky, his little coughs and smidges of reality, with the whole of the planet shaking around his ears, his people about to be destroyed, and we get the tiny dihs and dahs, the static creepy anemic beeps" (RR, 21). And of himself in the story "Heroes Are Gang Leaders": "It is the measure of my dwindling life that I returned to the book to rub out their image, and studied very closely another doomed man's life" (T, 69).

41   *Black World*, May 1973, p. 45.

42   Mention should be made of Baraka's ongoing efforts in one such area of synthesis: the reading of his poems to musical accompaniment. Recorded instances can be heard on the albums *New York Art Quartet* (ESP 1004), on which he reads "BLACK DADA NIHILISMUS," *Sunny's Time Now* (Jihad 663), on which he reads "Black Art" accompanied by drummer Sunny Murray's group, and his own *It's Nation Time* (Black Forum B-457L), on which he reads pieces from *Tales, In Our Terribleness, Spirit Reach*, and *It's Nation Time* against a background of music by African drummers, a choral group, a New Music combo, and an R&B group. In the interview conducted by Marvin X he spoke of his desire to write R&B lyrics: "Like I'm sure, for instance, that I could write a song for James Brown – that it will be as good a song as he's been singing (in terms of the words)." Hence the prayer/song "Come See About Me" (based on the Supremes' tune) on *It's Nation Time*, the poem "Beautiful Black Women" done to R&B choral accompaniment on a Jihad 45 rpm release and the Marxist songs he has written for a Newark soul band, the Advanced Workers.

CHAPTER THREE

1   Ralph Ellison, *Invisible Man* (New York: Random House, 1952), p. 438.

2   Clarence Major, *Swallow the Lake* (Middletown: Wesleyan University Press, 1970), p. 28. Hereafter referred to as SL.

3   Clarence Major, *The Dark and Feeling* (New York: Third Press, 1974), p. 134. Hereafter referred to as DF.

4   Clarence Major, *Symptoms & Madness* (New York: Corinth Books, 1971), p. 7. Hereafter referred to as SM.

5   Clarence Major, *All-Night Visitors* (New York: Olympia Press, 1969), pp. 58–59.

6 Clarence Major, *The Cotton Club* (Detroit: Broadside Press, 1972), p. 16. Hereafter referred to as CC.

7 Clarence Major, *Private Line* (London: Paul Breman, 1971), p. 19. Hereafter referred to as PL.

8 Robert Kelly, *The Mill of Particulars* (Los Angeles: Black Sparrow Press, 1973), p. 11.

9 Charles Olson, *Muthologos: The Collected Lectures and Interviews*, Volume I (Bolinas; Four Seasons Foundation, 1978), p. 123.

10 LeRoi Jones, *Black Magic* (Indianapolis and New York: Bobbs-Merrill, 1969), p. 41.

11 LeRoi Jones, *The Dead Lecturer* (New York: Grove Press, 1964), p. 30.

CHAPTER FOUR

1 Robert Duncan, *An Interview* (Toronto: Beaver Kosmos/Coach House Press, 1971), no pagination. Hereafter referred to as I.

2 The statement from which these two fragments are taken appears on the back cover of Duncan's *Roots and Branches* (New York: New Directions, 1964). Hereafter referred to as RB.

3 Quoted by Ann Charters in her introduction to Charles Olson's *The Special View of History* (Berkeley: Oyez, 1970), pp. 9–10.

4 *The Collected Poems of Charles Olson* (Berkeley: University of California Press, 1987), p. 172.

5 Duncan, *Bending the Bow* (New York: New Directions, 1968), p. 78. Hereafter referred to as BB.

6 *Towards A New American Poetics*, ed. Ekbert Faas (Santa Barbara: Black Sparrow Press, 1978), p. 74. Hereafter referred to as TNAP.

7 Robert Duncan, *The Years As Catches* (Berkeley: Oyez, 1966), pp. ix–x.

8 *Stony Brook 3/4* (Fall 1969), 340.

9 *A Caterpillar Anthology*, ed. Clayton Eshleman (Garden City: Doubleday, 1971), pp. 56–57.

10 William Carlos Williams, *Paterson* (New York: New Directions, 1963), p. 52. Hereafter referred to as P.

11 William Carlos Williams, *Pictures from Brueghel* (New York: New Directions, 1962), p. 132.

12 William Carlos Williams, *Selected Essays* (Norfolk, Conn.: New Directions, 1954), pp. 137, 139, 143.

13 Charles Olson, *Call Me Ishmael* (San Francisco: City Lights Books, n.d.), pp. 113–19.

14 Tuzo Wilson, "Continental Drift," *Scientific American* (April 1963), 86–100.

15 *A Caterpillar Anthology*, p. 23.

16 Robert Duncan, *Fictive Certainties* (New York: New Directions, 1985), pp. 179–180.

17 *A Caterpillar Anthology*, p. 66.

18 Robert Duncan, *The Opening of the Field* (New York: New Directions, 1960), p. 43.

19 *Parable, Myth and Language*, ed. Tony Stoneburner (Cambridge, Mass.: The Church Society for College Work, 1968), p. 17.

CHAPTER FIVE

1 *Stony Brook*, 3/4 (Fall 1969), 360–363.
2 Robert Duncan, *Ground Work: Before the War* (New York: New Directions, 1984), pp. 116–117. Hereafter referred to as GW.
3 Robert Duncan, *Bending the Bow* (New York: New Directions, 1968), pp. i–iv. Hereafter referred to as BB.
4 William Carlos Williams, *Paterson* (New York: New Directions, 1963), p. 271. Hereafter referred to as P.
5 Charles Olson, *Muthologos: The Collected Lectures and Interviews,* Volume 1 (Bolinas: Four Seasons Foundation, 1978), p. 66.
6 *A Caterpillar Anthology*, ed. Clayton Eshleman (Garden City, N.Y.: Doubleday, 1971), p. 62.
7 Robert Duncan, "Nights and Days," *Sumac*, I, 1 (Fall 1968), 111.
8 Wilson Harris, *Explorations: A Selection of Talks and Articles, 1966–1981* (Mundelstrup: Dangaroo Press, 1981), p. 47.
9 "The Practice of Outside," in *The Collected Books of Jack Spicer*, ed. Robin Blaser (Los Angeles: Black Sparrow Press, 1975), pp. 285, 277.
10 Alan Bass, " 'Literature'/Literature," *Velocities of Change*, ed. Richard Macksey (Baltimore: Johns Hopkins University Press, 1974), p. 349. Hereafter referred to as VC.

CHAPTER SIX

1 Robert Creeley, *Contexts of Poetry: Interviews 1961–1971* (Bolinas: Four Seasons Foundation, 1973), p. 112. Hereafter referred to as CP.
2 Robert Duncan, *An Interview* (Toronto: Beaver Kosmos/Coach House Press, 1971), no pagination. Hereafter referred to as I.
3 Denise Levertov, *The Poet in the World* (New York: New Directions, 1973), p. 239.
4 Charles Olson, *Letters for Origin* (New York: Cape Goliard/Grossman, 1970), pp. 22, 63. Hereafter referred to as LO.
5 Charles Olson, *Additional Prose* (Bolinas: Four Seasons Foundation, 1974), p. 47.
6 Charles Olson, *Human Universe and Other Essays* (New York: Grove Press, 1967), p. 127. Hereafter referred to as HU.
7 *The Collected Essays of Robert Creeley* (Berkeley: University of California Press, 1989), p. 466. Hereafter referred to as CE.
8 Robert Graves, *The White Goddess* (New York: Noonday, 1966), p. 110.
9 *New American Story*, ed. Donald Allen and Robert Creeley (New York: Grove Press, 1965), p. 263.
10 Alain Robbe-Grillet, *For a New Novel* (New York: Grove Press, 1965), p. 19.
11 "What I tried to do was to show certain inner 'movements' by which I had long been attracted. . . . These movements, of which we are hardly cogni-

zant, slip through us on the frontiers of consciousness in the form of un-definable, extremely rapid sensations. They hide behind our gestures, be-neath the words we speak, the feelings we manifest, are aware of experiencing, and able to define. They seemed, and still seem to me to constitute the secret source of our existence, in what might be called its nascent state." Nathalie Sarraute, *Tropisms* (New York: George Braziller, 1967), p. vi.

12 Charles Olson, *Mayan Letters* (London: Cape/Grossman, 1968), p. 68.

13 Warren Tallman, *Three Essays on Creeley* (Toronto: Beaver Kosmos/Coach House Press, 1973), no pagination.

14 See, for example, John D. Hammond's "Solipsism and the Sexual Imagi-nation in Robert Creeley's Fiction" in *Critique*, Vol. 16, No. 3, 59–69. Hammond's hardheaded talk of "solipsism," "delusion," "distorted reality," and "compensatory imagination" seems intent on denying Creeley and his characters the liminal, indeterminate space in which "objective" and "sub-jective," "public" and "private," and other such pairs penetrate one another. The word *solipsism* rests upon a static prying apart of these pairs, upon what Creeley himself calls "a useless fight" between inside and out. There can be no answer to Hammond's charge except to say that he speaks a language Creeley's tales declare dead.

CHAPTER SEVEN

1 *Boundary* 2, Vol. III, No. 3 (Spring 1975), 541. Hereafter referred to as B.

2 Charles Olson, *Human Universe and Other Essays* (New York: Grove Press, 1967), pp.3–4. Hereafter referred to as HU.

3 Robert Duncan, "A Preface," *Maps 6: Robert Duncan*, 2.

4 George Quasha and Charles Stein, "Ta'wil or How to Read: A Five-Way Interactive View of Robert Kelly," *Vort*, Vol.2, No. 2, 119.

5 Robert Bly, "Looking for Dragon Smoke," in *Naked Poetry*, ed. Stephen Berg and Robert Mezey (Indianapolis and New York: Bobbs-Merrill, 1969), p. 163.

6 William Carlos Williams, *Selected Essays* (New York: New Directions, 1969), pp. 339–340. Hereafter referred to as SE.

7 William Carlos Williams, *Selected Poems* (New York: New Directions, 1969), p. 40.

8 William Carlos Williams, "Letters to Denise Levertov," *Stony Brook*, 1/2 (Fall 1968), 163.

9 Charles Olson, *Selected Writings* (New York: New Directions, 1966), p. 5. Hereafter referred to as SW.

10 Charles Olson, "Project (1951): "The Art and the Language of Mayan Glyphs,'" *Alcheringa*, 5 (Spring–Summer 1973), 95. Hereafter referred to as A.

11 Michel Foucault, *The Order of Things* (New York: Random House, 1970), p. 9.

12 *The Complete Works of Ralph Waldo Emerson*, Centenary Edition (Boston and New York: Houghton Mifflin, 1903–1921), I, 25.

13 Hugh Kenner, *The Pound Era* (Berkeley and Los Angeles: University of California Press, 1971), pp. 105, 231.

14 Ernest Fenollosa, *The Chinese Written Character as a Medium for Poetry* (San Francisco: City Lights, 1964), p. 8.

15 *The Writings of Henry David Thoreau*, Walden Edition (Boston and New York: Houghton, Mifflin, 1906), V, 232.

16 *The Collected Poems of Charles Olson* (Berkeley: University of California Press, 1987), p.106. Hereafter referred to as CP.

17 Charles Olson, *The Maximus Poems* (Berkeley: University of California Press, 1983), p. 40. Hereafter referred to as MP.

18 Robert Kelly, "Texts: 1," *Wch Way*, 2 (Fall 1975), no pagination.

19 Louis Zukofsky, *Prepositions* (Berkeley: University of California Press, 1981), p.13. Hereafter referred to as P.

20 Charles Olson, *Letters for Origin* (New York: Cape Goliard/Grossman, 1970), p. 109. Hereafter referred to as LO.

21 Charles Olson, *Muthologos: The Collected Lectures and Interviews*, Volume 1 (Bolinas: Four Seasons Foundation, 1978),p. 64.

22 Matthew Corrigan, "Charles Olson: Materials for a Nexus," *Open Letter*, Second Series, 2 (Summer 1972), 23.

23 Robert Kelly, *The Mill of Particulars* (Los Angeles: Black Sparrow Press, 1973), p.104. Hereafter referred to as M.

24 William Bronk, *The World, The Worldless* (New York: New Directions/San Francisco Review, 1964), p. 13.

25 *The New American Poetry*, ed. Donald M. Allen (New York: Grove Press, 1960), pp. 420–421.

26 LeRoi Jones, *The Dead Lecturer* (New York: Grove Press, 1964), p. 10.

27 Charles Olson, *Additional Prose* (Bolinas: Four Seasons Foundation, 1974), pp. 50–51.

CHAPTER EIGHT

1 Wilson Harris, *Tradition, the Writer and Society* (London and Port of Spain: New Beacon, 1967), pp. 13–20. Hereafter referred to as TWS.

2 Edward Brathwaite, *The Arrivants: A New World Trilogy* (Oxford: Oxford University Press, 1973), pp. 7–8. Hereafter referred to as A.

3 Two examples of the digging song, "Bahl 'Oman Bahl" and "Georgie Lyon," can be heard on the record album *Caribbean Island Music* (Nonesuch Explorer H-72047).

4 Pablo Neruda, *The Heights of Macchu Picchu*, trans. Nathaniel Tarn (New York: Farrar, Straus & Giroux, 1966), pp. 56–59.

5 Brathwaite's liner notes to record one of the two-record Argo recording of his reading of *Rights of Passage* (PLP 1110 and 1111).

6 *The Complete Poems of Paul Laurence Dunbar* (New York: Dodd, Mead and Company, 1913), p. 71.

7 See Walter Rodney, *The Groundings with My Brothers* (London: Bogle-L'Ouverture, 1975): "a sitting down together to reason, to 'ground' as the Brothers say. We have to 'ground together.'"

8   Mingus's spoken introduction to "Folk Forms, No. 1" on the album *Charles Mingus Presents Charles Mingus* (America 30 AM 6082).

9   Octavio Paz, *The Other Mexico: Critique of the Pyramid* (New York: Grove Press, 1972), pp. 81–82, 90.

10 Liner notes to the Argo recording.

11 Roland Barthes, *Mythologies* (New York: Hill and Wang, 1975), pp. 158–159.

CHAPTER NINE

1   Federico García Lorca, "Theory and Function of the *Duende,*" *The Poetics of the New American Poetry*, ed. Donald Allen and Warren Tallman (New York: Grove Press, 1973), pp. 91–103.

2   Wilson Harris, *Tradition, the Writer and Society* (London and Port of Spain: New Beacon, 1967), p. 33. Hereafter referred to as TWS.

3   Wilson Harris, *The Eye of the Scarecrow* (London: Faber, 1965), p. 95. Hereafter referred to as ES.

4   Robert Kelly, *Flesh Dream Book* (Los Angeles: Black Sparrow Press, 1971),

5   Wilson Harris, *The Secret Ladder* (London: Faber, 1963), p. 26. Hereafter referred to as SL.

6   C.L.R. James, *Wilson Harris: A Philosophical Approach* (St. Augustine, Trinidad: University of the West Indies, 1965), p. 15.

7   David Lowenthal, *West Indian Societies* (New York: Oxford University Press, 1972), p. 5.

8   "The Unresolved Constitution," *Caribbean Quarterly*, 14, 1/2 (1968), 43–47. Subsequent quotations in Section I of the essay are taken from this source unless otherwise noted.

9   *Caribbean Quarterly*, 16 (1970), 1–32. Subsequent quotations in Section II of the essay are taken from this source unless otherwise noted.

10 Charles Olson, *The Special View of History* (Berkeley: Oyez, 1970), pp. 35–36.

11 Wilson Harris, *Ascent to Omai* (London: Faber, 1970), pp. 103–104.

12 Wilson Harris, *The Waiting Room* (London: Faber, 1967), p. 47.

13 Wilson Harris, *Explorations: A Selection of Talks and Articles 1966–1981* (Mundelstrup: Dangaroo Press, 1981), p. 43. Hereafter referred to as E.

14 Wilson Harris, *The Sleepers of Roraima* (London: Faber, 1970), p. 24. Hereafter referred to as SR.

15 Wilson Harris, *The Age of the Rainmakers* (London: Faber, 1971), p. 26. Hereafter referred to as AR.

16 C.G. Jung, *Psychology and Alchemy* (Princeton, N.J.: Princeton University Press, 1969), p. 18.

17 Wilson Harris, *Palace of the Peacock* (London: Faber, 1960), p. 147. Hereafter referred to as PP.

18 Wilson Harris, *The Whole Armour* (London: Faber, 1962), p. 116.

19 Wilson Harris, *Companions of the Day and Night* (London: Faber, 1975), p. 58.

20 Edward Brathwaite, *The Arrivants: A New World Trilogy* (Oxford: Oxford University Press, 1973), pp. 265–66.

CHAPTER TEN

1 Marcel Griaule, *Conversations with Ogotemmeli: An Introduction to Dogon Religious Ideas* (London: Oxford University Press, 1965), p. 73.

2 George E. Marcus and Michael M.J. Fischer, *Anthropology as Cultural Critique: An Experimental Moment in the Human Sciences* (Chicago: University of Chicago Press, 1986), pp. 8–9.

3 Ibid., p. 9.

4 John La Rose, "Self-Discovery and Self-Reconstruction in the Poetry of the Caribbean," *Encrages,* 15 (Winter 1986), p. 105.

5 *Writing Culture: The Poetics and Politics of Ethnography,* ed. James Clifford and George E. Marcus (Berkeley: University of California Press, 1986), p. 10.

6 Wilson Harris, *The Whole Armour and The Secret Ladder* (London: Faber and Faber, 1973), p. 145. Subsequent references will be cited in the text of the essay.

7 Wilson Harris, *Explorations: A Selection of Talks and Articles 1966–1981* (Mundelstrup: Dangaroo Press, 1981), p. 74.

8 Wilson Harris, *Tradition, the Writer and Society* (London: New Beacon, 1967), p. 29.

9 Richard Price, *First-Time: The Historical Vision of an Afro-American People* (Baltimore: Johns Hopkins University Press, 1983).

10 *Maroon Societies: Rebel Slave Communities in the Americas,* ed. Richard Price (Garden City: Doubleday Anchor, 1973), p. 28.

11 Ibid., p. 293.

12 Kenneth Ramchand, *An Introduction to the Study of West Indian Literature* (Middlesex: Thomas Nelson and Sons, 1976), p. 165.

13 See, for example, Kimberly W. Benston's "I Yam What I Am: The Topos of Un(naming) in Afro-American Literature" in *Black Literature and Literary Theory,* ed. Henry Louis Gates, Jr. (New York: Methuen, 1984, pp. 151–172).

14 Edward Kamau Brathwaite, *Mother Poem* (Oxford: Oxford University Press, 1977), p. 121. See also *X/Self* (Oxford: Oxford University Press, 1987), p. 127, and "Gods of the Middle Passage: A Tennament," *Caribbean Review,* XI, 4 (Fall 1982), p. 18.

15 Toni Morrison, *Sula* (New York: Knopf, 1973).

16 Ibid.

17 Toni Morrison, *Song of Solomon* (New York: Knopf, 1977).

18 See Henry Louis Gates, Jr.'s *The Signifying Monkey: A Theory of African-American Literary Criticism* (New York: Oxford University Press, 1988) for a discussion of the African-American uses of this term.

19 The image of Poseidon, "eyes inverted, brow pointing down," seen through the inverting telescope of Fenwick's spirit-level, initiates their second encounter (p. 180).

20 Alejo Carpentier, *The Lost Steps,* trans. Harriet de Onís (New York: Avon Books, 1979), p. 237. The novel was originally published in Spanish in 1953. The first English translation appeared in 1956. Harris comments upon it in

the essay "Some Aspects of Myth and the Intuitive Imagination" in *Explorations*, pp. 97–106.

21   L. Sprague de Camp, *Lost Continents: The Atlantis Theme in History, Science, and Literature* (New York: Dover Publications, 1970), pp. 28–29.

22   Janheinz Jahn, *Leo Frobenius: The Demonic Child* (Austin: African and Afro-American Studies and Research Center, University of Texas, 1974), p. 6.

23   Ibid., p. 11.

24   Wilson Harris, *Explorations*, p. 115.

25   W. K. C. Guthrie, *The Greeks and Their Gods* (Boston: Beacon Press, 1954), p. 94.

26   Dick Hebdige, *Cut 'n' Mix: Culture, Identity and Caribbean Music* (London: Methuen, 1987), p. 83.

27   Timothy White, *Catch a Fire: The Life of Bob Marley* (New York: Holt, Rinehart and Winston, 1983), p. 230.

CHAPTER ELEVEN

1   This is the argument of Hena Maes-Jelinek in the essay "The True Substance of Life: Wilson Harris's *Palace of the Peacock*," in *Common Wealth* (Papers delivered at the Conference of Commonwealth Literature, Aarhus University, Aarhus, Denmark, 26–30 April 1971), ed. Anna Rutherford (Aarhus: Akademisk Boghandel, n.d.), pp. 151–59.

2   Wilson Harris, *Palace of the Peacock* (London: Faber, 1960), p. 152. Hereafter referred to as PP.

3   The choice of a Metaphysical poet hardly seems arbitrary when one considers Harris's remark in the essay "History, Fable and Myth in the Caribbean and Guianas": "Haitian *vodun* – like West Indian and Guianese/Brazilian *limbo* – may well point to sleeping possibilities of drama and horizons of poetry, epic and novel, sculpture and painting – in short to a language of variables in art which would have a profoundly evolutionary cultural and philosophical significance for Caribbean man. Such new resources . . . are not foreign to English poetry except in the sense that these may be closer to the 'metaphysical poets' – to a range and potency of association in which nothing is ultimately alien – of which Eliot speaks in his famous essay on 'dissociation of sensibility' " (*Caribbean Quarterly*, 16 [1970], 14–15).

4   This phrase appears in Harris's essay, "The Phenomenal Legacy," in *Explorations: A Selection of Talks and Articles 1966–1981* (Mundelstrup: Dangaroo Press, 1981), pp. 43–48.

5   Wilson Harris, *The Eye of the Scarecrow* (London: Faber and Faber, 1965), p. 15. Hereafter referred to as ES.

6   Wilson Harris, *Tradition, the Writer and Society* (London and Port of Spain: New Beacon, 1967), p. 29. Hereafter referred to as TWS.

7   Harris seems most impressed by and concerned with human resilience and durability. He speaks of "the transforming imperative to endure (which is the highest moral principle)" and remarks: "We have aged overnight in the knowledge that man lived on this planet twenty million years ago. The fact of our survival becomes increasingly one of both miraculous protection from

wild animals and plants, and miraculous insight into the living void of the present or future as this unrolled itself in the heavens and within the catastrophic premises of the earth" (TWS, 42, 63–64). Relatedly, the crash throws the narrator and L– into what's called "a jungle of miraculous survival" (ES, 85).

8 Kenneth Ramchand, *The West Indian Novel and Its Background* (New York: Barnes and Noble, 1970), pp. 9–10.

9 For example: "I was *pushing* her (was aware of a contrary rebuke and stillness in the heart of crude action) – *pushing* her, nevertheless, even as I had involuntarily pushed him, her son, into the canal" (ES, 45). The later novel *Black Marsden*, between *The Eye of the Scarecrow* and which many parallels and continuities exist, perpetuates this motif of the involuntary push: "Everybody claims he is being *pushed*. Nobody ever does the pushing but everybody is being pushed" (Wilson Harris, *Black Marsden* [London: Faber and Faber, 1972], p. 73; hereafter referred to as BM).

10 Henri Corbin, *Avicenna and the Visionary Recital* (New York: Pantheon, 1960), pp. 19–20.

11 For example: "Poetry, if it is anything, is a revelation of the 'essential heterogeneity of being,' eroticism, 'otherness.' . . . the vision of our estrangement." "If the word is the double of the cosmos, the realm of spiritual experience is language." "All of us are alone, because all of us are two. The strange one, the other, is our double. Again and again we try to lay hold upon him. Again and again he eludes us. He has no face or name, but he is always there, hiding" (*The Bow and the Lyre* [New York: McGraw-Hill, 1975], pp. 77, 70, 117; hereafter referred to as BL).

12 Harris, "History, Fable and Myth in the Caribbean and Guianas," p. 20.

13 Alain Robbe-Grillet, *For a New Novel* (New York: Grove Press, 1965), pp. 153–54.

14 Wilson Harris, *Ascent to Omai* (London: Faber and Faber, 1970), p. 96.

CHAPTER TWELVE

1 Wilson Harris, *The Whole Armour* (London: Faber and Faber, 1962), p. 70. Hereafter referred to as WA.

2 Wilson Harris, *The Eye of the Scarecrow* (London: Faber and Faber, 1965), pp. 47–48. Hereafter referred to as ES.

3 Wilson Harris, *Ascent to Omai* (London: Faber and Faber, 1970), p. 42. Hereafter referred to as AO.

4 Roland Barthes, *Mythologies* (New York: Hill and Wang, 1972), pp. 43, 45. Hereafter referred to as M.

5 Wilson Harris, *Tradition, the Writer and Society* (London and Port of Spain: New Beacon, 1967), p. 29. Hereafter referred to as TWS.

6 Wilson Harris, *Explorations: A Selection of Talks and Articles 1966–1981* (Mundelstrup: Dangaroo Press, 1981), p. 12. Hereafter referred to as E.

7 James Hillman, *Re-Visioning Psychology* (New York: Harper and Row, 1975), p. ix. Hereafter referred to as RP.

8 Wilson Harris, *Black Marsden* (London: Faber and Faber, 1972), p. 54.

9   *Caribbean Quarterly*, 14, No. 1–2 (1968), 43–47.
10 W.B. Yeats, *A Vision* (New York: Collier, 1966), p. 25.

CHAPTER THIRTEEN

1   Examples of *gisalo* and other varieties of Kaluli song can be heard on the album *The Kaluli of Papua Niugini: Weeping and Song* (Musicaphon BM 30 SL 2702).

2   Orlando Patterson, *Slavery and Social Death: A Comparative Study* (Cambridge: Harvard University Press, 1982).

3   Victor Zuckerkandl, *Sound and Symbol: Music and the External World* (Princeton: Bollingen Foundation/Princeton University Press, 1956), p. 371. Hereafter referred to as SS.

4   Stephanie A. Judy, " 'The Grand Concord of What': Preliminary Thoughts on Musical Composition and Poetry," *Boundary 2*, VI, 1 (Fall 1977), 267–85.

5   Louis Zukofsky, *Prepositions* (Berkeley: University of California Press, 1981), p. 19.

6   Octavio Paz, *The Bow and the Lyre* (New York: McGraw-Hill, 1973), p. 37.

7   Julia Kristeva, *Desire in Language: A Semiotic Approach to Literature and Art* (New York: Columbia University Press, 1980), p. 31.

8   Steven Feld, *Sound and Sentiment: Birds, Weeping, Poetics and Song in Kaluli Expression* (Philadelphia: University of Pennsylvania Press, 1982), p. 34.

9   Robert Farris Thompson, *Flash of the Spirit: African and Afro-American Art and Philosophy* (New York: Vintage Books, 1984), p. xiii.

10 LeRoi Jones, *Tales* (New York: Grove Press, 1967), p. 77.

11 Charles Mingus, *Beneath the Underdog* (New York: Penguin Books, 1980), p. 262.

12 Nathaniel Mackey, *Bedouin Hornbook* (Charlottesville: Callaloo Fiction Series/University Press of Virginia, 1986), p. 1.

13 Michael Taussig, *The Devil and Commodity Fetishism in South America* (Chapel Hill: University of North Carolina Press, 1980), p. 4.

14 Josef Skvorecky, *The Bass Saxophone* (London: Picador, 1980), p. 109.

15 Quoted by Lawrence W. Levine in *Black Culture and Black Consciousness: Afro-American Folk Thought from Slavery to Freedom* (New York: Oxford University Press, 1977), p. 85.

16 Jean Toomer, *The Wayward and the Seeking* (Washington, D.C.: Howard University Press, 1980), p. 123.

17 Quoted by Charles W. Scruggs in "The Mark of Cain and the Redemption of Art," *American Literature*, 44 (1972), 290–291.

18 Jean Toomer, *Cane* (New York: Liveright, 1975), p. 12. Hereafter referred to as C.

19 LeRoi Jones, *Black Music* (New York: Morrow, 1967), p. 66.

20 William Carlos Williams, *Paterson* (New York: New Directions, 1963), pp. 144–145. Hereafter referred to as P.

21 William Carlos Williams, *Selected Poems* (New York: New Directions, 1969), p. 115.

22 Norman O. Brown, *Hermes the Thief: The Evolution of a Myth* (New York: Vintage Books, 1969), p. 82.

23 Robert D. Pelton, *The Trickster in West Africa: A Study of Mythic Irony and Sacred Delight* (Berkeley: University of California Press), p. 80.

24 Paule Marshall, *Praisesong for the Widow* (New York: Dutton, 1984), p. 243.

25 Levine, pp. 405–406.

26 Ralph Ellison, *Invisible Man* (New York: Vintage Books, 1972), p. 8. Hereafter referred to as IM.

27 Charles Olson, *Human Universe and Other Essays* (New York: Grove Press, 1967), p. 3.

28 Theodore Thass-Thienemann, *The Subconscious Language* (New York: Washington Square Press, 1967), p. 96n.

29 Quoted by Paul L. Mariani in "Williams's Black Novel," *The Massachusetts Review*, XIV, 1 (Winter 1973), 68. This article is part of "A Williams Garland: Petals from the Falls, 1945–1950," edited by Mariani, which includes *Man Orchid*, 77–117. Subsequent citations of Mariani's article and of *Man Orchid* are incorporated into the text, referred to as MO.

30 See, for example, "This is what it's called" by Albert Saijo, Lew Welch, and Jack Kerouac in *The Beat Scene*, ed. Elias Wilentz (New York: Corinth, 1960), pp. 163–170.

31 Edward Kamau Brathwaite, *History of the Voice: The Development of Nation Language in Anglophone Caribbean Poetry* (London and Port of Spain: New Beacon, 1984), p. 31.

32 Paul Blackburn, *The Collected Poems* (New York: Persea Press, 1985), p. 316.

33 Wilson Harris, *The Angel at the Gate* (London: Faber and Faber, 1982), p. 109. Hereafter referred to as AG.

34 Wilson Harris, *The Womb of Space: The Cross-Cultural Imagination* (Westport: Greenwood Press, 1983), pp. 130–131.

35 Wilson Harris, *Explorations: A Selection of Talks and Articles 1966–1981* (Mundelstrup: Dangaroo Press, 1981), pp. 43–48.

36 Wilson Harris, *Da Silva da Silva's Cultivated Wilderness and Genesis of the Clowns* (London: Faber and Faber, 1977), pp. 8–9.

37 Wilson Harris, *Palace of the Peacock* (London: Faber and Faber, 1960), p. 83. Hereafter referred to as PP.

38 "The eye and its 'gaze' . . . has had a lockhold on Western thought," notes, as have others, Paul Stoller in "Sound in Songhay Cultural Experience," *American Ethnologist*, 11, 3 (1984), 559–570.

CHAPTER FOURTEEN

1 This essay was first presented as respondent comments at "A Symposium of the Whole: Towards A Human Poetics" at the Center for the Humanities, University of Southern California, March 1983.

2 See Nathaniel Tarn, "Dr. Jekyll, the Anthropologist Emerges and Marches into the Notebook of Mr. Hyde, the Poet," *Conjunctions*, 6 (Spring 1984), pp. 266–281.

3 Robert Duncan, "Rites of Participation," *A Caterpillar Anthology*, ed. Clayton Eshleman (Garden City, N.Y.: Doubleday, 1971), p. 39.

4 Jay Wright, *The Double Invention of Komo* (Austin and London: University of Texas Press, 1980), pp. 29, 6, 48.

5 Édouard Glissant, "Free and Forced Poetics," *Ethnopoetics: A First International Symposium*, ed. Michel Benamou and Jerome Rothenberg (Boston: Alcheringa/Boston University, 1976), p. 100.

6 Charles Olson, *Human Universe and Other Essays* (New York: Grove Press, 1967), p. 3

7 Amiri Baraka, "Pfister Needs To Be Heard!," in Arthur Pfister, *Beer Cans, Bullets, Things & Pieces* (Detroit: Broadside Press, 1972), p. 4.

8 Ishmael Reed, *Mumbo Jumbo* (Garden City, N.Y.: Doubleday, 1972), p. 211.

9 *Narrative of the Life of Frederick Douglass, An American Slave* (Cambridge: Harvard University Press, 1960), p. 59.

10 Maurice Blanchot, *The Gaze of Orpheus and Other Literary Essays* (Rhinebeck, N.Y.: Station Hill Press, 1981), p. 134.

11 Jerome Rothenberg, "Pre-Face," in *Technicians of the Sacred*, ed. Jerome Rothenberg (Garden City, N.Y.: Doubleday, 1968), p. xix.

12 Wilson Harris, *The Eye of the Scarecrow* (London: Faber and Faber, 1965), p. 102.

CHAPTER FIFTEEN

1 This essay was first presented as a lecture as part of "Otherness: A Symposium on Cultural Diversity" at the Detroit Institute of Arts, March 1991.

2 LeRoi Jones, *Blues People: Negro Music in White America* (New York: Morrow, 1963), p. 143. Hereafter referred to as BP.

3 Dick Hebdige, *Cut 'n' Mix: Culture, Identity and Caribbean Music* (London: Methuen, 1987), p. 12.

4 LeRoi Jones, *Black Music* (New York: Morrow, 1967), p. 66. Hereafter referred to as BM.

5 Liner notes, *Coltrane Live at the Village Vanguard Again!* (Impulse! Records AS-9124).

6 Zora Neale Hurston, *Their Eyes Were Watching God* (Urbana: University of Illinois Press, 1978), pp. 9–10.

7 Zora Neale Hurston, *The Sanctified Church* (Berkeley: Turtle Island, 1981), pp. 49–68.

8 Ibid., pp. 69–78.

9 Garrison, Allen, Spaulding, Armstrong, and Ludlow quoted in Eileen Southern, *The Music of Black Americans: A History* 2nd Edition (New York: Norton, 1983), pp. 191–194.

10 Ed Roberson, "Taking the Print," *Hambone, 9* (Winter 1991), p. 2.

11 Aimé Césaire, *The Collected Poetry*, trans. Clayton Eshleman and Annette Smith (Berkeley: University of California Press, 1983), pp. 368–371.

12 James Clifford, *The Predicament of Culture: Twentieth-Century Ethnography, Literature and Art* (Cambridge: Harvard University Press, 988), pp. 175–181.

13 Edward Kamau Brathwaite, *X/Self* (Oxford: Oxford University Press, 1987), pp. 129–130. Hereafter referred to as X.

14 Edward Kamau Brathwaite, *Mother Poem* (Oxford: Oxford University Press, 1977), p. 121.

15 Edward Brathwaite, *The Arrivants: A New World Trilogy* (Oxford: Oxford University Press, 1973), pp. 265–266.

16 Edward Brathwaite, *The Development of Creole Society in Jamaica 1770–1820* (Oxford: Oxford University Press, 1971), p. 237.

17 Edward Kamau Brathwaite, *Sun Poem* (Oxford: Oxford University Press, 1982), p. 56. Hereafter referred to as SP.

18 Ira Gitler, *Swing to Bop: An Oral History of the Transition in Jazz in the 1940s* (New York: Oxford University Press, 1985), p. 153. Hereafter referred to as SB.

19 Edward Brathwaite, *Other Exiles* (London: Oxford University Press, 1975), pp. 12–16.

20 LeRoi Jones, *Home: Social Essays* (New York: Morrow, 1966), pp. 173–178.

21 Liner notes, *The Complete Blue Note Recordings of Thelonious Monk* (Mosaic Records MR4-101).

22 Liner notes, *Thelonious Monk Live at the It Club* (Columbia Records C2-38030).

23 "My Sweet Hunk O'Trash."

24 Charles Mingus, *Beneath the Underdog* (New York: Penguin, 1980), p. 7.

25 Liner notes, *Black Bone* (Soul Note Records SN 10550).

26 Artistic othering pertains to intracultural as well as intercultural dialectics. The will to change whereby African-American culture reflects critically upon the dominant white culture is intertwined with its impulse to reflect critically upon itself, the will to change whereby it redefines, reinvents, and diversifies itself. Bebop, for example, was a reaction to the datedness of the music played by black swing musicians as well as to its appropriation by white musicians. No last word, no seal of prophecy, bebop in turn became dated, subject to the changes initiated by Ornette Coleman, Cecil Taylor, Albert Ayler, and others during the late fifties and early sixties. An aspect of intracultural dialectics that we should not overlook is the role of eccentric individuals whose contributions come to be identified with the very culture that may have initially rejected them. Think of Ornette Coleman being beaten up outside a Baton Rouge dance hall in 1949 for interjecting "modern" runs into an R&B solo (A.B. Spellman, *Black Music: Four Lives* [New York: Schocken Books, 1970], p. 101). The recent ascendancy of cultural studies in academia tends to privilege collectivity and group definition over individual agency and self-expression, to see the latter as a reflection of the former. In relating the two, however, we should remember that in matters of artistic othering individual expression both reflects and redefines the collective, realigns, refracts it. Thus it is that Lester Young was in the habit of calling his saxophone's keys his people. Bill Crow reports that when the keys on his horn got bent during a Jazz at the Philharmonic tour Young went to Flip Phillips for help. "Flip," he said, "my people won't play!" (*Jazz Anecdotes* [New York: Oxford University Press, 1990], p. 272).

27 Wilson Harris, *Explorations: A Selection of Talks and Articles 1966–1981* (Mundelstrup: Dangaroo Press, 1981), p. 139.

28 Wilson Harris, *The Four Banks of the River of Space* (London: Faber and Faber, 1990), pp. 140–141.

29 Art Sato, "Interview with John Gilmore," *Be-Bop and Beyond*, Vol. 4, No. 2 (March/April 1986), 21.

30 Jacques Attali, *Noise: The Political Economy of Music* (Minneapolis: University of Minnesota Press, 1985), p. 57. Hereafter referred to as N.

31 Ellen B. Basso, *A Musical View of the Universe: Kalapalo Myth and Ritual Performances* (Philadelphia: University of Pennsylvania Press, 1985), pp. 69–70. Hereafter referred to as MV.

32 Robert C. Toll, *Blacking Up: The Minstrel Show in Nineteenth-Century America* (New York: Oxford University Press, 1974), p. 51. Hereafter referred to as BU.

33 *Complete Minstrel Guide* (Chicago: The Dramatic Publishing Company, no date), pp. 49–50.

34 Alexander Saxton, "Blackface Minstrelsy and Jacksonian Ideology," *American Quarterly*, Vol. 27, No. 1 (March 1975), 12. Subsequent references will be cited in the text of the essay.

35 Quoted in Elizabeth Sprigge, *Gertrude Stein: Her Life and Work* (New York: Harper, 1957), pp. 124–125.

36 Gertrude Stein, *Three Lives* (New York: Viking Penguin, 1990), pp. 85–86. Hereafter referred to as TL.

37 Carolyn Copeland, *Language and Time and Gertrude Stein* (Iowa City: University of Iowa Press, 1975), p. 24. Subsequent references will be cited in the text of the essay.

38 Janice Doane, *Silence and Narrative: The Early Novels of Gertrude Stein* (Westport: Greenwood Press, 1986), p. 52.

39 For a discussion of Stein's racist view of black people and of "Melanctha" as "the signpost of modernism's discourse on the nonwhite," see Aldon Lynn Nielsen, *Reading Race: White American Poets and the Racial Discourse in the Twentieth Century* (Athens: University of Georgia Press, 1988), pp. 21–28.

40 Wilson Harris, "In the Name of Liberty," *Third Text*, 11 (Summer 1990), 15.

41 Hurston, in "Characteristics of Negro Expression": "After adornment the next most striking manifestation of the Negro is Angularity. Everything that he touches becomes angular."

42 John Clellon Holmes, *The Horn* (New York: Thunder's Mouth Press, 1988), p. 8. Subsequent references will be cited in the text of the essay.

43 Henry Dumas, *Play Ebony Play Ivory* (New York: Random House, 1974), p. 52.

Index

Continued from the front of the book

LOS ANGELES

625 S BONNIE BRAE ST.

ENTRE LA 6TH ST. Y WILSHIRE BLVD.

(A UNA CUADRA DEL MACARTHUR PARK)

1 800 581 4141

MATRIMONIO BLINDADO

MATRIMONIO BLINDADO

SU MATRIMONIO A PRUEBA DE DIVORCIO

Renato y Cristiane Cardoso

Obra editada en colaboración con Editora Planeta do Brasil Ltda - Brasil

Título original: *Casamento blindado*

Traducción: 2013, Ágatha Parras, Jorge Olveira Paz (por el prefacio y las notas)

© 2012, Thomas Nelson Brasil, Vida Melhor Editora SA
Rua Nova Jeresaléj, 345, Bonsucesso
Río de Janeiro, RJ, 21402-325
www.thomasnelson.com.br
© Textos: Renato Cardoso, Cristiane Cardoso

De esta edición:
© 2013, Editorial Planeta Mexicana, S.A. de C.V.
Bajo el sello editorial PLANETA M.R.
Avenida Presidente Masarik núm. 111, 2o. piso
Colonia Chapultepec Morales
C.P. 11570, México, D.F.
www.editorialplaneta.com.mx

Primera edición impresa en México: agosto de 2013
Segunda reimpresión: septiembre de 2014
ISBN: 978-607-07-1804-5

Impreso en los talleres de Litográfica Ingramex, S.A. de C.V.
Centeno núm. 162-1, colonia Granjas Esmeralda, México, D.F.
Impreso en México – *Printed in Mexico*

A todas las parejas que valoran su matrimonio lo suficiente como para blindarlo. Y a los solteros inteligentes que saben que más vale prevenir que lamentar.

SUMARIO

PARTE II
EMOCIÓN VS. RAZÓN

PARTE III
DESMONTANDO Y REMONTANDO EL AMOR

PARTE IV
HACIENDO EL BLINDAJE

PREFACIO

«Defense! Defense!»

Es probable que al comenzar a leer este prefacio espere encontrar un texto con varias referencias al básquet, deporte que me ha reportado muchas victorias, luchas, alegrías, conflictos y recompensas. Bien, para ser franco, quiero hablar sobre otro ámbito de mi vida que también me ha dado muchas victorias, luchas, alegrías, conflictos y recompensas, aunque mucho más profundas y significativas: mi matrimonio. Y, para ser todavía más franco: si no fuese por la solidez de mi unión con Cristina, es posible que tuviese muchas menos cosas que contar, incluso en lo referente a mi vida como atleta.

Cristina y yo nos casamos hace más de treinta años y nos conocemos desde hace casi cuatro décadas. Sé que parece una frase bastante común, pero no puedo evitar pensar, y tengo la certeza de que usted estará de acuerdo conmigo, que se trata de toda una vida juntos. Imagine cuántas cosas suceden durante toda una vida. Días de sol, agradables, buen clima; aunque también días de lluvia e incluso de tempestad. Simplemente se trata de una relación con unos buenos cimientos para resistir el azote del vendaval que lo desbarata todo.

Si nos remontásemos cuarenta años atrás, cuando yo era mucho más ingenuo (me faltaba creer en el Conejito de Pascua), podría decir que basta solo con el amor para resolver todos los problemas de un matrimonio. Está claro que es un elemento fundamental en cualquier unión, ninguna pareja logra ser feliz y permanecer unida sin amor, pero puedo garantizarle que hay otros muchos factores que intervienen en un matrimonio. Puedo simplemente explicarle cómo una persona como mi esposa, Cristina, llegó a renunciar a un título universitario, cuando apenas le quedaban tres meses para obtenerlo, para mudarse conmigo a Europa, lugar al que fui a jugar a los seis meses de casarnos. Fue ella la que, durante aquellas primeras semanas, mantuvo la fortaleza cuando el equipo en el que yo jugaba tuvo un mal comienzo de campeonato. No importaba el tiempo que tuviese que entrenar o si debía concentrarme más, Cristina nunca descuidó la casa. Sin ella, quizá hubiera desistido. Con ella, regresé de allí victorioso, años más tarde.

En básquet (está bien, terminé hablando de básquet), un equipo que se valore solo consigue un buen resultado cuando todos se preocupan por todos. Quien sabe encestar baja también para defender, para proteger al resto del equipo. En Estados Unidos los fanáticos gritan: «*¡Defense! Defense!*» He descubierto que esto funciona de forma muy parecida en el matrimonio. El que ama avanza, progresa, gana, pero también se preocupa por proteger no solo al cónyuge sino la relación en sí. Por respeto a Cristina he dejado de llevar a muchas admiradoras en el coche. No se trataba solo de preservarla de un disgusto, se trataba también de preservar nuestra unión, nuestro amor, nuestra relación.

Por lo tanto, me ha hecho muy feliz que me invitaran a escribir el prefacio del libro de Renato y Cristiane Cardoso. He leído algunos libros sobre el matrimonio y he oído hablar de otros, pero es la primera vez que doy con uno que llega a la raíz de la cuestión: el que ama de verdad, blinda el matrimonio. Y blindar quiere decir activar todas las defensas, para evitar que cualquier cosa pueda comprometer la relación. No solo se incluyen los ataques externos, sino también los internos: los reproches por tonterías, las crisis (y no hay nada que hacer, siempre aparecen), la falta de humildad para saber cuándo hay que ceder por amor (o tomar medidas por amor), la incapacidad de adaptarse a las virtudes y los defectos de la otra persona, los chantajes y los jueguitos emocionales... Una lista interminable.

Renato y Cristiane aprendieron eso tras años de ofrecer consejos a muchas parejas, pero la mejor formación que han tenido fue la propia escuela de la vida. Fue así como descubrieron el poder del blindaje, que se vuelve mucho más fuerte y sólido cuando se basa en principios y valores cristianos. Y ahora ellos comparten dichas experiencias y orientaciones en este libro. Se trata de una fantástica oportunidad tanto para el que descubre que su matrimonio es vulnerable y necesita un escudo, como para aquellos que ya han blindado su unión y conocen lo importante que es reforzar la protección. Léalo y blinde también su matrimonio.

Oscar Schmidt

El mejor jugador de básquet brasileño
de todos los tiempos, casado con Cristina
y padre de Felipe y Stephanie

INTRODUCCIÓN

Nadie se casa por odio. Hasta el día de hoy no he encontrado a alguien que le haya pedido matrimonio a otra persona diciendo: «Te odio, ¿te quieres casar conmigo?». Las personas se casan por amor; sin embargo, el índice de divorcios continúa aumentando cada año. En algunos países, como en Estados Unidos, la mitad de los matrimonios acaba en divorcio. En América Latina, más de la mitad de los matrimonios se han disuelto y la estadística ha ido en aumento durante 2012. De cada tres matrimonios, uno fue deshecho. Vamos de mal en peor. Eso muestra que el «amor» que une a las personas no ha sido suficiente para mantener el matrimonio. Preocupante, ¿verdad? ¿Se imagina que aquel amor que siente el uno por el otro no pueda ser suficiente en los momentos de crisis?

El problema no ha sido la falta de amor y sí la falta de herramientas para resolver los problemas inherentes a vivir en pareja. Las personas se embarcan en el matrimonio prácticamente sin habilidades para resolver problemas de convivencia. Por algún motivo, eso no se ha enseñado en lugar alguno, al menos no con la claridad y la practicidad necesarias. Antiguamente, esa enseñanza procedía de los padres. Cuando los matrimonios eran más sólidos y ejemplares, los hijos tenían en los padres un modelo natural de cómo comportarse en una relación. Actualmente, los padres muchas veces son un ejemplo de lo que no hay que hacer...

Tenemos otro gran problema: la ignorancia sobre lo que es el amor. Muchas veces he escuchado esta frase de maridos y esposas frustrados: «El amor se acabó. Ya no siento lo que antes sentía por él/ella».

Otros dicen que su matrimonio fue un error, que se casaron con la persona equivocada, que se precipitaron o se vieron forzados a casarse por las circunstancias, como en el caso de un embarazo no deseado. Sin embargo, en realidad, hay mucha más gente infeliz en el matrimonio porque hace lo incorrecto que por haberse casado con la persona equivocada. Las personas hacen demasiadas cosas erradas, acumulan muchos problemas que no se resuelven, lo que provoca que el amor quede sofocado, fracturado y sin fuerzas, eso si no muere antes de nacer. Los sentimientos buenos acaban dando lugar al rencor, a la indiferencia e incluso al odio.

Pero es posible rescatar el amor e incluso aprender a amar a alguien a quien usted nunca amó. Observe lo que he dicho: «Es posible aprender a amar». El primer paso es saber que la única manera de amar a una persona es saber más acerca de ella.

Muchos piensan, erróneamente, que el amor es un sentimiento. El amor produce sentimientos buenos, sí, pero no es un sentimiento en sí. Si usted ve a una persona por primera vez y siente algo bueno por ella, pero después no aprende a amarla por quien es, aquel «amor a primera vista» no permanecerá. Amar no es sentir. Amar es conocer a la otra persona, admirar lo que sabe de ella y mirar sus defectos positivamente. Podemos aprender a amar prácticamente a cualquier persona o cosa si nos esforzamos en ello.

Considere el caso de Dian Fossey, por ejemplo. En su sepultura se lee el siguiente epígrafe: «No one loved gorillas more» (Nadie amó más a los gorilas). Dian fue una zoóloga americana, famosa y respetada por sus estudios sobre los gorilas de África Central. Durante muchos años, hasta su muerte causada por cazadores furtivos, Dian vivió entre los gorilas, en las montañas de Ruanda. Vivía en una cabaña de madera, en condiciones primitivas, y dedicó más de dieciocho años de su vida a los animales, a quienes amaba más que a todo en la vida. ¿Y cómo fue que Dian comenzó a amar a los gorilas?

A los 31 años, de safari por África, Dian tuvo su primer encuentro con los gorilas y con los estudios de conservacionistas que trabajaban por la preservación de los primates. Allí comenzó a descubrir más sobre ellos, su comportamiento, cómo se comunican, sus hábitos, su dieta, la amenaza de extinción y mucho más. Dian es conocida por cambiar la imagen que tenían los gorilas desde que la película *King Kong* los pintó como animales agresivos y salvajes. Sus estudios mostraron que, en realidad, son «animales pacíficos, gentiles, muy sociables y con fuertes lazos familiares», poniéndolos así en una buena posición frente a muchos hombres...

Mi argumento es que ella *aprendió* a amar a los gorilas. Cualquier persona que ama algo o a alguien comienza a amarlo por el conocimiento adquirido sobre aquello que ama. Hay quienes aman a los animales, otros a las estrellas y astros, unos terceros a los soldaditos de plomo, otros a la arquitectura... Pero todos comenzaron a amar a partir del estudio, del aprendizaje, del conocimiento de aquello o de aquellos a quienes aman. Nadie ama lo que no conoce.

Desgraciadamente, muchas parejas nunca han aprendido a amarse. Se unieron debido a un sentimiento, una pasión u otra circunstancia, pero no aprendieron a estudiarse, a explorarse el uno al otro y descubrir lo que los hace felices. Cuando no se conoce bien a la otra persona es imposible amarla. No se sabe lo que la agrada o irrita, cuáles son sus sueños y luchas, ni lo que piensa. Por eso, probablemente, se cometerán muchos errores en la relación, lo que generará incontables problemas. Estos problemas los alejarán, aunque estén casados y hayan estado enamorados un día.

Si usted se ha preguntado:

- ¿Acaso aún amo a mi marido/esposa?
- ¿Acaso me casé con la persona equivocada?
- ¿Por qué mi compañero es frío conmigo?
- ¿Por qué nos amamos, pero no soportamos estar juntos?
- ¿Cómo puedo tener la seguridad de que mi matrimonio va a durar?
- ¿Cómo convivir con una persona tan difícil?
- ¿Por qué nuestros problemas van y vuelven, cada vez peores?
- ¿El matrimonio es solo tristeza o algún día voy a tener alegría?

¡Anímese! Usted va a comenzar a aprender el amor inteligente y cómo ser feliz con su cónyuge aunque él/ella sea un King Kong...

LOS AUTORES

Cristiane y yo nos casamos en 1991 y tenemos un hijo adoptivo. Yo provenía de un hogar deshecho por la infidelidad y el divorcio. Mis padres fueron la razón de la indignación que sentí en mi vida cuando tenía trece años. En esa época, una serie de acontecimientos provocaron su separación, que fue muy traumática para mí. Sentí como si el mundo se hubiera caído sobre mi cabeza. Consideraba a mi padre mi héroe, pero supe que había traicionado a mi madre y me entró la desesperación. Pasé a cuestionar el porqué había sucedido todo aquello. Quería morir. Llevado por ese sufrimiento, conocí la fe y me convertí al Señor Jesús. Más tarde, esa fe también alcanzó a mis padres y ellos, después de muchos años de sufrimiento, pudieron restaurar sus vidas. Aprendí a no tener una fe religiosa, sino una fe que sirve para resolver problemas; por eso decidí dedicar mi vida a compartir lo que había aprendido, a ayudar a las personas a vencer sus dificultades. Yo no podía callarme aquello que, literalmente, salvó mi vida y la de mis padres.

Más tarde, me casé con Cristiane. Siendo ella hija de pastor, compartía conmigo los mismos objetivos. Teníamos todo lo necesario para encarar un matrimonio sin conflictos, pero no fue tan sencillo. Enfrentamos muchos problemas, de los cuales hablaremos más en el transcurso del libro.

Fortalecer matrimonios, educar parejas y solteros, luchar para que menos matrimonios terminen en divorcio, se convirtió en una misión en mi vida. Hoy sé que el dolor que sentí en mi adolescencia con la separación de mis padres, y más tarde en mi matrimonio, podría haber sido evitado. Si mis padres hubieran tenido acceso a la información que usted va a obtener en este libro, no habrían pasado por todo aquello. Si Cristiane y yo hubiéramos sabido antes de casarnos lo que usted va a leer aquí, no nos habríamos hecho sufrir el uno al otro.

Lamentablemente, las personas sufren por falta de conocimiento. Hoy en día existen escuelas para todo tipo de formación, pero no para matrimonios. Aún en el medio cristiano, hay mucha teoría sobre lo que es el amor, el noviazgo y el matrimonio, pero, en la práctica, las personas, –de forma general– no saben cómo actuar. Los conocimientos útiles y la educación matrimonial son raros. Por eso, he ahí la doble razón por la que nos dedicamos a transmitir esos conocimientos a las parejas: 1) para que los novios y recién casados eviten cometer los errores que pueden comprometer la relación y 2) para que quienes ya tienen un matrimonio turbio sepan cómo resolver los problemas y vivir felices.

Cristiane y yo hablamos, tanto a partir de las experiencias personales en nuestro matrimonio, como de los años como consejeros de parejas. En nuestro trabajo, hemos aconsejado a miles de parejas en cuatro continentes, desde adolescentes hasta sexagenarios (parece que después de los setenta las parejas se dan cuenta que la vida es muy corta para seguir discutiendo...). Y, debido a la demanda, nuestra labor con las parejas se ha intensificado mucho en los últimos años.

A finales de 2007, fuimos a trabajar a Texas, Estados Unidos. Fue allí donde nació el curso «Matrimonio blindado», cuyo resultado ha sido este libro. Allí nos sentimos estimulados a compartir nuestras experiencias debido al hecho tan alarmante de que, de cada diez matrimonios, casi seis acaban en divorcio.

Las parejas americanas que nos buscaban ya habían pasado por varias relaciones y continuaban con problemas. Muchos ya estaban en la tercera, cuarta, hasta quinta relación y, claramente, no estaban aprendiendo nada con el cambio de compañeros. Nos vimos en la obligación de ayudarlos, de transmitirles lo que aprendimos. Con los resultados obtenidos, nos dimos cuenta de que, a pesar de que somos conscientes de que nuestras experiencias y enseñanzas no son el descubrimiento de la pólvora, han sido un poder transformador en la vida de muchas parejas.

Creo que eso se debe a la combinación única de los factores que reunimos: 1) experiencia personal, 2) experiencia con miles de parejas en cuatro continentes, y 3) el uso de la inteligencia espiritual. Déjeme explicar brevemente este tercer factor.

El matrimonio fue idea de Dios. Fue Él quien decidió que el hombre y la mujer fueran «una sola carne». Además de eso, la Biblia dice que «Dios es amor»;[1] por lo tanto, si buscamos el mejor funcionamiento de la vida en pareja, es inteligente que volvamos a los orígenes donde todo comenzó y a la Fuente del amor. Por eso las enseñanzas que impartimos están fundamentadas en la inteligencia de Dios, en aquello que Él determinó que funciona. No quiere eso decir que este libro tenga por objetivo convertirle, en caso de que usted no sea una persona cristiana. No vamos tampoco a estar hablando de la Biblia todo el tiempo, aunque algunas veces, inevitablemente, hagamos referencia a ella. Quiero decir aquí abiertamente que, sin la base de los principios determinados por Dios para un buen matrimonio, sus esfuerzos por construir uno serán en vano. Hemos visto que las parejas que han abrazado ese hecho son las más felices y exitosas en sus esfuerzos por restaurar y mantener su matrimonio.

Un factor adicional del gran éxito de nuestras enseñanzas es que nosotros centramos nuestra ayuda en dos puntos principales: resolver

---

[1] 1 Juan 4:8.

los problemas y prevenir que acontezcan de nuevo. La mayoría de los problemas matrimoniales son recurrentes; por lo tanto, no basta que usted sepa resolver el problema de hoy, es necesario cortar el mal de raíz para que no surja de nuevo en el futuro. Estamos absolutamente convencidos de que si usted lee este libro con una mente abierta y está dispuesto a por lo menos intentar aplicar las herramientas que vamos a enseñarle aquí, tendrá un matrimonio sólido y muy feliz. Recuerde: de la práctica provienen los resultados.

P.D.: Algunos capítulos terminan con una sugerencia a través de una tarea para que usted aplique lo que ha aprendido. No subestime el poder de ejecutar estos ejercicios. Creemos que si usted va a leer este libro es para ver resultados y estos solo vienen cuando usted pone a prueba lo que ha aprendido. Es tan serio que le invitamos a hacer público su esfuerzo. Si usted está en una red social, comparta su compromiso a través de cada tarea para que otros le motiven en su jornada. ¿Qué tal comenzar ahora?

Publique en nuestra página www.facebook.com/MatrimonioBlindado para que podamos acompañar sus progresos (allí tenemos también videos para ayudarle en las tareas..., ¡revíselos!). En Twitter, no se olvide de añadir @matrimonioblind y el *hashtag* #matrimonioblindado.

/MatrimonioBlindado

Publique esto:
Comienzo hoy a
blindar mi matrimonio.

@matrimonioblind

Tuitee esto:
Comienzo hoy a
blindar mi matrimonio
#matrimonioblindado
@matrimonioblind

PARTE I

ENTENDIENDO AL MATRIMONIO

CAPÍTULO 1
POR QUÉ BLINDAR SU MATRIMONIO

Algunos diputados mexicanos, preocupados con el aumento de divorcios en el país, propusieron una ley: el matrimonio renovable. Creían haber encontrado la solución ideal para evitar las graves crisis conyugales, infidelidades y todos los inconvenientes del divorcio. Cada dos años, la pareja podría evaluar la relación y decidir si querían continuar juntos y renovar el matrimonio o si preferían desistir y seguir cada uno por su lado. Además de la firma de un contrato temporal, la propuesta planteaba también que los novios podrían protejerse contra un hipotético divorcio. Para ello, decidirían, antes de casarse, quién se quedará con la custodia de los niños y cuánto pagaría cada uno de pensión alimenticia, en caso de separación. La propuesta, que plantea el Congreso, tiene un gran apoyo entre los mexicanos que quieren acabar con los altos costos de las separaciones y de las pensiones alimenticias. Al fin y al cabo, las estadísticas en la ciudad de México son poco alentadoras respecto al matrimonio: cinco de cada diez uniones terminan en divorcio.

Si la ley se retomara y aprobara en el futuro, una conversación como esta entre los alumnos en el colegio no sería ficción:

—¿Y dónde vas a pasar las vacaciones? –pregunta un joven a un compañero.

—Bueno, depende. Si mi padre renueva el contrato con mi madre, a fin de año iremos a Disneylandia. Si no, voy a tener que ver cuál de los dos se quedará conmigo y, por las notas que estoy sacando, probablemente me van a mandar a casa de mi abuela.

No quiero ser portador de malas noticias, pero aquí está un hecho: el matrimonio como institución está fallando bajo los pesados ataques de varias fuerzas de la sociedad. Lo que se estaba proponiendo en México es tan solo un síntoma de lo que los gobernantes están intentando hacer para lidiar con el alto número de divorcios. Y no es solo allí. No conozco un solo caso en ningún país, cultura o sociedad en el mundo donde el matrimonio esté siendo fortalecido, ni siquiera en las culturas tradicionales y sumamente religiosas. En Estados Unidos, el gran dictador de la cultura para el resto del mundo, la mayoría de los bebés nacidos de mujeres de hasta treinta años de edad ya nacen fuera del matrimonio. Renombrados sociólogos americanos también argumentan que la figura del padre no es necesaria en una familia.

¿Se da cuenta de hacia dónde estamos yendo?

Incluso donde los índices de divorcio publicados son más bajos, solo apenas esconden una realidad: menos personas se están casando, pues optan por la «unión libre» y por eso cuando se separan no se registra como divorcio. Muchos de los que se mantienen en la relación –por falta de opciones o por fuertes presiones religiosas– siguen siendo infelices.

Cuando veo esta realidad me quedo pensando en cómo estarán las cosas de aquí a cinco, diez o veinte años. ¿La extinción del matrimonio será consumada? ¿Las personas todavía creerán que el matrimonio para toda la vida es posible? ¿Serán los conceptos de fidelidad conyugal y lealtad a una sola persona, aspectos tan solo de museos y de películas históricas?

Aquí va una alerta para los que todavía no se han despertado: las fuerzas de la sociedad conspiran contra el matrimonio y la familia, y sus ataques son cada vez más fuertes.

LA METAMORFOSIS DEL MATRIMONIO

Los medios de comunicación en general (películas, novelas, internet, libros, etc.), la cultura, la política, las leyes, las celebridades, la enseñanza en los colegios y universidades, en fin, todos los mayores poderes de influencia en la sociedad están volviéndose (o ya son) predominantemente anti-matrimonio.

¿Qué significa esto en la práctica?
- El número de matrimonios disminuirá considerablemente.
- La «unión libre» o «estable», marcada por un concepto de que el compromiso duradero y absoluto no es posible, será más y más común.
- La infidelidad y las traiciones aumentarán (sí, aún más) y se harán más tolerables.
- Los encuentros casuales con terceros solo para fines sexuales serán más aceptados.
- Hombres y mujeres se volverán aún más 'depredadores'.
- El hombre será más prescindible para las mujeres, quienes se verán más independientes.
- Las mujeres oscilarán entre la incredulidad total en el amor (y en los hombres) y la búsqueda de la felicidad, a costa de su propia devaluación.

Nota: todo lo arriba indicado YA ESTÁ sucediendo en nuestra sociedad. Es la metamorfosis del matrimonio y el tiempo solo continuará acelerando ese proceso.

Tal vez usted no pueda hacer nada para cambiar esa situación en el mundo; pero en *su* mundo, en *su* matrimonio, usted puede, y debe. No es una cuestión de *si* su relación podrá ser atacada y sí de *cuándo*.

La pregunta es: ¿sabrá cómo protegerla de los ataques cuando vengan? Si no es que ya están sucediendo.

EL MATRIMONIO EN LA ERA DE FACEBOOK

Nuevos desafíos como internet, por ejemplo, las redes sociales, las tecnologías de la comunicación como SMS y MSN, la proliferación de la pornografía, la cultura anti-matrimonio, la facilidad del divorcio o el avance de la mujer en la sociedad, son solo algunos fenómenos recientes que están afectando a las parejas del siglo XXI. Y muchos no están preparados para lidiar con estos nuevos desafíos. Las parejas de hoy están enfrentando una nueva realidad, un mundo que sus padres no conocieron; de hecho, ninguna generación anterior a esta lo conoció. Pregúntele a su abuela cuáles eran las señales que buscaría para detectar si su marido estaba teniendo una aventura y, probablemente, le dirá que estaría atenta a las manchas de lápiz labial en la ropa, al olor de perfume de mujer y cosas de ese tipo. Hoy en día, traicionar al compañero es mucho más fácil.

Mark Zuckerberg, creador de Facebook, es uno de los mayores 'destructores de hogares' en Gran Bretaña. Según un estudio divulgado por la web especializada en divorcios Divorce-Online, Facebook es citado como el motivo de la separación en una de cada tres separaciones en el país. Cerca de mil 700 de los 5 mil casos mencionaron que los mensajes inadecuados a personas del sexo opuesto y comentarios de ex novias(os) en Facebook fueron causa de problemas en el matrimonio. En Estados Unidos, la Asociación Americana de Abogados Matrimoniales (American Academy of Matrimonial Lawyers) divulgó, en 2011, que Facebook es citado en uno de cada cinco divorcios.

Para tener una idea de la gravedad de la situación, se lanzó recientemente en Brasil una red social exclusiva para personas casadas que «viven un matrimonio sin sexo y quieren encontrar a otras personas en la misma situación». Hombres y mujeres comprometidos son el blanco de la web que facilita una «manera discreta de tener una aventura». En menos de seis meses, la web ya tenía más de trescientos mil usuarios en el país, haciendo de Brasil el segundo país en número de usuarios, por detrás solamente de Estados Unidos, donde la web ya existe desde hace algunos años. La web ofrece una cuenta de email privada y cobro con tarjeta de crédito sin que aparezca el nombre en el extracto, todo para facilitar los encuentros sexuales casuales, sin dejar vestigios para el compañero traicionado. Su eslogan es: «El verdadero secreto para un matrimonio duradero es la infidelidad». En España, páginas como Ashley Madison o Victoria Milan también están en auge.

Insólito, ¿verdad? Pues eso no es nada.

¿Sabe cuál es el negocio que más crece en el mundo, con una facturación mayor que Google, Apple, Amazon, Netflix, eBay, Microsoft y Yahoo juntas? Se llama pornografía. En 2006, las rentas de esta industria fueron 97.060 millones de dólares. Las películas pornográficas se producen en todo el mundo en mayor número que las de cualquier otro género, con gran diferencia. Son en promedio 37 películas por día, más de 13.500 por año. Brasil es el segundo mayor productor de esas películas, por detrás de Estados Unidos. Un estudio informó que siete de cada diez hombres de entre dieciocho y treinta y cuatro años visitan webs pornográficas en internet. Las mujeres, antiguamente más reservadas con ese tipo de actividad, tienden cada vez más a recurrir a la pornografía, muchas para intentar agradar al compañero. «Ah, pero, gracias a Dios, nosotros somos cristianos y eso no nos afecta». No se precipite.

Una investigación entre cristianos en Estados Unidos reveló que un 50 % de los hombres y un 20 % de las mujeres tienen el vicio de la pornografía. Otra investigación, solamente entre pastores, reveló que un 54 % habían visto pornografía en los últimos doce meses y un 30 % en los últimos treinta días anteriores a la investigación. ¿Quién está inmune?

HOMBRE VS. MUJER: LA BATALLA FINAL

Los hombres, por primera vez en la historia de su especie, están sintiéndose desubicados y perdidos dentro del matrimonio. Con el avance de la mujer, en casi todas las áreas de la sociedad, esta se ha convertido en rival del hombre, en lugar de ocupar su tradicional papel de auxiliadora. El hombre era el exclusivo cazador, proveedor y protector de la familia; ahora, ve su papel dividido y, muchas veces, suplantado por la mujer. Ella se ha convertido también en cazadora.

La mayoría de las mujeres, actualmente, trabajan y contribuyen a la economía del hogar. En muchos casos, la mujer incluso gana más que el marido, y esta tendencia aumentará, teniendo en cuenta que, en muchas facultades, ya hay más mujeres estudiantes que hombres.

¿Qué es lo que esto ha causado en el matrimonio? He aquí algunas consecuencias: la mujer se ha vuelto más independiente y menos tolerante con las peculiaridades masculinas, tomando decisiones sin tenerlo en cuenta y provocando el «choque» con él; el hombre, en un intento de agradar a la mujer, se ha vuelto más sensible, desplazándose de su lugar en el matrimonio, sintiéndose despreciado por la mujer y, a veces, desechable. Es decir, la mujer se ha vuelto más como el hombre y el hombre más como la mujer. Desorden y confusión total de los papeles.

Y no es solo en el campo laboral donde la mujer ha avanzado y competido con el hombre. Un estudio de la Universidad de São Paulo reveló un dato preocupante para los hombres casados. La infidelidad femenina está creciendo aterradoramente y, cuanto más joven se es, más se traiciona. De las 8.200 mujeres entrevistadas en diez capitales del país, apenas el 22 % de las mayores de setenta años confesaron haber tenido alguna relación extramatrimonial. El índice sube al 35 % para las mujeres entre cuarenta y uno y cincuenta años y asciende al 49,5 % entre las de dieciocho a veinticinco años. Es decir, la mitad de las jóvenes casadas traicionan a su marido. La salida de la mujer de simple ama de casa hacia un papel más activo en la sociedad, en la facultad, en el trabajo..., ha facilitado situaciones que hacen proliferar la infidelidad.

Además de todo esto, hay que añadir el flujo constante de mensajes directos y subliminales en nuestros medios atacando las bases del matrimonio: telenovelas, películas, revistas, blogs, noticias, moda, música, grupos y fiestas «culturales»..., todos estos cañones apuntando y disparando sin tregua: ¿para qué casarme? Un pedazo de papel no va a marcar la diferencia... Se juntan pero no se unen de verdad... Si no sale bien, se divorcian y se casan con otro... Tanto el hombre como la mujer hacen lo mismo... No existe el amor, el amor es fantasía. El matrimonio es una prisión... ¿Cómo se puede aguantar a la misma persona veinte, treinta, cincuenta años? No, el matrimonio es cosa del pasado...

Cada día se crea un nuevo argumento derogatorio y anti matrimonio.

Si aprecia su relación y no quiere convertirse en una estadística más, blinde su matrimonio, es fundamental para su supervivencia. Es hora de defender y proteger su mayor inversión antes de que sea demasiado tarde. Vamos a luchar.

Si está realmente empeñado en blindar su matrimonio, entonces comience a seguir los consejos y tareas que le vamos a recomendar en este libro.

TAREA

¿Cuáles son los peligros que amenazan a su matrimonio actualmente? Identifique esas amenazas para tener en mente qué áreas de su vida necesitará fortalecer con mayor urgencia.

¡Espere! Antes de escribir su tarea aquí, piense si tal vez va a prestar este libro a alguien después de leerlo. Imagino que no va a querer que otros sepan sus reflexiones y luchas en su matrimonio... Una sugerencia es que apunte sus tareas en otro lugar, como una agenda, un diario o la computadora. Haga lo que mejor le parezca, yo simplemente he pensado que podría tener esto en cuenta.

/MatrimonioBlindado

Publique esto:
Identifiqué las actuales amenazas en mi matrimonio.

@matrimonioblind

Tuitee esto:
Identifiqué las actuales amenazas en mi matrimonio #matrimonioblindado @matrimonioblind

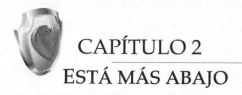

CAPÍTULO 2
ESTÁ MÁS ABAJO

Si yo fuese una mosca en la pared de su living o de su habitación cuando usted y su pareja estuviesen discutiendo algún problema, ¿qué vería? Tal vez una frialdad a la hora de hablar, groserías, un tono de rabia en las palabras, irritación, uno interrumpiendo al otro, acusaciones, críticas y cosas así. Un día ustedes discuten sobre la disciplina de los hijos, otro día sobre por qué el marido acepta a su ex novia en su Facebook, otro día sobre la interferencia de la suegra en el matrimonio. La cuestión es que el verdadero problema no es aquello que usted ve, el problema está más abajo.

El marido tiene un vicio, por ejemplo. La esposa lo ve en aquel vicio y piensa que aquello es el problema. Ella se irrita, lo critica, intenta conversar y pedirle que cambie, pero no cambia. ¿Por qué? Porque el vicio no es el problema. Hay una raíz, algo más profundo que causa aquel vicio. Ella no sabe lo que es y posiblemente ni él. Pero los dos discuten en círculo sobre aquello que ellos ven.

Los problemas visibles son como las hojas, ramas y tronco de un árbol; en cambio, las verdaderas causas son menos aparentes, difíciles de detectar y entender. Sin embargo, la única razón de que los problemas que se ven existan es la raíz que los alimenta. Si no hubiese raíz, el árbol no existiría.

Cuando usted descubra la raíz de los problemas en su matrimonio, entenderá por qué su pareja y usted hacen lo que hacen. La lucha contra las hojas y las ramas de los problemas disminuirá –y mucho– así como también será amenizado el ambiente desagradable que acostumbra a formarse entre ustedes. ¡La eliminación de apenas una mala raíz podrida dará como resultado la solución de muchos de los problemas de una sola vez, y de forma permanente! Así es el poder del cambio de objetivo. Saber concentrar su atención y energía en el verdadero problema puede transformar su matrimonio, pues todo, incluso nuestro comportamiento, depende de cómo miramos, hacia dónde miramos y cómo interpretamos lo que miramos.

Stephen Covey menciona un acontecimiento en su vida a través del cual aprendió la importancia de esto.

Cuenta que un día estaba en el metro, sentado, leyendo tranquilamente su periódico. El vagón no estaba lleno, todo estaba tranquilo y había algunos asientos vacíos. En una de las estaciones, entró un padre con dos hijos muy traviesos y se sentó junto a él. Los niños no paraban, saltaban, corrían de allá para acá, hablaban alto, e inmediatamente acabaron con la paz que había en el vagón. El padre, sentado con los ojos cerrados, parecía no prestar atención a lo que estaba sucediendo. Covey entonces no resistió la indiferencia del padre e, irritado, le miró y le preguntó por qué no hacía algo para controlar a sus hijos. El padre, como dándose cuenta de la situación por primera vez, respondió: «Es verdad, discúlpeme, acabamos de salir del hospital porque su madre acaba de fallecer. Yo no sé qué hacer y parece que ellos tampoco lo saben...». Covey se disculpó y empezó a consolar al hombre. Inmediatamente, toda su irritación en contra del padre de los niños desapareció y dio lugar a la empatía.

Pero ¿qué transformó el comportamiento anteriormente irritado de Covey? Fue la manera en la que pasó a mirar la situación. Antes de recibir la información del padre, Covey solo veía la escena a través del lente de sus propios valores y principios. «¿Cómo puede un padre permitir que sus hijos sean tan maleducados? Si fuesen *mis* hijos...» Pero después de la información, su manera de ver lo cambió todo. Dese cuenta que no hubo alteración en las personas: ni los niños pararon de comportarse mal ni el padre los controló. Solo la óptica de la situación cambió, y con ella el comportamiento de Covey.

Así también sucede en el matrimonio. Juzgamos al otro, exigimos que él cambie, porque lo vemos con la lente de nuestras experiencias, valores y conceptos. Pero todo ese conflicto ocurre porque no entendemos, ni prestamos atención a lo que realmente está detrás de cada situación. Por eso, una de las primeras actitudes que usted tiene que adoptar para transformar la realidad de su matrimonio es cambiar su percepción de las cosas, hacia dónde mira, cómo mira y cómo interpreta lo que ve. El desafío es saber hacia dónde mirar, pues no siempre la raíz es tan fácil de identificar. Déjeme ayudarle, usando otra analogía.

UNA SOLA CARNE, DOS CONJUNTOS DE PROBLEMAS

Cuando dos personas se casan, ambas llevan al matrimonio sus propios problemas y cuestiones personales. Lo que usted no ve en la invitación a la boda son cosas como esta:

«Juan, adicto a la pornografía, fue víctima de *bullying* cuando era niño, extremadamente inseguro, se va a casar con María, de la que abusaron en la infancia, una bomba de tiempo ambulante dispuesta a cualquier cosa para salir de la casa de sus padres».

El historial de los novios no viene escrito en la invitación de matrimonio, es más, en ningún lugar. Pero nadie se casa sin llevar su equipaje dentro del matrimonio. Por ejemplo, en el caso de este matrimonio, Juan y María, ¿se puede imaginar uno cómo será el futuro de esta unión?

En el día de su boda usted conoce entre el 10 y el 20 % de la persona con la que se está casando, en la mejor de las hipótesis, y la mayor parte que usted conoce es apenas el lado bueno. Esto es porque la mayoría de nosotros sabemos esconder muy bien nuestros defectos cuando estamos saliendo como novios. Digo «esconder» no porque queramos intencionadamente engañar a la otra persona, sino que es un proceso natural de la conquista. Forma parte del cortejo intentar con todas sus fuerzas dar una buena impresión de sí mismo a la otra persona. Usted siempre se viste con la mejor ropa, mide sus palabras, se aparta para soltar gases, sale para comer en un restaurante... De hecho, la cena típica de un restaurante ilustra bien este punto.

Él escoge el restaurante que a usted le gusta, se sientan a la mesa y piden la comida. Entre miradas de admiración uno por el otro, sobran elogios para el cabello, la ropa, y los dos aprovechan aquel momento al máximo. Al final, él paga la cuenta sin protestar, y claro, ustedes salen felices.

Después de casados, la escena cambia un poquito. La cena es en la mesa de la cocina, sin muchos detalles. Él comenta algo sobre que el arroz no está de la manera que le gusta; y usted, por primera vez, se da cuenta de que él hace un ruido irritante con la boca cuando mastica..., sin contar otros ruidos acompañados de olores no tan agradables. Al terminar, usted se da cuenta de que ni siquiera lleva el plato hasta la tarja, mucho menos lo lava..., y es entonces cuando se pregunta: «¿Cómo es que me casé con esta cosa?».

¡Bienvenidos al matrimonio! Ahora es cuando comienzan a conocerse de verdad. Y con el conocimiento de este «nuevo lado» del matrimonio, surgen los problemas.

Por esta razón, yo insisto en que en el noviazgo sean muy transparentes y abiertos respecto a sus personalidades y pasado, con el fin de disminuir las sorpresas más adelante. No se queden encantados con la otra persona como si tuviese solo el lado bueno. El noviazgo es un periodo para descubrir todo sobre la persona con quien se va a casar. Cosas como el pasado del pretendiente, la familia, cómo fue criado, la relación que tenía con los padres, etcétera.

El matrimonio no es el lugar, ni el tiempo, para sorpresas sobre la otra persona. No es después de seis meses de casados cuando la esposa quiere descubrir por la ex novia del marido que él tiene un hijo. No es en la luna de miel cuando la mujer debe explicar al marido que, debido a un abuso que sufrió en la infancia, tiene dificultades para entregarse sexualmente. Cuanto más sepan el uno del otro, menos oportunidad habrá de sorpresas desagradables.

Una vez aconsejamos a un joven que nos buscó determinado a dejar a su esposa, tras unas semanas de casado. La razón que dio fue que había descubierto en la luna de miel que ella no era virgen, como le había hecho creer. Él se sentía traicionado porque ella había omitido ese hecho y también tenía dificultades para superar el dolor emocional de pensar que ella había tenido relaciones sexuales con otros hombres. Lo que para muchos puede parecer una tontería, para él fue razón suficiente para contemplar la separación. Costó mucho convencerlo para que la perdonara y venciera las emociones negativas. Ellos permanecieron casados, pero los primeros años de su matrimonio estuvieron marcados por serios problemas.

No es que el pasado negativo de alguien sea motivo para que usted no se case con él o ella. Quien no tiene esqueletos en el armario, que tire la primera piedra... Pero es imprescindible que usted sea consciente de que su pasado puede afectar el presente y el futuro.

Considere, por ejemplo, cuánto un marido, cuya esposa sufrió abusos sexuales cuando era niña, tendrá que ser paciente y comprensivo con ella. Para saber cómo tendrá que lidiar con eso, él tiene que ser consciente de toda la situación.

Cuando dos personas se casan, el pasado de ambas se junta. Y son ellos, esos pasados, los que determinan el comportamiento de cada uno dentro del matrimonio. Por eso, usted no puede mirar solamente hacia la persona con la que está hoy, aunque ya lleven años de casados. Usted tiene que saber quién es esa persona desde su raíz, de dónde vino, quién es, cuáles son sus circunstancias y las personas que la influenciaron e hicieron de ella la persona que hoy es, y todo lo que contribuyó a eso. Solamente así podrá entender bien la situación y cómo actuar con eficacia.

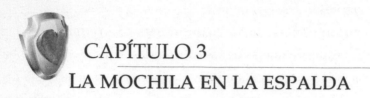

CAPÍTULO 3
LA MOCHILA EN LA ESPALDA

Imagínese esto: el novio y la novia están en el altar de la iglesia, vestidos debidamente delante de los invitados. El oficiante conduce la ceremonia. En la espalda de cada uno de los prometidos, por encima del vestido blanco de ella y del traje alquilado de él, hay una mochila grande y pesada. Dentro de la mochila de cada uno está todo su pasado, el equipaje que están introduciendo en el matrimonio, cuyo contenido ambos comenzarán a descubrir en breve: la crianza y las enseñanzas que absorbieron de los padres, las experiencias antiguas, los traumas, el miedo al rechazo, las inseguridades, las expectativas... Por eso, quien todavía se está preparando para casarse debe actuar como un guarda de seguridad de aeropuerto: «¡Abra la maleta, quiero ver lo que lleva adentro!».

He visto a muchas parejas que decían: «Tu pasado no me interesa, yo solo quiero saber de nosotros de aquí en adelante». Por supuesto que suena muy romántico, pero esa actitud no impedirá que ambos introduzcan el pasado en la relación presente. Su pasado forma parte de usted, es imposible librarse de él. Pero sí es posible aprender a lidiar con él, sea lo que sea. Sin embargo, si no conocen el pasado el uno del otro, ¿cómo sabrán actuar cuando surja más adelante, cuando estén casados?

Permita que le demos un ejemplo personal de cómo al principio del matrimonio ese equipaje afecta a la pareja.

5.6 SEGUNDOS DE LIBERTAD

Cuando Cristiane y yo nos casamos, comenzamos a tener problemas debido a la falta de atención que ella sufría por mi parte y las consecuentes exigencias que ella me hacía. Seis días a la semana yo iba temprano al trabajo y regresaba muy tarde, cansado e incluso trayendo trabajo extra para terminar en casa. El sábado, nuestro supuesto día de descanso, yo volvía voluntariamente al trabajo por lo menos media jornada de mañana. Por ser muy joven, queriendo afirmarme en mi trabajo, entendía que necesitaba dedicarme a ello.

Continué trabajando como cuando estaba soltero, pero no era consciente de que ahora tenía una esposa. No tenía ningún equilibrio en relación con el trabajo y la familia. Cristiane se quedaba en casa la mayor parte del tiempo, y cuando yo llegaba por la noche, ella venía con aquella preguntita: «¿Cómo fue tu día?». La última cosa de la que yo quería hablar a aquellas horas era sobre mi día, pues estaba exhausto. Entonces yo respondía con dos palabras: «Fue bueno». Ella, insatisfecha, insistía: «¿Pasó algo?». Y yo le daba tres palabras más: «No, todo normal». Obviamente (no tan obvio para mí por aquel entonces), ella se sentía excluida de mi vida. Unido al hecho de que yo solo quería saber de comer, terminar algún trabajo que había traído para hacer en casa, y después caerme muerto de sueño en la cama. He ahí una receta perfecta para una esposa infeliz.

Pero eso era solo durante la semana. El sábado era peor. Mi querida esposa pensaba: «Bueno, por lo menos el sábado vamos a salir». ¡Qué lástima! Como el principal día de la semana en mi trabajo era el domingo, mi preocupación el sábado era planear y dejar listo todo para el día siguiente.

El poco tiempo que quedaba por la tarde y noche del sábado, yo quería solo descansar; sin embargo, ella quería ir al cine, pasear. Y como durante la semana no daba tanta importancia a mi falta de atención, el sábado estaba más decidida: «¿Adónde vamos a salir hoy? ¿Vamos a ver una película? ¿Vamos a almorzar afuera? ¿Vamos a llamar a unos amigos para salir juntos?».Y yo, con «aquella» cara, decía: «¿Tú estás loca? ¿Es que no entiendes que este es el único momento que tengo para quedarme en casa y descansar?». Creía que era muy pesada, que no me entendía. Mi defensa era: «Tú sabías cuál era mi carga horaria antes de casarnos, siempre fue así, estás creando un problema por nada». Realmente, mis días y horarios de trabajo no habían cambiado. Solo que yo me olvidaba de que cuando éramos novios, yo sacaba tiempo el sábado por la tarde para salir con ella. En realidad, el que había cambiado era yo.

Cristiane:

Soy hija de pastor. Mi vida consistía en estar en casa o en la iglesia. Cuando me casé, a los diecisiete años, fue como si mi mano derecha estuviera esposada a la izquierda de mi padre y allí, en el altar, él abriese la esposa de la muñeca y la colocase en la muñeca de Renato, y la cerrase de nuevo y le entregara la llave a él.

Fueron 5,6 segundos de libertad cronometrados... Claro, en el momento no parecía eso. Yo pensaba que, cuando me casase, todo cambiaría en mi vida, porque, cuando éramos novios, salíamos a pasear, Renato me llamaba siempre, dedicaba un día exclusivamente para mí, era muy romántico, vivía escribiéndome cartas de amor, es decir, yo me sentía dueña de la situación...

Sin embargo, mis expectativas se fueron por el desagüe. En primer lugar, ni bien nos casamos, Renato fue trasladado a Nueva York; allí yo estaba lejos de mi familia y de todas mis amigas. Vivíamos a una hora de distancia de su trabajo, lo que restaba un poco más del escaso tiempo que pasábamos juntos.

Siguiendo el ejemplo de mi madre, yo quería ser una buena esposa para Renato, hacerlo muy feliz. Me dedicaba mucho al hogar, cuidaba su ropa prácticamente todo el día, cocinaba diariamente algo nuevo y siempre me esforzaba en estar bien arreglada para cuando llegara por la noche a casa. Pero todo eso era difícil, pues yo era muy joven y acababa de salir de la escuela. La comida no me salía bien, planchaba sus camisas de lino tres veces y, aun así, no quedaban bien, los productos de limpieza dañaban mi piel..., y al final, pensaba: «Renato va a llegar más tarde y va a valorar todo mi sacrificio». Pero ¡nada que ver!, no se daba cuenta de nada.

Renato fue mi primer novio y era todo lo que siempre soñé. Pero yo hice de mi matrimonio un problema. Comencé a entristecerme, a reclamar, a llorar y a exigir mucho. Y él siempre decía que él era así y que yo debía aprender a convivir con su forma de ser, que debía adaptarme a aquella vida... Yo solo salía para ir a la iglesia los miércoles y viernes por la noche. ¡Eran los días más especiales de la semana! No es de extrañar que las demás noches, cuando él llegaba a casa, yo lo esperase ansiosamente: era el único amigo que tenía para conversar. Pero él no se daba cuenta de mi necesidad y no decía nada. Llegué al punto de creer que mi marido ya no me amaba.

A causa de mi inexperiencia, por ser muy joven y nunca antes haber tenido otra relación, todo era motivo de desconfianza. A veces llegaba a la iglesia, veía a Renato aconsejando a una mujer (eso formaba parte de su trabajo), y sentía celos. «¿Cómo puede prestar tanta atención a esa persona que ni conoce y yo, que soy su esposa y hago todo por él, ni se entera que existo?». Le hacía ese tipo de comentarios y ya está; mi marido se encerraba en sí mismo aún más. Me daba el famoso «tratamiento de silencio» que a veces duraba tres días. Con todo el mundo conversaba con normalidad, sonreía, pero conmigo..., era como si yo no existiera. Aquello, obviamente, no me ayudaba a lidiar con todas las inseguridades que había llevado al matrimonio, al contrario, solo aumentaba aún más nuestro problema.

Mi educación fue muy diferente de la que tuvo él. En mi familia hablábamos abiertamente de todo lo que sentíamos ante cualquier situación. Yo hacía lo mismo en casa con Renato, pero él, en lugar de enfadarse conmigo, mandarme a volar y después volver a la normalidad, simplemente no decía nada, me lanzaba aquella mirada de desprecio y dejaba de hablar conmigo durante varios días. Esa diferencia en la forma de lidiar con nuestros problemas empeoraba aún más los conflictos, pues además de las dificultades del trabajo —debido a sus responsabilidades—, cuando llegaba a casa, él enfrentaba otras. Por ser todo eso algo novedoso para mí y debido a no tener a nadie con quien conversar, yo quería encontrar en él un amigo, pero solo conseguía un marido fracasado, que me consideraba una pesada.

Solamente cuando yo cambié y dejé de reclamar su atención, vi el resultado. Él pasó a hacer lo que a mí me gustaba y agradaba sin que yo tuviera que pedírselo. Hoy conversamos bastante, somos nuestros mejores amigos y nos sentimos realizados el uno con el otro. Pero solo conseguimos eso cuando aprendimos a lidiar con el equipaje el uno del otro.

Yo me daba cuenta de sus celos y me quedaba irritado, pero no conseguía descubrir la raíz de ese sentimiento. No tenía ni idea de lo que ella traía en el equipaje. Así que, cuando ella reclamaba, presionaba o acusaba de algo, yo me cerraba a cualquier discusión. Fue en ese momento cuando ella comenzó a conocer un poquito de mi equipaje también.

Crecí viendo a mi padre lidiar con los problemas entre él y mi madre cerrándose con ella. Toda mi infancia fue así. Si mi madre hacía algo que lo disgustaba, mi padre la «castigaba» a través de su indiferencia. Dos, tres, cinco días. El periodo más largo, créalo si quiere, fue de ocho meses.

Si ser indiferente fuera un deporte de competición, mi padre sería el campeón y *recordman* único...

Yo odiaba aquello. Veía a ambos callados el uno con el otro, mi madre intentando hacer las paces, buscando agradarlo, y él atado a lo que había sucedido, que casi siempre era una tontería. Aquello creaba un ambiente horrible también para nosotros, los cuatro hijos. Yo me decía a mí mismo que cuando me casase, jamás sería así.

Sin embargo, cuando me casé, hacía exactamente lo mismo con Cristiane. En definitiva, la experiencia es mejor profesora que la teoría. Yo sabía que lo que estaba haciendo estaba mal, pero en la práctica solo sabía hacer aquello que había visto durante toda mi infancia y juventud. Era el peso de mi mochila.

EXCESO DE EQUIPAJE

La verdad es que nosotros hacemos solamente lo que aprendemos. Yo no tenía una referencia mejor que aquella. Usted acaba repitiendo los errores de sus padres, pues su comportamiento (no las palabras) fue su escuela. No me gustaba ser así, pero era como si ya estuviese programado para actuar como mi padre. Aunque Cristiane me pidiera disculpas, yo no cambiaba mi comportamiento.

En el matrimonio, tenemos que desaprender las cosas malas para, después, aprender las cosas buenas. Tenemos que identificar los malos hábitos, aquello que no funciona, y eliminarlos de nuestro comportamiento, desarrollando mejores hábitos. Reconocer eso es muy doloroso, pero es imprescindible para el cambio.

Como puede ver, ya desde el principio de nuestro matrimonio Cristiane y yo tuvimos muchos problemas, debido a los equipajes que traíamos con nosotros. Yo no era una mala persona, tampoco ella; pero la mezcla de nuestro equipaje no resultó positiva. Así sucede en todos los matrimonios. Todo ser humano lleva en su equipaje un conjunto de principios, valores, experiencias, cultura, visión del mundo, opiniones, hábitos, pasado, traumas, influencias de la familia, escuela o amigos, sueños y mucho más.

Cuando dos personas se juntan, a través del matrimonio, la mayor parte de sus problemas provienen de las cosas que traen en su equipaje, que pelean entre sí. Por lo tanto, conocer a la otra persona profundamente, descubrir sus raíces, es fundamental para comprender el porqué de este o aquel comportamiento. Es más: conocerse y entenderse a uno mismo es igualmente esencial, pues eso le ayudará a buscar maneras de lidiar con sus propias raíces y, así, resolver las diferencias y conflictos.

Fue eso lo que sucedió conmigo y con Cristiane. Años más tarde, pude darme cuenta de nuestros equipajes y entender por qué nos comportábamos de aquella manera. Ella llevaba en su equipaje altas expectativas de la familia perfecta con la que creció; la imagen del padre ejemplar, la inseguridad de no haber tenido nunca un novio (en cambio, yo venía de un noviazgo roto); la infancia y la adolescencia sin prácticamente nada de diversión ni vida social. Todo esto explicaba por qué Cristiane esperaba tanto de mí, tenía celos de mujeres por quien nunca me interesé, exigía mi atención y valoraba mucho salir a pasear.

LOS OPUESTOS SE REPELEN

Lo interesante es que su equipaje chocaba frontalmente con el mío. Es típico de los matrimonios: los polos opuestos se atraen pero, después de casarse, se repelen..., enloquecen el uno al otro.

Mi familia era considerablemente diferente a la de ella. En casa éramos tres hermanos y una hermana. Nosotros no tratábamos a la niña así, cómo decirlo... con tanta delicadeza. Éramos brutos. Mi madre, siempre sirviéndonos a mi padre y a nosotros, raramente exigía algo para sí misma. Vivía para él y para sus hijos. Y mi padre... bueno, ya dije cómo era. Tener el conjunto de eso como fondo me hacía ver a Cristiane un poco ingenua, muy exigente, pegajosa, reclamando teniéndolo todo, un chicle en mi pelo. Yo tenía la imagen de una mujer fuerte, grabada en mi mente por lo que conocía de mi madre, una mujer que aguantaba todo, y eso no me ayudaba en la percepción de mi mujer. Esa era la razón de que tratase a Cristiane tan fría y duramente.

Otro pedacito de mi equipaje: yo crecí en medio de mujeres. Tenía una hermana, primas, muchas tías, amigas en la vecindad, amigas en la escuela, amigas en la iglesia, novias por aquí y por allá. No veía ninguna diferencia entre tener amigos y amigas. Después de casado, esto no ayudó a la inseguridad de Cristiane. Tampoco mi manera fría de ser con ella. Esto explica sus celos.

Y en casa, siempre fuimos una familia con mucho trabajo. Mi padre se levantaba a las cinco de la mañana incluso los domingos. A los doce años, él nos indujo a mi hermano mayor y a mí a trabajar. El trabajo duro siempre estuvo en nuestra sangre. Cuando comencé a trabajar en la iglesia, antes de casarme, ese concepto aumentó, pues ahora no era por dinero y sí para ayudar a otras personas. Sumado al hecho de que me casé con una hija de pastor, yo pensaba que ella comprendería muy bien mi entrega al trabajo. Sin embargo, estaba volviendo loca a Cristiane. Ella no me entendía, ni yo a ella. Y vivimos años intentando cambiarnos el uno al otro en vano.

¿Cuándo y cómo superamos nuestras diferencias? Solamente cuando comprendimos lo que estaba detrás de nuestro comportamiento e hicimos ajustes para lidiar con la raíz de cada conflicto.

Yo entendí que el problema que ella tenía de sospechas y celos era también responsabilidad mía. No podía hacerla cambiar, pero podía reducir las razones que yo le daba para alimentar su inseguridad. Vi que podía ayudarla a tener más confianza en ella misma y en mí. Dejé de discutir y culparla por los celos, comencé a apartarme de mis amigas mujeres y a limitar el contacto solo a lo necesario. Puse distancia y aprovechaba cualquier oportunidad para hacerle sentir la seguridad de que era la única mujer de mi vida. Mi objetivo pasó a ser transmitir seguridad a mi esposa.

ATENCIÓN AL SEXO OPUESTO

Dicho sea de paso, muchos matrimonios tienen dificultades para tomar esta decisión. No quieren dejar las amistades que ejercen una influencia negativa sobre el matrimonio. Como regla general, aprendí que no es aconsejable que el hombre casado tenga amistades femeninas muy íntimas, ni que la mujer tenga tales amigos. Mantener amistades muy cercanas con el sexo opuesto es jugar con fuego. Normalmente nos resistimos a la idea de que hay algo malo en esto porque, en el fondo, nos gusta la atención. Pensamos también que si no tenemos una mala intención, de traicionar o de tener una aventura con la otra persona, no hay problema. Confiamos demasiado en nosotros mismos. Nos olvidamos de que no controlamos nuestros sentimientos ni los de la otra persona. Por eso, entienda: ninguna amistad es más valiosa que el matrimonio. En lugar de mantener amistades íntimas con el sexo opuesto, aprenda a hacer de su pareja su mejor amigo.

Cristiane:

Yo ya había aprendido esa lección en la escuela, por experiencia propia. Hubo una época en que me cansé de amistades femeninas, que vivían chismeando, y empecé a andar con amigos en lugar de con amigas del colegio. Era muy bueno, porque ellos me respetaban y no se quedaban hablando de la vida de los demás. Pero algunos empezaron a verme con otros ojos, sin que yo me diera cuenta. Cuando descubrí que estaban enamorados de mí, tuve que distanciarme de todos y me dije a mí misma que nunca más tendría amistad con chicos...

Cuando me casé y vi a Renato teniendo amistad con mujeres, ¡enloquecí!

Comencé a tener miedo de que le nacieran sentimientos hacia ellas, así como mis amigos del colegio los tuvieron por mí. Al principio vivía pidiéndole explicaciones, condenándole; en fin, usaba todas las armas para combatir aquellas amistades.

No fue fácil vencer mis inseguridades en ese sentido, pero lo conseguí. Lo que me ayudó en ese desafío fue prestar atención a lo que yo estaba haciendo mal, en lugar de centrarme en lo que él estaba haciendo.

A veces, la mujer puede hasta tener la razón, pero la forma de resolver el problema la hace perderla y dificulta todo en la relación. Cuando comencé a cambiar mis actitudes, centrándome más en mí, me convertí en una esposa más agradable y Renato ya no desconectaba más mi canal.

Lo bueno es que cuando invertimos más en nosotros mismos pasamos a ver las cosas que no estábamos haciendo bien. Yo, por ejemplo, descubrí que también tenía un llamado y ese llamado no era quedarme detrás de mi marido, auxiliándolo de lejos, y sí a su lado. Empecé a vencer mis propias debilidades, principalmente mi timidez. Mi vida ya no giraba alrededor de él, pero si con él, y alrededor de un solo objetivo: trabajar para Dios.

A veces la mujer no se da cuenta de que, cuando se vuelve improcedente, el hombre se aparta. El marido difícilmente aceptará ser desafiado. Cuando Cristiane cambió su comportamiento, se volvió más deseable para mí. De repente comencé a interesarme más por ella, a estar más cerca, a llamarla para salir.

Fue ahí cuando me sentí motivado para equilibrar mi tiempo entre el trabajo y mi matrimonio. Empecé a prestarle más atención a mi mujer, pues entendí que ella necesitaba eso. En fin, cuando los dos entendimos las raíces de nuestro comportamiento e hicimos lo que era necesario para lidiar con ellas, se acabaron los problemas.

EL MATRIMONIO FELIZ REQUIERE TRABAJO

Nosotros, hombres adictos al trabajo, debemos entender que el matrimonio también es un tipo de trabajo, una empresa. Si no trabaja en su matrimonio, inevitablemente se irá a pique.

Los matrimonios felices dan trabajo y no lo son por casualidad. Cuando vea un matrimonio unido durante muchos años y viviendo bien, sepa que no es fruto de la suerte. No es porque ellos «fueron hechos el uno para el otro» ni porque «congenian bien». Si mirásemos mas de cerca, veríamos cómo ese matrimonio trabaja constantemente en su mantenimiento. Después de veintiún años de matrimonio, Cristiane y yo continuamos trabajando, actuando en nuestro matrimonio. Un descuido, un poco de pereza en hacer algo, un despiste de algo importante, ya es suficiente para que los problemas surjan; por eso, nunca descuidamos ese trabajo.

Desgraciadamente, muchos matrimonios se dan por conquistados el día de la boda. Es como si el esfuerzo por conquistar a la otra persona hubiese acabado cuando se van de luna de miel. ¡Bien, ya estamos casados! ¡Hecho y consumado!

Los hombres, sobre todo, estamos acostumbrados a hacer eso. Para nosotros, el periodo comienza con la primera conversación y llega hasta la luna de miel, es lo más interesante para nuestra naturaleza competitiva. Es emocionante saber que ella ha aceptado salir, ver que está deslumbrada por nosotros y que piensa que somos lo máximo..., todo esto es como si fuese un juego para nosotros (mujeres, estamos siendo honestos... es nuestra naturaleza. Usted va a entender más sobre esto más adelante en este libro). Por eso, el día de nuestro matrimonio es como la entrega del trofeo.

Cuando el campeón recibe el trofeo, lo pone en el estante y aquello ya forma parte del pasado. Y así es como actuamos muchos hombres con nuestras mujeres después del matrimonio. Pensamos que el juego acabó, que aquel trabajo de la conquista ya ha terminado. Tenemos hasta el papel para probarlo: ¡el acta de matrimonio!

Compañeros, aquí va un aviso: ¡el juego apenas ha comenzado! Si dejamos de trabajar para mantener nuestro matrimonio, perderemos el juego...

TAREA

¿Cuáles son los principales ítems en su equipaje, y en el de su pareja, que afectan o pueden afectar su relación en el futuro? Tómese algunos minutos para pensar en los principales acontecimientos que marcaron sus vidas o les formaron el carácter o engendraron los principios y valores que rigen su comportamiento. Esta tarea requiere un viaje al pasado, meditación cuidadosa, esmero y, probablemente, una conversación con su pareja para descubrir las respuestas de él/ella. Escriba lo que consiguió identificar, pero quédese a gusto y libre de aumentar la lista conforme vaya descubriéndolas.

/MatrimonioBlindado

Publique esto:
Ya comencé a revisar
nuestro equipaje.

@matrimonioblind

Tuitee esto: Ya
comencé a revisar
nuestro equipaje
#matrimonioblindado
@matrimonioblind

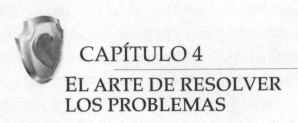

CAPÍTULO 4
EL ARTE DE RESOLVER LOS PROBLEMAS

Nuestro equipaje, diferencias de personalidad, gustos, expectativas, etc., preparan el escenario para que los problemas aparezcan en la relación. Cuando estos aparecen y usted no sabe cómo lidiar con las diferencias, quedan mal resueltos y el matrimonio se deteriora. Si nada cambia, dentro de pocos años vendrá el divorcio. A propósito, ¿es el divorcio una señal para huir de los problemas conyugales que el matrimonio nunca consiguió resolver?

Matrimonios que se aman acaban separándose, o viviendo juntos como dos extraños dentro de casa, porque no consiguen resolver los conflictos en la relación. La verdad es que ellos insisten e intentan cambiar a la otra persona. Piensan así: «Si yo consigo que mi marido/esposa sea como yo, entonces los problemas estarán resueltos». Y entonces critican, acusan, señalan los errores del otro, y defienden y justifican sus actitudes. Dando vueltas sin llegar a ningún lugar. Cuando uno finalmente se cansa de esa insana relación, decide separarse.

Vivir un matrimonio feliz es un arte: el arte de resolver problemas. Existen por lo menos siete mil millones de problemas en el mundo de hoy: cada ser humano tiene por lo menos uno, probablemente muchos más. Aun así, estamos sobreviviendo a pesar de ellos. Algunos conseguimos resolverlos y con otros aprendemos a convivir hasta que encontramos la solución. Los problemas forman parte de la vida. Quien es más hábil en resolver problemas, tiene más éxito; quien es menos hábil, fracasa más. En el matrimonio no es diferente. Si usted quiere blindar su matrimonio, debe comenzar con la decisión de convertirse en un experto en resolver problemas.

Observe: resolver problemas no es resolver personas. Su objetivo tiene que ser resolver los conflictos entre ustedes, cambiar la situación, y no luchar contra la otra persona. Es un error suyo el pensar que la otra persona cambiará a su gusto. No, usted no lo conseguirá, pero acabará pensando que el problema es la otra persona; y por lo tanto, tiene que separarse de ella y encontrar otra persona. Eso quiere decir que usted no aprendió a resolver problemas en el primer matrimonio, y comienza el segundo sin esas habilidades, encontrándose con los mismos problemas e incluso con otros más, y continúa fracasando en el matrimonio. ¿Acaso es una novedad que el índice de divorcios, para la persona que se casa por segunda, tercera vez..., vaya en aumento?

Nuestro método es más eficaz: ayudarle a ver el verdadero problema, a encontrar la raíz, eliminarla y evitar que regrese.

Una de las cosas que nos intrigaron fue descubrir que el índice de divorcios no varía mucho entre las personas de orientación cristiana y personas no religiosas. La creencia en Dios, el autor del matrimonio, parece no ser suficiente para evitar que una persona se divorcie. Esto es algo curioso, pues si hay un grupo que al menos debería de ser más hábil para mantener el matrimonio, sería el grupo de las personas que creen en Dios. Pero ¿por qué no ocurre esto? Porque la mayoría de esas personas no consiguen o no saben cómo aplicar sus conocimientos teóricos sobre el amor en el día a día de sus relaciones. Una cosa es que yo sepa que Dios es amor, y otra cosa es saber qué hacer cuando la persona que yo amo por ejemplo me miente. El cristianismo de una persona comienza a ser realmente probado cuando se casa.

ESPEJITO, ESPEJITO

El matrimonio nos sirve como un espejo. Cuando se arregló hoy por la mañana, usted se habrá mirado en el espejo como mínimo cinco veces (si usted es mujer, unas veinte...). ¿Por qué nos miramos en el espejo siempre que tenemos oportunidad? Porque nuestros ojos no nos dan una visión clara de cómo nos ven los demás. Si no existiesen espejos, ni cámaras de fotos o vídeo, nunca sabríamos cómo está nuestra cara, ni algunas partes de nuestro cuerpo, especialmente la parte de atrás (a pesar de que algunos piensen que eso no sería una mala idea). Pero gracias al espejo podemos ver un reflejo fiel de cómo somos, inclusive de las partes ocultas a nuestros propios ojos.

Así es el matrimonio. Nuestra pareja se vuelve un espejo porque refleja exactamente lo que somos, tanto nuestro lado bueno como el malo. Cuando se mira al espejo, usted ve una imagen de su cuerpo, cosas que le gustan y cosas que no. Cuando se pone una ropa que le sienta bien, usted se queda admirándose y diciéndose a sí mismo: «Me queda bien esta ropa, ¡qué bien! Estos zapatos combinan bien con este cinturón...». Pero también hay ciertas partes que a usted no le gusta mirar. Si encuentra su nariz torcida o muy grande, sus dientes muy separados o sus caderas muy anchas, usted se siente mal solo con mirarse. Yo conozco a una persona que, cuando va a sacarse una foto, coloca su cabeza en un ángulo de 45 grados en relación a la cámara para que su rostro salga de lado, porque piensa que tiene la cabeza muy grande... ¡Quiere decir que cada uno lidia con lo que el espejo le muestra de la manera que puede! Pero una cosa es cierta: de nada sirve insultar o pelear con el espejo. La culpa no es de él, pues solo está mostrando la realidad.

Cuando se coloca delante del espejo del matrimonio, usted comienza a descubrir defectos suyos que desconocía. Cuando me casé, mi temperamento fuerte se manifestó. Yo no había notado ese problema antes, pues cuando era soltero nunca tuve que convivir tan de cerca con alguien en el papel de marido. Cuando éramos novios, estábamos cerca, pero no tan cerca como en el matrimonio. Cuanto más cerca del espejo, más clara y nítida es nuestra imagen. Es eso lo que sucede con los matrimonios.

El problema es que, hasta el matrimonio, solíamos oír de la otra persona lo maravillosos que éramos. «Eres linda», «Me gusta mucho tu honestidad», «Me haces sentir tan bien que me olvido de mis problemas». Solo elogios. Por eso, pensamos: «Esta persona me hará muy feliz. Voy a casarme con ella». Es decir, en el matrimonio esperamos oír solo cosas buenas sobre nosotros. Pero el espejo no miente. Después de casados, estamos muy cerca de nuestro espejo, y la otra persona comienza a mostrarnos nuestros defectos... En lugar de aprovechar aquello y cambiar, comenzamos a proyectar nuestros defectos sobre la otra persona y a apuntar dónde ella necesita cambiar. «Él es tan irritante», «Ella es muy mimada, llora por todo», «Yo no quiero ser así, pero me provocas». Es decir, culpamos al espejo.

Es natural ponerse a la defensiva cuando nuestras fallas son señaladas. A nadie le gusta. Pero no es una actitud inteligente. Si usted decidiese no mirarse más al espejo porque le muestra algo desagradable, no estaría mejorando en nada. En lugar de defender su manera de ser o su comportamiento delante de su pareja, use su *feedback* positivamente. Aproveche esa información para mejorar.

Mientras me irritaba porque Cristiane decía algo negativo sobre mí, no mejoraba como marido, ni como persona. Pero cuando usé mi cabeza y entendí que mi esposa era mi desafío personal para mejorar, entonces comencé a utilizarla como espejo para lidiar con mis defectos. Usted también puede hacerlo.

Entienda una cosa, ya desde el principio: *Nadie cambia a nadie. Las personas solo cambian cuando ellas mismas deciden cambiar.*

Por eso mismo, cuando alguien nos fuerza a cambiar, nuestra reacción natural es resistir. Es una manera de proteger nuestra identidad, nuestro derecho a ser como queremos ser, aunque no le agrade a alguien. Lo sé, parece una locura, pero el ser humano es así.

«Entonces, ¿no hay esperanza para mí?», se preguntará usted. «¿Mi marido nunca va a cambiar? ¿Mi esposa siempre será así?» Fíjese bien, no estoy diciendo que él o ella no vayan a cambiar nunca. Estoy diciendo que no será usted quien le hará cambiar. Pero hay una buena noticia: usted podrá influenciar e inspirar a esa persona para el cambio. Es para aprender cómo hacer eso que está usted leyendo este libro.

Todo comienza centrándose en uno mismo en lugar de señalar los errores de su compañero. Recuerde: si usted resuelve solo sus cuestiones personales, la mitad de los problemas conyugales serán resueltos antes de que su compañero cambie un poco.

Cuando usted cambie y pare de exigir que el otro cambie, dará el primer paso para inspirar el cambio en la otra persona sin necesidad de reclamar nada de ella. En lugar de eso, mire hacia su interior, reconociendo sus propios errores. Abra su equipaje y saque de adentro lo que está pesando mucho. No se preocupe por el equipaje de él o ella por ahora, su objetivo será entenderse a sí mismo primero, para después entender a los demás.

Tal vez usted haya empezado a leer este libro pensando en descubrir técnicas para cambiar a su marido o esposa. La verdad es que usted aprenderá cómo cambiarse a sí mismo. Si se embarca en esta misión de ser una persona mejor, entonces su matrimonio mejorará, incluida su pareja. Pero si su misión es cambiarlo, puede parar aquí. Nosotros no podemos ayudarle. Nadie puede.

¡ALTO AL FUEGO!

Si usted está realmente empeñado en blindar su relación, entonces comience a seguir los consejos y tareas que vamos a recomendarle en este libro.

La primera tarea es declarar un «¡Alto el fuego!».

Cuando dos países están en guerra y buscan una solución, el primer paso es declarar un alto el fuego, para negociar un acuerdo de paz. Paran los ataques como voto de confianza, una señal de buena voluntad.

Si usted ha atacado a su pareja de alguna forma, aunque sea esporádicamente, debe detener de inmediato este tipo de trato. Por ejemplo, comentarios irónicos, respuestas sarcásticas, acusaciones, ataques verbales, mencionar los errores del pasado, son también formas pasivas de ataque, como ser indiferente, omitir informaciones importantes, tratar con indiferencia, permanecer fuera de casa y cosas de ese tipo.

Piense: ¿cómo podrá usted blindar su relación de ataques externos si insiste en los ataques internos? No es sabio. Los ataques externos que usted tiene que combatir ya son suficientes, ustedes no necesitan ser enemigos uno del otro. Los enemigos son los problemas que ustedes enfrentan, no ustedes mismos.

Por lo tanto, si su matrimonio ahora está en pie de guerra, ¡pare! Dé tregua a su pareja. A partir de ahora, mientras lea este libro, usted va a tratar a su pareja con respeto y educación. Eso le dará la oportunidad de respirar y concentrarse en nuevos caminos para la solución de los problemas.

Otra razón por la cual el alto el fuego es importante: que usted no sabotee sus esfuerzos de blindar su matrimonio. Piense: si mientras usted lee este libro continúa atacando a su pareja, los problemas solo aumentarán. Llegarán a un punto en que usted mirará la portada de este libro y se dirá a sí mismo algo como «¡No está sirviendo de nada! No voy a leer más este libro inútil», seguido de un pensamiento donde usted se ve lanzando el libro a la garganta de su pareja... ¡Nada bueno!

Entonces, esta es su primera tarea para blindar su matrimonio: ¡alto el fuego!

TAREA

Escriba aquí (o en otro lugar, si no quiere guardar el libro) cómo ataca normalmente a su compañero. Piense en todas las maneras, de mayor a menor, e inclúyalas abajo.

_____

_____

_____

_____

Me prometo a mí mismo que no trataré más a mi compañero de esta forma y me esforzaré en actuar con respeto, dominio de mí mismo y consideración.

/MatrimonioBlindado

Publique esto:
Comienzo hoy mi
«alto el fuego».

@matrimonioblind

Tuitee esto:
He completado la
primera tarea para
blindar mi matrimonio
#altoelfuego
 @matrimonioblind

PARTE II

EMOCIÓN VS. RAZÓN

CAPÍTULO 5

EL MATRIMONIO COMO UNA EMPRESA

Vivir feliz en el matrimonio es un arte: el arte de resolver problemas. Quien es más hábil para resolver problemas, tiene más éxito en el matrimonio. Quien es menos hábil, fracasa más. Si usted quiere blindar su matrimonio, debe comenzar con la decisión de convertirse en un experto en resolver problemas.

Lo que normalmente sucede con los problemas en el matrimonio es que son eludidos, ignorados, pospuestos, en lugar de ser resueltos. El ciclo acostumbra a ser así: el matrimonio tiene un malentendido, debate sobre el asunto, sin progresar mucho, los ánimos se caldean, uno acaba ofendiendo al otro con palabras, o por su posición inflexible; los dos se cansan de debatir, pues no consiguen llegar a un acuerdo, desisten por el cansancio y la frustración, y pasa el tiempo hasta que nuevamente surge el conflicto.

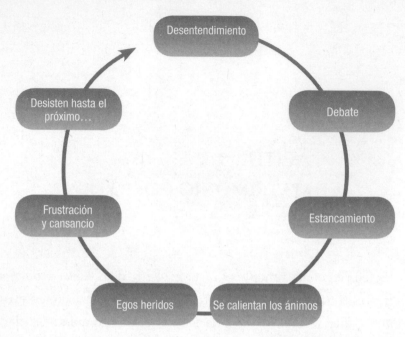

Las siete etapas del ciclo de los problemas no resueltos en el matrimonio.

En este ciclo nada se resuelve. El problema se retrasa o apenas se evita de manera temporal, pero después regresa, y casi siempre peor. Muchos matrimonios piensan que el tiempo resolverá sus problemas. «Vamos a dar tiempo al tiempo» es una expresión que a muchos les gusta usar cuando se justifican por no resolver el problema en el momento. Pero los problemas en el matrimonio no son como el vino. No mejoran con el tiempo. Cuando se trata de simples roces en el matrimonio, un problema que se posterga es un problema empeorado. En este caso, el tiempo se vuelve enemigo del matrimonio.

Una de las principales razones por las que las personas deciden no lidiar con el problema en el matrimonio es el hecho de que la experiencia es extremadamente dolorosa. La falta de habilidad en la comunicación, los ataques verbales, la irritación, hacen que el matrimonio evite el asunto en lugar de resolverlo. Eso se hace especialmente real en el caso de los hombres. Muchos hombres huyen de una conversación seria con una mujer porque no consiguen dialogar al mismo nivel. Las mujeres, por su parte, se frustran porque parece que nunca consiguen que el hombre las entienda.

Pero no es necesario que así sea. Hay una manera eficaz de que hombres y mujeres puedan resolver sus problemas conyugales y prevenir que se repitan, sin que nadie salga herido en el proceso. Yo lo llamo de esta manera: «Tratar su matrimonio como una empresa».

LOS OBJETIVOS DE UNA EMPRESA

¿Por qué alguien comienza una empresa? ¿Cuál es su objetivo? Puede haber muchos. Ganar más dinero es uno de los obvios. Ser su propio jefe, y así tener más independencia, es otro. Muchos sienten la necesidad de desarrollar su potencial y ven en la creación de una empresa un medio para ello. Otros quieren marcar la diferencia en el mundo en que viven, ayudar al prójimo. Una cosa es cierta: toda empresa tiene por lo menos un objetivo. Ningún negocio existe por existir. Siempre hay una búsqueda de resultados. Y esos resultados se convierten en el centro de todos los asuntos de esa empresa, especialmente de los dueños. Si no hay resultados, no hay razón para que la empresa exista.

El matrimonio también es una empresa. Nadie se casa sin objetivos, ni sin buscar resultados. Cuando los novios piensan en casarse, en realidad piensan en objetivos, sueños realizados, entre ellos: formar una familia, tener hijos, hacer a la otra persona feliz y ser feliz, estar siempre al lado de quien se ama y sentirse amado; conquistar juntos metas materiales; tener a alguien que les apoye en la realización de sus sueños; alcanzar el placer sexual, tener en el compañero un amigo verdadero, etcétera.

Cristiane:

Cuando me casé con Renato, aunque tenía los mismos objetivos que él, también tenía algunas expectativas que no estaban de acuerdo con las suyas. Fue exactamente con esas diferencias, que no estaban alineadas, con las que tuvimos problemas. Es muy importante que los cónyuges sepan todas las expectativas que ambos tienen para el matrimonio. Si nos hubiésemos sentado a conversar sobre eso antes de casarnos, seguramente hubiéramos sabido qué esperar después el uno del otro.

A veces los matrimonios incluso llegan a conversar sobre sus metas, pero con el paso del tiempo, las expectativas superan los objetivos iniciales. Si no se hace un ajuste y un mantenimiento de los objetivos, la frustración les llevará a reclamar el uno del otro: «Pero siempre dijiste esto o aquello, ¿ahora quieres cambiar?». En lugar de bailar conforme con la música, el matrimonio comienza a bailar músicas diferentes y allí es donde empieza todo a complicarse.

Recientemente, hemos divulgado a través de nuestro programa *Escuela del amor* la Caminata del Amor, en todo Brasil y en todo el mundo. Fueron alrededor de diez mil personas las que se reunieron con un solo objetivo: conocer mejor a su pareja a través del diálogo. Esa idea vino justamente por una experiencia que tuvimos hace algunos años, cuando Renato me invitó al parque a dialogar.

Ya llevábamos más de quince años de casados y fue entonces cuando por primera vez conciliamos todo lo que pensábamos y queríamos en una conversación. Él supo todos mis sueños, mis preocupaciones, mis dificultades, lo que yo quería y lo que no, y viceversa. Fueron horas preciosas que fortalecieron, y mucho, nuestra unión. Después de esa conversación, yo sabía exactamente lo que él esperaba de mí. Sabía qué iba a hacer para apoyarlo y cómo hacerlo.

A veces usted piensa que está al lado de su pareja y, en realidad, está muy distante debido a la ignorancia que ambos tienen de lo que quieren el uno del otro.

El matrimonio también tiene objetivos y existen para producir resultados, igual que una empresa...

¿Por qué es importante que usted entienda este paralelismo?

Son los objetivos de una empresa los que guían todo lo que se hace en ella en el día a día. Las decisiones que toman, a quién se contrata, los cursos a los trabajadores, los productos que crean, la publicidad que hacen, todo es movido y guiado por los objetivos y resultados, esos resultados que la empresa quiere alcanzar.

Cuando trasladamos ese pensamiento al matrimonio, nos damos cuenta de que, desgraciadamente, la mayoría de los matrimonios no piensan así. Ellos se perjudican con el transcurso de la vida, se pierden en los sentimientos y enseguida pierden de vista los objetivos por los cuales se casaron. Cuando los objetivos se olvidan, entonces las decisiones que toman y todo lo demás que se hace dentro de la relación ya no contribuye a la realización y al éxito del matrimonio.

Cuando el marido empieza a involucrarse con una amante, por ejemplo, es porque claramente ha perdido de vista los objetivos de su matrimonio. Pero eso no sucede apenas en el momento de la traición. Fue algo que comenzó con la primera decisión de mirar con interés a otra mujer. Aquella mirada ya fue un desvío del camino que buscaba los objetivos de su matrimonio. Es decir, él perdió el objetivo de su empresa. Su persistencia en ese rumbo, inevitablemente llevará a aquel matrimonio a la ruptura.

Si uno de los cónyuges entra en el matrimonio con la idea de que aquella unión no durará hasta que la muerte los separe, entonces esa persona acabará haciendo cosas para arruinar el matrimonio, causando su fin. Si por otro lado, la persona se ve al lado de la otra hasta que la muerte los separe, hará de todo para mantener esa relación. Es decir, la meta de llegar al objetivo dicta nuestro comportamiento.

Al inicio de mi matrimonio, cuando yo tenía algún desentendimiento con Cristiane, mi objetivo principal era ganar la discusión. Yo quería probarle que era ella la que estaba equivocada, y yo tenía razón. Y como yo soy mejor argumentador que ella, casi siempre salía ganando. Pero ese era el objetivo equivocado. Yo ganaba la discusión, pero perdía la intimidad y amistad que tenía con mi esposa. Es lo que muchos matrimonios hacen: prefieren tener la razón a ser felices.

Cuando aprendí que mi matrimonio es una empresa, entendí que incluso las decisiones y actitudes más pequeñas tienen que estar unidas a nuestros objetivos a largo plazo. Hoy, cuando hay algún desentendimiento, me pregunto: ¿cuál es el resultado que yo quiero obtener con esta conversación? En ese momento pienso en mi objetivo, y dirijo la conversación para lograrlo.

¿CÓMO RESUELVEN LOS PROBLEMAS LAS EMPRESAS?

¿Usted cree que Steve Jobs no enfrentó problemas cuando comenzó su empresa Apple? Claro que sí. Desde Apple hasta el carrito de palomitas en la esquina de la avenida, toda empresa comienza con sueños y objetivos, pero inmediatamente encuentra problemas. Y no solo al principio. Por más exitosa que sea una empresa, debe enfrentar y resolver cuestiones diariamente. La supervivencia de cualquier negocio depende de la solución de sus problemas. Si no se resolvieran, la empresa se iría a pique. Es cierto que si usted es un empleado, esa es la razón por la cual fue contratado: para resolver problemas (¿o usted cree que fue porque les gustó su currículum...?).

Sea cual sea el número de trabajadores, dos, dos mil o veinte mil, las empresas con éxito consiguen alcanzar sus objetivos resolviendo sus problemas. Y lo curioso es que la relación entre los trabajadores no es precisamente de amor. Muchas veces es lo contrario. No es muy común oír a los trabajadores decir «¡amo a mi jefe!», ni verlos escribiendo cartas de amor para el compañero del Departamento de Contabilidad. Pero si ellos consiguen tener éxito en esas condiciones, es porque deben de estar haciendo algo que trae buenos resultados.

La pregunta es: *¿Por qué las parejas, que pasan por pequeños problemas, se aman y muchas veces no consiguen vencer los desafíos en la relación?*

La respuesta es: porque han usado la herramienta equivocada para resolver los problemas: la emoción. El secreto de las empresas de éxito es no usar la emoción para resolver los problemas, y sí la razón. Ellos entienden que no se resuelve nada usando los sentimientos. El lugar de trabajo es un espacio de inteligencia y actitud, no de sentimentalismo, ni de sentir esto o aquello. Por eso, ellos alcanzan sus objetivos independientemente de los sentimientos de los trabajadores, e incluso cuando a un trabajador no le cae bien otro. En esas empresas se aprende a separar el trabajo de las personas, y no mezclar las dos cosas. Piensan: «A mí puede no agradarme mi jefe, pero él me ha mandado hacer algo, y yo dependo de él para recibir mi salario. Entonces, voy a hacer lo que debe hacerse». Es decir, separan los sentimientos de las actitudes y las personas del trabajo, y se centran en los resultados deseados. Usan la razón, no la emoción. Grabe esta frase en su mente:

La emoción no es una herramienta para resolver problemas.

Compruebe: cada vez que usted ha tomado una decisión basada en una emoción, falló. Todos los que dirigen sus negocios a través de las emociones, acaban fracasando. Ya habrá escuchado el dicho: «Amigos son amigos, los negocios aparte». Resume bien el lema de los empresarios con éxito. «No importa quién es usted, si a usted le caigo bien o si usted no me cae bien. Lo que importa es que nosotros tenemos este problema aquí, y necesitamos resolverlo para alcanzar nuestros objetivos; por lo tanto, ¿qué vamos a hacer para resolverlo?».

Este es el objetivo de las empresas: ¿qué vamos a hacer?

¿Qué podemos hacer para aumentar las ventas? ¿Qué haremos para disminuir nuestros gastos? ¿Qué haremos para superar a la competencia?

Hacer, hacer, hacer. No sentir, sentir y sentir.

El sentimiento no es una herramienta para resolver los problemas.

EL DESCUBRIMIENTO EN EL LABORATORIO

Tenemos un apartado en nuestro programa *Escuela del amor* llamado «el Laboratorio». Consiste en grabar a una pareja mientras discuten los problemas de la relación. Después, Cristiane y yo observamos a la pareja e identificamos las fallas en su comunicación y comportamiento, y damos sugerencias para que mejoren. Antes de conectar las cámaras, dejamos a la pareja a solas en el estudio, sentados uno enfrente del otro, y les pedimos que comiencen a conversar sobre cualquier asunto que tenga que ver con ellos y que, crean, necesita resolverse. Es entonces cuando conectamos las cámaras. Es una experiencia... Por eso el nombre de «Laboratorio».

Uno de nuestros descubrimientos observando a las parejas discutiendo sus asuntos fue exactamente la cantidad de emociones que hay en la conversación y la ausencia de objetivos en lo que hay que hacer para resolver el asunto. Movidos por los sentimientos de irritación, rabia, dolor, desprecio e incomprensión, las parejas se quedan la mayor parte del tiempo haciendo la «lista de quién es peor». Es más o menos así:

Ella: Eres muy desordenado, dejas las cosas en cualquier lugar.

Él: El problema es que quieres las cosas en el momento. Si yo no guardo inmediatamente los zapatos o pongo el plato en la tarja, ya comienzas a sacarme de quicio.

Ella: Pero qué falta de consideración por tu parte, ¿no ves que yo había limpiado toda la casa?, lo mínimo que podrías hacer es no desordenarla. Sabes que a mí me gustan las cosas organizadas.

Él: Tú tampoco eres muy organizada. El otro día abrí los cajones de tu escritorio y las cosas estaban todas desordenadas. ¿De qué sirve? La mesa está limpia, pero los cajones están todos desordenados.

Ella: Sí, pero si me ayudaras más en la casa ibas a saber cómo me siento yo.

Él: ¿Que yo no ayudo?

Y continúa, continúa... Diez, veinte, treinta minutos, pasando de un problema a otro. Observe que la conversación nunca se enfoca en el problema ni en lo que van a hacer para resolverlo. A causa de las emociones, uno se queda intentando demostrarle al otro que no es tan malo, o que el otro no es tan santo como cree. El sucio hablando del mal lavado.

Lista de quién es peor

Sucio	Mal lavado
Desordenado	Quiere todo en el momento
Desorganizado	Colma la paciencia
No tiene consideración	No es tan organizada
No ayuda en casa	No reconoce la ayuda

Cuando la conversación se acaba, normalmente la lista es muy extensa, equilibrada, y los egos resultan estar más heridos. Y claro, nada se ha resuelto. No es de extrañar que muchas parejas no dialoguen más. ¿Para qué dialogar? ¿Para oír de la persona amada una lista de todos sus defectos? No, muchas gracias. Prefiero la televisión.

Sin embargo, si ellos usaran la razón en vez de la emoción, se centrarían en cómo resolver el problema. Al final de la conversación habrían llegado a una conclusión y ambos sabrían exactamente qué hacer para que el problema no se repitiese. Y nadie saldría herido.

Ahora imagínese si en las empresas las personas actuaran como la pareja anterior a la hora de resolver los problemas. El jefe llama al gerente de ventas a su oficina y le dice:

Jefe: Juan, nuestras ventas están cayendo.

Juan: Claro, si usted se levantara de esa silla tan cómoda y me ayudara, tal vez las ventas no continuarían tan bajas.

Claro que la conversación nunca comenzaría en ese nivel emocional tan elevado, pues en ese caso acabaría inmediatamente con un «Juan, está usted despedido. Pase por el Departamento de Recursos Humanos». Como Juan no quiere ser despedido, ni el jefe quiere perderlo, los dos deben enfocarse en estrategias para mejorar las ventas. Usarían la inteligencia y la razón, y no los sentimientos ni la emoción, aunque estos últimos sean reales y estén presentes.

La emoción es la herramienta equivocada para resolver problemas en el trabajo y en el matrimonio también. Lo que yo siento sobre un problema no importa. Lo que importa es lo que yo voy a hacer en relación con el problema.

Nadie «siente» la solución de un problema. Juan no se presenta ante el jefe y le dice: «Déjelo en mis manos, ya estoy sintiendo que las ventas van a subir». Si lo hiciera, sería enviado nuevamente al Departamento de Recursos Humanos. La solución se encuentra pensando, razonando, llegando a una conclusión y actuando sobre ella, nunca sintiendo.

Usando la razón y no la emoción para resolver problemas, las empresas mantienen a decenas, centenas, y hasta millares de empleados unidos en un solo objetivo –incluso sin amarse. Con certeza, una pareja que se ama inteligentemente también puede beneficiarse de esa misma herramienta para mantenerse juntos y resolver sus problemas.

SUPERVIVENCIA DE UN NEGOCIO: DOS REGLAS

Todo negocio, toda empresa, tiene que seguir dos reglas básicas para su supervivencia. Si usted rompe una de esas reglas, no puede permanecer en el empleo o mantener sus negocios. ¿Cuáles son esas dos reglas?

1. Definir, resolver y prevenir. Definir el problema (entender lo que realmente es, y qué lo causa), resolverlo, y si es posible prevenir que no suceda otra vez, es el pan de cada día de las empresas de éxito.

Por ejemplo: varios clientes han reclamado sobre los grandes atrasos en la entrega del producto. La empresa tiene que descubrir el problema que causa los atrasos, resolverlo e implementar normas y métodos que eliminen la posibilidad de que los atrasos se repitan.

2. No llevar nada al terreno personal. En los negocios, las cosas tienen que permanecer en el ámbito racional. Quien es sentimental y suele llevar todo al lado personal no es eficaz y normalmente no dura mucho tiempo en el trabajo. Su vida personal, sus sentimientos, lo que pasa en casa o sobre los compañeros de trabajo no interesan a la empresa. Usted tiene que saber separar las cosas. La meta en la empresa son los objetivos y lo que debe hacerse para alcanzarlos. Su jefe espera que usted sea un adulto y no un niño mimado, que hace rabietas cuando algo no le gusta.

Enfocándose en el problema y rechazando la emoción, así es como las empresas sobreviven y prosperan; y así también su matrimonio podrá vencer todos los desafíos.

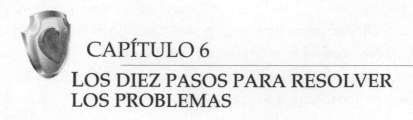

CAPÍTULO 6
LOS DIEZ PASOS PARA RESOLVER LOS PROBLEMAS

Guiadas por las dos reglas básicas descritas en el capítulo anterior, las empresas de éxito prosperan y avanzan todos los días resolviendo desde problemas pequeños y fáciles hasta los mayores y más complejos.

Podemos dividir este arte de resolver problemas en diez pasos diferenciados, que se adaptan muy bien al matrimonio. Cualquier persona con éxito en el trabajo, jefe o empleado, ya sigue estos diez pasos, aunque no piense en ellos de esta forma estructurada. Es algo instintivo, pues el foco en los resultados sumado al uso de la inteligencia, en vez de la emoción, exigen que la persona siga este proceso natural de solución de los problemas.

La mente empresarial está acostumbrada a seguir este proceso automáticamente sin pensar mucho en él, así como los músculos de nuestras piernas se acostumbran a subir y bajar escaleras sin que los ojos necesiten mirar hacia los escalones.

Pero como en un matrimonio las emociones entran en juego, parece que ellas ciegan nuestras facultades mentales, de modo que lo que es tan claro y lógico en el trabajo no lo es en la relación. Por eso, vamos a desmontar este proceso para ayudarnos a ver cómo debe aplicarse en las situaciones conyugales.

Vamos a hacer una comparación usando dos ejemplos típicos de un problema empresarial y otro matrimonial. Así usted podrá ver cómo los mismos pasos que usamos para resolver problemas en el trabajo también pueden ser utilizados para resolver problemas en la relación.

Supongamos que usted es gerente de Recursos Humanos en la empresa «Aparatos, S. A.» (es solo un ejemplo, fue el nombre que me vino a la cabeza). Usted es responsable de todos los aspectos relacionados con la gestión de empleados. Un síntoma de algún problema ha llamado su atención: ha habido una gran inestabilidad en el puesto de recepcionista de la empresa. En los últimos tres meses, cuatro recepcionistas han entrado y salido del cargo, y ahora la empresa recibe a la quinta. Altos costes de contratación y entrenamiento, caída en la moral de los empleados y la falta de secuencia en el cargo son solo algunos de los efectos negativos. Es su responsabilidad resolver ese problema. Su jefe quiere resultados.

Mientras tanto, en su empresa «Matrimonio, S. A.» también enfrentan un síntoma que los lleva al problema: él reclama que añora tener sexo más veces y ella cree que la regularidad actual es más que suficiente. Eso es lo que a veces ha afectado los ánimos de los dos, haciendo que él se disguste con ella y ella se sienta presionada por él. Ustedes dos quieren un resultado satisfactorio para ese callejón sin salida.

Vamos ahora a los diez pasos para resolver esos problemas:

1. Reunirse e iniciar comunicación inmediatamente

En la empresa: Lo primero que usted hace es reunirse inmediatamente con las personas relacionadas con ello e iniciar una comunicación con ellas para descubrir lo que realmente está aconteciendo. Hago énfasis aquí en la palabra «inmediatamente». Es decir, usted no pospone el problema porque sabe que un problema aplazado es un problema aumentado. En el mundo de los negocios sabemos que la velocidad de actuación es una gran ventaja sobre la competencia. Por eso, usted no pierde tiempo. Convoca inmediatamente una reunión con todos los que pueden darle informaciones útiles sobre la situación: el responsable de personal, el encargado de despidos, el gerente de la recepción, etc. Usted hace eso independiente de los sentimientos, suyos o de cualquiera de los involucrados en el asunto. Lo que se debe hacer, ha de hacerse.

En el matrimonio: Aquí ya comienzan los errores de la mayoría de las parejas. Generalmente, cuando surgen problemas, ambos se alejan, evitando resolver sus conflictos. Creen que el aplazamiento de la discusión supuestamente resolverá algo. Normalmente, los hombres son más culpables en esto, dependiendo del tipo de problema que deba ser resuelto. La mujer suele ser la persona que da a conocer el problema, que presenta el asunto con la esperanza de que el marido participe en la solución. El hombre tiende a ser más simplificador, menos preocupado con los detalles y con poca paciencia para discutir una cosa que él muchas veces ni cree que es un problema. En el afán por no enfadarse, por querer quedar bien, evita hablar sobre el asunto y se equivoca al intentar aplazar o darle rápidamente un giro a la cuestión. Siempre inventa excusas para no oír a la esposa: «Ahora no, estoy cansado, déjalo para otro día» (a veces el hombre hace eso pensando que la mujer va a acabar olvidándose del asunto y dejarlo en paz. ¡Qué ingenuos somos!).

Cuando surge un problema en el matrimonio, usted tiene que actuar en el momento para resolverlo. Recuerde, los problemas no son como el vino, que mejora con el tiempo. Por lo tanto, a la primera oportunidad, deben reunirse e iniciar la comunicación para exponer el problema, ya que deberá ser resuelto tarde o temprano, mejor temprano, porque tarde podría haber aumentado. Así que actúe rápido.

En este caso en cuestión, o sea cual sea el caso, la pareja debe reunirse sin demora y exponer el problema que ambos están enfrentando en la cama. No importa lo que sientan al respeto, pues el sentimiento no resuelve problemas. Lo que importa es que está habiendo un conflicto y la empresa de ustedes no puede prosperar con un problema mal resuelto. Por lo tanto, la mejor hora para resolver un problema, salvo raras excepciones, siempre es inmediatamente.

2. Oír

En la empresa: El segundo paso, después de reunirse con su equipo, es que usted oiga a los involucrados (responsable de personal, el encargado de despidos, el gerente de la recepción, etc.) para averiguar por qué hay recepcionistas que no permanecen en el puesto. Usted quiere oírlos porque es un profesional y un jefe inteligente. Uno de los peores tipos de jefe que usted puede tener es el sabelotodo. ¿Ya ha trabajado para alguien así? Cuando él o ella saben de un problema, se presentan delante de sus subordinados con una orden y una solución prefabricada: «A partir de ahora ustedes van a hacer así y así». No quiere saber ni oír a nadie, porque, claro, ya lo sabe todo y los subordinados son... solo subordinados. Pero usted no es así. Usted sabe que las mejores informaciones sobre el problema solo pueden venir de aquellos que están directamente involucrados en él. Por eso, usted quiere –necesita– oírlos atentamente. Usted inicia la comunicación hablando poco y oyendo más.

En el matrimonio: El segundo paso también suele comenzar mal entre las parejas con problemas, y justamente a causa de las emociones. Un cónyuge inicia la comunicación señalando un problema y el otro inmediatamente se ofende y se pone a la defensiva.

¿Se acuerda de la «Lista de quién es peor» que las parejas suelen hacer en el Laboratorio? Es ahí donde ellos pecan. En vez de escucharse atentamente el uno al otro, se ponen a la defensiva hasta que se cansan y desisten de la conversación. Mientras un cónyuge está hablando, el otro, en vez de escucharlo, ya comienza a formular en su mente una respuesta o represalia. Al hacer eso, deja de escuchar. Hay una explicación psicológica y natural de por qué ocurre eso. Cuando nos sentimos atacados, nuestro instinto es luchar o correr. Ese es un instinto tan básico que puede ser observado en cualquier animal. Si usted ataca a un perro, por ejemplo, el instinto de autodefensa y supervivencia del animal lo hará atacar de vuelta o huir de usted. El ser humano opera a partir de este mismo instinto para todo. Por eso, quien inicia la conversación tiene el poder de determinar la reacción del compañero, si va a ser buena o negativa. Una conversación iniciada en tono acusatorio o crítico inevitablemente provocará una reacción de pelear o huir de la conversación. Lo ideal es que el problema sea expuesto de forma separada de la persona. Por ejemplo, si el marido dice: «Estás fría, nunca quieres estar conmigo», la esposa se sentirá atacada personalmente e intentará responderle a la altura: «Tú eres un animal, solo te importa el sexo». Listo, el combate está armado. Ninguno va a escuchar al otro, excepto con la intención de atacar o defenderse. Pero si él comienza así: «Amor, ¿qué puedo hacer yo para que los dos tengamos una vida sexual más satisfactoria?», la reacción será otra. ¿Ha notado la diferencia? La manera en que el hablante inicia la conversación determina si el oyente se quedará con ganas de dialogar o no.

Cuando su cónyuge comience a exponer el problema, resista a la tentación de defenderse o justificarse. Inicialmente, solo oiga para reunir toda la información, dejando a la persona libre para expresarse. No presuma que ya sabe cuál es el problema, pues probablemente la otra persona tenga una visión muy diferente de la suya sobre lo que realmente está pasando. Por lo tanto, sea inteligente: oiga.

3. Preguntar

En la empresa: Con el objetivo de identificar y comprender la raíz del problema, usted hace preguntas que le aporten esta información. ¿Sabemos las razones de la salida de cada una de las cuatro recepcionistas? ¿Desde dónde fueron incorporadas? ¿Quién hizo la selección y qué criterios usó? ¿Cuál es el salario que se les paga? ¿Es compatible con el mercado? ¿Cuáles son las responsabilidades que el puesto implica? ¿En qué fase de selección de la próxima aspirante estamos? Es decir, usted hace preguntas enfocadas en lo que necesita para entender mejor el problema, y sigue oyendo atentamente las respuestas. Note que estas preguntas no son acusativas ni tienen como objetivo hallar un culpable, solo buscar las informaciones relevantes.

Una técnica desarrollada por profesionales japoneses dice que, si usted define un problema y pregunta por qué está ocurriendo, hasta cinco veces, probablemente encontrará la raíz de ese problema. Por ejemplo:

- La casa está fría. (Problema). ¿Por qué?
- Porque el sistema de calefacción está roto. ¿Y por qué?
- Porque no se ha hecho el mantenimiento periódico. ¿Por qué?
- Porque yo no quería gastar dinero. ¿Por qué?
- Porque soy muy tacaño y no me gusta gastar dinero salvo cuando ya no hay otra opción. (¡Raíz del problema!)

La solución inmediata para el problema de que la casa esté fría es, obviamente, reparar el sistema de calefacción. La solución permanente, sin embargo, es un cambio en mi mentalidad en relación con el dinero. Yo necesito reajustar mis pensamientos y comprender el concepto fundamental de «gastar ahora para economizar más tarde». Si yo realizo el mantenimiento del sistema de calefacción periódicamente, gastaré algo de dinero ahora, pero no tanto como cuando el sistema se estropee por falta de mantenimiento.

Está claro que yo puedo decidir reparar solo la calefacción ahora, y no preocuparme por la raíz del problema. En ese caso, debo ser consciente de que el problema se repetirá en el futuro... Preguntar «¿por qué?» de manera inteligente es una buena forma de encontrar la raíz de sus problemas y así procurar una solución permanente.

En el matrimonio: Hacerle preguntas a su cónyuge cuando él o ella le hablen de un problema pendiente de resolver es una manera óptima no solamente de entender mejor la situación, sino también de demostrar que usted realmente está oyendo y se interesa por comprender a la otra persona. De la misma forma que lo hace en el trabajo, enfoque las preguntas en el descubrimiento de la raíz del problema. ¿Se considera realizado/a sexualmente? ¿Por qué? ¿Qué hago que te gusta/no te gusta? ¿Qué importancia tiene el sexo para ti dentro de nuestro matrimonio? ¿Por qué? ¿Qué hago yo que te hace sentir presionada? ¿Cuándo el acto es placentero para ti? ¿Cuándo no lo es? ¿Hay algún momento del día/noche que prefieres reservar para que estemos juntos? ¿Alguno que no? ¿Qué regularidad del acto conyugal sería ideal para ti? Es decir, esas preguntas ayudan a explorar lo que está detrás del problema, y seguramente las respuestas generarán otras preguntas. Observe nuevamente el tono no acusatorio y el objetivo de descubrir las causas del problema sin atacar a nadie.

4. Enfocar los hechos

En la empresa: En los negocios trabajamos con hechos, números, datos, evidencias. Claro que intuición, experiencia, personalidad, principios, y otras características más abstractas influencian nuestras decisiones. Sin embargo, la base inicial y más confiable de nuestras decisiones en el trabajo es aquello que es tangible, sólido, real e indiscutible. Por lo tanto, sus consideraciones sobre lo que está ocurriendo en la recepción de la imaginaria empresa Aparatos, S. A. se basan principalmente en los hechos factibles en vez de en las opiniones o suposiciones. Si alguien del sector de la contabilidad simplemente dice: «La última recepcionista no me caía bien», eso no es suficiente para tenerse en cuenta. Más importantes son las informaciones sólidas, como las que su encargado de despidos dice: «Las cuatro últimas recepcionistas alegaron que dejaban el trabajo para ganar más dinero en otro lugar». Eso es un hecho. «Varios departamentos de la empresa suelen dar trabajos extras a las recepcionistas, y ellas acaban no pudiendo hacerse cargo tanto del trabajo de la recepción como de los otros extras», dice el gerente de la recepción. Eso es otro hecho.

En el matrimonio: Una escena típica en la empresa Matrimonio, S. A.: el marido llega del trabajo, se quita los zapatos, los calcetines y otras prendas y las deja esparcidas por la casa que la esposa ha pasado todo el día limpiando y arreglando. Juega en el suelo de la sala con el perro y en cinco minutos consigue poner patas arriba lo que ella tardó horas en hacer. La esposa, exasperada, entra en la sala y dice: «¡No tienes ninguna consideración!». Aunque ella honestamente diga y sienta eso, no es necesariamente un hecho. Aún no he encontrado un marido que de camino del trabajo a casa maquinase maquiavélicamente contra la esposa: «Ojalá que la casa esté arreglada, porque cuando yo llegue, voy a desordenarlo todo, ja ja...». El hecho no es que él no tiene consideración. Eso es lo que parece, lo que ella siente. Pero los hechos observables son simplemente que «él deja la ropa fuera de su sitio ni bien llega del trabajo; parece valorar el relajamiento y el estar cómodo después de un día de trabajo, por encima del arreglo de la casa». No entra en cuestión aquí, de momento, lo correcto o errado, sino simplemente el hecho observable por cualquier persona que viera la escena, no solamente la esposa.

Tenemos que tener cuidado para no tener espíritu de juez con nuestro cónyuge. De hecho, si realmente quisiéramos ser un juez, la primera cosa que deberíamos aprender es exactamente a enfocarnos en los hechos, en las evidencias. El buen juez ignora los sentimientos y mira los hechos, nada más; sin embargo, la mayoría de las veces que juzgamos a nuestro cónyuge, somos pésimos jueces, y siempre damos una «sentencia» favorable a nosotros mismos...

Enfocar los hechos es más una forma de separar sentimiento y razón, separar las emociones del problema.

En el caso de la pareja con problemas en el lecho conyugal, los hechos observables pueden incluir, por ejemplo: el último mes tuvieron relación solo dos veces; el marido buscó a la esposa diez veces y todas ellas recibió un no; la esposa a veces siente dolores durante la relación; la pared que separa el cuarto de ellos y el de su hijo no ofrece privacidad; ella confiesa que no ve el sexo como prioridad en el matrimonio y añora la amistad que tenían al principio del matrimonio; ella añade que se siente usada cuando él la presiona a tener sexo cuando no siente deseo.

Hechos son hechos, informaciones verificables por cualquier observador e independientes de opiniones. Este paso es imprescindible para continuar la conversación de forma eficaz y llegar a una buena solución del problema.

5. Explorar ideas

En la empresa: Observe que hasta aquí, en los cuatro primeros pasos, usted solo ha cosechado informaciones para entender y definir el problema. Ahora está listo para comenzar a explorar posibles soluciones. En el mundo corporativo este proceso es conocido como *brainstorming,* una discusión libre en grupo con el objetivo de generar ideas y maneras de resolver un determinado problema. Todos son invitados a contribuir con sus ideas, mientras más, mejor, hasta que las mejores ideas son seleccionadas, y la mejor propuesta es entonces escogida para ser ejecutada.

Tal vez su encargado de despidos sugiera aumentar el salario del puesto y equipararlo con lo que se paga en el mercado. Alguien da la idea de pagar hasta más de lo que se ofrece en el mercado laboral y aumentar las responsabilidades. Otro sugiere que se haga una descripción de funciones y se le explique claramente a la próxima recepcionista, y que se avise a los departamentos de lo que ella no está autorizada a hacer. El gerente de recepción da la idea de que tal vez un plan de carrera puede ser ofrecido como incentivo para que la recepcionista permanezca en el cargo, ya que ella verá la posibilidad de crecer en la empresa. Todas las ideas son recibidas y debidamente consideradas.

En el matrimonio: Este proceso democrático de permitir la sugerencia de ideas es muy importante en el matrimonio. Muchas parejas pecan porque insisten en querer imponer uno al otro su propia solución. El buen líder en el trabajo sabe involucrar a sus compañeros y subordinados en la búsqueda de soluciones, no solo por el beneficio político, sino porque sabe que dos cabezas piensan mejor que una. Así también la pareja debe actuar en la búsqueda de la solución que mejor resuelva el problema, no necesariamente la que agrade a uno más que al otro.

Mirando el problema, que a estas alturas ya debe haber sido definido por los cuatro primeros pasos, la pareja se pregunta: ¿cómo podemos resolver este problema y prevenir que ocurra de nuevo?

Esta práctica es enfatizada por la creatividad y cantidad de ideas. La pareja debe ser creativa y sentirse libre para sugerir soluciones sin criticar, condenar o ridiculizar las ideas propuestas. Incluso porque realmente hay más de una manera de pelar una piña. La esposa sugiere, por ejemplo: «Tal vez puedas esforzarte para que pasemos más tiempo juntos, como hacíamos antes. Eso me hace sentir más cercana a ti. Reconozco que tengo que ser más sensible a tus necesidades también, no rechazarte tantas veces. Voy a esforzarme para valorar más la intimidad física, pues sé que es importante. Si pudieras hacer algo con la pared de nuestro cuarto, yo estaría más dispuesta. La privacidad es muy importante para mí».

Él puede dar otras sugerencias, como: «Podemos ir juntos a un médico para ver esos dolores que tienes. Reconozco que a veces te digo cosas que no debería cuando me enojo. Voy a tener más cuidado con mis palabras. ¿Dónde podemos ceder ambos para equilibrar mejor nuestras necesidades, sin que las impongamos el uno al otro? Yo quiero priorizar tu placer, y pido que me ayudes a descubrir lo que te excita. También puedo informarme más sobre el asunto y buscar ayuda profesional».

No se debe descartar la posibilidad de que ninguno de los dos tenga la solución ideal. Por eso, una idea puede ser buscar ayuda externa profesional, que pueda mostrar la solución para la pareja.

6. Proponer una solución

En la empresa: Entre las varias ideas exploradas, usted tiene que ver cuáles serían las más factibles y eficaces para resolver el problema ahora y, si no es permanentemente, por lo menos durante un largo plazo. Después de todo lo que han oído, digamos que usted y su equipo llegan a la siguiente propuesta: equiparar el salario de la recepcionista con el valor de mercado; proponer un plan de carrera para ella dentro de la empresa y mantener contacto con la nueva recepcionista semanalmente durante los primeros tres meses para identificar las señales de insatisfacción en el trabajo con tiempo, a fin de accionar una solución a tiempo y así minimizar la posibilidad de renuncia. Esa propuesta es elegida porque parece alcanzar las causas principales del problema.

En el matrimonio: Para llegar a una propuesta de solución, tenga en mente que la mejor respuesta a cualquier problema conyugal siempre será aquella en que los dos salen ganando. Si uno pierde, los dos pierden. Por lo tanto, acuérdese aquí de los objetivos de la empresa, del equipo, y no solamente de los individuos. Como en la empresa, proponga lo que mejor parezca alcanzar las causas del problema.

La pareja concluye entonces, por ejemplo, que va a buscar ayuda externa de un médico y otra fuente de conocimiento sobre cómo estimular el placer femenino; los dos se esforzarán más para atender con más equilibrio a las expectativas sexuales del otro, cediendo cuando y donde sea necesario, sin imponerlo indebidamente el uno al otro; se aislará acústicamente la pared del cuarto de la pareja.

7. Concordar un plan de acción

En la empresa: Ahora que tienen una propuesta, todos deben creer en ella, en su viabilidad. Nada será hecho si no hubiera acuerdo entre los responsables. La pregunta que debe responderse es: ¿todos creen y están de acuerdo en que la propuesta podrá resolver el problema? Todos los involucrados tienen que creer y apoyar la propuesta.

En el matrimonio: Si es imprescindible que la propuesta tenga el apoyo de todos en el ambiente de trabajo, mucho más en el matrimonio. No necesitan estar de acuerdo en todo. A veces tendrán que «concordar en discordar» de algunas cosas. Si eso sucede, comiencen buscando puntos en común.

Den pasos cortos. Hay problemas que no se resuelven de una vez, y usted tendrá que repetir ese proceso muchas veces. Pero no dejen que las discordias sobre algunos puntos les impidan actuar en otros donde hay acuerdo. Este paso tiene que concluir con los dos diciendo: estoy de acuerdo en que, si hiciéramos eso, podríamos solucionar el problema.

8. Definir quién hará qué, y hacerlo

En la empresa: ¿Quién va a hacer qué, cómo y cuándo? En las empresas de éxito, nadie sale de una reunión sin decidir esos tres puntos. Las tareas tienen que ser definidas y distribuidas a los responsables, para que cada uno sepa su papel en la solución del problema. Por ejemplo, en la solución propuesta en el paso anterior, usted, como gerente de Recursos Humanos, buscará la aprobación de la dirección para aumentar el salario de la recepcionista.

El responsable del entrenamiento y desarrollo de personal va a preparar un posible plan de carrera para la recepcionista dentro de la empresa. El gerente de la recepción mantendrá contacto con la nueva recepcionista semanalmente para detectar cualquier problema. Los plazos son acordados.

En el matrimonio: Ella buscará al médico, él la acompañará; él buscará un buen libro que le aclare hechos importantes sobre el placer sexual de la mujer; él dejará de presionarla; ambos tendrán más cuidado con las palabras hirientes; él llamará a un profesional para el aislamiento de la pared del cuarto; él será paciente con ella, y ella cederá más con él. Está claro que el «hacer» es la parte más importante de todo eso. Una vez más necesitarán ignorar el sentir, la propia voluntad, y simplemente hacer lo que es correcto y preciso para llegar a la solución. Como en los negocios, con seguridad, los directores no sienten ganas de pagar un salario mayor a la recepcionista, por ejemplo. Pero si eso es necesario para evitar gastos aún mayores con la rotación de personal en aquel puesto, entonces tiene que hacerse.

9. Ver si está funcionando

En la empresa y en el matrimonio: Aunque mucho adelanto ya se haya alcanzado hasta aquí, el problema aún no está resuelto, pues hasta ahora ha sido solo conversación. Por lo que, tanto en la empresa como en el matrimonio, después de que todo ha sido acordado y del debido tiempo para ejecutar el plan de acción, los resultados tienen que ser monitoreados. No abandone el proceso en el octavo paso, que es donde la mayoría cree que ha conseguido resolver el problema. Acompañe paso a paso si la solución propuesta está funcionando.

En la empresa, el buen resultado será que la nueva recepcionista contratada permanezca en el cargo mucho más tiempo y crezca en la compañía.

En el matrimonio, la pareja tendrá mayor satisfacción sexual, menos frustración y ánimos alterados, y la experiencia los habrá hecho aproximarse más el uno al otro.

10. ¿Sí? Continuar. ¿No? Repetir el proceso

En la empresa y en el matrimonio: Siguiendo estos diez pasos, usted probablemente conseguirá resolver el problema, si no totalmente, por lo menos en parte. Si no se resuelve por completo, no se desanime, es absolutamente normal. Puede ser necesaria más de una tentativa. En realidad, este proceso nunca acaba, pues nuevos problemas van surgiendo día tras día, en los negocios y en casa, y tenemos que hacernos expertos en implementar esos pasos a medida que avanzamos.

Muchas veces oigo a las personas decir: «Ya intenté de todo, no hay esperanza para mi marido» o «Mi esposa nunca va a cambiar, yo ya hice por ella todo lo que te puedas imaginar, pero ella no ha cambiado. No hay manera». Alto ahí. Analice estas palabras. ¿Ya intentó de todo? ¿Ya hizo todo lo que se pueda imaginar? No creo. Usted puede haber intentado tres, cinco, diez formas diferentes de resolver la situación, pero no diga que ya intentó de todo. Siempre hay algo diferente que usted aún no ha hecho. «Ya intenté de todo» son palabras de la emoción. Pero la razón rechaza aceptar que no haya solución para un problema.

Por eso, no desista del proceso si al final de un intento el problema aún parece estar ahí. Repita los diez pasos, y ahora con el conocimiento de lo que no funcionó. Es así como lo hacemos en el trabajo.

Los diez pasos

1. Reunirse e iniciar comunicación inmediatamente	Descubrir el problema
2. Oír	
3. Preguntar	
4. Enfocar los hechos	
5. Explorar ideas	Buscar la solución
6. Proponer una solución	
7. Concordar un plan de acción	
8. Definir quién hará qué, y hacerlo	Ejecutar el acuerdo
9. Ver si está funcionando	
10. ¿Sí? Continuar. ¿No? Repetir el proceso	

Preste atención a estos diez pasos y fíjese en la ausencia de emociones en ellos. Es un proceso lógico y racional, no emotivo.

La belleza de este proceso está en el hecho de que ya lo practica diariamente en su trabajo (nadie conseguiría mantener una empresa o un empleo sin practicarlo). Usted ya sigue estos diez pasos instintivamente, aunque no piense en ellos como diez pasos distintos; pero usted los practica varias veces al día, cada minuto.

Es decir, seguramente no necesita aprender esos diez pasos porque ya los domina. Tan solo necesita *transferir* ese conocimiento a su matrimonio y aplicarlo cuando vaya a resolver problemas.

LA PRUEBA DEL TELÉFONO

Normalmente, cuando explico la idea de tratar su matrimonio como una empresa, algunas personas dicen directamente que nunca les va a funcionar. Lo justifican: «Yo tolero a las personas en el trabajo porque no tengo que dormir con ellas. No estoy implicado con ellas sentimentalmente, entonces, es más fácil». Sin embargo, observando con mayor detenimiento, comprobamos que no es así.

Seamos honestos: la verdadera razón por la que controlamos nuestras emociones en el lugar de trabajo no tiene nada que ver con que nos gusten o no las personas y sí con el dinero. Usted no insulta a su patrón y no le da una patada al empleado simplemente porque eso le costaría dinero. Tan es así que, cuando a una persona ya no le preocupa el trabajo, es capaz de «soltar los perros» sobre cualquiera, porque ya planeaba irse de todas maneras. Por lo tanto, controlamos nuestras emociones, la verdad, motivados por el hecho de no querer perder dinero. Ahora responda: ¿no podemos controlar nuestras emociones motivados por el hecho de no querer perder el matrimonio?

Ahí está otro beneficio de ver su matrimonio como una empresa: entender que es su mayor inversión. Las personas casadas, normalmente, son más estables económicamente y en todas las demás áreas de su vida como la salud, la espiritualidad y la familia. No tiene sentido que usted sacrifique sus emociones para tener éxito en el trabajo, pero no en su matrimonio. ¿De qué sirve tener éxito profesional sin ser feliz en el amor? ¿De qué sirve tener tantos bienes sin ser feliz con la familia?

Déjeme plantearle un panorama común en la lucha de la pareja. Marido y mujer están en casa discutiendo sobre algo, con dimes y diretes de allá para acá. Los ánimos están exaltados. De repente, suena el teléfono. El dueño del celular mira quién está llamando, ve que es una llamada importante y decide contestar. Sin embargo, antes, con voz de rabia, grita al marido o a la mujer: «¡ESPERA UN MOMENTO, TENGO QUE ATENDER ESTA LLAMADA!». Entonces, atiende la llamada y, en cuestión de uno o dos segundos, cambia la voz y dice en tono amable y suave: «¿Sí? Hola, Fulano, ¿qué tal? Dime...». La persona del otro lado jamás imaginaría que, dos segundos atrás, quien le atendió la llamada, ¡estaba gritando con rabia! En otras palabras, ¿podemos o no podemos controlar nuestras emociones en medio de una discusión de pareja?

TAREA

¿Vamos a practicar los diez pasos? Identifique un problema que todavía no haya sido resuelto entre ustedes. Tal vez sea mejor no empezar con nada demasiado serio, por ahora; hasta que gane más confianza y dominio sobre sus emociones. Piense en algo que no sea muy sensible, pero que necesite ser resuelto. Empiece definiendo el problema, escriba lo que es en tan solo una o dos frases. Ahora, póngase de acuerdo con su cónyuge un momento, sin distracciones, para tratar el asunto.

/MatrimonioBlindado

Publique esto:
Empecé a usar los
Diez Pasos Para
Resolver Problemas.
@ matrimonioblind

@matrimonioblind

Tuitee esto:
Empecé a usar los
Diez Pasos Para
Resolver Problemas
#matrimonioblindado
@matrimonioblind

CAPÍTULO 7
INSTALANDO UN PARARRAYOS EN SU MATRIMONIO

En el siglo XVIII, cuando las construcciones de edificios más altos se volvieron más comunes, el riesgo de que fueran alcanzados por rayos aumentó. Se comprobaba que, cuanto más alto era el edificio, mayor era el riesgo. El problema causaba incendios y muertes; y nadie conseguía encontrar una solución ni entender por qué los rayos eran atraídos por ciertos edificios.

Religiosos desprovistos de conocimientos decían que los rayos eran las «flechas del juicio de Dios» o provocados por demonios. Sin embargo, curiosamente, los edificios más propensos a ser alcanzados por un rayo eran las iglesias, debido a sus altas torres. El campanario era, generalmente, la primera víctima... El problema era tan serio que las autoridades aconsejaban a la población buscar refugio durante las tormentas «en cualquier lugar menos dentro o cerca de una iglesia». Nadie entendía por qué, según los religiosos, el Todopoderoso se centraba en Sus propios templos o permitía a Satanás hacerlo; sin contar con que, los días de lluvia, nadie iba a la iglesia...

Sin embargo, la verdadera razón no tenía nada que ver con Dios ni con el diablo. Benjamín Franklin descubrió, en 1752, que los rayos trasmitían electricidad. Partiendo de ese conocimiento, Franklin inventó el pararrayos: una barra metálica que, instalada en la parte más alta del edificio y unida por un solo hilo conductor, absorbía la carga eléctrica del rayo y la descargaba en la tierra, librando así del peligro al edificio y a sus ocupantes. Dios lo agradeció y el diablo se rió de los religiosos, que se quedaron con cara de bobos.

La emoción es una forma de energía, como la electricidad. Cuando los ánimos está alterados entre la pareja, el riesgo de «rayos» aumenta. Si las emociones no se controlan, el resultado serán las explosiones de temperamentos, que pueden llevar el matrimonio a la destrucción. Y así como ciertos edificios eran más propensos a ser alcanzados por los rayos, ciertas personas tienen un genio más fuerte y son más difíciles de lidiar por dejarse controlar por las emociones.

No obstante, el mal genio no es una buena excusa, como tampoco lo es culpar a Dios o al diablo de sus emociones negativas. Todos estamos sujetos a las emociones, pero también estamos dotados de inteligencia para controlarlas.

No estamos abogando aquí por reprimir las emociones. Nadie es un robot. El matrimonio es una de las mayores pruebas de nuestro temperamento. No es razonable esperar que, simplemente, vayamos a «tragar sapos» y más sapos y no sufrir ningún tipo de diarrea después... Antes o después, los sapos tendrán que salir por algún sitio.

En vez de reprimir las emociones, tiene que encontrar otro recipiente para ellas que no sea su compañero. Benjamín Franklin descubrió que no era posible evitar los rayos, pero sí cambiar su dirección hacia otro lugar donde no causarían daños. Es decir, tenemos que instalar un pararrayos en nuestro matrimonio para descargar nuestras emociones en otra cosa. Pero ¿cómo?

ANTES DE LOS PARARRAYOS

Al principio de nuestro matrimonio, no teníamos pararrayos. Cristiane y yo soltábamos chispas cuando los ánimos se alteraban. Sus rayos se manifestaban en forma de reclamos, insistencia, celos y palabras duras.

Los míos eran básicamente frialdad en la forma de hablar y el famoso «tratamiento de silencio» que le daba.

Cuando mis emociones afloraban, no sabía cómo lidiar con ellas. Por ser mi naturaleza tranquila, yo era de quedarme callado, acumulando sentimientos negativos dentro de mí. No explotaba, sino que hacía implosión; por no querer discutir con Cristiane, me detenía. Sin embargo, por dentro me quedaba pensando en todo lo que quería decirle, imaginando un diálogo, pero guardando todo dentro de mí mismo (si hubiera podido volcar hacia fuera por lo menos un 10 % de la conversación imaginaria que formaba en mi cabeza, habría resuelto el problema mucho más rápido... Más tarde, aconsejando a otros matrimonios, descubrí que no estaba loco, pues ¡no era el único que hacía eso!). Estaba reprimiendo mis emociones. Los rayos estaban incendiándome por dentro y mi ira incendiaba a Cristiane.

El resultado era que me quedaba con rabia hacia ella durante días y la trataba con el silencio. Algunas veces, de tanto acumular sentimientos negativos, acababa explotando y comportándome como un caballo psicótico preso en un establo en llamas. Da para imaginar, ¿no? Nada bonito.

No hay forma de no sentir emociones. Al fin y al cabo somos de carne y hueso. Pero tenemos que saber y creer que también somos seres inteligentes, no solamente animales que siguen sus instintos. Si por un lado estamos sujetos a las emociones, por otro, podemos sujetar nuestras emociones a nuestra inteligencia.

Fue eso lo que aprendí y empecé a poner en práctica en mi matrimonio. Hoy en día, casi no hay ninguna situación en la que Cristiane y yo provoquemos el temperamento del otro. Pero las pocas veces en que hay algún roce o surge una irritación, mi pararrayos ha sido preguntarme: «¿Cuál es mi objetivo en esta situación? ¿Cuál es el resultado que quiero alcanzar después de resolver este asunto?».

Y luego, pienso: «Quiero estar bien con ella..., dormir abrazado a ella..., haber resuelto el problema de forma favorable para los dos..., no quiero quedar mal, en silencio, callado durante dos o tres días en casa..., etc.».

Entonces, enfocado en esos objetivos, uso mis emociones como energía para resolver el problema racionalmente. Es decir, descargo mis emociones, destilo mis sentimientos en mi razón y me enfoco en los resultados que quiero. Ese proceso me ayuda a controlar lo que siento, en vez de dejar que mis sentimientos me controlen.

Una vez que pongo mis emociones bajo el control de mi inteligencia, inicio el proceso de resolver la cuestión junto a Cristiane. A estas alturas ya no hay rayos, porque fueron conducidos por mi razón en dirección a mis objetivos en lugar de hacia Cristiane. Está claro que eso, a veces, requiere que emplee algunos minutos para organizar mis pensamientos. Si usted tiene un problema semejante, también tendrá que aprender a no entrar en combate impulsivamente y no dejar que sus emociones utilicen su boca.

El mensaje es: encuentre algo para descargar sus emociones que no sea su cónyuge. Lo que describí arriba es lo que me funciona a mí, y usted tiene que averiguar lo que le funciona a usted. Cristiane, por ejemplo, tiene un pararrayos completamente diferente al mío, pero muy eficaz.

Cristiane:

Cuando me altero mucho por algo, yo no consigo hacer lo que Renato hace sin primero orar. Mi pararrayos es la oración. Entro en mi habitación o en otro lugar privado y descargo mi rabia en Dios —no contra Él, sino como un desahogo—. He descubierto que la oración es un canal por el que puedo llevar cualquier frustración a Dios. A fin de cuentas, Él es el Todopoderoso, por lo que puede soportar la furia de una mujer..., al contrario que mi marido. Cuando empecé a practicar eso, Dios me hizo ver que si yo insistiese y siguiese hacia adelante con un determinado asunto, queriendo pelear con Renato, no estaría agradándole a Él, a mi Dios. Entonces, cuando oro, no solamente descargo mis emociones en Dios, sino que también recobro mis fuerzas para decidir no hacer de esa cuestión un problema. Tomo la decisión de relevar y desistir de crear una tempestad, pues esta solo atraerá más rayos de emociones... Por lo tanto, decido sacrificar mis emociones.

Usando la oración, dejé de reclamarle a mi marido y pasé a reclamarle a Dios; dejé de desconfiar de mi marido y pasé a confiar en Dios; dejé de hablarle duramente a mi marido y pasé a hablar abiertamente con Dios. Eso ha sido mi pararrayos desde entonces. Funciona, y yo aconsejo a todas las parejas que experimenten eso, especialmente a la mujer.

Nosotras, las mujeres, solemos ser más emotivas y menos racionales; por eso, la oración es una manera óptima de tomar el control de nuestros sentimientos y actuar de forma más racional. Si nunca lo ha probado, hágalo.

Fíjese que no estoy hablando de un rezo, ni de un ritual religioso, sino de una conversación franca que no podemos tener con nadie —ni con el marido, ni con el padre o con la madre, ni con la amiga—, pues, probablemente, no iban a comprendernos. Pero Dios, que nos hizo como somos, sabe exactamente lo que pasa dentro de nosotros, nos comprende y nos da fuerzas para actuar sabiamente.

Lo mejor de todo es que, al llevarle un problema a Dios en primer lugar, ya estamos yendo directamente a la Fuente. Si no podemos cambiar o hacer que nuestros compañeros nos entiendan, Dios puede. Hay cosas que solo Dios puede hacer; esas son, generalmente, aquellas que pensamos que no tienen solución.

Me acuerdo de una vez que yo tenía la razón y él estaba equivocado, pero no servía de nada, él no lo aceptaba. Cuanto más intentaba explicarle la situación, más me condenaba y se alteraba conmigo. Aquel sentimiento de «pobre y perjudicada» se apoderó de mí, pero decidí dejar de pelear de frente con él y darme un baño. En la ducha, hablé en serio con Dios: «Tú sabes que está equivocado, Tú sabes lo que realmente sucedió, ahora, haz justicia, porque no hay nada más que yo pueda hacer. No quiero enfadarme con Renato, no quiero hacer lo mismo que él está haciendo conmigo, Te pido, Señor, que me justifiques». Cuando salí del baño, Renato todavía estaba con aquella cara de quien iba a guardar aquel episodio durante varios días. No dije nada más, simplemente me fui a dormir, confiando en que Dios me justificaría, tarde o temprano. A la mañana siguiente, la primera cosa que sucedió fue que Renato me abrazó y me pidió perdón.

GENERANDO ANSIEDAD

Cuando nuestras emociones no se desbordan en algo donde puedan ser utilizadas sabiamente, explotarán sobre nuestros cónyuges o serán reprimidas. Esa represión de las emociones es lo que genera la ansiedad, que es una emoción en estado avanzado. La ansiedad es ese sentimiento de constante preocupación, nerviosismo, inquietud y malestar, causado por la inseguridad respecto a lo que va a pasar. Todo ser humano está sujeto a eso.

Esa es una de las razones por las que Dios ha creado la oración, para que podamos lanzar sobre Él nuestra ansiedad. Si lo hacemos, Él promete que cuidará de nosotros.[2] Ese cuidado incluye el alivio de la carga emocional y, también, la dirección para lidiar con la situación.

Usted puede darse cuenta de que la fe no es algo religioso, sino algo extremadamente inteligente. Cuando aprende a usar su fe con inteligencia, usted consigue sacar provecho de ella para resolver los problemas cotidianos.

Por lo tanto, puede estar seguro: habrá días nublados, de lluvias y tempestades en su matrimonio. Cuando lleguen, traerán con ellos los rayos de las emociones. Eso es inevitable. Pero usted puede instalar un pararrayos en su matrimonio para descargar sus emociones en algo que no sea su compañero. El pararrayos, para unos, es contar hasta diez, para otros es la oración, para algunos es dar un paseo... en fin, encuentre el suyo, lo que a usted le funcione.

Y nunca lo olvide: la emoción es la herramienta equivocada para resolver los problemas.

---

[2] Pedro 5:7.

TAREA

¿Qué va a usar como pararrayos?

Defínalo y empiece a practicarlo ya.

/MatrimonioBlindado

Publique esto:
Ya instalé el
pararrayos en mi
matrimonio.

@matrimonioblind

Tuitee esto:
Ya instalé el
pararrayos en mi
matrimonio
#matrimonioblindado
@matrimonioblind

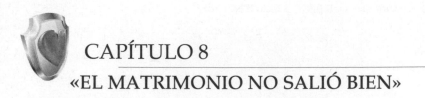

CAPÍTULO 8
«EL MATRIMONIO NO SALIÓ BIEN»

«Mi marido es un hombre fantástico fuera de casa, trata a todo el mundo bien y es admirado por todos; pero, conmigo, es un demonio», se desahogó una esposa durante nuestra sesión de asesoramiento. Sus palabras reflejan las de muchas esposas y maridos que se frustran al ver las dos caras de sus cónyuges. Este síndrome de las dos caras, en realidad, es provocado por la falla de la persona al procesar correctamente sus emociones negativas.

Cuando no descargamos nuestras emociones de forma útil y positiva, se van acumulando y acabamos arrojando todo encima de nuestro compañero. Conseguimos sujetar nuestras emociones en el trabajo porque pensamos que los extraños no tienen la obligación de soportar nuestras frustraciones; sin embargo, creemos, erróneamente, que nuestro cónyuge sí tiene la obligación de escuchar y entender, sin importar cómo nos comportemos. Por eso, vomitamos toda nuestra basura sobre la pareja, sin tener la consideración que tenemos con los extraños. Somos educados con los de fuera pero, dentro de casa, somos una peste.

No es necesario decir que esa actitud va desgastando la relación, causando profundas heridas y, por eso, muchos matrimonios se van distanciando y se va enfriando el amor.

Entienda una cosa: la persona que usted es en casa es quien usted realmente es.

Las personas con el síndrome de las dos caras acostumbran profundizar todavía más en el error cuando se dan cuenta de lo siguiente: en casa, el compañero se siente siempre infeliz y vive protestando por su comportamiento; pero afuera, todos los amigos y compañeros le aprecian y admiran (porque no conocen su otra cara). La conclusión a la que llegan es: «El problema es de mi compañero. A todo el mundo le gusto, pero a él/ella no. Tengo que salir de este matrimonio».

Sin embargo, el problema, claramente, no es el compañero. Si tratasen al compañero con la misma educación y consideración con la que tratan a los extraños, también tendrían su admiración y respeto.

La persona que somos en casa es quien realmente somos. Por eso, incluso si nos divorciamos de aquella persona que creemos que es el problema y nos casamos con otra que nos parece maravillosa y que nos admira tanto, esta persona también empezará a ver nuestra otra cara y a hacer los mismos reclamos que la primera. La verdad es que somos nosotros los que estamos equivocados. Muchos no consiguen ver eso y se van casando y separando intentado encontrar a «la persona adecuada». El problema no es que no encontremos a la persona adecuada; el problema es que no estamos «haciendo las cosas bien» dentro de casa con aquella persona. Estamos actuando racionalmente con los de fuera, pero emocionalmente en casa, arrojando nuestras emociones negativas encima de nuestro compañero.

Por eso, muchos tienen un éxito total en el trabajo pero un fracaso terrible en el amor.

«ME CASÉ CON LA PERSONA EQUIVOCADA»

Cuando la relación empieza a salir mal y la persona no consigue que el compañero sea como quiere –alguien que acepte toda su basura emocional y atienda a todos sus caprichos–, la conclusión obvia viene a su mente: «Me casé con la persona equivocada».

«El matrimonio no salió bien» o «Me casé con la persona equivocada» o «No somos almas gemelas» son expresiones que nos eximen totalmente de culpa cuando la relación se derrumba hacia el fracaso. ¿Qué sucede con el sentido de la responsabilidad?

En los viejos tiempos, un matrimonio fracasado era una vergüenza individual. Cuando las parejas tenían problemas y alguno recurría a la familia o amigos, reclamando el uno del otro, el consejo que generalmente escuchaban era: vuelve, conversen y resuélvanlo. El mensaje estaba claro: lucha por tu matrimonio. Si el matrimonio fracasa, el fracaso es de ustedes.

Hoy, quien da los consejos suele asumir los dolores de la otra persona y decir: «¿Cómo él se atreve a hacer eso contigo? Tú mereces algo mejor, ¡dale una patada!» o «Hay mujeres a montones por ahí, ¿por qué vas a tolerar eso? No salió bien con esa, ¡busca otra!».

Es decir, la culpa es del matrimonio, que salió mal, o de la otra persona por no ser la «adecuada». Es la nueva moda de transferencia de la culpa y el eximirse de la responsabilidad personal por hacer que el matrimonio funcione. Es como si el matrimonio fuese una persona con voluntad propia que pudiese ser el responsable del éxito o del fracaso de la unión o como si solamente la otra persona pudiese garantizar un matrimonio feliz.

La verdad es que la culpa es de los individuos. El matrimonio no es una persona. Son las personas, dentro del matrimonio, las responsables del éxito o el fracaso de la unión.

EL MITO DEL ALMA GEMELA

Una de las cosas que han ayudado a las personas a esquivar cualquier responsabilidad por el éxito o el fracaso del matrimonio es el mito del alma gemela; la idea de que todos tenemos un alma gemela, alguien que nos completará y nos hará perfectamente felices. Pero ¿de dónde salió esa idea? Vino de la mitología griega.

Según el mito, el ser humano, originariamente, tenía cuatro brazos, cuatro piernas y una cabeza formada por dos caras. Pero Zeus, el llamado todopoderoso dios griego, temía el poder de los humanos y los dividió por la mitad, condenándolos a pasar el resto de sus vidas buscando la otra mitad que los complementaría.

Desde entonces, la mayoría de las culturas han idealizado la idea de que cada persona tiene su alma gemela, alguien que comparte con ella una afinidad profunda y natural en el campo afectivo, simpático, amoroso, sexual y espiritual. Este concepto implica que las personas son la mitad de un alma y que deben encontrarse con la otra para ser felices.

La lógica del mito sugiere, por lo tanto, que si la persona con la que me casé no me «completa», no me hace feliz, no me comprende y no me hace sentir como me siento cuando como chocolate, no es mi alma gemela. Por lo tanto, es en vano seguir con la relación intentando conseguir lo que nunca será posible lograr con aquella persona –la persona inadecuada–. La solución es separarse y continuar la búsqueda del alma gemela –la persona adecuada–.

Después de leer esto, tal vez encuentre esta historia un tanto ridícula e increíble, pero le aseguro que ese mito está profundamente enraizado en la mente de la mayoría de las personas. Impregna la gran mayoría de las obras dramáticas, desde Hollywood hasta las novelas, películas infantiles y libros románticos. ¿Quién no ha visto una escena típica de película en que la novia entra en la iglesia y ve al novio en el altar, pero está llena de dudas porque sabe que ese no es su «otra mitad»? Y todos nosotros, telespectadores, somos empujados a creer que, en realidad, su alma gemela está ahí, entre los invitados (o en el aeropuerto, preparado para tomar un avión y marcharse, dependiendo de la película que vea), y nos quedamos deseando que ella no cometa la tontería de casarse con la persona equivocada. De hecho, ella, al final, se da la vuelta y sale corriendo, abandonando al pobre chico en el altar para unirse a «su otra mitad».

Incluso en el medio cristiano, a pesar de no existir una base bíblica para esta creencia de que Dios habría creado un alma gemela para cada persona, muchos viven orando para encontrar a su «querida mitad»... Y se quedan solteros durante mucho más tiempo del que deberían, porque nunca están seguros si esta o aquella persona es la correcta, tal vez porque no han sentido «aquella química». Muchos viven aterrorizados por la idea del matrimonio. La duda y el miedo están siempre presentes: «No sé si es él/ella».

El mito del alma gemela ha tenido gran aceptación en todas las culturas, e incluso en religiones, por ser muy romántico y atractivo. La idea de que solo existe una persona en el Universo capaz de completarle y de que Dios creó una persona solamente para usted, es muy bonita. (Parece que nadie piensa: ¿y si, por ejemplo, esa persona vive en Kazajistán?)

No es difícil de entender lo que hace esa idea tan irresistible. Es porque elimina la necesidad de esforzarnos por nuestra parte y nos exime de responsabilidad cuando el matrimonio no sale bien. «Ella no era mi alma gemela». Listo. La culpa no fue suya. Es que usted solamente todavía no encontró a su querida mitad...

Las personas no quieren tomarse trabajo, quieren las cosas rápidas. Es el carácter del ser humano. Microondas, café instantáneo, pastillas para adelgazar... Felicidad con un chasquido de dedos.

En esa línea de pensamiento, las personas actúan emotivamente y no por la razón. Cuando están pasando por problemas crónicos en la relación, empiezan a pensar en tirar la toalla. «Ya lo intenté, pero no salió bien». «Es muy difícil, no voy a aguantar».

Ahora bien, ¿qué hacemos en el trabajo cuando intentamos resolver un problema y fracasamos? Está claro, lo intentamos de nuevo. ¿Y si fallamos de nuevo? Lo seguimos intentando, de varias maneras, hasta encontrar la solución, porque de ella depende la supervivencia de la empresa y nuestra fuente de sustento. No desistimos. No echamos la culpa a los demás. Asumimos nuestra responsabilidad y vamos en busca de una solución. Dejamos lo que sentimos de lado y usamos nuestra inteligencia, creatividad y perseverancia para resolver el problema. Y, si no conseguimos resolver el problema, encontramos una manera de no dejar que afecte al resto de la empresa. Hacemos la debida compensación. Pero ¿desistir? Jamás.

Es más: ese espíritu de perseverancia, de enfrentar los problemas sin miedo y de encontrar una solución cueste lo que cueste es la principal razón del éxito de una persona en su trabajo o empresa. Las personas de éxito no huyen del problema: lo enfrentan. Saben que todo desafío es provechoso, que todo problema representa una oportunidad. Entonces encaran las dificultades con naturalidad y pasan a recibir más confianza con más responsabilidades en el trabajo, siendo ascendidas a cargos mayores.

Cuando usted es conocido en el trabajo como la persona que resuelve problemas, todo el mundo acude a usted. Usted es la persona. Todos saben que, si quieren que algo se lleve a cabo, tienen que ponerlo en sus manos. Y eso le va dando más experiencia, más respeto, y va creciendo como persona dentro de la empresa.

En cambio, cuando no asume la responsabilidad de resolver los problemas de su trabajo, sino que se pone a dar excusas y a echarles la culpa a los demás, nadie quiere tratar con usted. Nadie quiere oír excusas. Usted no fue contratado para dar excusas, para limitarse a señalar el error de los demás o lamentarse.

Cristiane me desafió a ser una persona mejor. Tuve que aprender a resolver problemas que nunca había tenido antes. Tuve, también, que reconocer mis defectos y ser humilde para cambiar. Pero fui perseverante, pues los cambios no fueron rápidos. Tuve que intentarlo de varias maneras y siempre resistir a la idea de desistir.

Es eso lo que debemos hacer en el matrimonio. Lo que está aprendiendo en este libro son cosas que funcionan y que pueden cambiar su relación, e incluso a usted como persona; pero no debe esperar un cambio inmediato; es necesario tiempo para que los frutos empiecen a aparecer. Es una inversión a largo plazo, principalmente si está luchando prácticamente solo/a para salvar el matrimonio y la otra persona está endurecida o escéptica de que usted pueda cambiar. No espere que solamente porque empezó a actuar de forma diferente ayer, hoy la otra persona va a creer en su cambio. Es necesario rescatar la confianza. Sea constante. La otra persona necesita ver que su cambio es verdadero y permanente. Acepte el desafío; por el matrimonio y por usted mismo.

PERSONA CORRECTA VS. ACTITUDES CORRECTAS

La clave para un matrimonio feliz no es encontrar a la persona adecuada, es hacer las cosas adecuadas.

Si hace lo que es correcto para la relación, el matrimonio sale bien. Si hace lo que está equivocado, sale mal.

Cuando Dios creó al hombre y a la mujer, no los creó como «almas gemelas». Después de crear al hombre, Dios decidió crear una «auxiliadora»[3] para el hombre, que lo ayudase. No dijo nada de completarse el uno al otro, ni los puso bajo la responsabilidad de hacer al otro feliz. Habló de «ayudar». La pareja debe verse como auxiliadores uno del otro, personas que están comprometidas a ayudarse la una a la otra. Está claro que un subproducto de esta asociación es la inevitable felicidad de los dos y la percepción de que los dos son uno solo, «una sola carne».

Por eso, dejará el hombre a su padre y a su madre y se unirá a su mujer, volviéndose los dos una sola carne.[4]

Obsérvese que los dos solo se volverán una sola carne después de que se unan. No eran «dos mitades» antes de casarse, como si ya estuviesen predestinados a unirse, no. El milagro de la fusión de los dos individuos sucede cuando ambos se unen en un solo propósito de hacer con que el matrimonio funcione, sin importar lo que venga.

---

[3] Génesis 2:18.
[4] Génesis 2:24.

Claro que si usted todavía está soltero (o soltera) y está considerando a alguien para casarse, debe buscar la mejor persona que pueda (no se va a casar con un psicópata y pensar que «con amor puedo cambiarlo»). Pero la verdad es que un matrimonio feliz no depende tanto de que la persona sea la «adecuada» como de que los dos hagan las cosas correctas.

Lo que hace que la relación funcione es la obediencia a ciertas leyes de convivencia. Cuando Dios creó al hombre y a la mujer, Él estableció ciertas leyes que regulan esa relación. Si respetan esas leyes serán felices; si no, no hay alma gemela que aguante quedarse con usted.

El negocio con las leyes es el siguiente: usted obedece, ellas le protegen; usted las desobedece, ellas le castigan. Si usted salta de un edificio de diez pisos, seguramente va a morir. La ley de la gravedad se asegurará de eso. Si va a un safari y sale del coche para sacar una fotito a un león, porque es tan bonito y parece tan tranquilo, probablemente usted se convierta en su almuerzo. La ley de la selva garantiza eso. Quiera o no creer en esas leyes, está sujeto a ellas.

Las leyes de las relaciones establecidas por Dios no son desconocidas por nadie. Cosas como perdonar, tratar al otro como se quiere ser tratado, tener paciencia, servir, ayudar, oír, no ser egoísta, decir la verdad, ser fiel, respetar, tener buenos ojos, quitar la viga del propio ojo primero, cuidar, agradar, etc., cosas básicas para que haya una relación. Eso es lo que las personas saben que deben hacer, pero no lo hacen. Quebrantan esas leyes y cosechan las consecuencias de ello.

Si obedece las leyes de las relaciones, ellas le protegen; si las desobedece, le castigan. Así de simple.

No hay otro camino. Pueden intentar culpar al matrimonio como institución, facilitar el divorcio, inventar relaciones alternativas, vivir buscando el alma gemela... pero la única manera de que una relación sea exitosa es respetando las leyes que la rigen. Y este poder está en sus manos. Es su responsabilidad. Entender eso fue el punto decisivo en mi matrimonio, lo que sucedió durante una llamada de teléfono.

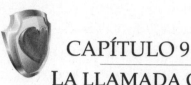

CAPÍTULO 9
LA LLAMADA QUE SALVÓ NUESTRO MATRIMONIO

Cristiane y yo nunca tuvimos un matrimonio que alguien pudiese llamar conflictivo. Al contrario, vivíamos bien la mayor parte del tiempo. Quien nos veía desde fuera podía jurar que éramos un matrimonio perfecto. No vivíamos peleando, nunca hubo una infidelidad y teníamos los mismos objetivos. Sin embargo, de vez en cuando, más concretamente cada cuatro o seis meses, teníamos una gran discrepancia sobre algún tema. Era como si la cosa se quedase rumiando en el estómago de nuestra relación durante meses hasta que volvía a la boca y era vomitada; cosas que no habían sido nunca verdaderamente digeridas y procesadas entre nosotros; raíces de problemas que no conocíamos y, por lo tanto, nunca habían sido cortadas.

A veces, la discrepancia era en relación con los celos, sobre mi falta de atención hacia ella, sobre el trabajo que hacíamos, sobre cómo sentía que me faltaba al respeto y otras vertientes. Todo hojas y ramas. No veíamos las raíces de los problemas.

Cuando teníamos esas grandes desavenencias, nos quedábamos durante horas intercambiando palabras en la habitación. A veces, los ánimos se calentaban. Ella lloraba y, si elevaba la voz, yo la elevaba más todavía. Llegaba un punto en el que nos cansábamos y ahí, por lo menos para mí, el objetivo ya no era resolver el problema que fuese, sino solo salir de aquella desagradable situación. Rodeábamos la situación, pero nada se resolvía. Yo me mantenía en silencio con ella durante algunos días y ella se quedaba con los ojos hinchados de llorar. Todo volvía a la «normalidad» por lo menos durante cuatro o seis meses más. Y así fueron los primeros doce años de nuestro matrimonio.

En mi mente, yo pensaba: «El problema es ella. Yo no estoy haciendo nada mal. Es ella quien tiene una cabeza dura e imposible de entender. Yo tengo que mantenerme firme en esta línea porque, algún día, ella va a tener que ceder y cambiar». Y eso no era un secreto. Varias veces le dije a Cristiane: «¡Tú eres quien tiene el problema! Yo estoy bien, no estoy haciendo nada malo. Es mejor que resuelvas tus pensamientos porque yo no tengo tiempo para eso». Y ella respondía con lágrimas, con insistencia en su punto de vista.

Yo no estaba queriendo ser malvado. Realmente pensaba de esa manera. Dura cosa es estar sinceramente equivocado. Un día horrible, que se volvió bonito, tuvimos una de esas peleas y la discusión se prolongó más de lo normal. Ya era de madrugada y no había un final a la vista, hasta que Cristiane tuvo una idea: «Voy a llamar a mi padre». Me pareció excelente. Agarré el teléfono y se lo puse en la mano. «¡Llama ahora! ¡Vas a ver como tengo razón!».

Por lo que sabía de su padre, a quien respeto mucho, y por el asunto que estábamos discutiendo, tenía la seguridad de que él iba a confirmar que ella estaba equivocada. Como él nunca fue parcial, ni por ella ni por mí, yo lo tenía por la voz de la razón. Por eso, a pesar de la vergüenza y de no gustarme tener que llevarle aquel problema, vi su decisión como una buena opción.

Salí de la habitación y dejé que ella hablase con su padre. Transcurridos unos cinco minutos, salió de la habitación, mucho más calmada, me pasó el teléfono y me dijo: «Quiere hablar contigo».

«Sí, señor», atendí.

Él fue directo a la yugular, alto y claro: «Renato, déjame que te diga una cosa. Ese problema ES TUYO. ¡RESUÉLVELO!».

Aquello me agarró por sorpresa. No era lo que yo esperaba. Creía que él iba a mostrar empatía hacia mí, decirme que había hablado con ella y, ahora, ella me iba a entender mejor y que yo debía tenerle paciencia. Sin embargo, aquellas palabras, «ese problema es tuyo, ¡resuélvelo!», fueron como un hierro de marcar ganado clavándose en mi mente.

Él no dijo nada más. Me quedé mudo y, después de algunos segundos, respondí: «Puede estar seguro de que nunca más recibirá una llamada como esta, porque lo voy a resolver». Le di las gracias y colgué el teléfono.

«Ese problema es tuyo, ¡resuélvelo!». Las palabras se quedaron resonando en mi mente. De repente, la venda se me cayó de los ojos. «Ese problema es mío. ¡Soy yo quien tiene que resolverlo!». Todo empezó a aclararse.

Hasta entonces yo estaba golpeando en la misma tecla, diciéndole a Cristiane: «Tú eres quien tiene el problema». Aquel modo de pensar me hacía lanzar el problema sobre ella y culparla por fallar en resolverlo. Automáticamente, me eximía de la culpa y me «lavaba las manos». Si este matrimonio falla, no va a ser mi culpa, pensaba.

Esa mentalidad, además de hacerme pensar que la responsabilidad no era mía, empeoraba la situación de dos maneras: 1) dejaba el poder totalmente en manos de Cristiane para hacer lo que quisiera con la situación (desistir del matrimonio, luchar por él, continuar como estaba) y 2) le daba a ella la impresión de que no me preocupaba por ella y no estaba dispuesto a hacer nada para cambiar la situación.

Si ella hubiera sido otro tipo de mujer, habría tomado aquel poder que yo, inconscientemente, ponía en sus manos, le uniría el sentimiento de desprecio que le trasmitía con mi actitud y habría puesto fin a nuestro matrimonio. Y hoy entiendo que yo habría sido el máximo responsable. ¿Por qué? *Porque yo no había cumplido mi papel de líder y cabeza en mi matrimonio.*

Lo que aquella llamada me hizo entender fue que, como marido, todo y cualquier problema que ocurra en mi matrimonio es también mi problema. No puedo separar algunos problemas para mí y otros para mi esposa. Todos los problemas son nuestros. Si ella tiene un problema, yo tengo un problema. Si ella está enferma, yo estoy enfermo. Si ella hace un reclamo, yo debo ver lo que es y actuar rápido en la fuente del problema, aunque me parezca que es «cosa de mujer». Ese concepto cambió mi visión sobre nuestros problemas conyugales.

Veo que los hombres, en general, tienen esa tendencia a echar el problema sobre su mujer y continuar viviendo su propia vida como si todo fuese normal. La naturaleza del hombre tiende a hacerle evitar o huir de la mujer cuando está alterada; por eso, cuando ella lo enfrenta con un problema, él enseguida quiere apuntar con el dedo de nuevo hacia ella y dejar la conversación. De ahí provienen los hábitos típicamente masculinos de quitar el centro de atención de la mujer y ponerlo en el trabajo, el fútbol, la televisión, los videojuegos, etc. como una forma de escape. Esos hombres necesitan entender que evitar o huir del problema no lo va a resolver. Repito, el problema no es como el vino.

El hombre tiene que tomar las riendas de la situación y, como un buen líder, buscar la solución del problema juntamente con su mujer. Y fue eso lo que yo hice inmediatamente después de aquella llamada.

LA LISTA

Con la bendición de su padre, y con mi nueva visión de que el problema era mío y era mi responsabilidad resolverlo, entré de nuevo en la habitación con Cristiane y fui pragmático: «Vamos a hacer una lista de todo lo que está mal en nuestro matrimonio. Quiero que me digas todas tus quejas y vamos a escribirlas. Después me toca a mí. A partir de ahí vamos a trabajar juntos para eliminar cada punto de la lista». Y comenzamos. El resultado final fue 6 x 11, seis ítems de ella sobre mí, y once míos sobre ella. Uno más y yo doblaba la ventaja, ja ja... Pero lo interesante es que, cuando nos sentamos para hacer esa lista, tuvimos más progresos en treinta minutos que en los doce primeros años de nuestro matrimonio. Es increíble hasta qué punto el uso de la razón es eficaz en la solución de problemas, especialmente en el matrimonio. Aquel ejercicio fue un acto de lucidez, inteligencia, y cero por ciento de emoción. Por eso los resultados fueron positivos. Yo no voy a hablar aquí de cuáles fueron los ítems en la lista, pero puedo decir que se resumían en dos categorías:

- Cosas malas que ya no íbamos a hacer, que entristecían o herían uno al otro.
- Cosas buenas que íbamos a comenzar a hacer por el otro, cosas que agradarían y harían a la otra persona feliz.

Así de sencillo. Esa lista nos ayudó a dejar de quedarnos mirando los defectos uno del otro y comenzar a mirar hacia nosotros mismos, hacia aquello que debíamos hacer para mejorar la relación. Ahora, con la lista, teníamos una meta clara y objetiva. Ambos entendimos que, si trabajábamos juntos para eliminar cada ítem de la lista, cada uno haciendo su parte sin quedarse señalando los defectos del otro, no tendríamos nunca más aquellos problemas. Y aquella perspectiva, de no volver a pasar por aquellas experiencias dolorosas cada seis meses, nos motivó bastante. Yo estaba determinado a hacer todo lo que aún no había hecho para resolver aquel problema de una vez por todas. En definitiva, si no se resolviera nada, el fracaso sería más mío que de ella, ya que yo era el líder y cabeza de mi matrimonio.

Sin embargo, yo sabía que necesitaba ayuda de lo alto. No era suficiente solamente confiar en mis propias habilidades, pues la lista era grande, diecisiete ítems en total, sin contar las derivaciones de todos ellos... No iba a ser fácil. Por eso, hacia las dos y media de la mañana, en aquella misma noche, cuando terminamos la lista y acordamos que íbamos a trabajar en ella, yo me metí la lista en el bolsillo, entré en el coche y fui a la iglesia donde trabajaba. No podía esperar al amanecer.

Era ahora o nunca. Entré en la iglesia, estaba todo apagado, y me dirigí al altar. No había nadie allí, solo Dios y yo. Allí derramé mi alma delante de Él. Admití mis errores, pedí perdón, pedí fuerzas y dirección para mi vida y mi matrimonio. Yo no aceptaba que lo que había acontecido en el matrimonio de mis padres fuera a acontecer en el mío. Jamás iba a aceptar aquello, y por eso estaba allí, pidiendo a Dios que colocara su mano sobre mí y Cristiane. Levanté la lista hacia Él y le pedí ayuda. Fue una verdadera limpieza espiritual, un momento muy íntimo y real que tuve con Dios. Salí de allí liviano y fortalecido.

Nada había cambiado aún en la práctica, pero la verdad es que todo comenzó a cambiar a partir de ahí. Volví a casa, abracé a Cristiane y dormimos juntos. Mañana sería otro día. El primer día de nuestro nuevo matrimonio. Las cosas no cambiaron de golpe, pero fuimos aplicándonos. No tardó mucho. En algunas semanas, ya percibíamos que nuestro matrimonio había renacido. Aún hoy yo conservo esa lista y cuando escribía este capítulo fui a echarle un vistazo, solo por curiosidad. Fue una alegría ver una vez más que todas las metas que escribimos ya se habían alcanzado, y mucho más. El círculo vicioso de problemas había sido roto; las raíces, cortadas. Es el poder de entender: «Ese problema es SUYO. Es usted quien tiene que resolverlo».

Ahora que usted entiende esto, voy a dejar a Cristiane contar en el próximo capítulo cómo fue la conversación de ella con su padre durante y después de aquella llamada y cómo eso produjo el cambio.

TAREA

La lista funcionó para nosotros, y tengo la certeza de que puede funcionar para usted. Muchas veces subestimamos el poder de escribir, de colocar algo en el papel. Por eso, hoy quiero animarlo a escribir su propia lista. Pregunte a su compañero/a lo que lo/la hace ser una persona difícil con la que tratar. Escriba una lista, independientemente de cómo se sienta. Si su compañero/a está haciendo lo mismo, dele su opinión para que él/ella pueda escribir su lista también. Importante: esta no es una oportunidad para atacar a su compañero/a o para desenterrar difuntos... Ni es hora de quedarse a la defensiva. Su objetivo en esta tarea es reunir una lista de cosas en las que usted comenzará a trabajar para resolver en su relación. Mire con frecuencia esta lista y vaya actuando sobre cada punto de ella hasta terminarla.

Decisión
A partir de ahora voy a trabajar en cada ítem que acordé con mi cónyuge que necesitamos cumplir/eliminar. Estos problemas son MÍOS, y yo voy a resolverlos.

/MatrimonioBlindado

Publique esto:
Hice «la lista» con
mi esposo/a.

@matrimonioblind

Tuitee esto:
Hice «la lista» con
mi esposo/a
#matrimonioblindado
@matrimonioblind

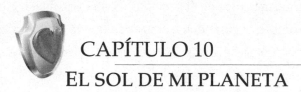

CAPÍTULO 10
EL SOL DE MI PLANETA

Cristiane:

Cuando mi padre atendió el teléfono, intenté explicarle la situación. Estaba llorando, no conseguía ni hablar bien, porque cuando hablamos con nuestros parientes sobre problemas, es entonces cuando nos derrumbamos solo de la emoción. Él simplemente se quedó escuchando y, después de unos minutos, todo lo que dijo fue: «Dale el teléfono a Renato, déjame hablar con él». Usted ya conoce el resto de la historia.

Aquella llamada fue el punto de partida para el cambio en nuestro matrimonio; sin embargo, lo que realmente me llevó a cambiar fue la continuación de esa conversación que tuve con mi padre algunos días después. La lista que Renato y yo hicimos renovó nuestro compromiso de luchar para cambiar y hacer lo que fuese necesario para agradar al otro, pero dentro de mí había un problema más profundo, que ni yo misma sabía que existía. Solamente lo descubrí cuando mi padre vino a visitarme y me preguntó cómo estaba después de aquella llamada.

Él nunca se entrometió en nuestro matrimonio, pero, debido a lo que había sucedido, era de esperar que quisiera saber. Le respondí que estaba «intentando» cambiar. No entré en detalles, solo le dije eso. Para ser sincera, en aquel momento yo no estaba muy segura de si las cosas habían cambiado o no. Muchas veces, en el pasado, me había dicho a mí misma que iba a cambiar, pero pasaban algunos meses y estaba haciendo las mismas cosas. ¿Quién me garantizaba que ambos pondríamos de nuestra parte para cumplir aquella lista?

Así que mi padre, dándose cuenta de mi duda, fue directo al grano. Nunca me olvido de aquel día. Estábamos en el jardín, se volvió hacia mí y me dijo: «Hija mía, a ningún hombre le gusta que su mujer se quede implorando su atención. Pierdes tu valor como mujer. Ocúpate en ayudar a las personas, haz algo con tus talentos, desarrolla tu llamado».

Fue eso lo único que me dijo. Era todo lo que necesitaba oír. Descubrí que, en todos aquellos años de matrimonio, estaba realmente haciendo de Renato el sol de mi planeta.

Como esposa de pastor, iba a la iglesia, ayudaba en lo que se me confiaba, hacía lo «máximo» que podía hacer, pero, al final del día, mi centro de atención siempre recaía sobre Renato. Todo lo que quería era llamar su atención, conseguir su aprecio, sentir su compañía, ser importante a su lado, lo que no era pedir demasiado, pero cuando eso es todo para alguien, es otra cuestión, pues se acaba haciendo todo en función de aquella persona y, si esa persona no le da la debida importancia, todo lo que uno ha hecho no sirve de nada para uno.

Aunque en aquella época no fuera consciente totalmente de eso, fue lo que descubrí sobre mí misma. Durante todos aquellos años, en vez de estar al lado de mi marido, me había puesto detrás de él. Está claro que él no iba a quedarse mirando hacia atrás, viendo lo que yo estaba haciendo allí. En realidad, yo cargaba con una mentalidad equivocada de lo que la mujer representaba para su marido.

Escuchaba a muchas mujeres hablar de que nosotras somos el soporte del portarretratos, ahí escondidito. Mientras nuestros maridos estaban en pie, ahí, al frente, nosotras, las mujeres, teníamos que estar detrás de ellos, dándoles el soporte necesario. Una idea anticuada y sin ninguna base fundamental. Creo que, por esas y otras ideas, muchas mujeres han defendido el feminismo. Si yo no hubiera despertado a la realidad, también habría hecho lo mismo. Llega un momento en el que cansa quedarse solo entre bastidores, sentirse menos importante que el propio compañero y permanecer en su dependencia para suplir su valor.

Fueron aquellas palabras que me dijo mi padre por las que yo, finalmente, me embarqué en una jornada interesante, llena de aventuras y muy productiva. Me conocí mejor.

PRESENTANDO: CRISTIANE 2.0

Empecé a desarrollar talentos que estaban escondidos o adormecidos, invirtiendo no solamente en ayudar a otras personas, sino también en mí. Cada vez que hacía algo nuevo, diferente y productivo, mi autoestima lo agradecía. Ayudaba a los demás y, en la medida que eran ayudados, me valoraban y, como consecuencia, eso me ayudaba a vencer toda esa inseguridad que llevaba dentro de mí.

Dejé de hacer las cosas para llamar la atención de Renato. Pude entenderle mejor porque ahora estaba en el mismo barco, trabajaba con los mismos objetivos que él, solo que en sociedad con él y no entre bastidores. Dejé de enfocarme en él para enfocarme en mí y en cómo podía también desarrollar mis talentos y, con ellos, ayudar a otras personas. Salí de mi capullo. Es increíble cómo un simple cambio en el punto de mira lo transforma todo. Los problemas que anteriormente me hacían llorar y protestar se volvieron tan ínfimos que no valían ya ni un solo centavo de mi atención.

Un ejemplo fue el tema de que Renato no salía conmigo a pasear con mucha frecuencia. Antes, yo incluso intentaba fingir, durante un tiempo, que no me importaba; pero llegaba un momento en el que ya no aguantaba más, y listo, teníamos otra pelea. Después de ese cambio de objetivo, eso ya no merecía llamarse problema o falta de consideración. Me adapté a su forma de ser casera. Cuando llegaba nuestro día de descanso ya no me quedaba con la expectativa de qué haríamos, al contrario, encontraba algo que hacer en casa. Hacía videos en la computadora, leía libros, alquilaba una película, me hacía una limpieza de cutis, en fin... ¿Y sabe lo que sucedió? Me convertí en una mujer mucho más agradable.

No pasó mucho tiempo sin que que Renato observase ese cambio en mí y me encontrara más interesante. Lo que antes era algo raro se convirtió en algo diario entre nosotros. Nuestras conversaciones eran divertidas, compartíamos ideas, hablábamos de nuestras experiencias diarias sin que yo necesitara pedirlo. Aparté el foco de Renato, dejé de criticarlo por todo lo que no me daba, y lo puse en mí misma. Fue entonces cuando conseguí observarme y ver lo que me faltaba.

Durante todos aquellos años, todo lo que Renato necesitaba de mí era una compañera. Y yo, honestamente, pensaba que era esa compañera hasta ese momento en el que descubrí que ser compañera no es correr detrás del compañero y sí a su lado. Por eso, él no estaba interesado en compartir su día conmigo, por eso no me incluía en sus planes diarios. Yo no estaba en el mismo barco y sí en un barquito por detrás, intentado llegar cerca de su yate. Lo interesante es que él ya había comentado que me implicase más en lo que él hacía...

Una cosa es que su compañero le diga lo que usted debe cambiar, otra completamente diferente es que usted descubra en qué usted tiene que cambiar. Un simple ajuste de enfoque transformó nuestro matrimonio. Y cuando yo ya me había acostumbrado al modo casero de Renato, él se adaptó a mí. Empezamos una competencia saludable: ¡quién agrada más al otro!

Veo ese problema casi todos los días en el trabajo que hago con las mujeres. Parece que tenemos esa tendencia a enfocarnos más en los otros que en nosotras mismas. Vamos de un extremo al otro. Unas se detienen en el tiempo, debido a la vida amorosa, y otras dejan la vida sentimental de lado para seguir una carrera, como si no fuésemos capaces de tener las dos cosas al mismo tiempo y ser felices.

Es así como muchas mujeres inteligentes acaban convirtiéndose en mujeres frustradas. Por muy importante que sea la carrera, necesitamos a nuestro compañero para aprovecharla de verdad. Y, por mucho que la vida sentimental sea importante, necesitamos ser independientes de ella para no convertirnos en insoportables para la persona que amamos. Si depende de alguien para ser feliz, nunca conseguirá hacer feliz a nadie.

Su compañero no tiene la menor oportunidad de ser su sol. Él tiene defectos, no siempre la podrá iluminar ni suplir todo lo que necesita; por eso, no es sabio ponerlo en esa posición. Usted puede estar haciéndolo todo bien, era lo que yo creía, pero, incluso así, no va a cambiar la situación en la que está. Sus ojos tienen que estar enfocados primero en usted para que, de esta forma, haya un cambio real y concreto en su relación.

Nunca me olvido de una frase que escuché en una reunión en la iglesia: «Mientras usted mire hacia las demás personas a su alrededor siempre va a tener problemas».

LUZ PROPIA

Me acuerdo de una mujer que solo después de casi veinte años de casada descubrió que su marido nunca la había amado. Su mundo se derrumbó, cayó sin paracaídas, hasta que, finalmente, despertó y se apegó a la fe. Muchas, en su lugar, habrían convertido sus vidas en un desastre; pero su historia puede ilustrar lo que acabamos de escribir.

Imagine a una bonita mujer, inteligente, con mucho talento, llena de los valores que todo hombre de verdad busca. Durante todos los años de matrimonio vivía corriendo detrás del marido, que no daba ningún valor a todo lo que ella hacía. Con el tiempo se adaptó a la extraña forma de ser de él; ni siquiera pensó nunca en una posible separación en el futuro. Se había casado para el resto de su vida y, por eso, soportó todo y un poco más. Hasta que un día, de la nada, él finalmente le reveló con palabras que no la amaba.

En vez de haberse percatado de eso mucho antes, desde el principio del matrimonio, ella se sorprendió, como si él hubiese cambiado de la noche a la mañana. ¿Por qué no se había dado cuenta de eso antes?

La mujer que hace de su marido su sol tiene esa desventaja. no se valora y, por eso, no pone ciertos límites. Cuando convierte a otra persona en alguien más importante que usted mismo, se disminuye y se desvaloriza ante ella. El otro tiene todo el poder en la relación; si quisiera herirle, puede hacerlo cuantas veces quiera porque sabe que usted nunca —jamás— le dejará. Su vida gira alrededor de esa persona en vez de invertir en usted misma, en sus valores y talentos; guarda todo en un baúl dentro de sí, bajo siete llaves.

Hasta conocer a su marido, esa mujer era aquella joven llena de vida, con sueños y planes de futuro; una joven muy interesante que cautivó el corazón del muchacho hasta el punto de que él pensara: «Quiero pasar el resto de mi vida a su lado». Después de casarse, guardó todo dentro del baúl y pasó a ser una molestia. Vivía reclamándole cuentas, imponiendo su voluntad y encontrando defectos en todo lo que él hacía.

Ella no hacía eso a propósito —nadie lo hace—. Yo, por ejemplo, no me daba cuenta de lo que hacía; al contrario, pensaba que ese era mi papel. Debe ser nuestra naturaleza de madre, siempre queriendo arreglar las cosas, proporcionarles una ayudita a nuestros hijos, haciendo de ellos los mejores en todo. Solo que nuestros maridos no son nuestros hijos.

No estoy sugiriendo que el marido de esa mujer la dejó de amar debido a esa actitud, pero eso puede haber contribuido, y mucho. El hombre tiene la naturaleza de conquistar, como vamos a explicar en los próximos capítulos. Cuando su mujer deja de ser una conquista diaria, él es capaz de buscar otras conquistas. Es decir, ella no puede, ni debe, dejarle sentir que es el centro de su atención.

El valor de la mujer está en su misterio, su discreción, su forma de hacer florecer una situación. Es exactamente lo que mi padre me indicó: al hombre no le gusta la mujer fácil, aunque sea su propia mujer. Cuando me ocupé en ayudar a otras personas, desarrollando nuevos talentos en el proceso, Renato empezó a sentir la falta de mi constante atención. Obviamente, me volví una nueva conquista para él. Pasé a tener luz propia.

No hay forma de que su matrimonio florezca con los años si usted, como mujer, no florece cada día. Con cada conquista que hago, cada libro que escribo, cada proyecto que creo, más autoconfianza tengo en mí y más interesante resulto para Renato. Vuelvo a ser aquella joven que Renato conoció, llena de sueños, muy divertida y una óptima compañía para el resto de su vida. Eso sí es tener una sociedad, sí es ser un equipo.

Cuando Renato escuchó por primera vez que yo lo hacía mi sol en el pasado, preguntó, con la cara de quien pierde una posición muy importante: «¿Puedo por lo menos ser tu luna?». A fin de cuentas, todo marido quiere su debida atención... No es porque ellos no puedan ser nuestro sol que vamos a dejarlos de lado y vivir nuestra propia vida. No fue eso lo que yo hice y, si usted hace eso, puede olvidarse de todo lo que ha aprendido en este libro, pues su matrimonio estará destinado al fracaso.

Lo que queremos decir es que, si usted no está bien consigo misma, si no se conoce ni conoce su propio valor, la tendencia es a hacer de su compañero ese sol, su puerto seguro. Eso no es inteligente.

Aunque su compañero no quiera ya invertir en el matrimonio, e incluso esté con otra persona, no deje de florecer tan solo porque él ya no se encuentra en su vida. Esa mujer cuyo marido la dejó después de casi veinte años hoy está mucho más bonita en todos los sentidos, parece hasta que la partida de él le hizo bien. Lo adecuado sería que usted mejore mientras están juntos y, quién sabe, incluso logre reconquistar el corazón de la otra persona.

HOMBRE EMPALAGOSO

La mujer tiende a hacer, de la persona que ama mucho, su sol; sin embargo, ella misma odia ser el sol. Lo sé, lo sé, nos encanta recibir atención, pero cuando esta es exagerada y pegajosa, da asco. A ninguna mujer le gusta un hombre pegajoso.

Para nosotras, mujeres, el hombre tiene que mostrarnos fuerza, cierta independencia y liderazgo. Podemos no mostrar eso muchas veces, especialmente cuando estamos chocando con alguna de sus decisiones o cuando reclamamos que él siempre hace lo que quiere. Pero, por otro lado, si él empieza a hacer todo lo que queremos... la relación se deteriora.

Conversando con una amiga el otro día, me pareció interesante lo que ella dijo al respecto de su actual relación:

—Este novio es de verdad, Cris, tiene lo que los demás no tenían. Es difícil. Me quedé intrigada y quise saber más...

—¿Cómo es eso?

—¡Ah! Los otros hacían todo lo que yo quería. La relación era aburrida. Este es así: yo digo: «Vamos por aquel camino, que no hay tráfico», y él dice: «No, quiero ir por el camino que me gusta».

Pude darme cuenta de una cosa que nunca había pensado antes: a nosotras, las mujeres, nos gusta probar nuestros límites, ver hasta dónde podemos llegar. Y si el hombre nos da una libertad ilimitada, ¡perdemos totalmente el interés! No es que nos guste ser dominadas, pero... tampoco nos gusta que todo sea tan fácil. Dejamos de sentir el respeto que queríamos tener por nuestro amado. Por eso, hombres, por favor, no nos alimenten con uvas frescas mientras nosotras estamos recostadas teniendo todo a nuestros pies. Esa idea de Cleopatra no es buena.

Además, dicho sea de paso, los hombres que no ven los defectos de sus mujeres y, por eso, no las ayudan a mejorar como personas, son fácilmente manipulados por ellas. Cada vez que yo me he equivocado, tuve en Renato al compañero que necesitaba, que me mostró mis errores y me puso de nuevo en el camino. A la mujer le gusta eso.

TAREA

¿Dónde y de qué manera puede usted estar succionando la energía de su compañero y volviéndose alguien inconveniente? Aparte algunos minutos, ahora, para pensar en eso. Escriba cómo hará para comportarse de manera más equilibrada en esas situaciones. ¿Qué talentos y actividades saludables podría desarrollar para disminuir su excesiva atención colocada sobre su compañero/a?

_____

_____

_____

_____

Me prometo a mí mismo/a que dejaré de hacerle/a el sol de mi planeta.

/MatrimonioBlindado

Publique esto:
Él/ella ya no es el sol
de mi planeta.

@matrimonioblind

Tuitee esto:
Él/ella ya no es el sol
de mi planeta
#matrimonioblindado
@matrimonioblind

PARTE III

DESMONTANDO Y REMONTANDO EL AMOR

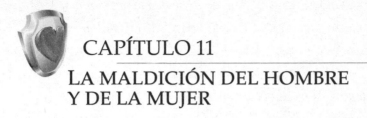

CAPÍTULO 11
LA MALDICIÓN DEL HOMBRE Y DE LA MUJER

Como prácticamente todos los problemas de la humanidad, la relación de amor y odio entre el hombre y la mujer comenzó en el Jardín del Edén. (Yo espero que Adán y Eva tengan un lugar especial en el cielo, bien reservado y protegido, porque le garantizo una cosa: va a haber mucha gente pidiéndoles explicaciones...). Diría que la desobediencia de ambos resultó ser una maldición que afectó directamente a su relación y a la de todos sus descendientes. Primeramente, vamos a entender lo que sucedió allí. Sé que conoce la historia, pero tal vez no desde este ángulo.

Antes de que «la vaca fuera al pantano»[5], allí, en el Edén, Adán y Eva vivían muy bien, en todos los sentidos. Habían recibido del Creador una posición privilegiada en la Tierra, con autoridad para hacer y deshacer:

... y ejerza dominio sobre los peces del mar, sobre las aves del cielo, sobre los ganados, sobre toda la tierra, y sobre todo reptil que se arrastra sobre

---

[5] Para nuestros lectores más jóvenes: si una vaca decide dar un paseo y acaba en un pantano esto supondrá auténtico problema, porque difícilmente conseguirá salir de él ella sola. La pobre vaquita quedará atrapada en un terreno pantanoso y, si nadie la encuentra, acabará muriendo de hambre o de sed. Tan solo un tractor y mucha paciencia pueden ayudar a sacar al animal del atolladero. Perder una vaca implica perder futuros becerros, leche y sus derivados; algo nada bueno para el criador. Ni para el animal, claro.

la tierra. Creó, pues, Dios al hombre a imagen Suya, a imagen de Dios lo
creó; varón y hembra los creó. Y los bendijo Dios y les dijo: «Sed fecundos y
multiplicaos, y llenad la tierra y sojuzgadla; ejerced dominio sobre los peces
del mar, sobre las aves del cielo y sobre todo ser viviente que se mueve sobre
la tierra». Y dijo Dios: «He aquí, Yo os he dado toda planta que da semilla
que hay en la superficie de toda la tierra, y todo árbol que tiene fruto que
da semilla; esto os servirá de alimento. Y a toda bestia de la tierra, a toda
ave de los cielos y a todo lo que se mueve sobre la tierra, y que tiene vida,
les he dado toda planta verde para alimento». (Génesis 1:26-30).

El hombre fue puesto sobre todos los seres, animales y vegetales, y
sobre toda la Tierra. Esta autoridad era compartida, también, con la mujer: «*... y les dijo...*». Esa posición significaba que toda la naturaleza fue
puesta como sierva del hombre y de la mujer. La función de la naturaleza
era la de servirles y suplir todas sus necesidades.

Con todo ese poder y toda esa armonía, sumados a la Compañía de
Dios, el bonito matrimonio vivía en el paraíso, literalmente. No tenían
cuentas que pagar ni defectos que señalar el uno del otro. Adán tenía
la mujer que pidió a Dios, y Eva, el hombre que... Bien, el único que estaba disponible; de cualquier forma, era un matrimonio sin problemas.

Pero la vaquita tenía que ir a dar un paseo y, para empeorarlo, aquel
día estaba una serpiente allí, en el pantano. Eva desobedeció a Dios y
llevó a su marido a hacer lo mismo. Hora de ajustar cuentas.

Dios llamó primero a Adán y este se dio prisa en echarle la culpa a Eva.
El Señor, sin embargo, «no compró la idea», reforzando que el líder es el responsable de todo lo que sucede bajo su responsabilidad. Recuerde el capítulo
9: «¿Es ese su problema?». Adán tuvo que aprender eso amargamente. Consecuencia de su fracaso y su desobediencia, Dios determinó para el hombre:

Por cuanto has escuchado la voz de tu mujer y has comido del árbol del
cual te ordené, diciendo: «No comerás de él», maldita será la tierra por

tu causa; con trabajo comerás de ella todos los días de tu vida. Espinos y abrojos te producirá, y comerás de las plantas del campo. Con el sudor de tu rostro comerás el pan hasta que vuelvas a la tierra, porque de ella fuiste tomado; pues polvo eres, y al polvo volverás. (Génesis 3:17-19).

Eva, a su vez, echó la culpa a la serpiente. Pero no era un buen día para las excusas:

A la mujer dijo: «En gran manera multiplicaré tu dolor en el parto, con dolor darás a luz los hijos; y con todo, tu deseo será para tu marido, y él tendrá dominio sobre ti». (Génesis 3:16).

Es interesante que, como resultado de la maldición, hombre y mujer fueron sometidos a los elementos de los que salían, de donde fueron creados: el hombre se quedó sujeto a la tierra y la mujer, al hombre. Y aquí empezó la maldición[6] de los dos. Entendamos ahora las consecuencias y el impacto de esta maldición en el matrimonio.

ESCLAVO DEL TRABAJO

La maldición que afectó al hombre estuvo directamente relacionada con su trabajo. Mientras que antes había una relación armoniosa y de total cooperación entre el hombre y la tierra, después de la maldición, la tierra se volvió enemiga del hombre. No habría más cooperación, pero sí una lucha, una labor, una contienda entre la naturaleza y el hombre. Era como si la tierra, de mala gana, comenzara a darle los frutos al hombre y, muchas veces, espinos en vez de frutos.

---

[6] Permítame aclarar aquí que un análisis cuidadoso del texto bíblico revelará que Dios no maldijo a Adán y Eva. El texto dice que el Señor maldijo la tierra y a la serpiente, pero no al ser humano. Queda claro que, aun no siendo maldecidos directamente, recibieron las consecuencias de dichas maldiciones, a las que me refiero aquí en singular: «La maldición del hombre y de la mujer».

Esa condenación perduraría hasta el fin de la vida del hombre, cuando este, finalmente, perdería la batalla y volvería al lugar del que vino: el polvo. (Fíjese que, hasta este momento, no había muerte; el hombre fue creado para vivir para siempre, pero su pecado limitó su tiempo de vida en la tierra. Por lo tanto, cuando Dios unió a Adán y a Eva, el plan no era «hasta que la muerte os separe», sino para toda la eternidad).

Considere un agravante: el hombre fue designado como el proveedor de su familia. Es decir, no hay manera de que él huya de esa maldición. Él tiene que trabajar –y trabajar para sacar el sustento de una tierra que se volvió su enemiga–. La presión de sustentar a la familia, de ser el cazador, de no dejar a la familia pasar necesidades, hace que el hombre se cobre a sí mismo el resultado de su trabajo. Es una cuestión de honra, de amor propio, de satisfacción a los padres de la mujer e incluso del sentido del propio valor. Este impulso de querer probar el valor propio, a través de su trabajo y de sus conquistas, está en el ADN del hombre.

Por eso, la mayor frustración que un hombre puede pasar es el fracaso profesional. Un hombre puede perder su matrimonio, vivir lejos de los hijos, incluso vivir con una deficiencia; todo eso puede superarlo, siempre que se sienta útil y tenga éxito en su trabajo. No quiero decir que será feliz, pero su ego estará más satisfecho de las conquistas en su trabajo que de cualquier otra cosa. Esa es su maldición, su carga.

La maldición le hace sentirse siempre insatisfecho, no importa lo que haya conquistado. Difícilmente verá a un hombre diciendo: «Estoy realizado, conseguí todos mis sueños, voy a dejarlo aquí». Si trabaja día y noche por un objetivo, pone todas sus fuerzas y alcanza un buen resultado, normalmente dice: «Podría haber sido mejor». Nunca piensa que llegó. Está siempre exigiéndose.

Es un hecho conocido que muchos hombres, cuando se jubilan, caen en depresión; algunos se enferman e incluso mueren poco después. Es como si el trabajo fuese su vida. Muchos no quieren jubilarse y siguen trabajando mientras la salud se lo permita.

Además de esa insatisfacción, él todavía se compara con los otros hombres de más éxito, siempre queriendo superarlos o sintiéndose inferior por no ser tan bueno como ellos. Su espíritu competitivo es inigualable. No es extraño que la mayoría de los que aparecen en el Guinness –Libro de los Récords– sean hombres, especialmente en los hechos competitivos. Para que se haga una idea, hay una categoría en ese libro donde dieciséis récords fueron superados por hombres, uno de ellos por un equipo de doce gimnastas alemanes... ¿El hecho? «Más saltos mortales en calzoncillos en noventa segundos». Están invictos desde el 2000, con 94 saltos... Ese es el tipo de cosas en el que usted no encontraría a doce mujeres dispuestas a competir.

¿Y cómo afecta eso en la relación?

Ya lo debe de haber adivinado. ¿No es el tiempo que el hombre pasa en el trabajo una de las cuestiones clásicas que la mujer le reclama? ¿No es la «tendencia a gastar» (el dinero que él sudó para ganar) una de los principales reclamos del hombre hacia la mujer? Ahora usted sabe el porqué.

Al principio de la relación, durante el noviazgo, el hombre ve a la mujer como una conquista, es decir, un trabajo. Es como si fuese una competencia. ¿Quién va a ganar a la chica? ¿A quién va a elegir para que sea su novio? Entonces, eso lo motiva para trabajar por su atención y su corazón. Pero cuando, finalmente, la conquista y se casa, traslada su atención al próximo desafío, que siempre tiene que ver con algún trabajo. Por eso, se concentra en el trabajo y deja a la mujer casi muriéndose de falta de su atención en casa. Es entonces cuando ella reclama, él la mira perplejo y pregunta: «¿Pero no ves que tengo que trabajar, que lo hago por ti?». Con la primera mitad de la frase, acertó; pero, en la segunda, no fue sincero. Él trabaja más por sí mismo que por ella.

La maldición del trabajo hace al hombre esclavo del sentimiento de realización, la cual raramente consigue obtener. En esa búsqueda, va sacrificando a la familia, la mujer, la salud y otras cosas, igual o más importantes. Pídale al marido que hable con la mujer sobre la familia y la relación y no tendrá nada que decir. Pídale que hable con sus amigos sobre el trabajo y no parará.

La mujer, sin entender su comportamiento, piensa que no la ama porque no pasa tiempo con ella, no hablan y le parece que siente más placer trabajando y con los amigos que con ella y con las cosas relacionadas con ella. Pero es un error llevar eso al plano personal, pensando que hay algo equivocado en él o en ella. ¿Qué puede hacer ella? ¿Cómo debe lidiar con esa maldición y ayudar a su marido? Primero, es importante entender la maldición que cayó sobre ella.

ATENCIÓN DEL MARIDO

La maldición que afectó a la mujer está relacionada con su dependencia de la atención y aprobación del marido. Dejando a un lado los dolores de parto, los cuales este libro no se propone solucionar (¡lo siento mucho, mujeres!), la segunda parte de la maldición determinó para la mujer que «...*tu deseo será para tu marido, y él tendrá dominio sobre ti*». Es decir, usted estará deseando algo de su marido siempre y él será su líder. Así como el hombre se quedó esclavo del trabajo, sujeto a la tierra, ella quedó dependiente de la aprobación del marido y de tener en él a la persona que cumplirá sus deseos y sueños.

Hasta aquel momento, hombre y mujer no se preocupaban de «quién mandaba en quién». Era una unión armoniosa que, simplemente, funcionaba sin resistencia de uno ni imposición del otro. Los dos eran uno. Pero ahora, debido al error de la mujer, ella fue, a propósito, puesta bajo los cuidados y el liderazgo del marido, como para recordarle el error que cometió al inducirle al pecado.

Sé que este concepto es anatema para la mayoría de las mujeres, pero en realidad podría haber sido mucho peor. Piénselo bien, mujer: ¿quedar sujeta al hombre que ama? Lo malo sería haber sido condenada a quedar sujeta a uno a quien *odiase*... De cualquier forma, el concepto de sumisión es un asunto para un capítulo posterior, que aclarará mucho más la cuestión y sacará el veneno que la ideología feminista ha inyectado en la palabra.

Lo que esta maldición resultó para la mujer fue el deseo de conseguir la atención total del marido. Quiere ser la princesa, la escogida, la mujer por encima de todas las mujeres; aquella por quien él arriesga la vida y deja a las personas y a las cosas que más le gustan para estar a su lado. Sin embargo, raramente consigue esa atención durante mucho tiempo. Él, bajo los efectos de su propia maldición, está siempre mirando al trabajo, la próxima conquista, y además se queda resentido con ella cuando le reclama atención. La ve como una interferencia para sus objetivos. Se molesta porque ella no «entiende» que él tiene que trabajar y le parece que ella no le aprecia por ser un hombre tan trabajador y dedicado.

En su búsqueda de la atención del hombre, la mujer, inconscientemente, se desvaloriza, pues empieza a hacer todo lo que puede para que sus ojos se vuelvan hacia ella. Invierte en ropa atractiva y sensual, en la belleza física, en la estética, en el pelo... pero eso es solo el comienzo. También llora, dramatiza, se hace la víctima o la pobre, crea situaciones de celos, le reclama al marido, hace chantaje emocional, deja de hacer las cosas en casa, compite con la suegra, con el perro... Hoy en día, muchas mujeres comprometidas, pero infelices en el matrimonio, son capaces incluso de tener una aventura tan solo para llamar la atención del marido.

Esa búsqueda desesperada es lo que está detrás de muchas mujeres consideradas muy inteligentes profesionalmente, pero que acaban sometiéndose a hombres canallas a cambio de un poquito de atención. Es el caso de Roseane, a quien aconsejamos recientemente en nuestro consultorio.

Roseane es contadora. A los treinta y cuatro años, es el orgullo de la familia por llegar hasta donde ha llegado. Abrió su despacho contable hace apenas dos años, y ya tiene más de cincuenta clientes y cinco empleados. Es una mujer ágil, decidida, pero lo que le sobra de determinación y autoconfianza para los negocios, le falta para el amor.

Hace cuatro años que Roseane vive una mala relación con Roger. Él, de treinta y un años, sin ninguna realización, es la encarnación del perfecto canalla: guapo, 1,80 m de altura y voz de terciopelo, que sabe decir lo que toda mujer quiere oír.

Roger no tiene trabajo fijo, ni profesión –por lo menos hasta el día en que ser canalla gane ese derecho–. Si dependiese de él, ya tendría hasta un sindicato. Su talento es contar historias en las que él es el protagonista y la víctima al mismo tiempo. La mamá siempre pagándole el apartamento hasta que «aquel» trabajo llegue. El papá le da el coche, pues «el pobre tiene que moverse».

Y Roseane le da amor, comida caliente cuando la visita, sexo y, para colmo, todavía le compra algo de ropa. Su novio tiene que vestirse bien.

A cambio, Roger ya le ha sido infiel por lo menos tres veces, que ella sepa. No está «preparado» para el matrimonio. Vive apareciendo en el despacho de Roseane para contarle una de sus historias y, entre abrazos y besos, la convence para que le dé un cheque que –jura– es todo lo que necesita para empezar un negocio muy prometedor.

Roseane es una de las muchas mujeres súper inteligentes que no consiguen ver las barbaridades que hacen en el amor.

¿Por qué cree usted que se someten a eso? Es la maldición de la mujer.

DOS POR EL PRECIO DE UNA

Las dos maldiciones –la del hombre y la de la mujer– son en realidad una sola: la inseguridad.

La esencia, en el fondo de todo eso, es que el hombre está inseguro de sí mismo. Algunos muestran esa inseguridad, sin duda, más que otros; pero todos sufren del mismo mal; incluso los hombres que aparentan bravura y coraje inmensos, o temperamentos fuertes; muchos usan esos comportamientos como máscaras para esconder la inseguridad. Consciente o no, es el peso del rechazo que sufrió allá en el Edén, cuyo principal culpable fue él mismo.

El miedo al fracaso, la pobreza, el sentimiento de insuficiencia, lo hacen matarse trabajando. La voz de reclamo de un padre o de una madre extremadamente exigente durante la infancia todavía resuena y le hace sentir que nunca responde a las expectativas, no importa el éxito que tenga.

El orgullo, que le impide reconocer los errores y aprender con los demás, se ve todavía más fortalecido cuando ve que otros hombres tienen éxito donde él ha fracasado. La rabia, la agresividad, los vicios, la mentira y otros comportamientos autodestructivos son las formas en que lidia con la inseguridad en lo más profundo de su interior. Todo eso son las hojas de parra para cubrir la desnudez de su inseguridad.

La inseguridad de la mujer, por ser emocionalmente más abierta que el hombre, es más fácil de percibir. Conozco a mujeres guapas que se ven feas, solamente porque una parte de su cuerpo no coincide con los patrones de belleza de las revistas femeninas. Otras tienen celos de todo respecto al marido: celos del trabajo, del fútbol, de la cuñada, del coche, de la mujer de la parada del colectivo, de la compañera de trabajo, de la exnovia... de todo a lo que el marido le presta atención, e incluso de aquello a lo que no, y todo debido a su inseguridad.

La autoestima de la mayoría de las mujeres es, de forma natural, baja; y de la misma manera que muchos hombres utilizan el machismo, la fuerza y el temperamento fuerte para enmascarar su inseguridad, muchas mujeres se rebelan contra su propia maldición y se declaran independientes de los hombres. «No necesito a un hombre para ser feliz», «Los hombres son todos iguales, solo cambia el domicilio», «A mí no me manda un hombre» y otras frases del mismo estilo que establecen su credo; aunque, en el fondo, permanecen infelices.

Resumiendo: son dos inseguros, desesperadamente necesitados de la seguridad y la afirmación el uno del otro (Un aplauso aquí para Adán y Eva. Estuvo bien, ¿eh?).

Ahora, la pregunta más importante: ¿cómo librarse de esa maldición?

CAPÍTULO 12
LA LIBERACIÓN

Buena noticia y mala noticia. Vamos con la mala: la primera cosa que el hombre y la mujer necesitan entender es que no van a cambiarse el uno al otro. El hombre siempre se moverá por las conquistas en su trabajo y la mujer siempre se moverá por el deseo de tener toda la atención del hombre. No sirve de nada rebelarse contra estos hechos. Los que se rebelan caen en el extremo opuesto, que no es nada mejor. El hombre desiste de ser un conquistador, se vuelve débil, «un blandengue, una vergüenza para sí mismo y para la familia»; la mujer que se rebela contra el hombre se vuelve amargada, endurecida, inalcanzable para cualquier hombre y, en consecuencia, solitaria. No sirve de nada rebelarse contra la maldición, usted simplemente tiene que saber lidiar con ella; la suya y la de su cónyuge.

Ahora, la buena noticia: hay formas eficaces de lidiar con la maldición. Se compone de dos partes: una, que puede hacer usted, y, otra, que solo Dios puede.

Vamos con lo que el hombre puede hacer sobre la suya y cómo la mujer puede ayudarle.

LA ESTRATEGIA PARA EL HOMBRE

A lo largo de toda la Biblia, Dios le proporciona al hombre consejos para el éxito que pueden resumirse en estas palabras: «Trabaje en sociedad conmigo». Uno de los pasajes más claros al respecto está en el Salmo 127:1-2:

Si el Señor no edifica la casa, en vano trabajan los que la edifican; si el Señor no guarda la ciudad, en vano vela la guardia. Es en vano que os levantéis de madrugada, que os acostéis tarde, que comáis el pan de afanosa labor, pues Él da a su amado aun mientras duerme.

¡Ahí está el secreto! Dios deja bien claro que el hombre tiene que trabajar en unión con Él. Su éxito depende de su relación con el Creador. Aunque tenga que trabajar no debe confiar tan solo en sus propias habilidades, sino que también debe depender de Dios. Cuando el hombre trabaja en sociedad con Dios, se queda tranquilo respecto al resultado. A fin de cuentas, ¡el Socio que tiene trabaja incluso cuando él duerme! Por eso no se produce una auto exigencia excesiva, ni inseguridad, ni depresión ante un resultado aparentemente insatisfactorio. El hombre ya no es esclavo de su trabajo porque entiende que Su Socio es el mayor interesado en que él crezca. Hay confianza, paz y certeza de que el futuro será bueno.

La mujer puede ayudar al hombre aquí recordándole la importancia de esta dependencia. Además de orar por el éxito de su trabajo, debe, con sabiduría, influir en su marido para que tenga una relación con Dios, pues ella misma se beneficiará de ello. El mensaje que debe pasarle, con sus propias palabras, es: «¡Solo, consigues lo que es posible! ¡Con Dios, consigues lo imposible!».

Otro concepto que el hombre tiene que absorber y practicar para neutralizar los efectos de su maldición es el equilibrio. Nosotros, los hombres, debemos recordar que el trabajo siempre va a existir y que, por mucho que trabajemos, nunca se va a acabar. Si trabajamos veinticuatro horas sin parar, al día siguiente habrá más trabajo. El hombre, especialmente el casado, tiene que recordar que debe atender otras cosas importantes en la vida, como a la mujer, por ejemplo; por eso, es equilibrado.

La Biblia dice que Dios creó el sábado para «el hombre».[7] Creo que Él se refirió más específicamente al hombre que a la mujer, porque si no hubiese determinado el sábado como día de descanso, el hombre trabajaría siete días a la semana. Dios no necesitó mandarle al hombre que trabajase; sin embargo, necesitó mandarle descansar...

La mujer entiende muy bien el concepto de sábado. Que lo diga Cristiane... Si no fuese por ella, recordándome y planeando lo que vamos a hacer para relajarnos al menos algunas horas a la semana, yo solo pararía para dormir y comer. Al principio del matrimonio me resistí a sus intentos; yo era desequilibrado, trabajaba prácticamente siete días a la semana, y le decía que tenía que aceptarlo y acoplarse a mi rutina, conformarse. Ella quería un poquito de mi atención, pero yo le daba prácticamente cero e incluso me enfadaba con ella porque quería que sacase tiempo para nosotros.

El hombre debe aceptar esa ayuda de la mujer, pues ella es un recurso que Dios usa para ayudarle a tener equilibrio. Hombre, si su mujer le está reclamando que no pasa tiempo con ella ni con sus hijos, que está trabajando demasiado, etc., probablemente tiene razón. Escúchela. Sea equilibrado.

Y la otra cosa con la que todo hombre debe tener mucho cuidado para no empeorar la maldición es la de compararse con los otros. Un poco de competitividad es bueno, tener mentores y ejemplos para inspirarse es positivo, pero ¡cuidado con las comparaciones! Estar continuamente comparándose con otros hombres, midiendo su éxito en función de los otros, es la mejor receta para la frustración y la inseguridad.

Tenemos que confiar y desarrollar los talentos que tenemos, no querer ser iguales a los demás. Conózcase a sí mismo, desarrolle su propia identidad, identifique sus talentos y trabaje con ellos. Aprenda a celebrar el éxito de los otros y el suyo también. Aprenda a felicitarse por sus realizaciones. ¿No fue eso lo que Dios hizo cuando creó el mundo? El relato de la Creación dice que, al final de cada día, Dios contemplaba

---

[7] Marcos 2:27.

Sus obras y veía que «lo que había hecho era bueno».[8] (E incluso siendo Dios, sacó un día al final de la semana para descansar). Nosotros, los hombres, tenemos que practicar eso, pues es un fuerte antídoto contra la maldición.

La mujer tiene aquí uno de sus papeles más importantes para ayudar al marido. Primeramente, ella nunca –jamás– debe compararlo con otro hombre. Decirle: «Tendrías que ser como mi padre...» o «El marido de Fulana sí que es genial...». Mujer, nunca conseguirá el resultado que quiere. Usted piensa que con esas palabras va a motivarlo para mejorar, pero en realidad son como clavarle un cuchillo en su autoconfianza y en su amor propio. Vale la pena repetirlo, pues es muy importante: nunca compare a su marido (ni a su hijo) con otro hombre, ni en sueños.[9]

En vez de compararlo, reconozca y elogie abiertamente sus cualidades y realizaciones. No lo critique negativamente ni señale sus fallas, sea la voz alentadora que muestra confianza en sus habilidades. Eso es esencial en los buenos tiempos y mucho más en los malos. Nada hunde más al hombre que tener un fracaso profesional. ¿Quiere ver a un hombre deprimido? Despídalo de su empleo, o ni eso, es suficiente con que señale un fracaso suyo en el trabajo. Con seguridad, ese día él se irá directo al bar o a vegetar frente a la televisión sintiéndose la peor criatura. Muchos hombres, cuando son despedidos, no se lo cuentan ni a su mujer y salen por la mañana como si fuesen a trabajar, pero en realidad están intentando encontrar otro trabajo. En una situación así, la mujer puede levantar o acabar de enterrar a su marido.

Me acuerdo aquí de Cristina, esposa del gran baloncestista brasileño Oscar Schmidt. Ella nos contó, durante la entrevista con el matrimonio

---

[8] Génesis 1:18.

[9] Una guerra civil que azotó durante años Israel comenzó cuando el rey Saúl sufrió una comparación negativa con David por parte de las mujeres de Israel. Tras haber derrotado a Goliat, y a continuación al ejército de los filisteos, David regresaba a Jerusalén con Saúl y su ejército. Recibidos con una gran fiesta, las mujeres cantaban: «Saúl mató a mil, David a diez mil». El inseguro rey Saúl no pudo soportar aquello, algo que precipitó su ruina.

en *Escuela del amor*, que, faltándole tres meses para graduarse en Psicología, decidió botar los cinco años de facultad para acompañar a su marido cuando fue contratado para jugar en Italia. Cristina dijo que una de las cosas que la motivó fue pensar en las luchas y desafíos que el marido seguramente iba a enfrentar en el nuevo país. La posibilidad de que su marido pasara por momentos difíciles mientras ella estaba lejos de él, en Brasil, terminando sus estudios, hizo que priorizase el matrimonio. Lo abandonó todo, fue a Italia con él y nunca se graduó. Como si ella lo hubiese adivinado, Oscar perdió los siete primeros partidos que jugó. Pero, con su mujer al lado, se levantó y tuvo trece años de una carrera brillante en Italia, sin contar los títulos internacionales que ganó para Brasil. Fue el jugador de baloncesto con más puntos marcados, un éxito absoluto, no solo en el campo sino también en casa. Él atribuye el mérito a su mujer: «Sin su apoyo nunca habría hecho lo que hice», afirma. El matrimonio está unido desde hace más de treinta y siete años.

Cristiane:

Es muy común para nosotras, las mujeres, pensar que si elogiamos a nuestros maridos su ego va a atravesar el techo. Es el miedo que la mujer tiene de hacer a su marido arrogante y autosuficiente. Pero ese miedo se debe a nuestra propia inseguridad. Nos parece que un elogio puede hacerles pensar que son mejores que nosotras. Es por eso que muchas mujeres incluso admiran a sus maridos, pero casi nunca verbalizan esa admiración.

Con ese entendimiento de que el hombre está siempre corriendo detrás de una conquista, de un reconocimiento, de una auto aprobación, usted entiende lo importante que es su papel a su lado.

Una de las cosas que siempre vi en mi madre fue su aprecio y admiración hacia mi padre; no era que fingiese que no veía sus errores, pero sus elogios eran tantos que los errores de mi padre se volvían irrelevantes e insignificantes. Eso contribuía a que nosotras, sus hijas, también lo admirásemos y respetásemos, además de dejarnos el ejemplo para hacer lo mismo con nuestros maridos. Y, en eso, Renato no tuvo que reclamar...

Cuando la mujer se convierte en la fan número uno de su marido, ella también gana –y mucho–. Es como en un partido de fútbol, él mete el gol e, inmediatamente, corre hacia los brazos de ella para celebrarlo. Él pierde el partido y, también, corre hacia sus brazos, sabiendo que no va a criticarlo por eso, al contrario, va a darle una palabra de apoyo y, además, tendrá aquella mirada amorosa que desvanece cualquier tristeza. Ahora bien, ¿quién no quiere eso de su jugador favorito? ¡Nuestra naturaleza femenina adora esa «dependencia» masculina!

Muchas mujeres se equivocan en eso, no porque quieran, sino porque piensan que necesitan ser duras con sus maridos, ya que ellos se hacen los duros. Usted le dice que está guapo y él aparta la mirada como si no necesitase ese elogio. Si cree en esa «dureza» masculina, va a pensar que no lo necesita y es ahí donde se equivoca. Él necesita eso, y mucho. El hombre se puede hacer el duro, pero, en el fondo, anhela sus elogios, aunque solo sea porque ¿quién le va a dar eso aparte de usted y de su suegra? ¿Sus compañeros de trabajo?

Solamente porque ellos no reaccionen igual que nosotras, no quiere decir que no les guste. Todo el mundo puede criticarle, pero si usted lo critica, le va a doler mucho más. Su palabra de esposa tiene un peso mucho mayor, no se olvide de eso.

Si usted, mujer, apoya a su marido en sus conquistas, e incluso en las derrotas, él nunca la abandonará, a menos que sea realmente un burro (en ese caso le estará haciendo un favor).

LA ESTRATEGIA PARA LA MUJER

La maldición de ella hace que espere que el marido la haga feliz, realizada, en todas las formas y maneras. Vamos a aclarar aquí una cosa: *Ningún hombre es capaz de satisfacer todas las necesidades y expectativas de una mujer*. No hay hombre en este mundo que consiga hacer eso, aunque fuese proyectado y creado por una mujer (pues el resultado sería otra mujer, a quien ella encontraría incompleta también).

La verdad es que ningún hombre puede satisfacer todas las necesidades de una mujer, ni ninguna mujer satisfacer todas las necesidades de un hombre. Eso es utopía. Escucho a muchas personas que dicen: «Estoy buscando a alguien que me complete» o «Mi marido no me completa». Alto ahí. Esa persona que le «completa» no existe. Nuestra vida se completa por una combinación de cosas, no solo por una persona. Es así, por más completa que sea la vida de alguien, tendrá sus problemas.

Mujer: no le exija a su marido lo que él no puede darle. Su marido no es el responsable de hacerla feliz, así como usted no es la responsable de hacerle feliz a él. Por otra parte, si usted todavía está soltera y está leyendo este libro como preparación para casarse, pero se cree una persona infeliz, por favor, ¡no se case! Libre a otra persona de una vida miserable. Primero tiene que resolver sus infelicidades, volverse una persona feliz y, ahí sí, casarse para compartir su felicidad con otra persona. Y esta felicidad, en el matrimonio, viene de un conjunto de cosas en las que su marido ciertamente está incluido. Pero hay cosas que él no puede hacer por usted. Por ejemplo, yo no puedo dar a mi mujer lo que Dios le da. Yo no soy Dios. Él le da a Cristiane cosas que, en un determinado momento, yo no puedo ni imaginar que necesita, tales como consuelo, sabiduría y paz. Yo no puedo darle un consejo de madre. Eso es algo que recibe solamente de su madre. Yo no puedo hacerla sentir útil y valorada más allá de lo que yo reconozco y le digo; pero, cuando recibe *feedback* de su trabajo de ayudar a otras personas, su percepción de valor propio aumenta. Entonces, todo eso va sumándose y haciendo de ella una persona feliz en sí misma, de modo que no depende de mí para ser feliz.

La mujer debe entender que esperar que todos sus deseos sean cumplidos y satisfechos por el hombre es la propia maldición en sí. Por lo tanto, no debe correr al encuentro de la maldición. Usted, mujer, tiene que buscar la satisfacción también en otras cosas, como en su relación con Dios, en su trabajo, en su valor. Eso hará que deje de sofocar a su marido y la volverá una persona más interesante y atractiva para él.

Aparte la excesiva atención de su marido, no sea como el polvo, agarrándose a él con todos los tentáculos. No sea asfixiante (una de las quejas más comunes que escucho de los maridos).

Todo lo que es demasiado fácil, no tiene valor. Nadie corre detrás de lo fácil. Cuando la mujer es demasiado fácil, fastidia y recibe lo contrario de lo que busca: el desprecio de él. Pero cuando se controla un poco y da solo con medida, mantiene en él el interés de la conquista. No insista en que la lleve a pasear, por ejemplo. Puede revelar sus gustos y deseos, pero no mendigue su atención. La mujer sabia hace que el hombre trabaje para conquistarla. Para el hombre, la relación tiene que tener la motivación y el gusto de la conquista de un trabajo. A veces es bueno que él la persiga.

La liberación de la maldición debe tener como objetivo la vuelta al estado original, antes de la caída allá en el Edén: el hombre volver a dominar la tierra, en vez de ser su esclavo, y la mujer volver a la posición de auxiliadora y compañera de equipo del hombre.

Cuando ella se hace su auxiliadora, ayudándole a alcanzar sus objetivos, se vuelve preciosísima para él. Y es exactamente entonces cuando recibe lo que más quiere: su atención. Hay mujeres que quieren competir con el marido en vez de entrar en su equipo, quieren hacer el foco principal de su vida algo que no ayuda al marido en nada. Entonces, no sirve. Cuando la mujer no ayuda y, encima, da trabajo, realmente es una piedra en el zapato. Se vuelve indeseable para él.

Cristiane:

Nuestro problema es no creer en nosotras mismas. Siempre nos autodestruimos con palabras y pensamientos. Muchas mujeres, incluso, piensan que eso es ser humilde; lo que no tiene nada que ver. Esa «humildad» es irritante y solo perjudica sus relaciones.

Si usted, como mujer, no aprende a valorarse, no sirven de nada los esfuerzos externos. No consigue valorar nada más en su vida y, realmente, se vuelve una persona con la que es difícil convivir. Ya he pasado por eso. Tenía todo, el matrimonio de mis sueños, una familia ejemplar, salud e incluso belleza natural, pero no me valoraba. Entonces todo eso era manipulado por mí misma. Constantemente encontraba problemas en mi matrimonio porque Renato no me prestaba la atención suficiente, decía que no me amaba y un día llegué al colmo de preguntarle si quería el divorcio.

No conseguía ver mi propia belleza. Vivía cambiando de *look*, intentando diferentes estilos, y nunca me sentía cómoda. Tengo fotos de esa época y me pregunto qué pasaba por mi mente para ponerme aquella ropa. Es increíble cómo incluso una cosa tan fútil como la ropa y el pelo reflejan nuestras inseguridades. Cuando me acuerdo de esa época, no entiendo por qué tanta ceguera de mi parte.

Solamente cuando aprendí a valorarme de verdad, como describí mejor en el capítulo 10, todo cambió. Es como si mis ojos hubieran estado cerrados hasta ese momento. Logré ver mi potencial —¡y qué potencial!—. Si la mujer supiese su potencial, no se desvalorizaría tanto como lo hace en los días actuales...

Mujer virtuosa, ¿quién la hallará? Su valor supera en mucho al de las joyas. (Proverbios 31:10).

Usted puede ser esa mujer virtuosa, a quien me gusta llamar «Mujer V». Es suficiente con que crea e intente mostrar su valor en lo que hace y es.

¿Cómo puede el marido ayudar a su mujer a librarse de la maldición? Tiene que pasarle seguridad de todas las maneras posibles. Por ejemplo: no prestar atención a otras mujeres, exaltar sus cualidades, notar y comentar su belleza, ponerla por encima de todo y de todos, intentar valorar su opinión, invertir en sus talentos, ayudarla a desarrollar su potencial; en fin, todo lo que puede levantar la autoestima de su mujer. No puede esperar a que ella lo resuelva por sí misma, sin su ayuda. Dejar a su mujer sola con sus problemas y luchas no es inteligente. A veces, la mujer va a buscar ayuda en terceros porque el marido no la ayuda (entonces, él se resiente con ella; pero la negligencia fue suya). El apoyo y el reconocimiento genuinos del marido son mucho más valiosos que los de cualquier otra persona; pero si ella ve que él es muy atento con los demás, pero no con ella, la inseguridad solo aumentará.

El marido necesita entender que invertir en la mujer es ganancia para sí mismo. Hay un versículo interesante en Proverbios que dice:

No habiendo bueyes, el granero está limpio, pero por la fuerza del buey, hay abundancia de cosechas.[10]

Es decir: si no tiene bueyes, no tendrá excrementos de buey que limpiar; pero tampoco tendrá cosecha. Si quiere tener mucha cosecha, también tiene que limpiar los excrementos de los bueyes... Es una manera de entender el matrimonio. Da trabajo, a veces huele mal, tiene que limpiar la suciedad, pero el resultado final es muy bueno. Un matrimonio feliz da trabajo. Hombres: eso debería de ser una buena noticia para nosotros... El trabajo va con nosotros, ¿verdad?

COMPENSANDO

Ahora que entiende la maldición inherente al hombre y a la mujer, puede entender mejor por qué usted y su cónyuge hacen las cosas que hacen. Es ahora cuando entienden lo que los dos enfrentan y deben ayudarse el uno al otro, llevando a cabo las correspondientes compensaciones.

Los matrimonios maduros y de éxito son aquellos que aprenden a calibrar eso y trabajan en equipo, ayudándose el uno al otro.

---

[10] Proverbios 14:4.

TAREA

Medite en lo que ha leído en este capítulo y en el anterior. ¿Qué efectos de esta maldición percibe en usted y en su cónyuge? Escriba cuáles son y cómo va a lidiar con ellos a partir de ahora, en vez de lo que ha estado haciendo.

/MatrimonioBlindado

Publique esto:
Ya tengo el antídoto
para cancelar la
maldición.

@matrimonioblind

Tuitee esto:
Ya tengo el antídoto
para cancelar la
maldición
#matrimonioblindado
@matrimonioblind

CAPÍTULO 13
LA RAÍZ DE TODOS LOS DIVORCIOS Y MATRIMONIOS INFELICES

Si preguntamos a un grupo de personas divorciadas cuál fue el motivo que condujo a sus matrimonios al fin, obtenemos varias respuestas diferentes. Muchos dirán que fue por la infidelidad de su pareja, otros culparán a la «incompatibilidad de caracteres», otros responsabilizarán a los problemas económicos o a la falta de compromiso del compañero. Si pedimos a los que viven infelices con su matrimonio que hagan un listado de las razones de esta infelicidad, dirán cosas del tipo «él no me presta atención», «ya no confío en él», «discutimos mucho», «ella es obstinada» y otras similares. Está claro que no todo matrimonio es infeliz por las mismas razones y no todo divorcio se produce por los mismos motivos, pero todos ellos tienen una única raíz principal. Los motivos que dan los matrimonios son tan solo consecuencias de un problema mucho más profundo, que es la raíz de todos los matrimonios infelices y divorcios. Y quien nos revela esta raíz no es un psicólogo ni un terapeuta de parejas, sino el propio Autor del matrimonio.

Entender esta raíz y cortarla es algo tan eficaz que, si usted hace tan solo eso, de todo lo que ha aprendido en este libro, podrá transformar su matrimonio.

IMPOTENTE PARA IMPEDIR EL DIVORCIO

Para descubrir esta profunda raíz le traigo dos informaciones de la Biblia que pueden parecer incoherentes a primera vista. La primera, que el divorcio está permitido según la Ley dada por Dios a Moisés, en el principio del Antiguo Testamento.[11] La segunda, que en el último libro del Antiguo Testamento encontramos la información de que Dios odia el divorcio.[12] La palabra utilizada es esa misma: «odia». Uno no encuentra muchas veces en la Biblia a Dios diciendo que odia algo. Él no usa ese término a no ser que esté siendo literal. Él realmente *odia* el divorcio. ¿Por qué el divorcio provoca el odio de Dios?

Cuando la pareja se divorcia es como si dijese a Dios: «Mira, has cometido un error. Este asunto del matrimonio no funciona». El divorcio es una afrenta a Dios, ya que fue Él quien estableció la alianza del matrimonio; es una anomalía que nada tiene que ver con lo que Él tenía en mente cuando unió a la mujer y al hombre.

Pero, si esta es la opinión de Dios respecto al divorcio, entonces, ¿por qué hizo una excepción haciendo que fuese permitido por la ley que Él mismo creó? Y, siendo tan poderoso, ¿por qué parece incapaz de impedir una cosa que odia?

Fue esta la duda que los religiosos trajeron a Jesús. Al contrario que usted, ellos no querían realmente saber la respuesta, solo lanzar un señuelo para ver si conseguían alguna declaración que pudiesen usar contra Él en el tribunal –literalmente–. Como siempre, les salió mal, y el resultado fue una revelación maravillosa del Señor Jesús respecto a este asunto tan controvertido.

Se acercaron a Él algunos fariseos para probarle, diciendo: «¿Es lícito a un hombre divorciarse de su mujer por cualquier motivo?» Y respondiendo Él,

---

[11] Deuteronomio 24:1.
[12] Malaquías 2:16.

dijo: «¿No habéis leído que aquel que los creó, desde el principio los hizo varón y hembra, y añadió:"por esta razón el hombre dejará a su padre y a su madre y se unirá a su mujer, y los dos serán una sola carne"? Por consiguiente, ya no son dos, sino una sola carne. Por tanto, lo que Dios ha unido, ningún hombre lo separe». (Mateo 19:3-6).

Al responder, Jesús señala el plan original de Dios y revela el sentido real del matrimonio. En la matemática de Dios, 1+1=1, es decir, el hombre y la mujer, unidos por el matrimonio, se convierten en una sola persona. Hay una fusión de dos individuos, que se transforman en una persona diferente. Yo ya no soy más la persona que era cuando estaba soltero, ni tampoco Cristiane. Quien nos conoció solteros y nos conoce hoy puede ver eso claramente. Nos volvimos personas diferentes (y mucho mejores) en virtud de nuestro matrimonio. Hubo una fusión de nuestras personalidades. Solemos hacer una analogía con el puré de papas, que ilustra muy bien este proceso. Antes de hacer el puré, tenemos dos papas aisladas. Al amasarlas y cocinarlas con leche, se funden y se transforman en un tercer elemento: el puré. El puré ya no es ni leche ni papa... No hay manera de separarlo. Exactamente eso es lo que Jesús quiso decir con *«ya no son dos, sino una sola carne».*

La palabra hebraica para «se unirá», en el texto original, significa «pegar como pegamento», en el sentido de fundir los dos objetos de manera que no se pueda separarlos sin producir un gran daño. Imagine rasgar su propia carne. Eso es el divorcio. Causa heridas profundas y difíciles de cicatrizar; violenta a los que lo sufren. El matrimonio fue ideado para que hubiese una fusión y el surgimiento de un tercer elemento, con la intención de no ser derogado jamás.

Muchos se quieren casar y, sin embargo, permanecen igual que cuando eran solteros. Se resisten a la fusión y nunca se vuelven una sola carne. Los dos continúan como individuos distintos y no maleables dentro de la relación. Así, nunca va a funcionar. No estoy diciendo que deba abdicar de su personalidad y dejar de ser usted mismo; la idea es mejorar, aceptando las influencias positivas de la otra persona y amoldándose a ella. Es como un hijo del matrimonio. Tiene características del padre y de la madre –nariz de uno, ojos de otro, pelo de uno, color de la piel del otro, etc.– pero, aun así, también tiene su propia personalidad. Así es el matrimonio. Ustedes acaban volviéndose un producto de su unión; por eso, cuando se casa, usted tiene que empezar a pensar más como «nosotros» y menos como «yo».

Cuando, para justificarse ante su compañero por algún error, usted dice: «Yo nací así, crecí así, viví así, voy a ser siempre así... Es mi manera de ser», en realidad, Gabriela (o Gabriel), usted está queriendo mantener su individualidad a costa de su matrimonio. Si su manera de ser no es buena para su relación, tiene que cambiar su manera de ser –o no va a haber una solución para ustedes dos.

«Yo soy así, esta es mi manera de ser» era una de las frases de moda que utilizaba para acabar con cualquier callejón sin salida que tuviera con Cristiane. Yo preguntaba: ¿por qué quieres ahora cambiarme, si yo ya era así cuando me conociste? Esa era la voz de mi individualidad resistiendo la idea de volverme una sola carne con ella. Muchos escuchan esa voz hasta que, finalmente, se separan. ¿Por qué esa obstinación? Debido a la maldita raíz que enseguida que Jesús reveló.

CORAZÓN DE PIEDRA

Ellos le dijeron: «Entonces, ¿por qué mandó Moisés darle carta de divorcio y repudiarla?». Él les dijo: «Por la dureza de vuestro corazón, Moisés os permitió divorciaros de vuestras mujeres; pero no ha sido así desde el principio». (Mateo 19:7,8).

Esa es la verdadera raíz de todos los divorcios y matrimonios infelices: el corazón endurecido. El divorcio no estaba en los planes de Dios. No era una opción cuando creó el matrimonio; sin embargo, por el corazón petrificado del ser humano, tuvo que tolerar –e incluso permitir– algo que Él tanto odia. ¿Puede imaginarlo? Cuando usted endurece su corazón, ¡ni Dios puede impedir el divorcio! Pero ¿no es que Él puede todas las cosas? ¿Cómo es que no evita algo que tanto odia? Y peor, ¡además lo legaliza! ¿No lo podría haber prohibido de una vez? Dios no es un tirano. Respeta nuestras elecciones, no va a invadir nuestro corazón y obligarnos a cambiar. Ni siquiera Dios le puede ayudar cuando usted endurece su corazón, ¡qué decir de su cónyuge! Solamente usted puede hacer algo para evitar el desastre.

Pero, primero, necesita entender lo que es un corazón de piedra. ¿Qué hace que se endurezca el corazón de una persona? ¿Será que su corazón está petrificado y no lo sabe?

Hay muchas cosas que pueden endurecer su corazón. Cuando hablamos de corazón nos referimos al centro de las emociones y sentimientos. Todo sentimiento negativo que no es debidamente procesado y eliminado del corazón acaba volviéndose una piedra. Uno de las principales es el orgullo.

El orgullo es el cemento de los corazones. La persona orgullosa está ciega ante sus errores. En general, se cree muy humilde y le parece que el error siempre está en los demás. Ella es la víctima incomprendida, tiene alergia a admitir sus fallas y prefiere sacarse un diente sin anestesia que pedir perdón. El orgulloso, por creer que siempre tiene razón, se queda esperando a que la otra persona se rebaje y ceda. Es incapaz de ver lo importante que es, para la persona herida, ver a la otra reconocer su error y pedir disculpas. Muchos problemas se resolverían si el orgulloso simplemente dijese: «Discúlpame, me equivoqué, no voy a hacerlo más». Pero prefiere endurecer todavía más su corazón.

Me acuerdo de una pareja mayor, que se habían casado cuando ella tenía catorce años. La familia, preocupada por el hecho de que ella tenía una personalidad muy fuerte, creía que el matrimonio sería una buena forma de «domesticarla». ¡Pobre muchacho! En la primera discusión, ya en la luna de miel (¿creía que iban a tardar más que eso?), él dijo una tontería, afirmando que la única mujer a la que había amado en la vida había sido una noviecita de la infancia a la que le regalaba las frutas cuando tenía diez años. Dolorida con aquella «revelación» fuera de lugar, ella se guardó durante décadas la información: «Él no me ama y nunca me va a amar». Él, pensando que ella estaba equivocada, nunca le pidió perdón. Ella, sintiéndose dañada, se empeñó en hacerle la vida un verdadero infierno.

¿Qué ganaron con eso? Un matrimonio en ruinas, una familia despedazada, años de sufrimiento inútil. Él encontró en la calle el aprecio que no tenía en casa y ella se tragó las diversas traiciones del marido, acumulando rencor hacia «la otra». Ninguno de los dos daba su brazo a torcer, aunque se amasen. La vida pasó muy rápida y solamente cerca del final se dieron cuenta de que habían perdido la oportunidad de ser felices durante todos aquellos años que estuvieron juntos.

¡Cuántas oportunidades está perdiendo el orgulloso! No sabe que si fuese menos duro sería mucho más feliz. Podría aprender cosas nuevas, descubrir una manera diferente de ver la vida... ¿Por qué cree que Dios determinó que dos criaturas tan diferentes como el hombre y la mujer viviesen juntas?

Pensándolo bien, el matrimonio parece incluso una broma de mal gusto de Dios. Puedo imaginar al Padre, al Hijo y al Espíritu Santo riéndose y frotándose las manos mientras dicen: «¡He tenido una idea! Vamos a crear al hombre. Va a ser así y así... ¡Listo! Ahora vamos a crear a la mujer...; ella será..., ¡exactamente lo opuesto! ¡Vamos a ver qué pasa! Van a tener que vivir en la misma casa. ¡Ah!, y algo más: ¡no pueden separarse!». ¡Parece broma! Pero está claro que, felizmente, hay un propósito.

Dios permite que dos personas, totalmente diferentes, estén juntas, no para torturar a Sus criaturas, sino para que una desafíe a la otra para ser mejor persona. Él nos hizo tan diferentes para que podamos complementarnos, pero solo es posible mejorar como persona, a través de la convivencia como cónyuge, si su corazón está abierto y es maleable. Es necesaria una buena dosis de humildad para matar esa raíz y aprovechar lo mejor que tiene el matrimonio.

Volvamos al ejemplo de aquella pareja mayor. El problema empezó con una tontería dicha por el marido. Si él se hubiese tragado su orgullo y pedido perdón sinceramente a su mujer, habría evitado cincuenta años de infierno en su vida. O si, por lo menos, ella no se hubiese tomado en serio la tontería que él dijo y hubiese tratado a su marido con respeto y cariño, él no habría tenido otro remedio que hacerla feliz.

Pariente del orgullo es el egoísmo, también capaz de petrificar un corazón. El pensamiento del egoísta es esencialmente guiado por estas máximas: «Lo que yo quiero, lo que es bueno para mí, mis deseos primero». La persona egoísta no se preocupa por el punto de vista de la otra persona. Ella escucha, pero no oye; pues la voz de su yo habla más alto y oculta la voz de su compañero.

Al principio de mi matrimonio, no estaba preocupado por las necesidades de mi mujer; con tal de que yo estuviera satisfecho con mi trabajo, estaba bien. Me parecía que, mientras no faltase nada en casa, ella no tenía por qué protestar. Si cree que su cónyuge se queja por nada, porque usted le da esto, hace aquello..., entienda una cosa: no sirve de nada dar mucho de algo que la persona ya tiene lo suficiente y no dar nada de aquello que ella realmente necesita y sintiendo que le falta.

Conocí a un joven que creía que su mujer era muy feliz. Se espantó cuando, un bonito día (no tan bonito para él), la mujer le anunció que se iba de casa. Teorías conspiratorias invadían su mente. ¿Quién le habría «lavado el cerebro» a aquella mujer perfecta y sumisa con quien vivía desde hacía seis años? ¿Un hermano? ¿Una amiga? ¿Un pastor? ¿El hijo de su primer matrimonio, con quien nunca se llevó bien? Era injusto, él, un excelente marido, «que siempre le dio todo», siempre estuvo a su lado, con quien se llevaba tan bien; ser abandonado, ahora, sin mayores explicaciones.

Lo que él no imaginaba era que ella se había sentido postergada la mayor parte de esos años de matrimonio. Me confesó que todo lo que el marido hacía y decía era en función de él mismo. Jamás se interesó en saber lo que a ella le gustaba, lo que quería. No se comunicaban. Él se creía mucho más inteligente –o por lo menos era así como ella lo interpretaba– y le imponía paseos culturales que no le interesaban. Ella también estaba equivocada, ya que nunca dejó que él supiese que nada de lo que hacían le agradaba. Pero si él hubiese mirado menos su propio ombligo, se habría dado cuenta de que, a su lado, había una mujer anulada e infeliz.

Entienda esto: usted perdió el derecho de pensar solamente en sí mismo el día en que firmó el certificado de matrimonio.

NO VOY A CAMBIAR

La dureza de corazón es básicamente una obstinación, insistir en algo que no funciona. Es lo que le hace al marido decir que no va a cambiar, incluso viendo el matrimonio irse río abajo. Es lo que hace a la esposa insistir en su manera de ser y permanecer sorda a los pedidos de su marido. Si su forma de ser no es buena para su matrimonio y no quiere cambiar, sepa que su destino es morir solo.

Muchas veces endurecemos nuestro corazón por autodefensa. Después de sufrir mucho, tal vez seguido de alguna traición, mentira, palabras duras u otra experiencia dolorosa a manos de nuestro compañero, es normal que nuestro corazón se endurezca. Nos apartamos, nos desligamos emocionalmente para que nunca más aquella persona nos vuelva a herir. El problema es que levantar murallas para proteger nuestro corazón no es inteligente, a no ser que quiera quedarse atrapado allí dentro, solo, con todos aquellos sentimientos malos, como un prisionero en la casa de los horrores. Quien construye murallas acaba en una prisión construida por sí mismo.

Piense en esto: si su pareja está realmente determinada a herirle y cree que no hay nada más por lo que luchar en ese matrimonio, entonces salga de él de una vez por todas. Pero si todavía está intentándolo es porque cree que hay esperanza, así que tiene que derrumbar esas murallas y ablandar su corazón. Vivir al lado de su compañero y mantener las murallas entre ustedes es disfrutar con el sufrimiento. Recuerde: si la dureza de corazón permanece, ni Dios podrá ayudarle.

Vea si estas piedras están en su corazón:

- Orgullo.
- Egoísmo.
- Inflexibilidad en su forma de ser.
- Estar siempre a la defensiva.
- Permanecer preso de un punto de vista.
- Ser incapaz de perdonar.
- Resistirse a la intimidad física.
- Falta de deseo de cambiar.
- Pensar que nunca está equivocado.
- Le gusta recibir, no dar.
- Permanecer preso del pasado.
- Ha construido murallas que su compañero no puede atravesar.
- No es sincero, oculta sus sentimientos.
- Acostumbra a enfocarse en los puntos negativos del compañero.
- Raramente pide disculpas.
- No se preocupa por los sentimientos del compañero.
- No quiere oír.
- Intenta imponer cambios al compañero.
- Tiene una opinión formada (que es la única correcta, claro).
- Hace chantajes emocionales.
- Intenta controlar al compañero.
- Utiliza «esa es mi forma de ser» como excusa para todo.
- No reconoce que necesita ayuda para sus problemas personales.
- Emplea palabras hirientes.

- Frialdad y distancia emocional.
- No consigue abrirse y compartir con el compañero.

Analícese a sí mismo en función de los puntos anteriores. Haga un examen honesto de su corazón. ¿No hay algunas piedras que necesitan ser rotas? ¿Qué diría su cónyuge al respecto, si alguien le preguntase? Mientras mantenga la dureza de corazón, nunca podrá ser feliz en su vida sentimental.

Cristiane:

Para complicar todavía más la situación, existen dos tipos de corazones duros: aquel que está claramente a la vista, que todos ven, cuya dureza se nota fácilmente, y aquel que piensa que es la víctima. Ambos están endurecidos y ambos están acusándose el uno al otro.

Así sucedía conmigo y con Renato. Durante los primeros doce años de nuestro matrimonio yo le culpaba por no ser el marido que necesitaba que fuese. Su forma de resolver nuestros problemas era terrible. Permanecía con cara de enojado durante días y, al final, era yo quien tenía que pedir perdón. Yo se lo pedía, porque si no el matrimonio no seguía adelante; pero, en realidad, no pedía disculpas de corazón. Continuaba pensando que él era el problema, tanto es así que vivía orando por él (era justa a mis propios ojos). Me veía como una esposa desaprovechada, porque le daba todo de mí y recibía poco. Llegué hasta a componer una canción muy triste y sentimental para la banda sonora de nuestra historia de «amor». Hasta que llegamos a la época de la llamada telefónica, que explicamos en el capítulo 9. Cambié mucho, me enfoqué más en lo que podía hacer y descubrí que, durante todos aquellos años, yo también había tenido un corazón duro. El mío era aquel que se llamaba víctima.

Sí, Renato me debía la atención de marido. Sí, no debería castigarme durante días sin hablar conmigo por cualquier cosa que no le gustaba que hiciera. Pero, ¿de qué sirve saber que su cónyuge no hace lo que debería, si usted tampoco hace lo que debería hacer?

Al principio, me asusté con esa revelación. Siempre me había considerado una óptima esposa para Renato, siempre dándole lo mejor. ¿Cómo podía yo también estar siendo dura y mala con él? Es por eso por lo que muchos continúan en el círculo vicioso del desamor. Amar es dar. Pero cuando llega el punto en el que ambos dejan de dar para ver quién da primero, ¡se acabó! Permanecen dando vueltas y más vueltas, ¡un verdadero «cambio» de 360 grados! Cambian los primeros meses pero, en poco tiempo, vuelven a estar en el punto de partida.

Mi corazón duro insistía en demandar el cambio de Renato. Le reclamaba constantemente. Cuando hacía algo que él me había pedido, enseguida esperaba ver lo que él iba a hacer por mí. Y, cuando no veía nada en el horizonte, volvía a reclamarle. Y usted sabe que hay varias formas de reclamar. Reclama, pone mala cara, suelta algún comentario verde para ver si él cosecha algo maduro, hace chantaje emocional, hace comparaciones y así sucesivamente. Todas esas cosas derivan de un corazón duro que cree ser la víctima.

Yo creo que ese es el peor de los corazones duros, porque no conseguimos verlo. Pensamos que tenemos la razón, izamos la bandera de «¿Hasta cuándo tendré que dar?», pero ¿de qué sirve dar con una mano mientras se cobra con la otra?.

Yo tenía ese corazón duro y por eso nuestros problemas duraron más de lo que deberían. Soy totalmente consciente de eso, tan es así que ni bien ablandé mi corazón, Renato cambió y mi matrimonio se transformó; como si yo hubiera estado bloqueando todas mis oraciones y nuestros intentos de cambio.

Mi cambio fue bien sencillo. Por cierto, creo que, para la víctima, el cambio no es tan complicado como para el «culpable». Simplemente dejé de imponer. Sacrifiqué lo que yo creía que él debería hacer, dejé de señalar, dejé de reclamar. ¡Ya ve qué simple!

Solamente eso fue suficiente. Y lo que yo gané a cambio... ¡estamos aquí escribiendo un libro sobre ese tema para que usted pueda ver cómo vale la pena!

Quien cede primero tiene el privilegio de decir lo que yo digo hoy: yo cambié primero para que mi marido cambiase. Eso no es para cualquiera.

LIBRÁNDOSE DE LAS PIEDRAS

Si reconoce que hay piedras y murallas en su corazón y quiere cambiar, el primer paso es pedir ayuda a Aquel que odia el divorcio. ¿Se acuerda de Él? Ahora podemos concluir que, si Dios odia el divorcio y la dureza de corazón es la responsable de los matrimonios destruidos, entonces Dios le quiere ayudar a vencer eso. Mire lo que Él dice:

Además, os daré un corazón nuevo y pondré un espíritu nuevo dentro de vosotros; quitaré de vuestra carne el corazón de piedra y os daré un corazón de carne. (Ezequiel 36:26).

Para que Dios pueda ayudarle, necesita asumir su error. Puede empezar haciendo una oración sincera, con humildad: «Mi Dios, quiero cambiar de corazón. Saca mi corazón de piedra y dame un corazón de carne. Muéstrame cómo tengo que ser. Ayúdame a ser la persona que Tú quieres que sea».

Si le parece que «no está bien así» y quiere continuar haciendo las cosas a su manera, olvídelo. Ni Dios puede ayudar a quien no quiere renunciar a su corazón petrificado. Si tiene ese deseo sincero de entregarse y permitir que Dios le moldee en la persona que debe ser, Él le ayudará a quebrar su corazón, recuperar su matrimonio y evitar, incluso, un futuro divorcio.

Pero no piense que tener la ayuda de Dios significa que podrá quedarse de brazos cruzados mientras Él trabaja. No funciona así. La acción de Dios exige sociedad. Él le va a ayudar en aquello que no puede conseguir solo, pero su esfuerzo es necesario en este proceso. Dios le dará las herramientas para que usted mismo quiebre su duro corazón. Quebrar piedras nunca es una tarea fácil, pero le vamos a decir qué hacer –y qué no hacer– para conseguirlo.

Reconocer sus errores es muy doloroso, pero tendrá que hacerlo para empezar. Sienta ese dolor ahora y tendrá un alivio durante toda la vida. La alternativa es aferrarse a sus errores y hundirse con ellos, sintiendo dolor en cuotas durante años. ¿Cuál prefiere?

TAREA

Ustedes tendrán una conversación. Haga la siguiente pregunta a su cónyuge: ¿qué me hace una persona difícil para convivir? Anote las respuestas. Después cambien: usted responderá a la pregunta y su cónyuge anotará sus respuestas. Aunque su cónyuge no quiera hacer esta tarea, acuérdese de las principales quejas que suele oír y anótelas. No lo olvide: el más inteligente es el que da el primer paso para el cambio. Atención a las reglas: papel, lapicero, oír y escribir. No debe rebatir, ni defenderse ni cuestionar. Cero sentimientos en esta tarea. Apenas explore el punto de vista de la otra persona, aunque esté en desacuerdo con ella. Lo importante es entender lo que él (ella) está sintiendo.

No lo lleve hacia el lado personal. Acuérdese de guardar sus emociones en el cajón antes de empezar esta tarea. Aunque no esté de acuerdo, respire hondo y continúe. No ataque al carácter, intente expresarse de manera que enfoque el problema. Guarde esta lista con toda su vida. No la pierda. Demuestre a su cónyuge que lo está tomando en serio.

Si aparta la emoción y sabe mantener la atención, tendrá en esta lista algo muy útil para ayudarle a cambiarse a sí mismo. No es una competencia. No se preocupen por cuál lista será la más larga. Lo que importa es sacar todo hacia fuera. Otro punto crucial: a partir de este ejercicio ya no va a señalar más esos ítems a la otra persona, ni reclamarle que haga algo con la lista. Usted es responsable tan solo de su propio trabajo.

Manos a la obra, agarren sus martillos. Hoy empezarán a quebrar las piedras.

/MatrimonioBlindado

Publique esto:
Comencé a quebrar
las piedras de mi
corazón.

@matrimonioblind

Tuitee esto:
Comencé a quebrar
las piedras de mi
corazón
#matrimonioblindado
@matrimonioblind

CAPÍTULO 14
EL ORDEN DE LAS RELACIONES

En el colegio aprendemos que «el orden de los factores no altera el producto». Eso puede servir muy bien a la hora de la multiplicación, pero no siempre esa máxima puede aplicarse en nuestra vida. Dentro del matrimonio el orden de los factores altera –y mucho– el producto. Después de una competencia olímpica, los vencedores se sitúan en el podio por orden de importancia y reciben las recompensas de acuerdo con sus posiciones finales. Nadie daría la medalla de oro al tercer lugar ni, mucho menos, dejaría al primer lugar con la de bronce, pero usted puede estar haciendo eso en su casa en este momento, simplemente por no saber a quién pertenece cada una de las tres posiciones del podio dentro del matrimonio.

ESTE JUEZ NO ES LADRÓN

Dios dejó bien claro que Él debe estar en primer lugar en la vida de todos nosotros. Eso no es egocentrismo de Su parte, Él sabe lo que está haciendo, conoce muy bien al ser humano y sabe por qué el caos es inevitable cuando esa regla no se sigue. Si no pone a Dios en primer lugar, naturalmente, quien ocupa ese lugar es usted mismo. Y, cuando usted se pone en primer lugar en su vida… ¡Prepárese! Nadie lo aguanta. Hace un montón de tonterías y acaba cayendo en el egoísmo del que hablamos en el capítulo anterior, endureciendo su corazón y echándolo todo a perder. Dios sugiere que Lo coloquemos en primer lugar para que haya un árbitro en nuestra vida. En el matrimonio es esencial tener un árbitro entre ustedes dos.

Sin lugar a dudas, puedo atribuir mi matrimonio al hecho de que, nosotros dos, ponemos a Dios en primer lugar. Si no fuese así, no estoy seguro de que estuviésemos juntos. El matrimonio es la unión de dos personas completamente diferentes; por lo tanto, es natural que, a pesar del amor, haya momentos en los que no estén de acuerdo. Uno va a decir A, el otro va a decir Z, y los dos van a pensar que tienen razón. ¿Cómo resolver esta situación? Solo hay una solución: alguien por encima de ustedes, establecido como árbitro, juez. Es Su ley, imparcial, la que va a decidir.

Hubo veces en las que tuve que retirar mis razones y Cristiane también tuvo que apartar las suyas y dejar que las razones de Dios prevalecieran. Ya no era lo que yo quería, lo que me parecía correcto o lo que a ella le parecía adecuado, sino lo que Dios dice y determina que debe ser. Usted no puede imaginar cómo eso simplifica la vida del matrimonio, resuelve una parte de los problemas.

¿No fue eso lo que Jesús determinó cuando se Le inquirió sobre cuál era el mandamiento más importante de todos? *Amarás al Señor tu Dios de todo tu corazón, con toda tu alma y con todo tu entendimiento. Este es el gran y primer mandamiento. Y, el segundo, semejante a este, es: Amarás a tu prójimo como a ti mismo.*[13] Primero, Dios, después, su prójimo, en este orden. ¿Y quién es la persona más próxima a usted? ¿No es su marido o su mujer?

Cuando trabajábamos en Texas la deficiencia espiritual era muy visible. Algunos matrimonios se entusiasmaban mucho con el curso Matrimonio blindado, se lo contaban a todos sus amigos e, incluso, veían cambios en la relación. Sin embargo, esos cambios no conseguían transformar sus matrimonios de forma permanente. Aunque la mayoría perteneciesen a alguna iglesia, ya que el estado es prácticamente evangélico, no man-

---

[13] Mateo 22:37-40.

tenían una relación real con Dios. Hay una gran diferencia. Mantener una relación real con Dios, tratarlo como la persona más importante en su vida y con actitudes, no tiene nada que ver con la religión o las prácticas religiosas. Me gustó la forma en que mi compañero Marcus Vinícius habló sobre cómo el matrimonio debe mirar hacia Dios, en uno de nuestros cursos en São Paulo:

Al mirar a Dios, intente quitar el preconcepto religioso. Vea a Dios como la justicia, como la verdad. No su verdad, ni la de su cónyuge, sino como la verdad que les va a ayudar a los dos a superar juntos el problema. No tiene nada que ver con religión y sí con los verdaderos valores que todo ser humano necesita y aprecia. No es inteligente no tenerlo en primer lugar en su vida. Si la justicia de su compañero es una y la suya es otra, ¿cuál se va a imponer al final? Solamente la justicia que viene de lo Alto, es decir, la justicia perfecta es la que puede traer el verdadero equilibrio y justicia para ustedes, ya que sin justicia no puede haber amor.

Si no hubiera esa justicia mayor mediando en los conflictos, se acaba atado a las especulaciones. ¿Quién tiene la razón? Ella cree que es ella, él cree que es él; pero creer no significa nada, no prueba ninguna cosa. Por eso, todo deporte tiene reglas, todo país tiene su constitución. Usted no puede ir a trabajar en bermudas –a menos, claro, que sea salvavidas–. Es decir, las cosas están organizadas o se forma un lío. ¿Por qué en el matrimonio sería diferente? Pueden no gustarle las reglas, pero existen para regular las relaciones.

Si no hubiese un juez en el campo de fútbol, el juego nunca se acabaría, las faltas no se reconocerían y la confusión sería inevitable. Los dos equipos jugarían hasta la extenuación, nunca llegarían a un acuerdo. Inclusive no gustándole el juez, los equipos (y los hinchas) entienden que él es necesario para mantener el orden. Cuando Lo tenemos en primer lugar en nuestras vidas, Él se convierte en el Juez de nuestro matrimonio.

Es muy importante en aquellos momentos en los que no conseguimos llegar a un acuerdo... Es entonces cuando buscamos saber lo que Dios cree al respecto y hacemos Su voluntad, con la confianza de que será lo mejor. A fin de cuentas, Él no es un juez ladrón. Es muy difícil tener un matrimonio feliz sin obedecer las reglas establecidas por Dios.

Y LA MEDALLA DE PLATA ES PARA...

Con Dios recibiendo la medalla de oro, ahí está usted, con la medalla de plata en las manos, esperando ponerla en su propio cuellito, en el cuellecito de su hijo, en el cuello de su madre. La respuesta está en el pasaje bíblico que cita la creación del matrimonio. ¿Se acuerda de él?

Por tanto dejará el hombre a su padre y a su madre, y se unirá a su mujer, y serán una sola carne (Génesis 2: 24).

El matrimonio viene con esa reglita en el manual de instrucciones. Para que el hombre (y la mujer) se casen, primero tienen que dejar a su padre y a su madre, salir del nido. Si debemos dejar a los padres que son los más influyentes en nuestras vidas, ¡cuánto más a los hermanos, amigos, el Facebook de la ex novia! «Y serán una sola carne» muestra el inicio de una nueva familia. Cuando se casa, deja a su familia de origen y forma una nueva familia. Su nueva familia es su cónyuge. Sus padres y hermanos, toda su familia de origen, se convierten en parientes como en el diagrama siguiente:

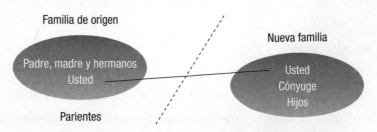

Después de que usted se case los miembros de su familia de origen pasarán a ser sus parientes.

No estoy diciendo que sus padres y hermanos dejarán de ser importantes, pero usted ha emigrado para hacer su propio nido y, ahora, tiene una nueva familia –es necesario establecer unos límites claros para mantener una relación saludable con todos–. Si esa línea no queda bien clara, comienza a haber interferencias.

Uno de los errores comunes cometidos por los recién casados y sus parientes es creer que, mientras el matrimonio no tenga un hijo, no se es visto como una familia. Es muy común oír: «Ahora sí, nuestra familia está completa», con la llegada de un bebé; pero eso es despreciar el hecho de que la familia ya estaba completa desde el día en que se casaron. Tener hijos es una elección y no un paso obligatorio en la relación (y, por favor, nunca tome esa decisión con el objetivo de resolver algún problema entre ustedes o de completar alguna laguna. No funciona).

El hombre se une a su compañera y se convierten en una sola carne. La familia está creada, completa y cerrada, sin espacio para la intromisión de terceros. Quitando a Dios, en su vida no existe otra cosa ni persona que pueda ser más importante para usted que su marido o su mujer. Si son una sola carne, cuando cuida de su cónyuge está cuidando su propio cuerpo. Al priorizar al otro, se está priorizando a usted mismo, a su parte más importante.

Por desgracia, muchas mujeres piensan que ese es el tipo de relación que deben tener exclusivamente con sus hijos, que son sangre de su sangre. Llevan a los bebés durante nueve meses dentro de sí y se sienten unidas a ellos para el resto de sus vidas, más que hasta al propio padre del niño. Pero esas criaturas, que salieron de adentro de ellas, crecen y van a querer vivir sus propias vidas y formar sus propias familias. No tiene sentido volverse una sola carne con alguien que, inevitablemente, se irá de su casa en pocos años. Es receta para la frustración y el sufrimiento. Los hijos necesitan encontrar una base firme en el matrimonio de sus padres para formar sus propias bases en el futuro.

La fuerza de la relación está en la unión de la pareja, y la única manera de conseguir eso es estableciendo las prioridades correctamente. Quien pone el trabajo por encima del cónyuge crea un abismo en su relación. El problema es que es muy fácil dejar que otras cosas o personas se instalen por encima de su marido o su mujer, aunque usted no admita eso verbalmente. Con seguridad, si alguien le pregunta, usted siempre va a decir que su cónyuge es más importante pero, en la práctica, ¿cómo demuestra quién –o qué– está en primer lugar?

El grado de importancia de algo o de alguien en su vida se mide en función del tiempo que le dedica y por lo que hace, no por lo que dice. Observe sus actitudes. ¿A quién le ha dedicado la mayor –o mejor– parte de su tiempo, esfuerzo, atención y pensamientos? Su tiempo debe ser, preferentemente, para su cónyuge. Si tiene más tiempo para estar en casa de mamá, de los amigos o en el trabajo y pone esas cosas por delante de su compañero, está poniendo a su matrimonio en riesgo y sin equipo de protección. Eso exige mucha atención de su parte, día a día. Mida sus actitudes.

Yo le decía a mi mujer: «Te amo»; pero la manera como la ignoraba y no le prestaba atención invalidaba mis palabras. Era lo que yo hacía lo que le mostraba que, en mi vida, lo más importante era mi trabajo. En mi caso, es todavía más difícil porque mi trabajo es servir a Dios. Es mucho más fácil mezclar las estaciones y creer que, si Dios está en primer lugar, todo lo que está relacionado con Él también debe estarlo. No confunda a Dios con la Obra de Dios.

Incluso trabajando como pastor, sirviendo a Dios, no podía poner el trabajo para Dios por encima de mi mujer. Es lo que Él deja claro cuando habla de los pastores, de los obispos, de los que Le sirven, al decir que deben estar bien casados, cuidar primero de la casa para, después, cuidar de la iglesia. Dios no Se está contradiciendo al afirmar que el pastor debe cuidar, primero, de su familia. Él continúa en primer lugar, pues la Obra de Dios no es Dios. ¡Observe cómo Él valora su matrimonio! Él no quiere que haga Su obra si dentro de casa no da ejemplo y no hace de su cónyuge la primera oveja. El matrimonio, en realidad, sirve como un termómetro que mide nuestra relación con Dios. Si estoy bien con Dios, tengo que estar bien en mi matrimonio; si estoy mal en mi matrimonio, no puedo estar bien con Dios.

Para que un matrimonio funcione es necesario que ambos, marido y mujer, se preocupen el uno por el otro, por encima de todas las demás personas y cosas; si eso no sucede, de hecho, no hay matrimonio. En la posición correcta en el podio, la mujer se siente especial por haber sido escogida por encima de todas las demás mujeres. Si se la pone en un rincón, será una mujer amargada e infeliz. Una mujer infeliz hace un hogar infeliz y −estamos de acuerdo− no es eso lo que usted desea. El marido, puesto en el lugar correcto, se siente respetado por su responsabilidad de cuidar a su mujer como si fuese su propio cuerpo.

Ahora que usted sabe todo esto, y siendo los dos una sola carne, saque de la ecuación a los terceros. Ustedes tienen que estar tan juntos que parezcan pegados, inseparables. No puede haber una tercera persona entre ustedes, ni siquiera el propio hijo.

Salvo raras excepciones, por supuesto. Supongamos que su marido es agresivo, consumidor de drogas; este comportamiento genera un riesgo para toda la familia. En este caso, usted y sus hijos −si existieran− se convierten en la prioridad, pues las actitudes de su marido hacen que se haya convertido en un riesgo para la seguridad de la familia. En esta situación puede ser necesaria una separación temporal para que él se ponga en tratamiento. Está claro que si Dios estuviese en primer lugar en la vida de este marido, él no sería toxicómano, pero eso es un tema para otro libro.

Con el primero y el segundo lugar debidamente ocupados por Dios y su cónyuge, el tercer lugar queda para el resto de la humanidad: sus hijos, parientes, amigos y demás personas. Organícenlos ahí.

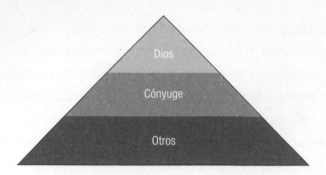

El orden de las relaciones según está determinado por Dios.

¿QUÉ HACER CON LOS CURIOSOS?

No es fácil trazar las líneas que sus amigos y parientes no podrán atravesar, principalmente si ellos ya tenían la costumbre de entrometerse en su vida antes de que usted se casara. Pero, antes de pedir cuentas a sus familiares, deje de alimentar la intromisión. Cuando usted lleva sus problemas a parientes o amigos, les da la autorización para realizar juicios respecto a su cónyuge, formarse opiniones parciales y tratar su vida como si fuese la de ellos. Si expone su vida como la novela de las ocho a todos sus parientes, no sirve de nada protestar después.

Si su relación ha sido invadida por parientes entrometidos, ¿qué hacer? No sirve de nada pelear, ni patalear. Actúe con la mente. Aquel que no pertenecía a la familia de origen –y que está siendo visto como el invasor– necesita entender que los parientes serán siempre parientes. No es inteligente pelear contra ellos, ya que estará atacando a los orígenes de su compañero y creará un problema todavía mayor. Lo ideal es tratarlos de la mejor manera posible e intentar conquistarlos.

Corte el mal de raíz y no lleve nada hacia el lado personal. Muchas veces, la raíz del mal humor de la suegra con la nuera, por ejemplo, está en la inseguridad. Si trata bien a la madre de su compañero, dejando claro que no está ahí en el papel de rival y que su objetivo es hacer de él la persona más feliz del Universo, le transmitirá seguridad y eliminará los problemas. Ella debe ser una aliada suya, alguien a quien ama y respeta, nunca una enemiga. Aprenda a amar a su suegra, aunque en este momento crea que será misión imposible. Si usted leyó este libro hasta aquí, sabe que no lo es. ¿Se acuerda de Dian Fossey y los gorilas?

Si son sus parientes a quienes les gusta entrometerse en su matrimonio, debe saber priorizar a su nueva familia y mostrar eso en sus actitudes. Sea educado, no agreda a nadie, pero establezca unos límites claros para que los parientes sepan que su familia es sagrada y que quien habla de ella, habla de usted. Aquel a quien le caiga usted bien tendrá que aprender a que le caiga bien su cónyuge, pues ahora son uno.

Los casos en los que la pareja quiere ayudar a un pariente que necesita ayuda económica tienen grandes probabilidades de generar conflictos; sin embargo, si antes de decidir, ambos conversan y se ponen de acuerdo, no hay ningún problema. La pareja debe ser equilibrada y priorizar sus necesidades para, después, ayudar a quien lo necesita.

Conocemos a una pareja que pasó por serios problemas económicos. Después de casarse, ambos contrajeron una deuda. Tras tres años de matrimonio, todavía estaban esforzándose por pagar. En esa época, la mujer se compadeció de la madre, que tenía varias cuentas atrasadas, y, llevada por la emoción, convenció al marido para hacerle un préstamo bastante alto para ayudarla. Fue hasta él con el tema decidido, sin alternativa, valiéndose del viejo chantaje emocional. Incluso no pudiendo, el marido cedió, pero aquella actitud –además de aumentar la deuda– provocó un gran deterioro en la relación. El marido se sintió desvalorizado al ver que la mujer no había priorizado las necesidades de la nueva familia, ni consideró el esfuerzo de él en quitar la deuda inicial.

Muchos matrimonios hacen lo que está bien, pero en el orden equivocado. No está mal ayudar a la familia de origen, siempre que sea hecho en el momento adecuado y de la manera correcta, sin pasar por encima del otro. Si eso hace que su compañero se sienta despreciado, usted sembrará problemas.

Cristiane:

Nunca voy a olvidar lo que mi padre, que celebraba mi ceremonia de matrimonio, me dijo en el altar: «Ahora no tienes más madre, ni padre, hija mía. Tus problemas tendrán que ser resueltos entre tú y Renato». De todo lo que él dijo aquella noche, eso fue lo que se me quedó más grabado; pienso que se debió al hecho de ser muy joven todavía y de estar muy apegada a mi familia.

Aquella palabra dura y directa me llevó a aprender sobre el nuevo orden en el que yo estaba entrando al casarme. Ahora mi familia era Renato, y su familia era yo. Nuestros padres se convirtieron en nuestros parientes. Los problemas que tuvimos al principio de nuestro matrimonio quedaron entre nosotros dos. Eso no es nada fácil, especialmente para nosotras, mujeres, que tenemos la necesidad de sacar hacia fuera lo que sentimos…

No es tan difícil de entender que, cuando estamos formando una nueva familia, tenemos que dejar la anterior; pero hoy en día ese hecho ha sido uno de los mayores problemas de los matrimonios. No era tan habitual hace algunos años. Las personas ya se casaban con el objetivo de formar su familia; tanto es así que la mujer que no se casaba estaba mal vista, no solamente por la sociedad, sino también por la propia familia.

En aquella época, muchos matrimonios se realizaban sin ningún sentimiento. Era un deber casarse, y punto. No siempre se amaba a la persona con la que se casaba. Con los años, muchos matrimonios que se habían casado sin sentimientos desarrollaban el verdadero amor porque partían de la base de que, ahora, eran una familia y debían actuar como tal. Es decir, actúe como alguien que ama a su marido o mujer, y serán un matrimonio. Y si en ese matrimonio se tratan el uno al otro como el primero en sus vidas, se volverán una familia y nadie podrá meterse en medio para separarlos.

TAREA

¿Qué ajustes tendrá que hacer para seguir el orden correcto en sus relaciones? Escriba lo que va a poner en práctica, especialmente lo que hará de diferente para que su cónyuge se sienta la persona más importante para usted, después de Dios.

/MatrimonioBlindado

Publique esto:
Puse en orden
mis relaciones.

@matrimonioblind

Tuitee esto:
Puse en orden
mis relaciones
#matrimonioblindado
@matrimonioblind

CAPÍTULO 15
CÓMO FUNCIONAN LOS HOMBRES Y LAS MUJERES

Para empezar este capítulo hice una rápida averiguación a fin de ilustrar cómo la mente de los hombres funciona de forma diferente a la de las mujeres. Paré de escribir durante un momento, salí del despacho y fui a la habitación donde Cristiane estaba secándose su bonito pelo mientras en su iPad se escuchaba una canción. Sin que supiera lo que yo estaba haciendo, entré como si nada, me lavé las manos, la miré en el espejo y le pregunté:

—¿Qué estás pensando?

Sin dudar, ella respondió:

—Estoy pensando que Rafaela no puso en mi blog la reseña de la película que vimos la semana pasada. Tengo que mandarle un email. Estoy pensando también en que esta canción es buena para que la usemos en el programa *La Escuela del amor,* solo que, probablemente, no haya un clip oficial en YouTube, pues es muy antigua. Entonces, pensé que nuestro equipo de producción podría usar imágenes de entre bastidores para montar un clip. Y, pensando en nuestro equipo, me acordé de que cuando entré en su oficina, antes de ayer, me di cuenta de que necesitan más sillas, siempre hay alguien que tiene que trabajar de pie. ¡Ah!, también estaba pensando que mi pelo está reseco y que prefiero pagar a alguien para que me peine a quedarme aquí haciéndomelo yo misma».

—¿Algo más? —me atreví a preguntar.

—No, solo eso.

Solo eso. Mi esposa estaba pensando en cinco cosas al mismo tiempo y la canción ni siquiera había acabado… Y yo aquí, pensando solo en una cosa: ¿cómo voy a escribir este capítulo?

Uno de los hechos más ignorados por los matrimonios es la diferencia entre los sexos y cómo afecta a la relación. Los hombres lidian con sus mujeres como si ellas fuesen ellos. Las mujeres hablan con sus maridos como si ellos fuesen mujeres. Y cada experiencia de esas abre una latita de lombrices.

Cuando ambos entienden esas diferencias todo cambia sin cambiar nada al mismo tiempo. Cambia porque empiezan a ver que su cónyuge no está haciendo esto o aquello porque él es malo o porque ella ella quiere irritarlo; están siendo simplemente lo que son: hombre y mujer. No malos, sino muy diferentes.

Cristiane:

«De haber sido yo en lugar de él, no lo habría hecho así», es lo que yo pensaba, de vez en cuando, respecto a Renato. Además, vivía criticando a los hombres cuando veía en ellos la falta de la tan querida consideración hacia los demás. Entraba en un lugar cargada de bolsas, cada una más pesada que la otra, y los hombres que estaban allí ni se fijaban en lo necesitada que estaba de ayuda, así que pensaba: «¡Ah, si los hombres fuesen un poquito más caballeros!».

Vivía comparándome con Renato y viendo lo grandes que eran las diferencias. Usted puede imaginarse la constancia de esos pensamientos. Él no se daba cuenta de mi ropa nueva mientras que mis amigas lo veían desde lejos. ¿Cómo puede ser? Yo le preguntaba y él no conseguía entender por qué aquello era tan importante para mí. ¡Parecía que éramos de planetas diferentes! Hasta que, un día, descubrí que estaba siendo injusta al querer que él pensase como yo. A fin de cuentas, él es un hombre.

Ese es un defecto horrible del ser humano, querer que los demás piensen como usted. Incluso en nuestros gustos: cuando alguien no tiene los mismos gustos nos parece horrible, como si eso importase. ¿Importa algo si a mí me gusta su color de pelo si el pelo no es mío? Pero es eso lo que hacemos con nuestro compañero, siempre lo criticamos por no pensar como nosotras y no hacer las cosas como las haríamos nosotras.

En esta batalla, en el mejor de los casos, nadie sale ganando, sino que, al contrario, el matrimonio se llena de roces. Yo quería que él tuviese conmigo la misma consideración que yo tenía con él y él quería que yo fuese tan fuerte como él para aguantar las cosas. Él quería que yo fuese un hombre y yo quería que él fuese una mujer.

Está claro que, al principio, no nos dimos cuenta. ¡Nunca pensé que estaba pidiendo a mi marido que fuese una mujer! Pero, si hiciese una lista de todo lo que yo idealizaba respecto a él, con seguridad sería una versión mía en masculino. Incluso parece que yo iba a aguantarme a mí misma.

Pura realidad. Pida a cualquier mujer que describa al «hombre ideal» y describirá a otra mujer…

El hombre y la mujer difieren de muchas formas. Genéticamente, el cromosoma 23 determina la diferencia de los sexos. Físicamente, el cuerpo masculino y el femenino son, de un modo obvio, distintos. Pero una de las diferencias más determinantes está en el cerebro de ambos.

El cerebro masculino es en promedio un 10 % más grande que el femenino y con un 4 % más de células. Pero antes de que usted, hombre, empiece a fanfarronear por tener un cerebro mayor que el de la mujer, sepa que el cerebro femenino tiene más células nerviosas y conectoras sinápticas, lo que la posibilita para tener un cerebro más eficiente y eficaz. Esto significa que, de modo general, los hombres tienden a realizar las tareas utilizando el lado izquierdo del cerebro, que es el lado lógico y racional. Las mujeres, a su vez, tienden a usar los dos lados simultáneamente debido a su habilidad para transferir la información más rápidamente entre el lado izquierdo y el derecho del cerebro. El resultado es que los hombres tienden a centrarse más en cosas, sistemas y en resolver problemas, mientras las mujeres son más sensibles a los sentimientos de todos a su alrededor y más creativas. Los estudios al respecto reconocen que hay excepciones y es posible, a veces, que un hombre tenga un cerebro «más femenino» y viceversa –lo que no tiene que ver necesariamente con la sexualidad de cada uno, ¡no se preocupe!–. Tan solo significa que hay hombres que son más emotivos y mujeres que son más racionales, pero no son la mayoría.

Louann Brizendine, en su libro *The female brain (El cerebro femenino)*, habla sobre cómo los dos cerebros son muy diferentes ya desde el nacimiento. La bebita se convierte en una niña a quien le encanta hacer amistades y relacionarse con sus compañeras. Consigue, incluso, darse cuenta cuándo las cosas no van bien en casa. Pero, cuando el bebote se convierte en un niño, no es así. Quiere jugar y, si hace daño a alguien en el proceso, no le preocupa , pue adora los desafíos y las aventuras. Él es un conquistador ya desde pequeñito y ella, una compañera cariñosa.

UNA CAJITA PARA CADA COSA

La forma como Mark Gungor expresa esas diferencias es mi preferida. Él explica que es como si el cerebro masculino estuviese formado por varias cajitas. En su cabeza hay una cajita para cada asunto de su interés: una para el coche, una para el trabajo, una para usted, otra para los niños, otra para la suegra en algún lugar del sótano y sellada con un aviso de «¡Peligro!»...Y un detalle muy importante es que esas cajitas no se apoyan las unas en las otras. Cuando un hombre quiere discutir sobre algo, saca tan solo la cajita de aquel asunto, la abre, discute solamente sobre lo que está dentro de aquella cajita y, cuando termina, la cierra y la pone en el mismo sitio –con mucho cuidado para no tocar ninguna otra.

Y aún hay más: ¡mujeres, mucha atención a esta información!

Dentro del cerebro del hombre hay una cajita que la mayoría de las mujeres desconoce. Esa cajita no tiene nada dentro. De hecho, se llama «cajita de la nada». Y, de todas ellas, esa cajita es la favorita del hombre. Siempre que tiene oportunidad, corre a esa cajita. Es por eso por lo que los hombres son capaces de entretenerse durante horas con actividades que exigen prácticamente cero uso del cerebro, tales como entretenerse con videojuegos, pescar, quedarse cambiando de canal frente a la televisión sin ver nada. Si nos dejan, cuando no estamos trabajando, totalmente concentrados en algo, gravitamos, automáticamente, hacia la cajita de la nada.

La mujer no consigue entender eso pues, simplemente, no consigue quedarse sin pensar en nada. Cuando ve a su marido en ese estado vegetativo, callado, ido, como un muerto viviente, se queda intrigada y no resiste preguntar:

—¿En qué estás pensando?

Y él responde, sin ninguna expresión:

—En nada.

—Con seguridad estás pensando en *algo*. No es posible que no estés pensando en nada.

—Te lo estoy diciendo, no estaba pensando en nada –insiste él, en vano.

—Me estás mintiendo. Lo que no quieres es decírmelo. ¿Por qué no me lo cuentas?

Todo hombre ya ha tenido esta conversación y le da miedo el resultado porque sabe que no hay forma de que termine bien. No importa lo que diga, ella no le va a creer. Si dice que no estaba pensando en nada, ella no cree que eso sea posible. Si inventa que estaba pensando en alguna cosa solamente para satisfacerla, ella cree que no era eso exactamente lo que estaba pensando (sin saber que, ahora, ella tiene razón, no es en eso en lo que estaba pensando).

Lo que ella no entiende es que, cuando el hombre está estresado o, simplemente, apartado de su trabajo, la manera de relajarse es correr a la cajita de la nada. Quiere estar en paz, sin hablar, quedarse callado durante algunos instantes. La última cosa que quiere hacer es hablar sobre sus problemas y frustraciones. El hombre solo le cuenta sus problemas a otro hombre si cree que le puede ayudar a resolverlos. Si no, se queda callado. Sin embargo, la mujer, cuando está estresada, tiene que hablar con alguien, no necesariamente porque esté buscando un consejo, sino porque, si no, su cabeza explota...

UNA BOLA DE CABLES ENMARAÑADOS

Si el cerebro del hombre está formado por cajitas desconectadas, el cerebro de la mujer es como una bola de cables, un enmarañado de cabos, todos entrelazados. Todo está conectado con todo: el coche está unido a su trabajo, que está unido a los hijos, que están unidos a su madre, que está relacionada con la gotera en el baño... Todo está unido entre sí, y nada es por casualidad. Y la energía que corre por esos cables se llama emoción. Es por eso por lo que la mujer se acuerda de todo, de los detalles de una conversación que el hombre jura que nunca ocurrió. Es que cuando usted junta un acontecimiento con una emoción aquello funciona como un rayo láser que imprime aquel recuerdo en el cerebro, y la persona no se olvida nunca más de aquel hecho. El hombre también tiene esa capacidad, pero la verdad es que casi nunca la usa porque la mayoría de las veces él ni se preocupa por los pequeños acontecimientos. Por su parte, la mujer se preocupa por todo...

Cuando ella está estresada y necesita a alguien con quien desahogarse; el hombre, erróneamente, piensa que tiene que resolverle los problemas (los de ella). Ella dice:

—No sabes lo que me ha pasado hoy. La caradura de Pamela se ha llevado todo el reconocimiento por el trabajo que yo había hecho.

—¿Quién es Pamela? – pregunta el «desconectado».

—Amor, ¡es mi compañera de oficina! –le explica ella por vigésima vez. Y continúa–: Va al jefe, le da el proyecto que yo había entregado hace dos semanas, matándome para hacerlo, solo lo firma y da a entender que ella lo ha hecho todo.

—Ups, tienes que hablar con ella y decirle que eso no se hace. O, si no, busca una manera de informar al jefe de que también tú participaste. Y, si no, olvídalo, no te enojes por eso.

Aquí, el marido piensa que está siendo magnífico dándole un gran consejo a su mujer. En realidad, está haciendo que ella se sienta una idiota, como si no supiese lo que podría hacer en esa situación. Lo que realmente necesita no es un consejo, sino tan solo un oído. Necesita hablar porque en su mente están ese y otros muchos pensamientos y frustraciones. En ese preciso momento lo que el hombre debe hacer es tan solo cerrar la cremallera los labios y oír. Si no tiene esa sabiduría y paciencia, ella recurrirá a su madre, hermana, amigas, o –lo que es peor– al «Don Juan» de la oficina. Si la mujer entiende el cerebro del hombre y, él, el de ella, los dos podrán ajustarse y no irritarse el uno al otro o frustrarse con la forma de ser de su compañero.

¿SERÁ QUE ES SORDO?

Debido a esas diferencias, las mujeres suelen ser multitareas –hacen varias cosas al mismo tiempo–. Los hombres suelen ser monotareas –hacen una sola cosa a la vez–. Nuevamente esto es fuente de irritación, pues la mujer, muchas veces, culpa al hombre de no prestar atención a lo que le dice, por ejemplo. El marido está leyendo el periódico mientras ella está preparando el desayuno, vigilando al niño haciendo los deberes de casa y hablando por teléfono al mismo tiempo. En un determinado momento ella finaliza la llamada y le dice al marido: «El sábado que viene es la fiesta de cumpleaños de mi sobrina. Tenemos que estar a las tres de la tarde». Él murmura desde el living: «Ajá».

Pasa una semana, ve a su mujer arreglándose y le pregunta: «¿Dónde vas?». Ella ya responde frustrada: «Te olvidas de todo, ¿no? O no prestas atención a lo que te digo». La verdad es que él estaba totalmente concentrado en la lectura del periódico cuando usted le habló. No quiere decir que a él no le importe usted, tan solo significa que así funciona su cerebro. Si quiere disminuir este tipo de frustración, asegúrese de que su marido está totalmente concentrado en usted cuando le esté hablando. Esto es, mirándola sin hacer nada más. Si no, espere el momento adecuado.

Pero las diferencias entre los sexos van mucho más allá de estas reglitas de convivencia y comunicación. A lo largo de los siglos, hombres y mujeres fueron naturalmente programados para esperar cosas específicas el uno del otro. Por desgracia, hoy más que nunca esas expectativas no siempre están tan claras entre los dos. Ahora usted va a entender cómo se desarrollaron y cuáles son, y cómo cumplirlas.

CAPÍTULO 16
NATURALMENTE PROGRAMADOS

Desde el principio de la humanidad, la diferente estructura física, genética y mental del hombre y de la mujer determinó otras diferencias entre ellos, de relación y culturales. La fuerza física del hombre, así como sus habilidades naturales para construir armas y navegar lo cualificaron para ser el proveedor y protector de la familia. Las características inherentes a la mujer la hicieron la cuidadora y organizadora del hogar.

Desde el principio, durante millares de años, los papeles de los dos estaban bien diferenciados, claros y específicos. La rutina típica de un matrimonio era más o menos como describo en los siguientes párrafos.

Antes de que amaneciera, el hombre salía con sus armas para cazar, solo o en grupo, arriesgando su vida para traer el alimento a la casa. La mujer se quedaba en casa, esperando ansiosamente a que él volviese al final del día, no tan solo con la comida, sino sano y salvo. Él era su héroe, que arriesgaba su vida por ella y por sus hijos. Mientras cazaban, los hombres no hacían un gran uso de la comunicación verbal, también porque un pequeño barullo les podía costar la caza. Tenían que moverse furtivamente y comunicarse por gestos. No podían tener miedo a matar —ni a fieras ni a otros hombres, en caso de ser atacados—.

Por su parte, la mujer, al quedarse en casa en compañía de los hijos y las vecinas, desarrolló una mejor habilidad de comunicación verbal.

Como organizadora y enfermera de la familia se convirtió en experta para percibir los detalles y expresiones faciales, siempre unida al estado físico y emocional de las personas. Se volvió la arquitecta de las relaciones, el pegamento entre su familia y la comunidad.

Ahora entiende por qué el hombre se volvió menos emocional, no tan apto para «leer los sentimientos» de los demás como la mujer, naturalmente lo hace; menos hablador que ella y más directo en las palabras.

Además de las tareas domésticas, la mujer era considerada por la habilidad, casi divina, de generar hijos. Cargaba en sí la simiente de la vida; por eso, el hombre la protegía y valoraba. Ella, a su vez, lo respetaba como líder natural de la familia y lo cubría de valoración por el riesgo que corría diariamente para la supervivencia de ella y de los hijos.

Todo eso dejaba bien claro cuál era el papel del hombre y el de la mujer en relación uno con el otro. No había discusión entre ellos sobre eso, ni competitividad. Cada uno sabía bien cuál era su papel y no existía el sentimiento de que uno fuera mejor que el otro. Y así fue durante miles de años. A través de los siglos, esos papeles no cambiaron mucho. Tradicionalmente, el hombre fue siempre el proveedor y protector de la familia, y la mujer, la cuidadora del hogar y la arquitecta de las relaciones.

Sin embargo, algunos factores han ido cambiando esta realidad desde hace unos cincuenta años para acá. Podríamos citar varios, pero mencionaremos tan solo los dos principales y sus efectos en el matrimonio.

LOS PAPELES SE CONFUNDEN

Dos fenómenos, compañeros el uno del otro, han transformado el concepto tradicional del papel del hombre y de la mujer en la sociedad: el movimiento feminista y la Revolución Industrial. Está fuera del alcance de este libro entrar en detalles sobre esos dos puntos. Siéntase libre de investigar más, si quiere. En resumen, para nuestros fines, aquí está lo principal y por qué nos importa:

La Revolución Industrial

La mujer empezó a salir de la casa hacia el trabajo, aunque tímidamente, a mediados del siglo XIX. El desarrollo de la tecnología maquinaria dio origen a las fábricas, que abrirían oportunidades de empleo, hasta entonces inexistentes, para las mujeres. Pero no fue hasta el siglo pasado, especialmente a partir de la Segunda Guerra Mundial, cuando la mujer empezó a ganar su espacio en el mercado de trabajo. Se mostró tan capaz como el hombre en muchas profesiones. Conquistó iguales derechos y superó en número a los hombres en las universidades. Con la explosión del crecimiento de las grandes industrias, de la tecnología, del funcionariado público y los servicios de salud, la mujer, hoy, es una parte esencial de la economía global. El nuevo poder adquisitivo de la mujer, unido al del marido, posibilita al matrimonio el acceso a una vida material mucho mejor que la de sus padres y abuelos. La actual cultura consumista –la publicidad incansable de productos y bienes que prometen la «felicidad» de quienes los consumen– prácticamente imposibilita a un hombre de ingresos medios o bajos para sustentar a su familia sin el ingreso extra de la mujer. Esto significa que la mujer ya no es la madre y esposa que tan solo cuidaba de la casa y recibía al marido al final del día con una torta calentita esperando en el horno. Ella es tan activa como él, allí fuera, gana tanto o más que él, siendo, por lo tanto, muy diferente de la mujer tradicional. Ella se está volviendo cazadora también.

El movimiento feminista

La americana bell hooks,[14] una activista feminista con gran influencia, define bien la esencia del feminismo: «El feminismo es una lucha contra la opresión machista». Sin duda, muchos hombres a lo largo de la historia hicieron una gran descortesía, no solamente a las mujeres, sino también a todo el género masculino. Por lo tanto, la lucha por los derechos de la

---

[14] No escribe su nombre con mayúsculas de forma deliberada. Curiosamente, a los cincuenta y nueve años, hooks sigue soltera.

mujer tiene un valor innegable; sin embargo, a pesar de que las feministas han conseguido grandes avances en la búsqueda del equilibrio de los sexos, un subproducto de eso ha sido el sentimiento casi de odio contra los hombres. El feminismo ha llevado a muchas mujeres a ver al hombre, de modo general, como un opresor, un enemigo que está listo para oprimirlas a la primera de cambio. Mientras eso puede ser verdad en algunos casos, esta generalización conduce a que muchas mujeres se resistan al papel tradicional del hombre como proveedor y protector por miedo a quedar por debajo de él. Además, izando la bandera de la igualdad de los sexos, el movimiento genera confusión entre la igualdad de derechos e igualdad de géneros. Y es precisamente cuando la mujer empieza a mirar al hombre como su igual, especialmente dentro del matrimonio, cuando los innumerables conflictos empiezan a existir.

Quiero dejar clara una cosa: estoy totalmente a favor de la igualdad de derechos entre los sexos; pero decir que los hombres y las mujeres son iguales en su naturaleza y forma de ser es un error gravísimo que ha tenido serias consecuencias en las relaciones sentimentales. Una cosa es tener los mismos derechos, otra cosa es querer cumplir los mismos papeles. Hombres y mujeres siempre tuvieron los mismos derechos a ojos de Dios, ya que Él no creó a uno mejor que el otro; pero los papeles que les fueron asignados son muy diferentes. El problema comienza cuando la mujer quiere llevar a cabo el papel del hombre en el matrimonio y en la familia.

Esos dos factores se resumen en uno solo: el ascenso de la mujer. Y, como resultado, los papeles no están tan claros, definidos y específicos como lo estaban hace poco tiempo atrás. Por primera vez en la historia de la humanidad, el hombre empieza a tener una crisis de identidad.

¿QUIÉN SOY? ¿DÓNDE ESTOY?

¿Quién es esta «cazadora» que está a mi lado? Los hombres todavía no han conseguido situarse dentro de este nuevo escenario. Son exactamente esos nuevos cambios los que están causando problemas en el matrimonio. Las mujeres se han vuelto independientes; por lo tanto, menos inclinadas a implicar a sus maridos en sus decisiones; chocan de frente con ellos –a fin de cuentas, ellas «pueden»–. Los hombres se han sentido intimidados ante el crecimiento de la mujer, se han retraído y, en algunos casos, incluso se sienten inferiores a ella. La firmeza ha dado lugar a la indecisión o a hacer cualquier cosa que no desagrade a la mujer, con tal de mantener la paz. Ella, a su vez, se frustra con la falta de iniciativa de él y termina poniéndose al frente, completándose así el círculo vicioso. En fin, ella acaba pareciéndose a él, y él a ella.

Las consecuencias de eso pueden verse en el paralelismo que hay entre el ascenso de la mujer y el gran aumento en el número de divorcios de los últimos cincuenta años. ¿Cómo puede algo tan bueno para las mujeres ser tan malo para nuestras relaciones?

No estamos sugiriendo que el avance de la mujer sea malo ni queremos que la sociedad retroceda. Tan solo queremos señalar el hecho de que, aunque la sociedad haya cambiado, las necesidades naturales de los hombres y de las mujeres continúan siendo las mismas de hace miles de años. El hombre todavía es hombre y, la mujer, no dejó de ser mujer. Fuimos creados así y nuevos derechos y maneras de vivir no van a cambiar nuestro ADN. Estamos naturalmente programados, es decir, tenemos una predisposición para esperar ciertas cosas de nuestro cónyuge.

Hombre y mujer pueden crecer y evolucionar en la sociedad. Que la mujer gane más que el hombre no es el problema, ni que el hombre lave los platos o ayude a cambiar los pañales. Lo que los dos necesitan saber hacer es atender las necesidades básicas el uno del otro. Es decir, sin tirar por la ventana el progreso y avance conquistado por la mujer, vamos a rescatar los valores y principios que rigen un matrimonio feliz.

Cristiane:

Yo estoy a favor de que la mujer tenga derechos; a fin de cuentas, a mí me gusta conquistar también. El problema es que necesitamos saber cómo lidiar con nuestros hombres ante tantos cambios en la sociedad.

Mis padres ya pasaron los cuarenta años de casados y su manera de pensar es muy distinta de la de las parejas que se casan hoy. Cuando mi padre se casó con mi madre, él tenía en mente trabajar duro para mantenerla. Hoy en día, muchos hombres ya no tienen esa preocupación. La mujer también trabaja y, a veces, puede incluso mantenerlo. Eso, en el pasado, era humillante para el hombre, pues mostraba su debilidad. Si sacaba a una mujer de la casa de sus padres, tenía la obligación de cuidarla y proveerla de todo lo que necesitase.

Mientras tanto, la obligación de ella era cuidar de su marido, su casa y criar a los hijos. A ella le gustaba eso, lo que ya no se ve tanto hoy en día. La mujer actual no siempre siente placer en cuidar de su marido y, mucho menos, de la casa. Si tiene hambre, que se las arregle. Los hijos pueden quedarse la mayoría del tiempo en la escuela, en clubs deportivos, para que ella tenga más tiempo para su carrera y otros intereses. Y, cuando llega a casa, no quiere tener el trabajo de cocinar, ni de limpiar nada; entonces se molesta con su marido por haber dejado los zapatos en medio del living. Es decir, cosas que en el pasado no eran un problema, hoy son motivo de conflicto.

Hombre y mujer no fueron creados para competir el uno con el otro. Somos muy diferentes y nuestras diferencias son precisamente para mejorar la vida el uno del otro, no para empeorarla.

Los medios de comunicación, para contribuir con este desastre, también ponen la imagen del hombre allí abajo. Reflexione solamente en la mayoría de las comedias, y en algunos otros géneros de películas, donde el hombre es siempre aquel personaje débil que teme a la mujer, que lo hace todo mal, que no tiene mano dura, ni da ninguna seguridad, mientras la mujer es muy inteligente, sabe lo que quiere, hace todo bien y es siempre el brazo fuerte de la familia.

Esta imagen acaba haciendo un lavado de cerebro en las personas: el hombre es débil, la mujer es fuerte; el hombre es bobo, la mujer es inteligente. El resultado en los hogares es que los hijos no tienen respeto a sus padres, las mujeres no respetan a sus maridos, y el pobrecito acaba huyendo de aquella familia. La mujer rápidamente lo acusa de alguna incapacidad y los hijos se decepcionan con él, diciéndose a sí mismos que nunca se van a casar.

Ahí tiene una foto de lo que ha sido la familia del siglo XXI. Si la sociedad no valora el papel del hombre en la familia, el hombre, a su vez, tampoco valora el de la mujer y lo que sucede es lo inevitable: nadie valora a nadie, cada uno por sí mismo, Dios por todos y abundan las actitudes egoístas en el día a día.

Si quiere formar parte de la cultura del matrimonio feliz y duradero no podrá seguir las normas de la cultura actual. Tendrá que andar a contracorriente y crear su propia cultura dentro de su relación. Cristiane y yo tenemos la nuestra y ya determinamos que nada del exterior que sea nocivo podrá entrar. Por eso, conseguimos mantener los valores y principios que necesitamos para conservar nuestra intimidad, y no nos olvidamos de satisfacer las necesidades básicas del otro, predeterminadas por nuestras naturalezas distintas.

Y usted ¿sabe cuáles son esas necesidades? Vamos a conocer más de ellas.

LAS NECESIDADES BÁSICAS NATURALMENTE DETERMINADAS

Estamos programados por nuestra naturaleza humana a tener ciertas necesidades cubiertas. Y no hay necesidades más básicas que comer, beber, vestirse y tener vivienda. Saque esto del ser humano y su comportamiento se vuelve como el de un animal. Eso puede observarse cuando los grandes desastres naturales afectan a una ciudad. De repente, las personas se ven sin alimentos, agua, abrigo y seguridad. Si no hay una intervención rápida de los servicios de emergencia, caen en la desesperación y adoptan un comportamiento incluso agresivo por la supervivencia. La búsqueda por el qué comer o beber y dónde vivir hace que las personas actúen como si volviesen a la época de las cavernas. Cuando las necesidades básicas se ven afectadas, afloran las reacciones primitivas.

Minutos antes de que sucediese el desastre, la mayoría estaba preocupada con banalidades, tales como si el dobladillo del pantalón está demasiado alto, si el mejor color para las paredes de la habitación es el beige o el blanco, si va a hacer un *upgrade* del celular, etc.; tras la catástrofe, a nadie le importa ya eso. La única preocupación es salvar la propia vida. Lo que las personas antes veían como «necesidad» queda reducido al más alto capricho frente a las cosas más básicas como el agua, el pan y el abrigo. Personas que nunca robaron, nunca agredieron a nadie ni violaron las leyes son capaces de hacerlo. Es el instinto natural del ser humano, y ¿cuál es la mejor manera de contener ese comportamiento animal? Satisfaciendo nuevamente las necesidades básicas de esas personas.

Hay otra cosa muy importante que usted debe saber al respecto:

No se discute sobre las necesidades básicas de una persona. La única cosa que se puede hacer es satisfacerlas.

A nadie se le culpa de tener hambre. Nadie es malo por querer dormir una noche. Nadie es delincuente por tener sed. Nadie puede ser acusado por querer tener un lugar donde vivir. Malo es quien puede suplir esas necesidades de alguien pero no lo hace.

Ahora, traslade ese hecho hacia el interior de la relación. Hombre y mujer también tienen, por sus naturalezas masculina y femenina, sus necesidades básicas que necesitan ser satisfechas. Para que un matrimonio funcione, hay ciertas cosas mínimas que deben existir. Muy bien, el marido no puede ser tan romántico como un personaje de Robert Redford; la mujer no puede ser la más perfecta dama de un cuento de hadas; pero ambos tienen que ofrecer, el uno al otro, por lo menos lo esencial.

Las necesidades básicas, del hombre y de la mujer, son de extrema importancia. Si no son cubiertas, su marido o mujer empezará a actuar irracionalmente.Y no sirve de nada criticar o preguntarse «¿por qué él es así?» o «¿por qué ella actúa así?» Lo mejor que puede hacer al respecto de las necesidades básicas de su pareja es satisfacerlas. Sobre necesidades no se discute. Cuando se tiene hambre, la única cosa útil que se puede hacer al respecto es comer.

Cuando usted adopta una mascota, la primera cosa que hace, antes incluso de llevarlo a casa, es averiguar lo que come, bebe, le gusta y no le gusta. No discute con quien le dio el animal, ni intenta cambiar al bichito después de llevárselo a casa. Si quiere un animalito feliz, tan solo satisfaga sus necesidades, por más molestas que sean. Para tener un marido o mujer feliz descubra sus necesidades básicas y cúbralas. No discuta.

CAPRICHOS Y COMPARACIONES

Una aclaración: estamos hablando aquí de necesidades básicas, no de caprichos ni fantasías. Para las mujeres, un aviso: amor verdadero no se resume en un romance o un beso cinematográfico. Es un gran error de la mujer comparar al hombre real con el hombre de la pantalla. Cierta vez una mujer casada dejó un comentario en uno de nuestros videos en YouTube sobre lo que esperaba de un hombre ideal:

> ... *me gusta el hombre que se cuida, se preocupa por los sentimientos, que sea romántico, al estilo de Brad Pitt o Tom Cruise; pero que sea un galán como James Bond y proveedor y protector como Conan el Bárbaro o los hombres del Viejo Oeste. Pienso que el hombre ideal es aquel vampiro de* Crepúsculo. *Me gusta aquel hombre de* Lo que el viento se llevó, *o aquel bailarín de* Cantando bajo la lluvia..., *ah, sería un poco de cada uno. También están los samuráis...*

Mi primer consejo para aquella mujer fue: ¡deje de ver películas!

Si usted no sabe lo que quiere, ¿cómo exigirle a su marido que lo sepa? Esta ilusión del amor hollywoodiense ha llevado a muchos matrimonios al fracaso. Ese amor, de guión, ensayado, con el director dirigiendo al actor, no existe en la vida real. En la vida real aquel galán de la novela, seguramente, ya se casó tres o cuatro veces; tiene una vida sentimental infeliz y, tal vez, incluso le haya pegado a su mujer. No podemos vivir la realidad basada en la fantasía.

Una de las peores cosas que puede hacer es comparar a su cónyuge con alguien, sea ese alguien real o imaginario. Esto es capaz de matar el matrimonio. Si compara a su marido con el de la televisión, prepárese para frustrarse.

Lo mismo se aplica a los hombres. Usted, hombre, pasará por lo mismo si se embarca en la plaga llamada «pornografía». Dejando a un lado la parte moral de la cuestión, el resultado de ese vicio es que muchos hombres ya no consiguen ser estimulados por sus mujeres, sino solo por la pornografía y la masturbación. Es decir, aquello que es real, la intimidad con la mujer, ya no sirve. Deja de ser ese hombre que su mujer necesita, se frustra porque su mujer no es aquella que vio en un video producido, y acaba viviendo de fantasías, creando así una fecha de vencimiento para su matrimonio.

A ninguna mujer le gusta ser comparada de esta forma, para ella es humillante saber que su marido solo se siente realizado viendo este tipo de videos. Ella no se excita como él y ambos no logran llegar a la intimidad total. El hombre que se vuelve dependiente de ese estímulo está desmoralizando a su mujer, haciendo que se sienta insuficiente para él, exactamente lo contrario de la necesidad más básica que ella tiene.

PARTE IV

HACIENDO EL BLINDAJE

CAPÍTULO 17
NECESIDADES BÁSICAS DE LA MUJER

¿Cuáles son las necesidades más básicas de una mujer? Podemos resumirlas en una frase: ser valorada y amada. Fue así como la inteligencia espiritual definió la principal responsabilidad del marido respecto a su mujer:

Maridos, amad a vuestras mujeres, así como Cristo amó a la Iglesia y Se dio a Sí mismo por ella. Así también deben amar los maridos a sus mujeres, como a sus propios cuerpos. El que ama a su mujer, a sí mismo se ama (Efesios 5: 25-28).

Observe que, al principio, se hace una comparación entre el amor del marido hacia la mujer y el amor de Cristo hacia la Iglesia; es decir, Su amor es utilizado como modelo a seguir. Nuestro modelo de amor hacia nuestra mujer no debe proceder de películas, libros, padres, parientes o amigos. El Autor del matrimonio señaló el amor de Jesús por nosotros como referencia para los maridos. Y ¿qué tipo de amor fue el Suyo? Un amor marcado por la entrega de Sí mismo, el sacrificio, el cuidado y la renuncia –no por la emoción.

Enseguida, el hombre es llevado a entender que amar a su mujer es amarse a sí mismo. Si yo trato bien a Cristiane, en realidad estoy cuidando de mí. Si me gusta maltratarla, es como si me estuviese haciendo daño a mí mismo. ¿Recuerda la idea de que los dos «serán una sola carne»? El hombre necesita ver a su esposa como la extensión de sí mismo y no descuidar sus necesidades.

La mujer es un regalo de Dios para el marido.[15] Dios creó a la mujer para el hombre y, en la forma en que Dios creó al hombre, también hizo de él un complemento para la mujer. Si el marido rechaza, maltrata o repudia a la esposa es como si estuviese rechazando el regalo de Dios (lo mismo sucede cuando la mujer rechaza al marido). Cuando se desprecia a la mujer diciendo que la «mujer solo quiere gastar» o se habla mal del hombre, diciendo que «todos los hombres son iguales», en realidad se está hablando mal de Dios, del Creador de ambos.

La mujer está bajo los cuidados del marido. El origen de la palabra «marido» en inglés (*husband*) se refiere a «cuidador, administrador». Este significado concuerda bien con el papel del marido, pues, cuando el hombre se casa, se convierte en el responsable de su mujer, de todo lo que sucede con ella y de cuidar de ella. Eso, en verdad, es amor. Amar es más una actitud que solamente sentir. El mundo dice: «Se acabó el sentimiento, se acabó el amor». Ese tipo de amor-sentimiento es lo que genera monógamos en serie –se acaba el amor hacia uno, se va con otro; se acaba de nuevo, va con otro, etc.–. El verdadero amor no se basa en el sentimiento, sino en el cuidado que el marido debe a la mujer por el compromiso que asumió con ella.

VALORARLA Y AMARLA, PERO ¿CÓMO?

En la práctica, la mujer se siente valorada y amada cuando:

El marido le ofrece seguridad. No se refiere tan solo a seguridad física o económica, sino seguridad en todos los sentidos de la palabra. El diccionario define la seguridad como:

---

[15] Proverbios 18:22.

Conjunto de acciones y de recursos utilizados para proteger algo o a alguien; disminuir los riesgos o los peligros; garantizar; aquello que sirve de base o que da estabilidad o apoyo; amparo, sentimiento de fuerza interior o de creencia en uno mismo; certeza, confianza, firmeza; fuerza o convicción en los movimientos o en las acciones.[16]

Hay varias formas de que el hombre transmita seguridad, o no, a la mujer. Cuando es fiel, por ejemplo. Una necesidad básica de ella es saber que el marido al ir al trabajo, o a cualquier lugar, se mantendrá fiel. Cuando el hombre empieza a coquetear con otras mujeres, quizá por ser muy extrovertido, transmite inseguridad a la esposa. Ese hecho de ser juguetón que, muchas veces, genera amistades inapropiadas con otras mujeres, tal vez deberá ser cambiado para transmitir seguridad a la esposa (los celos de la esposa, a veces, son consecuencia de la falta de seguridad que el marido le transmite). Si es irresponsable, inmaduro, indefinido, tiene un temperamento fuerte, gasta con facilidad o tiene un vicio… genera, también, inseguridad. A veces él quiere que ella confíe en él, mientras no le pasa ninguna firmeza a través de su comportamiento. El hombre que habla alto, grita, golpea la puerta, se altera, etc., puede creer que se está mostrando fuerte y seguro; sin embargo, ocurre lo contrario; si no muestra control de sí mismo ¿qué dirá del resto de la familia y de la situación? Muéstreme un marido «descontrolado», que vive lleno de rabia, y yo le mostraré una mujer insegura, desvalorizada y mal amada.

Cuando la mujer no se siente segura, inmediatamente levanta murallas para protegerse de lo que aquella inseguridad puede traerle. Su instinto dice que, si él no la está cuidando ni protegiendo, tiene que hacerlo ella por sí misma. Eso también genera un círculo vicioso donde él no se siente respetado, se retrae y, ella, entonces, se ve en la obligación

---

[16] Diccionario Priberam de la Lengua Portuguesa © 2012.

de tomar decisiones, iniciativas y luchar por sí misma, aumentando así la falta de respeto hacia él.

El hombre debe ser equilibrado, seguro en todos los sentidos. Para proteger y cuidar de su mujer, tiene que ser fuerte, de la manera adecuada. No puede ser un vicioso o un indefinido. Ahora quiere una cosa, luego quiere otra. Si es inmaduro, irresponsable y no muestra un liderazgo firme, puede estar seguro: ella acabará poniéndose al frente, por su propia supervivencia… Hombres, ¡despierten!

Él la escucha: Eso es muy difícil para el hombre ya que, generalmente, no le gusta prestar atención ni escuchar detalles. Le gusta resolver los problemas y no solo oírlos; lo que, normalmente, la mujer hace cuando está con sus iguales. Que su desahogo sea escuchado por una amiga ya es suficiente para que se sienta bien. He ahí otro problema: usted quiere que su mujer comparta todo con usted pero no quiere oírla. Por eso, a veces, ¡la mujer tiene más intimidad con sus amigas que con el propio marido!

Es frecuente que el hombre se moleste al descubrir que su mujer ha contado algo que él considera privado a otra persona. ¿Qué puede hacer si el marido no quiere escuchar lo que tiene que decir? Ella se equivocó, pero él también. Si no encuentra oídos disponibles en casa, existe una gran probabilidad de que se abra hacia los oídos solícitos en la calle. Eso representa un gran peligro. Una mujer carente, con sus necesidades más básicas descuidadas… es un blanco fácil para el conocido «sinvergüenza», aquel muchacho del trabajo, siempre tan simpático y atento, que conoce intuitivamente esas necesidades y que ha dado a muchas de esas mujeres casadas lo que sus maridos no tienen tiempo de darles: oídos. Sin atención, esas mujeres caen como crías de foca en manos del depredador.

Hombres: límpiense los oídos, no la desprecien, especialmente si ella se está descargando. No intenten resolver sus problemas, solo oigan. Como ya explicamos anteriormente, la mujer lidia con el estrés de forma muy diferente a como lo hacemos nosotros, los hombres. Necesita hablar y sacar para afuera todo lo que la atormenta por dentro. Eso no quiere decir que necesite ninguna orientación sino, tan solo, unos buenos oídos y un abrazo para transmitirle la seguridad de que está a su lado.

La intimidad del matrimonio empieza por escucharse el uno al otro. Si no dialogan ni conversan, probablemente tienen una intimidad muy débil porque, esta, no se constituye solamente del sexo. La intimidad está mucho más allá del sexo. Y otro consejo para los hombres: para evitar problemas después, cuando ella esté hablando, deje lo que está haciendo y ¡preste atención! Peor todavía que no escucharla es fingir que la está oyendo… Si no puede prestarle atención ahora, avísele, si no, eso se va a volver contra usted después.

Yo tuve que aprender a escuchar. A mí no me gustaba quedarme oyendo ni contando detalles. Cuando mi mujer me preguntaba: «¿Cómo fue tu día?», lo máximo que respondía era: «Fue bueno», dando por terminada allí nuestra conversación de la noche. Aquello estaba matando nuestra intimidad…, entonces, empecé a involucrarla más en mi vida para que se sintiera partícipe de mi jornada.

Se siente la escogida. Ella tiene la necesidad de sentir que, de entre todas las mujeres del mundo, usted la escogió y que es la única para usted. Hay muchas mujeres que podría haber escogido, pero la escogió a ella. Está por encima de la madre, los hijos, hermanos y amigos. Cuando visite a sus parientes, aunque exista un familiar al que no le guste su mujer, llegarán agarrados, tomados de la mano, demostrando que ella es importante y que la defenderá a cualquier precio. Si hay una mujer en su trabajo o en su círculo social que le hace a su mujer sentirse insegura, por cualquier razón, es su responsabilidad transmitirle seguridad con sus actitudes (no solo con palabras). Un marido que conozco hizo de eso una pequeña regla: no llevar en el auto a otra mujer, por respeto a su esposa. ¿Imagina cómo se siente ella con eso? Como mínimo como la destinataria de esta bonita carta de Graciliano Ramos a su futura mujer:

He observado, en los últimos tiempos, un fenómeno extraño: las mujeres murieron. Creo que hubo una epidemia entre ellas. Desde diciembre, han ido desapareciendo, desapareciendo y, ahora, no hay ninguna. Veo, la verdad, personas vestidas con falda por las calles pero, tengo la seguridad, de que no son mujeres (…) Murieron todas. Y ahí se explica la razón por la que tengo tanto apego a la única sobreviviente (Cartas de amor a Eloísa, de Graciliano Ramos).

La mujer necesita sentirse única. Normalmente es bastante insegura por naturaleza. La sociedad también contribuye a ello bombardeando su imagen con lo que es bonito y feo en la mujer, siempre comparándola con lo que es aceptable: el cuerpo ideal, el pelo, la piel, el estilo de ropa, etc. No se ven los mismos ataques a los hombres, porque los hombres, normalmente, no se preocupan tanto con la apariencia como la mujer. Si un amigo le dice que está gordo, se ríen juntos; si una amiga le dice lo mismo a otra, automáticamente entra en la «lista negra»…

Es por eso que la mujer no se cansa de preguntarle a su marido si está bonita o si la ama. El hombre, que no entiende el razonamiento que hay detrás de eso, le dice: «Si me casé contigo es porque te amo, si cambia alguna cosa te aviso». Parece evidente para usted, pero para ella no es tan sencillo. Cuidado con la manera como habla a su mujer, eso también puede contribuir a su inseguridad respecto a usted.

Está siempre en su radar. El hombre debe mantener a su mujer siempre en su radar, es decir, estar siempre consciente y atento de cómo y dónde está, con quién, qué le preocupa, qué está haciendo o necesitando. El radar de él está normalmente en el trabajo, las cuentas, proyectos y preocupaciones; pero, aunque su objetivo esté en esas cosas, de vez en cuando mueva el puntero del radar y acuérdese de ella.

Si al terminar el día no se ha acordado de ella en ningún momento, cuando llegue a casa, seguramente, lo recibirá con cara fea. Como protector de ella, usted tiene que conocer todos sus pasos; no porque la esté espiando o controlando, sino para cumplir su papel de cuidador.

Muchos matrimonios están caminando hacia el divorcio precisamente porque se alejaron el uno del otro. No se preocupan por lo que el otro hace o dónde va. Viven indiferentes el uno del otro. Y así es como el amor se enfría. Toda relación necesita una inversión constante. Si él se olvida, debido al trabajo o a los nuevos proyectos, ella se siente desvalorizada y, muchas veces, no amada. Muchas mujeres viven sumergidas en celos y la raíz no es que el hombre le haya dado a entender que la está traicionando sino que no la ha hecho sentirse valorada.

Si está enferma, él espera que su madre o sus amigas la cuiden, mientras lo adecuado es que lo haga él, siempre que sea posible. Si ella tiene nuevos proyectos, su responsabilidad es saber cómo están esos proyectos. Ella es su responsabilidad y no puede dejarla como si fuera cualquier mujer del mundo.

Cierta vez, una mujer nos contó que su marido no tenía nunca tiempo para ella debido a su trabajo. Entonces, decidió preparar unas vacaciones para los dos, con tres meses de antelación, con el consentimiento de él. La semana anterior a las vacaciones, él le dijo que no podía ir debido al trabajo y ella tuvo que irse con una amiga y los niños. Ahora bien, ¿cómo cree que se sintió aquella mujer al ver que su marido ponía el trabajo en primer lugar?

Se siente atractiva. Cuando hace aquella pregunta que todo hombre teme: «¿Te parece que estoy gorda?», usted, hombre, no va a mentir, pero debe ser diplomático... La mujer tiene la necesidad de sentirse atractiva porque la competencia es grande: revistas, periódicos, televisión, mujeres por la calle... La presión es tan fuerte que incluso muchas modelos que son los referentes de la belleza se sienten feas. Esa necesidad la acompaña desde la infancia. A la muchacha le encanta el elogio, mientras que el joven no se preocupa por eso. La mujer necesita elogios; no se deben escatimar.

Debe tener un lenguaje que la haga sentirse mujer. Si se siente fea, tendrá una baja autoestima y eso no es bueno; ni para ella, ni para él. Cuando Cristiane engorda un poquito y me pregunta lo que me parece, siempre le digo: «¡Genial, así tengo más de ti para amar!».

Siempre va a haber una mujer más bonita que otra, no hay forma de ganar sola el trofeo de la mujer más bella del mundo, eso es imposible –incluso porque la belleza es algo muy subjetivo–. Pero, para los ojos del marido, su mujer tiene que ser la más bella del mundo. Debe tener ojos solamente para ella.

El marido tiene que aprender a ser amante de su mujer, mirando más allá de los defectos. Si hace eso, la mujer puede ser considerada «fea» ante los patrones de la sociedad e, incluso así, sentirse la más sexy del mundo debido a cómo su marido la hace sentirse. El hombre inteligente hace que su mujer se sienta atractiva para él.

Recibe afecto. El contacto físico es fundamental para la mujer. Muchos hombres tienen dificultades para tener contacto físico debido a su historia familiar. El niño crece con las expectativas de ser fuerte, no llorar, no necesitar de nada ni de nadie para crecer; pero el hecho es que la mujer no es así; el afecto significa mucho para ella.

La proximidad física del hombre y de la mujer habla mucho más que las palabras. Muchos matrimonios con el paso del tiempo se van separando, duermen en camas separadas, viven respetuosamente en la misma casa como hermanos pero son indiferentes el uno con el otro. Cuando quieren sexo, el hombre lo acuerda con la mujer y, por la noche, solo dice: «¡Vamos!». Entonces quiere que esté preparada mientras que durante todo el día, la semana o el mes entero no le dio ningún cariño.

A veces, el hombre se avergüenza de besar y abrazar a su mujer en público. A otros no les gusta ni darle la mano. La mujer siente esa necesidad, principalmente cuando está estresada, y, cuando él le niega

SU MATRIMONIO A PRUEBA DE DIVORCIO

ese contacto físico, se siente rechazada. Si usted quiere tener una mujer que se sienta valorada y amada, y loca por usted en la cama, debe saber que ese contacto físico tiene que estar siempre presente en su relación, principalmente en las horas en las que están en la cama.

Como consecuencia de traumas del pasado a algunas mujeres no les gusta el contacto físico. Casos así necesitan ser tratados específicamente.

Cristiane:

Siempre escuché decir que nosotras, las mujeres, somos complicadas, que no sabemos lo que queremos, que, para agradarnos, el hombre tiene que, prácticamente, dejar de ser hombre; pero, ahora, usted puede entender el porqué de ese mito. Muy bien, somos un poco complicadas (ok, bastante), pero eso se debe a nuestra inseguridad, que ya explicamos de dónde procede. Está en nuestro ADN. Sin embargo, no es por eso por lo que somos difíciles de agradar. El problema es que somos muy diferentes de los hombres. Lo que para un hombre no es tan importante, para la mujer sí lo es, y viceversa. Es fácil decir que la mujer no sabe lo que quiere. La cuestión es: ¿no sería eso una razón para darle mayores cuidados en vez de críticas?

Como mujer, ya vencí muchas inseguridades, pero, lamentablemente, por naturaleza tengo que luchar contra ellas casi a diario. Esa es una batalla femenina que nunca acaba. No sirve de nada que el marido crea que, solamente porque le dio un poco de cariño un día de la semana pasada ya hizo su parte. Amar es valorar a su mujer, es un conjunto de cosas que necesitan hacerse para que ese amor realmente se transmita a través de usted.

Cuando la mujer ama, se entrega. Además, adora entregarse a los demás, siempre piensa en todos, incluso en las personas a las que no gustan de ella. Usted, marido, gana mucho con esa manera de ser femenina; pero, cuidado, cuando la mujer se cansa de darse, puede ser demasiado tarde para que usted cambie.

TAREA

PARA EL MARIDO

¿Qué necesidades básicas de su mujer debe suplir con más dedicación? ¿Qué va a hacer al respecto a partir de ahora para que se sienta valorada y amada?

PARA LA MUJER

¿Cómo podría ayudar a su marido a entender sus necesidades más básicas, sin exigir ni imponer?

 /MatrimonioBlindado

Hombres, publiquen esto:
Ya sé qué hacer para que mi mujer se sienta valorada y amada.

 @matrimonioblind

Hombres, tuiteen esto:
Ya sé qué hacer para que mi mujer se sienta valorada y amada #matrimonioblindado @matrimonioblind

Mujeres, publiquen esto:
Ahora entiendo al hombre y lo que él realmente quiere.

Mujeres, tuiteen esto:
Estoy ayudando a mi marido a entender qué es lo que más necesito de él #matrimonioblindado @matrimonioblind

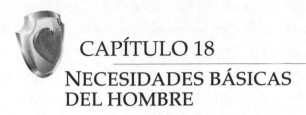

CAPÍTULO 18

NECESIDADES BÁSICAS DEL HOMBRE

Antes de hablar sobre lo que los hombres realmente quieren (consejo de antemano para las mujeres: no es solo sexo), vamos a volver a nuestros amigos «edénicos», Adán y Eva. Ya vimos anteriormente cómo Dios los creó con autoridad compartida sobre toda la Tierra. No se les dio a entender que el hombre fuese mayor que la mujer, ni que ella fuese menor que él. La idea inmediata cuando Dios idealizó a la mujer fue hacerla una socia, más específicamente, auxiliadora del hombre, alguien útilmente adecuada[17] para él. Es decir, los dos juntos estarían más capacitados y serían más felices que solos.

Al crear a la mujer, Dios le dio atributos peculiares que el hombre no tiene: femineidad, delicadeza, sensualidad, el poder de ser madre, emociones más agudizadas, dulzura, ser el imán de la familia, detallista, organizadora nata –por citar solo algunas–. La combinación de todos los atributos únicos y primordialmente femeninos hace que la mujer tenga un atractivo natural para el hombre. Él quiere tenerla a su lado. Cuando Adán vio a Eva por primera vez, no resistió y exclamó: «¡Por esta vale la pena dejar al padre y a la madre!».[18] Hasta aquel momento él no había

---

[17] Génesis 2:18, 20.
[18] Génesis 2:24.

visto nada igual… Naturalmente, no quería perderla. Por eso todo hombre, dentro de sí, tiene un deseo natural de agradar a la mujer. Cuando la ama se queda embobado por ella. Y cuando la mujer no es sabia, eso puede ser algo muy peligroso –no solo para él, sino para los dos–. A fin de cuentas, lo que sucede con él la afecta también a ella.

Fue entonces cuando Eva, con sus modito de mujer, consiguió convencer y llevar a Adán a hacer lo que era malo. Obviamente, Dios enseguida vio que aquel poder necesitaba ser controlado. Si era capaz de llevar al hombre a tomar tal actitud y él no era capaz de resistirse, algo tenía que hacer para lograr el equilibrio. Es decir, Dios reconoció que la mujer, en realidad, era más fuerte que el hombre. Su aparente debilidad, sumada al hecho de ser deseada por él, la puso en una posición de gran poder e influencia sobre su marido; por eso, parte de la maldición que le cayó fue: «… y él te gobernará».

Nació entonces, allí, el concepto de que el hombre sería la cabeza de la mujer y ella, su cuerpo; es decir… (bajo música siniestra de una película de terror…) sumisa a él. Mujer, antes de cerrar este libro y tirarlo a la basura con rabia, déjeme explicar lo que eso realmente quiere decir. Sumisión al marido, probablemente, no es lo que usted piensa. Hago ahora uso del modito de la mujer y le paso la bomba a mi mujer para que la desarme…

EL ENVENENAMIENTO DE UNA PALABRA

Cristiane:

¡Muchas gracias, querido esposo!

Mujeres, lean con atención las palabras dirigidas a nosotras:

Las mujeres estén sometidas a sus propios maridos como al Señor. Porque el marido es cabeza de la mujer, así como Cristo es cabeza de la Iglesia, no dominando, sino cuidando; pues ella es Su cuerpo. Pero, así como la Iglesia está sujeta a Cristo, también las mujeres deben estarlo a sus maridos en todo (Efesios 5: 22-24).

«Someterse», en el pasado, no tenía la connotación negativa que tiene hoy gracias al veneno inyectado en la palabra por hombres y mujeres que poco entendían del concepto. Algo que era perfectamente positivo y virtuoso se convirtió casi en una palabra maldita para las mujeres. Decir que la mujer debe ser sumisa al marido, hoy en día, implica ser llamado troglodita. Si las personas piensan que la sumisión al marido significa que la mujer debe ser su tapete, que él es el macho y que, por eso, puede darle con un palo en la cabeza y arrastrarla por los pelos cuando quiera, entonces concuerdo con ellas en que realmente no deben someterse. Sin embargo, sumisión, en el sentido original de la palabra designado por Dios, no tiene nada que ver con eso.

Sumisión al marido no es ser una sufrida esposa, tampoco lo es la idea machista de mandar sobre la mujer; es, tan solo, una manera inteligente de lidiar con la sociedad del matrimonio. En la Biblia, la palabra está relacionada con humildad, suavidad, complicidad, confianza en el liderazgo, maleabilidad, docilidad y respeto. Es lo contrario de desafiante, rebelde, inflexible y testaruda. Quiero decir que la mujer necesita ciertas cualidades para trabajar en sociedad con su marido, a quien debe respetar como líder. ¿Se ha fijado en el versículo de arriba, cuando dice que la mujer debe dejar que su marido la lidere? ¡Mire solamente nuestro poder! Somos tan fuertes que Dios nos orientó para que «permitiésemos» que nuestros maridos nos lideren. Sí, permitir, porque si no acabamos mandando… Pero Él quiere que usemos nuestra fuerza de manera diferente, más sabia.

Primero tiene que entender que ser sumisa no quiere decir que sea inferior a su marido. Es tan solo un rol que usted debe cumplir para el funcionamiento de esa sociedad llamada matrimonio. En todo lugar donde dos o más personas se proponen trabajar juntas con un objetivo común, alguien tiene que liderar y alguien tiene que someterse. Todos los países tienen un gobernante, todo equipo deportivo tiene un capitán, toda empresa tiene un gerente, todo colegio tiene un director. En todo lugar, los conceptos de liderazgo y sumisión trabajan juntos. Eso no quiere decir que el líder sea mejor que el liderado como persona. Simplemente tienen papeles diferentes.

Ahora mismo, sea cual sea su situación como mujer en la sociedad, está sometida a varias autoridades y líderes –muchas de las cuales no conoce y, probablemente, no le gustan–. Pero tiene que someterse para el buen funcionamiento de la sociedad o del grupo al que pertenece. Esta es la parte práctica de la sumisión. Es algo necesario en toda sociedad con objetivos comunes. Ahora, observe qué extraño: ¿somos motivadas para someternos a todos esos líderes que ni conocemos pero, al mismo tiempo, a rebelarnos contra nuestros maridos, que nos aman? Vamos a usar nuestra inteligencia. Sumisión es una manera inteligente de lidiar con la sociedad del matrimonio.

Pero usted pregunta: «¿Por qué tengo que someterme yo y no él?». Sea honesta: ¿se sentiría realizada convirtiéndose en la líder de su marido, mientras que él se resigna a la posición de flojo en el matrimonio? No tendría un hombre a su lado. A ninguna mujer le gusta un hombre que no toma la iniciativa, que necesita ser mandado y dirigido todo el tiempo y que no tiene un brazo fuerte; es más, ella desprecia a los hombres así.

Créalo: nosotras no necesitamos liderar. Tenemos otra fuerza que es la influencia. Con ella podemos conseguir lo que queramos de nuestros maridos. Esta influencia no es más que la sumisión llevada a cabo con inteligencia. Acuérdese, el hombre ya está «vendido» para la mujer. Él anhela agradarla. Por eso, el marido puede ser el cabeza, pero la mujer es el cuello. Y, si es sabia, puede girar la cabeza hacia donde quiera… Es tan temible que debemos tener mucho cuidado con ese poder para no destruir a nuestros maridos y a nosotras mismas.

Una de las cosas que más escuchaba cuando atendíamos a los matrimonios en Houston era esa frustración de la mujer: «Mi marido no lleva las cosas adelante, soy yo quien tiene que resolverlo todo, ¡no lo aguanto más!». Mal sabían que la culpa era de ellas...

La mujer que no se somete a su marido acaba castrándolo, sin querer. No es su intención, pero lo hace un don nadie. Sin respeto, el hombre pierde su esencia masculina. Cuando no le cede ese papel en el matrimonio, él no se siente respetado y deja de cumplir su papel de hombre de la casa.

EL VERDADERO LÍDER

La otra cara de la moneda es que la sumisión bíblica de la mujer presupone el liderazgo bíblico del marido. Es decir, la mujer no está obligada a someterse a un líder que le haga mal, sino a uno que se sacrifica y se entrega por ella, que la trata como una extensión de sí mismo —el líder tipificado por el Señor Jesús—. El verdadero líder quiere el bien de sus liderados. Por eso, al emplear su liderazgo, intenta hacer lo que es mejor para quienes lidera. El marido sabio, que espera la sumisión de su mujer, debe dirigirla así. Debe hacerse digno de ser seguido.

El verdadero líder no es un dictador. Intenta escuchar las opiniones y necesidades de sus seguidores. Sus decisiones son para beneficiar a todos, no solamente a sí mismo. Por eso, su liderazgo gana respeto y no necesita ser impuesto por la fuerza. Hay una armonía en la relación: el líder busca lo mejor para sus liderados y estos, a su vez, confían en su liderazgo y, con alegría, se someten sin resistencia. Fue así como Dios lo designó: hombre y mujer, cabeza y cuerpo, en perfecta armonía.

Sin embargo fíjese bien: es la mujer quien tiene mayor poder para crear esa armonía en el matrimonio. Es ella la que es invitada a «dejar» al marido que lidere. Es decir, el poder está en las manos de ella y, si ella sabe usar ese poder, no querrá otra cosa. Lo que pocas entienden es que son raras las veces que la mujer verdaderamente sumisa se somete. Yo, por someterme a Renato, son raras las veces que hacemos las cosas solamente a su manera. La mujer que se somete al marido consigue todo de él. Él se queda tan feliz por el respeto que ella le da que su deseo es agradarla y, así, acaba haciendo lo que ella quiere. Mujer, si su cabeza está dándole vueltas ahora porque lo que está leyendo aquí es muy diferente de todo lo que ya oyó, respire un poco, pare y léalo de nuevo. ¡Este es uno de los secretos más simples y más despreciados en la historia de la humanidad!

Sin embargo, no tenga duda: así como es un sacrificio para el hombre mostrarle sus sentimientos a su mujer, también es un sacrificio para la mujer dejar a su marido que la dirija. Va en contra de su naturaleza y es ahí donde muchas han perdido en el amor. No quieren «salir perdiendo» en la relación; mientras que, en realidad, la mujer que se somete es la que sale ganando.

Es a tiempo: si usted, marido, no es un buen líder para su mujer, no le da seguridad, es egoísta con sus decisiones, se muestra irresponsable con su comportamiento (como cuando se deja llevar por los vicios, por ejemplo), no atiende sus necesidades, ni la cuida con todas sus fuerzas, ¿cómo espera que ella se someta? Por eso, la sumisión de la mujer al marido está limitada por el momento en que él comienza a actuar de manera que la hiera. Si insiste en ser un mal líder y quiere caminar hacia el pozo, ella no puede seguirlo. Tiene que dejarlo ir solo.

Por lo tanto, si el marido atiende las necesidades básicas de la mujer, que se resumen en hacerla sentir valorada, amada y segura a su lado, ella, a su vez, será sumisa a él como algo natural –aunque, a veces, tenga que frenarse a sí misma para dejarlo dirigir–. Ahora podemos entender y explorar la necesidad más básica del hombre: respeto.

EL HOMBRE QUIERE SU PAN DE CADA DÍA

En mis andanzas por las tierras del asesoramiento de matrimonios he visto casi de todo («casi» porque siempre hay alguien que nos sorprende con algún comportamiento que nunca habíamos visto). Pero, tratándose de hombres, específicamente, llegué a la conclusión de que el hombre es mucho más simple y fácil de agradar. He visto hombres aceptar de sus mujeres, sin protestar, falta de sexo, tener que comer afuera todos los días porque ella no quiere cocinar, hacer de niñera mientras ella sale con las amigas, gastar todos los ingresos dejándolo endeudado, crisis de SPM e, inclusive, ver con ella un espectáculo de Celine Dion. Verdaderos héroes. Pero hay una cosa que todavía no he visto: hombres que aceptasen no ser respetados por su mujer.

Quítele todo al hombre, pero no le quite el respeto. Es su pan de cada día en la relación. Pensándolo bien, no pide mucho. Pero muchos no han recibido ni eso de sus mujeres. Y usted ya sabe lo que pasa cuando una necesidad básica no es cubierta. El sujeto se convierte en un animal y sale a la lucha por la propia supervivencia.

Cuando el marido no tiene el respeto que necesita dentro de su casa, va a buscarlo afuera. Y existen dos cosas principales que él normalmente busca para llenar ese vacío: el trabajo u otra mujer.

El éxito en el trabajo llena la necesidad de respeto de un hombre. Todos lo admiran, reconocen su valor, se hace necesario, y todo eso le hace sentirse apreciado. Por eso se entrega más al trabajo, para recibir más de ese respeto. Y, si aparece otra mujer, como acostumbra a aparecer para esos hombres de éxito, y ella lo aprecia de la forma en que no lo hace su mujer, tenemos la fórmula para el fin del matrimonio.

Por eso, la mujer sabia no discute ni es reacia sobre esa necesidad básica del marido, se limita a cubrirla. Y es así como ella lo hace, observe:

Exalta la fuerza del marido. Cuando la mujer hace al hombre sentirse fuerte, demuestra respeto hacia él. Por desgracia, muchas han caído en la agenda «hollywoodiana» de destruir la imagen masculina. Le critican por no ser «sensible», le ridiculizan públicamente, denigran su imagen y no hacen ningún secreto de ello. Hay mujeres que hacen ciertos comentarios y chistes maliciosos sobre sus maridos delante de los demás, hasta avergonzarlos delante de los hijos. Muchos hijos ya no respetan a su padre al ver que ni su madre lo respeta. Es decir, sin querer, muchas mujeres le han quitado al hombre su fuerza.

Viéndose como un débil, ni siquiera intenta tomar iniciativas más osadas porque su mujer lo influyó a para pensar que es incapaz. Así, a la mujer le «sale el tiro por la culata». Él, con la autoconfianza destruida, se vuelve un fracasado. Las palabras le ofenden y entristecen hasta el punto de hacerle sentirse derrotado, debilitado. ¿Cómo puede un hombre así darle seguridad a ella?

La mujer sabia hace que su marido se sienta un héroe, como si él pudiese conquistar todo el mundo. Dentro y fuera de casa, lo levanta con palabras y actitudes, exaltando sus cualidades más fuertes. Así, lo prepara para el mundo y cosecha con él los beneficios de sus conquistas.

Le deja ser el cabeza. Ella practica el concepto de sumisión inteligente del que hemos hablado anteriormente. Las pocas veces en que no hay acuerdo entre ellos y una decisión de él la contraría, ella permite que él tenga la palabra final (claro, nada que la hiera). La mujer debe respetar ese derecho de que él diga «sí» o «no». Incluso cuando sabe, o cree saber, cuál será la decisión de él, le consulta antes de hacer cualquier cosa, para reforzar la idea de que su decisión es valiosa e importante para ella.

Un problema común en los matrimonios actuales es el del marido anulado, que desiste. Debido a que nada de lo que dice, ella lo respeta, acaba dejando de opinar y de liderar. Si él está de acuerdo, o no, en alguna cosa, ella no le hace caso. Si ella quiere hacer algo, no importa lo que él piensa. Entonces él asume la siguiente posición: «Sigue adelante, haz lo que quieras. No importa lo que yo opino. Si estoy de acuerdo o no, lo vas a hacer de cualquier modo. Entonces, hazlo». Con reticencia y pesar, delega las decisiones en ella. La mujer piensa que está ganando pero, en realidad, está castrando al marido. La ironía es que tales mujeres viven reclamando que sus maridos no toman la iniciativa y no participan.

Mujeres, entiendan: a ningún hombre le gusta meterse en ninguna situación sabiendo que *siempre* va a perder. Simplemente, deja de participar.

La mujer sabia consigue prácticamente todo de su marido. Consiste solo en dejarle pensar que la idea fue suya… ¡Cristiane ya domina eso como un arte! El secreto está en llevarle la cuestión, darle la información que necesita para tomar la decisión y dejar que decida. Y si por casualidad la decisión no es la que esperaba, acátela, incluso así. La semilla está plantada. Más adelante, el deseo de agradar a la mujer le pasará la factura para que él haga algo por usted.

Es su admiradora número uno. Ella admira a su marido, inclusive con todos sus defectos, como una verdadera fan. Lo que caracteriza a un verdadero admirador es que, incluso cuando el equipo se está hundiendo, sigue apostando por él. Es como el equipo de su corazón, por ejemplo. El equipo puede perder diez juegos seguidos, parecer un chiste y ser descendido a divisiones inferiores; aun así, continúa apoyándolo, esperando que un día gane. Eso es ser admirador y seguidor.

Todo hombre carece de admiración, ya que sus realizaciones son muy importantes para él. Y, como todo hombre, también tiene sus defectos. Pero la mujer sabia no lo critica ni resalta sus defectos; en vez de eso, encuentra razones para admirarlo. Esa admiración trabaja en el subconsciente de él y acaba llevándolo a ser el hombre que ella siempre quiso. Ella exalta las cualidades positivas y finge que no ve las negativas. No hay nada más desmoralizante para un hombre que tener a su mujer como su crítica principal.

Lo reconoce delante de todos. A la mujer, de forma natural, le gusta desahogarse, contar la razón de su estrés a su amiga, madre u otra confidente. Ahí está el peligro: revelar los puntos negativos de su marido a otras personas. En vez de eso, sea una embajadora de su marido. Represéntelo bien y refuerce, así, el respeto por él.

Procura ser atractiva para él. Es una necesidad básica del hombre sentirse atraído físicamente por la mujer. El hombre se siente mucho más atraído por lo visual que la mujer y, por eso, la mujer debe cuidar su apariencia física. Lo interesante es que, antes de casarse, las mujeres son mucho más cuidadosas a este respecto que después, como si solo por el hecho de haber conquistado a un hombre, ahora, no necesiten más mantener la conquista. Si a él le gusta verla maquillada, debe maquillarse por amor, para mantener la química entre ellos. A veces, por saber que la mujer es sensible, el marido no le pide esas cosas; pero le corresponde a ella conocer las necesidades de él. La mujer tiene que cuidarse para mantener la llama de la atracción física. Sin embargo, debe hacerlo para su marido y no para otras mujeres, como suele ocurrir. Intente saber lo que le gusta a su marido. A veces la mujer quiere ser flaquísima debido a la moda, cuando al marido no le gusta eso. Si la revista tal dice que la última moda es hacer desaparecer todas las arrugas y expresiones del rostro con bótox, ella lo sigue fielmente; pero si el marido le dice que le encantaría verla con un labial rojo, rápidamente le dice que no le gusta.

Lo que para muchas revistas femeninas y sus lectoras es muy importante estéticamente, no siempre lo es para el marido. Un ejemplo clásico de eso es la celulitis. La mujer tiene «paranoia» con ella, y la mayoría de los hombres ¡no sabe ni lo que es!

Cristiane:

Nosotras, mujeres, no debemos querer competir con las modelos «photoshopeadas» de las revistas. Debemos, sí, invertir en nuestra feminidad, que también llama mucho la atención de nuestros maridos. La feminidad forma parte de la belleza de la mujer, incluso aunque la moda ya no acentúe eso.

Hace algunos años, vivía quejándome de mi nariz solamente porque me di cuenta de que no era el tipo de nariz «perfecta», respingada, como la de las modelos. Empecé a indagar sobre la posibilidad de «arreglarla». Pero solo pensé en eso después de casarme, demasiado tarde. Renato nunca me dejó y, con el tiempo, me hizo que me gustase mi propia nariz. Descubrí que quería cambiarla por culpa de la sociedad y no porque realmente lo necesitara, también porque Renato siempre dice que ifue una de las cosas que más le llamaron la atención de mí!

A veces nosotras, mujeres, queremos embellecernos por motivos equivocados y acabamos ignorando lo que realmente interesa a nuestros maridos. Hace algunos años descubrí que lo que Renato encuentra más sexy de mí es mi autoconfianza, que no siempre estuvo alta. Es decir, en la época en la que me veía sin gracia y vivía intentando cambiar mi estilo de peinado o de ropa y mi maquillaje, iestaba dejando de ser sexy!

Con todas aquellas inseguridades, toda la inversión física no estaba consiguiendo nada para mi matrimonio.

La mujer segura se convierte en una caza interesante para el hombre; a fin de cuentas, él es cazador. Imagínese un cazador en el bosque, todo camuflado, con el rifle apuntando, moviéndose furtivamente en dirección a la caza… todo aquel ritual. De repente, el venado percibe al cazador y, en vez de huir, corre en su dirección diciéndole: «¡Mátame con ese rifle, mátame, llévame a casa!». Yo le garantizo algo: ¡el cazador perdería todo el interés! La gracia de cazar está en la dificultad.

De la misma manera, el misterio en la mujer es lo que encanta a su marido. Tiene que notarla segura de sí misma para motivarse a cortejarla. Segura, mujeres, no demasiado difícil.

Le deja su espacio. El hombre necesita espacio, un tiempo para relajarse y procesar su estrés. Se trata de la famosa «cajita de la nada», citada anteriormente. Muchas mujeres no les dan tiempo a sus maridos ni para que respiren. Tan pronto llegan a casa ya les arrojan todo el estrés del día. La esposa sabia escoge el momento adecuado para hablar, qué hablar y cómo hablar. Eso tiene un gran valor para el hombre. Se hace más atractiva para él, pues ve en eso el respeto que la mujer le tiene y la autoconfianza de no estar atrás de él todo el tiempo.

Está claro que ese espacio tiene un límite. El marido que está siempre queriendo espacio y nunca tiene tiempo de conversar con su mujer está dejando su matrimonio morir poco a poco. Eso la hará sentirse insegura y frustrada y no podrá ser la esposa que necesita y quiere. Hombres, espacio es una cosa, pereza por cuidar la relación es otra. ¡Hay vida afuera de la cajita!

NADIE MERECE

Quiero enfatizar que lo que acabamos de contar en este capítulo hasta aquí son maneras de suplir la necesidad más básica del hombre, que es tener el respeto de su mujer. Tal vez usted, mujer, tenga un marido que no sea merecedor de ese respeto actualmente, por las cosas negativas que hace.

Sin embargo, acuérdese de una cosa: *La mejor cosa que se puede hacer sobre las necesidades básicas de alguien es suplirlas.*

La verdad es que nadie «merece» nada. La mujer puede decir que su marido no merece su respeto o el hombre puede decir que su mujer no merece su atención, pero el hecho es que si ustedes todavía están juntos y quieren blindar el matrimonio, tienen que cumplir sus deberes el uno con el otro. No espere a que él o ella lo merezcan, haga lo que *usted tiene que hacer* y verá que la otra persona acabará volviéndose merecedora.

Mujer: Respete a su marido porque así conseguirá todo de él.

Marido: Haga a su mujer sentirse amada y valorada y cosechará los frutos de esta entrega durante toda su vida.

CUANDO LAS NECESIDADES BÁSICAS DE ÉL SON LAS DE ELLA Y VICEVERSA

En uno de nuestros cursos en Houston, una mujer nos preguntó después de la clase en la que explicamos las necesidades básicas del hombre y de la mujer: «Yo creo que soy el hombre de la relación. Lo que dicen que yo necesito es lo que él quiere y lo que yo vivo insistiendo que él me dé, es respeto. ¿Qué hago?». Era una policía, acostumbrada a ser dura y poco sentimental y se había casado con un marido al que le gustaba… recibir atención.

Parece que este panorama se ha vuelto más común actualmente. No es difícil de entender, con todo el proceso de emancipación de la mujer y de la feminización del hombre en las últimas décadas. Lo que hemos visto es que, cuando el hombre es muy emotivo, la mujer acaba teniendo que ser la más racional, ya que dos emotivos no llegan a ningún lugar. Pero eso es algo de lo que ella misma acaba lamentándose, pues incluso a la mujer dura e independiente le gusta, en ciertos momentos, tener un hombre fuerte a su lado.

Este nuevo fenómeno ha dificultado todavía más la relación de algunos matrimonios. El hombre emotivo quiere respeto, pero no hay forma de dárselo, y la mujer racional quiere seguridad, pero tampoco encuentra cómo confiar en su marido…

Quien tiene una relación así, atención:

- Si usted es un marido sentimental, necesita vencer sus inseguridades para hacer a su mujer feliz; ser menos emotivo y más racional; intentar transmitir firmeza y madurez a su mujer.
- Si usted es una mujer muy independiente, racional, tal vez incluso mandona, necesita equilibrio en su manera de ser y dejar a su marido ganar más espacio en la relación. Invítelo a tomar decisiones junto con usted. Déjele tener la última palabra.

Si cada uno se pone en su lugar, los dos podrán andar juntos el resto de su vida.

Cristiane:

Yo soy más detallista que Renato y pienso en las cosas que él se olvida de pensar, mientras él es más racional que yo, piensa en cosas en las que yo, por mi manera impulsiva de pensar, no reparo. Él es fuerte. Cuando estamos en situaciones difíciles, yo quiero llorar y esconderme en un rincón; él, con su fuerza, me abraza y me hace sentirme protegida.

La mujer sabia reconoce los atributos de su marido y viceversa.

Yo nunca habría imaginado que el capítulo sobre las necesidades básicas del hombre sería más largo que el de las de la mujer... ¿Por qué será? Esa es su fuerza, mujer. Necesita más palabras para convencer... Úselas con inteligencia.

TAREA

PARA LA MUJER

¿Qué necesidades básicas de su marido necesita cubrir con más dedicación?

¿Qué va a hacer respecto a eso a partir de ahora que él se sienta respetado?

PARA EL MARIDO

¿Cómo puede ayudar a su mujer a comprender sus necesidades básicas, sin exigir ni imponer?

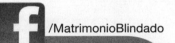

f /MatrimonioBlindado

Hombres, publiquen esto:
Estoy ayudando a que mi mujer entienda lo que más necesito de ella.

t @matrimonioblind

Hombres, tuiteen esto:
Estoy ayudando a mi mujer a entender lo que más necesito de ella
#matrimonioblindado
@matrimonioblind

f

Mujeres, publiquen esto:
Ahora entiendo lo que el hombre realmente quiere.

t

Mujeres, tuiteen esto:
Ahora entiendo al hombre y lo que él realmente quiere
#matrimonioblindado
@matrimonioblind

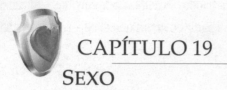

CAPÍTULO 19
SEXO

Antes de nada, quiero dar la bienvenida a los hombres que decidieron leer este libro: este es, probablemente, el primer capítulo que a ustedes les va a interesar leer. Y también a las mujeres que están frustradas sexualmente: hay una luz casi al final del túnel. Me gustaría, eso sí, recordarles que hay una razón especial por la que este capítulo está al final del libro. La práctica de todo lo que fue enseñado en los capítulos anteriores es lo que le proporcionará una vida sexual óptima. Si ignora lo que hemos hablado hasta aquí, probablemente sacará tan solo un provecho parcial de este capítulo; por lo tanto, haga el servicio completo y vuelva al principio del libro. ¡Le garantizo que valdrá la pena!

La vida sexual saludable es una de las principales herramientas de blindaje del matrimonio. Y nunca está de más enfatizar eso. La manera más rápida de descubrir la salud de la relación de pareja es intentar saber cómo les va en la cama. Si mi mujer y yo tuviésemos derecho a hacer una única pregunta para descubrir la situación de una pareja en nuestro consultorio matrimonial, sería: «¿Cómo está la vida sexual de ustedes?».

El sexo en el matrimonio es como un pegamento que mantiene al matrimonio unido. Es el misterio que hace que los dos se vuelvan uno –literalmente y también en todos los demás sentidos–. El sexo habla, y mucho. Comunica sentimientos y pensamientos que las palabras no pueden expresar. Cuando usted no busca a su compañero sexualmente, esa actitud habla en la mente de él o de ella cosas como: «No soy suficiente para mi marido/esposa... ¿Por qué me rechaza? ¿Será que tiene a otra persona? Tal vez haya algo malo en mi apariencia... Él/ella ya no me quiere cerca». Por otro lado, cuando el matrimonio mantiene una vida sexual activa y saludable, los mensajes no verbales son: «Mi marido me encuentra atractiva... Mi mujer está satisfecha conmigo... Somos suficientes el uno para el otro... No hay motivo para que mi marido/esposa mire a otra persona». Las consecuencias de esos mensajes en su mente pueden apuntalar o destruir su matrimonio. Ignore esto bajo su propia responsabilidad.

El sexo no solo habla, también cura muchos males. Está científicamente probado que la actividad sexual actúa como una limpieza, una desintoxicación mental y física en la pareja. Por eso, cuanto menos lo practican ustedes, más distantes se sienten y más oportunidades dan para que haya problemas entre ustedes. En un matrimonio sin sexo, cualquier problemita se multiplica por mil. Por otro lado, es raro que una pareja tenga una mañana alterada después de una óptima noche en la cama... Cosas pequeñas se revelan, pues los dos tienen crédito suficiente en las cuentas emocionales –donde el sexo es la moneda más fuerte–.

Es posible detectar cuándo un matrimonio está bien y es activo sexualmente o no, observando sus temperamentos. Irritación, mal humor, frialdad y falta de consideración del uno hacia el otro son señales seguras de que la cama ha sido usada tan solo para dormir. Tal es el poder del sexo.

El recado es: practiquen sexo, practíquenlo bien y regularmente. Pero, para muchas parejas, es más fácil hablar que hacer. Vamos a develar este misterio.

DÓNDE COMIENZA Y TERMINA

Al contrario de lo que muchos piensan, el sexo no es solamente lo que sucede cuando el marido y la mujer se desnudan y mantienen relaciones sexuales. Para entenderlo mejor, piense en un sándwich. Cuando quiere comer un sándwich, piensa si va a quererlo de pollo, carne, chorizo, etc.; pero no piensa solo en lo principal que va dentro, piensa también en el tipo de pan, en la cebolla, lechuga, tomate, mostaza…, en todo lo que va a complementar y realzar el sabor de aquella carne. La carne pura en sí es comestible, pero con el resto del sándwich es mucho mejor.

Así es el sexo. Está claro que son dos cuerpos físicos que se involucran en el acto, pero el acto en sí tan solo es la carne del sándwich. Es lo que va en el medio. Sin embargo, antes y después es donde está el verdadero inicio y el fin de lo que llamamos un óptimo sexo. El antes y el después es trabajo de la mente. Sí, el sexo empieza y termina en la mente. El acto físico es el vehículo de expresión, pero la mente es su conductor y destino al mismo tiempo. La mujer generalmente hace eso mejor que el hombre. El sexo para ella está conectado con todo. ¿Se acuerda de los hilos conductores del cerebro femenino? Ella puede excitarse por cosas que nunca excitarían a un hombre, simplemente porque ella asocia todo con todo.

Por lo tanto, no se espante, marido, si usted un día saca la basura fuera de casa sin ella pedírselo, por ejemplo, y cuando vuelve ella le mira como si quisiera ir a la cama en aquel momento. No intente entenderlo, ¡simplemente aproveche!

Por su parte para el hombre, el sexo es algo muy simple. Para que él tenga deseo, es suficiente con que ella esté presente. El hombre es como si tuviese un único botón de encender y apagar para practicar sexo. La mujer es como una cabina de un Jumbo 787, llena de botones, y el hombre no sabe por dónde empezar. ¡Ha presionado un botón equivocado, apriétese el cinturón de seguridad y póngase la máscara de oxígeno!

Por eso, corresponde poner aquí un consejo especialmente para los hombres:

El sexo empieza del cuello hacia arriba.

Acostumbro a oír a los hombres que nos buscan para el asesoramiento decir: «Mi esposa nunca está dispuesta... Siempre con una excusa... Parece que solo a mí me gusta el sexo, a ella no... No quiero que se sienta como si me estuviese haciendo un favor... Para ella una vez al mes es suficiente, y ya está...».

Queridos míos: el sexo para la mujer es algo muy, muy diferente que para nosotros, hombres. El error de muchos maridos es pensar que la mujer ve el sexo como ellos, es decir, un placer físico, asociado a aliviar la tensión. Para usar otra analogía gastronómica (de aquí a poco me va a dar hambre), el sexo para la mujer es una fresa en la torta de la intimidad. Es una expresión de cuán íntimos, amigos y amantes son ustedes –no solo en la cama, sino durante todo el día–.

No sé si usted ha comido alguna vez una fresa sola, sin la torta. Es un poco ácida y sin gracia, ¿no? No satisface y, luego, apetece comer otra cosa para quitarse aquel gusto. Así es como la mujer entiende el sexo que no es precedido de intimidad. Ácido y sin gracia. No es algo que ansía hacer de nuevo. Pero cuando la fresa viene encima de la torta, entonces es diferente. La torta es lo principal y la fresa realza el sabor. Óptima combinación.

La torta es la intimidad que precede a la cama. Dígase de paso que, cuando la mujer escucha la palabra «intimidad», piensa principalmente en «conversación»; el hombre, sin embargo, piensa en poner las manos en ciertos lugares. Ella piensa en descubrir lo que el hombre está pensando, especialmente respecto a ella; y también le encanta cuando toda su atención está en ella, en lo que dice. Eso sí es lo que fortalece la intimidad de la pareja.

Por lo tanto, si usted solo le ha dado la fresa a su mujer, ahora entiende la reacción ácida de ella. Sea mejor amante con su mujer volviéndose mejor oyente y mejor conversador. Esmérese en la torta. Conéctese con ella.

No estoy diciendo que se convierta en un canalla, que utiliza una pequeña charla solamente para conseguir lo que quiere. Esté seguro de que ella va a notar su falsedad y, ahí, ni fresa ácida va a tener… Estoy hablando de un sincero interés en la persona que está dentro del cuerpo de su mujer.

Si entiende eso, que el sexo para la mujer empieza por encima del cuello, serán mucho más felices en la cama y en otros lugares. Y ahí les va a faltar torta para tanta fresa.

NO ME GUSTA EL SEXO

Esta frase es casi tan imposible como decir que «no me gusta el aire». La única diferencia es que nadie se muere por falta de sexo, pero decir que no le gusta el sexo no es algo plausible. A no ser que haya algo físicamente mal en usted, el sexo *es bueno y óptimamente delicioso*. Fue creado por Dios, y Dios no hace nada malo. Si alguien dice que no le gusta el sexo es porque nunca supo lo que es o lo sabe, pero el compañero/a no. Por lo tanto, si al marido le gusta pero a la mujer no, es responsabilidad de él ayudarla a descubrir cuán bueno es para ella. Enfatizo aquí «para ella» porque el objetivo del acto sexual es dar placer al compañero. Por eso, a muchas mujeres no les atrae el sexo; porque se sienten usadas por los maridos tan solo para su propio placer.

Quiero dejar algo bien claro aquí: el orgasmo de la mujer es obligación del marido. El sexo es para dar placer a su pareja y no solamente para buscar el propio placer. Es esa actitud egoísta la que lleva a muchos a decir «no me gusta el sexo». A todo el mundo le gusta el sexo cuando se practica de la forma designada por Dios: para llenar al compañero de placer.

Para que eso suceda los dos tienen que poner el placer del otro como prioridad. El orden obvio y lógico de esta prioridad es el placer de la mujer primero y, después, del hombre. Debido a que ella, normalmente, es más lenta que él, si él busca primero su propio placer, ella se quedará esperando en vano.

Así que concluyendo el sexo es a la vez la necesidad y el placer que fortalece y protege al matrimonio. ¿Cuáles son los consejos para una óptima vida sexual? Tenemos cinco para usted.

CINCO INGREDIENTES PARA UNA ÓPTIMA VIDA SEXUAL

1. Limpie la mente. Primero limpie su mente de cualquier pensamiento sucio respecto al sexo. Tal vez tenga que desinfectar su mente de información contaminada que recibió en círculos de amigos/as, revistas, material pornográfico y otras fuentes dudosas. Hay mucha suciedad, distorsión y desinformación rodando por ahí al respecto. Entienda una cosa: cuando Dios creó al hombre y a la mujer, no necesitaron revistas pornográficas ni manuales para practicar el sexo. Él proyectó el sexo también para el placer de la pareja y les capacitó a ambos para satisfacerse el uno al otro sin la necesidad de la interferencia de terceros. Usted y su cónyuge son suficientes entre sí para alcanzar el placer sexual mutuamente. Por lo tanto, no vea el sexo como algo sucio ni prohibido. Es un regalo de Dios para ustedes. Es una de las únicas cosas que son exclusivas entre los dos. La amistad no es exclusiva del matrimonio, tampoco la fidelidad (puede ser fiel en su trabajo, por ejemplo), pero el acto sexual es algo exclusivo de la pareja; por eso, trátelo con la importancia, la pureza y el valor que merece.

2. Use la mente para conectar. Acuérdese de que el sexo, especialmente para la mujer, está unido a todo lo que antecede al acto. El sexo empieza y termina en la mente. Separe un tiempo en su mente para fijarse en las cualidades que admira de su cónyuge. Eso es una decisión consciente y voluntaria que tiene que tomar; si no, las preocupaciones sobre lo que no tiene que ver con su compañero ocuparán sus pensamientos. El estrés es el mayor generador de impotencia y frigidez. Tiene que separar un tiempo en su mente para conectarse con su compañero, no importa lo ocupado y estresado que pueda estar por el trabajo o cualquier otra razón. Desconéctese de lo que le está robando la atención a su cónyuge. Coméntele acerca de su ropa, su belleza natural, la parte del cuerpo que más le gusta; pregúntele sobre lo que está pensando, sus planes y proyectos, sus preocupaciones –oiga atentamente– y ofrézcale apoyo, seguridad y valor. La mujer no debe esperar que el hombre sea tan abierto como ella sobre sus pensamientos, él no necesita eso para sentirse «conectado». Pero debe regar su día con un comentario de admiración aquí y allí, un toque físico en un momento inesperado, una mirada sensual, un elogio sobre una característica masculina –como su fuerza, firmeza e inteligencia para los negocios–. Todo eso es el pre-sexo.

3. Enfóquese en su compañero. El placer de llevar a su compañero al placer debe ser tan placentero para usted como su propio placer. Guau… ¡intente decir esta frase con la boca llena de comida! Realmente aquí está uno de los principales secretos para conseguir que su marido o su mujer esté loco por usted. El objetivo es la otra persona, ¡no usted! Si ella alcanza el placer, el suyo será una consecuencia. Por eso, tenga en cuenta lo que es importante para la otra persona. Un punto crucial, que normalmente difiere entre el hombre y la mujer, es la cuestión de la privacidad. A él no le preocupa tanto si alguien en la habitación de al lado escucha gemidos y suspiros. Para él eso aumenta su virilidad. Sin embargo, a ella, si no le da un ataque de corazón al saberlo, nunca más va a mirar a la cara a aquella persona por vergüenza. Y ni mencione si el niño entra en la habitación para saber por qué están haciendo tanto ruido en la cama. Por lo tanto, hombres, enfóquense en lo que es importante para ella. La mujer tiene que sentirse absolutamente segura de tener privacidad para soltarse. Póngale llave a la puerta de la habitación. Invierta en aislamiento acústico en las paredes de la habitación si fuera necesario. Respétela y sea discreto. Además, la mujer tiene que sentirse segura no solamente respecto a la privacidad, sino también respecto a usted. Si acostumbra a mentirle, esconderle información, actuar irresponsablemente con el dinero y tener un temperamento imprevisible, no se sentirá cómoda ni segura con usted. ¿No le avisamos de que el sexo para ella está unido a todo? Ahora, un consejo para las mujeres: si su marido realmente se esfuerza para llevarla a las nubes, entonces, enseguida, llévelo a ver las estrellas. Es su turno de centrarse en él...

4. Descúbranse y explórense entre sí. Nadie es igual a nadie. Lo que a una mujer le parece lo máximo, otra lo detesta. Por eso, deben ser amantes el uno del otro, descubrir lo que les excita. ¿Qué partes del cuerpo le gusta que le toque? ¿Cuáles no le gusta? Trate de descubrir con su propia mujer, pregunte, explore, no confíe en fuentes externas como sitios web y revistas. Eso es algo muy personal. Algunos hombres quieren que sus mujeres se sometan a las cosas que les gustan (o que leyeron en algún lugar que a «las mujeres le gusta»); por eso algunas mujeres se sienten incómodas con la práctica sexual. Es muy común encontrar en las portadas de revistas cosas como «Siete maneras de enloquecer a un hombre en la cama». Eso vende, pues las personas son ignorantes al respecto y, así, abren la mente para muchas barbaridades. Cuidado con lo que introduce en su mente y en su habitación. No todo lo que está en las revistas (es más, casi nada) es bueno para usted. El placer sexual empieza aprendiendo a explorar a la persona con la que está casado. No me interesa si la revista habla de que a la mujer le gusta esto o aquello. ¿Y si a mi mujer no le gusta? No todas las mujeres son iguales. No son robots ni fueron creadas en serie. La pareja tiene que dialogar, conversar, descubrir lo que a uno le gusta, lo que no le gusta, y adecuarse. También es importante saber cuál es la frecuencia ideal para su cónyuge. Por ejemplo, la mujer puede no sentir necesidad de practicar sexo, una vez a la semana está bien para ella. Sin embargo, el marido quiere todo el día. En ese caso, los dos deben encontrar un término medio. Tal vez ella tenga que ceder un poco más para que puedan relacionarse sexualmente tres veces por semana. Y él también tendrá que sacrificarse para que tres veces por semana sean suficientes. O dos. O cuatro. Lo importante es buscar ajustarse teniendo en cuenta al otro. No imponga algo sobre la otra persona, especialmente en el sexo. Si es forzado, si no es natural, no será placentero. Si no es bueno para uno, no lo será para ninguno. Respete los límites de la otra persona. Si a usted le gusta practicar el sexo oral, pero a su compañera no le gusta, no se lo imponga.

5. Invierta en los preliminares: ¿Cuál fue la última vez que se besaron apasionadamente, que le dio un largo masaje a su compañero, que tocó a su mujer con verdadero cariño, que pasó los dedos por sus cabellos, que le acarició el cuello, culminando con un abrazo? Todo el romance que se desarrolla durante el día y en las horas anteriores al sexo culmina en el momento en el que los dos de hecho se implican en el acto. Ese momento requiere un gran dominio propio del hombre. Los estudios indican que, en promedio, al hombre le lleva de dos a tres minutos eyacular después de la penetración. Por su parte, la mujer necesita, en promedio, de siete a doce minutos para llegar al orgasmo. ¿Puede ver el problema? Por lo tanto, el hombre necesita subir a la montaña con calma para no llegar a la cumbre mientras la mujer está todavía poniéndose las botas… Llegados a este punto, el hombre que es inteligente, que viene practicando todos los pasos explicados hasta aquí, lleva ventaja. La mujer que ha sido preparada veinticuatro horas al día por él no va a necesitar tanta preparación en el momento del acto sexual.

Aun así, él necesita controlar y acompañar el paso de ella, en vez de imponerle su paso. Mujer, usted podrá ayudar a su marido en ese punto manteniendo relaciones con él más periódicamente. Si él solo tiene sexo con usted una vez al mes, o menos, va a resultarle difícil controlarse cuando estén juntos.

ESPERE, ¡TODAVÍA NO TERMINÓ!

Hablamos de que el sexo empieza y termina en la mente y que el acto físico en sí no es más que la carne del sándwich. Eso quiere decir que, donpués de que los dos hayan tenido sus respectivos orgasmos (sí, ese es el objetivo), el sexo todavía no se ha acabado. Está claro que, a estas alturas, los dos estarán físicamente cansados; el hombre, principalmente, va a querer darse vuelta y dormir. ¡Pero no el hombre que leyó *Matrimonio blindado*! Este sabe que en el momento inmediatamente posterior al acto sexual es cuando la mujer se está sintiendo más próxima y conectada a él. Por lo tanto, este es el momento de mantener el contacto físico, el cariño, las palabras dulces y los elogios. Él no permite, de ninguna manera, que su mujer se sienta usada. Sabe que este es el mejor momento para hacerla sentirse amada y –honestamente– también para empezar a prepararla para la próxima vez.

LA SUEGRA QUE LE PEDÍ A DIOS

Cristiane:

Poco antes de casarme, muy joven e inexperta, mi madre me comentó algo sobre el sexo que he guardado siempre conmigo: «No siempre vas a tener el deseo de hacer el amor con tu marido, pero no actúes por lo que tú sientes. Hazlo incluso así. Una vez que empieza, acabas teniendo deseo. Nunca le digas que no para que no se sienta rechazado».

¡Y, hasta hoy, Renato lo agradece!

Tanto al hombre como a la mujer les gusta el sexo. Yo no creo en ese mito que dice que a la mujer le gusta menos que al hombre. El problema es que muchos hombres no saben cómo ve una mujer el sexo. Para ella, el sexo es el clímax de un día de amor productivo: el diálogo, las caricias, el cuidado, el mirar, la paciencia; en fin, todo lo bueno derivado del amor que presenció de su marido durante el día. Si el hombre practica eso, la mujer es capaz de querer tener más sexo que él…

Pero la verdad es que no todos los días estarán regados de romanticismo. Habrá días malos y días normales. No espere que todas las noches o todos los encuentros íntimos entre ustedes estén marcados por el fuego de la pasión. No es así. No viva de las fantasías de las películas. Muchas veces tendrán que empezar el acto sin estar muy excitados el uno por el otro. Otras veces su compañero la buscará y usted no estará preparada. Pero, cuando eso sucede, decida entrar en el clima. No le dé lugar a la pereza. Vaya adelante y participe. Nunca rechace a su compañero o compañera. Acuérdese, el sexo habla. Un rechazo sin una buena razón puede empezar a crear monstruitos en la cabeza de su cónyuge. Es por eso por lo que los matrimonios deben hacer el amor incluso cuando están cansados. Con el estilo de vida atareado en el que vivimos hoy, ¿quién no está cansado al final del día? Una cosa es segura: cuanto más lo hace, más lo quiere hacer; cuanto menos lo hace, menos lo quiere hacer.

El asunto es tan serio que la Biblia dice[19] que usted no tiene derecho a decir que no a su marido o mujer cuando él (o ella) quisiera mantener relaciones sexuales. Mujer, no se trata de volverse una esclava sexual de su marido. La explicación dada es mucho más bonita y profunda: su cuerpo no es suyo, es de él, y el cuerpo de él, no es de él, es suyo. Se pertenecen el uno al otro. Si uno niega el placer al otro, estará rompiendo la alianza del matrimonio, además de dejar espacio al diablo. (Hay muchos que le están abriendo las puertas del matrimonio a causa de eso).

La insatisfacción sexual porque uno de los dos no está nunca disponible para el cónyuge muchas veces culmina en adulterio, que es una de las principales causas de los matrimonios deshechos. Claro que si la razón para negarle el sexo a su cónyuge tiene que ver con dolores o con alguna otra dificultad física, conversen y busquen juntos un médico.

FASES Y ÉPOCAS

Una señal de aviso a las parejas en el camino de la sexualidad: permanezcan atentos a las fases y épocas del matrimonio y de su vida. Hay ciertos acontecimientos, factores y cambios que, inevitablemente, van a

---

[19] Corintios 7:3-5.

afectar a su vida íntima. No quiero decir que será necesariamente malo, pero tendrán que adecuarse y ser más comprensivos el uno con el otro. Una obvia consideración es que el sexo a los cincuenta años no será como a los veinte. Otra es si hay una gran diferencia de edad –él cuarenta y cinco, ella treinta y cinco, por ejemplo–.

Inmediatamente después de un embarazo, la mujer no estará dispuesta a tener sexo como antes. El marido tendrá que entender que la llegada del niño cambia todo en el matrimonio, y uno de esos cambios es el cansancio de la mujer por cuidar del bebé (si no lo cree, intente cuidarlo durante 24 horas y verá), el cambio en su cuerpo, la falta de dormir lo suficiente. El marido tiene que entender y disminuir sus expectativas respecto a la mujer en ese sentido. La mujer, sin embargo, no debe dejar que eso se convierta en una excusa. Su deseo sexual puede haber disminuido, pero el de él sigue igual... El bebé la necesita, pero también a un padre. No descuide a su marido.

El hombre que pasa por momentos difíciles en el trabajo también acostumbra a disminuir su libido. El fracaso profesional es desmoralizante para el hombre y puede, incluso, causar impotencia. La mujer debe, con sabiduría, apoyar al marido y hacerlo sentir «hombre», con su constante admiración, apoyo y aliento.

Cambios en los horarios de trabajo (dificultando que los dos estén juntos), viajes largos y cuestiones de salud son otros factores que pueden afectar su actividad sexual. El consejo es que estén atentos a las señales y hagan las debidas compensaciones para no permitir que eso les afecte.

¿ESTÁ PERMITIDO?

Pocos asuntos conyugales generan más dudas y preguntas que el sexo. Constantemente se nos pregunta si se puede esto o aquello en el acto sexual. En vez de detallar tales preguntas aquí, quiero plantear un punto importante para las parejas, como una guía general.

Las parejas más fracasadas sexualmente son aquellas que se preocupan demasiado con el asunto. Normalmente son aquellas mujeres que están súper preocupadas en vestir lencerías sensuales (una redundancia, pues, para la mayoría de los hombres, prácticamente cualquier lencería es sensual), visitar la sex shop, queriendo saber lo que esta o aquella revista dice sobre sexo, extremadamente preocupadas con una lonjita extra que apareció y qué es lo que el marido va a pensar. O aquellos hombres que cayeron en el vicio de la pornografía y masturbación, y dejaron de ser amantes de la mujer real que tienen al lado para fantasear con mujeres que ellos nunca tendrán en la realidad.

Querido lector: no se guíe por personas que no son ejemplo ninguno de felicidad conyugal. Las celebridades y los supuestos expertos en relaciones tan glamourizados por los medios de comunicación son, en su mayoría, personas infelices en el amor. Casados por tercera o cuarta vez, divorciados, traicionan y son traicionados, o nunca encontraron un verdadero amor. Si hay alguien de quien usted *no* quiere recibir consejos para su vida amorosa es de esas personas. Por lo tanto, no deje que la confusión de este mundo complique lo que Dios hizo simple. Siga estas reglas de sentido común: sea amante de su marido o esposa. Descúbranse el uno al otro. No impongan ni exijan nada que al otro no le guste. No hagan nada contrario a la naturaleza (como sexo anal). Enfóquense en el placer de la otra persona y no sean egoístas. El resto, ustedes mismos lo llevarán a la práctica entre los dos.

TAREA

¿Necesito decirla?

CAPÍTULO 20
LAS 27 HERRAMIENTAS

A lo largo de nuestro matrimonio, y también aconsejando a matrimonios con toda clase de problemas conyugales, Cristiane y yo desarrollamos lo que llamamos herramientas para lidiar con las diversas situaciones. Algunas las creamos para nosotros mismos, otras las aprendimos o adquirimos de otras sabias parejas. Seleccionamos las mejores y las hemos puesto aquí para que las tenga a su disposición.

Toda casa necesita una caja de herramientas, pues son útiles para colgar algo en la pared, ajustar un cajón o para destapar alguna cosa. Todo matrimonio necesita también ciertas herramientas de auxilio. Estas 27 herramientas le ayudarán a arreglar y a mantener su matrimonio. No todas se aplican a su situación actual, pero esta información le ayudará a armar la cajita de herramientas que le será útil en una situación de emergencia en su matrimonio. Cualquier caja de herramientas es así, no necesita todos los artículos que contiene para llevar a cabo el trabajo, pero siempre es bueno tenerlos pues nunca se sabe cuándo serán necesarios.

Muchas de esas herramientas son cosas que usted ya sabe, pero que no practica. Su fuerza está en la práctica conjunta con otras herramientas. Puede ser que ya haya intentado usar solo una de ellas sin resultado. Renueve sus fuerzas para volver a aplicarla de nuevo junto a otras. Puede que no haya tenido resultado antes de leer este libro porque, entonces, no sabía lo que sabe ahora. Siga adelante y abra su caja, ponga las herramientas allí dentro, una a una, y aprenda en qué situación usarlas.

1. No se vaya a dormir con el problema

No se vaya a la cama con un problema no resuelto entre ustedes. Creer que se solucionarán más tarde solo hará que los problemas se agraven. La Biblia aconseja: «*Airaos, pero no pequéis; no se ponga el sol sobre vuestro enojo, ni deis lugar al diablo*».[20] Es decir, no está mal enfadarse y sí dejar que ese enojo siga al día siguiente, hasta el punto de hacer tonterías por su causa. Dicen que el tiempo lo sana todo, pero eso casi nunca es verdad. Una herida abierta solo empeora con el tiempo. Un problema es como un monstruito verde recién nacido: frágil, pequeñito y aparentemente inofensivo que se alimenta del silencio, de la indiferencia y que crece durante el sueño. Si nadie hace nada al respecto, en poco tiempo tendrán un enorme monstruo verde como mascota, que masticará su matrimonio y les hará pedazos a los dos. Cuanto antes lo mate (preferentemente, en el huevo), menor será el estrago que cause. Es muy fácil identificar si mataron o no a tal monstruito. Si se acuestan dándose la espalda el uno al otro, en habitaciones separadas o sin tocarse, significa que el problema aún no se solucionó y que el monstruito está agonizando. Vuelvan a conversar hasta que lleguen a la reconciliación. Esa herramienta fue algo que desarrollé con Cristiane para solucionar el problema del tratamiento del silencio. Nos pusimos de acuerdo: «A partir de ahora, cuando tengamos un problema, vamos a hablar sobre él y no nos vamos a dormir hasta que se quede solucionado». Claro que eso tuvo como resultado que muchas noches fuésemos a dormir a las tres de la madrugada, pero abrazaditos. Nos despertábamos bien al día siguiente, sin arrastrar ninguna carga negativa del día anterior. Cuando empezamos a ser bien rígidos con esa herramienta, el tratamiento del silencio se acabó. Yo aprendí a

---

[20] Efesios 4:26, 27.

solucionar el problema al instante. Problema ignorado es problema empeorado. Muchos matrimonios pasan por esa situación. Su compañero quiere solucionar el asunto, pero usted no quiere porque piensa que ya se solucionó, o porque está enfadado. Ignore sus emociones y haga lo que es correcto. Usar los «Diez Pasos para Solucionar los Problemas» explicados en el capítulo 6 le ayudará. La frase «no deis lugar al diablo», del versículo escrito arriba, es reveladora. Cuando la ira queda mal resuelta, está dando lugar al diablo. En cualquier momento de la relación usted está en la presencia de Dios o en la presencia del diablo. Sea consciente de eso. Debe desarrollar la sensibilidad de discernir cuándo está en la presencia de uno o de otro. Preste atención a las señales. Es fácil saberlo. Cuando Dios está presente, la relación está bien. Cuando el diablo está presente, las cosas se traban; es decir, él encontró una brecha. Así que, sin demora, vaya y cierre esa brecha, ¡ya!

¿Cuándo usar esta regla? Siempre que haya algo mal resuelto, «en el aire», entre ustedes; cuando tiene algo dentro de usted en contra de su pareja; cuando uno está despreciando al otro.

2. El amor nunca hiere

No existe justificación para herir a su cónyuge, ya sea de manera física, verbal o emocional. Estar enojado no es motivo para dañar a la pareja. ¿Cuántas veces nos enfadamos por algo que sucedió en el trabajo? Y ¿qué hacemos cuando eso sucede? ¿Golpeamos al jefe, pateamos la silla? No, aprendemos a administrar esa rabia sin herir al otro. Porque si herimos a nuestro jefe (o a cualquier otra persona en la empresa), probablemente nos quedaremos sin trabajo. Usted aprende a administrar esa rabia para evitar una situación desagradable con los compañeros de trabajo. Lo mismo debe hacer con la persona amada. Nunca actúe con agresividad. No es excusa decir que es nervioso o que tiene poca paciencia, pues el verdadero amor no lastima. Eso también incluye ciertas malas palabras que, a veces, a la hora de la pelea, se dicen el uno al otro. Se insultan y dicen palabrotas como si la otra persona no representase nada. No se trata así a quien forma parte de nuestro propio cuerpo. Mantenga un alto nivel, no insulte, no ataque al carácter.

Las parejas felices adoptan un patrón elevado de tratamiento el uno con el otro. Se rehúsan a aceptar un comportamiento dañino. Cuanto menor es la tolerancia al mal comportamiento en una relación, más feliz será la pareja con el paso del tiempo. Si la mujer insulta al marido, por ejemplo, y él responde, ambos rompieron las reglas del comportamiento civilizado. Si no arreglan aquel hecho, disculpándose y comprometiéndose a no actuar más de aquella manera, ¡listo! Aceptó que se cruzara la línea una vez, la próxima vez será cruzada nuevamente, hasta alcanzar una línea todavía más peligrosa. Atendemos a muchas parejas que, al contarnos la discusión que tuvieron, usan la siguiente frase: «Perdona, pero tengo que ser sincero y decir lo que siento». No siempre lo que se siente tiene que ser dicho. Las emociones nos hacen pensar en disparates. Muchas veces lo que siente no es lo que verdaderamente piensa. Si exterioriza algo llevado por el impulso, causará un daño del cual su cónyuge puede no curarse.

¿Cuándo usar esta regla? Cuando sus emociones fluyan y quiera explotar con la otra persona. Guarde esta frase: «El amor nunca hiere». Actúe civilizadamente. Si la otra persona le está hiriendo, insista —con respeto, sin avivar aún más el fuego— en mantener el alto patrón entre ustedes. Puede ser que tenga que señalar eso más tarde, después de que los ánimos se calmen, pero no lo deje pasar.

3. No generalice

No importa cómo completaría estas frases: «Tú nunca…» o «Tú siempre…». Ambas causarán problemas. No use el pincel de una situación para pintar todo el carácter de su compañero. «*Siempre* haces lo que quieres, *nunca* lo que yo quiero», «*Nunca* me oyes». Esa clase de afirmaciones raramente son verdaderas y solo sirven para enojar a su compañero. Lidie con las situaciones de forma individual y resista la tentación de relacionar el problema actual con un problema pasado. Cuidado con las palabras *nunca, siempre, nada, todo* y *siempre que,* pues son palabras absolutas que no dejan opción. Evítelas. La mayoría de las veces, este es un problema femenino. La mujer *siente* determinada actitud del marido *como* si él siempre hiciese aquello, recordando todas las veces que ya pasó por aquella sensación. Ella expresa lo que está *sintiendo* y no propiamente el hecho en sí. El problema es que si la mujer dice: «Nunca sales conmigo», el hombre, automáticamente, se acuerda de que la llevó por ahí una vez, dos meses atrás, y contesta: «¿Nunca? Pero si te llevé a ver aquella película…» y el foco se vuelve hacia ella. Cuando usted generaliza, la persona no lidia con el problema que usted trajo, sino que tiende a acordarse de algo que contraríe lo que usted está diciendo.

Si está oyendo generalizaciones, ¿cómo lidiar? Entienda que ella no está diciendo que «nunca», o que «siempre», sino que está expresando la sensación que tiene ante aquella situación. Oiga: «Siento como si nunca me llevases a pasear», en vez de «Nunca me llevas a pasear». Sea paciente. No se enfade y mantenga el foco de atención en el problema que le está planteando.

¿Cuándo usar esta regla? En toda comunicación entre ustedes. Si se escapara alguna de esas palabras en algún momento, discúlpese y rehaga la frase. Si su pareja generaliza, apunte el error para no repetirlo en el futuro, pero céntrese en lo que él o ella está queriendo decirle realmente y lidie con aquello.

4. Deje de reclamar y comience a orar

Su pareja insiste en hacer algo equivocado, no quiere cambiar, usted ya viene reclamando desde hace años y nada sucede. ¿Se ha dado cuenta de que no sirve de nada reclamárselo a Él? Reclámeselo a Dios. Pídale que toque en el corazón de su pareja y que le dé sabiduría para combatir aquello. Es natural que, si le ataca, él/ella no consiga ver el error que le señala, ya que está empeñado en defenderse. Pero Dios puede hacer que vea el error dentro de sí. La oración tiene mil y una utilidades. Más allá de ser una herramienta capaz de producir el cambio que usted no lograría solo, también le ayuda a lidiar con el estrés, al colocar la ansiedad en Dios. Él aguanta la frustración, la rabia, el mismo asunto, una y otra vez, durante el tiempo que sea. Por su parte, el cónyuge puede reaccionar no muy bien. Piense en eso, así, ¡usted está acudieno a quien creó el matrimonio para solucionar su problema, está reclamando directo a la fábrica! Como si llamara al servicio de atención al cliente de una empresa y pudiese hablar directamente con el dueño. Pero sea perseverante. No siempre la respuesta viene a la mañana siguiente. Insista en la oración a Dios. Ore por usted también, para no formar parte del problema. Pida sabiduría para lidiar con la situación.

Cristiane:

Cuando me di cuenta de que mi marido no estaba cambiando a través de los constantes reclamos que yo hacía, concluí que no podría lidiar con aquella situación sola y busqué a Dios. Esa herramienta es el cambio de dirección: dejar de actuar por la emoción y pasar a actuar por la fe, a través de la confianza en Dios. Pero no se engañe, Dios no hace magia, no hace todo Él solo. Él actúa cuando usted hace su parte, para sumar con la de Él. Y si usted no sabe cuál es su parte, pídale orientación a Él. Nosotras, las mujeres, somos propensas a reclamar demasiado y nos volvemos molestas, pensamos que lograremos solucionar el problema protestando. Yo empecé a orar a Dios pidiéndole que cambiase mi comportamiento. Quería dejar de llorar y empezar a actuar por la fe y, a través de la oración, lo logré. Solo Dios puede hacer que el marido o que la mujer cambie. Solo Él puede cambiar el interior de una persona. Antes, yo oraba para cambiar a Renato, pero después de preguntar a Dios la dirección, que me mostrase lo que debía hacer, empecé a buscar el cambio primero en mí, y fue así como comencé a ver el resultado en él. Dios no solo nos da consuelo y paz, sino que, además, nos da la dirección para saber qué hacer. Funciona en todas las situaciones de nuestra vida.

¿Cuándo usar esta regla? Cuando todo lo demás falle.

5. Muestre aprecio

Muchas personas casadas se sienten tentadas de tener una relación extraconyugal simplemente porque encuentran a alguien que los aprecia más que su cónyuge. Cuando percibe a su pareja distante o usted mismo se siente distante, necesita esforzarse conscientemente para demostrar consideración hacia ella. Por ejemplo, cocine algo que le guste, haga una cena especial, dúchese y perfúmese para esperarlo, esté en casa cuando llegue. Intente saber cómo está, llámela por teléfono durante el día, note su ropa nueva, salgan para hacer algo que a ella guste. Es muy fácil descuidarse después de estar muchos años juntos.

Existen varias situaciones que apartan el objetivo de la pareja haciendo que se olviden el uno del otro con el paso de los años y que entren en la fase de la indiferencia. Después de la llegada de los hijos, estos consumen toda la energía de la pareja, la mujer vive solo para ellos y el marido se siente desplazado. O los dos están luchando para que crezca la empresa, o para pagar las deudas. O los hijos finalmente se casan y la pareja se queda como si fueran dos desconocidos, sin saber cómo relacionarse porque pierden aquello que los conectaba. La herramienta de mostrar el aprecio es muy útil en este momento. Identificar la fase de la indiferencia es fácil. Observe a su pareja. Ya no forman juntos una unidad. Cada uno vive en su mundito. Uno frente a la televisión, el otro pegado a la computadora. Uno se va a acostar antes que el otro. Salen solos, viven vidas independientes, tienen muy pocas cosas en común. La pareja que vive así raramente muestra aprecio, pues para apreciar a alguien necesita darse cuenta de que la otra persona está ahí. Es posible revertir ese cuadro, inclusive después de varios años de indiferencia, basta con querer. ¿Se acuerda de las cositas que hacían durante el noviazgo y al principio del matrimonio? ¿Del cuidado que tenían el uno con el otro? Es eso lo que usted tendrá que rescatar. Le repito la frase que usted ha encontrado muchas veces en este libro (porque no puede ser olvidada): el matrimonio feliz da trabajo. Hasta hoy tengo que invertir en mi matrimonio. Es un trabajo continuo y que compensa enormemente.

Una frase que me gusta que las parejas se graben es: ¿Qué es lo que mi cónyuge necesita de mí ahora? Si no lo sabe, pregúntele o intente descubrirlo. (No siempre se lo dirá. O puede decir «nada» cuando, en realidad, tendría una lista que leer, en orden alfabético). Pregúntese: «¿Qué puedo hacer por él(ellaa)?». *Ella p*uede estar estresada, o deprimida, necesitando de su compañía, de ánimo, de saber que hay alguien fuerte a su lado. A veces basta una palabra, o apoyo silencioso, señalando que todo saldrá bien, que es una fase y que ustedes vencerán. Si está enferma, necesita sentirse cuidada o, por lo menos, saber que usted se preocupa, en el caso de que otra persona haga ese trabajo.

Mujeres, no piensen que esta es una tarea solo para los hombres. A veces, el hombre está pasando por una situación en la que se siente derrotado y necesita una palabra que le demuestre que usted aún lo ve fuerte. Un aviso: la mayoría de los hombres no saben recibir elogios, pero eso no significa que no les guste. Puede que usted ya haya pasado por eso. La mujer elogia la ropa y él levanta los hombros. ¡No se intimide! Créalo, es solo que no quiere perder «la pose»… Eso es muy común e involuntario, casi como un defecto de fábrica. Aunque la persona no sepa recibir elogios, no deje de elogiarla. No se preocupe, causará efecto.

El psicólogo John Gottman, respetado especialista en relaciones, condujo un estudio que lo llevó a concluir lo siguiente: por cada experiencia negativa que la pareja tiene, son necesarias cinco experiencias positivas para compensarla. Digamos que la pareja haya tenido un intercambio de palabras desagradables que dañaron al otro; para nivelar esta situación negativa, tendrá que practicar cinco acciones positivas para poner a cero la ecuación. El índice de Gottman nos lleva a creer que las malas experiencias son cinco veces más poderosas que las buenas. Es por esa razón por lo que si el marido hace algo que lleva a su mujer a perder la confianza, un mes después ella aún se acuerda del hecho. Cuanto más aprecio muestre, más impresiones positivas acumulará en su relación...

¿Cuándo usar esta regla? Siempre, especialmente cuando note cierta distancia e indiferencia entre ustedes.

6. Lo que su cónyuge le pida, va al principio de la lista

Mucho del estrés en la relación se debe al pensamiento de que no se es tan importante para el compañero como otras cosas o personas; entonces, cuando su compañero le pida algo, póngalo al principio de su lista, haga de eso una prioridad para que no necesite pedírselo nuevamente. Es una reglita simple, pero vale oro.

El marido pide: «Amor, cómprame una maquinita de afeitar, la mía ya no afeita bien». La mujer responde con un «Ah, bueno» pero no le estaba prestando atención. Al día siguiente, él busca la maquinita y no está. Él se molesta un poco y lo deja pasar; entonces, la mujer se disculpa y promete comprarlo la próxima vez. Y la historia se repite al día siguiente. ¿Es algo tonto? Sí, las parejas discuten por cosas tontas, pero ¿por qué discuten? Porque aquella cosita tonta está diciendo algo muy grave al oído de la persona, del tipo: «Yo no soy importante para ti», «Si tu madre te pide algo, dejas todo, corres y lo haces al instante, pero, cuando lo pido yo, no lo haces». Ese es el verdadero problema. El problema no es la maquinita de afeitar sino el mensaje oculto tras la actitud. Esta es una regla que debe absorber en su día a día. Él/ella le pidió algo, entonces hágalo rápido y fortalecerá la idea de que ustedes son los primeros en la vida uno del otro. Piénselo bien. Cuando su jefe le pide algo, ya tiene el hábito de hacerlo rápido. Sabe que aquella persona es importante porque tiene influencia sobre usted. ¡Muchísimo más el matrimonio! Su marido/mujer es mucho más importante. Quizá exista algo que su cónyuge le haya pedido hace mucho tiempo y usted no hizo todavía. Desde la cosa más pequeña hasta una conversación seria que necesitan tener. Realícelo ahora mismo, como prioridad, como prueba de consideración.

¿Cuándo usar esta regla? Siempre que él(ella) le pida alguna cosa.

7. Cuide su apariencia

Muchos que se preocupaban por cuidar bien de su apariencia antes, durante el noviazgo, ven el matrimonio como un «permiso para andar feos». En realidad es precisamente después del matrimonio cuando debe cuidarse como nunca. No menosprecie a su compañero creyendo que ya lo conquistó. Procure estar siempre bonita para su cónyuge, controle su peso, fíjese en la manera de vestirse, utilice maquillaje si a él le gusta. La limpieza y el orden de su casa también son muy importantes.

A algunas mujeres no les gusta maquillarse, pero a sus maridos les gustaría que se pintasen los labios o los ojos. La mujer cree que tiene que gustarle a su marido al natural: «Es así que yo soy». Claro que no me va a gustar Cristiane por sus aretes o maquillaje, pero si la mujer sabe lo que le gusta al marido debe esforzarse un poco para agradarlo. Lo mismo sucede con la comida: si a usted algo no le gusta pero a él sí, le hará esa comida para agradarlo.

El matrimonio es eso, vivir para agradar al otro, para hacerlo feliz. Está bien, estoy de acuerdo en que no es justo exigirle a la persona que sea alguien que no es, pero hacer algún esfuerzo en la dirección de aquello que agrada a su cónyuge no es demasiado, es muy válido y con toda seguridad le hará sentirse mejor. En mi trabajo, tengo que ponerme traje, corbata, camisa, pantalón de vestir y zapatos. En mis momentos libres, me gusta ponerme sandalias, pantalón corto y playera, pues casi nunca me pongo ese tipo de ropa. Al principio, cuando íbamos al cine, iba de pantalón deportivo y sandalias, quería estar muy cómodo. Para ella, aquel era un momento especial y salía muy arreglada. ¡Imagine qué pareja! Ella no me decía nada, pero sentía vergüenza de mí. Cuando finalmente me dijo: «Con esa ropa, parece que desististe de la vida», primero me enojé pero, después, lo entendí. Nosotros salimos muy poco, así que, cuando vamos a salir, tengo que honrarla, estar a su altura. Hago un esfuerzo por amor a ella, porque a ella le gusta. ¡Pero por mí iría en sandalias!

Aconsejamos a una pareja cuyo marido estaba insatisfecho sexualmente. Se quejaba de que siempre que buscaba a su mujer era rechazado. Mientras él hablaba nos dimos cuenta de que ella estaba avergonzada. Les pedimos que se retirase uno para hablar con cada uno de ellos con más privacidad. Entonces ella se desahogó: «Él dice que yo nunca quiero que me toque, ¡pero si por lo menos él se bañara todos los días!». La mujer debía de ser una heroína para aguantar momentos íntimos con alguien que no tenía una buena higiene. Él estaba tan acostumbrado a la falta de higiene que ni siquiera imaginaba que ese era el motivo del abismo entre los dos. ¡Algo tan fácil de solucionar! ¡Jabón, agua, toalla y listo! Fin de los problemas de aquella pareja.

Cristiane:

Usted representa a su cónyuge; por eso, después de casarse, su responsabilidad con la apariencia es aún más grande. La apariencia dice mucho respecto a cómo se siente, si es feliz, si está realizada, va a mostrar eso en su exterior. Si ama, respeta y valora a su marido, es natural que muestre eso en su exterior. Puede sentirse mal por dentro y estar bien por fuera, pero de ninguna manera conseguirá estar bien por dentro y mal por fuera. Si está bien en su interior, tiene que demostrarlo en su exterior, no solo en la forma de arreglarse sino en su semblante, la sonrisa, la mirada cariñosa... La mujer que recibe al marido en casa malhumorada, ¿está feliz? La mujer que sale con mala cara, desarreglada, ¿está feliz? Si el marido mira a su mujer y ve a una mujer amargada y descuidada, ¿cómo se sentirá? Si usted está irritada debido a aquel periodo delicado del mes, avísele a su marido, no permita que piense que el problema es él o que usted no es feliz. La apariencia no es todo en mi vida, pero si me amo, ¿por qué no voy a cuidarme? Y más ahora que tengo a alguien a quien representar.

¿Cuándo usar esta regla? Siempre. E intente averiguar lo que le agrada a su cónyuge respecto a la apariencia. También comuníquele sus preferencias, pero no imponga nada.

8. Nunca ridiculice su pareja

Ya sea de forma privada o pública. Tener buen humor no es lo mismo que burlarse. ¡Cuidado con los chistes de mal gusto! No exponga los defectos y las debilidades de su cónyuge ante terceros. «El amor *cubre* todas las transgresiones», dijo el sabio rey Salomón.[21] El amor cubre los defectos de la otra persona. Aunque su pareja esté equivocada, demuéstrele su apoyo, en vez de exponer sus errores. Ridiculizar es faltar al respeto. No haga comentarios que disminuyan a su cónyuge o que expongan algo que él mismo aún no había expuesto para los demás. «Ah, Roberto no sabe ni hacer una suma. ¿Sabías que solo terminó la primaria?». ¿Qué aporta eso a su matrimonio? Sarcasmo, ironía y desprecio son fatales también para la relación. «¿Harás una lista para no olvidarte? Y ¿desde cuándo eres bueno con las listas?». Esas actitudes generalmente demuestran que la persona piensa que es superior a la otra. Acuérdese, el amor no hiere.

¿Cuándo usar esta regla? Siempre. Preste doble atención cuando esté en medio de una discusión acalorada o entre amigos.

---

[21] Proverbios 10:12.

9. Beba del agua santa

Hay una historia de un vecindario donde los desentendimientos conyugales aumentaban desenfrenadamente. Cansada de las peleas con su marido, una mujer fue a pedir consejo al sabio del lugar: «¿Qué debo hacer para acabar con las discusiones con mi marido?», le preguntó. El viejo sabio le dio una botella con agua y le dijo: «Esta agua es santa. Cada vez que su marido empiece a discutir, beba un poco; pero es necesario que la mantenga en la boca durante diez minutos antes de tragarla. Y dígales a todos sus vecinos y amigos que tengan el mismo problema que hagan lo mismo». En poco tiempo, ya nadie discutía en aquel vecindario. Invitaciones para discutir siempre llaman a la puerta del matrimonio. Entienda que no está obligado a aceptarlas todas. Si su cónyuge ha hecho un comentario que le invita a contestarle, tengo una buena noticia: puede decir no y decidir no presentarse a esa pelea. No es que vaya a ignorar el problema pero tendrá dominio propio, principalmente si decide controlar su lengua. Los ánimos se calmarán y habrá evitado una discusión innecesaria que solo serviría para alejarlos a los dos. ¿No es excelente? Ganar una discusión no es tan importante como solucionar el problema. Si percibe que su pareja está alterada, respire hondo y cierre la cremallera de sus labios. Nunca me olvido de un matrimonio de Singapur que acudía a nuestra iglesia en Londres. El día que hicimos una oración especial por sus cincuenta años de casados les preguntamos cuál había sido el secreto de una vida juntos tan duradera y el marido nos contestó: «Cuando yo estaba nervioso, ella se callaba. Cuando ella estaba nerviosa, me callaba yo». Eso realmente funciona.

¿Cuándo usar esta regla? Cuando se sienta con el deseo de devolver palabras duras con otras más duras todavía.

10. Inicie la conversación suavemente

Si sus conversaciones ya empiezan en un tono grosero, inevitablemente terminarán en pelea, aunque haya muchos intentos de calmar los ánimos después. Algunos ejemplos clásicos: Si el marido pregunta: «¿Necesitas dinero?» (Empezó bien). La mujer contesta: «Solo para las cuentas que deberías haber pagado la semana pasada» (Empezó mal). Los cuchillos de la acusación y del sarcasmo empiezan a volar. Cuando la conversación empieza bien, son grandes las probabilidades de terminarla bien. Elija cuidadosamente sus palabras, pruebe la frase mentalmente y vea si suena bien. Si piensa que la persona puede no entenderlo, cambie el orden de la frase, elija otras palabras. La conversación será más tranquila y tendrá tiempo de pensar para no decir ninguna tontería. Si se da cuenta de que empezó a perder la paciencia, respire hondo, pida perdón y empiece de nuevo.

Cristiane:

Una manera eficaz de comunicación es hablar de cómo le hace sentir su cónyuge, en lugar de tratarlo como si él fuera la personalización del problema. Por ejemplo, si su marido es grosero con usted, no es sabio llamarle grosero, pues así empieza el asunto con el ataque y, con total seguridad, él se defenderá. Pero puede hablar de cómo usted se siente cuando él habla con usted...: «Mi amor, cuando estás ocupado y te pregunto algo, a veces la manera como me respondes me hace sentir mal». ¿Nota la diferencia? No es él quien la hace sentir mal, es la manera en que él le responde la que hace eso. Concéntrese en lo que usted piensa y siente al respecto en vez de en lo que usted piensa de la persona en relación al problema.

¿Cuándo usar esta regla? Siempre que vayan a tratar algún asunto delicado entre ustedes.

11. El cajón de los problemas perpetuos

Siento tener que informarle de que ciertas cosas que nos irritan y que consideramos «defectos» en nuestra pareja, para nuestra tristeza, nunca cambiarán. Quizá él sea para siempre. Es posible que siempre esté apegada a su mamá. En fin, hay cosas en cada uno de nosotros que forman parte de nuestra identidad y que no cambiarán. En lugar de frustrarse y quedarse siempre discutiendo con la otra persona sobre ello, tome ese problema y póngalo en el cajón de los problemas perpetuos –un lugarcito de su cerebro reservado para recordarle que es en vano seguir debatiendo sobre aquel tema y que, por eso, lo mejor que puede hacer es aprender a lidiar con él–. Ponga más cestos de ropa en lugares estratégicos de la casa. Recoja sin protestar la ropa que él –aun así– la tirará al suelo. Acepte la amistad de su mujer con su suegra, ¡únase a ellas! Si es un problema tolerable, que le da para gestionarlo, entonces use esa herramienta.

Desista de cambiar a la otra persona, pues eso no es posible. Como ya dijimos al comienzo: usted solo puede cambiarse a sí mismo. Quite su foco de atención de los defectos del otro, de lo que no hizo y que, a su parecer, está mal. Valore las cualidades de su cónyuge y el contenido del cajón tendrá cada vez menos importancia en su relación.

¿Cuándo usar esta regla? Cuando identifique un problema perpetuo.

12. Borre los últimos diez segundos

A veces necesitamos dejar pasar algunas cosas. Una palabra fuera de contexto, un comentario innecesario en un momento de ira… Evalúe la situación y vea si vale la pena enojarse con eso. Algunas veces, su mujer pisará en su callo y va a querer explotar, pero acuérdese: no *necesita* explotar.

Cuando usa una cámara de video y no le gusta lo que acaba de grabar, regresa y graba nuevas imágenes encima de las imágenes innecesarias; de la misma manera, use este mecanismo mental de «para, regresa y borra», diciéndole a su cónyuge: «Está todo bien, voy a fingir que no vi ni escuché lo que acaba de suceder. Empezamos con el pie izquierdo, vamos a volver a empezar». Esa herramienta de borrar los últimos diez segundos también es de mi invención. Me di cuenta de que, a veces, Cristiane actuaba por impulso o movida por una frustración, decía lo que no quería decir y vomitaba lo que estaba sintiendo. En lugar de pelear empecé –inclusive de buen humor– a darle señales de que no debería haber dicho aquello. Si ella suelta algo que me da una cuchillada, digo: «Espera, déjame rebobinar la cinta. Ok, toma 2. ¡Acción!». Cuando ella escucha eso, entiende que lo que dijo estuvo mal y tiene la oportunidad de hablar nuevamente. A propósito, si ha fallado en la herramienta de empezar la conversación suavemente, tiene otra oportunidad con esta herramienta para borrar los últimos diez segundos. Use esta herramienta con buen humor y cambie la situación. Ayude a la otra persona, perdone, dele otra oportunidad.

¿Cuándo usar esta regla? Cuando la otra persona pisó la pelota y su voluntad es hacer que él se trague la pelota.

13. No deje que el lenguaje no verbal cancele sus palabras

Los especialistas en comunicación afirman que más del 90 % de la comunicación es no verbal. Fíjese en ese número. ¡Más del 90 %! Cosas como el comportamiento, el tono de la voz, la mirada, las expresiones faciales y el lenguaje corporal son las responsables de casi todo lo que transmitimos. Nuestras palabras aportan menos del 10 % de nuestra comunicación a la otra persona. Preste atención en su día a día y verá cómo esa información es verdadera. Si usted dice: «Vale, yo te perdono», mientras su rostro (y aquel giro en los ojos) dice: «Solo estoy diciendo eso porque lo pediste pero, en el fondo, sé que nunca cambiarás» (sí, usted puede decir todo eso tan solo con una mirada), eso hará que su perdón no parezca sincero. Más allá de la expresión facial y corporal, algo que habla más que sus palabras es su comportamiento reciente. Si dice: «Voy a cambiar», pero su comportamiento dice que ya lo prometió cien veces y nunca lo ha cumplido… sus palabras no tendrán ninguna credibilidad para la otra persona. No sirve de nada reclamar.

Preste atención a las señales que envía sin palabras. Es muy común, durante la conversación, que el marido cruce los brazos y diga: «Muy bien, puedes hablar». En realidad está diciendo: «Yo preferiría estar en cualquier otro lugar y no tener esta conversación pero, después, no podrás culparme por no oírte». Todo eso puede decirse sin abrir la boca. Una expresión corporal más abierta y receptiva es el secreto para una buena comunicación. No quiera tener un buen resultado en una conversación en la que mantiene una postura cerrada y defensiva, un tono de voz sarcástico, suspiros audibles. Mantenga siempre en mente que su pareja no es el enemigo y que su objetivo es terminar la conversación bien. Estar abierto al diálogo es imprescindible para que eso suceda. Procure comunicarse con su cónyuge de forma cariñosa, placentera y pacífica. Lo que quieren es una buena relación ¿no es así? Desee eso con todas sus fuerzas, con todo su cuerpo –literalmente.

¿Cuándo usar esta regla? En toda la comunicación.

14. Reconstruir la confianza es trabajo de a dos

Si hubo infidelidad o se quebró la confianza en su relación, sea usted el culpable o la víctima, ambos tendrán que trabajar duro –y juntos– para reconstruir la confianza. Un error común es que la persona herida le eche toda la culpa encima a la otra, que le traicionó: «Quien cometió el error fuiste tú, estoy desconfiado porque me diste motivos». Ella cree que el otro, exclusivamente, es el que tiene que trabajar para rescatar la confianza. Siento tener que informarle de que no es así. Los dos tienen que trabajar en eso.

Eso vale para cualquier situación en que haya pérdida de confianza. Por ejemplo, la mujer se gastó el dinero que no debería haber gastado; ahora, el hombre no le confía nada de valor. En el caso de la infidelidad, el dolor y la desconfianza –«¿ocurrirá de nuevo?»– estarán siempre como un fantasma en su cabeza.

El culpable tendrá que actuar de modo diferente para demostrar que hubo, de hecho, un cambio. No pida cuentas, simplemente haga lo que tiene que hacer. Es el precio a pagar por su infidelidad. Elimine el teléfono secreto, no borre los mensajes del celular, permita el acceso a los correos electrónicos y a Facebook. Entre las cosas que ya no pertenecen a su realidad están: salir y no decir a dónde va, tener momentos del día en los que el otro no sabe con quién o dónde está, tener secretos, esconder información. Mantener esas actitudes solo continuará alimentando la desconfianza. Para que la confianza sea rescatada, la persona que traicionó tendrá que grabar en su mente la palabra «transparencia». Cuando se es transparente, no hay nada que esconder y empieza a ser digno de confianza.

Sea transparente en todo y no reclame. No venga con la historia de «¿Y mi privacidad?» o «Ya no hago más eso, tienes que confiar en mí». Usted renunció a su privacidad el día en que se casó. Y si su cónyuge le está otorgando el perdón y una nueva oportunidad, es su transparencia la que le servirá de puente para la reconstrucción de la confianza, no sus promesas. Es como el ciudadano que comete un crimen y es llevado al tribunal. Por ser la primera vez, recibe el beneficio de la fianza. El juez plantea algunas restricciones: no puede viajar, tiene que presentarse mensualmente durante un determinado tiempo –pero no lo envía a la cárcel–. La persona que cometió un crimen y recibe esa clase de sentencia se pone muy feliz. Piensa: «Tendré que comportarme bien, controlarme algunas veces, ¡pero por lo menos no estoy en la cárcel!». Aprecia esa oportunidad. Del mismo modo, el que traicionó tiene que apreciar la nueva oportunidad, y la única manera de hacer eso es siendo transparente.

Si usted fue la víctima, deje de recordar a su cónyuge lo que dejó en el pasado y evite alimentar desconfianzas. No suponga ni saque conclusiones precipitadas. Lidie con los hechos en el presente. Si su pareja no cambia, usted puede advertirle que no habrá una tercera oportunidad, pero, mientras no demuestre lo contrario, no se quede volviendo al pasado innecesariamente. Si se comprometió a cambiar, no se convierta en detective, investigando lo que no existe, ni insinúe que todavía le sigue traicionando. Es muy irritante y frustrante intentar cambiar y ver que el otro nunca cree en el cambio.

Es común para quien fue traicionado empezar a ver cosas que no existen. Se trata del miedo controlándole. Pero sea racional. Las paranoias no sirven. Haga planes y prepárese ante la posibilidad de que el otro no cambie, pero deje el plan «en el cajón» para ponerlo en práctica solamente en caso necesario. Así, ya tiene la respuesta para el miedo, si lo peor sucediese.

Entierre el pasado y pase con el coche por encima veinte veces, para que ni siquiera sea posible saber dónde fue enterrado. No vuelva allí para llevar flores o escupir en la tumba. Olvídese. Auxilie a su pareja en esa reconstrucción, es un trabajo en equipo. ¿Es difícil? Lo es, nadie dijo que fuera fácil, pero solo así comenzarán a reconstruir la confianza perdida.

¿Cuándo usar esta regla? Cuando haya traición, mentiras o cualquier ruptura de confianza en la relación y hayan decidido darse una segunda oportunidad.

15. Duerma antes del problema

No se trata de una contradicción con la herramienta número 1, donde se le aconseja no irse a la cama dejando un problema no solucionado para el día siguiente. Aquella orientación es para ayudarlo a lidiar con problemas que *ya ocurrieron*. Esta enseña a lidiar con el estrés *antes* de que el problema llegue. Muchos de los problemas del matrimonio se originan por situaciones de estrés en uno o ambos. Si está atento para detectar el problema ANTES de que suceda, podrá evitarlo.

Observe el lenguaje corporal, el tono de voz y el nivel de estrés de su cónyuge. Dele espacio suficiente. Las personas encaran de manera diferente el estrés. Como regla general, los hombres necesitan espacio y las mujeres necesitan hablar. Claro, hay excepciones, existen mujeres que también necesitan silencio y hombres que quieren desahogarse. Lo importante es entender que, si uno está en un nivel de alta irritabilidad, no sirve de nada que el otro quiera solucionar el problema en aquel momento.

Incluso, un añadido a la primera regla: si ya ocurrió el problema y ve que la persona está peligrosamente alterada, entonces es mejor dar una pausa y esperar a que los ánimos se calmen. No tendrán una buena conversación si las personas están funcionando en base a la emoción y la irritabilidad. Esa herramienta es semejante a la regla del «time out» en el básquet. Cuando el equipo empieza a perder muchos puntos seguidos, el técnico pide tiempo y reúne a sus jugadores para darles instrucciones. Es estratégico, principalmente porque rompe la ventaja del adversario.

Acuérdese de que, en su matrimonio, también hay un adversario. No le dé brecha al diablo. Si insiste en quedarse provocando a su cónyuge cuando los ánimos están alterados, entonces le está dando ventaja al adversario. Dé una pausa. Decidan hablar más tarde sobre el asunto.

A pesar de que el nombre de la herramienta sea «Duerma antes del problema», eso no significa, necesariamente, que tenga que dormir –a pesar de que una buena noche de sueño es una de las mejores maneras de hacer una higiene mental y emocional–. También puede ser una pausa de veinte minutos o de una hora. La idea es darle tiempo a su pareja para recobrar las fuerzas y el equilibrio emocional.

¿Cuándo usar esta regla? Tenga esta herramienta siempre a mano para detectar las señales de estrés en la pareja, o en sí mismo, y valerse de una pausa, u otra forma de calmarse, antes de que genere problemas.

16. Ensaye para la próxima vez

En el matrimonio raramente se tiene un nuevo problema. No discreparán solo una vez sobre el dinero, ni sobre la educación de los niños. Lo más común es tener que enfrentarse con problemas reciclados, que vuelven de tiempo en tiempo. Cuando se encuentra con un problema recurrente, ¿qué puede hacer? Primero, resuelva el conflicto inmediato, usando aquellos diez pasos que enseñamos en el capítulo 6. Enseguida, pregúntese: «¿Cómo podemos evitar que eso suceda?» o «¿Qué haremos si eso vuelve a ocurrir?» Entonces, así como los guionistas planean lo que pasará en la próxima escena de una película o novela, escriba su propio «guión» para la próxima vez. ¿Qué harán cuando una situación similar suceda? Decida lo que pasará, cuál será el papel de cada uno y pónganse de acuerdo. Cuando la situación surja, ambos sabrán qué hacer, sin exaltar los ánimos.

¿Cómo es eso en la práctica? Por ejemplo, el marido se olvida de la fecha del aniversario de boda. No es bueno recordando fechas y la mujer se irrita mucho con eso. Por la forma de ser de él, existe una gran probabilidad de que se olvide nuevamente el próximo año. Algunas personas no están conectadas con las fechas, es un defecto de fábrica (herramienta 11 aquí, ¿quizás?). La pareja debe solucionar el problema de que la mujer esté enfadada ahora pero, también, deben ponerse de acuerdo en cómo van a encarar eso las próximas veces.

La mujer puede apuntarlo en la agenda del marido a principios de año (simple, ¿no?), avisarle con alguna anticipación, pegar recordatorios por la casa… «¡Pero, así, no tiene gracia!», dice ella. Entienda una cosa muy importante: nuestras altas expectativas pueden llevarnos a querer que nuestra pareja sea como somos nosotros, que lo importante para nosotros sea importante para él (ella), pero no siempre es así. Es necesario que haga un ajuste en sus expectativas para evitar problemas recurrentes. Hay un abismo entre lo real y lo ideal. Cuanto más grande es el abismo, más grande es la frustración y los problemas llegarán.

Olvide lo ideal y lidie con lo real. Aunque lo real no sea suficiente, es eso lo que tiene, es sobre eso sobre lo que tendrá que trabajar para conseguir un resultado mejor.

Esta herramienta se aplica en todas las situaciones. Muchos discuten respecto a la educación de los hijos. Uno es más estricto, el otro más flexible, y los hijos perciben esto y empiezan a hacerlos que se enfrenten el uno con el otro. Entonces, tienen que ensayar eso para la próxima vez. Pónganse de acuerdo, por ejemplo, en que la próxima vez que el marido diga que no al hijo y el niño vaya a la mamá queriendo cambiar lo que él ha decidido, la mujer confirmará lo que el marido dijo, aunque piense que fue muy duro. Ustedes pueden incluso conversar sobre eso después, sin el niño, pero jamás dejen que el hijo se dé cuenta de que uno estaba en desacuerdo con la decisión del otro.

Otra situación clásica es el problema respecto al dinero. Esperaba que su cónyuge le consultase antes de gastar tanto dinero, pero no lo hizo. ¿Y ahora? Algunas parejas se sientan y se ponen de acuerdo: «Hasta tal cantidad, puedes gastarlo, pero desde esa cantidad, hablaremos y lo decidiremos juntos». Eso es hacer el guión. Cuando la situación aparezca, ya sabe cómo solucionarlo, debido al *script* previo.

Nuevamente retomamos la comparación con el mundo corporativo. En la empresa, usted tiene que solucionar problemas y prevenir que vuelvan a ocurrir. Es exactamente el razonamiento a seguir de esta herramienta. Verá una reducción considerable de los problemas.

¿Cuándo usar esta regla? Siempre que identifique un problema resucitando de entre los muertos. Generalmente acompañado del pensamiento: «Ya he visto esa película antes».

17. Proteja sus noches

¡Últimas noticias! La noche es un momento para relajarse. Si generalmente discute los problemas y expone sus tristezas cuando su compañero llega del trabajo, por ejemplo, se arriesga a echar a perder el clima ideal para tener un agradable momento de unión e intimidad –léase «Sexo». Una pareja encaró esa situación llegando al acuerdo de no hablar más sobre los problemas después de las ocho de la noche. A ellos les funcionó y usted debe descubrir lo que les funciona a ustedes. No se olvide de que si se van a acostar peleados no dormirán como si fueran uno. Esa es la hora del día en la que deben invertir más en su relación, al contrario de lo que muchos han hecho. Esperan ansiosos a que llegue su pareja para quejarse por las cuentas que tienen que pagar o por lo que la profesora dijo de los niños.

En el cuadro del «Laboratorio» de *Escuela del amor*, tuvimos una pareja con ese problema. A la hora de la cena, ella demandaba que él tardaba mucho en comer y él le pedía un tiempo para relajarse. En un determinado momento ella le dijo: «¿Para qué te relajas a la hora de la cena? Hay muchas cosas que hacer, lavar los platos, ¿quién tiene tiempo para relajarse?». Debido a las muchas cosas que hay que hacer, las noches de esa pareja están alteradas. ¿Cómo podrán invertir en la intimidad al final del día si no pueden ni ponerse cómodos? Proteger la noche es proteger las horas que anteceden a los momentos íntimos entre ustedes. Muchas parejas se quedan días, semanas e incluso meses sin relacionarse sexualmente por descuidar las noches. La persona está pensando que va a tener una noche agradable pero, debido a una palabrita en la cena, los planes se van río abajo. No se olvide de que el sexo empieza en la mente. Cuando no protege los momentos anteriores al de estar con su pareja en la cama, elimina el clima y mata cualquier posibilidad de una noche agradable bajo las sábanas.

¿Cuándo usar esta regla? Todas las noches y en otros momentos que anteceden el acto sexual.

18. Rescate a su compañero(a)

Todos nos sentimos sobrecargados alguna que otra vez. La mujer puede llegar a casa, después de un día terrible en el trabajo, y todavía tener decenas de tareas que hacer antes de, finalmente, poder apagar las luces y dormir. Un marido dedicado debe ser sensible a esta situación y ayudar a aliviar su carga siempre que sea posible. Él viene a socorrerla: «Yo guardo las compras mientras miras las tareas del colegio de los niños…» o «Yo arreglaré la ropa y sacaré la basura mientras preparas la cena». ¡Arreglar sus propias cosas también ayuda! De la misma manera, la mujer debe ser auxiliadora del marido y entrar en escena cuando él estuviere sobrecargado. Amar significa cuidar.

Eso puede venir junto con la herramienta 17. La mujer, estresada, llega a casa y quiere descansar su cabeza, el marido se da cuenta de que ella está muy cansada y pide una pizza para que no tenga que preparar la cena. Ella se siente valorada y cuidada. De la misma manera, si el marido estuviera estresado y la mujer decide dejarlo descansar en su cajita, también estará ayudando. Usted se da cuenta de que su cónyuge no está bien, entonces, si no hace lo que normalmente haría, hágalo usted. No cree una tempestad, esté allí cuando más lo necesita. Es una herramienta para emergencias. Socorrerse el uno al otro cuando uno está soportando más de lo que puede. Acuérdese de la pregunta: ¿Qué es lo que mi cónyuge necesita de mí ahora? ¿Ánimo, cuidados médicos, orientación, ayuda práctica o, simplemente, mi presencia?

Cristiane:

Nunca me gustó imponer los quehaceres de casa a Renato, siempre fui el tipo de mujer chapada a la antigua, reina del hogar, cuyo marido no necesita preocuparse con nada. Sin embargo, un día, ya no aguantaba más, estaba sobrecargada con responsabilidades en casa y fuera. Vivíamos con otros dos matrimonios y, cuando me tocaba preparar la comida, cocinaba para un batallón de personas. Después, tenía que limpiar la cocina y el resto de la casa, y, además, ocuparme de la merienda por la tarde y de la cena… Llegaba el fin del día y ¡yo estaba extremadamente cansada! Fue cuando tuve una gripe terrible, me quedé en cama y nadie me ayudó.

Nunca me olvido de lo que Renato hizo por mí: me vino a socorrer. Siempre me hablaba de contratar a una persona para limpiar la casa dos veces por semana pero, por no conocer a ninguna y tener aquel pensamiento de que iban a hacer mal el trabajo, nunca tomaba la iniciativa. Él llamó por teléfono a la persona, firmó un contrato con ella de dos semanas y lo organizó todo para mí. Recuerdo haberme sentido apreciada y valorada por aquel simple gesto. ¡Él me socorrió cuando yo más lo necesitaba!

El asunto de los quehaceres domésticos merece un comentario especial. La sociedad cambió mucho, pero la mentalidad de algunas aún está allá atrás. Si tiene discusiones constantes sobre la casa, hagan una lista y definan quién será responsable de qué cosas. ¿Quién sacará la basura? ¿Quién va a cortar el césped? ¿Quién limpiará la habitación? ¿Uno de los dos? ¿El hijo? ¿Mejor contratar a alguien? En una empresa, todo el mundo sabe quién hace qué, quién hace el café, quién limpia la sala de reuniones… Todo debe estar bien definido. Si uno piensa que otro lo hará, nadie hace nada. Defina las tareas semanales, diarias y mensuales de la casa y pónganse de acuerdo sobre quién hará y qué hará. Si tienen hijos, ellos pueden ayudar, la familia será un equipo en el cuidado de la propia casa. Pegue la lista en la heladera, para que nadie se olvide. Es una manera práctica de solucionar esos problemas.

¿Cuándo usar esta regla? Siempre que observe a su cónyuge sobrecargado o sin condiciones de ejecutar sus tareas.

19. No haga ataques personales

«Eres un mentiroso…», «Eres grosero…», «Eres una testaruda…». Cuando dice cosas de ese tipo a su cónyuge, es señal de que su relación bajó a los niveles más bajos de la falta de respeto, un viaje del cual es difícil regresar. Los ataques personales muestran que ha perdido de vista a su verdadero enemigo, que es el problema, no su pareja. Cuando insulta a su cónyuge, se está insultando a sí mismo, ¡ya que fue usted quien eligió casarse con él!

No imagine que su pareja le está mintiendo. Dos personas pueden ver la misma escena y atestiguar versiones diferentes. No quiere decir que estén mintiendo, sino tan solo contando su punto de vista. Llamar a su cónyuge mentiroso por no coincidir con su versión de los hechos puede ser una gran injusticia; por eso, mantenga el foco de atención en el problema y no parta hacia acusaciones contra su carácter. No es inteligente.

No puedo vestir a Cristiane con el problema y atacarla como si ella fuera el propio problema. Tengo que saber separar las cosas. Yo odio el problema, pero sigo amando a Cristiane. Lo que debe tener en mente es que son amigos y van a trabajar juntos contra la adversidad a la que están haciendo frente. Fueron víctimas del problema, ambos se volvieron enemigos de él y, ahora, deben descubrir cómo solucionarlo, tomados de la mano.

¿Cuándo usar esta regla? En cualquier conversación, especialmente cuando su pareja le irrita.

20. No proyecte

Si tuvo una mala experiencia en el pasado, ya sea con su padre, madre o en una relación anterior, se vuelve muy fácil proyectar injustamente sus inseguridades del pasado en su pareja actual. Por ejemplo, una mujer que haya sufrido abusos por parte del padre puede tener traumas no solucionados, lo que hace que reaccione mal ante cualquier figura de autoridad, incluso el propio marido. O un hombre que tuvo una mala experiencia en la relación anterior y que piensa que, ahora, su mujer le será infiel como lo fue su ex mujer.

Si fui traicionado en el pasado y proyecto mis experiencias traumáticas en mi mujer, cuando haga alguna cosa que me recuerde el comportamiento de la otra, voy a atacarla con celos, con desconfianza y, ella jamás entenderá el porqué. Ella es inocente pero yo la estoy atacando como si hubiera hecho lo mismo que me hizo la otra. Está echando un recuerdo sobre otra persona como si fuera culpable.

El ejemplo que dimos arriba, de la mujer que sufrió abusos y tiene traumas que solucionar, merece un poco más de atención. Puede ser que no esté satisfecha con la relación debido al abuso, que tenga asco del acto sexual. El marido no tiene la culpa, no fue él quien abusó de ella, pero ella no logró solucionar la situación. Este problema tiene dos lados, el del proyector y el de la pantalla que está recibiendo la proyección.

¿Cómo alguien traumatizado consigue lidiar con la situación? Ahí entra el poder de la fe. Psicólogos y psiquiatras, con seguridad, pueden ayudar, pero la sabiduría humana y la medicina tienen límites. Sin embargo, la fe en Dios no tiene límites y puede curar las heridas más profundas. Dios le capacita para perdonar e, inclusive, para –literalmente– olvidarse. Él mismo usa ese poder. Dice en Isaías 43: 25: «*Yo mismo soy el que borro tus transgresiones, por amor de mí y de tus pecados no recuerdo*».

Dios, que tiene la capacidad de lidiar con cualquier hecho, decide voluntariamente no acordarse más de nuestros pecados porque sabe que no es una información útil, ni práctica. Si la persona se arrepintió y quiere cambiar de vida, Él hace el proceso de limpieza mental y no hay necesidad de volver al pasado. Si no logra hacer eso solo, busque la ayuda de Dios. También vale la pena recordar que la otra persona no tiene la culpa de lo que pasó. Entonces, sea justa. Si está luchando con alguien que pasó por esa situación, sea paciente. Sabiendo del equipaje que trae, sabiendo con quién está lidiando, consigue comprender, dar la ayuda necesaria y no reaccionar mal. Use la mente para ayudar a quien todavía está preso de las emociones.

¿Cuándo usar esta regla? Tan pronto identifique un trauma o hecho del pasado como la raíz de algún problema en su relación.

21. Pónganse de acuerdo respecto a cómo educar a los niños

Cuando no hay un frente común edificado sobre la educación de los hijos, crea un alto nivel de estrés en el matrimonio, sin hablar de la confusión y frustración de sus hijos. Y jamás discutan delante de ellos. Si no están de acuerdo en alguna cosa, hablen en privado. Uno puede ser muy duro con los niños debido a su educación, y el otro puede ser mucho más tolerante, también debido a su niñez. Ambos métodos funcionan, dependiendo de la ocasión, dosifique un poco de los dos. No menosprecie a su pareja por educar a los hijos de una manera diferente a la suya, simplemente pónganse de acuerdo previamente respecto a cómo lo harán.

Niño es niño (adolescente es un niño con un cuerpo más desarrollado), no piensa, se guía por las emociones, pues su mente aún no se ha desarrollado por completo. Por desgracia, por el proceso natural, sus hijos no están tan maduros emocionalmente como a usted le gustaría. Llegarán a eso, pero hasta que eso suceda necesitan rutina y disciplina: límites, hora de levantarse, para dormir, de sentarse a la mesa para comer junto con la familia, hora de llegar a casa (en el caso de adolescentes), saber cuándo hablar y cuándo quedarse callado. Los niños siempre intentarán presionar los botones, probar los límites. Claro, hay que dejarles que descubran las cosas, pero no es saludable dejarlos totalmente a su voluntad. Los padres son los responsables de establecer esas reglas, sin violencia, con diálogo. Acuérdense de la herramienta 16 sobre hacer los guiones previamente. Los hijos no pueden recibir indicaciones contradictorias.

En el caso de que uno de ellos empiece a reclamar del padre o de la madre, jamás desvalorice la imagen de su marido o mujer delante de sus hijos. Para entrenar a sus hijos para el mundo, debe ponerles límites, consecuencias y recompensas. Es como conducir un coche, no puede excederse del límite de velocidad, la ley determina consecuencias para ese comportamiento: la multa. Si recibe una multa de tránsito en su casa y tiene que pagarlo por violar la ley, la próxima vez tendrá más cuidado e intentará no exceder el límite establecido. Muchos padres se olvidan de establecer consecuencias a los hijos. No estoy hablando de nada muy severo; sea equilibrado, no es miedo lo que quiere generar en el niño. La cuestión no es castigar, sino entrenarlo para que cambie su comportamiento, eso es posible estableciendo consecuencias debidas un comportamiento errado y recompensas cuando hacen las cosas bien. ¿Esta semana no se ha retrasado para ir al colegio? Merece ir al cine el fin de semana. La vida es así. Si trabaja bien, espera que el jefe le reconozca, ¿no es así?

Si eso ocurre, se siente más motivado para seguir haciendo bien el trabajo y perfeccionarse aún más.

Si su hijo ya es adulto y todavía vive con usted, no puede llevar una vida de eterno adolescente. Él también debe contribuir, ayudar con las cuentas, arreglar la casa, tener consecuencias. Por desgracia, muchos padres hoy en día están creando marginales por miedo a ser juzgados por la cultura que pone a los hijos en contra de los padres. Acaban creando hijos totalmente sin preparación para vivir en sociedad. Antiguamente, un chico de dieciocho años ya era un hombre, estaba preparado para tener sus propias responsabilidades y dirigir a su familia. Hoy en día, un chico de dieciocho años no sabe nada de la vida porque los padres están dejando que sea la sociedad quien eduque a sus hijos. Tiene que establecer una cultura propia dentro de su casa, de su cultura. Piénselo bien, si incluso entre los delincuentes hay reglas (algunas bastante rígidas), ¿por qué ustedes no van a tener reglas?

¿Cuándo usar esta regla? Desde que toman la decisión de ser padres, diariamente, ajustando su comportamiento al hecho de educar a sus hijos. Acuérdese: esta es una gran responsabilidad, están formando un ser humano.

22. Acuérdese de que ambos están en el mismo equipo

¿Qué es más importante, ser feliz o tener razón? ¿Estar bien en el matrimonio o demostrar que tiene razón? Las personas individualistas son pésimos cónyuges. Las parejas deben aprender a trabajar en equipo, porque son uno. Algunas veces tendrán que estar de acuerdo o en desacuerdo. Discrepar no implica tener que discutir. Únanse en contra de los problemas, jamás dejen que ellos los dividan. Nunca se olvide de que lo importante es que el equipo salga ganando y no tan solo uno de sus jugadores.

¿Cómo trabaja un equipo? Uno de los fundamentos del básquet es lo que se denomina «entendimiento en el equipo» y consiste en pasar la pelota de mano en mano entre los jugadores hasta que llegue a alguien que pueda encestar. Fíjese en que el objetivo *personal* de cada jugador es, naturalmente, encestar mucho y convertirse en el mejor del equipo; sin embargo, cada jugador deja de lado cualquier objetivo personal por el éxito de su equipo. En aquel momento no es importante cuál de los jugadores, individualmente, va a encestar sino que se adopte la mejor estrategia para que el jugador mejor colocado logre acertar el blanco y aumentar la puntuación del equipo. Si el último en recibir la pelota no encesta, no es criticado por los demás. Todos están comprometidos en el esfuerzo conjunto y saben que el trabajo del equipo sigue.

Otro aspecto de un equipo es reconocer los puntos fuertes y débiles de cada jugador. Cada uno hace aquello en lo que es mejor y todos se complementan. Cristiane es mejor organizadora y realizadora que yo y óptima contadora. Ella lidia con las finanzas. Yo soy mejor estratega y planificador, pienso más en los detalles. Ambos combinamos nuestras fuerzas para el bien del matrimonio.

¿Cuándo usar esta regla? Desde el primer día del matrimonio hasta que la muerte los separe. Principalmente en las discusiones en que haya desacuerdos, señales de individualidad y problemas que los dividan.

23. Problemas con dinero son problemas de confianza

Cuentas de banco separadas, retener información sobre ingresos y gastos de su pareja, decisiones de compra sin consultarse el uno al otro, son algunas de las señales de que hay un serio problema de confianza en su relación. Descubra por qué no consigue confiar en su cónyuge o por qué él no confía en usted respecto al dinero y lidie con la situación. Ahí está la raíz. Las cuestiones relacionadas con el dinero son una de las principales causas de divorcio.

No estamos hablando de problemas económicos sino de problemas entre ustedes sobre el dinero. El marido piensa que la mujer gasta demasiado o la mujer reclama que el marido no logra ahorrar. Ustedes van a discutir hasta la vejez si no solucionan la raíz. ¿Cómo puedo ayudar a mi mujer a aprender a gastar con más sabiduría? Quitarle la tarjeta de crédito no solucionará el problema. Si yo le quito la tarjeta, ella sigue con el problema y aún añade otro más: el resentimiento debido a mi actitud. Debo preguntarme: «¿Qué es lo que realmente quiero?». Yo no quiero quitarle la tarjeta, quiero que me ayude a confiar más en ella. ¿Cuáles son las opciones para lidiar con la raíz de ese problema? ¿Tendremos que sentarnos y hacer un presupuesto de la casa juntos? ¿Poner un límite para los pequeños gastos hasta que desarrolle esa habilidad? Yo siendo el cabeza tengo que ayudarla.

Por otro lado, si admite que no logra controlar sus impulsos consumistas o tiene un vicio que agota el dinero y no sabe cómo controlar lo que pasa por sus manos, acepte la ayuda de su cónyuge, por el bien del equipo. Trabajando juntos para solucionar esta situación encontrarán la mejor salida para equilibrar las cuentas y eliminar esa fuente de desgaste de su relación.

¿Cuándo usar esta regla? Si cuestiones relacionadas con el dinero se vuelven una fuente de estrés en su matrimonio, busquen la raíz de la desconfianza.

24. No interrumpa a su compañero

Cuando tengan un desentendimiento, permita que su cónyuge explique su punto de vista antes de empezar a hablar. Resista la tentación de defenderse o contraatacar. Eso mantiene la discusión en un nivel racional en lugar de emocional. Es también importante concentrarse en UN PUNTO cada vez. No salga de un tema hasta que haya sido solucionado; sólo entonces prosiga con el próximo tema.

Es el problema de los dos cerebros nuevamente. El hombre hace eso naturalmente, sacando la cajita que corresponde. La mujer ya ve las conexiones con todo unido a aquel problema. Rápidamente la discusión camina por tópicos paralelos y sube al nivel irracional. *«¿Sobre qué estamos discutiendo al final?*» Oiga todo primero. No piense que ya entendió antes de que el otro termine de hablar. No se quede pensando en lo que va a contestar antes de terminar de oír. No es una disputa, no tiene que defenderse, ni tiene que ganar en argumentos. Debe entender el problema (no pensar que lo entendió) y, solo después, hablar. Si su interés es solucionar el problema, deje a la persona hablar.

Claro que eso no es una excusa para que usted que habla mucho domine la conversación. He visto muchas parejas en que uno es el orador nato y el otro tiene dificultades para expresarse. Es muy desagradable ver a esa pareja discutir porque uno domina la conversación y el otro no consigue ni abrir la boca.

Algo muy bueno para no perder el foco es tomar un papel y escribir cuál es el problema que ustedes necesitan solucionar. Por ejemplo: «Nuestra casa se está cayendo a pedazos y ya te lo dije varias veces». Es eso lo que quieren discutir; entonces, no se dispersen hacia la suegra, ni hacia el coche o el perro. Permanezcan en aquel tema, en un solo punto. Soluciónenlo y, solo después, solucionen el siguiente.

¿Cuándo usar esta regla? En cualquier discusión, cuando le entren ganas de interrumpir o de dominar la conversación.

25. Tenga sentido del humor

Estimule el sentido del humor de su compañero. Intenten reírse lo máximo posible. Si no se hacen reír el uno al otro con frecuencia, ¡considere la alternativa! Pienso que una de las cosas que mantienen nuestro matrimonio muy agradable es el buen humor. Es la manera de aliviar la tensión y mantener la cosa interesante entre los dos. Ustedes están casados para una larga jornada: que esta jornada sea estimulante, y no aburrida.

Cristiane y yo tenemos una rutina sin mucha vida social. Incluso así, nunca nos aburrimos cuando estamos juntos, precisamente debido al buen humor. Bromeamos el uno con el otro, comentamos algo gracioso, siempre con ligereza, varias veces al día. Existen parejas a quienes no les gusta estar juntos, les resulta tan aburrido quedarse el uno al lado del otro que se acaban cansando. En nuestro caso, la convivencia es tan ligera y divertida que no conseguimos estar separados.

Tenemos juegos y chistes que nunca vamos a compartir con nadie o de los cuales nadie se reiría porque son chistes privados. A propósito, mujeres, un consejo más: a los hombres, generalmente, les gusta contar chistes. No tienen el mismo tema de conversación que las mujeres, ustedes son normalmente más serias. Cuando se encuentran no hablan del pelo, la ropa, les gusta reír. El marido puede estar muy frustrado porque intenta aportar humor a la relación y la mujer lo ve como un tonto sin gracia (y lo peor: se lo dice a él), después protesta porque se queda viendo la televisión. ¿Dónde está la gracia de conversar con alguien que lo disminuye solo porque usted está a gusto y lo obliga a mantenerse tenso y serio todo el tiempo? Aunque su humor sea diferente, usted, mujer, tiene que aprender a apreciar el humor de su marido. A tiempo: responsabilidad y madurez nada tienen que ver con la cara seria. Al contrario, una reciente investigación realizada por Accountemps, especializada en reclutamiento en las áreas financiera y contable, mostró que el 79 % de los directores financieros creen que el buen humor es fundamental para que el empleado se adapte a la empresa. Si eso fuera indicativo de irresponsabilidad o falta de seriedad, ¿cree que ejecutivos expertos lo considerarían como algo importante a la hora de contratar el personal?

No olvidando que las ventajas van más allá del trabajo y de la salud de su relación, ya se sabe que el buen humor mejora el funcionamiento del sistema inmunológico, estimula la creatividad, la memoria y, además, ayuda a disminuir la sensación de dolor. ¡Sin contar con el aumento en la autoestima! Es muy bueno cuando tiene a otra persona riéndose de sus chistes. Eso da intimidad. ¡Su cónyuge puede que prefiera quedarse con los amigos porque ellos se ríen de sus chistes! Si usted no suma nada, no es una persona agradable y desprecia lo que le dice, ¿por qué iba a preferir su compañía?

¿Cuándo usar esta regla? Mientras esté respirando. Tenga cuidado para no ofender a su pareja con un humor que él(ella) no aprecia o en momentos inapropiados.

26. Asegúrese de que tiene toda su atención

Esta es una herramienta específicamente para el uso de las mujeres. Mencionamos anteriormente que, debido a las diferencias entre los cerebros femenino y masculino, las mujeres tienden a ser multitareas y los hombres monotareas. Ella consigue hacer muchas cosas al mismo tiempo, él lo hace mejor enfocando toda su atención en una sola cosa cada vez. Por eso, mujer, cuando quiera hablar algo muy importante con su marido, ¡asegúrese de que la esté mirando y libre de cualquier otra tarea! Pero, cuidado, eso, normalmente, quiere decir que usted tendrá que interrumpir su atención en lo que fuera que esté haciendo. Elija bien el momento, hable suavemente y, aun así, esté preparada para, si es realmente crucial, recordárselo nuevamente más tarde.

¿Cuándo usar esta regla? Siempre que necesite que el cerebro opuesto registre algo importante.

27. Mantenga el romance vivo

Un matrimonio no se basa en emoción y sí en mucho esfuerzo y perseverancia; sin embargo, un poco de romance ayuda bastante. Es muy importante que el marido y la mujer hagan siempre cosas especiales el uno para el otro. Si no somos cuidadosos, el trabajo, los hijos, y otras responsabilidades y presiones ocuparán todo nuestro tiempo. Asegúrense de tener momentos a solas. Llevar el trabajo a casa regularmente, pasar horas frente a la televisión, permitir que los hijos tengan todo su tiempo y atención son comportamientos que hacen que las parejas se distancien. Ustedes necesitan tener esos momentos «a solas». Planéelo con anticipación.

Hollywood nos hizo creer que el romance es una cosa complicada, elaborada y costosa, pero no lo es. El romance puede ser definido simplemente como «hacer algo fuera de la rutina, que muestre su amor por la otra persona». No necesita que sea algo grande, la mayoría de las veces el romanticismo está en los detalles. Usted, hombre, puede que no se considere romántico, pero la cosa es muy simple, se trata solo de hacerlo con naturalidad. No necesitará siempre gastar dinero para ser romántico. He aquí algunas ideas: llame por teléfono en medio del día, preguntando a su mujer como está, déjele una notita inesperada, una cartita como las que escribía cuando eran novios (puede ponerla bajo la almohada o junto a los cepillos de dientes, dentro de la maleta cuando vayan a viajar). Regalar flores es muy común y no siempre funciona. Si tienen un gato, por ejemplo, tenga en cuenta su temperamento. Si ataca el ramo y destroza las flores, puede no resultar muy romántico. Si decide arriesgarse, aun así, elija flores que los gatos puedan comer (nunca se sabe, ¿verdad?). Puede apagar los teléfonos, hacer palomitas de maíz, alquilar un DVD que a ella le guste y verlo abrazaditos en el sofá (no se duerma durante la película, eso no es romántico). En fin, sea creativo, haga algo diferente, pero simple, que muestre que piensa en su cónyuge en los momentos más triviales. Para ayudar, su tarea de casa es hacer algo romántico para su pareja este fin de semana. ¿Vamos a empezar a practicar?

¿Cuándo usar esta regla? Como mínimo una o dos veces al mes y siempre que la rutina haga que la relación sea aburrida. Esta es una herramienta de mantenimiento. Sorprenda a su cónyuge.

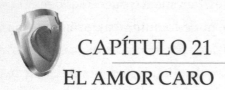

CAPÍTULO 21
EL AMOR CARO

Un matrimonio cumplía cincuenta años de casados y decidió celebrarlo. Al preguntarle sobre el secreto para permanecer casado durante tanto tiempo y en armonía, el marido respondió:

—¿Conoce el piquito del pan? Es mi parte favorita. Durante cincuenta años, todas las mañanas, le he dado ese piquito a ella.

Respondiendo a la misma pregunta, la mujer dijo:

—¿Conoce el piquito del pan? ¡Lo odio! Pero durante cincuenta años lo he aceptado sin protestar...

Esta pequeña historia revela el gran secreto de la base del matrimonio, en una palabra: sacrificio. Durante 50 años él renunció a aquello que le gustaba por amor a ella, y ella también renunció a su voluntad por él. Piense en la base de una casa o edificio, es la que sustenta aquella estructura. Así es el sacrificio en el matrimonio. Y lo que nadie consigue ver de la pareja, desde fuera, es su mayor felicidad resultado de los sacrificios que hacen el uno por el otro.

DIECINUEVE AÑOS EN COMA

Desde que supe de este caso, nunca lo he olvidado. Para mí es uno de los mejores ejemplos de lo que es el amor verdadero, el amor-sacrificio. Jan Grzebski era un ferroviario polaco. En 1988 sufrió un fuerte golpe en la cabeza mientras intentaba enganchar dos vagones de tren, y entró en coma. Jan fue desahuciado por los médicos, quienes, posteriormente, encontraron un cáncer en su cerebro. Según ellos, la recuperación era imposible y no sobreviviría. Gertruda Grzebska, mujer de Jan, ignoró aquella palabra derrotista y decidió llevarlo a casa y cuidar de él sola.

Jan no hablaba, no caminaba, no se comunicaba de ninguna manera ni interactuaba. Toda la relación que habían tenido ya no existía, el marido fuerte con quien había convivido durante tantos años era ahora un bebé totalmente dependiente de sus cuidados. Ella terminó de criar sola a sus hijos, mientras se esforzaba por mantener vivo a su marido, que tan solo era capaz de realizar los movimientos más básicos como respirar, tragar, abrir y cerrar los ojos. Aun así, ella se indignaba cuando alguien la sugería la eutanasia (con la excusa de «interrumpir el sufrimiento»), pues creía que lo correcto era darle la oportunidad de recuperarse. Todos los días, Gertruda hablaba con su marido como si él pudiese escucharla, cuidaba de que no se quedase mucho tiempo en la misma posición en la cama girando su cuerpo para evitar las temidas úlceras de contacto, comunes en las personas que están mucho tiempo en la cama, que pueden llevar incluso a la muerte por infección. Los hijos fueron creciendo, se casaron y les dieron nictos. Gertruda llevaba a su marido a todas las fiestas principales de la familia como si él pudiese participar.

La incansable Gertruda tuvo su recompensa en 2007. Después de diecinueve años en coma, Jan finalmente despertó, a los sesenta y cinco años. Los médicos adjudicaron su recuperación a su mujer, que optó por el camino más arduo. Jan estaba todavía más unido a ella, pues se acordaba de que Gertruda estuvo a su lado cuando más lo necesitaba. Ella hizo lo que era más correcto y mejor para él, renunciando a su propia vida para cuidar de su marido, sin cobrar nada por eso. Creyó cuando los médicos no creyeron, esperó, perseveró…, y fue recompensada.

Durante el coma, Gertruda describía a su marido como «un cadáver viviente»; incluso así, permaneció a su lado. No hubo sentimiento en lo que hizo, ni romance, fue puro sacrificio, verdadero amor. Sin embargo, ¿consigue usted pensar en una actitud más romántica? Ninguna historia de amor es más bonita que las que implican el amor sacrificial. Gertruda recibió una merecida medalla de honor al mérito, del presidente polaco, por su dedicación y sacrificio; tremenda es la rareza de ese tipo de amor en los días actuales.

Ante la realidad que Gertruda vivió durante diecinueve años, las preguntas son inevitables: ¿Qué habría hecho usted en el lugar de ella? ¿Qué problemas ha encarado en su matrimonio? ¿Cómo desistir de su cónyuge?

Solamente el amor-sacrificio es capaz de vencer todo. Es el amor caro, genuino.

Cuidado con las imitaciones baratas.

PERDER PARA GANAR

Sacrificio es la manera de poner en práctica todo lo que hemos enseñado hasta aquí. En realidad, toda persona de éxito está bien familiarizada con el concepto de sacrificio. En cualquier área de la vida, si alguien conquistó algo de gran valor, realizó grandes hechos, obtuvo grandes victorias, con seguridad cruzó el puente del sacrificio. Este es el camino más corto para el éxito, pero claro, no es el más fácil.

¿Qué es el sacrificio? Digamos que hace un frío extremo y tengo dos abrigos, y alguien a mi lado está congelado. Le ofrezco uno y yo me quedo con uno solo. Eso no es sacrificar, es dar. Pero si yo tengo un solo abrigo y se lo entrego, estoy sacrificando. Es perder ahora porque tiene la seguridad de que va a ganar algo de mucho más valor más tarde. Y, a veces, ese algo de mucho más valor es su propia consciencia de saber que hizo lo correcto y no lo que sintió ganas de hacer. Es lo que hizo Gertruda.

El amor verdadero es el amor marcado por el sacrificio. Es caro. Como ya dijimos aquí, amor no es sentimiento. Incluye sentimientos, pero no está definido por ellos. El mundo ha asociado al amor con el sentimiento en una receta bastante indigesta: une a la palabra «amor» la voluntad de estar juntos, los celos, la codicia, el deseo sexual…, junta todo y –a través de la cocción con la música, las películas, el arte en general– hace al público creer que eso es amor. No lo es. Es pirata. Lo que define al amor son dos cosas conectadas:

Hacer lo que es mejor para la otra persona. Tengo que ser correcto con la persona que amo. Haré lo adecuado por ella, independientemente de lo que siento o dejo de sentir, de lo que creo o dejo de creer y de cuánto me va a costar.

Sacrificio. Si su amor se reduce a una sensación placentera, no sobrevivirá a las tempestades. El único amor que sobrevive a todo es el que no se basa en sentimientos, sino en sacrificio. Quien dice que «el amor se acabó» es porque no conoce el amor. El verdadero amor jamás se acaba.

El egoísmo de los días actuales impide a muchas parejas poner ese concepto en práctica, creyendo que se perjudicarán al sacrificar; pero quien ha escogido trillar ese camino por amor no se arrepiente.

No quiero que piense que deberá sufrir o que su matrimonio será una cruz a cargar eternamente. El sacrificio no es un fin en sí mismo, es un medio para conquistar algo mayor. Como la persona que tiene como meta ganar un disputadísimo concurso público, para ganar un sueldo tres veces mayor que el actual; si no sacrifica, abandonando el placer por horas de estudio, tal vez un curso preparatorio o días preparándose de manera integra, difícilmente conseguirá algún resultado. Empiece a sacrificar por su matrimonio y cosechará una relación maravillosa, llena de paz, comprensión, compañerismo y fidelidad…, que compensa todo el sufrimiento que tuvo que encarar al principio. Por el resultado alcanzado, haría todo de nuevo. Haga la prueba.

Tal vez diga: «¿Pero no hay limites? ¿Y si mi cónyuge no me corresponde? ¿Estoy preso por el resto de mi vida?».

Sin duda hay personas que no quieren el amor de otras. Hay quien rechaza hasta el amor de Dios; por eso, es imposible tener una relación con tales personas. Ni siquiera Dios fuerza a nadie a amarlo o a seguirlo. Él sacrificó por todos, pero no todos aceptaron Su sacrificio ni las condiciones para tener una relación con Él.

El amor es incondicional respecto a la comprensión de las debilidades de la otra persona; pero una relación, un matrimonio, no es, y nunca puede ser, incondicional. Para que dos personas vivan juntas tienen que cumplirse ciertas condiciones. Yo amo a mi mujer, pero si ella me traiciona no veo la forma de continuar mi relación con ella. Sé que ella siente lo mismo con respecto a mí. La fidelidad es una condición para que nuestro matrimonio funcione. ¿Dar una nueva oportunidad ante un arrepentimiento sincero? Tal vez. Cada caso es un caso y cada uno tiene su fe y sus límites, pero una cosa es cierta: una buena relación exige la participación de ambas partes. Si la otra persona no lo quiere, entonces, tal vez, su sacrificio esté mejor invertido en otra persona.

CÓMO SE PRACTICA EN EL MATRIMONIO

Pongo aquí una lista con algunos ejemplos (hay muchos más) de sacrificio en el matrimonio para que entienda cómo y cuándo se aplica en la práctica:

Sacrificio en la comunicación. Tuve que aprender a comunicarme más con Cristiane, no era mi forma de ser llegar y conversar, generalmente estaba muy cansado y quería quedarme callado. Me comunicaba con monosílabos. Por amor, sacrifiqué esa forma de actuar respondiendo a sus preguntas. Hasta hoy, me hace preguntas y yo me veo haciendo un esfuerzo porque no quiero hablar sobre aquello, no le encuentro sentido a hablar de ello pero pienso: No importa lo que yo siento, voy a hacer lo que es importante para ella. Si el marido es más callado y la mujer se comunica mucho, es un sacrificio para el hombre ser más comunicativo con su mujer. Por otro lado, la mujer que habla demasiado, exige, reclama, impone… es insoportable. Nadie la aguanta. Se volverá una persona más agradable para su marido si sacrifica disminuyendo el ritmo y eliminando las exigencias.

Si los dos hacen eso, alcanzarán el equilibrio saludable, pero si tan solo lo hace uno, se resolverá la mitad del problema… y la otra mitad acabará siguiendo el modelo y se solucionará también, antes o después.

Sacrificio de humildad. Usted sacrifica cuando se traga el orgullo, da su brazo a torcer y admite que el otro tenía razón. Eso es sacrificio porque duele, pero como usted no quiere alimentar un corazón duro, entonces sacrifica su orgullo y asume el error.

Sacrificio en el ocio. Usted sacrifica si a su mujer le gusta salir y sale con ella para agradarla, o si a uno de los dos no le gusta salir y el otro se queda en casa, sin protestar. Su marido adora el fútbol y usted no entiende cuál es la gracia de ver a un montón de hombres corriendo tras una pelota. Incluso así, se sienta a su lado y se esfuerza por aprender a admirar aquel deporte, viéndolo con los ojos de su marido, porque es importante para él. Es feliz con la felicidad de su cónyuge.

Sacrificio en el sexo. Cuando usted es egoísta y no sacrifica en el sexo, su objetivo es obtener satisfacción y punto final. A partir del momento en el que aprende lo que es el sacrificio, consigue poner el placer del otro en primer lugar. Nunca quedará uno insatisfecho porque su meta será satisfacer a la otra persona y no estará satisfecho mientras ella no lo esté. Solamente a través del sacrificio es posible alcanzar el placer mutuo.

Sacrificio en el temperamento. Tolerar hábitos que le irritan pero que usted va a ignorar conscientemente. Razone: comparado al conjunto de cosas que compone la relación, aquello es insignificante. No va a convertir algo pequeño en un problema.

Sacrificio de las emociones. Este, tal vez, sea uno de los mayores sacrificios, pues se refiere a algo directamente unido al corazón. Impulsividad y sentimientos llevan a las parejas a explotar hasta el punto de dañarse, alimentar la rabia y dormir en habitaciones separadas. Es necesario el sacrificio para controlar los instintos emotivos que los lleva a cometer actos sin pensar. No dejaré que la emoción me haga insultar a mi mujer, tengo que respetarla. No irritaré a mi cónyuge con un sinfín de quejas, que desembocan en una pelea inútil e innecesaria. Cristiane dejó de pedirme cuentas a mí para pedírselas a Dios, pidiendo un cambio en mi comportamiento. Sacrificó sus emociones por la dependencia de Dios.

Sacrificio de los objetivos. Muchas veces, cuando su objetivo personal excluye su matrimonio, es necesario sacrificar. Cuando uno pone sus objetivos individuales por encima de la relación, eso daña la relación. Ese es el motivo por el que muchos matrimonios de celebridades terminan en divorcio. Si pone la carrera por encima de la unión, por ejemplo, el compañero se siente mero accesorio. Es difícil soportar esa situación durante mucho tiempo. Tienen que sacrificar sus objetivos personales para encontrar objetivos comunes.

Sacrificio de las amistades. Si alguien ha sido una influencia negativa en su matrimonio, una persona en la que su cónyuge no confía o con cuya amistad se siente incómodo, tendrá que sacrificarlo por su matrimonio. Amistades del sexo contrario que generan celos, a veces incluso algunos parientes, tendrán que mantenerse a distancia.

PERDÓN: EL MAYOR DE TODOS LOS SACRIFICIOS

Si su cónyuge le ha causado mucho dolor y decepción y están intentando seguir adelante, es necesario que apriete el botón de «reiniciar» en su relación. Cuando su computadora se bloquea tiene que reiniciarla para que termine con lo que estaba provocando el problema, ¿verdad? De la misma manera, para que su matrimonio funcione tiene que reiniciarlo a través del perdón.

El perdón no es algo que tenemos *voluntad* de hacer. Su voluntad es la de castigar a la persona. Cree que perdonar hace que la persona no sufra las consecuencias de sus actos, entonces guarda rencor como forma de venganza. Existe un dicho que dice que guardar rencor es como tomar veneno para ratas y esperar que el ratón se muera. Piénselo bien, ¡el ratón no va a morir! Es usted quien se está tomando el veneno, es usted quien se va a morir mientras que el ratón continuará viviendo la vida, corriendo de acá para allá, haciendo sus ratonadas y royendo todo lo que encuentre en su camino. ¿Quién pierde con eso?

El rencor esclaviza, es un peso y por eso no concuerda con la inteligencia. ¿Para qué cargar con un peso que no necesita cargar? La otra persona ya se olvidó y sigue hacia adelante, pero usted está ahí, rumiando el pasado. Perdone, no porque la otra persona lo merezca, sino para no cargar con algo con lo que ni ella está cargando. El rencor es una basura emocional. Cuando alimenta el rencor, está comiendo basura. Ingiere la comida más podrida y tóxica de lo que pueda imaginar, carga en la espalda la bolsa de la basura orgánica en descomposición que le servirá de comida y se agarra a ella cuando alguien le pide que deje aquello atrás.

Sé exactamente lo que es eso. Yo tenía rencor de una persona de mi familia que tuvo, en parte, culpa de la separación de mis padres. En la adolescencia me prometí a mí mismo que en el momento adecuado le daría el castigo para que pagara por lo que había hecho. Cuando empecé a concurrir a la iglesia y oí al pastor hablar sobre perdonar a los enemigos, mi primer pensamiento fue: «Usted no conoce a la persona que destruyó a mi familia. Es fácil para usted decir eso porque no sabe lo que yo pasé». Tal vez sea lo que le pasa por su cabeza cuando lee acerca del perdón. Yo tampoco lo entendí al principio, pero con el paso del tiempo me di cuenta de que ella no estaba pagando nada con mi rencor, era yo quien lo estaba pagando. Cuando entendí que debía perdonar para mi bien, me interesé por saber cómo podría hacer eso, ya que no tenía ningún deseo.

ENTONCES, ¿CÓMO PERDONAR?

La primera cosa que debe saber respecto al perdón es que no surge de un deseo, sino de una decisión. Decidir perdonar no fue tan difícil, ya que yo lo había entendido: era lo correcto por hacer. Necesitaba ahora lograr seguir adelante. El segundo paso era empezar a orar por tal criatura, pedir a Dios por ella. Muchos, que continúan cargando su basura emocional, dicen orar por sus enemigos; sin embargo, lo que expresan en sus oraciones no encaja en esa categoría. Por ejemplo, no espere un resultado positivo contra el rencor si usted dice: «Señor, haz que Juan pague por lo que hizo», o «Dios, pon Tu mano sobre María». ¡Eso no es orar por sus enemigos! Eso es arrojar su rencor sobre algo que Dios no va a escuchar. La Biblia nos orienta para bendecir a los que nos persiguen[22] y lo refuerza: «Bendecid, no maldigáis». Ese es el punto.

Al principio, mi oración no era sincera. Empezaba a orar por ella, pedía a Dios que la bendijera, pero deseaba pedirle que mandara un rayo sobre su cabeza. Ignorando mi voluntad de verla partida en millones de pedacitos, continuaba mi oración sin gracia. Con el tiempo, aquella piedra de mi corazón se deshizo y empecé a ver a aquella persona con otros ojos. La oración me ayudó a cambiar la manera de verla. Entonces di el tercer paso: empecé a mirar hacia adelante. Me di cuenta de que tenía que ser práctico, mirar hacia atrás no era inteligente. Lo que ella hizo, ya estaba hecho. Si tenía que pagar alguna cosa, lo pagaría delante de Dios, yo ya no tenía nada más que ver con eso. Me di cuenta de que yo también estaba lleno de fallas; no podía exigirle perfección, pues yo no soy perfecto. Si Dios, que es perfecto, me viese con el mismo rigor con el que yo miraba a la persona, ¡estaría perdido! Pero si recibí Su perdón, ¿cómo no iba yo a perdonar también? *Perdona nuestras deudas así como nosotros perdonamos a nuestros deudores.*[23] Si usted no perdona, ni el Padre Nuestro puede orar, ¿lo había pensado? Es injusto que yo quiera algo que no estoy dispuesto a dar.

Ahí está la diferencia entre el amor verdadero y el amor-sentimiento. Su corazón, el centro de las emociones, estará siempre pidiéndole hacer

---

[22] Romanos 12:14.
[23] Mateo 6:12.

lo que a usted le apetece hacer en vez de hacer lo que es necesario. Usted sabe que lo correcto es ir a hablar con su marido, pero no tiene ganas. Su corazón hace que su mente lo justifique diciendo: «¿Por qué tengo que hablar yo? ¡Es él quien está equivocado!» Pero si utiliza la mente y domina su corazón para no vivir en función de sus emociones, va a hacer lo que es correcto, incluso aunque vaya en contra de su voluntad.

Es una guerra constante. No puedo prever lo que voy a sentir, nadie tiene ese control. El sentimiento viene. Pero yo tengo el control de mi mente, puedo determinar lo que voy a pensar, cómo voy a reaccionar ante aquel sentimiento. Tengo que usar mi inteligencia cuando mi corazón está usando los sentimientos en mi contra.

¿Le parece difícil? Pero ya hace eso todas las mañanas, principalmente los lunes, cuando el sacrificio es naturalmente mayor. No quiere levantarse de la cama. Su voluntad es seguir acostado. Programa el despertador para «cinco minutitos más» y regresa de nuevo al mundo de los sueños; pero, cuando suena de nuevo, su mente dice: «No, no puedes faltar. No puedes llegar tarde de nuevo. Tienes que trabajar». Usted se levanta, se arrastra hasta el baño, luchando contra sí mismo. Si es necesario se mete debajo de la ducha helada tan solo para mostrar a su corazón quién manda. Resignado, él no insiste más y usted consigue tomarse el café e irse al trabajo. Si no hiciese eso, no tendría trabajo, ¿no es verdad? Es así como se vence esa guerra que está dentro de su matrimonio. Es un sacrificio, sí, pero perfectamente ejecutable. Todo lo que es bueno, es caro.

TAREA

¿Qué sacrificios necesita empezar o continuar haciendo por su relación?

/MatrimonioBlindado

Publique esto:
Yo no quiero un amor
barato; por eso,
sacrifico.

@matrimonioblind

Tuitee esto:
Yo no quiero un amor
barato; por eso,
sacrifico
#matrimonioblindado
@matrimonioblind

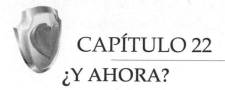

CAPÍTULO 22
¿Y AHORA?

Esperamos que usted haya despertado al hecho de que el matrimonio en el siglo XXI no es el mismo que tradicionalmente fue. Estamos en un mundo nuevo, envueltos en una cultura de relaciones sin compromiso y rodeados por un conjunto de nuevas amenazas que hace apenas unos años no existían. Para quien todavía quiere casarse y permanecer casado, el blindaje de la relación no es un lujo, sino una necesidad.

Y lo que hemos hecho en este libro, hasta aquí, ha sido exactamente lo contrario de lo que el mundo está haciendo. Mientras que las palabras de moda incluyen progresismo, avanzar, modernidad, disfrutar, relación sin compromiso, «disfrutarse pero no unirse», etc., nosotros volvimos al principio de todo, fuimos allá atrás, al Jardín del Edén, y seguimos los pasos del hombre y de la mujer hasta aquí. Descubrimos, así, lo que es el matrimonio en su esencia, lo que funciona, lo que es el amor marcado por lo que hace y no por lo que siente, cuáles son las maldiciones particulares del hombre y de la mujer, cómo afectan a la relación entre los dos y cómo lidiar con ellas. Entendimos también las diferencias fundamentales entre los sexos y sus conflictos inherentes. Aprendimos a buscar la raíz de los problemas y a resolverlos usando la razón en vez de la emoción. Encontramos decenas de herramientas prácticas que usted puede usar en el día a día de su matrimonio para resolver y prevenir problemas.

Usted conoció un poco más de Cristiane y de mí, y esperamos que nuestras luchas y experiencias hayan contribuido positivamente para su matrimonio. Intentamos transmitirle una idea realista de lo que es el matrimonio, sin rodeos, revelando sus dificultades pero también sus alegrías y su belleza. Matrimonio feliz da trabajo, sí, pero ¡el salario vale la pena!–. Queremos izar la bandera del amor verdadero, desbancar los mitos y la desinformación que maldice las relaciones de hoy en día y mostrar que es posible estar casado y ser muy feliz. Sinceramente, creemos que la felicidad total solamente es conocida por quien está bien casado, pues para eso fuimos creados. Y es posible. No deje que nadie le diga lo contrario.

Cristiane y yo no nos consideramos «suertudos». La felicidad de nuestro matrimonio se debe totalmente a nuestras decisiones, muchas veces en contra de nuestros sentimientos, y a la práctica de la inteligencia espiritual, que es la obediencia a los consejos de Dios. Si no hubiésemos hecho eso, y continuásemos haciéndolo, seríamos una estadística más. Cualquier persona, incluido usted, que quiera practicar esos consejos también puede tener un matrimonio muy feliz. Respecto a eso, no podemos prestar poca atención. Es solamente por la fe práctica que estamos aquí. Nuestra inteligencia hace que nos rehusemos a creer que es posible ser feliz en el amor sin conocer el Verdadero Amor, que es Dios. Todo lo que usted quiera realizar en su vida, no solo en su matrimonio, es posible a través de su fe en Él, inclusive las respuestas que usted puede no haber encontrado en este libro. Por eso, nuestro consejo principal en respuesta a la pregunta «¿Y ahora?» es este:

Busque conocer personalmente al Dios de la Biblia a través del Señor Jesús. Él no quiere que usted se vuelva un religioso, sino que desarrolle una relación con Él.

Además, tenemos la más absoluta certeza de que los principios y enseñanzas prácticas que ha aprendido en este libro funcionan. No son siempre fáciles de practicar, pero son certeros. Difícil no quiere decir imposible y la demora de los resultados no quiere decir que no vayan a llegar nunca. Sea paciente y perseverante. No espere que el cambio total venga en cuestión de días, ni reclame eso de su compañero. Empiece por el primer paso y siga trabajando.

Le sugerimos que se centre en algunos puntos, al principio: uno, dos o tres puntos principales que le marcarán, que sabe que son los que necesitan un cambio más urgente. Trabaje en esos puntos hasta que estén integrados en su vida; después, vuelva a los demás capítulos y trabaje en otras áreas. Es como una reeducación alimenticia. Usted quiere adelgazar pero sabe que no sirve de nada cortar drásticamente las calorías y pasar hambre, eso no funciona; pero si cambia su alimentación poco a poco y realiza más ejercicio el resultado llegará naturalmente y de una manera permanente. Enfóquese en el cambio, realice esfuerzo continuo y alcanzará su objetivo. No desista. Como dice el dicho: «Una caminata de mil kilómetros empieza con un primer paso». A través de la práctica llegarán los resultados.

Cristiane y yo realmente queremos ser un impacto positivo en su vida. Nos gustaría sugerirle algunos pasos que puede seguir a partir de ahora para maximizar los resultados en su relación e, incluso, ayudar a otras personas a su alrededor. Aquí van algunos consejos:

Relea las partes de este libro que llamaron su atención o que le parece que necesita entender mejor. Se sorprenderá con cuánto le ayudará a absorber y guardar los puntos más importantes. Le ayudará a acordarse de lo que aprendió y a saber cómo actuar en situaciones futuras.

Si no cumplió alguna de las tareas, todavía hay tiempo. Vuelva y trabaje en ellas. No subestime el poder de implementarlas. Sintiendo ganas o no ¡hágalo!

Mantenga el contacto con nosotros a través de nuestros sitios y blogs. Nos gustaría mucho recibir su *feedback* y continuar ayudándole. Siga, deje un comentario, vea nuestros videos, cuéntenos sus experiencias:

- Blogs: www.renatocardoso.com y www.cristianecardoso.com
  Facebook: www.facebook.com/MatrimonioBlindado

- Twitter: *@matrimonioblind*
  Email: libro@matrimonioblindado.com
  Conviértase en un alumno de The Love School (La Escuela del Amor).
  Véanos de lunes a viernes, a las 11:00 hrs. en www.iurdtv.com y los sábados al mediodía por la Red Record. Los horarios están sujetos a cambios, por lo tanto compruebe siempre en nuestra página de Facebook la última información: www.fb.com/EscoladoAmor.

Hágale un bien a alguien regalándole un ejemplar de este libro. Tal vez conozca a alguien que se va a casar pronto y que necesita aprender temprano para hacer lo correcto en el futuro. Con seguridad conoce a personas casadas que necesitan blindar sus relaciones. Agasájelos con un libro. Se lo van a agradecer de todo corazón y jamás se olvidarán de usted.

De vez en cuando, Cristiane y yo hacemos el «Curso del Matrimonio Blindado» para grupos seleccionados de matrimonios. El curso en directo es divertido y muy práctico. Las enseñanzas del libro salen del papel hacia la vida y tiene acceso a mucha información extra. Considere participar. Los detalles sobre los próximos cursos aparecen en www.matrimonioblindado.com.

Le aconsejamos que guarde su ejemplar de este libro para volver a leerlo dentro de seis meses. Los cambios llevan tiempo y necesitan perseverancia. Por eso, busque en su calendario la fecha para dentro de seis meses desde hoy y márquela: «Releer el libro *Matrimonio blindado*». Las personas que hagan eso verán muchos más resultados muchos mayores.

Considere ir a la Caminata del Amor con su cónyuge, siempre que pueda, al menos una vez al año. Explicamos más sobre lo que es en este link: www.renatocardoso.com/es/the-love-walk/

¡Feliz matrimonio blindado!
Renato & Cristiane Cardoso

AGRADECIMIENTOS

Antes de nada, al inventor del matrimonio, a Dios. Para los menos entendidos, el hecho de crear al hombre y a la mujer, tan diferentes el uno del otro, y hacer que convivan puede parecer una broma de mal gusto. Pero Él siempre sabe lo que hace. Le agradecemos el habernos brindado a cada uno la vida del otro. Renato no sería Renato sin Cristiane, y a su vez, Cristiane no sería Cristiane sin Renato. Es difícil de explicar.

A los problemas que hemos atravesado durante nuestro matrimonio. Han sido duros, pero también los mejores maestros.

Al obispo Macedo y a la Sra. Ester, quizá la pareja más sólida y feliz que hemos conocido y que más nos ha influenciado. Gracias por las enseñanzas, muchas de las cuales están presentes en este libro.

A David y Evelyn Higginbotham, que nos han ayudado a desarrollar este trabajo en Texas, siempre con un excelente *insight*.

A Ágatha Cristina y Raquel Parras, que han investigado, revisado, leído y releído este libro más veces de las que se deberían permitir a cualquier persona.

Y a todo nuestro equipo y alumnos de Matrimonio Blindado y de *The Love School*. Su contribución a esta obra ha sido enorme. ¡Alégrense con nosotros!

Renato y Cristiane Cardoso

REFERENCIAS BIBLIOGRÁFICAS

Capítulo 1

http://www.ionline.pt/mundo/uniao-termo-certo-mexico-quer-casamento-renovavel-dois-dois-anos

http://noticias.r7.com/videos/mexico-cria-casamento-renovavel-para-solucoes-conjugais/idmedia/4e85e84f
3d146409c15fb55a.html

http://www.nytimes.com/2012/02/18/us/for-women-under-30-most-births-occur-outside-marriage.html?_r=1

https://www.hcfr.org/pressroom/journal-news-releases/do-children-need-both-mother-and-father

http://www.theatlantic.com/magazine/archive/2010/07/are-fathers-necessary/8136/

http://www.dailymail.co.uk/femail/article-2080398/Facebook-cited-THIRD-divorces.html

http://www.dailymail.co.uk/news/article-1334482/The-marriage-killer-One-American-divorces-involve-Face-
book.html

http://internet-filter-review.toptenreviews.com/internet-pornography-statistics.html

http://www.safefamilies.org/sfStats.php

ChristiaNet, Inc. "ChristiaNet Poll Finds that Evangelicals are Addicted to Porn." Marketwire, 7 Aug. 2006. Web.7

Dec. 2009. <http://www.marketwire.com/press-release/Christianet-Inc-703951.html>

Pastors.comsurvey.@td.im "Wounded Clergy." Hope and Freedom Counseling Services, Media A-Team, Inc.,
March

2002 Web. 7 Dec. 2009. <http://www.hopeandfreedom.com/hidden-pages/private/wounded-clergy.html>

http://noticias.r7.com/vestibular-e-concursos/noticias/mulheres-sao-maioria-nas-universidades-do-mun-
do-20111022.html

http://www.terra.com.br/istoe-temp/edicoes/2037/artigo116712-1.htm

Capítulo 2

En el libro *The 7 habits of highly effective people*, 1.ª parte [*Los siete hábitos de las personas sumamente
eficientes*].

Capítulo 4

http://www.reuters.com/article/2009/07/14/idUSSP483675

http://www.barna.org/barna-update/article/15-familykids/42-new-marriage-and-divorce-statistics-released

Capítulo 6

http://en.wikipedia.org/wiki/5_Whys

Capítulo 7

Peter Ahlwardts, *Reasonable and theological considerations about thunder and lightning* (1745).

http://www.evolvefish.com/freewrite/franklgt.htm

Capítulo 8

http://en.wikipedia.org/wiki/soulmate

Capítulo 11

http://www.lexiophiles.com/portugues/e-a-vaca-foi-para-o-brejo

Capítulo 15

http://www.thirdage.com/love-romance/the-male-vs-the-female-brain?page=1

http://web.sfn.org/index.aspx?pagename=brainfacts

Louann Brizendine, *The female brain*, Three Rivers Press, 2007.

Mark Gungor, *Laugh your way to a better marriage*, Atria Books, 2008.

Capítulo 16

Bell Hooks, *Feminist theory: from margin to center,* Cambridge, South End Press, 2000, p. 26.

Consulte solo la causa de ello en Brasil: «1977: Se aprueba la ley del divorcio (n.º 6.515), una antigua reivindicación del movimiento feminista». http://www.brasil.gov.br/linhadotempo/epocas/1977/lei-do-divorcio

Capítulo 17

Merriam-Webster's Collegiate Dictionary: «Etymology of husband, husbandry: ORIGIN late Old English (in the senses "male head of a household" and "manager, steward"), from Old Norse *húsbóndi,* "master of a house", from *hús,* "house" + *bóndi,* "occupier and tiller of the soil". The original sense of the verb was "till, cultivate"».

Capítulo 20

http://marriagegems.com/tag/five-to-one-ratio/

http://accountemps.rhi.mediaroom.com/funnny-business